W9-CQZ-472

ELECTRONIC MEDIA AND GOVERNMENT

The Regulation of Wireless and Wired Mass Communication in the United States

F. LESLIE SMITH
UNIVERSITY OF FLORIDA

MILAN MEESKE
UNIVERSITY OF CENTRAL FLORIDA

JOHN WRIGHT
UNIVERSITY OF FLORIDA

 Longman Publishers USA

Electronic Media and Government: The Regulation of Wireless and Wired Mass Communication in the United States

Longman, 10 Bank Street, White Plains, N.Y. 10606

Associated companies:
Longman Group Ltd., London
Longman Cheshire Pty., Melbourne
Longman Paul Pty., Auckland
Copp Clark Longman Ltd., Toronto

Acquisitions editor: Kathleen M. Schurawich
Production editor: Linda W. Witzling
Cover design: Delgado Design Inc.
Cover photo courtesy of AT&T Archives
Text art: Fine Line Inc.
Production supervisor: Richard Bretan

Library of Congress Cataloging-in-Publication Data

Smith, F. Leslie, Date.
    Electronic media and government: the Regulation of Wireless and
Wired Mass Communication in the United States / by F. Leslie Smith,
Milan D. Meeske, John W. Wright, II.
        p. cm.
    Includes bibliographical references and index.
    ISBN 0-8013-1142-X
    1. Telecommunication—Law and legislation—United States.   2. Mass
media—Law and legislation—United States.   I. Meeske, Milan D.
II. Wright, John W., II.   III. Title.
KF2765.S63   1994
343.7309′9—dc20
[347.30399]   94-1163
                                                                CIP

1 2 3 4 5 6 7 8 9 10-MA-9897969594

CONTENTS

CHAPTER 15   **LIBEL, PRIVACY, AND INTELLECTUAL PROPERTY**   **412**

CHAPTER 16 REPORTING EFFORT   487

PREFACE

A business of almost any type must deal with the government. Incorporation, building permits, code compliance, environmental and safety regulations, taxes—the list goes on and on. If the business is a medium of communication such as a newspaper or a magazine, it faces an additional layer of concern with government. That layer consists of free speech/free press issues and is usually identified by terms such as *law of the press* and *media law.* If the business is an *electronic* medium of communication, it faces yet a third layer of concern with government. This layer is usually labeled "regulation," is peculiar to the electronic media, and is central to the very existence of those media. Complicated and, to the novice, arcane, the importance of government regulation is often not fully comprehended even by students of free speech/free press issues.

In the present volume we sort out and explain that peculiar-to-electronic-media layer of regulation. It features a *content* or *horizontal* approach to the subject—that is, chapters focus on major regulatory areas or concerns that affect all electronic mass media. We feel that this is the most logical approach and provides for opportunity to discern contrasts and commonalities across media.

We wrote this book for two audiences—those hoping to go into, and those already working in, the electronic media. The second group includes everyone from the radio station general manager to the TV station news director to the cable system access channel supervisor. People in this group can utilize the book as a one-stop key to the plethora of rules and regulations, a logical presentation of what they are supposed to be doing and why they are supposed to do it.

With respect to the first audience, those involved in education for electronic media, this book aims to serve as the text for a one-term college course in law and regulation of electronic media at the graduate and undergraduate levels. For students in such courses it provides information needed to work and to make decisions in the electronic media, to understand legal rights and responsibilities as working professionals, and to understand the concepts and implications of electronic media regulation.

Instructors will find that the book adapts easily to most teaching situations. The first few chapters lay the groundwork—the structural, historical, and constitutional bases for regulation of public communication. The majority of the chapters deal with law and regulation that pertain specifically to radio and television—nature and composition of the Communications Act and other laws; makeup and operation of the Federal Communications Commission; structure of the various regulated media; criteria for and limitations on facility ownership; acquisition and retention of a radio or television facility; development and meaning of "the public interest"; requirements for political content and the once-and-future Fairness Doctrine; prescriptions and proscriptions on programming; and regulation of networks.

Some of these chapters are particularly rich in detail. We believe this feature to be especially useful in a classroom situation. Since the book explains the complexities of regulation, the instructor is free to devote class discussion time to those topics that so readily lend themselves to exploration, debate, and argument, the large issues out of which these complexities arise. One caveat: Please avoid rote memorization of details. Most persons in an academic setting would find the ability to recite the requirements of each of the classes of AM radio stations, for example, to be of little use; more important would be the fact that classifications exist, the rationale for their existence, and—in *general* terms—the manner in which those classifications are set up.

The last two chapters review general law-of-the-press topics, material often missing from radio-television regulation texts. Individual sections deal with defamation, privacy, copyright, obscenity, access to government information, shield laws, and free press/fair trial conflict. Many of the legal decisions in these areas come from cases that involve newspapers and magazines. Such cases are cited and fully explained. However, in drawing conclusions and stating principles based on those decisions, the language aims directly at radio and television; it tells the meaning of the decisions for persons who report with cameras and recorders, who edit film and videotape, who write scripts, who deal with moving pictures, rather than persons who report with pencils, who edit newspapers, who write print copy, or who deal with still pictures.

In this book the generic term *electronic media* (or sometimes *radio and television*) is used rather than the more restrictive *broadcasting*. The use is intentional. "Broadcasting," despite the more catholic earlier meanings of the term (to scatter over a large area; to spread; to inform many people) has come to denote specific forms of electronic mass media. The FCC has even provided an official definition: radio (i.e., over-the-air) communication intended for reception by the general public (which therefore excludes, for example, cable television). This book, however, deals with regulation of many different forms of radio and television. Certainly it focuses on broadcasting and cable. However, since the 1970s entire industries have formed based on new entertainment- and information-handling technologies. Consumers may choose from a multiplicity of services and devices that utilize such technology. Graduates of radio-TV academic programs seek jobs in these new fields. So, where relevant, the book will also discuss the legal aspects of such areas.

We have, each of us, both worked in the electronic media and, for years, taught the regulation course, and we have brought our experience from the workplace and the classroom to the authorship of this text. The book has been written to be understood. It describes and explains as completely and simply as possible. A straight narrative style is used, not a casebook approach. However, full legal citation is provided for each case, law, and regulation mentioned so that readers who wish to examine the full text may go to the proper page of the proper volume of the proper source quickly and easily. Legal and technical terms are defined as they occur in the text.

We extend our thanks to our excellent reviewers for their invaluable and thoughtful critique of our manuscript:

Sandra Braham, University of Illinois

Susan Brinson, Auburn University

Charles Clift, Ohio University

Bruce Drushel, Miami University

David Goff, University of Southern Mississippi

David Jaffe, University of Oklahoma

Jeremy Lipschultz, Univeristy of Nebraska, Omaha

Michael McGregor, Indiana University

Alan Richardson, Ball State University

Loy A. Singleton, University of Alabama

Thanks to Kathy Schurawich, communications editor, Longman Publishing, for her encouragement and positive reinforcement. Special thanks go to Bill F. Chamberlin, Joseph L. Brechner Eminent Scholar of Mass Communication at the University of Florida, for his oh-so-appreciated support, both moral and scholarly. The toughest road is made easier with good advice and good friends.

Finally, we would greatly appreciate feedback. People making their living in the electronic media, professors, students, anyone—we are interested in what you think about this book. Please let us know what you found to be good about it, what needs improvement, why you read it, how you used it. All comments and all suggestions are welcome and encouraged. Write to any or all of us at our respective institutions. Or drop us an E-mail note on the Internet. Either way, you'll hear from us.

Les Smith
(LESMITH@NERVM.NERDC.UFL.EDU)

Mike Meeske
(MEESKE@UCF1VM.CC.UCF.EDU)

John Wright
(JWRIGHT@JOU.UFL.EDU)

1

STRUCTURE OF LAW AND REGULATION

Born in the giddiness and prosperity of the 1920s, radio brought mass entertainment and mass confusion to the public's airwaves. At first radio was a novelty. But as audiences quickly grew, more and more entrepreneurs saw in radio the potential for profit. The number of applications for radio frequencies exploded. Manufacturers turned out receiving and transmitting equipment—but with no common standards. The novelty turned to chaos, and the federal government was forced to step in, first with the Radio Act of 1927 and then with the Communications Act of 1934.

From that time to the present, governmental bodies have formulated regulatory policies affecting almost every aspect of radio and television. Today the electronic media exist within a complicated matrix of law and regulation. This chapter begins an examination of that matrix.

The chapter begins with a review of the major sources of law in the United States, then discusses institutions that establish that law—the U.S. Constitution, the Congress, the court system, and administrative agencies. Relevant publications of governmental agencies and court decisions are identified, along with explanations and examples of citations to assist the reader in locating and researching documents relevant to the regulation of electronic media.

1.1   FOUR SOURCES OF LAW

Law and policy affecting the electronic media evolves from four primary sources—the Constitution, laws passed by Congress, the common law, and administrative law.

Legal scholars disagree as to the precise number and categorization of the sources of law. Four generally recognized sources—constitutional law, statutory law, common law, and administrative law—are particularly relevant to regulations affecting the electronic media. The U.S. Constitution grants powers to Congress, which writes statutes and delegates regulatory authority to the Federal Communications Commission and other administrative agencies. The courts review statutes and FCC policies and decisions to determine whether they are in the scope of authority delegated by Congress, whether they are arbitrary or capricious, and whether they are constitutional.

1.1.1 Constitutional Law

Constitutional law evolves as judges interpret the Constitution but is also impacted by actions of Congress and the executive branch of government.

Constitutional law is not easily defined. Of course, constitutional law evolves—directly or indirectly—from the actual content of the U.S. Constitution. Interpretations of the Constitution by the executive branch and Congress certainly contribute to the development of constitutional law. But most constitutional law is generated by the judicial branch, especially the Supreme Court, as judges make decisions and write opinions in attempts to interpret the meaning of the Constitution.

The power of judicial review, not expressly granted by the Constitution and somewhat controversial among legal scholars, has been practiced by the courts since the landmark decision *Marbury* v. *Madison*.[1] Judicial review gives the courts enormous interpretive power to declare any statute or action by a governmental agency null and void. Most electronic media cases in which judicial review is exercised involve the First Amendment. For example, in 1984 the Supreme Court struck down a portion of the Public Broadcasting Act of 1967 that prohibited editorializing by noncommercial broadcast stations if they received grants from the Corporation for Public Broadcasting,[2] holding that it violated the First Amendment.[3] The U.S. Constitution will be discussed in greater detail later in this chapter.

1.1.2 Statutory Law

Statutory law is that created by a legislative body.

Most laws affecting electronic media are federal laws. The most important legislation is the Communications Act of 1934. The 1934 act, which will be discussed in detail in Chapter 3, is the basis for electronic media regulatory policy.

---

[1] Cranch 137; 2 L. Ed. 60 (1803).
[2] 45 U.S.C. § 399, 95 Stat. 730 (1981).
[3] FCC v. League of Women Voters of Cal., 468 U.S. 364 (1984).

It created the Federal Communications Commission and provides the basis and authority on which all FCC policies are enacted. Congress has passed other laws specifically addressing the regulation of cable television,[4] children's programming on television,[5] and obscene or indecent speech.[6] The first of these two *amended* (changed; in this case added to) the original Communications Act; the third removed provisions from the Communications Act and transferred them to the Criminal Code.

Statutory law is recorded in codes and law books. For example, the Communications Act of 1934 can be found in Volume 47 while the Criminal Code is found in Volume 18 of the *United States Code*.

1.1.3   Common Law

Common law is created by judges as they render decisions on questions not covered by statutory law.

Common law, also called judge-made law or case law, is created by judges as they decide cases and write opinions. Common law can be distinguished from constitutional law in that it is based on custom and practice, not on judicial interpretations of constitutions. Also, there are no official codes for common law since it is not officially recorded as is statutory law.

Two terms must be defined before we go on with our explanation of common law. First, a *precedent* is a court decision on a question of law that gives authority (permission or power to act) or direction on how to decide a similar question of law in a later case with similar facts. Second, an *opinion* or *judicial opinion* is a judge's statement of the decision that judge has reached in a case. Now, with that in mind, we can say that common law is an accumulation of judicial precedent, typically formulated by consideration of a number of opinions. It can be found only in case books containing those opinions.

An important concept relevant to common law is that of *stare decisis*, a Latin term that means "let the decision stand." Once a decision is made, it establishes "precedent" for that court and lower courts that other judges, in theory, follow. Of course, a court may refuse to follow precedent. And, if no precedent exists on a particular question, the court may make a ruling that establishes new precedent. In most cases, courts either follow precedent or modify it to meet circumstances of a particular case.

Perhaps the best example of common law affecting mass media is the law of privacy, discussed in detail in EMG 15.2. Most privacy law, as is the case in all common law, is state law.

---

[4] Cable Television Consumer Protection and Competition Act of 1992, Pub. L. No. 102-385, 1992 S. 12, 106 Stat. 1460 (1992).

[5] Children's Television Act of 1990, Pub. L. No. 101-437, 1990 H.R. 1677, 104 Stat. 996 (1990).

[6] 618 U.S.C.A. § 1464.

1.1.4 Administrative Law

Administrative law consists of rules, policies, and regulations created by administrative agencies.

Administrative agencies are created by legislative bodies to formulate and enforce policies. For example, Congress passed the Communications Act of 1934, which created the Federal Communications Commission. The Communications Act also provides a legal framework for the regulation of wire and wireless interstate communication, but the FCC has the responsibility to formulate and enforce specific rules, policies, and regulations to carry out the intent of the act. The Federal Communications Commission has direct jurisdiction over interstate electromagnetic communication, and so the FCC's rules, policies, and regulations constitute the primary body of administrative law for such media as broadcasting, cable systems, long-distance telephone carriers, and communication satellites.

The FCC's personal attack rules are a good example of administrative law. The rules require broadcast stations to allow persons who are verbally attacked during any issue-oriented programming an opportunity to respond (see EMG 11.3.1). The rules do not appear in the Communications Act of 1934 and were promulgated solely by the FCC. The authority and role of administrative agencies in the regulation of electronic media will be discussed briefly in EMG 1.6; the FCC is the subject of Chapter 4; other administrative agencies impacting electronic media are discussed in Chapter 5.

1.2 UNITED STATES CONSTITUTION

The U.S. Constitution is the supreme law of the land. Ratified in 1788, it is the oldest written national constitution in the world and has served as the model for most others created since then.

1.2.1 Framework for Government

The U.S. Constitution establishes the framework for government and assigns powers to the various branches.

Our Constitution, an agreement between the people of the United States and those they select to govern, establishes our nation as a constitutional democracy and divides powers among the executive, judicial, and legislative branches of government. All actions on the part of the government must take place within the framework of this people/government agreement.

The Constitution serves as the primary basis on which all governmental actions—the making of statutes and administrative agency rules, regulations, and decisions—are scrutinized by the courts. If, in the opinion of the court, the action falls within the intent of that people/government agreement, the court rules the action constitutional; if not, the court rules it unconstitutional. In the 1969 *Red Lion* case, for example, the Supreme Court considered whether the FCC's personal attack rules were authorized by Congress and whether they violated the First Amendment. The rules were, on both counts, upheld.[7]

All 50 states also have written constitutions, but the federal Constitution takes precedence in the event of conflicts. Constitutions are not easily changed. It requires ratification by three-fourths of the states' legislatures to pass an amendment to the U.S. Constitution, and many state requirements are equally stringent. There are 26 amendments to the U.S. Constitution, but the first 10, the Bill of Rights, are often considered part of the original document. The Bill of Rights, originally proposed by James Madison as amendments to the main body of the Constitution, were approved by the very first Congress and ratified in 1791.[8] It could be said, therefore, that in over 200 years the Constitution has been amended only 16 times. Still, the Constitution has been significantly impacted by informal means, such as executive actions, legislative enactments, and judicial interpretations.

1.2.2 The First Amendment

The First Amendment to the U.S. Constitution sets forth the principles of freedom of the press and freedom of speech.

The intellectual and philosophical climate of the seventeenth and eighteenth centuries provided ideal conditions for the growth of faith in pure reason and natural rights. The individual was thought to be a rational being, one who could listen to all arguments, weigh their merits, and, through the power of reason, make an intelligent choice. Given the power to reason, continued this line of thought, the people needed no lawgiving absolute ruler; they could govern themselves. But if they were to govern themselves efficiently, they needed *access to the greatest possible flow of information and opinion*—to an uninhibited free *marketplace of ideas*.

Yet, when the U.S. Constitution emerged from the federal convention in 1787, it contained no declaration of natural rights. Such a clamor arose that 10 amendments were proposed and the famous *Bill of Rights* was ultimately added to the Constitution. Included was the First Amendment, which provides that "Congress shall make no law . . . abridging the freedom of speech, or of the press." The First Amendment survives today as a powerful protector of free speech.

Still, although the language of the First Amendment suggests that *no* law shall be passed, in reality Congress and state and local governments have passed numerous statutes restricting freedom of expression. Statutes have been passed, for example, to prohibit perjury, libelous speech, and advocacy of the violent overthrow of the U.S. government. The First Amendment offers some protection for broadcasters, but the Supreme Court has ruled that protection of the listening

---

[7] Red Lion Broadcasting Co. v. FCC, 395 U.S. 367 (1969).
[8] Edward L. Barrett, Jr., and William Cohen, *The Structure of Government* (Mineola, NY: Foundation, 1981) 17–24.

and viewing public is of greater concern. The First Amendment is discussed in greater detail in Chapter 2.

1.3   CONGRESS

Under the Constitution's commerce clause, Congress has the ultimate responsibility to regulate interstate electronic communications. In the Communications Act of 1934, Congress delegated broad regulatory powers to the Federal Communications Commission.

Article I, Section 8 of the Constitution describes the powers of Congress. Included are the powers to collect taxes, to provide for the general welfare of the United States, and to make all laws necessary and proper to execute the powers assigned. Also included is the commerce clause, which gives Congress the power to regulate interstate commerce. Early on, the U.S. Supreme Court ruled that Congress's power extends to all kinds of commercial dealings involving more than one state and to the formulation of rules to regulate those dealings.[9] Later, the Court ruled that the term *commerce* includes electronic communications[10] and that all radio communication is considered "interstate."[11]

Congress wrote the basic law of radio, but it also created an independent agency and delegated to it the authority to make specific rules and regulations. A federal court ruled in 1929 that Congress has the power to establish such an agency.[12] Five years later Congress passed the Communications Act, which created the present agency, the Federal Communications Commission. Since 1943, Congress has amended that Communications Act many times, and the FCC, acting under the authority delegated to it by Congress, has created, changed, and deleted a myriad of rules and regulations that have the force of law. The Communications Act as amended, together with the FCC's rules and regulations, account for the vast majority of regulations affecting radio, television, cable, and satellite communications. The Communications Act is discussed throughout the text, with a detailed discussion found in EMG 3.2.

1.4   STATE LAWS

Since the regulation of electronic media is largely a matter of federal jurisdiction, state laws have little impact on the regulatory process.

By far, most regulations affecting the electronic media are promulgated and enforced at the federal level. State and local authorities have passed legislation af-

---

[9] Gibbons v. Ogden, 9 Wheat. 1 (1824).
[10] Pensacola Tel. Co. v. Western Union Tel. Co., 96 U.S. 1 (1878).
[11] Federal Radio Comm'n v. Nelson Bros. Bond & Mortgage Co., 289 U.S. 266 (1933).
[12] General Electric v. Federal Radio Comm'n, 31 F.2d 630 (1929).

fecting business matters, advertising, and libel and privacy. But under the supremacy clause of the U.S. Constitution (Article VI, Section 2), any state regulation that conflicts with federal law, including rules and regulations of administrative agencies, is preempted.

In 1980, the state of Oklahoma determined that the state's ban on advertising of alcoholic beverages applied to cable television. This meant that Oklahoma cable operators would have to monitor programming originating from out of state and delete all wine commercials. The Supreme Court ruled that the Oklahoma ban conflicted with the FCC's authority to regulate cable and with federal copyright laws prohibiting cable operators from deleting commercials from distant signals.[13]

State law also affects the electronic media because ownership of media outlets falls under the province of state business and corporate laws. States and municipalities also tax businesses, and city zoning and safety ordinances affect location of studios, headends (EMG 6.7.1), and towers. Cable operators, dependent as they are on local franchising, are especially subject to city, county, and state regulation. A local government authority issues the franchise and adopts legislation that will govern cable operations within its jurisdiction. Some states have also adopted cable legislation, and a few have established cable television commissions or councils to ensure uniform franchising and regional planning.

1.5   JUDICIAL SYSTEM

The courts, as they settle disputes and interpret statutes and policies, have a profound effect on the regulation of electronic media.

There are 52 different court systems in the country, including the federal court system and one for each of the 50 states and the District of Columbia. Each system consists of trial courts and appellate courts. The trial courts are courts of *original jurisdiction.* This means that the trial courts are where the facts of a case are presented and the first decision is rendered. Appellate courts lack original jurisdiction. They may, if a trial court decision is appealed, review the law affecting the facts of the case but not the facts themselves. The primary task of the appellate courts is to determine whether the law has been properly applied in a particular decision.

1.5.1   State Courts

State courts typically have little impact on most issues relevant to the regulation of electronic media.

State court decisions can and do have an impact on matters related to libel and privacy, access to governmental records and proceedings, shield laws protecting reporters, and issues pertaining to the trial process itself. But for the most part,

---

[13] Capital Cities Cable v. Crisp, 467 U.S. 691 (1984).

BOX 1.1   The State Court Reporters

The nine state reporters and their abbreviations are listed below.

1. *Atlantic Reporter* (A. & A.2d)
2. *California Reporter* (Cal. Rptr.)
3. *New York Supplement* (N.Y.S. & N.Y.S.2d)
4. *North Eastern Reporter* (N.E. & N.E.2d)
5. *North Western Reporter* (N.W. & N.W.2d)
6. *Pacific Reporter* (P. & P.2d)
7. *Southern Reporter* (So. & So.2d)
8. *South Eastern Reporter* (S.E. & S.E.2d)
9. *South Western Reporter* (S.W. & S.W.2d)

---

issues pertaining to FCC regulations are beyond the jurisdiction of state courts. Not all state court decisions are reported, but those that are can be found in West's National Reporter System. The state reporters are listed in Box 1.1.

1.5.2   Federal Courts

At the federal level, the trial courts, or courts of original jurisdiction, are called federal district courts. The first level of appeal is to the U.S. Circuit Courts of Appeal, and the highest court is the U.S. Supreme Court.

These are not the only federal courts. And they are not the only courts in which individuals and businesses involved in the electronic media would ever find themselves party to a case. During the economic problems of the early 1990s, for example, many broadcast licensees became intimately acquainted with tax and bankruptcy courts. However, most decisions affecting the regulation of electronic media do come from the federal appeals courts and the U.S. Supreme Court.

Judges in the federal court system are appointed by the president and confirmed by the Senate. Once confirmed, judges are appointed for life.[14] The confirmation process is not always automatic. When Justice Lewis Powell retired from the Court in 1987, President Reagan nominated Robert Bork, a U.S. Appeals Court judge, to replace him. The Senate, in part because of concern over Bork's positions on civil rights and civil liberties, voted to deny confirmation.

1.5.2.1   U.S. District and Appeals Courts.
The majority of cases involving the electronic media originate in the FCC and not in federal district court. Exceptions include cases dealing with state and local regulations. For example, after the

---

[14] Appointed for life, that is, unless impeached and removed from office. However, only four federal judges have ever been impeached.

city of Miami passed an ordinance regulating indecent programming on cable television, a suit was filed in federal district court to have the ordinance struck down. Selected district court decisions are published in the *Federal Supplement* (cited as F. Supp), and the citation for the district court's decision in the Miami case, *Cruz* v. *Ferre,* is 571 F. Supp. 125 (1983).

The intermediate appellate courts are called the U.S. courts of appeals. There are 11 numbered appellate circuits, each representing a particular geographic region of the country. The twelfth circuit, the District of Columbia, hears a large number of cases involving electronic media.

Since the Supreme Court rejects most cases submitted for appeal, the courts of appeals are the last appeal for most litigants. Parties dissatisfied with decisions by the FCC commissioners appeal them to the U.S. court of appeals.

Each court of appeals has at least nine judges. Typically, three judges hear and vote on each case. Decisions in which *all* judges of a particular circuit will sit in on a case are called *en banc* decisions. Appellate judges, just like justices on the Supreme Court, write opinions to accompany decisions, including concurring and dissenting opinions (EMG 1.5.2.2). Appeals court decisions are published in the *Federal Reporter* (cited as F. and F.2d). The citation for the appeals court decision in the *Cruz* v. *Ferre* case mentioned above is 755 F.2d 1415 (1985).

1.5.2.2   U.S. Supreme Court

Most cases reach the Supreme Court on what is called a *writ of certiorari*. The Court agrees to hear a case only when at least four justices feel it has sufficient importance. The decision of the Court reflects the position taken by the greatest number of justices. Opinions are written statements by the justices explaining the legal bases on which they do or do not support the decision of the Court.

The Supreme Court has the power to exercise both appellate and original jurisdiction, but is principally an appellate court. There are three ways a case may reach the Supreme Court. The most rarely utilized method is by *certification.* This occurs when a lower court of appeals, not a litigant, refers a case upward to have particular questions of law answered. The entire record of the case may be referred up to the high court for a decision. The Supreme Court does not accept certification questions from trial courts.

The Supreme Court also rarely accepts cases on *direct appeal.* Although certain litigants have a statutory right to carry an appeal directly to the Supreme Court, most cases are rejected.

The vast majority of cases that reach the Supreme Court do so on a *writ of certiorari.* Litigants losing a lower court decision petition the Court for an appeal. A writ of certiorari is granted when at least four justices perceive the issues raised in the case to be of sufficient importance to merit consideration. Cases are accepted, for example, when at least four justices believe they involve fundamental constitutional questions that need to be resolved.

All other legal remedies must be exhausted before a writ of certiorari will even be considered. Still, fewer than 5 percent of petitions for a writ of certiorari are accepted. When a case is rejected by the Supreme Court the decision of the lower court is allowed to stand. This does not mean that the Supreme Court affirms or agrees with the lower court decision.

Once a case is accepted by the high court, the justices study legal briefs filed by the litigants and hear oral arguments. Justices retire to the privacy of chambers to discuss the case and reach a decision. No one is allowed to be present, not even clerks and secretaries. Once a decision is reached, the opinion or opinions must be written. If the chief justice votes with the majority, he or she writes the opinion or selects another justice to do so. When the chief votes with the minority, the majority associate justice with highest seniority selects the author.

A *majority opinion* is rendered when at least five justices agree with the decision *and* the opinion as it is written. The *Red Lion* decision was unanimous, with all voting justices joining in the opinion.[15] *Red Lion,* therefore, is a majority opinion. Often, however, justices write *concurring* and *dissenting* opinions. A concurring opinion is written when a justice agrees with the majority decision, but for reasons other than those stated in the written opinion. If fewer than five justices agree with the majority opinion, a *plurality* decision is rendered. Plurality decisions typically have much less precedential influence than majority opinions. For example, in the libel case *Rosenbloom* v. *Metromedia,* a 5–3 decision (see EMG 15.1.5.2), only three justices joined in Justice Brennan's opinion, with two writing concurring opinions, three dissenting, and one taking no part in the decision.[16] It is not too surprising that the *Rosenbloom* plurality decision was overturned just three years later.[17]

Sometimes Supreme Court decisions are issued by the Court as a whole rather than by individual justices. These *per curiam* decisions are drafted by majority justices and are published unsigned. Concurring and dissenting opinions sometimes accompany per curiam decisions.

It takes a long time for the Supreme Court to accept and fully dispose of a case. In the *Red Lion* case, the controversy resulted from a personal attack during a radio broadcast on November 27, 1964. The individual verbally attacked during the broadcast, author Fred Cook, promptly demanded an opportunity to respond. But the Supreme Court did not render a final decision, a decision that did allow Cook response time, until June 9, 1969. Cases often take significantly longer.

1.5.3   Legal Terms

Over the years, attorneys have developed their own jargon, a sort of pseudo-Latin, to refer to parties and procedures involved in legal proceedings. If you understand some of the more commonly used jargon words, you will be much better able to

---

[15] Justice Douglas did not hear the oral arguments in the case and took no part in the decision, thus the 8-0 vote. However, Douglas later spoke out strongly against the Fairness Doctrine. *See* CBS v. DNC, 412 U.S. 94 (1973).

[16] 403 U.S. 29 (1971).

[17] Gertz v. Welch, 418 U.S. 323 (1974).

pick up a legal decision and understand the opinion. What follows is a summary of some commonly used terms.

The party initiating a suit at the trial level is called the *plaintiff.* The action is brought against the *defendant.* If the case is appealed, the *petitioner* or *appellant* initiates the appeal against the *respondent* or *appellee.* The name listed first in a lawsuit is the party initiating the litigation.

Sometimes litigants' names are reversed as the case proceeds through the courts. For example, when Sheriff Thomas Houchins refused to allow television station KQED's reporters and cameras access to a California county jail, KQED appealed to the U.S. Court of Appeals. In *KQED* v. *Houchins,* KQED was the petitioner or appellant, Houchins the respondent or appellee. The appeals court held that KQED had a First Amendment right to enter the jail.[18] When Sheriff Houchins appealed the decision to the U.S. Supreme Court, the case became *Houchins* v. *KQED,* with Houchins the petitioner and KQED the respondent.[19] The Supreme Court reversed the lower court, holding that the First Amendment provides KQED no special right to gather news and that the news media have no greater right of access to the jail than the general public (EMG 16.1.1.2).

A few other terms are often used in lawsuits involving the media. A *tort* is a civil or private wrong—as opposed to a criminal wrong—committed against an individual. Tort law includes statutes protecting individuals from libelous statements and some forms of invasion of personal privacy.

Sometimes a plaintiff or defendant can file a motion for *summary judgment.* This is done when the pretrial discovery process reveals that the two sides virtually agree on the facts of the case so that the only issues left to resolve are matters of law that the court can decide. If summary judgment is granted the case does not go to trial. Sometimes the defendant will file a *demurrer* or a motion to dismiss. In so doing, the defense argues that even though the plaintiff's claims against the defendant are true, no legal wrong has occurred and the case should be dismissed.

Sometimes relevant information is submitted to the court in briefs filed by persons who are not parties of record in the case. These persons are called *amicus curiae.* In the *Red Lion* case amicus curiae briefs were filed by the American Civil Liberties Union and the Office of Communication of the United Church of Christ, an organization that will figure prominently in cases discussed later.

Several other legal terms are relevant to the study of electronic media and government. Federal appeals courts sometimes order a case back to a lower court or to the FCC on *remand.* When this occurs, the court is ordering the lower court or Commission to reconsider the case, usually regarding some specified issue.

If a completely new trial is granted by a judge it is sometimes referred to as a *trial de novo.* A decision made in a judge's chambers or in a courtroom with the public excluded is an *in camera* decision.

Statements made in a judge's opinion that are not essential or necessary to decide the case at hand are called *dicta,* or *obiter dicta.* One famous "dictum" was

[18] KQED v. Houchins, 546 F.2d 284 (1976).
[19] Houchins v. KQED, 438 U.S. 1 (1978).

advanced by Justice Powell in the landmark libel decision *Gertz* v. *Welch.*[20] Powell argued that "under the First Amendment there is no such thing as a false idea," interpreted to mean that statements of opinion would receive greater First Amendment protection than statements of fact. But the facts of the *Gertz* case did not even involve false assertions of opinion, so Powell's statement is considered an example of dicta. Any statements characterized as dicta do not have the same precedential power as those made as part of the actual opinion.

Finally, the *voir dire* is the process of interviewing and selecting jurors. The *venire* is a list of potential jurors for a case (or the jurors themselves), and a *venireman* is a person actually serving on a jury.

1.6   REGULATORY AGENCIES

Administrative agencies are granted considerable power in that they are authorized to perform executive, legislative, and judicial functions. The federal regulatory agencies, including the Federal Communications Commission and Federal Trade Commission, are examples of administrative agencies.

The hundreds of administrative agencies that operate at the state and federal levels function under statutory mandate. We are primarily concerned with regulatory agencies at the federal level.

Administrative agencies, and particularly regulatory agencies such as the FCC, are created to handle matters too complex, time consuming, and laborious for Congress or other governmental bodies to handle directly. They are, as mentioned in EMG 1.1.4, the source of administrative law. Gellhorn and Byse offer four reasons for the establishment of administrative agencies:

1. the need for special expertise in a particular area;
2. the need for specialization and continuity of regulation;
3. the desirability of regulation by a sympathetic administration;
4. the large number of cases litigated.[21]

Administrative agencies have the power to perform legislative, executive, and judicial functions. The administrative agency of greatest concern to this text is the Federal Communications Commission. Created by Congress in the Communications Act of 1934, the FCC's existence and purpose is discussed in much of this text and is the sole subject—concerning its structure, powers, and procedure—of Chapter 4. Other regulatory agencies such as the Federal Trade Commission and Securities and Exchange Commission are involved peripherally in the regulation of

---

[20] 418 U.S. 323 (1974).

[21] Walter Gellhorn and Clark Byse, *Administrative Law: Cases and Comments* (Mineola, NY: Foundation, 1974) 6–7.

electronic media. These other agencies, along with other nonregulatory agencies that impact the electronic media, are discussed in Chapter 5.

1.7 LEGAL RESEARCH AND THE ELECTRONIC MEDIA

Whether you want to read about a new statute passed by Congress, find the actual text of a court decision, or look up a new FCC policy, a number of valuable resources are readily available. Those resources range from government publications to computer services. A list of legal sources is provided in Box 1.2.

1.7.1 Researching Federal Statutes

To research federal statutes, begin with the *United States Code Annotated*. It provides the text of all statutes as well as the legislative history of the law and related court decisions. Other publications track bills as they make their way through committees, publish the names of committee members and their voting records, and provide summaries of entire legislative sessions.

All federal statutes can be located in the *United States Code* (U.S.C), which is actually a topical compilation of what is published in the *Statutes at Large*. A citation to the *U.S. Code* contains the number of the code title, the abbreviation for the code (U.S.C), the section of the statute, and the year of enactment. The term *title* is used here much as we normally use the word *chapter.* A title is merely a topical division of the code. You can find laws affecting the broadcast media, including the Communications Act of 1934, in Title 47 of the *U.S. Code.* For example, the code citation for broadcast licensing requirements is 47 U.S.C. § 307(c) (1982).

A citation to *Statutes at Large* contains the name of the act, the public law or chapter number, the volume number, the abbreviation (Stat.), the page on which the statute begins, and the year of enactment. The Communications Act is cited in *Statutes at Large* as Communication Act of 1934, 48 Stat. 1064 (1934).

Two unofficial or commercial versions of the code are also published. *The United States Code Annotated* (U.S.C.A.) publishes the text of all statutes, but it is the annotations that make *U.S.C.A.* perhaps the *best* place to research federal legislation. The annotations provide the legislative background of statutes, summaries of relevant court cases, and for selected cases, citations to law review articles or other sources of discussion about the statutes.

Citations to *U.S.C.A* include the number of the title and section number corresponding to the statute as it appears in the *U.S. Code.* The Communications Act would be cited as 47 U.S.C.A. § 151 et seq. (meaning section 151 and the following sections). The cover of *U.S.C.A.* contains "pocket parts," which are printed updates of statutes. *United States Code Service* (U.S.C.S.), the other unofficial publication, is similar to *U.S.C.A.* in content (including the annotations) and organization.

BOX 1.2   Sources for Researching Federal Statutes, Court Decisions, and Regulatory Matters

Sources for Federal Statutes

> *United States Code* (U.S.C.)
> *Statutes at Large*
> *United States Code Annotated* (U.S.C.A.)
> *United States Code Service* (U.S.C.S.)
> *United States Code Congressional and Administrative News* (U.S.C.C.A.N.)
> *Congressional Index*
> *United States Congressional Record*
> *Congressional Quarterly Almanac* (CQA)

Sources for Federal Court Decisions

> *United States Reports* (U.S.)
> *Supreme Court Reporter* (S. Ct.)
> *United States Supreme Court Reports, Lawyer's Edition* (L. Ed. or L. Ed. 2d)
> *Federal Reporter* (F. and F.2d)
> *Federal Supplement* (F. Supp.)
> *Media Law Reporter* (Media L. Rep.)
> *United States Law Week* (U.S.L.W.)
> *Shepard's Citations*

Sources for FCC and Other Regulatory Agency Rules and Decisions

> *Federal Communications Commission Reports* (F.C.C. and F.C.C.2d)
> *Federal Communications Commission Record* (F.C.C.R.)
> *Pike & Fischer's Radio Regulation* (Rad. Reg. and Rad. Reg. 2d)
> *Federal Register* (Fed. Reg.)
> *Federal Register Index*
> *CIS Federal Register Index*
> *Code of Federal Regulations* (C.F.R.)
> *List of CFR Sections Affected* (LSA)

Both unofficial versions of the code are printed much more quickly than the official version. *U.S.C.* runs as much as two years behind Congress. All three versions of the code consist of 50 subject titles.

The *United States Code Congressional and Administrative News* offers information on pending legislation, including the full text of bills enacted and the perspectives of various interest groups on the proposed statutes. Another excellent source of the status of current legislation is the *Congressional Index*, published by the Commerce Clearing House (CCH). This looseleaf service is supplemented weekly and includes notes on legislative history of statutes, the names of congressional committee members, and voting records. The *United States Congressional Record* publishes edited transcripts of congressional deliberations.

Finally, the *Congressional Quarterly Almanac*, published after each session, contains summaries of legislative developments, organized by subject matter. *CQA* is an excellent, permanent source of information on bills introduced during a particular session.

1.7.2   Finding Federal Court Decisions

The full text of federal court decisions affecting electronic media are published in what are called court reporters. There is at least one reporter for each federal court.

All decisions of the Supreme Court are reported in three court reporters. The official publication of the full text of a case is found in *United States Reports* (cited as U.S.). The *U.S. Reports* citation is considered the "proper" or "official" citation for a case. Unfortunately, *U.S. Reports* runs months behind in publishing decisions of the Court.[22]

There are two unofficial court reporters. The *Supreme Court Reporter* (cited as S. Ct.), a West Publishing Company series, contains the full official text of decisions as well as editorial features and headnotes that outline key aspects of the case. The *United States Supreme Court Reports, Lawyer's Edition,* is found in two series cited as L. Ed. and L. Ed. 2d., and presents the official text of each case along with editorial comments and headnotes. Additionally, for more important cases, annotations or brief interpretive summaries and essays on significant legal issues are included. The annotations are helpful in gaining quick insight into the significance of important cases. Both of the unofficial reporters publish Supreme Court decisions much more quickly than *U.S. Reports.*

A *parallel citation* for a case includes all three reporters. The parallel citation for the *Red Lion* case is Red Lion Broadcasting v. FCC, 395 U.S. 367, 89 S. Ct. 1794, 23 L. Ed. 2d 371 (1969). As you can see, the citation first provides the name of the litigants. Then, for each of the three reporters the citation provides, in this order, the volume number of the reporter, the name of the reporter (abbreviated), and the page number of the decision. The year of the decision is included last.

---

[22] Early versions of *U.S. Reports* were published under the names *Dallas, Cranch, Wheaton, Peters, Howard, Black,* and *Wallace.*

Media Law Reporter also publishes the text of some court decisions dealing with electronic media (and general media law). In fact, opinions are published more quickly in *Media Law Reporter* than in any of the other court reporters. A typical issue of *Media Law Reporter* will include other useful information including special reports and news notes on important issues. A citation for *Media Law Reporter* contains the volume number, the abbreviation Media L. Rep., and the page number. If a year appears with the citation it is the year the case was decided. The citation for the *Red Lion* case is 1 Media L. Rep. 2053 (1969).

United States Law Week (cited U.S.L.W.) publishes Supreme Court decisions as soon as they are handed down. Also, a review and analysis of the most important decisions of the week is included in the "Summary and Analysis" section of *U.S.L.W. U.S.L.W.* also publishes selected decisions of lower courts, administrative agency rulings, and congressional statutes. A citation for *U.S.L.W.* contains the volume number, the abbreviation (U.S.L.W.), the page number, and the year of the decision.

It is critical to know whether particular cases affecting electronic media have been cited in subsequent decisions and, if so, whether those decisions have affirmed or overturned policies or legal principles established in the original case. "Citators" allow the researcher to trace the history of a case and determine how and when subsequent courts have referred to the decision. Also, ascertaining the number of times a case has been cited indicates its precedential value. The most comprehensive citator series, published by McGraw-Hill, is called *Shepard's Citations*. The series includes citations for federal courts, courts of all 50 states, the federal and state constitutions, federal, state, and local statutes, and administrative agencies.

Generally, each series of *Shepard's* contains tables of cases. Beneath each case is a list of all subsequent decisions in which it is mentioned. Abbreviations indicate whether each of the later decisions have affirmed, modified, superseded, reversed, or vacated the original decision.[23]

1.7.3   Researching Federal Regulatory Agencies

Much like decisions of the Supreme Court, administrative agency policies, rules, and decisions can be found in a number of publications.

The first official publication of the Federal Communications Commission was called *Federal Communications Commission Reports* (F.C.C. and F.C.C.2d). It contains all FCC decisions, reports, and other actions through September 1986. Beginning October 1, 1986, *FCC Reports* was replaced by the *Federal Communications Commission Record* (F.C.C.R.). The *FCC Record* is issued every two weeks and publishes all FCC decisions, reports, public notices, and other documents.

Perhaps the best source for researching FCC activities is *Pike & Fischer's Radio Regulation* (Rad. Reg. and Rad. Reg. 2d). *Pike & Fischer* (P & F) is comprehensive,

---

[23] Effective use of *Shepard's Citations* would require additional reading. (For example, see *How to Use Shepard's Citations*, published by McGraw-Hill, Colorado Springs.)

BOX 1.3   How to Use *Pike & Fischer*

Pike & Fischer consists of three different sets of looseleaf binders entitled "Current Service," "Digests," and "Cases." "Current Service" consists of two "Finding Aids" volumes. The first contains the "Master Index" to all subject matter. The "Master Index" is a good starting point for researchers using *P & F.* FCC documents are indexed by *P & F's* own paragraph numbering system, which corresponds roughly, but not exactly, to sections of the 1934 Communications Act. It is important when using *P & F* to start with the "Master Index" to determine the correct paragraph number. The first "Finding Aids" volume also contains copies of all major forms used by the FCC. Volume 2 contains the text and legislative history of the Communications Act and a citator for cases found in *P & F.*

In addition to the "Finding Aids," "Current Service" also consists of "star" volumes so named because of differing numbers of stars appearing on the cover. The one-star volume includes statutes related to telecommunications law. Volumes with two through seven stars contain current versions of all FCC rules and proposed rules. Proposed rule changes are printed on green paper.

---

well indexed, and updated biweekly; it also has excellent cross-referencing with *FCC Reports* and the *Code of Federal Regulations. P & F* includes relevant court cases and statutes as well as all significant FCC actions. Despite its qualities, *P & F* can be intimidating and frustrating for the novice to use without guidance and patience. For those who want to try, Box 1.3 contains a discussion of how to use *Pike & Fischer.*

All federal agency rules and regulations, including those of the FCC, are published in the *Federal Register* (Fed. Reg.). The *Federal Register* publishes agency rulings every business day, in chronological order. Any ruling of any federal agency including the FCC must be published in the *Federal Register* before it becomes legally effective. Citations for the *Federal Register* include the volume number, the abbreviation (Fed. Reg.), the page number on which the document begins, and the year.

Federal Register Index is printed monthly and is organized by agency, not by subject. Most electronic media policies will, therefore, be indexed under the Federal Communications Commission. *CIS Federal Register Index* is published weekly by the Congressional Information Service. Subject matter is typically indexed within three weeks of appearing in the *Federal Register.*

Agency rulings can also be found in the *Code of Federal Regulations* (C.F.R.). The *C.F.R.* is a codification of all rules published in the *Federal Register*, organized by subject matter. The *C.F.R.* contains 50 titles. FCC rulings and policies are located in Title 47. Citations include the number of the title, the abbreviation (C.F.R.), and the section number of the document. The citation for the personal attack rules, 47

C.F.R. § 73.123, refers to Title 47, Section 73.123 of the *C.F.R.* The *List of CFR Sections Affected* (LSA) is published monthly to allow a researcher to determine if a particular rule or decision has been amended or affected in any way since its publication in the *Code of Federal Regulations.* Additionally, the last issue of each month of the *Federal Register* includes "CFR Parts Affected," which allows the researcher to check for recent changes.

1.8   COMPUTER-ASSISTED LEGAL RESEARCH

For the researcher so fortunate as to have access to a computerized database, the ability to conduct legal research is greatly enhanced.

Access to one of two computer-assisted services greatly facilitates the process of researching documents relevant to the regulation of electronic media. LEXIS and WESTLAW offer the researcher computerized access to court cases, administrative agency rulings including those of the FCC, and statutes. The two services are quite similar, one major difference being that WESTLAW offers editorial materials and the West Key Numbers and headnotes. Both services also allow the legal researcher computerized access to citators (EMG 1.7.2) in order to trace the history of a particular case and determine whether courts have subsequently affirmed or reversed decisions.

DISCUSSION QUESTIONS

1. What is common law and how is it formulated? What is the difference between common law and constitutional law?
2. To what source would you go to find out information about a federal statute?
3. Why do states play such a minor role in the regulation of electronic media?
4. What is a writ of certiorari? Under what circumstances is such a writ granted?
5. Distinguish between a majority and minority decision of the Supreme Court.
6. Compare and contrast the various sources one might use to find out about decisions of the Supreme Court.
7. What types of governmental power are exercised by administrative agencies?

SUGGESTED READINGS

Barrett, Edward L., Jr., and William Cohen. *Constitutional Law: The Structure of Government.* Mineola, NY: Foundation, 1981.

Bryner, Gary C. *Bureaucratic Discretion: Law and Policy in Federal Regulatory Agencies.* New York: Pergamon, 1987.

Commission on the Bicentennial of the United States Constitution. *The Bill of Rights and Beyond, 1791–1991.* Washington, DC: Commission, 1991.

Harris, Richard A., and Sidney M. Milkis. *The Politics of Regulatory Change: A Tale of Two Agencies.* New York: Oxford UP, 1989.

Jacobstein, J. Myron, and Roy M. Mersky. *Legal Research Illustrated: Abridgment of Fundamentals of Legal Research.* Mineola, NY: Foundation, 1987.

Leahy, James E. *The First Amendment, 1791–1991: Two Hundred Years of Freedom.* Jefferson, NC: McFarland, 1991.

Marshall, Burke, ed. *A Workable Government: The Constitution after 200 Years.* New York: Norton, 1987.

Shiffrin, Steven H., and Jesse H. Choper. *The First Amendment: Cases—Comments—Questions.* St. Paul: West, 1991.

Wren, Christopher G., and Jill Robinson Wren. *The Legal Research Manual: A Game Plan for Legal Research and Analysis.* 2d ed. Madison, WI: A-R Editions, 1986.

Chapter 2

ELECTRONIC MEDIA AND THE FIRST AMENDMENT

The First Amendment holds an exalted position in American political theory because it guarantees the right of free speech and press. The traditional view of the First Amendment is media oriented in that the press is viewed as a watchdog of government. The printed press, called the Fourth Estate, has long accepted its role. The broadcast media, the Fifth Estate, occupy a somewhat different position. Congress has specified that broadcast stations are entitled to First Amendment protection, but it is also clear that broadcast stations do not enjoy the same level of First Amendment protection as their print brethren. Broadcasters argue that they should enjoy the same level of constitutional protection to air programs as newspapers do to print stories. The emerging technologies raise even further questions. We will see these issues throughout the remaining chapters of this book, but first we will look at the emergence of First Amendment concerns and the theories used to apply the free press guarantees to the electronic media.

2.1 ORIGINS AND AUTHORITY

Much political thought in the United States has its roots in England, and that is certainly true of the concept of freedom of the press. In the 1400s, England, like much of Europe, was affected by the invention of the printing press and the subsequent spread of knowledge. Suddenly, the masses had access to information about economics and politics heretofore denied them. Once the English authorities, both the church and state, recognized the threat posed by the printed word, government censorship was instituted.

2.1.1   Prior Restraint in England

English authorities sought to restrict free expression that represented criticism of church or state.

Three forms of censorship were instituted: licensing, taxation, and seditious libel laws. Although these controls were used in different ways, and with differing levels of severity, they nevertheless represented illustrations of prior restraint (censorship imposed before publication) on the printed word.

2.1.1.1   Licensing

Under the licensing plan, printing was controlled by the government and printers had to have a government license to operate a printing press.

Once printing was introduced in England, it was quickly viewed as a state matter that was subject to control by the authorities. In 1530 a licensing plan was instituted, a plan that operated until 1697. Under the licensing plan, any published criticism of the church or government was subject to harsh penalties. To carry the plan further, anything published without a license violated the law.

Those who violated the licensing laws were taken before the infamous Court of the Star Chamber, a court that met behind closed doors to issue decrees and order punishments. The court could not issue the death penalty, but it did issue prison terms, fines, seizure of printing presses, and various physical abuses. The Star Chamber ceased operating in 1641, but Parliament set up a Board of Licensers to continue its policies against printers.

2.1.1.2   Taxation

A government stamp act required English publishers to pay taxes on printed material and to register their activities with the government.

The next form of control of the press was a stamp act, which Parliament passed in 1712. The act imposed a tax on newspapers, pamphlets, advertising, and even on the printing paper. This form of harassment impacted the press in two ways: it forced publishers to register with the government, thus making publishers easier to control, and made publishers pay for the right to print. Taxation continued until 1855.

2.1.1.3   Seditious Libel

Sedition or seditious libel was defined as printing criticism of those in authority. To publish criticism of the government was considered a crime against the state.

The last of the controls on the press made criticism of those in authority a crime. While sedition is technically not prior restraint because the punishment comes after publication, it is nevertheless considered a form of prior censorship, since the penalties were so severe that printers were frequently frightened into following the rules. It is unclear just when the crime of seditious libel was instituted, but the law remained in force until the 1840s.

2.1.1.4 *Easing of Prior Restraint*

Opposition to prior restraint increased as English citizens gained more freedom and as intellectuals spoke out against the repressive aspects of prior restraint.

During the English Civil War, debate began over whether prior restraint should continue. At that time, the poet John Milton added his views to the debate, and gave a preview of the modern view of truth being tested in a "marketplace of ideas." Milton wrote:

> And though all the winds of doctrine were let loose to play upon the earth, so Truth be in the field, we do injuriously by licensing and prohibiting to misdoubt her strength. Let her and Falsehood grapple; who ever knew Truth put to the worse in a free and open encounter?

Nevertheless, Milton and other philosophers were not ready to remove all controls on the press. John Locke in his 1689 *Letter Concerning Toleration* argued that government needed to be intolerant of opinions contrary to the moral rules necessary to preserve human society, but maintained that prior government censorship was not the proper form of punishment.

Thus, freedom of the press from licensing came to be recognized as a natural or common law right. The English jurist Sir William Blackstone summarized that view in a now famous passage:

> The liberty of the press is indeed essential to the nature of a free state; but this consists in laying no previous restraint upon publication, and not in freedom from censure for criminal matter when published. Every freeman has an undoubted right to lay what sentiments he pleases before the public; to forbid this is to destroy the freedom of the press; but if he publishes what is improper, mischievous, or illegal, he must take the consequences of his own temerity.[1]

2.2 FREE PRESS IN AMERICA

Licensing of printing presses was never a major policy in the American colonies, but stamp acts were imposed on printers, and seditious libel was considered a crime.

The American colonies did not require newspapers to be licensed, but some did permit government censorship. Stamp acts were also imposed on colonial print-

---

[1] William Blackstone, *Commentaries on the Laws of England,* Book 4 (London: Gifford, 1820), Sections 151–152.

ers, although they were vigorously opposed. Seditious libel laws were also enforced, but the famous trial of John Peter Zenger did much to change that. As publisher of the *New York Weekly Journal,* Zenger printed criticisms of Governor William Crosby. A grand jury refused to indict Zenger, but Crosby prevailed on the colony's attorney general to bring charges of seditious libel.

Zenger, who was defended by Alexander Hamilton, surprised the prosecution by admitting he had published the critical comments. This could have been construed as a plea of guilty, since the prosecution only had to show who had printed the comments, but Hamilton argued that truth should be a valid defense. The jury agreed that the comments were true and acquitted Zenger.

2.2.1   Birth of the First Amendment

Significant factors in the American approach to free expression were the Blackstonian doctrine that free press consists of no prior restraint but accountability for misdeeds after publication, and the trial of John Peter Zenger that established truth as a defense to seditious libel. The founding fathers viewed freedom of the press as important but did not explain how the press was to relate to government.

Certainly, the English experience played a major role in the political thinking of our founding fathers, who gave free press the preeminent position in the Bill of Rights. The all-important subject of free expression was protected in the First Amendment, which states: "Congress shall make no law . . . abridging the freedom of speech, or of the press. . . ."

There has been much debate about what the founding fathers meant by "freedom of the press." Neither the Articles of Confederation nor the Constitution defined the proper relationship between government and the press.[2] There is no official record of either the Constitutional Convention or the First Congress's committees, which met in secret and fashioned the first 10 amendments to the Constitution. Many believe that the term *freedom of the press* meant no prior restraint, but that viewpoint is not certain.

2.3   INTERPRETATIONS OF "FREE PRESS"

The Supreme Court which has the final word in interpreting the Constitution, has advanced several theories of what the founding fathers actually meant by freedom of the press.

Interpretations of what the founding fathers had in mind concerning freedom of the press have largely come from the U.S. Supreme Court, the final arbiter on the meaning of the Constitution. Four major definitions of freedom of expression have been advanced.

---

[2] Paul L. Murphy, "The Meaning of a Free Press," in *This Constitution—Our Enduring Legacy* (Washington, DC: Congressional Quarterly, 1968) 202.

2.3.1   Marketplace of Ideas

The marketplace of ideas theory holds that all ideas, good and bad, should be admitted to the marketplace. The people should be free to debate these ideas and determine which ideas are valid.

The marketplace concept was first enunciated by John Milton in 1644, but was more prominently the view of Supreme Court Justice Oliver Wendell Holmes, who served on the Court during and after World War I. The marketplace theory holds that the First Amendment provides protection so that ideas may freely enter the marketplace where the public can pick and choose. From this kind of competition, it is hoped that truth will emerge. Although little used after Holmes was on the Supreme Court, the theory was used to substantiate the decision in *Red Lion Broadcasting Co.* v. *Federal Communications Commission,* a decision that we will frequently refer to throughout this book.

2.3.2   Political Speech

Alexander Meiklejohn advanced the notion that political speech should be absolutely protected from government interference.

Professor Alexander Meiklejohn argued that political speech, as opposed to private speech, should be absolutely protected by the First Amendment. Meiklejohn felt that political speech included any speech related to the sciences, the arts, and morality—any speech that has something to do with the self-governing process.[3]

Although his ideas were criticized, Meiklejohn's concepts were visible in two prominent Supreme Court decisions. In the 1964 landmark libel case, *New York Times Co.* v. *Sullivan,* Justice William J. Brennan, Jr., in his majority opinion, stated that a libel suit against the newspaper had to be considered "against the background of a profound national commitment to the principle that debate on public issues should be uninhibited, robust and wide open."[4] In *Red Lion Broadcasting Co.* v. *FCC,* in 1969, a unanimous Supreme Court held that "the right of the people to receive suitable access to social, political, aesthetic, moral, and other ideas and experiences" could not be constitutionally abridged.[5]

2.3.3   Absolutism

The absolutist viewpoint argues that all forms of expression should be protected from government interference, absolutely.

---

[3] *See* Alexander Meiklejohn, *Political Freedom: The Constitutional Powers of the People* (New York: Harper, 1960), and "The First Amendment Is an Absolute," *Supreme Court Review* (1961) 245.

[4] 376 U.S. 254 (1964).

[5] 395 U.S. 367 (1969).

Another school of thought held that all expression, without exception, should be protected from government interference. This position was most vigorously advocated by two prominent members of the Supreme Court, Justices Hugo L. Black and William O. Douglas. Justice Black gave his view on First Amendment protection of the press in a separate opinion in the famous *Pentagon Papers* decision:

> Both the history and language of the First Amendment support the view that the press must be left free to publish news, whatever the source, without censorship, injunctions or prior restraints.[6]

Black and Douglas agreed that all ideas should be expressed, no matter how unpopular, unorthodox, repulsive, or offbeat. Apparently the absolutist view was too extreme, for it was never favored by the majority of the Supreme Court.

2.3.4 Access Theory

Access theory suggests that the First Amendment includes the right of the people to gain access to the communications media to present or broadcast their own viewpoints.

In the mid-1960s, a number of legal theorists became concerned that the diminishing number of daily newspapers, and the excessive cost of getting on a broadcast station, required a public access view of the First Amendment, one that emphasized the public's rights instead of the rights of media owners and operators. Jerome Barron, a major proponent of access, argued that media-imposed self-censorship threatens our free society more than government censorship. He believed that it was necessary to find a way to present diverse views and ideas. Since he blamed commercialism and monopoly control of the media for repressing diverse views, he argued for a right of access to be achieved through congressional statute confirmed by a "sympathetic court."[7]

Barron quoted Alexander Meiklejohn, whose view of access to the media was not that everyone should have access but that everything worth saying be said. Thus, Meiklejohn's view was of idea-oriented access, and not access conferred on any particular person or group.[8]

Barron's viewpoint received some support, but the Supreme Court rejected the idea when it was applied to newspapers.[9] However, access theory has been a major stimulus of broadcast regulation. As we will see in Chapters 11 and 12, the FCC has previously used access theory in both the Fairness Doctrine and in political broadcasting rules. The FCC's elimination of much of the Fairness Doctrine marked a weakening of the access idea in broadcast regulation, but two major access com-

---

[6] *See* New York Times v. United States, and United States v. Washington Post Co., 403 U.S. 714 (1971).
[7] Jerome Barron, "Access to the Press—A New First Amendment Right," 80 *Harv. L. Rev.* 1667 (1967).
[8] *Id.* at 1676; *see also* Meiklejohn at 25–28.
[9] *See* Miami Herald v. Tornillo, 418 U.S. 241 (1974).

ponents of the doctrine still exist, and the application of access theory to political broadcasting remains unchanged.

The four theories just described guide the courts in giving meaning to the First Amendment. One should remember that the First Amendment means what the Supreme Court says it means, so we will now see how the Supreme Court, and lower courts, have utilized tests to apply guarantees of free speech and press.

2.4   FIRST AMENDMENT TESTS

Since government interests often conflict with free speech rights, courts over the years have used a number of tests to help decide whether a particular law or policy restricting free speech violates the First Amendment.

To decide whether a particular type of speech—such as burning a draft card or choosing which television stations or programming services to carry on a cable system—is protected by the First Amendment, the courts have employed a number of tests. When the court applies a "test" it looks at the facts in a given case and applies a set of criteria or principles that constitute the test. Whether the court considers a particular act to be protected by the First Amendment may well depend on which test the court employs.

Despite the seemingly direct language of the First Amendment, an early test, the *bad tendency test,* provided almost no free speech protection at all. Under this test government could punish a speaker if the speech had "any" tendency to cause a substantive evil. If, for example, a speech by an anarchist had even a slight possibility of causing a disturbance, the speech was not protected. The bad tendency test was eventually ruled unconstitutionally vague and has not been used since the early twentieth century.

2.4.1   Clear and Present Danger

The clear and present danger test operated on the belief that the constitutional right of free expression should be waived in circumstances where the expression posed a threat to society.

The clear and present danger test provides more protection for communication because under this test the dangerous consequences are supposed to be *imminent and likely.* The test first appeared in Justice Oliver Wendell Holmes's opinion in *Schenck* v. *United States.*[10] In this case, two socialists were convicted of violating the Espionage Act of 1917 by distributing antidraft circulars during World War I. Holmes compared distributing the circulars to the kind of danger created by crying fire in a crowded theater. He said:

---

[10] 249 U.S. 47 (1919).

[I]n ordinary times the defendants in saying all that was said in the circular would have been within their constitutional rights. But the character of every act depends upon the circumstances in which it is done. The most stringent protection of free speech would not protect a man in falsely shouting fire in a theater and causing a panic. [The] question in every case is whether the words used are used in such circumstances . . . as to create a clear and present danger that they will bring about the substantive evils that Congress has a right to prevent.

Holmes's analogy was a dubious one, as there was never any evidence that even one recruit was influenced by the circulars.

In subsequent decisions, the Court has refined what it means by "clear and present danger." In *Abrams* v. *United States*,[11] immigrants were convicted of circulating leaflets criticizing the sending of troops to Russia as an attempt to thwart the Russian revolution. Interestingly, Justice Holmes dissented in this case, arguing that the leaflets presented no imminent danger:

It is only the present danger of immediate evil or an intent to bring it about that warrants Congress in setting a limit to the expression of opinion where private rights are not concerned. Congress certainly cannot forbid all effort to change the mind of the country. Now nobody can suppose that the surreptitious publishing of a silly leaflet by an unknown man, without more, would present any immediate danger. . . .

Still, as late as 1951, cases were being decided more or less on the basis of the reasoning of the majority in *Schenck* and *Abrams*. In *Dennis* v. *United States* several defendants were convicted of distributing communist literature.[12] The Court held that even though the danger was not imminent, "an attempt to overthrow the Government by force, even though doomed from the outset . . . is sufficient evil for Congress to prevent." Justice Douglas dissented, arguing that freedom of speech should be sacrificed only when the evil advocated is imminent.

Then, in 1957, the Supreme Court in *Yates* v. *United States* for the first time interpreted "clear and present danger" more literally and overturned a conspiracy conviction because the danger was too far removed.[13] And in 1969, the Court ruled that even speech by the Ku Klux Klan is protected unless it is "directed to inciting or producing imminent lawless action."[14] The notion of "incitement" or "producing imminent lawless action" has been referred to as the *Brandenburg* test, which is considered by some to be a new version of the clear and present danger test. As we will see in Chapter 12, the FCC has adopted the clear and present danger test in

---

[11] 250 U.S. 616 (1919).
[12] 341 U.S. 494 (1951).
[13] 354 U.S. 298 (1957).
[14] Brandenburg v. Ohio, 395 U.S. 444 (1969).

determining whether comment by political candidates can be removed from the airwaves.

2.4.2 Preferred Position

The preferred position rests on the assumption that when First Amendment rights are weighed against other rights, the First Amendment rights must be preferred.

This notion, which was widely used in the 1940s, holds that the First Amendment is preferred over other rights. In *Murdock* v. *Pennsylvania,* the Court stated that "freedom of press [and] speech . . . are in a preferred position."[15]

The essence of this concept is that the First Amendment is not a means to an end, but that free speech and press is the crucial ingredient in obtaining our other basic rights and liberties. Thus, when we balance rights, the First Amendment must be preferred.

The preferred position is especially important when legislation interferes with political freedoms, such as freedom of expression. The Supreme Court noted in one case that such legislation should not be presumed constitutional when it threatens a basic freedom. As a result, the government cannot restrict a preferred freedom such as free expression without showing a compelling need for the legislation to inhibit the freedom.[16]

The preferred position has not been widely accepted, although the First Amendment continues to enjoy a unique, although not preferred, position in constitutional matters. As we will see in Chapter 11, the FCC used the preferred position in justifying its decision to abolish the Fairness Doctrine.

2.4.3 Balancing Interests

When First Amendment rights conflict with other rights, such as property rights, then the rights must be balanced to decide which right will win out in a given situation.

The balancing of interests test has been most commonly used by the Supreme Court in deciding First Amendment issues since the 1950s. The notion here is that when other rights conflict with the First Amendment—for instance, property rights or right of privacy—speech and press interests must be balanced against personal and social interests.

The courts have used two approaches to balancing. In *ad hoc balancing* the courts use no single standard for judging First Amendment issues, but treat each case separately. Thus, the press might be free to report the departure of troops on a foreign mission for the United Nations, but the need for secrecy about a secret spy plane might take precedence over freedom of expression.

---

[15] 302 U.S. 105 (1943).
[16] United States v. Carolene Products, 304 U.S. 144 (1938).

In *definitional balancing* the courts establish the parameters of free expression before balancing the concerns in an individual case. For example, in libel cases brought by public figures, the Supreme Court has ruled that the public figure must prove actual malice in order to prevail.[17] The concept of actual malice defines the First Amendment interest in advance, so ad hoc balancing will not be used in such a case. Definitional balancing offers more predictability than ad hoc balancing, since the deciding standard is known in advance.

A number of balancing tests have been used by the courts, but two used in media cases are the *O'Brien* and *strict scrutiny* tests. The *O'Brien* test evolved from the case *United States* v. *O'Brien.*[18] David Paul O'Brien was convicted of burning his draft card on the steps of the South Boston, Massachusetts, courthouse in 1966. He appealed, claiming that the act was protected symbolic speech. In fact, he had stated publicly that the act was intended to influence others to adopt his antiwar beliefs. The Supreme Court used a three-part test to balance the government's interest in maintaining a draft with O'Brien's right to free speech.

The Court ruled that the statute under which he was convicted was constitutional because

1. it furthered an important or substantial government interest;
2. the government interest was unrelated to the suppression of free expression; and
3. the restrictions imposed were no greater than necessary to meet the governmental interest.

The courts have used the *O'Brien* test in cases involving the electronic media. The U.S. court of appeals applied the *O'Brien* test when, in 1986, the FCC passed rules requiring cable systems to carry certain local television signals.[19] The court held that the FCC's stated governmental interest of protecting local television stations was not substantial, and even if it was, the broadly drafted rules were an over-inclusive response to the problem.[20] In other words, the restrictions imposed on cable operators were greater than necessary to achieve the interest.

The strict scrutiny test is similar to *O'Brien* but involves two major steps. First, the government interest must be compelling, and second, that interest must be achieved in the least restrictive manner.

Of the two tests, it is easier for government, in justifying a restriction on free speech, to meet the criteria of *O'Brien,* since an "important" or "substantial" governmental interest can be established more easily than a "compelling" one. In *City of Los Angeles* v. *Preferred Communications* a U.S. district court divided issues in the case on the basis of whether they placed an incidental or nonincidental burden

---

[17] *See* New York Times v. Sullivan, 376 U.S. 254 (1964).
[18] 391 U.S. 367 (1968).
[19] 1 F.C.C.R. 864 (1986).
[20] Century Communications Corp. v. FCC, 835 F.2d 292 (1987).

on free speech of cable operators.[21] By "incidental," the court meant a burden that did not directly affront First Amendment rights. On the other hand, a nonincidental burden *directly* conflicted with First Amendment rights. In the *Preferred* case, if the burden was incidental, the court applied the *O'Brien* test. If nonincidental, the court used the strict scrutiny test.[22]

Limiting a franchise area to one cable operator was defined as an "incidental" burden. The court, using *O'Brien*, held that the limit did achieve a substantial governmental interest—the minimizing of disruption and visual blight in the city. But the restriction still failed the *O'Brien* test and was ruled unconstitutional because the court considered it more restrictive than necessary to achieve the interest.

In contrast, the city's requirement that local persons participate in ownership and operation of cable systems was defined as nonincidental, since it favors the speech of local persons over others. However, the court judged the government interest in promotion of local interests to be compelling, so the strict scrutiny test was passed and the requirement was held constitutional.[23]

2.5   ELECTRONIC MEDIA AND THE FIRST AMENDMENT

The courts have consistently held that while the First Amendment does protect broadcasters and cable operators, it is the rights of listeners and viewers that are of greater concern. Recent FCC policy statements and court decisions suggest a possible change in this philosophy.

Generally, broadcasters and cable operators have been afforded limited First Amendment rights by the courts. The courts have reasoned that since the amount of spectrum space is limited, government may impose restrictions on broadcasters' freedom of speech. The issue was directly addressed by the Supreme Court in *Red Lion Broadcasting* v. *FCC*. Red Lion Broadcasting, Inc., owner of station WGCB in Red Lion, Pennsylvania, was challenging the FCC's authority to enforce the personal attack rules mentioned earlier in this chapter. A primary basis of the challenge was that the rules violated broadcasters' First Amendment rights. The Supreme Court disagreed. The Court held that where there are substantially more individuals who want to broadcast than there are frequencies available, it is permissible to limit First Amendment rights:

Because of the scarcity of radio frequencies, the Government is permitted to put restraints on licensees . . . [i]t is the right of viewers and listeners, and not the broadcasters, which is paramount.[24]

---

[21] Preferred Communications v. City of Los Angeles, U.S. Dist. LEXIS 18383 (1989).
[22] 68 Rad. Reg. 2d (P & F) 121 (1990).
[23] This case was on remand from the U.S. Supreme Court, which had refused to address the First Amendment issues (*see* 476 U.S. 488 (1986)).
[24] Red Lion Broadcasting Co. v. FCC, 395 U.S. 367 (1969).

The decision affirmed what is called the "scarcity rationale" or the notion that placing limitations on broadcasters' First Amendment rights is legitimized by the fact that the number of frequencies to allocate is limited.

Recent decisions by the FCC and the courts have raised questions about the scarcity rationale and traditional limited concern for broadcasters' First Amendment rights. The FCC, in eliminating its Fairness Doctrine rules, concluded that with the multiplicity of voices in the modern marketplace, scarcity is no longer a sufficient justification for abridging broadcasters' First Amendment rights.[25] In what is referred to as the "TRAC II decision," a federal appeals court held that distinguishing print and broadcast media on the basis of scarcity represents a "distinction without a difference,"[26] and the Supreme Court has expressed a willingness to reexamine the entire scarcity rationale.[27] Scarcity as a rationale for the FCC's regulation of broadcasting in the public interest will be discussed in greater detail in Chapter 9.

Cable presents some different First Amendment considerations than broadcasting. In *Home Box Office* v. *FCC* the court of appeals scuttled cable pay-TV rules.[28] In the decision, the court held that the First Amendment theory set forth in *Red Lion* could not be applied directly to cable, since two primary elements of the theory—physical interference and scarcity requiring government regulation—were not present with cable. Traditional cable does not use the airwaves, so a scarce resource is not involved. Nevertheless, the court said that the absence of scarcity would not automatically leave cable free of regulation, and identified certain instances, such as time, place, and manner of speaking, where regulations could be imposed. Whether the *Red Lion* rationale will apply to wireless cable and other cable technologies is less clear.

As we will see in the remainder of this book, broadcasters and, to some extent, cablecasters are required to carry certain types of content but are prohibited from carrying others. Both cable and broadcast, for instance, must adhere to the equal time provisions of the law and must satisfy certain aspects of the Fairness Doctrine. On the other hand, neither broadcast stations nor cable can carry obscene content, and other provisions restrict carrying indecent material. The industry has argued in many court tests that such requirements interfere with the licensee's programming freedom.

DISCUSSION QUESTIONS

1. How do broadcast stations compare with the print media in enhancing public communication?
2. Cite contemporary topics that represent Meiklejohn's notion of political speech related to the sciences, the arts, and morality.

[25] Syracuse Peace Council, 2 F.C.C.R. 5043 (1987).
[26] Telecommunications Research and Action Ctr. v. FCC, 801 F.2d 501 (1986).
[27] FCC v. League of Women Voters of Cal., 468 U.S. 364 (1984).
[28] 567 F.2d 9 (D.C. Cir. 1977), *cert. denied*, 434 U.S. 829 (1977).

3. Apply the marketplace of ideas theory to broadcast programming that is offensive but not obscene.

4. Some believe that television is such a powerful means of communication that it should receive more extensive regulation than radio. How would this notion fit within First Amendment theory?

5. For what purpose do the courts use the *O'Brien* and strict scrutiny tests? How do the tests differ?

6. Explain the nature of the First Amendment protection afforded broadcasters.

SUGGESTED READINGS

Barnouw, Erik. *A History of Broadcasting in the United States.* 3 vols. New York: Oxford UP, 1966.

Barron, Jerome. "Access to the Press—A New First Amendment Right." *Harvard Law Review* 80 (1967): 1667.

Caristi, Dom. *Expanding Free Expression in the Marketplace.* New York: Quorum, 1992.

"Colonial Intentions and Current Realities of the First Amendment." *University of Pennsylvania Law Review* 125 (1977): 737–760.

Emerson, Thomas. *The System of Freedom of Expression.* New York: Random, 1970.

Levy, Leonard W. *Emergence of a Free Press.* New York: Oxford UP, 1985.

Meiklejohn, Alexander. *Political Freedom: The Constitutional Powers of the People.* New York: Harper, 1960.

Powe, Lucas A., Jr. *American Broadcasting and the First Amendment.* Berkeley: U of California P, 1987.

Shiffrin, Steven H., and Jesse H. Choper. *The First Amendment: Cases—Comments—Questions.* St. Paul: West, 1991.

Sterling, Christopher H., and John M. Kittross. *Stay Tuned: A Concise History of American Broadcasting.* Belmont, CA: Wadsworth, 1978.

Stevens, John D. *Shaping the First Amendment: The Development of Free Expression.* Beverly Hills, CA: Sage, 1982.

Chapter 3

ELECTRONIC MEDIA AND THE COMMUNICATIONS ACT

U.S. broadcast stations are highly regulated by the government. In fact, the only way to operate a station legally is to get a license from the government and to periodically get government permission to renew the license. This situation is much different from that of newspapers, magazines, and motion picture theaters. Theoretically, anyone can operate one of these businesses, and a license from the government is not needed. Cable has some similarity to broadcasting, since cable operators must obtain a franchise from the city or county in which they operate. Still, a cable system does not have to obtain a license from the federal government as do radio and television stations. Broadcast regulation is all the more paradoxical when one considers that our political system is based on concepts that give government little power to regulate communication. How is government regulation justified within this framework? How did government obtain its regulatory authority over the broadcast industry? The early history of electronic communication in the United States provides an explanation for this apparent contradiction.

3.1 DEVELOPMENT OF RADIO LAW

The earliest form of electronic communication was telegraphy, which was followed by wireless radio. Both forms of communication presented problems that required government action.

In the late 1800s electronic communication in the United States was limited to telegraphy. The nation was interconnected with a system of wires and was connected to Europe by the Atlantic cable. This system permitted messages to be sent in Morse code from one telegraph station to another.

Wireless signals came next. Guglielmo Marconi, an Italian inventor and businessman, saw that wireless could have practical applications. With the help of the British government, he sent wireless signals across the English Channel in 1899, and in 1901 he sent a signal across the Atlantic. A year later, transatlantic wireless messages were exchanged.

Marconi's efforts had several results. First, he demonstrated that wireless was more than a toy; in fact, it emerged as a rival to telegraph systems. Second, Marconi set up worldwide companies to promote the use of his wireless systems to the exclusion of competing systems. His goal was to lease complete systems that forced wireless users to adopt his system or be shut out of wireless. The first applications of wireless were ship-to-shore communication, and an example of Marconi's monopolization efforts occurred when Prince Henry of Prussia tried to send a wireless thank-you message to President Theodore Roosevelt after a U.S. visit. British Marconi refused to relay his message because it came from a German ship using German wireless equipment.

Germany hosted a convention on wireless in Berlin in 1903, but it failed to reach agreements on wireless problems because the Marconi company was uncooperative. In 1906, Germany hosted the first International Radiotelegraph Convention, which led to the signing of an agreement by 27 countries that wireless would be available in times of emergency at sea.

The United States did not ratify the 1906 agreement until 1912, but the convention did set the stage for U.S. legislation to adopt the agreement and promote cooperation among its maritime interests.

3.1.1   Wireless Ship Act of 1910

The Wireless Ship Act of 1910 was enacted to regulate telegraphy but represented the first effort by the U.S. government to regulate electronic communication.

The first concern for the regulation of wireless was humanitarian, to save lives at sea. By 1910 many ships leaving U.S. ports had wireless gear. As a result, Congress passed the Wireless Ship Act of 1910, which paved the way for maritime communication.[1] The act required all large passenger vessels to carry workable wireless equipment capable of exchanging messages at a distance of 100 miles and ordered ships to have a skilled operator on board. Supervision of the act was assigned to the secretary of commerce and labor. Even though the Wireless Ship Act represented the first step toward regulation of radio communication, it did not envision or provide for the regulation of pioneer radio stations that were to begin broadcasting in the next decade. Tragically, the act also failed to ratify the provisions of the 1906 International Radiotelegraph Convention.

A disastrous event changed that. In April of 1912 the new transatlantic cruise ship *Titanic* struck an iceberg in the North Atlantic. Another ship was only

---

[1] Pub. L. No. 61-262 (1910).

15 miles away when the doomed ship radioed "We've struck an iceberg. Sinking fast."[2] Unfortunately, 24-hour wireless watches were not required and the wireless operator of the other ship had gone off duty less than an hour before the disaster. Over 1,500 people died in the tragedy.

3.1.2   Radio Act of 1912

> The Radio Act of 1912 was the first comprehensive radio regulation enacted in the United States. It gave the secretary of commerce authority to issue radio licenses and to assign frequencies, but gave the secretary no power to deal with signal interference problems.

The *Titanic* disaster did serve to generate public interest in the proper use of radio facilities on ships at sea, and it did stimulate Congress to pass the Radio Act of 1912.[3] As part of the act, Congress finally adopted the recommendations of the Berlin Convention of 1906, which provided for the use of the international "SOS" signal and the prevention of unnecessary interference with distress signals.

Of more significance for our purposes, the Radio Act empowered the secretary of commerce and labor to issue station licenses to U.S. citizens and to specify the frequencies to be used by stations. Thus, the Radio Act of 1912 represented the first comprehensive piece of radio regulation in the United States.

Almost as soon as the Radio Act of 1912 was passed, a serious defect was exposed when the U.S. attorney general ruled that the Radio Act had given the secretary of commerce no general regulatory power.[4] Congress had authorized the secretary of commerce to issue licenses to U.S. citizens "upon application." It did not make any provisions under which the secretary could reject applications. Radio was experiencing limited use in 1912 and Congress apparently felt that everyone who applied for a license had a good reason for wanting one. The result was that Congress gave the secretary no grounds to reject applications. This meant that the Radio Act, which remained in effect for 15 years, throughout the basic technical and economic development of the radio industry, provided for little more than a registration process and gave the government only limited control over radio. The years between 1912 and 1920 showed rapid growth of radio use as well as regulatory issues not addressed in the Radio Act of 1912. As radio technology improved, the public was able to listen to simple crystal sets for dramatic events in the use of radio. No longer was radio broadcasting confined to dots and dashes of Morse code. Music and voice could be transmitted as well. One radio pioneer broadcast recorded music from the top of the Eiffel Tower in Paris to listeners below. He also went to New York and presented live broadcasts

---

[2] Erik Barnouw, *A Tower in Babel* (New York: Oxford UP, 1968) 77, vol. 1 of *A History of Broadcasting in the United States.*

[3] Pub. L. No. 62-238 (1912).

[4] 29 Op. Att'y Gen. 581 (1912).

of the Metropolitan Opera. Yet another person broadcast live from a bathysphere submerged in the ocean. Even though some of these broadcasts were "stunts," they did demonstrate the capability of radio to entertain and inform, and radio began to grip popular imagination. Eventually, full-fledged broadcast stations, much like those we know today, began operating in many parts of the country.

But, as radio gained in popularity, technical problems became evident, problems the secretary of commerce had no authority to solve. As the number of stations grew, interference problems developed, since no one could control the amount of power with which a station broadcast. One problem was that stations receiving interference from the signals of other stations simply boosted their power in an effort to drown out their competitors. Often the signal of neither station was suitable for audience satisfaction. When such a problem developed, one of the stations usually moved to another frequency, hoping to find one that would be free of interference.

Yet another problem was that station transmitters were portable. If operators received too much interference in one location, they simply moved to another, possibly creating interference problems for listeners there as well. By 1920, the airwaves were so chaotic, and the interference problem was so bad, that many wondered if radio could serve the public in any meaningful way.

Secretary of Commerce Herbert Hoover attempted to resolve some of the problems. In 1921, he assigned all radio stations to two channels in the belief that broadcast stations were similar to maritime operators. News and entertainment stations were assigned 833.3 kilocycles (kc) and stations broadcasting crop and weather information were assigned 618.6 kc. In theory, the small number of stations then broadcasting could share frequencies, but as more stations began operating, the use of the two frequencies only added to the interference problem.

It was soon evident that the number of stations and the manner in which they operated would have to be regulated. However, the only authority granted to the secretary of commerce by the Radio Act of 1912 was to award a license to every applicant. A court in 1923 ruled that the secretary had discretionary authority only to specify the frequencies stations used, but that did not solve the problems that existed.[5] A court decision in 1926 totally subverted the secretary's ability to regulate radio. A Chicago station, WJAZ, owned by the Zenith Radio Corporation, was licensed to share time with a Denver station, but operated on frequencies other than those approved by the secretary of commerce. Hoover brought suit against the station, but a court ruled in favor of WJAZ.[6] The U.S. attorney general subsequently issued an opinion stating that the secretary of commerce was without regulatory power. The secretary had to issue licenses when requested and could do little more.[7]

---

[5] Hoover v. Intercity Radio Co., 286 F. 1003, 1007 (1923).

[6] United States v. Zenith Radio Corp., 12 F.2d 614 (1926).

[7] 35 Op. Att'y Gen. 126, (1926).

3.1.3   Radio Act of 1927

A series of national radio conferences failed to resolve interference problems. As a result, Congress passed the Radio Act of 1927, which set the pattern for present radio regulation.

In the early 1920s, it became clear that the growth of radio would have to be controlled if the industry would benefit the American people. Secretary of Commerce Hoover had hopes that the broadcasters would be able to solve their own problems and organized a series of national radio conferences to bring broadcasters together.[8] Between 1922 and 1925, four conferences were held, but the radio operators could not agree to discipline themselves, and in fact, each conference only served to reinforce their desire for government control of radio. Recommendations from the radio conferences actually formed the basis of the congressional bill that developed as the Radio Act of 1927.

Attempts to get Congress to refine the Radio Act of 1912 had been proposed as early as 1923, but Congress was slow to act. Part of the delay can be attributed to the fact that radio broadcasting had not yet been defined in such a way that Congress could recognize it as a viable resource deserving of regulation. Following the *Zenith* decision, however, numerous stations began operation, and without guidelines for operation, it became impossible in many cities to receive a dependable signal. Clearly, something had to be done to preserve the value of radio broadcasting.

In February of 1927, a new radio act was passed. The Radio Act of 1927 not only acknowledged the existence of broadcasting, but it set the pattern for regulation that exists today.[9] Considering that radio then was strictly standard broadcasting or AM, the Radio Act of 1927 did much to provide a framework for the introduction of FM and TV, which were eventually incorporated into broadcast regulation. In this way, the events of 1922–1927 ended the period of uncertain radio development and paved the way for orderly growth of broadcasting.

3.1.3.1   Provisions of the Radio Act of 1927

Congress left some regulatory authority with the secretary of commerce but created the Federal Radio Commission to solve the problems of signal interference.

The Radio Act was characterized by a number of provisions that made it different from and, ultimately, more effective than previous legislative attempts to regulate wireless transmissions. Among the most important of these provisions were the following.

1. Congress expected that most of the regulatory authority would be assigned to the secretary of commerce, just as the Radio Act of 1912 had done. Nevertheless, a five-member Federal Radio Commission (FRC) was

---

[8] Edward F. Sarno, Jr., "The National Radio Conferences," 13 *J. Broadcasting* 189 (1969).
[9] Pub. L. No. 69-632 (1927).

established, with members appointed by the president and approved by the Senate. Initially, it was thought that the FRC would solve the interference problems that existed, and that their work was to be greatly reduced after the first year. The nature of the regulatory problems were more complex than envisioned, and the FRC was made permanent in 1929.

2. All stations were required to have a license, but the licenses were good only for a specified time. Initially, the FRC limited the licenses of existing stations to 60 days. During that time the FRC planned to resolve the most pressing interference. The license period was eventually set at three years.

3. The FRC was given control over a number of operating conditions, including times of operation, power, and frequency. The Commission was also given authority over network broadcasting, which had been set up in 1926. Stations were expected to operate in "the public interest, convenience, and necessity."

4. The secretary of commerce was authorized to establish qualifications for station operation, thus eliminating one of the major shortcomings of the Radio Act of 1912, which required the secretary to give a license to any U.S. citizen who applied for one. The secretary of commerce never actually carried out this provision, since a series of amendments kept the FRC in operation until 1934.

5. The FRC was given quasi-judicial powers to make investigations into the performance of licensees.

6. The act gave the federal government control over radio broadcasting as interstate commerce. The signals of some radio stations stay within the borders of a given state, raising the possibility that the states might have regulated radio communication as intrastate communication. However, Congress has the power to regulate interstate commerce, commerce involving more than one state. Since the signals of many broadcast stations cross state lines, it made sense to place radio under the uniform, federal standards of interstate commerce.

7. Radio was given First Amendment status, meaning that the government, specifically the FRC, was prohibited from censoring what broadcasters said on their stations.

8. Provisions prohibiting monopolization were instituted. Congress feared that the public would not be served if an individual broadcaster could dominate a number of licenses, so the FRC was assigned to enact antimonopoly provisions.

9. Broadcasting was recognized as a unique form of radio communication, distinct from common carriers, which are designed as radio or interstate wire communication facilities for hire. Telephone and telegraph are examples of common carriers.[10]

---

[10] Section 153(b) defines *radio communication* as any transmission by radio of intelligence. Section 153(0) then defines *broadcasting* as radio communication intended for reception by the general

The FRC began carrying out its duties early in 1927. Initial actions were designed to standardize procedures and to bring some of the problems under control. The standard broadcast (AM) band was set from 550 to 1,500 kc, and a 10-cycle separation was provided between stations. A general reallocation of frequencies was implemented, and portable stations were eliminated, but the FRC was slow to limit the total number of stations in operation. About 700 stations were on the air, causing interference in some cities, and serious interference at night when sky wave interference was a factor. The FRC failed to solve all the radio problems within the year it had been empowered to operate, so Congress renewed its authority at regular intervals until 1934, when all regulatory authority was vested in the Federal Communications Commission.

3.1.3.2 Challenges of Radio Act Provisions

The validity of the Radio Act of 1927 was soon tested when some of its provisions were challenged in the courts.

It is not surprising that regulation of the radio industry was challenged by existing radio operators. Radio stations had been on the air for some time, and now they had to meet the requirements brought by regulation.

One of the challenges was to the authority of the FRC to deny a license. An early goal of the FRC was to eliminate the problems of signal interference, and this meant challenging stations that were causing the problem. In some cases, those stations had to be shut down. The Supreme Court used these words to explain the power of the government to delete licenses:

> That the Congress had the power to give this authority to delete stations, in view of the limited radio facilities available and the confusion that would result from interferences, is not open to question. Those who operate broadcasting stations had no right superior to the exercise of this power of regulation. They necessarily made their investments and their contracts in the light of, and subject to, this paramount authority.[11]

But while the power of the government to revoke or delete licenses was affirmed, there was a question about the way in which the FRC carried out its actions. Even though broadcasters used the public airwaves, their stations were private property and station operators were entitled to due process of law in FRC actions.[12]

Another challenge was directed not at action by the Commission but inaction by the government. As more stations went on the air, existing stations sometimes asked the FRC to provide economic protection by refusing to grant licenses to new

---

public. Section 303(b), which defines common carriers, emphasizes the sender of the message. The emphasis on reception by the general public clearly distinguishes broadcasting from other forms of radio communication.

[11] FRC v. Nelson Bros. Bond & Mortgage Co., 289 U.S. 282 (1933).

[12] *See* Westinghouse Elec. and Mfg. Co. v. FRC, 47 F.2d 415 (1931).

stations. These requests were based on the grounds that there was not enough business in the community to sustain more than one station. Neither the Radio Act or Communications Act addressed the issue of competition, so the FRC was faced with the following question: In a broadcasting system primarily supported by advertising, which best serves the public interest—licensing as many stations as the spectrum would permit or licensing a smaller number of secure, economically protected stations? The Commission wrestled with the issue through the 1930s until the Supreme Court issued guidance in *FCC* v. *Sanders Brothers,* a landmark broadcast case:

> Plainly it is not the purpose of the Act to protect a licensee against competition but to protect the public. Congress intended to leave competition in the business of broadcasting where it found it, to permit a licensee who was not interfering electrically with other broadcasters to survive or succumb according to his ability to make his programs attractive to the public.[13]

A basic constitutional question was whether the federal government had jurisdiction over interstate commerce. Article I, Section 8 of the U.S. Constitution gave Congress the power to regulate interstate commerce, but the question was whether radio broadcasting qualified as being both interstate and commerce. Radio communication had to satisfy both requirements if it were to be placed under the federal control of the interstate commerce clause of the U.S. Constitution. These questions were answered as follows:

> It does not seem to be open to question that radio transmission and reception among the states are interstate commerce. To be sure it is a new species of commerce. Nothing visible and tangible is transported. There is not even a wire, over which "ideas, wishes, orders, and intelligence" are carried. . . . The joint action of the transmitter owned by one person and the receiver owned by another is essential to the result. But that result is the transmission of intelligence, ideas, and entertainment. It is intercourse, and that intercourse is commerce.[14]

One of the provisions of the Radio Act that was quickly challenged was the right of the FRC to act against stations in the "public interest, convenience, and necessity." This issue was of particular importance in the Brinkley[15] and Shuler[16] cases, two instances where the FRC deleted station licenses. Although these cases will be discussed in detail in EMG 9.2.1 and 9.2.2, it should be noted that the cases

---

[13] 309 U.S. 475 (1940).
[14] United States v. Am. Bond & Mortgage Co., 31 F.2d 454 (1929).
[15] KFKB Broadcasting v. FRC, 47 F.2d 671 (1931).
[16] Trinity Methodist Church, South v. FRC, 62 F.2d 850 (1932).

raised an important issue: Was the power to delete a license because of content used on the air a violation of First Amendment rights?

In both cases, the courts held that the Commission was not engaged in censorship when it considered *past* programming conduct in determining whether the public's interest, convenience, and necessity would be served by license renewal. This view has remained the prevailing position on the Commission's ability to judge the appropriateness of program content without censoring.

It could well be argued that the approach to First Amendment privileges in the Brinkley and Shuler cases skirts the rights of broadcasters to engage in free speech. Powe contends that radio programming was not given stronger First Amendment protection because it was treated as entertainment, as opposed to news, and thus not part of the exposition of ideas entitled to First Amendment protection.[17] Alexander Meiklejohn has argued that radio had no claim to the principles of freedom of speech because it was engaged in making money, not in "enlarging and enriching human communication."[18] Broadcasters have long maintained that radio and television should enjoy the same First Amendment protection as newspapers, which certainly exist to make money as well as to disseminate information. Nevertheless, the Brinkley and Shuler cases established the prevailing approach to broadcasting and the First Amendment.

3.2   COMMUNICATIONS ACT OF 1934

> Shortcomings in the Radio Act of 1927 led to passage of the Communications Act of 1934, the first comprehensive legislation to bring both wire and wireless regulation under a unified, federal jurisdiction.

Passage of the Radio Act of 1927 left some major problems unresolved, especially the division of authority over the various facets of communications. The FRC had been given a limited role, since the Department of Commerce maintained responsibilities concerning wireless communication. Wireless communication, primarily used for commercial purposes, had logically been assigned to the Department of Commerce in 1912. But radio broadcasting was aimed at public consumption, so it made little sense to have the government treat it as "commerce." Passage of the Radio Act of 1927 had complicated the arrangement further by requiring the FRC to guard the public's interest in broadcasting, focusing FRC efforts on radio. Added to the problem was the fact that the Interstate Commerce Commission, which had responsibility for interstate wire communication, had major problems dealing with transportation. As a result, the ICC had neither the time nor the expertise to deal with wire communication. It was clear that wireless and

---

[17] Lucas A. Powe, Jr., *American Broadcasting and the First Amendment* (Berkeley: U of California P, 1987) 28.

[18] Alexander Meiklejohn, *Political Freedom: The Constitutional Powers of the People* (New York: Harper, 1960) 25.

wire communication, both interstate and foreign, should be under a unified federal jurisdiction. Congress attempted to pass such legislation in 1929, but failed. Finally, in 1934, President Roosevelt sent Congress a recommendation for a single federal agency with broad authority over communications. The result was the Communications Act of 1934.

Much of the Radio Act of 1927 was retained in the Communications Act. However, sections for control of interstate and foreign wire communication were added, and the name of the Commission was changed to the Federal Communications Commission. In view of the added responsibilities, the number of commissioners was changed from three to five. Finally, broadcasting was completely removed from the Department of Commerce. Thus, the Communications Act produced a new, more comprehensive agency, one better suited to handle the growth of radio and related communication industries.

3.2.1   Assumptions behind the Act

Congress based the Radio Act of 1927 on a set of assumptions that formed the philosophical basis of broadcast regulation. This philosophy was carried forward to the Communications Act.

One of the problems with radio regulation prior to 1927 was that the nature of radio broadcasting had not been defined. The Radio Act of 1927 did that, using a set of key assumptions that served as the philosophical underpinnings of regulation. The assumptions, which were carried forth into the Communications Act of 1934, are:

1. *The radio waves belong to the people.* The electromagnetic spectrum is viewed as a natural resource of the nation, much like our national parks.
2. *Licensees must serve the public.* Uncontrolled private use of the spectrum could destroy its value, so no one is allowed to "own" a frequency; it can be used for private goals only if such use will serve the public.
3. *All of the public should receive benefits.* Because radio waves belong to the people, everyone should receive benefits from them.
4. *Not all applicants are eligible to receive a license.* There are a limited number of channels available in the spectrum. To ensure that the public will be served, only those applicants who qualify by meeting certain tests will be granted a license.
5. *Broadcasting has distinct features.* Congress was especially interested in distinguishing broadcasting from common carrier communication, which is radio or wire service available for hire. Common carriers, such as telephone and telegraph, provide important services to the public, and the government closely regulates both their rates and services. Although radio and TV stations are licensed by the government, they compete in

the marketplace for advertisers and audience, which common carriers do not do.

6. *Broadcast expression is protected by the First Amendment.* The First Amendment prohibits the government from engaging in prior restraint of broadcast expression, but special limitations are imposed on certain types of expression such as obscenity, which is prohibited. Thus, broadcast speech is protected by the Constitution, within special limitations imposed by the requirement that stations serve public needs and interests.

7. *The government maintains discretionary regulatory authority.* Congress recognized that certain regulatory powers were needed but that the Commission had to have flexibility to deal with unanticipated situations. The criteria for this discretion are the "public interest, convenience, and necessity."

8. *Governmental authority is not absolute.* The government must use due process in making decisions on broadcast matters, and decisions can be appealed to the courts.

These assumptions have stood the test of time and remain the philosophical framework for the regulation of broadcasting in the United States. They have been tested in the courts and found consistent with the Constitution.

The Communications Act has been modified many times. Looking back, it seems remarkable that Congress was able to enact such a workable federal law regulating broadcasting. Part of the reason is that both before and after passage of the Radio Act of 1927, bills were introduced to solve the problems of radio regulation. These bills did not pass, but they accomplished much work in addressing matters that were later incorporated into the Radio Act of 1927 and Communications Act of 1934. Credit must also be given to Congress for including the discretionary standard, "public interest, convenience, and necessity." This phrase, which was incorporated into the Communications Act, has given the Commission flexibility in dealing with unanticipated matters that would otherwise have been topics for Congress.

3.2.2 Purposes of the Act

The Communications Act provided for the regulation of wire and wireless communication but also justified the need for regulation.

Congress largely wrote the Communications Act in general terms, allowing the Commission to make specific applications in its rules and regulations. However, the purpose of the act is quite specific and is stated in Section 1 as follows:

For the purpose of regulating interstate and foreign commerce in communication by wire and radio so as to make available, so far as possible, to all the people of the United States a rapid, efficient Nation-wide, and world-wide wire and radio communication service with adequate facilities at reasonable charges, for the purpose of national defense, for the purpose of promoting safety of life and property through the use of wire and radio communication, and for the purpose of securing a more effective execution of this policy by centralizing authority heretofore granted by law to several agencies and by granting additional authority with respect to interstate and foreign commerce in wire and radio communication, there is hereby created a commission to be known as the "Federal Communications Commission," which shall . . . execute and enforce the provisions of this Act.

This is the charge Congress has given the Commission. It provides for many factors that affect our lives. Additional sections of the Communications Act will be covered in subsequent chapters.

3.2.3   Major Changes in the Act

The Communications Act, Title 47 of the United States Code, has evolved through the amendment process, greatly expanding government involvement in electronic mass media.

The Communications Act itself consists of seven major divisions called titles.[19] Title I defines the purpose of the act and specifies terms, organization, duties, and general powers of the Federal Communications Commission. Title II covers communications common carriers, that is, radio or interstate wire communications facilities for hire. Telephone and telegraph are both examples of common carriers. Title III deals with radio and is divided into four parts. Parts I and IV apply directly to our area of concern—(I) radio licensing and regulation in general (including sections that deal specifically with broadcasting); and (IV) special provisions pertaining to noncommercial educational stations. Parts II and III apply to uses of radio on ships and boats. Title IV includes procedural and administrative provisions. Title V prescribes penalties and forfeitures for violators of law or FCC regulation; Title VI covers cable communication; and Title VII deals with unauthorized reception of communication and the powers assigned the president in the event of war or national emergency. Title numbers conform to these groupings; for instance, sections dealing with radio are numbered in the 300s. Our primary focus is on the general provisions that established the Federal Communications Commission, the radio provisions, and certain provisions pertaining to administration and procedure.

Amendments to the Communications Act have allowed the act to deal with circumstances not anticipated in 1927 or 1934. For example, Congress passed the Communications Satellite Act in 1962, which created the Communications Satellite

---

[19] Within each title are numbered paragraphs called "sections" (for which the symbol is §). Section numbers are keyed to title numbers. For example, all sections in Title II are numbered in the 200s; all in Title III, 300s; and so on.

Corporation (Comsat), a private corporation to oversee the long-term commercial uses of communications satellites.[20]

Amendments to the Communications Act also made significant provisions in the development of noncommercial broadcasting. In 1962 Congress included the Educational Television Facilities Act and in 1967 the Public Broadcasting Act. The facilities act provided money for station construction and the broadcasting act provided the first direct appropriation for noncommercial programming and established the Corporation for Public Broadcasting.

Another amendment in 1962 was significant to the growth of television. The all-channel receiver bill added Section 303(s) to the Communications Act. The bill gave the FCC the authority to require that all television receivers sold in the United States be able to pick up both UHF and VHF television channels. This requirement was important to the growth of UHF.

In the 1980s Congress amended Title 47 to change the FCC itself and some of its rules. A 1981 amendment lengthened the license term for broadcast stations from three years to five for television and seven for radio. Another amendment opened the door that allowed public broadcast stations to run commercials on an experimental basis. A 1982 amendment changed the number of FCC commissioners, which had been seven since 1934, to five. Yet another amendment grew out of the *RKO* case (EMG 8.1.4), a major case involving transfer of licenses. The licenses of a number of RKO stations were not renewed, but Section 331 was added to the Communications Act. It required the FCC to renew the license of any VHF station willing to relocate to a state with no commercial stations. After RKO agreed to move WOR-TV from New York City to New Jersey, its license was renewed.[21]

The Communications Act has also been amended in response to the growth of cable. The nature of cable franchising (EMG 8.3) had created friction between cable system operators and the cities. Cities awarded franchises on a competitive basis and, according to cable operators, made exorbitant demands for facilities and payments. To win big-city franchises, would-be operators felt forced to promise fantastic systems. Their investment was long-range at best. Capital outlay was so large that profit depended on subscribers opting for extra-charge tiers, multiple pay channels, and expensive ancillary services. Additionally, cable systems in cities had problems with high rates of subscriber turnover (churn) and theft of service (piracy), both of which lowered earnings. Further, contended the cable operators, the cities used their rate-regulation power primarily to *refuse* cable system requests for needed increases in subscriber charges.

The cities, on the other hand, looked on operators as opportunists. Here were a bunch of outsiders (with maybe a few local people included to make it look good) requesting permission to use city easements and rights-of-way (the basis of a franchise) to lay cable. They would have a monopoly to *sell* TV signals—something citizens really did not need and could already get for free. With demands for municipal services outstripping city resources, cable operators should be happy to pro-

---

[20] 47 U.S.C.§§ 701–744.
[21] Multi-State Communications, Inc. v. FCC, 728 F.2d 1519 (1984).

vide some of those services and pay a franchise fee in exchange for an *exclusive* franchise.

The FCC had little authority to deal with franchising. Congress would have to address this problem directly.

After several years of attempts, the National Cable Television Association, the National League of Cities, and the U.S. Conference of Mayors agreed on legislation. Congress enacted this legislation as the Cable Communications Policy Act of 1984, its first comprehensive cable law. The 1984 act deregulated cable systems. It spelled out obligations of the cable operator to the local franchising authority, and it limited demands the authority could make on the operator. It also allowed cable operators to raise subscriber rates for basic service without first having to get permission from the franchising authority, it made denial of franchise renewal more difficult, and it limited the franchise fee that local authorities could charge cable operators. Dissatisfaction with the cable act developed over several issues. Many cable operators drastically increased subscriber rates, many cable networks (which were often owned in whole or in part by large cable operators) refused to make programming available to competing technologies such as home satellite and wireless cable services, and cable conglomerates began to acquire large numbers of local franchises. Complaints eventually led Congress to pass its second major comprehensive cable legislation, the Cable Television Consumer Protection and Competition Act of 1992. The 1992 act reregulated cable. Among other things, the act put local franchising authorities back in the rate regulation business, ensured that programming would be available for competing technologies, and instructed the FCC to set limits on various forms of cable ownership.

3.3   RATIONALE FOR BROADCAST REGULATION

Five elements emerge out of the Radio and Communications Acts to justify the coexistence of First Amendment stipulations, extensive regulation of the broadcast medium, and licensing.

At the outset of this chapter we noted the rather contradictory circumstances of the broadcast medium—licensing, government regulation, yet First Amendment rights. We conclude the chapter with five concepts that are used to justify regulation, concepts that will appear at various points throughout the book. These concepts summarize some of the ideas from the two previous chapters and represent the most crucial ideas used to justify broadcast regulation.

1. *Public "Ownership" Concept.* As we noted previously, the philosophy of broadcast regulation begins with the notion that the public "owns" the airwaves. In turn, public ownership gives the public a voice in how this valuable resource will be used.
2. *Trustee or Proxy Concept.* A licensee is only a trustee for the public in that a public frequency cannot be owned. Since the First Amendment

permits the government to require certain things of a licensee, such as providing benefits to the public, the licensee functions as the public's proxy. This notion is the essence of the *Red Lion* case that will be discussed at various points.

3. *Scarcity Concept.* Not only are the airwaves a publicly owned resource, but there are not enough of them for all who might want to use one. This *scarcity* justifies regulation of radio and television, but the development of cable and other technologies is raising questions about the validity of the concept.

4. *Media Uniqueness Concept.* Broadcast messages are distinct from print messages, since they travel through the air. Once a consumer turns on a radio or TV receiver, that person becomes a "captive" listener or viewer who does not make as many deliberate decisions, such as selecting stories or pages, as a user of the print medium. It can be argued that turning a set on and off, or changing stations, are deliberate decisions similar to those made by the print medium user. Nevertheless, the theory holds that the user of the electronic medium is more of a captive of the medium than the print user.

5. *Pervasiveness Concept.* Not only are listeners or viewers "captives" of the electronic media, but the reach of the electronic media outlets makes them impossible to avoid. Every corner of the nation has access to a certain number of stations, and consumers can supplement that number with cable or home satellites to obtain even more outlets. The electronic media reach us wherever we go, and thus the potential for impact is great.

DISCUSSION QUESTIONS

1. According to the philosophy of broadcast regulation, the public should receive benefits from the operation of radio and television stations. What kinds of benefits do we receive?

2. The Radio Act of 1927 solidified the licensing of broadcast stations by the government. How important is licensing now? Are licensing laws still needed?

3. Radio broadcasts by "shock jocks" have led to substantial fines by the FCC. Do these fines interfere with the announcers' right of free speech? With that of the stations?

4. The philosophy of broadcast regulation states that a licensee cannot own a frequency. Is this just rhetoric or does the provision really alter the way broadcasters operate their stations?

5. The Communications Act states that not everyone is eligible to receive a broadcast license. Who should not qualify?

6. Is the media uniqueness concept valid? Analyze it.

7. Analyze the electronic media since 1950. What media developments would refute the notion of scarcity?

SUGGESTED READINGS

Archer, Gleason L. *History of Radio: To 1926*. New York: American, 1938.

Barnouw, Erik. *The Golden Web*. New York: Oxford UP, 1968. Vol. 2 of *A History of Broadcasting in the United States*. 3 vols.

Barnouw, Erik. *The Image Empire*. New York: Oxford UP, 1970. Vol. 3 of *A History of Broadcasting in the United States*. 3 vols.

Barnouw, Erik. *A Tower in Babel*. New York: Oxford UP, 1966. Vol. 1 of *A History of Broadcasting in the United States*. 3 vols.

Hilliard, Robert L., and Michael C. Keith. *The Broadcast Century: A Biography of American Broadcasting*. Boston: Focal, 1992.

Kahn, Frank J., ed. *Documents in American Broadcasting*. 4th ed. Englewood Cliffs, NJ: Prentice, 1984.

Sarno, Edward F., Jr. "The National Radio Conferences." *Journal of Broadcasting* 18 (1969): 189.

Sterling, Christopher H., and John M. Kittross. *Stay Tuned: A Concise History of American Broadcasting*. 2d ed. Belmont, CA: Wadsworth, 1990.

Chapter 4

FEDERAL COMMUNICATIONS COMMISSION

The Federal Communications Commission is an independent regulatory agency created by the Communications Act and charged with carrying out the intent of Congress as stated in that act. The agency consists of five commissioners assisted by a staff.

As we mentioned in the previous chapter, Congress derives its power to regulate wireless and interstate wire communications from Article I, Section 8 of the Constitution of the United States. Congress, of course, has other responsibilities and cannot devote its attention to such regulation on a day-to-day basis. Therefore, when Congress wrote the Communications Act, it did so for the most part in broad-brush strokes. This 1934 statute provided a framework for regulation, an indication of the manner in which Congress intended the regulated communications services to operate under law. At the same time, the statute created an agency to carry out the intent of Congress. That agency is the Federal Communications Commission, the FCC.[1]

The FCC was to build on the legal framework of the act in order to complete the regulatory structure. Of course the regulatory process is never really completed. Interstate wire and wireless communication change rapidly, and the regulatory mechanisms must change also. The FCC adds, deletes, and changes policies and rules continuously.

The FCC is one of a number of *independent regulatory agencies* created by Congress. It is independent because, although its members are appointed by the president, it does not fall under the executive branch (the Food and Drug Administration, for example, is *not* an independent agency because it answers ultimately to

---

[1] 47 U.S.C. § 151.

FIGURE 4.1 FCC organization
SOURCE: FCC.

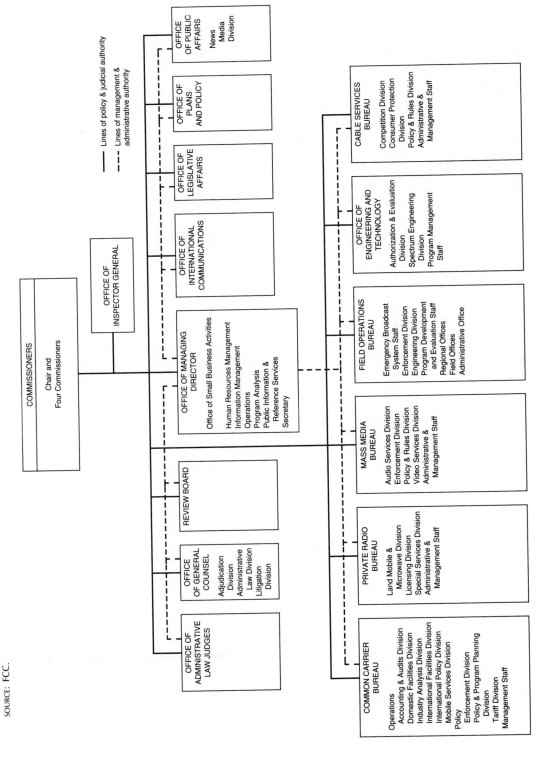

the secretary of Health and Human Services). Although independent, the FCC and its sister agencies are also *creatures of Congress*; that is, Congress passed the laws that created the agencies, and Congress can amend those laws to radically alter or even abolish the agencies.

Congress put most provisions pertaining to the nature and functioning of the FCC into Sections 4 and 5 of the Communications Act.[2] The act specifies that the FCC consists of five commissioners.[3] The act also allows the Commission to hire a professional staff to which it may delegate many of its functions. Thus, as shown in Figure 4.1, the FCC consists of five members who set policy within the parameters of the Communications Act and a staff that carries out that policy.

4.1 COMMISSIONERS

The president of the United States appoints the five commissioners with the advice and consent of the Senate. Commissioners must be citizens and have no financial interest in any industry the Commission regulates. No more than three commissioners may belong to the same political party. The act sets Commission terms of five years, staggered so that one ends each year, and fixes those terms. The president designates one commissioner to chair the FCC.

The phrase, "with the advice and consent of the Senate," means that the U.S. Senate is involved in the appointment process in at least two ways. First, when a vacancy occurs on the Commission, various individual senators recommend to the president names of people those senators would like to see appointed to the vacant FCC seat. Second, once the president has made the appointment, the Senate votes on whether to confirm that appointment. The formal confirmation process begins when the Senate Committee on Interstate Commerce holds a hearing on the appointment. At the hearing, the senators listen to testimony from the appointee and from any other interested parties, most often supporters of the appointee. The committee then votes on whether to recommend confirmation and sends its recommendation to the full Senate. The Senate's vote, in turn, usually follows the recommendation of the committee.

The ban against commissioners holding financial interest in regulated businesses is not really as hard and fast a prohibition as might be assumed. For example, an individual who holds shares of stock in a common carrier or in a corporate cable operator and who is appointed to the Commission does not have to sell off the stock to meet the letter of the law. Instead, the appointee is allowed to place that stock in a *blind trust*.[4] Supposedly, such an arrangement avoids

---

[2] 47 U.S.C. §§ 154, 155.

[3] Reduced from the original (1934) number of seven commissioners in the "Omnibus Budget Reconciliation Act of 1982," approved Sept. 8, 1982, effective July 1, 1983, 96 Stat. 763, H501.

[4] A *trust* is a formal and contractual arrangement by which money and investments are transferred to one person (the *trustee*) for the benefit of another (the *beneficiary*). In a *blind trust*, a public official is both *settlor* (the person who sets up the trust by providing the financial investments) and beneficiary;

conflict of interest. Critics, however, deny that. After all, the FCC must often make decisions on matters that affect the earnings or the value of stock of the regulated industries; a decision favorable to a particular company will often increase the value of investment in that company. Even with the stock in a blind trust, the increase in value will benefit the beneficiary. And if the beneficiary is an FCC commissioner, how could such a situation help but influence the commissioner's vote on the matter?

With respect to the three-to-a-party limitation, it is tempting to assume the reciprocal; that is, if there are three Republican commissioners, then the other two must be Democrats. But that is not so. In that particular case, the remaining commissioners could be anything *other* than registered Republicans. Rarely, however, are appointees anything but Democrats or Republicans; by 1993, during the FCC's nearly six decades of existence, 62 of the total 64 persons who had served as commissioners were registered with one or the other of the two major political parties; the other 2 were independents.[5]

Despite the three-to-a-party limitation, the president usually tries to appoint people to the Commission that reflect the administration's political philosophy and agenda. Thus, given enough commissioner resignations and expired terms, a Republican president might make appointments to the FCC so that its membership included (in addition to three Republicans) a Democrat who had supported the president in the last election and an independent who had, over the years, consistently voted Republican and espoused Republican causes.

Since the law stipulates *fixed terms*, it is entirely possible that a newly appointed commissioner may not serve a full five years. For example, if one individual leaves the Commission three years into a term, the president appoints the replacement for the remaining two years. When that term expires, the president then has the option to reappoint the replacement commissioner or to appoint someone else to the full term.

Each commissioner may choose a small personal staff, generally including secretarial and some combination of legal, engineering, and economics personnel. The Communications Act specifies that those personal staff people are not covered by civil service law; when the commissioner leaves, so does the staff—unless, of course, there is a vacancy for which they are qualified in the agency or on another commissioner's staff.

The individual designated by the president to chair the Commission gets a larger personal staff, presides at meetings of the commissioners, serves as chief executive of the Commission, and represents the FCC before Congress and other agencies and groups. In the event this individual leaves the Commission or will not or cannot serve, the other four commissioners may delegate one of themselves

---

the trustee controls the investments without the beneficiary's knowledge of how the affairs are being administered.

[5] The two independents were Ewell K. Jett, who served 1944–1947 and was interim chair in 1944, and Edward M. Webster, who served 1947–1956. Federal Communications Commission, *57th Annual Report Fiscal Year 1991* (Washington, DC: GPO, 1992) 3–4.

to chair the Commission, on a temporary basis, until the chair can be filled permanently.

4.1.1   Meetings and Business

The Communications Act requires that the Commission conduct its business in meetings and that it meet at least once a month at its Washington, D.C., headquarters. Three commissioners constitute a quorum. The Commission must submit a report to Congress every year and must request congressional reauthorization every two years.

The monthly meeting requirement is a minimum. Normally, the Commission meets once a week. The Commission may also hold special sessions in any part of the United States. When the need arises, the Commission can also take action between meetings "by circulation," which means that a document is submitted to each commissioner for approval.[6]

The Commission's annual report to Congress takes the form of a booklet published by the U.S. Government Printing Office. The law requires that the annual report contain general information of value in the regulation of interstate communication, a summary of FCC activities, an accounting of funds received and expended, and suggestions for legislation, including requests for appropriations.

In 1981, Congress changed the status of the FCC from a permanent agency to one that must be reauthorized every two years.[7] For the 47 years prior to that change, the Commission had to go before the appropriations committees of the House and Senate to support its request for funds to operate. With the change in status, the Commission must also go before the two commerce committees every other year to justify its very existence. The committees, then, recommend continuation to their respective chambers who, in turn, vote approval. Negative action, failure to act, delayed action—any of these could shut down the FCC, at least temporarily.

4.1.2   Responsibilities

The FCC summarizes its area of regulatory responsibility to include interstate and international communications by radio, television, wire, satellite, and cable. Its jurisdiction covers the 50 states and territories, the District of Columbia, and U.S. possessions[8] but not U.S. government communications.

Interstate wire communication includes physical conduits for electronic communication channels that cross state lines. The FCC would thus regulate, for example, a communications company whose telephone and telegraph wires cross from

---

[6] 47 C.F.R. § 0.5(d).

[7] 95 Stat. 738.

[8] FCC, *57th Annual Report* 5.

Georgia into Alabama, or a company that operates a multistate fiber optic network. The FCC would *not* regulate a local telephone company whose service area is completely within the boundaries of one state (*intrastate*); such a company would be regulated by the appropriate agency of the state in which it operates, typically a state public utilities commission.

The situation is different with respect to local cable systems, however. State and local governments are responsible for franchising and other areas of control, but a cable system—despite the fact that it crosses no state lines—is still subject to FCC regulatory authority in *certain* areas. Congress wrote this into law when it amended the Communications Act by passing the Cable Communications Policy Act of 1984 and the Cable Television Consumer Protection and Competition Act of 1992.[9]

Wireless communication occurs when someone operates a device that generates and emits radio waves. All such transmissions, no matter how low-power or short-range, are considered interstate by nature. Some examples of wireless communication include radio and television *broadcast* transmitters, radio amateur stations, communications satellites, cellular telephones, and two-way radios used by private firms and by state and local public safety departments. The FCC has classified wireless communications by use and, because they all transmit on the radio frequencies, refers to them collectively as the *radio services*.[10]

However, the FCC's authority also extends to noncommunication uses of radio frequencies. Any device that emits radio frequencies has the potential to interfere with other such devices. So the FCC must approve the design and manufacture not only of broadcast transmitters, microwave relay stations, cellular telephones, and satellite transponders but also of noncommunication emitters such as garage door openers, radio-controlled toys, personal computers, and certain medical equipment such as diathermy machines.

The FCC is concerned with *international* wired and wireless communications in several respects. It regulates those transmitted from within the United States but intended for reception in other countries. It regulates those originated in the United States but transmitted over communications facilities in other countries. And it regulates to ensure that U.S. communications facilities are operated in compliance with the various international agreements and treaties to which the United States is a party.

The FCC regulates users—the people or companies who control the communications channels—whether those channels are wired, wireless, or a mixture of the two. It does not regulate, for the most part, the customers of those users. Thus, the

---

[9] In this book, the term *station* refers to the originating point for wireless transmissions. Thus a *broadcast station* uses radio frequencies to transmit material intended for reception by the general public. A cable television facility is a *cable system*; its primary originating point is a *headend*; and its various programming services are *channels* or *services*. You may hear the term *cable station*, but technically there is no such thing. A TV superstation, for example, is simply a broadcast station whose programming has been picked up by and distributed to satellite receivers nationwide. A cable radio station is simply a cable audio channel that has been programmed as an aural (sound) service.

[10] Thus *radio broadcasting* is just one of a number of radio services.

Commission regulates as a common carrier the company that operates that multi-state fiber optic network mentioned several paragraphs above, a user of interstate wire communications; it does not regulate a firm that leases channels on that network to send messages back and forth among the firm's various branches. The Commission regulates as a broadcaster the local radio station, a user of wireless communication; it does not regulate an advertiser who pays to have the station air a commercial. The Commission regulates as point-to-point communication the radio amateur operator who lives next door, another user of wireless communication.

The wired/wireless dichotomy is not so clear-cut for many communications users, and this is where the "mixture," mentioned at the beginning of the previous paragraph, comes into play. Consider, for example, a long-distance telephone company. Many people might tend to associate such a company with telephone lines and consider the carrier a user of wired communication. In reality, it probably uses microwave and satellite, both forms of wireless communication, for its long-distance hops. Nonetheless, the Commission regulates that company not only as a licensee of wireless facilities but also as an *interstate common carrier*, a firm that makes its facilities available for hire to carry the communications of others; it does not regulate you or me, the company's customers, when we place a call across the country or around the world.

Further, the interstate/intrastate dichotomy is not always clear-cut, either. Consider, for example, a company that operates as a communications common carrier within the boundaries of one state and owns microwave relay stations to connect its various service areas within that state. Here, the state would regulate the company as a common carrier. But because microwave transmitters are a form of wireless communication, the FCC would regulate the company as a microwave licensee.

Since the U.S. Constitution vests in Congress the power to regulate interstate commerce (which by judicial definition includes radio transmissions),[11] the FCC regulates radio usage by state and local governments as well as by private citizens and businesses. Highway patrol, local police, fire departments, sheriff's offices, city and county utilities—radio use by all such activities must be licensed by and adhere to regulations of the FCC. The FCC does *not*, however, regulate radio frequency usage by units of the federal government. Instead, the needs and uses for spectrum space (another term for blocks of radio frequencies) of the Defense Department, the Treasury Department, and other federal agencies are coordinated through a branch of the Department of Commerce, the National Telecommunications and Information Administration (EMG 5.6).

4.1.3   Powers

Under the Communications Act, the Commission has the power to make rules and regulations for wireless and interstate wire communications, to license and to set up criteria for the licensing of wireless communication, and to make rules for cable

---

[11] FRC v. Nelson Bros. Bond & Mortgage Co., 289 U.S. 266 at 179.

television in specified areas. The act also lists other, more specific regulatory powers.

Section 303 directs the Commission to make rules and regulations necessary to carry out the intent of both domestic laws and all international agreements to which the United States is a party. "Domestic laws" refers to federal legislation; because radio emissions are interstate in nature, states and local governments are all but locked out of regulatory authority.

Sections 307–311 and 319 are critical to the FCC's effectiveness in regulating radio communication. A transmitter in any of the radio services must have a license to operate, and so licensing is one of the Commission's most important powers (FCC licensing is explained in Chapter 8). Further, the Commission's licensing power is *discretionary*. This means that under law the agency may set up criteria for determining who should get a license and under what conditions a license should be granted and, when those criteria are not met, refuse to grant the license. The lack of discretionary licensing power was a major weakness of the Radio Act of 1912 (EMG 3.1.2) and, therefore, a specific inclusion in the Radio Act of 1927 and its successor, the Communications Act of 1934.

Section 303 lists a number of other radio-related powers. Several center on traffic duties, that is, ensuring that stations operate so they do not interfere with each other. The FCC also has power to license operators, to inspect stations, to regulate network-affiliated stations, to require that stations keep certain records and paint and illuminate transmission towers, to assign and require stations to use call letters, and to require that new television receivers be equipped to pick up all channels. Section 303 also directs the Commission to study new uses and otherwise to encourage more effective use of radio in the public interest.

Other FCC powers granted by law impinge directly on program content. These are discussed in detail in subsequent chapters, as is the Communications Act's "public interest" standard, used in the past by the FCC as a broad empowerment to regulate areas not otherwise specified in law. Amendments to the Communications Act have added to the FCC's powers. In passing the two cable acts, for example, Congress amended the Communications Act to address directly the matter of cable television. The 1984 act was deregulatory in nature, its purpose mainly to get cable systems out from under the rate-setting and threat-of-franchise-nonrenewal thumb of the cities (EMG 3.2.3). That act gave the Commission relatively few rule-making chores. Nonetheless, those few responsibilities constituted the first legislative statement that the FCC *should* make rules for cable television. By contrast, the 1992 law was reregulatory and required a massive rule-making effort on the part of the Commission. Among the areas of cable television in which the FCC was to regulate were the following: subscriber rates, billing, and privacy; ownership of subscriber wiring; customer service standards; carriage of TV stations; program access; objectionable programming; ownership of systems and programming services; signal theft; signal quality; and equipment compatibility.

4.1.4 Rule Making

FCC rules and regulations have the force of law, but certain procedures must be followed in adopting them, and they may be challenged in court.

The FCC rule-making procedure is diagrammed in Figure 4.2. It works like this. Suggestions for new rules or revision of existing rules can come from almost any source—in or out of the Commission and in or out of government. All suggestions go to the appropriate FCC bureau or office and are evaluated to eliminate those that are "moot, premature, repetitive, or which plainly do not warrant consideration by the Commission."[12] A suggestion that survives staff screening goes to the Commission. The Commission then makes one of four determinations. Two of these end the procedure: a *Memorandum Opinion and Order* (MO&O), which results in no rules being adopted or changed, or a *Report and Order Adopting Change*, which makes editorial but nonsubstantive changes in existing rules.

The other two determinations continue the rule-making procedure. Both describe a problem or issue and ask for public comment. But a *Notice of Proposed Rule Making* (NPRM) spells out specific rules the FCC plans to adopt to deal with the problem, while a *Notice of Inquiry* (NOI) takes a more general approach and asks for suggestions on what rules are needed, if any. Whichever determination the FCC makes, the order or notice is published in the *Federal Register*[13] and made available in the FCC's News Media Division.

If the FCC chooses to issue an NPRM or NOI, interested parties or any member of the public may then file comments or replies to comments. The Commission may also decide or may be required (EMG 4.1.5) to hold oral arguments or hearings on the matter. Hearings or not, after everyone has had an opportunity to be heard and the record is closed, the FCC will consider all comments.

With respect to an NOI, the FCC now has two choices. It may decide that specific rules are needed and issue an NPRM. Or, it may decide that no rules are needed and end the inquiry by issuing an MO&O.

With respect to an NPRM, the FCC has three choices: adopt the proposed rules; change them, and adopt them as changed; or end the proceeding with no rule change. The Commission then announces its decision by issuing a "Report and Order" that is published in the *Federal Register*.

When rules are adopted, they go into effect 30 days after publication in the *Federal Register*. During that time, any interested party may file a petition for reconsideration.[14] Failing that, the rule may be challenged in court. If no one successfully challenges it, the rule stands as an enforceable FCC regulation until the FCC changes or repeals it or Congress overrides it with new legislation.

---

[12] 47 C.F.R. § 1.400(e).

[13] The *Federal Register*, a daily publication of the Government Printing Office, is the first place the rules and regulations of U.S. administrative agencies are published.

[14] 47 C.F.R. §§ 1.399–1.429.

FIGURE 4.2 FCC rule-making process

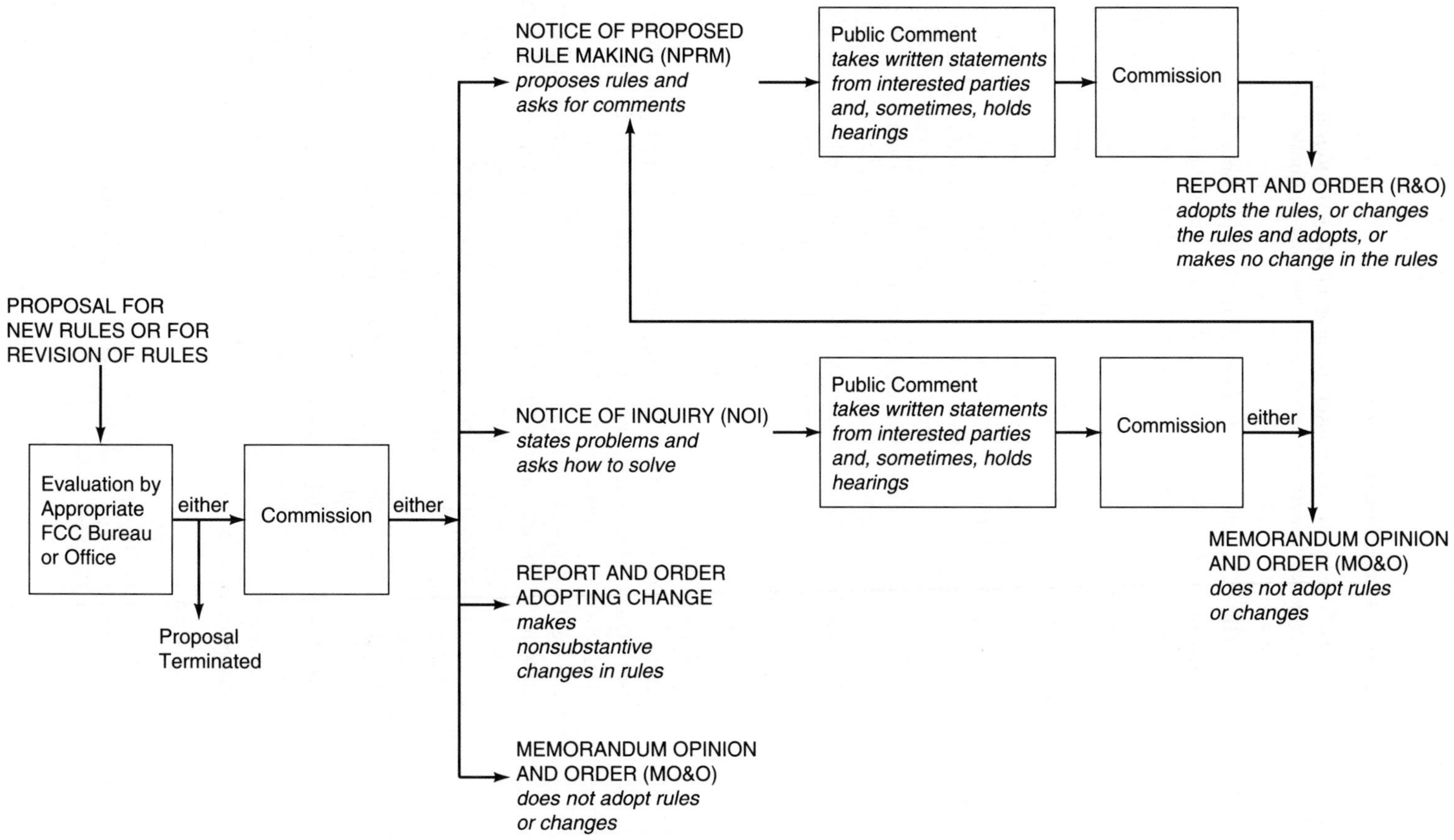

REPORT AND ORDER (R&O)
adopts the rules, or changes the rules and adopts, or makes no change in the rules

MEMORANDUM OPINION AND ORDER (MO&O)
does not adopt rules or changes

Commission

either

Commission

Public Comment
takes written statements from interested parties and, sometimes, holds hearings

Public Comment
takes written statements from interested parties and, sometimes, holds hearings

NOTICE OF PROPOSED RULE MAKING (NPRM)
proposes rules and asks for comments

NOTICE OF INQUIRY (NOI)
states problems and asks how to solve

REPORT AND ORDER ADOPTING CHANGE
makes nonsubstantive changes in rules

MEMORANDUM OPINION AND ORDER (MO&O)
does not adopt rules or changes

PROPOSAL FOR NEW RULES OR FOR REVISION OF RULES

Commission

either

either

Proposal Terminated

Evaluation by Appropriate FCC Bureau or Office

4.1.5 Hearings and Appeals

The Communications Act requires hearings in two instances: (1) during certain rule-making proceedings; and (2) in cases requiring adjudication. Adjudicatory hearings, held to make findings on designated issues, are presided over by an administrative law judge, whose initial decision may be appealed within the FCC and then to federal courts.

The purpose of a hearing is to ensure that all parties involved have a chance to make known their views before the FCC takes final action.[15] Some rule-making proceedings must, by law, be made on the record after opportunity for hearing. In those cases, the hearing is held before the Commission itself and is an integral part of the rule-making procedure (EMG 4.1.4).

Hearings must also be held in cases requiring adjudication as defined by law[16] (Box 4.1). For the sake of discussion, let us imagine a particular situation that requires an adjudicatory hearing. *Adjudication* means the formal giving, pronouncing, or recording of an opinion, so an *adjudicatory hearing* would be a hearing for the purpose of rendering an adjudication. Our hearing involves an application to renew a broadcast license. The Mass Media Bureau has found that the applicant's station had serious, recurring problems during the licensing period now concluding. These problems involved, among other things, an improperly lighted transmission tower, improper station identification, transmission at power levels greater than those authorized, and failure to have the transmitter operating within specifications. The station's signal has interfered with those of other stations in the area, and those broadcasters have complained to the FCC. The station had been cited and fined several times because of these problems but had apparently done little or nothing about them. Such practices seem to cast doubt on the applicant's ability to operate a station, so the matter of the renewal application is set for hearing.

The first step in the hearing process is for the Commission to issue an order for the hearing.[17] The Commission's order contains, among other things, the time, place, and nature of the hearing; a statement as to the reasons for the Commission's action; a statement as to the matters of fact and law involved; a statement as to the issues involved; and a statement of legal authority and jurisdiction under which the hearing is to be held.

The most important part of the order is the designation of issues. An issue is a single point in dispute; in the final decision, disposal of the issues determines the fate of the applicant. So various parties to the proceeding may petition to enlarge, change, or delete issues. The issues in our case deal with the problems themselves, whether the applicant was aware of them, and why nothing was done to correct them. The last issue asks whether, in the light of evidence received on the other issues, the public interest would be served by renewing the applicant's license.

---

[15] This section is adapted in part from F. Leslie Smith, *Perspectives on Radio and Television, Telecommunication in the United States*, 3d ed. (New York: HarperCollins, 1990).

[16] 5 U.S.C. § 554.

[17] 47 C.F.R. § 1.221.

BOX 4.1   Adjudicatory Hearings Required by the Communications Act

The Communications Act specifies that hearings must be held in the following adjudicatory situations:

When the Commission decides to deny an application for new, for renewal of, for modification of, or for transfer of license*

When a licensee whose station operation (i.e., frequency, power, or times of operation) the Commission proposes to change so requests[†]

When the FCC wishes to revoke a license or construction permit or to issue a cease and desist order[‡]

When a second party files a petition to deny an application for license (if the FCC finds the petition raises valid points)[§]

When two or more parties apply for the same frequency[¶] and

When an operator whose license has been suspended so requests[#]

---

* 47 U.S.C. § 309(e).
[†] 47 U.S.C. §§ 303(f), 316.
[‡] 47 U.S.C. § 312(c).
[§] 47 U.S.C. § 409(d).
[¶] 47 C.F.R. § 73.3593.
[#] 47 U.S.C. § 303(m)(2).

The order goes by mail to parties to the proceeding and is published in the *Federal Register*. The applicant and any other parties to the proceeding (which, in our case, include the neighboring stations that have complained) have 20 days to respond in writing that they will appear. If the applicant does not respond, the Commission dismisses the license-renewal application "with prejudice"; that is, the applicant loses all rights and cannot make another application. Other parties to the proceeding who fail to respond forfeit their right to be heard in the matter.

In our case, action on the part of the FCC's Mass Media Bureau has led to the hearing. The Mass Media Bureau thus becomes the applicant's adversary in the hearing and gives testimony and introduces evidence to oppose the applicant. This is common in broadcast and cable matters, since part of the Bureau's job is to examine applications and the applicants.

The hearing itself resembles a trial. An administrative law judge (ALJ) presides, as is the case in most adjudicatory hearings. ALJs are Commission employees.[18]

---

[18] 47 C.F.R. § 151.

They have authority to issue subpoenas, administer oaths, examine witnesses, and rule on admission of evidence.[19] An ALJ must render an impartial or independent opinion. This means the ALJ may not ask other employees and officers of the FCC for definitions, interpretations, and opinions on an informal basis. All such questions must be "on the record."[20]

After conclusion of the hearing, the ALJ issues an initial decision. Unless reviewed, the initial decision eventually becomes final and effective.[21] Review may result from appeal by one of the parties involved (for example, the applicant or the Mass Media Bureau) or by direction of the commissioners.[22] Most initial decisions go to the Review Board, a permanent body composed of three or more senior Commission employees.[23] The Board[24] issues a final decision, which, in turn, is subject to review by the five commissioners as a group. Some initial decisions, however, go directly to the five commissioners.

Section 405 of the Communications Act allows persons who are "aggrieved or whose interests are adversely affected" by a Commission decision to petition for rehearing. FCC decisions, however, may also be appealed directly to the federal courts,[25] and many are.[26]

The applicant in our imaginary case has lost all the way up the ladder. The ALJ's initial decision found that the violations were so serious and were repeated so often that the license should not be renewed. The applicant appealed, first to the Review Board, then to the five commissioners, but the decision was the same. So the applicant (whom we shall name Applicant Broadcasting, Inc.) decides to appeal the FCC decision to the federal court. Since the decision is to deny renewal of a license, Applicant Broadcasting must make its appeal to a specific appeals court, the U.S. Court of Appeals for the District of Columbia (Box 4.2). The case thus becomes *Applicant Broadcasting, Inc.* v. *FCC.*[27]

In its decision, the appeals court can either affirm or reverse the Commission decision. If the latter, it remands (that is, sends back) the case to the FCC to carry out the judgment. The party that loses the case may petition the U.S. Supreme Court to review the decision of the appeals court.

---

[19] 47 C.F.R. § 243.

[20] 5 U.S.C. § 554(d).

[21] 47 C.F.R. § 1.267.

[22] 47 C.F.R. § 1.276.

[23] 47 C.F.R. § 0.161.

[24] 47 U.S.C. § 155(c) provides for a panel of one or more commissioners to review an initial decision, but this is rarely done.

[25] 5 U.S.C. § 702.

[26] Once the five commissioners have reached their decision, that is the final decision of the Federal Communications Commission; therefore, the Mass Media Bureau, a component part of the FCC, will not appeal to the courts, even if the decision goes against it.

[27] However, to further complicate matters, a completely different party may appeal the case. For example, in the "sex talk radio" case, the Commission fined the broadcast licensee, Sonderling Broadcasting Corp. (27 Rad. Reg. 2d (P&F) 285, 1973), but two citizen groups petitioned for Commission reconsideration (41 F.C.C. 2d 777, 1973) and appealed the Commission's denial of that petition to the court (Illinois Citizens v. FCC, 515 F.2d 397 (D.C. Cir., 1975)). *See* EMG 13.1.1.3.

BOX 4.2   Courts of Appeals and FCC Decisions

Section 402 specifies that certain types of appeals must be made in the U.S. Court of Appeals for the District of Columbia. These include cases involving

> any party to whom the Commission has denied application for a construction permit or for new, renewal of, modification of, or transfer of license;
>
> any party to whom the Commission has denied application or revoked a permit to operate a broadcast studio or other place from which programs are transmitted or delivered to a radio station in a foreign country for the purpose of having them consistently reach the United States;
>
> any party who feels aggrieved or whose interests are adversely affected by a Commission grant or denial of any of the aforementioned applications;
>
> any party whose license or construction permit has been modified or revoked by the Commission;
>
> any party on whom the Commission has served a cease and desist order; and
>
> any radio operator whose license has been suspended.

This list may seem to include all possibilities, but, in fact, some important appeals do not have to go to the D.C. Court of Appeals. For example, appeals of FCC rules and regulations may be entered in any federal appeals court.

In our case, the appeals court affirmed the FCC's decision, so Applicant petitions the Supreme Court for review. The case remains *Applicant Broadcasting, Inc. v. FCC.* (If the Commission had lost at the appellate level and decided to petition for review, the case would have become *FCC* v. *Applicant Broadcasting, Inc.*) The Supreme Court may or may not grant certiorari (in effect, review the decision), depending on the principles involved. If it does not, the decision of the lower court stands.

4.1.6   Declaratory Ruling

> The FCC may issue a declaratory ruling, a legal device to terminate a controversy or remove an uncertainty.

The Administrative Procedures Act allows agencies to issue a declaratory ruling,[28] and the Commission has done so on occasion. For example, in the *Pacifica*

---

[28] 5 U.S.C. § 554.

"dirty words" case, the FCC issued a declaratory ruling in which it attempted to clarify its definition of the term *indecent* (EMG 13.1.1.3.1).

4.1.7   Enforcement

In mass media matters, the FCC has nine methods of enforcement: letter, consent order, cease and desist order, forfeiture, court action, conditional renewal, short-term renewal, denial of renewal, and revocation.

The Communications Act grants six, and the Commission has developed three. All nine are available to deal with a licensee or permittee[29] that violates law, Commission rules, or terms of license. The cease and desist order, the three methods having to do with renewal, and revocation apply only to broadcast stations and other services that use radio transmitters; the remainder apply also to cable television.

4.1.7.1   Letter

The FCC may send a letter to ask for an explanation or to admonish.

The letter is one of the "developed" enforcement methods (that is, not specified in the Communications Act). The Commission uses the letter to ask, in effect, "What about this? Please explain," or "What do you plan to do about this?" The letter can be prompted by what appears to be a valid complaint from the public or a problem on the license renewal application.[30] In fiscal year 1991, for example, the Commission used this letter technique—which some call the "raised eyebrow"—93 times to admonish broadcasters for technical and nontechnical violations and 227 times to admonish cable systems and broadcasters for EEO shortcomings.[31] Normally, such letters may not be challenged because they are not directly subject to the appeals process.

4.1.7.2   Consent Order

A consent order, which may be negotiated after a matter has been designated for hearing, is an agreement in which the consentee agrees to comply with specified laws, rules, or policies.

The process starts when an FCC bureau alleges that some party has violated statutes or Commission rules or policies. For example, let us say that the Mass Media Bureau has received well-documented complaints from several broadcasters in a certain city to the effect that a competing station has aired "teaser ads," a violation of the sponsorship identification requirement (EMG 10.1.1.4). The matter is set for

---

[29] A permittee is one to whom the FCC has issued a construction permit. *See* EMG 8.1.1.6. Normally, when you read in this book that certain conditions, rules, laws, or whatever apply to licensees, you can assume that they also apply to permittees.

[30] 47 C.F.R. §§ 1.89, 73.3566.

[31] FCC, *57th Annual Report* 25.

hearing to determine whether the allegations are true; the issues are designated and the order is drawn. The Bureau may then negotiate with the licensee, "where the interests of timely enforcement or compliance, the nature of the proceeding, and the public interest permit. . . ."[32] Either the Bureau or the licensee may initiate the negotiations. If unsuccessful, or if their agreement is rejected, the hearing proceeds. If successful, the two parties draw up an agreement that includes, among other things, a draft consent order, a statement that signing the agreement does not constitute admission of the alleged violations, and agreements by which the parties to the order (the Mass Media Bureau and the licensee) waive their rights to comment on and to appeal the order. The presiding officer for the hearing (or, if none is designated, the chief administrative law judge) signs or rejects the order or suggests further negotiation on specified parts of the agreement.

Those waivers do not totally eliminate the possibility for appeal or court challenge. Any party to the proceeding who has not signed the agreement (perhaps rival broadcasters in our example) may appeal the consent order, or the Commission on its own motion may review it. Appeal and review procedures for consent orders are the same as those for an ALJ's initial decision[33] (EMG 4.1.5).

Consentees violate consent orders at their own risk. Violators subject themselves "to any and all sanctions which would have been imposed . . . if all the issues in the hearing as originally designated had been decided against the consenting party and to further sanctions for violations as agreed upon in the consent order."[34] Consent order violation calls for a hearing, and the Commission bears the burden of showing that the violation occurred.

4.1.7.3 *Cease and Desist Order*

A cease and desist order commands a licensee to stop a specified action that violates license terms, communications law, FCC regulations, or a treaty. The FCC rarely uses this sanction.

Section 312(b) of the Communications Act gives the FCC authority to issue a cease and desist order. The Commission may issue a cease and desist order where it determines that a licensee has done any of the following:

1. failed to operate substantially as the license specifies;
2. violated some part of the Communications Act or sections 1304, 1343, or 1464 of the U.S. Criminal Code;[35]
3. violated any FCC rule or regulation or any treaty ratified by the United States.

---

[32] 47 C.F.R. § 1.93.

[33] 47 C.F.R. §§ 1.93, 1.94.

[34] 47 C.F.R. § 1.95.

[35] 18 U.S.C. §§ 1304, 1343, and 1464 regulate transmission of, respectively, lottery information (EMG 13.2.2), fraud, and objectionable language (EMG 13.1.1).

This sanction would seem ideal. The Commission could use it against an erring licensee whose transgression did not seem to warrant loss of license. However, when Congress amended section 312 in 1952 to authorize use of the cease and desist order, it attached the same cumbersome procedures required to revoke a license (EMG 4.1.7.9). So in 1960, Congress again amended the Communications Act, this time to allow the Commission to impose forfeitures. The FCC has used forfeitures more and cease and desist orders less than any of its other legislated sanctions.[36]

4.1.7.4 Forfeiture

The Commission may levy up to $25,000 for each day a violation occurs, $250,000 maximum, for violation of license terms, communication law, FCC regulations, a treaty, and violations of Communications Act sections 317(c) and 508(a).

Section 503(b) of the Communications Act allows the FCC to impose a forfeiture, in effect a fine. The act specifies five types of violations subject to forfeitures—the same three subject to cease and desist orders:

1. violation of license terms,
2. violation of the Communications Act or the Criminal Code,
3. violation of any FCC regulation or treaty,

plus two more:

4. failure to "exercise reasonable diligence" on the part of a broadcast licensee in getting (from employees, program syndicators, and others involved in preparing or supplying programs that the broadcaster or cable operator transmits) information necessary to make required sponsorship identification announcements [violation of section 317(c), EMG 10.1.1.4],
5. rigging or fixing of a broadcast promotional contest or quiz game [violation of section 508(a)].

That $250,000 limit applies to individual outlets. Therefore, a licensee who owns more than one station or a multiple-system cable operator may actually wind up owing more than the $250,000 maximum. For example, in late 1992 the FCC levied a record forfeiture of $600,000 against Infinity Broadcasting for violations of section 1464 of the Criminal Code that were alleged to have occurred over three Infinity-owned stations. The Commission cited 12 broadcasts in 1991 by Howard Stern, an announcer for Infinity, in which allegedly indecent language had been used over the three stations.[37]

---

[36] *See, e.g.,* FCC, *57th Annual Report* 25.

[37] The broadcasts had aired on Infinity's New York, Philadelphia, and Washington stations, plus at least one other station in Los Angeles (against whose licensee the FCC had already levied a $105,000 forfei-

To impose a forfeiture, the Commission must act within the current license term for broadcasters, within one year for all others. The FCC issues a *notice of apparent liability*. The notice sets forth all pertinent facts of the violation and is sent "to the last known address of [the party alleged to have committed the violation] by registered or certified mail."[38]

The notice of apparent liability procedure includes very little opportunity for respondent input and appeal. The FCC has the option on whether to hold a hearing before issuing a notice but usually chooses not to do so. Once issued, the targeted party has "a reasonable period of time [usually] thirty days from the date of the notice"[39] to pay or to explain to the FCC why the forfeiture should be reduced or eliminated. If the latter, the FCC considers the explanation and any other information it may have, then issues an order to cancel, reduce, or require payment in full. However, the only way to challenge a notice in court is to refuse to pay the forfeiture. The FCC refers unpaid forfeitures to the Department of Justice for recovery through civil suit.[40]

4.1.7.5   Court Action
Sections 401, 501, and 502 of the Communications Act authorize the FCC to prosecute violators in court.

Section 501 provides penalties up to $10,000 and one year in prison (two years for repeaters) for "willfully or knowingly" violating, or causing violations of, the Communications Act. Section 502 provides for a fine for violations of FCC rules and regulations, up to $500 per day for each day the violation occurs.

Section 401 deals with court enforcement. Upon application, a federal district court may issue any of the following:

1. a writ[41] or writ of mandamus commanding a party who has violated the Communications Act to comply with it;
2. an order commanding a party who has disobeyed an FCC order (other than for payment of money) to obey;
3. a writ of injunction[42] or other judicial process to force compliance (if a court order is ignored).

---

ture). This was a repeat violation by Infinity; a $6,000 fine for a 1988 broadcast by the same announcer was already pending. Joe Flint, "FCC Fines Stern $600K; OK's Deal," *Broadcasting,* 21 Dec. 1992, at 5–6.

[38] 47 U.S.C. § 503(b)(4)(B).

[39] 47 C.F.R. § 1.80(f)(3).

[40] 47 U.S.C. § 504.

[41] A writ is a judge's order that requires or orders that something be done outside the courtroom. A writ of mandamus is a judge's order to a public official or a lower court that requires, and allows no discretion in the performance of, some legal duty.

[42] A writ of injunction is a judge's order to do or to refrain from doing some specified thing. In this case, it would force compliance with the court order.

Section 401 also authorizes the Commission to call upon the Justice Department and its federal attorneys to prosecute enforcement and punishment proceedings in federal courts.

4.1.7.6 *Conditional Renewal*
The FCC may condition the renewal of a license on specific licensee behavior.

An example of the conditional renewal was the 1969 case involving KTAL-TV, Texarkana, Arkansas. The Commission granted the application for renewal with the condition that KTAL better serve its city of license. The station had programmed for and located facilities in the larger city of Shreveport, 70 miles away and across the state line in Louisiana. Texarkana citizens, unhappy over the lack of local service by their television station, prepared a petition to deny renewal of KTAL-TV's license. Citizens and station negotiated. In a policy statement, the station recognized the needs and problems pointed out by the Texarkana citizens and promised to take specified actions to meet those needs. In return, the citizens withdrew their petition. The FCC, then, renewed KTAL-TV's license, contingent upon the station's fulfilling the promises that it made to better serve Texarkana.[43]

The Commission has issued conditional renewals to licensees who have unsatisfactory records of employing minorities and women. The condition required that such licensees report on a regular basis the steps they have taken to ensure equal employment opportunities. The FCC has also conditioned renewal on transfer of station ownership and license within a specified period of time.[44]

The Communications Act seems to imply that the Commission has authority to grant conditional renewals. For example, section 309(h) says in part that licenses "shall be in such general form as [the Commission] may prescribe" and mentions that, in addition to legally required statements, the license may include "other provisions." However, while agencies such as the Civil Aeronautics Board and the Interstate Commerce Commission have *specific* authorization to impose conditions, the Communications Act does not grant such to the FCC.[45]

4.1.7.7 *Short-Term Renewal*
Section 307(d) of the Communications Act allows the FCC to renew a radio station license for less than seven years and a television station license for less than five.

The Commission uses the short-term renewal when it wishes to review a station's performance sooner than the normal five- or seven-year licensing period.[46] In fiscal year 1991, for example, the Commission granted six short-term renewals for

---

[43] KCMC, Inc., 19 F.C.C.2d 109 (1969).
[44] Barry Cole and Mal Oettinger, *Reluctant Regulators: The FCC and the Broadcast Audience* (Reading, MA: Addison, 1978) 197.
[45] *Id.* The Commission has codified the conditional renewal as 47 C.F.R. § 3592.
[46] 47 C.F.R. § 73.1020.

violations of the FCC's Equal Employment Opportunities rules.[47] Typical short-term renewals average six months to two years in length.

4.1.7.8 *Denial of License Renewal*

Section 307(d) of the Communications Act gives the FCC the option to deny application for renewal of license.

The Commission reserves this sanction for stations alleged to have knowingly committed some serious or continuing violation of law or regulation. The process begins when, near the end of its current licensing period, the station makes application to have its license renewed. At that time, the Commission notifies the licensee that there are problems and that the matter is being designated for hearing in order to determine whether the public interest would be served by renewing the license. Upon conclusion of the hearing, if the decision goes against the station, the license is not renewed, and the station must sign off the air when its current license expires.

4.1.7.9 *Revocation*

Section 312(a) of the Communications Act allows the Commission to revoke a license, to take it away before renewal time.

Again, the Commission uses this sanction when a station is alleged to have knowingly committed some serious or continuing violation of law or regulation. However, in the case of revocation, the Commission has determined that the allegations are serious enough that the matter cannot wait until renewal time. So the licensee is notified, and a hearing is set to determine whether the public interest would be served by continuing to allow the licensee to operate the station. A negative decision means that the station must surrender its license and cease broadcasting.

Both revocation and denial of renewal result in the removal of a broadcast license, so you may hear these two sanctions referred to collectively as *removals*. You may also hear them called the "death penalty." You should, however, be aware of the semantic considerations of that phrase. The "death penalty" reflects the broadcasting business's perception of the "injury" done to the licensee; that is, the licensee must give up the station. On the other hand, by the time a licensee has exhausted all avenues of appeal and really does have to cease broadcasting, quite often some other party has already gone through the process of acquiring a license for the to-be-vacated channel. So the losing licensee signs off and the new licensee signs on, and the public continues to receive programming service.

Three studies examined all license removals from the beginning of the FCC in 1934 through 1988.[48] They found that 147 licenses had been removed, and that 30

---

[47] FCC, *57th Annual Report* 25.

[48] John D. Abel, Charles Clift III, and Frederic A. Weiss, "Station License Renewal Revocations and Denials of Renewal, 1934–1969," 14 *J. Broadcasting*, 411 (1970); Frederic A. Weiss, David Ostroff, and

---

BOX 4.3   Violations Resulting in License Removals 1934–1988

Misrepresentation	60
Control Violations	47
Technical	37
Character Qualifications	17
Abandonment	13
Promise versus Performance	13
Report Violations	11

SOURCE: Hallock 92.

---

different types of violations were cited in those removals. The seven most frequently cited are listed in Box 4.3. The greatest number of violations stemmed from misrepresentation—that is, lying to the Commission. The second and third most frequent violations were engineering-type problems. The fourth was licensee character qualifications (EMG 7.1.2.2). The fifth resulted from licensees ceasing to broadcast without notifying the FCC; the sixth, from not programming substantially as promised in the preceding renewal application (EMG 9.3); and the last, from failure to submit required FCC reports in correct form.

The "common wisdom" is that the Commission rarely denies renewal of or revokes a license. Those three studies report the common wisdom to be correct. As Table 4.1 shows, license removals increased dramatically during the administrations of John F. Kennedy and his successor, Lyndon B. Johnson, and of Richard M. Nixon and his successor, Gerald Ford.[49] These figures must be considered in context. Although the averages seem high, and although these two administrations were considered, respectively, proregulatory and antimedia, these removals constituted less than one-tenth of 1 percent of the total number of stations authorized. So even in its most "punitive" years, the FCC removes so few licenses as to make the numbers insignificant.

During the 1970s, noncommercial stations lost their licenses for the first time. In 1975, the FCC denied renewal of licenses to the Alabama Educational Television Commission for eight television stations and a construction permit for a ninth. The FCC had found a pattern of underrepresentation or exclusion of minorities from overall programming in the Alabama system.[50] In 1978, the Commission denied

---

Charles E. Clift III, "Station License Revocations and Denials of Renewal, 1970–78," 24 *J. Broadcasting* 69 (1980); and Clay D. Hallock, "Station License Revocations and Denials of Renewal, 1981–1988: FCC Regulatory Sanctions and Philosophy in Perspective," thesis, U of Florida, 1989.

[49] Hallock demonstrated that increases in the number of removals could be tied to presidential administrations, a reflection of both the political agenda and the FCC appointees of the sitting president. He also suggested that the number of removals during the four-year Carter administration, although high compared with the Roosevelt, Truman, Eisenhower, and Reagan administrations, had started to decline and represented the opening of the so-called deregulatory era.

[50] 50 F.C.C.2d 46.

TABLE 4.1   Broadcast Licenses Removed, by Presidential Administrations

Administration		Averages Each Year of Administration		
Presidents	Total Removals	Removals	Stations Authorized	Percentage Removed
Roosevelt	12	1.0	802	0.12
Truman	15	2.1	2,801	0.07
Eisenhower	3	0.4	4,233	0.01
Kennedy/Johnson	42	5.3	6,285	0.08
Nixon/Ford	50	6.3	8,459	0.07
Carter	19	4.8	9,864	0.05
Reagan	6	0.8	11,677	0.01

SOURCE: Hallock 88, 90.

renewal of the license for the University of Pennsylvania's WXPN-FM. Listeners had complained that announcers used objectionable language. Though the university corrected the problem, the FCC denied renewal on grounds that the licensee had improperly abdicated control of the station to students.[51] The Commission did, however, allow both the Alabama agency and the university to reapply for their licenses.

4.2   FCC STAFF

The FCC staff is organized into five functional bureaus and a number of offices.

With respect to the FCC staff, the bureaucracy that handles the day-to-day operation of the agency, the Commission has a great deal of autonomy as to types of persons hired and organization. The Communications Act suggests inspectors, examiners, and engineering, accounting, legal, administrative, and clerical personnel. But the law also says the FCC may hire other employees as necessary to perform its functions. The Commission must organize its staff into bureaus along functional lines and provide each bureau with the staff needed to carry out that function. Otherwise, the Commission is free to organize the staff any way it deems necessary. In fact, the Communications Act requires only two specific employees—the managing director and the secretary to the Commission. Unlike the commissioners' personal staff members, most of the agency staff are covered by civil service laws and so have permanent positions.[52]

During the "deregulation" era of the 1980s, not only was the FCC itself reduced from seven to five members,[53] the staff was also cut. The theory was that

---

[51] 69 F.C.C.2d 1934; and 44 Rad. Reg. 2d (P & F) 747 (1978).

[52] 47 U.S.C. §§ 154(f)(1); 155(b), (d)(9), (f).

[53] *See* note 3.

deregulation had reduced the amount of paperwork, that the total workload on the agency had been thus reduced, and that therefore fewer persons were needed. That was not true, however. Even before the cuts, the agency had only just over 2,000 employees to deal with interstate common carriers, many of which were huge and complex corporations, the millions of licensees in the various regulated services, ranging from broadcasting to aeronautical mobile, and myriad other responsibilities such as equipment certification, operator licensing, and the few cable rules that were left. So when Congress cut over 350 staff positions, the work piled up and the regulated businesses complained about delays in the processing of applications. Congress gradually restored some of the previously eliminated positions, and by 1992, staff size was up to just over 1,800.

4.2.1 Bureaus

Each of the five bureaus has responsibility for one of the main areas of FCC concern. Three of the five—Mass Media, Private Radio, and Common Carrier—are charged with regulating specific segments of the communication services, while the fourth, Field Engineering, has duties that cut across all services.

The three "services" bureaus share certain responsibilities. Each bureau must, in connection with the services on which it focuses, develop and implement regulatory programs, process applications for licenses or other filings, analyze complaints, conduct investigations, and take part in FCC hearings. These responsibilities are in addition to the specific duties listed below.

During the 1950s through 1970s, the years of cable television's greatest growth, the Commission adopted several sets of rules covering the new medium and eventually created a separate cable television bureau. This brought the number of functional bureaus to five. Most of those cable rules were subsequently eliminated, and in 1982 the Commission went back to a four-bureau arrangement, folding both its broadcasting and its remaining cable activities into a new Mass Media Bureau. Ten years later, Congress passed the Cable Television Consumer Protection and Competition Act of 1992, which required the Commission to adopt numerous rules and take on continuing regulatory responsibilities dealing with cable. As a result, in 1994 the FCC resurrected its fifth bureau as the Cable Services Bureau. The Mass Media Bureau continues to exist but deals only with over-the-air mass communications matters.

4.2.1.1 Mass Media Bureau

The Mass Media Bureau is concerned with AM, FM, and television broadcast stations and related facilities; radio and television networks; and emerging video technologies.

During the 1980s and 1990s, "emerging video technologies" have included such developments as direct broadcast satellite, wireless cable, teletext, and interactive video. The Mass Media Bureau also carries out responsibilities of the United

States under international agreements and treaty obligations pertaining to broadcasting. And it processes applications for compensation of U.S. broadcasters who incur certain expenses as a result of interference from Cuban radio stations.[54]

4.2.1.2 Cable Services Bureau

The Cable Services Bureau has responsibility for regulation and rule making affecting cable television systems in the areas of signal carriage, consumer service, subscriber rates, and ownership.

One major concern of the Cable Services Bureau is consumer complaints, and the staff is especially organized to handle such complaints and to administer and enforce the FCC's cable regulations. Other matters handled by the Bureau include must-carry, retransmission consent, customer service, indecency, technical standards, home wiring, consumer electronics compatibility, mergers and horizontal and vertical integration in the cable business, and program access for competing media.[55]

4.2.1.3 Private Radio Bureau

The Private Radio Bureau regulates radio stations serving the communications needs of state and local governments, nonprofit organizations, businesses, individuals, aircraft, and ships.

The Private Radio Services include private land mobile, private operational-fixed microwave, aviation, marine, personal (which includes citizens band radio), amateur, and disaster. Licensees in the Private Radio Services use radio to promote safety of life and property, to increase industrial productivity, and to advance the science of telecommunications.[56] They are the local police department, the taxicab company, the pleasure boat owner, the airline company, the truck driver, and many, many more; they are literally millions in number.

4.2.1.4 Common Carrier Bureau

The Common Carrier Bureau regulates those organizations that provide interstate or foreign communications facilities for hire. Common carriers include such media as telephone, telegraph, and satellite companies.

The Common Carrier Bureau regulates all aspects of such carriers—services, facilities, rates, practices. This includes voice, record, data, video, and facsimile transmission using wire, satellite, radio marine cable, optical fiber, and other facili-

---

[54] 47 C.F.R. § 0.61; and FCC, *57th Annual Report* 8, 21.

[55] Kim McAvoy, "Hundt: New Bureau to Enforce Cable Act," *Broadcasting & Cable*, 20 Dec. 1993, at 55. An example of vertical integration is a multiple system operator who also owns or controls programming services. An example of horizontal integration is a multiple system operator who acquires many cable systems that together serve a significant percentage of cable subscribers. In either case, the possibility exists that the operator could do business in such a way as to suppress competition or otherwise illegally restrain trade.

[56] 47 C.F.R. § 0.131; and FCC, *57th Annual Report* 8, 57.

ties. The Bureau also licenses all radio facilities (such as microwave relay) used for such purpose, including those dedicated entirely to intrastate use. Intrastate wire communication, on the other hand, generally comes under the jurisdiction of the states; your local telephone company, for example, is probably regulated by your state public utilities commission[57]

4.2.1.5 Field Operations Bureau

The Field Operations Bureau maintains field offices nationwide. It performs technical investigative work, licenses operators, processes applications for transmission towers, and furnishes marine and aircraft finding aids.

The Field Operations Bureau maintains six regional offices, 40-some field installations, and a Public Service Branch at FCC headquarters in Washington. It performs all engineering activities in the field in regulating wire and radio communication. These activities include detecting violations of radio regulations, monitoring transmissions, inspecting stations, investigating complaints of radio interference, and issuing violation notices. The Bureau also examines and licenses radio operators; processes applications for painting, lighting, and placing antenna towers; and furnishes directional finding aids for ships and aircraft in distress.[58]

4.2.2 Offices

The offices perform management, auxiliary, and service functions.

The FCC changes the number and alignment of the support offices more frequently than they do the bureaus. As of 1994, the FCC's staff offices included managing director, plans and policy, engineering and technology, general counsel, international communications, legislative affairs, public affairs, inspector general, administrative law judges, and review board.

4.2.2.1 Managing Director

The managing director supervises the bureaus and offices; assists the FCC chair and advises the Commission on management and administrative matters; and handles public information, consumer assistance, small business, and minority enterprise functions.

The Office of the Managing Director was created in 1981. It replaced and assumed all the duties of the Office of Executive Director—duties that include responsibility for personnel matters, budget planning, data automation, health and safety, and records. However, the managing director has much greater discretionary and executive authority to run the agency than did the executive director.

The FCC chair appoints the managing director with the approval of the other members of the Commission. The managing director answers directly to the Com-

---

[57] 47 C.F.R. § 0.91; and FCC, *57th Annual Report* 8, 40.
[58] 47 C.F.R. §§ 0.111, 0.121; and FCC, *57th Annual Report* 8, 50.

mission and works under the supervision of the chair. The Commission establishes policies and objectives, within which the managing director supervises the bureaus and offices in management matters. In contemplating any proposed action or decision, bureau and office chiefs must consult with the managing director, whose review of such proposed activities has a major bearing on whether they are actually undertaken. The managing director ensures that the agency meets the objectives (that is, achieves the work goals) set by the Commission. When bureau and office chiefs hire personnel, the managing director must pass upon the hiring (subject to appeal to the Commission chair), and the managing director appraises performance of the chiefs and recommends bonuses for superior achievement.

In 1992, the FCC created the post of associate managing director for public information and reference services and an Office of Small Business Activities. The associate managing director handles information requests from the *public* (press relations are the responsibility of the Office of Public Affairs, EMG 4.2.2.6), manages the FCC's reference rooms and library, and oversees the consumer assistance and small business division. The Office of Small Business Activities works with small businesses, especially those operated by members of racial or ethnic minorities, providing guidance and information about the communications businesses.

The managing director gives general direction to the secretary of the Commission. The secretary maintains records of official Commission actions; prepares for printing the FCC's rules and regulations and material for *FCC Record* and the *Federal Register*; signs most correspondence and documents adopted by the Commission; maintains official dockets (records) of hearing and rule-making proceedings; officially receives all papers filed with the Commission; and acts as custodian of the FCC seal and records.[59]

4.2.2.2   *Plans and Policy*
The Office of Plans and Policy advises the Commission on economic and technical policy. It analyzes agenda items and develops long-term policy planning.

This office answers directly to the FCC, and the chief of plans and policy works under supervision of the chair. The office develops and evaluates long-range plans and policy recommendations. It also assesses long-term implications of FCC decisions and operations, provides policy analyses to the Commission; coordinates all policy research and development activities, recommends budgets and priorities for research programs, and manages accounts for research studies done under contract to the FCC.[60]

4.2.2.3   *Engineering and Technology and General Counsel*
The chief engineer advises the FCC on technical matters; the general counsel, on legal matters.

---

[59] 47 C.F.R. § 0.11.; 95 Stat. 738; FCC, *57th Annual Report* 5–6.
[60] 47 C.F.R. § 0.21; and FCC, *57th Annual Report* 6.

The chief engineer heads the Office of Engineering and Technology and provides the Commission with technical, engineering, and scientific recommendations. The general counsel provides the Commission with the legal guidance needed in establishing and implementing policy. The general counsel also handles legal questions concerning the agency's operation and represents the Commission in court. The chief engineer and the general counsel also act in regulatory matters that transcend the responsibilities of a single bureau and on international matters.

Included in the Office of General Counsel is the Adjudicatory Division. This division assists the Commission both in reviewing Review Board decisions (and sometimes the initial decision of administrative law judges; EMG 4.1.5 and 4.2.2.8) and in drafting final FCC decisions.[61] These duties had been handled by an Office of Opinions and Review, but in 1981 that office was merged into the Office of General Counsel.

4.2.2.4 International Communications
The Office of International Communications advises the FCC on international matters, coordinates among the FCC's bureaus where international communications are at issue, and maintains liaison with foreign and international communications officials.

Radio waves do not respect national boundaries, so coordination is needed at the international level for frequency usage and transmitter operation. The Office of International Communication assists the Commission and the staff in dealing with such matters. It oversees the integration of the FCC's international policy activities and ensures that these policies are uniform and consistent. This office, created in 1990, also keeps in contact with key communications officials in other countries and in international organizations (such as the United Nations and the International Telecommunications Union, EMG 5.3.3), and represents the FCC before international communications bodies.

4.2.2.5 Legislative Affairs
The Office of Legislative Affairs sustains the flow of communication between the FCC and Congress.

Congress created and must periodically reauthorize the FCC, makes and amends the laws within which the FCC regulates, and appropriates the funds that allow the FCC to operate. As a result, the FCC must maintain close and continuing contact with the Congress. The Office of Legislative Affairs, created in 1987,[62] is responsible for sustaining that contact.

The Office of Legislative Affairs informs Congress of FCC regulatory decisions. It coordinates the Commission's own efforts to have Congress pass or amend laws; it keeps the FCC informed of communications-related legislative activity; it assists in

---

[61] 47 C.F.R. §§ 0.31, 0.41; and FCC, *57th Annual Report* 7–8.
[62] 2 F.C.C.R. 6649.

preparing for Congress the FCC's budget request and annual report; and it responds and assists others to respond to inquiries for information from Congress and from the executive branch.[63]

4.2.2.6 Office of Public Affairs
The Office of Public Affairs is responsible for distributing information to and responding to questions from the news media.

The Office of Public Affairs prepares daily press releases, public notices, and other informational material. It also prepares the FCC's annual report to Congress.[64]

4.2.2.7 Inspector General
The Office of Inspector General is responsible for keeping FCC operations free of fraud, abuse, and inefficiency.

This office was added as a result of the Inspector General Act Amendments of 1988[65] to the Inspector General Act of 1978.[66] The inspector general answers directly to the FCC chair; however, the chair may not prevent the inspector general from carrying out duties of the office as mandated by law. Toward that end, the Office must recommend policies to prevent fraud, abuse, and inefficiency and must keep the FCC and Congress informed about the problems of the agency.[67]

4.2.2.8 Administrative Law Judges and Review Board
Administrative law judges preside over hearings and issue initial decisions. When initial decisions are reviewed, they generally go to the Review Board.

As explained in EMG 4.1.5, these two offices play important roles in the FCC's adjudicatory process. The chief administrative law judge, among other duties, sets times and places for hearings and assigns ALJs to preside over them.[68]

4.3 DELEGATIONS OF AUTHORITY

The Commission delegates its authority to act in certain matters to individual commissioners, to panels or boards of commissioners, and to the staff.

The Communications Act allows the Commission to delegate authority to act on various matters to boards or committees of commissioners, to individual

---

[63] 47 C.F.R. § 0.17.
[64] 47 C.F.R. § 0.15; FCC, *57th Annual Report* 6.
[65] Pub. L. No. 100–504.
[66] U.S.C. Appendix 3.
[67] 47 C.F.R. § 0.13; and FCC, *57th Annual Report* 7.
[68] 47 C.F.R. §§ 0.151, 0.161, 0.351.

commissioners, and to the staff.[69] The Commission delegates authority in three categories.[70]

One such delegation confers authority to act in matters that are minor or routine in nature or that require immediate action but that do *not* involve hearings. This category includes any special delegations to a single commissioner or to groups of commissioners, but most such delegations go to bureau chiefs and other staff members. For example, the chief of the Mass Media Bureau may act on requests for broadcast authorizations so long as those requests are routine and comply with all rules and regulations.[71] When the staff acts under delegated authority, the action has the same force and effect as a Commission action. However, the Commission may overrule a staff action. If the staff, when dealing with a matter under delegated authority, concludes that the matter is more appropriate for consideration by the Commission, it may refer the matter to the Commission at any time. The Commission may also direct the staff to refer a matter to it.[72]

The second type of delegation confers authority to rule on interlocutory matters (Box 4.4) in hearing proceedings; the third confers authority to review an initial decision. The FCC has delegated the second category to the ALJ who presides at a hearing and to the chief administrative law judge and both the second and third to the Review Board.[73] The Commission may also designate a panel of one or more of its own members to review an initial decision; this option is rarely used, however.

FCC regulations contain more than 35 sections that deal with delegation of authority. These regulations list each officer and group and the authority that has been delegated. Some of the more important of these delegations include those to individual commissioners, to the Board of Commissioners, and those designed to deal with national emergencies.

4.3.1 Individual Commissioners

The Commission chair has authority to take action as agency head in all routine matters, in all nonroutine matters that do not involve policy determinations, and in several other areas.[74] Also, one or more commissioners may be designated to preside at a hearing or to review an initial decision.[75]

4.3.2 Board of Commissioners

When the Commission needs to act on a matter but lacks a quorum, the chair can convene all commissioners present and able as a Board of Commissioners. This Board can act on all matters that the full Commission can, with the exception of

---

[69] 47 U.S.C. § 155(c).
[70] 47 C.F.R. §§ 0.201–0.204.
[71] 47 C.F.R. § 0.281.
[72] 47 C.F.R. § 0.5(c).
[73] 47 C.F.R. § 0.363.
[74] 47 C.F.R. § 0.211.
[75] 47 C.F.R. § 0.218.

BOX 4.4   Interlocutory Orders

"Interlocutory" means provisional or temporary. An interlocutory order is one made before a hearing has been concluded, an order that is not final and does not dispose of the entire matter. For example, a petition to amend, modify, enlarge, or delete issues in a hearing (EMG 4.1.5) would be an interlocutory matter, to be ruled on by the ALJ assigned to the hearing or, if no ALJ has been assigned, by the chief ALJ.

---

proceedings involving rule making, investigations, and appeals and reviews of various types. And even here, the Board can act in some of these situations if it first determines that the public interest would be harmed by waiting for a quorum.[76]

4.3.3   Delegations to Deal with National Emergencies

The Commission designates one commissioner as defense commissioner and two others as alternate defense commissioners. The defense commissioner directs the national defense activities of the Commission, including both internal preparations of the agency and external liaison with other agencies. In the event of attack or imminent threat of attack by an enemy, the defense commissioner assumes all duties and responsibilities of the Commission and its chair until relieved or augmented by other commissioners or staff members.

The managing director works with and under the general supervision of the defense commissioner in coordinating defense activities. The managing director also supervises and directs the Emergency Communications Division. This division develops plans for national emergencies including, among other things, use of common carriers, broadcast stations, and private radio services, and the continued operation of the Commission during such times. If conditions are such that the Commission cannot function at its Washington, D.C., offices, an Emergency Relocation Board convenes at the FCC's relocation headquarters and performs the functions of the Commission. The Board consists of all commissioners present and able. In the absence of any commissioners, FCC rules specify certain key staff members to compose the Board.[77]

4.4   CRITICISMS OF THE COMMISSION

Over the years, the Commission has been criticized for a number of weaknesses and shortcomings.

---

[76] 47 C.F.R. § 0.212.

[77] 47 C.F.R. §§ 0.181–0.186, 0.381–0.387.

As with all regulatory agencies, the FCC suffers from a number of problems. In the past, critics[78] have faulted the Commission with the following weaknesses.

4.4.1 Politically Motivated Appointments to the Commission

The commissioners are often not of the quality needed to guide the civilian communications policy of the United States. Individuals are appointed to the Commission not on regulatory qualifications but as political favors.

4.4.2 Decisions Made without Citizen Involvement

The Commission did not encourage citizen participation in licensing matters, rule-making procedures, and hearings until forced to do so by the federal court.[79] The agency now includes full-time personnel whose primary responsibilities are to facilitate public participation in the FCC's decision-making processes, to apprise the public of FCC policies, and to assist consumers (EMG 4.2.2.1).

4.4.3 Decisions Made under Pressure from Industry Lobbyists

The Commission, bombarded by myriad industry lobbying efforts, loses sight of the public interest. Commissioners find it hard *not* to adopt the point of view of the regulated industries; that is, let the trade run itself but regulate all competitors to the hilt. Broadcasters, large cable operators, the huge interstate common-carrier firms, and their lobbies and lawyers are in constant touch with the commissioners. They are always ready to provide information, help, and advice. They are the milieu within which commissioners work. Theirs is the viewpoint most often heard. Some FCC commissioners and staffers, after leaving the Commission, have taken high-paying jobs in the regulated industries.

4.4.4 Decisions Made with Inadequate or Biased Information

The agency is a bureaucracy. It consists of a hierarchy of chiefs and a staff of entrenched civil servants, many of whom are more interested in keeping pensions intact than in solving problems, making innovations, and clearing up backlogs. The commissioners must deal with matters and base decisions on information these

---

[78] Based on Smith 247–248. Critiques of the Commission that have often been quoted in the past include the following: Cole and Oettinger; Nicholas Johnson and John Dystel, "A Day in the Life: The Federal Communications Commission," 82 *Yale L. J.* 1575 (1973); and Erwin G. Krasnow, Lawrence D. Langley, and Herbert A. Terry, *The Politics of Broadcast Regulation*, 3d ed. (New York: St. Martin's, 1982).

[79] Office of Communication of the United Church of Christ v. FCC, 359 F.2d 994 (1966).

middle-level staff personnel put before them. These staffers often choose matters for FCC consideration based not on what will serve the public interest but on what will serve their own private interest. In addition, as electronic communication evolves and grows more technically complex, it is difficult for commissioners to educate themselves adequately in order to make competent technical judgments.

4.4.5 Unreasonable Delays in Resolving Matters

Efficiency is strangled in red tape. Huge backlogs of work build up, causing unreasonable delays. The Commission can take months, even years, to resolve a matter.

4.4.6 Decisions Made without Consideration of Precedent

In reaching a decision on a matter, commissioners may simply ignore past FCC decisions. As a result, decisions are inconsistent; that is, the Commission applies different principles in different ways in similar cases.

4.4.7 Sanctions Not Used; Policies Not Followed

The Commission does not follow its own guidelines or use the sanctions available to it. As a result, licenses are renewed routinely, irrespective of how well stations have met the public interest standard. Rarely are licenses removed (EMG 4.1.7.9), even for the most serious violations of law and regulation, and license transfers that are granted concentrate station control into fewer and larger corporate structures and create more and more absentee owners.[80]

4.4.8 Inability to Make Long-Range Policy

The Commission cannot seem to plan ahead. The heavy press of ongoing, everyday matters is so burdensome that little time is left for long-range planning. And when the Commission does attempt to make policy, it is buffeted from all sides—the executive, the legislative branch, and the regulated businesses. As a result, the FCC is reactive, taking matters as they come and allowing electronic interstate communication to develop willy-nilly with no plan or purpose. It has not been able to delineate an effective and coordinated long-range policy within which communication technologies can develop, evolve, and be regulated.

4.4.9 The Reagan FCC

The FCC's action during certain periods of its history have drawn particular criticism. For example, historian-critics now look askance at the Commission's 1934 report to Congress that channel reservations for noncommercial broadcast were

---

[80] Policies limiting station ownership are explained in EMG 7.1.3.

unneeded[81] and at the 1950s revelations of scandal and corruption in and around the FCC.[82] More recently, critics have taken aim at the FCC dominated by the appointees of President Ronald Reagan during the 1980s.

Reagan's FCC embraced the industry view—that electronic communications media should be free of regulation so they can make the maximum amount of money possible. As discussed in EMG 9.6.1, they turned that view into a guiding philosophy that they dubbed "marketplace regulation." They also redefined "the public interest" in terms of what business wanted. They had little use for citizen input and gave it short shrift. They declared that the concept of spectrum scarcity was simply an assumption that was no longer valid—despite the fact that there were still not enough over-the-air frequencies for everyone who wished to broadcast. They even convinced some key lawmakers, jurists, and other decision makers that this was a fact. They rejected nearly the entire precedential history of the FCC as no longer valid and wrote decisions to reflect their ideological aims. They suggested taking the radio frequencies out of the public domain and granting property rights for them to broadcasters and other licensees. They acted against the wishes of Congress, the body that had created the FCC in the first place.

Toward the end of this period, the Reagan FCC had so angered the legislative branch that Congress refused to move on nominations for two vacant Commission seats, leaving the FCC for months with only three members.[83] Congress also "micromanaged" the FCC,[84] writing into law instructions on matters before the Commission, matters that previously would have been left to the discretion of the commissioners. Even broadcasters were calling for an end to "deregulation" and a return to the public interest standard, the concept that broadcasters have a responsibility to program in response to the needs and interests of their local communities.[85]

Coming out of this period, the broadcasting business suffered financially. During the early 1990s, many licensees went bankrupt, and many stations went off the air.[86] Much of the problem derived from a failing national economy and increased competition from other media. But many analysts attributed at least part of the

---

[81] Erik Barnouw, *The Golden Web* (New York: Oxford UP, 1968) 26, vol. 2 of *A History of Broadcasting in the United States*.

[82] Erik Barnouw, *The Image Empire* (New York: Oxford UP, 1970) 126, vol. 3 of *A History of Broadcasting in the United States*.

[83] *See, e.g.,* "Plot Thickens at the Patrick FCC," *Broadcasting,* 29 Aug. 1988, at 27.

[84] "Micromanagement of the FCC: Here to Stay?" *Broadcasting,* 26 Dec. 1988, at 56.

[85] *See, e.g.,* "TOC's Public Interest Announcement," *Broadcasting,* 16 Feb. 1987, at 30; "A Pendulum Poised to Strike Back," editorial, *Broadcasting,* 16 Mar. 1987, at 106; "DSA Winner Umansky Champions Localism," *Broadcasting,* 6 Apr. 1987, at 76; "Deregulation Reduced to Four-Letter Word at NAB," *Broadcasting,* 11 Apr. 1988, at 34; "Padden Opts for Reregulation," *Broadcasting,* 25 Apr. 1988, at 42; "INTV's Padden Says Broadcasters Must Embrace Public Interest," *Broadcasting,* 27 June 1988, at 52; "Open Mike," *Broadcasting,* 4 July 1988, at 22; "Fritts Blasts FCC," *Broadcasting,* 31 July 1989, at 73.

[86] "Mass Media Bureau Has Come Up with Count of Broadcast Stations That Are Now Dark," *Broadcasting,* 1 Oct. 1990, at 96; "Financial Workouts: Growing Fact of Life in the 90s," *Broadcasting,* 15 Oct. 1990, at 65; "Majority of Radio Stations Operating at Loss," *Broadcasting,* 26 Aug. 1991, at 17.

problem to unfettered deregulation that had allowed stations to be bought and sold at ever-increasing debt loads.

DISCUSSION QUESTIONS

1. Compare the structure of the Federal Communications Commission with the overall structure of the federal government. Are there checks and balances? Is there a division of power? Does it work as it is supposed to? How is it supposed to work ideally?

2. Chapter 2 made the points that radio frequencies are scarce natural resources in the public domain and that the FCC must find that the public interest would be served before making a decision on licensing. In FCC hearings and appeals, who represents the interest of the public? In your answer, take into consideration the constant and persistent lobbying by the regulated industries at all levels of the FCC.

3. How would you change the FCC to have it function more effectively in all areas of responsibility, including making long-range national communications policy? Do not limit yourself to altering and retaining the existing body now known as the Federal Communications Commission.

4. How would you make the enforcement procedures the FCC now uses more effective? What would you do about the cease and desist order? How would you make it more "usable," and in what types of situations could it be used?

SUGGESTED READINGS

Bellamy, Robert V., Jr. "Constraints on a Broadcast Innovation: Zenith's Phonevision System, 1931–1972." *Journal of Communication* 38(4) (autumn 1988): 8–20.

Cole, Barry G., and Mal Oettinger. *Reluctant Regulators: The FCC and the Broadcast Audience.* Reading, MA: Addison, 1978.

Ferrall, Victor E., Jr. "The Impact of Television Deregulation on Private and Public Interests." *Journal of Communication* 39 (1989): 8–38.

Hallock, Clay D. "Station License Revocations and Denials of Renewal, 1981–1988: FCC Regulatory Sanctions and Philosophy in Perspective." Thesis. U of Florida, 1989.

Hilliard, Robert L. *The Federal Communications Commission: A Primer.* Boston: Focal, 1991.

Krasnow, Erwin G., Lawrence D. Longley, and Herbert A. Terry. *The Politics of Broadcast Regulation.* 3rd ed. New York: St. Martin's, 1982.

Lichty, Lawrence W. "The Impact of FRC and FCC Commissioners' Backgrounds on the Regulation of Broadcasting." *Journal of Broadcasting* 6 (1962): 97–110.

Lichty, Lawrence W. "Members of the Federal Radio Commission and the Federal Communications Commission 1927–1961." *Journal of Broadcasting* 6 (1962): 23–24.

Mosco, Vincent. "The Mythology of Telecommunications Deregulation." *Journal of Communication* 40(3) (summer 1990): 36–49.

Pennybacker, John H. "The Limits of Judicial Review: The FCC, the U.S. Court of Appeals for the District of Columbia, and the Supreme Court." *Journalism Monographs* 116 (Sept. 1989).

Ray, William B. *FCC: The Ups and Downs of Radio-TV Regulation.* Ames: Iowa State UP, 1990.

Starr, Michael F., and David J. Atkin. "The Department of Communications: A Plan and Policy for the Abolition of the Federal Communications Commission." *Com/Ent* (1990): 181–204.

Trauth, Denise M., and John L. Huffman. "A Case Study of a Difference of Communications: The DC Circuit Court of Appeals and the FCC." *Journal of Broadcasting and Electronic Media* 33 (summer 1989): 247–272.

Williams, Wenmouth, Jr. "Impact of Commissioner Background on FCC Decisions: 1962–1975." *Journal of Broadcasting* 20 (1976): 239–260.

5

OTHER DETERMINANTS OF REGULATORY POLICY

While the FCC is the primary agency to regulate radio and television, other entities also play major roles in regulating broadcasting and cable. Additional federal agencies and organizations and nongovernmental organizations also wield influence. In some cases the regulatory activities are direct; in other cases they are indirect. This chapter will introduce these organizations and explain the role they play in regulating the electronic media.

5.1 FEDERAL TRADE COMMISSION

The Federal Trade Commission protects consumers from deceptive advertising and enforces antitrust laws.

Broadcasting and cable carry advertising to generate revenue. As a result, these industries come into contact with the Federal Trade Commission (FTC), which regulates false, deceptive, and unfair advertisements. Some advertising regulation occurs under state law, and several other government agencies have some stake in the regulation of advertising. Nevertheless, the most significant regulation of advertising occurs at the federal level, and the Federal Trade Commission is the primary agency to regulate advertising. Since Congress did not give the FCC authority in the Communications Act to punish stations or cable operators for unfair advertising, the FCC leaves advertising regulation to the FTC.

Generally, the FTC brings actions against businesses, and often their advertising agencies, for misleading advertising practices. The FTC can bring direct actions against stations or cable systems for false or misleading advertising they originate, although such actions are relatively rare. Broadcast stations and cable operators must observe state laws that require the disclosure of such items as finance terms on the sale of automobiles (usually in very small print), state or local occupational license numbers for plumbers, roofers, and the like, and going-out-of-business registration numbers to indicate when a business is truly going out of business.

Stations and cable operators more often feel the indirect impact of FTC actions. If the FTC brings action against a class of businesses, as it did in 1992 when it restricted certain claims for weight loss clinics, the changes must be reflected in advertising run by the station or system. However, since such advertising copy is often prepared by an advertising agency, the station or system has little role in carrying out requests to eliminate inappropriate claims in such advertising.

Stations and cable systems feel FTC action more directly when the FTC seeks to ban the advertising of a product or limit the advertising of it. As we will see later in this chapter (EMG 5.1.4), the FCC did propose limits on advertising in children's programs. This ban was not implemented, but if it had been, stations would have experienced a loss of advertising revenue.

The FTC was created in 1914 and is structured much like the FCC. It has a five-member commission that is appointed by the president and approved by the Senate. Terms of office are seven years, and a person filling a vacancy is appointed to the unexpired time of the commissioner who had the position. No more than three members can belong to the same political party. A staff of more than 1,600 scientists, attorneys, and accountants issue reports, investigate product claims, and bring actions against advertisers.

When the FTC was first established, its responsibility was to prevent monopolistic business practices. The Commission primarily focused on antitrust policy, and the law did not specifically grant the FTC power to regulate advertising. In 1938, the Wheeler-Lea Amendment[1] granted the FTC power to protect consumers from deceptive advertising[2] and to control the advertising of food, drugs, cosmetics, and therapeutic devices.[3]

For many years the FTC budget was modest, and its accomplishments were largely unnoticed. It finally took the consumer movement of the 1960s to draw attention to the problems of advertising promise versus product performance. Consumer advocate Ralph Nader documented design and engineering flaws of the rear-engine Corvair, forcing General Motors to stop production of the car.[4] At the same time, he drew attention to the FTC and commented on the shortcomings of the agency. A 1969 American Bar Association study of the FTC's role in policing advertising soundly condemned FTC practices and suggested reforms.[5] A major benefit of the scrutiny was that Congress increased the budget of the FTC, and during the 1970s the FTC aggressively policed the advertising business. However, the 1980s

---

[1] H.R. Rep. No. 1613, 75th Cong., 1st Sess. 3 (1937).

[2] *See* Sec. 5(b), "Unfair methods of competition in commerce, and unfair or deceptive acts or practices in commerce, are declared unlawful," 15 U.S.C. § 45.

[3] 15 U.S.C. § 12.

[4] Ralph Nader, *Unsafe at Any Speed* (New York: Grossman, 1972).

[5] *Facts on File* 29 (11–17 Sept. 1969): 597; 30 (20–26 Aug. 1970) 608.

produced a turn of events. Businesses, Congress, and President Reagan all challenged the FTC. Eventually, the Reagan administration, with its emphasis on government deregulation, cut the FTC budget and limited the agency's power to challenge advertisements as deceptive. The administration of President George Bush made no major improvements in the FTC and had broad support from business. A spokesperson for President Clinton predicted the FTC under Clinton would not be an activist agency but would be responsible, perhaps with a tightening of regulation on both alcohol and tobacco.[6] However, a group of consumer advocates urged Clinton to clean house at the FTC. They urged Clinton to name a chair from the ranks of state and local consumer protection officials.[7]

Efforts to control deceptive advertising brought the FTC into conflict with some major businesses. The FTC had rulings against Sears appliances, Wonder and Profile breads, Warner-Lambert's Listerine, and Sterling Drug's pain relievers. These companies were often willing to fight the FTC, and in addition they applied political influence to ease agency restrictions.

5.1.1   Deceptive Advertising

Advertising is considered deceptive if there is an omission or misrepresentation that would cause a reasonable consumer to misunderstand an advertising claim, and if the misrepresentation is material.

Before the FTC can take action against an advertisement, it is necessary to show that the advertisement is deceptive or false. An investigation may be initiated by the FTC as a result of a staff investigation or as a result of consumer complaints alleging illegal activities. The means used by the FTC to define deceptive advertising are important both to the advertisers and to consumers. In a 1983 policy statement the Commission identified three elements that must exist if an advertisement is considered deceptive. First, there must be a misrepresentation, omission, or other practice in the advertisement that is likely to mislead consumers. Second, the advertisement must be considered from the perspective of a consumer acting in reasonable circumstances. Finally, the misrepresentation, omission, or practice must be material.[8] Let us examine each element further to see how they have been applied.

5.1.1.1   *Misrepresentation or Omission*

Misrepresentation is construed to be the tendency of an advertisement to deceive. Actual deception need not occur.

When the FTC staff considers an alleged misrepresentation, they look at the entire advertisement and the overall impression it creates. The basic consideration

---

[6] Steven W. Colford, "And the Clinton Era Begins, Transition Team Report; Don't Change the FTC," *Advertising Age*, 25 Jan. 1993, at 1.

[7] "Washington Watch," *Broadcasting*, 5 Apr. 1993, at 42.

[8] Trade Reg. Rep. (CCH) (Current) Section 50, 455, p. 56,079.

is capability or tendency of the advertisement to deceive. There need not be proof that the advertisement actually deceived anyone.

A classic case of misrepresentation occurred in 1965 when the Colgate-Palmolive Company used a false demonstration in a television commercial for Rapid Shave. The goal was to place Rapid Shave on sandpaper and, within a few moments, shave away the sand with a razor. The problem was that sandpaper could not be sufficiently moistened with Rapid Shave to shave the sand immediately. When the FTC tested the process, it took an hour to properly moisturize the sandpaper. To solve the problem, the producers of the commercial replaced the sandpaper with Plexiglas covered with sand, and the FTC termed that misrepresentation.

On appeal, the decision was reversed on the grounds that any mock-up could be considered deceptive. However, the Supreme Court agreed with the FTC that the mock-up was materially deceptive, although it stated that not all mock-ups or props would be considered deceptive. The Court noted that mock-ups could be used to overcome the technical distortions of television, as long as the mock-up is not used falsely to prove a product claim. For instance, the Court said that an advertiser could use mashed potatoes to represent ice cream in an advertisement for kitchenware, since the ice cream would melt quickly under hot lighting. On the other hand, mashed potatoes should not be used to depict the texture of ice cream.[9]

In another instance, Campbell Soup Company wanted viewers of its TV spots to see the meat and vegetables in its new Chunky Soups. But when bowls of the soup were prepared for the commercials, the heavier meat and vegetables sank to the bottom of the bowl. To make them visible, the producer of the spot placed a layer of clear, glass marbles on the bottom of the bowl with the meat and vegetables resting on top. The FTC also considered this to be misrepresentation.[10]

In 1992, the manufacturer of Volvo automobiles and its advertising agency were both ordered to pay $150,000 fines for misrepresenting the strength, structural integrity, and crashworthiness of Volvo automobiles.[11] In a TV ad, an oversized pickup was driven over a row of automobiles and crushed all the cars in the row except a Volvo station wagon. The FTC charged that some of the Volvos used in the demonstration were structurally reinforced, and structural supports in some of the competing cars were severed.[12]

There may be a serious problem with what the consumer is not told about the product. Such sins of omission can be severely damaging to the consumer, for information deleted from advertisements can have harmful effects. One major example is the warning labels placed on cigarette advertisements that inform consumers of the link between smoking and cancer. Without the warning label the message about the health risk is omitted. A second example involves deceptive advertise-

---

[9] Colgate-Palmolive Co. v. FTC, 380 U.S. 734 (1965).

[10] Campbell Soup Co., 77 F.T.C. 644 (1970).

[11] Volvo N. Am. Corp., 57 Fed Reg. 6328 (Feb. 24, 1992); Scali, McCabe, Sloves, Inc., 57 Fed. Reg. 6327 (Feb. 24, 1992).

[12] Volvo N. Am. Corp., 56 Fed. Reg. 43,782 (Sept. 4, 1991).

ments that deliberately attempt to mislead the public by omitting important data. As discussed later in this chapter, Profile bread was advertised as having fewer calories, when the only difference between it and other brands of bread was that it was sliced thinner. Naturally, the public was not told that they would get fewer calories per slice because the slices were thinner. That was an omission that the FTC felt the public should be informed about. Also, the FTC charged a fertility institute with misrepresenting the percentage of patients that achieve success in overcoming infertility.[13] The clinic's ads did not include the number of patients that gave birth or achieved pregnancy. The FTC also cited several rental car companies for not disclosing certain charges that were mandatory or not reasonably avoidable. For instance, the ads did not disclose mandatory airport surcharges based on the driver's age and they advertised unlimited mileage without disclosing geographical driving restrictions.[14]

5.1.1.2 *Reasonable Person Test*
The FTC judges whether an ordinary person would be deceived by a questionable advertisement. Such a person should be able to recognize and accept puffery in an advertisement.

The test of whether an advertising claim or presentation is misleading is to be judged from the viewpoint of a reasonable consumer. This means that advertising claims should be understood by "ordinary purchasers of the advertised goods or services at whom the advertising is directed or who can ordinarily be expected to read or view it."[15]

A reasonable person is expected to be able to endure a certain amount of "puffery" in advertising. Puffery is an exaggeration expressed in broad, vague, and laudatory language. This sales talk or puffing is thought to express the seller's opinion only, which is to be discounted as such by the buyer.[16] Explained less generously, puffing "amounts to a seller's privilege to lie his head off, so long as he says nothing specific. . . ."[17] The FTC gives advertisers latitude to exaggerate claims on subjective items such as smell, taste, feel, and appearance. The latitude exists simply because the FTC believes that reasonable people will recognize puffery and not take it seriously. For example, the FTC said it was reasonable for the makers of Bayer aspirin to claim that "Bayer works wonders."[18] At the same time, a court of appeals said Pennzoil's claim that its motor oil offered "better protection against engine wear" was common puffery.[19]

---

[13] Fertility Inst. of W. Mass., 56 Fed. Reg. 3479 (Jan. 30, 1991).

[14] *See* Dollar Rent-A-Car Sys., Inc., 57 Fed. Reg. 38,509; Value Rent-A-Car, Inc., 57 Fed. Reg. 38,513 (Aug. 25, 1992).

[15] George E. Rosden and Peter Rosden, *The Law of Advertising* (New York: Bender, 1979) 18.

[16] Castrol, Inc. v. Pennzoil Co. and Pennzoil Products Co., U.S. App. LEXIS 1778, at *18 (1993).

[17] W. Page Keeton (ed.), *Hornbook on the Law of Torts,* 5th ed. (St. Paul, MN: West, 1984) 756–757.

[18] Bristol-Myers Co., 102 F.T.C. 21 (1983), *aff'd,* 738 F.2d 554 (1984).

[19] U.S. App. LEXIS 1778, at *18.

Advertisements targeted at a specific audience are evaluated from the perspective of that audience. If advertising is aimed at the elderly, children, or non-English-speaking consumers, the advertising will be considered in terms of the likely effect it will have on a reasonable member of that group. In this instance, the FTC may consider advertising to be unfair as well as deceptive.[20] In one case, the FTC halted ads for General Foods showing naturalist Euell Gibbons eating berries and wild nuts. The ads were not false or misleading but the FTC was concerned that children might imitate Gibbons and poison themselves.[21] In another case, a court of appeals upheld an FTC cease and desist order against the S.S.S. Company for advertisements that led people to conclude that their tiredness was related to an iron or vitamin deficiency that could be remedied by the S.S.S. products. The court based its ruling on the fact that the advertising was aimed at the urban and rural poor "who are more likely to be uneducated and uninformed, and who are thus most likely to be victimized by improper self-medication resulting from false and misleading advertising."[22]

Despite the concern for the naive or gullible, an advertiser is not held responsible if a consumer simply has extremely limited knowledge of a product. As the Commission noted in one case, the FTC does not help the person who believes that all Danish pastry is made in Denmark.[23]

5.1.1.3 Likelihood of Deceit

The key to materiality is whether the advertisement is likely to deceive, or has a tendency to do so.

To be material, an advertising claim or practice must have a tendency to make a difference in a consumer's buying decision. The advertisement need not actually affect the consumer's decision, and the consumer does not have to lose money in the transaction.[24]

The FTC has specified certain categories of information as being significant in determining whether an advertising claim is material. These include:

1. information concerning the purpose, efficacy, or cost of the product or service;
2. claims about durability, performance, warranties, or quality;
3. information about the primary characteristics of the product or service;
4. claims or omissions that significantly involve health or safety; and,
5. specific claims about the attributes of the product.

---

[20] Section 5 of the Federal Trade Commission Act states that unfair competition and unfair or deceptive acts or practices in commerce are illegal. *See* 15 U.S.C. § 45(a)(1).

[21] General Foods Corp., 86 F.T.C. 831 (1975).

[22] S.S.S. Co. v. FTC, 116 F.2d 226 (1969).

[23] Heinz W. Kirchner, 63 F.T.C. 1282, 1290 (1963).

[24] Section 5 of the Federal Trade Commission Act defines false advertising as an advertisement, other than labeling, that is misleading in a material respect. 15 U.S.C. § 5.

Miles, Inc., manufacturer of One-A-Day vitamins, was cited by the FTC for falsely implying that the product protected the lungs against the adverse effects of air pollution, and that the product replaced Vitamin B depleted by everyday stress.[25] Finally, the FTC ruled as material a claim that Anacin and Arthritis Pain Formula relieved pain better than other pain relievers.[26] The concern was that the claim would affect the public's decision to buy the product.

5.1.2   Stopping Deceptive Advertising

Before the FTC can halt advertising believed to be deceptive, it must first determine if a violation has occured. If so, it can issue a consent decree, a cease and desist order, or an injunction.

The FTC cannot issue a formal complaint against an advertiser until it determines that illegal practices actually exist. The FTC staff makes this determination by investigating potential violations. Investigations may stem from complaints to the FTC by consumers or businesses, or from studies initiated by the FTC.

5.1.2.1   Consent Decrees

When a case is settled by a consent decree, the business, individual, or advertising agency involved signs a formal agreement specifying that the illegal practices will be discontinued or corrected.

If an FTC investigation concludes that a violation exists, the FTC staff submits a proposed complaint to the Commission. The Commission contacts the party involved in the challenged practice and offers it a chance to sign a consent decree.[27] The public is permitted to comment on the proposed consent order and the FTC may take the comments into account in issuing the final order.

The majority of FTC cases are resolved by consent decrees because there are distinct advantages for the advertiser. The consent decree stipulates what the advertiser must do to end the deception. If the advertiser agrees to the terms, the action ends. Signing a consent decree does not acknowledge wrongdoing and saves the advertiser the cost and negative publicity that could result from a formal FTC action. However, failure to honor the decree may subject the advertiser to a fine of $10,000 a day.

Mobil Oil Corporation accepted a consent order prohibiting the company from making unsubstantiated degradability and environmental benefit claims concerning plastic bags manufactured by the company.[28] The FTC said the bags were not biodegradable.

---

[25] Miles, Inc., 56 Fed. Reg. 8204 (Feb. 27, 1991).

[26] American Home Prod., 98 F.T.C. 136,368 (1981), *aff'd*, American Home Prod. v. FTC, 695 F.2d 681 (3rd Cir. 1982).

[27] Edwin S. Rockefeller, *Desk Book of FTC Practice and Procedure*, 3rd ed. (New York: Practising Law Inst., 1979) 105–109.

[28] Mobil Oil Corp., 58 Fed. Reg. 11,412 (Feb. 13, 1993).

5.1.2.2 Cease and Desist Orders

The FTC can issue an offending advertiser a cease and desist order if the advertiser chooses not to sign a consent decree.

If an advertiser decides not to sign a consent decree, the FTC may then file a formal complaint against it. If a formal complaint is issued, the case is assigned to an administrative law judge, who will hear the case. The FTC bears the burden of proof that the challenged practice is deceptive, and the administrative law judge has two options: either close the case because no substantial violation has occurred, or issue a formal complaint, along with a proposed cease and desist order.

A cease and desist order can be appealed to the FTC commissioners and then to a federal appeals court. Either the FTC or the advertiser may also appeal to the Supreme Court. Failure to adhere to a cease and desist order can lead to fines of up to $10,000 a day, although the fines are usually much less.

Appeals of an administrative law judge's ruling are rare because of the cost and bad publicity the business may suffer during the appeal. However, some cases are appealed, and may result in protracted legal battles. In fact, some companies may not wish to stop a successful advertising campaign and may feel the sales of a product may outweigh legal costs.

J.B. Williams Company, the maker of Geritol, battled for 14 years after an original cease and desist order was issued. The vitamin-and-iron product was advertised as being effective in reducing tiredness, loss of strength, and that "run-down" feeling. The FTC ruled the advertisement deceptive because tiredness is caused by factors not usually affected by Geritol. After 11 years of litigation the company was fined $800,000 for violating the FTC order, but a court of appeals granted a new trial.[29] Three years later the FTC won a $280,000 verdict against J.B. Williams.

Another case involved an FTC cease and desist order against *Reader's Digest.* The publication violated a consent order in which it publicized subscriptions with simulated checks and money that were supposedly redeemable for cash or a new automobile. In the 10 years of legal proceedings the magazine ignored two cease and desist orders. A district court penalized *Reader's Digest* $1,750,000 for violating the cease and desist orders, counting each advertisement as a separate act of deception. According to the court, *Reader's Digest* generated over $5 million in gross subscription funds from the deceptive advertising. A court of appeals upheld the lower court ruling.[30]

5.1.2.3 Injunctions

If advertisers continue to run deceptive advertising despite FTC pressure, the Commission can seek an injunction or restraining order in federal court to stop the advertising. A competing business can also seek a court injunction if its business is harmed by deceptive advertising.

---

[29] United States v. J.B. Williams Co., 498 F.2d 414 (2d Cir. 1974).
[30] United States v. Reader's Digest Ass'n, 662 F.2d 955 (1981); *cert. denied,* 455 U.S. 908 (1982).

In 1973 Congress passed legislation that enables the FTC to obtain temporary restraining orders and temporary injunctions to stop deceptive advertising.[31] Attorneys for the FTC can seek these orders in federal court. An injunction is a drastic step, but one the FTC can use to stop misleading advertising quickly. Commission policy is to use other administrative remedies unless there is a clear law violation or where there is no likelihood that the offending advertisement will soon cease running. Section 13 of the Federal Trade Commission Act also empowers the FTC to seek an injunction to stop deceptive advertising if public health is a concern.[32]

On one occasion, the FTC obtained a temporary injunction to block false and misleading statements about the relationship between eating eggs and heart and circulatory disease. The National Commission on Egg Nutrition claimed that there was no scientific evidence to show that eating eggs increases the risk of heart or circulatory disease. The FTC disagreed and a court of appeals upheld the decision.[33]

5.1.3 Changing the Content of Advertisements

In some cases, the FTC may let advertisers continue to run questionable advertising, but only after requiring changes in the content of the advertisement.

In addition to taking steps to get advertisers to halt questionable advertising, the FTC has the power to require advertisers to change the content of advertisements to make them accurate. The FTC can use either affirmative disclosure, substantiation of claims, or corrective advertising to prevent deception.

5.1.3.1 *Affirmative Disclosure*

If an advertisement does not state all facts about the product or service, the FTC may require the company to correct the false impression in future advertising.

At times advertisements make claims that do not tell the full story. Under such circumstances, the goal is to reveal the facts required to keep an advertisement from being deceptive, the facts left out in the initial advertisement. The Geritol case cited above was such an example. To avoid deception, the company was ordered to state in future advertising that the tonic would probably not correct a feeling of fatigue. Health warnings on cigarette packages and beer containers are other instances of affirmative disclosure. In addition, a court of appeals upheld an FTC ruling that a weight reduction product called "X-11" falsely reported that users of the product could lose weight without restricting their caloric intake and while they continued to eat the food of their choice. The manufacturer of the product was required to include the phrase "Dieting Is Required" in future ads for "X-11."[34]

---

[31] Pub. L. No. 93-153, 87 Stat. 576, at 591–92.
[32] *See* FTC v. Sterling Drug, Inc., 317 F.2d 669, 671 (1963).
[33] National Comm'n on Egg Nutrition v. FTC, 570 F.2d 157 (1977).
[34] Porter & Dietsch v. FTC, 605 F.2d 295 (1979).

5.1.3.2 *Advertising Substantiation*

The advertising substantiation program, located in Section 6 of FTCA, seeks to assist consumers in making rational buying decisions and pressures advertisers to have adequate data to back claims.

The goal of substantiation is to require advertisers to prove that the claims they make are true.[35] For example, if an automobile manufacturer claims a given car will get better mileage than its competitors, it must provide documentation to prove the claim. Firestone Tire and Rubber did not have evidence for its claim that its Sport Wide Oval Tires "corner better, run cooler, and stop 25 percent quicker." The tires did stop quicker on wet pavement, but Firestone had no data to prove the tires performed better on normal roads.[36] Similarly, Kraft failed to substantiate a comparative nutrient or calcium-content claim for cheese, substitute cheese, or imitation cheese.[37] The FTC felt the ads misrepresented the calcium content of the products.

5.1.3.3 *Corrective Advertising*

Corrective advertising has been used to correct deception in long-term advertising campaigns.

In instances where a long-term advertising campaign leads to misrepresentation, the FTC may turn to corrective advertising. The FTC applies corrective advertisements on a case-by-case basis only after surveys of the public measure the amount of exposure to the advertisements and the degree of persuasion generated by the claims.

The FTC first imposed corrective advertising in 1971 against ITT Continental Baking Company, bakers of Profile Bread. In a series of television commercials, Profile was touted as an aid in weight reduction. The FTC ruled that Profile advertisements left the misleading impression that Profile bread had fewer calories than other kinds of bread. In reality, Profile had the same number of calories per ounce as other kinds of bread. Thus, if the bread in any way contributed to weight reduction, it was because it was sliced thinner.

ITT Continental accepted a consent order requiring a corrective statement in all of its advertising the following year. The corrective statement was "Profile is not effective for weight reduction, contrary to possible interpretations of prior advertising."[38] Some critics of corrective advertising have maintained that the advertisements are too weak. Such criticism was leveled at the corrective advertisement ITT Continental ran for Profile Bread, the dialogue for which ran as follows:

---

[35] *See* Policy Statement Regarding Advertising Substantiation Program, 4 Trade Reg. Rep. (CCH) para. 39,060 (1984).

[36] Firestone Tire & Rubber Co. v. FTC, 481 F.2d 264 (6th Cir. 1973), *cert. denied,* 414 U.S. 1112 (1973).

[37] Kraft, Inc., 56 Fed. Reg. 8203 (Feb. 27, 1991).

[38] ITT Continental Baking Co., Inc., 79 F.T.C. 248 (1971).

I'm Julia Mead for Profile Bread. And like all mothers I'm concerned about nutrition and balanced meals. So I'd like to clear up any misunderstanding you may have about Profile Bread from its advertising or even its name. Does Profile have fewer calories than other breads? No, Profile has about the same per ounce as other breads. To be exact Profile has seven fewer calories per slice. But that's because it's sliced thinner. But eating Profile Bread will not cause you to lose weight. A reduction of seven calories is insignificant. It's total calories and balanced nutrition that counts. And Profile can help you achieve a balanced meal, because it provides protein and B vitamins as well as other nutrients.

A second application of corrective advertising came when the FTC ordered the Warner-Lambert Company, manufacturer of Listerine, to run statements to correct the impression that the use of Listerine would help prevent colds. Warner-Lambert fought the FTC all the way to the Supreme Court in a test of FTC authority.

Listerine had been on the market since 1879 and was one of the most widely sold mouthwashes. The FTC had examined the product's claims several times, but did not take action. In 1972, the FTC began another study, which concluded that Listerine actually did kill bacteria in the throat and mouth. The misleading aspect was that colds are caused by viruses, which are immune to the ingredients in Listerine. Thus, Listerine had no effect on colds.

The FTC issued a cease and desist order that required Warner-Lambert to stop advertising for Listerine that claimed to prevent colds. Moreover, it ordered Warner-Lambert to include in future advertising this corrective sentence: "Contrary to prior advertising, Listerine will not help prevent colds or sore throats or lessen their severity." Since Listerine had been advertised as a cure for the cold for so long, the FTC ordered Warner-Lambert to spend $10 million on advertising that included the corrective statement.

Warner-Lambert appealed to the U.S. court of appeals, contending that the penalty was excessive and that the ruling violated its First Amendment rights. A divided court ruled that the FTC had not exceeded its authority in ordering corrective advertising. Further, the court said false or misleading advertising does not warrant First Amendment protection.[39] The court did feel that the phrase "contrary to prior advertising" was unnecessary, so it was deleted from the corrective statement. Warner-Lambert appealed the case to the Supreme Court, which refused to hear the case. In the meantime, Warner-Lambert repositioned Listerine as a remedy for bad breath and incorporated the corrective statement in its advertising.

In a number of other cases the FTC has sought to use corrective advertising. These cases include Ocean Spray cranberry juice, which was advertised as having fewer calories than other juices;[40] Chevron gasoline, which claimed that its additive F-310 helped reduce air pollution;[41] and Coca-Cola, for claims made about the nu-

---

[39] Warner-Lambert Co. v. FTC, 562 F.2d 749 (D.C. Cir. 1977), *cert. denied,* 435 U.S. 950 (1978).
[40] Ocean Spray Cranberries, Inc., 70 F.T.C. 975 (1972).
[41] Standard Oil Co. of Cal. v. FTC, 577 F.2d 653 (9th Cir. 1978).

tritional qualities of its Hi-C fruit drinks.[42] In one case, a federal appeals court ruled that the FTC violated the First Amendment when it ruled that a finance company could not advertise loans as "instant tax refunds." The FTC had ruled that defining a loan as a tax refund misled consumers. The court said the company could refer to "instant tax refunds" in its ads as long as the messages clarified that the "refund" was actually a loan.[43]

Some critics of corrective advertising questioned whether the corrective advertisements actually removed the incorrect impressions from the minds of consumers. The advertising industry expressed strong displeasure with corrective advertising, and the business-oriented Reagan and Bush administrations also opposed it. As a result, the FTC has largely discontinued use of corrective advertising since the 1970s.

5.1.3.4 *Trade Regulation Rules*

Trade regulation rules enable the FTC to establish a rule applying to all advertisers of a given product or service.

In 1975, the Magnuson-Moss Warranty Federal Trade Commission Improvement Act gave the Commission the right to issue trade regulation rules or TRRs.[44] The impact of this legislation is dramatic, for it gives the FTC the power to issue rules defining and prohibiting deceptive acts and practices.

In the past the FTC had to pursue misleading advertisements one at a time. By issuing a TRR, the agency can issue a uniform rule that can apply to a given industry. The rule has the force of law. Thus, for example, the FTC can establish a rule pertaining to the advertising of headache remedies. All companies who manufacture headache remedies are bound by the rule, and if one such company breaks the rule, it may be asked to pay damages, refund money, return property, and pay civil penalties of up to $10,000 for each day of a violation.

The creation of a trade rule is not an arbitrary FTC action. The FTC first proposes a new rule, publishes it, and seeks input. Consumers, manufacturers, and advertisers can present testimony at hearings. Written comments are also accepted. All parties have 60 days to challenge a final rule in a federal appeals court.

Since 1975, the FTC has issued trade regulation rules for the advertising of eyeglasses,[45] cigarettes,[46] used cars,[47] home insulation,[48] vocational schools,[49] and others.

---

[42] 3 Trade Reg. Rep. (CCH), para. 19,351 (FTC, 1970).

[43] Beneficial Corp. v. FTC, 542 F.2d 611 (1976), *cert. denied,* 430 U.S. 983 (1977).

[44] Pub. L. No. 93-637, 88 Stat. 2183, 15 U.S.C. § 45 et seq. (1975).

[45] Advertising of Ophthalmic Goods and Services, 43 Fed. Reg. 23,992 (1978).

[46] FTC Trade Regulation Rule for the Prevention of Unfair or Deceptive Acts or Practices in the Sale of Cigarettes, 29 Fed. Reg. 8324 (1964).

[47] 16 C.F.R. § 455.

[48] 16 C.F.R. § 460.

[49] Proprietary Vocational and Home Study Schools, 43 Fed. Reg. 60,796 (1978).

The Trade Commission Act also gave the FTC the authority to bring suit in federal court on behalf of consumers who have fallen victim to violations of a TRR or a cease and desist order. Civil penalties of up to $10,000 a day can be imposed against violators.

5.1.4 Television Advertising Directed at Children

The FTC has been pressured both to protect children from television advertising and to refrain from instituting such rules.

Pressure groups have besieged both the FCC and FTC to act against television advertising directed at children. As a result of pressure by Action for Children's Television (ACT), the FTC as early as 1974 considered special protection for children. The Commission feared that advertising aimed at children would exploit their innocence and gullibility, so a ban on TV advertisements designed to entice children to buy cereals was proposed. The FTC considered the ban for over three years before deciding not to adopt it, but instead to deal with issues concerning children's advertising on a case-by-case basis.

In 1978 the FTC released a staff report that recommended the following trade regulation rule:

1. Bar all advertising from television shows seen by substantial numbers of children less than age 8
2. Ban the advertising of sugary foods that pose a dental health risk from television shows seen by significant numbers of children age 8 to 11
3. Allow continued television advertising of less hazardous sugared foods to the 8 to 11 age group, but only if the individual food advertisers fund messages concerning dental health and nutrition[50]

The Commission voted to issue the proposed TRR as a way of gaining feedback on the feasibility of the regulations. Since the TRR posed a direct threat to advertising revenue spent on television commercials aimed at children, the response was vociferous. Industry pressure led Congress to refuse funding for the FTC, and to enact veto power over TRRs the FTC planned to issue. As a result, Congress passed the Federal Trade Improvements Act of 1980, which prohibited the FTC from instituting the children's advertising rules.[51]

5.2 COURTS

Both the U.S. Court of Appeals for the District of Columbia Circuit and the U.S. Supreme Court conduct judicial review of decisions by the FCC. The Court of Ap-

---

[50] FTC Staff Report on Television Advertising to Children, at 348 (1978).
[51] Pub. L. No. 96-252, 14, 94 Stat. 388, 5 U.S.C.A. § 45 et seq (1980).

peals has overturned many FCC decisions, while the Supreme Court tends to side with the FCC.

Government administrative agencies, such as the FCC and the FTC, are permitted to make policy, but the courts are empowered to conduct judicial review of such policy. As a result, administrative agencies must make certain that their policies have been properly formulated. The courts that conduct judicial review are the U.S. Court of Appeals and the U.S. Supreme Court.

Judicial review may consist of either statutory review or constitutional review. Statutory review involves cases where the court must determine whether a given rule is in accord with governing law. For the FCC, this might mean comparing a newly adopted rule or regulation with the standards of a statute such as the Communications Act. Constitutional review involves claims that the FCC has violated the First Amendment's prohibition on abridging freedom of speech or press in a given decision. In recent years, a number of broadcast cases have involved constitutional challenges.

5.2.1   Court of Appeals

The U.S. Court of Appeals for the District of Columbia Circuit hears appeals from the FCC. The court has been accused of usurping the authority of the FCC by ruling against the Commission on constitutional issues.

Section 402(b) of the Communications Act specifies that appeals from FCC decisions must be filed with the Court of Appeals for the District of Columbia Circuit. The court normally hears appeals in panels of three judges, but cases of particular significance may require that all the judges of the circuit sit en banc on the same panel.

Until the late 1960s, the court of appeals mostly limited review of FCC decisions to cases of procedural shortcomings. However, in the early 1970s the court began an "activist" approach to judicial review in which it developed two concepts that went beyond procedural review. One, the "Hard Look" doctrine, examined indications that the agency had not taken a "hard look" at important problems and had not engaged in reasoned decision making. The other concept, one of "Court-Agency Partnership," developed the notion that agencies and courts collaborate in furthering the public interest.[52] Use of these concepts in an increased number of broadcast cases heard by the D.C. Circuit caused speculation that the court had usurped the regulatory power of the FCC, leading one observer to call the D.C. Circuit the "upper house of the FCC."[53]

---

[52] John H. Pennybacker, " 'Activism' v. 'Restraint': The DC Circuit, the FCC and the Supreme Court," 28 *J. Broadcasting* 153 (1984).

[53] Fred W. Friendly, *The Good Guys, the Bad Guys, and the First Amendment* (New York: Vantage, 1976) 161.

By the late 1980s some believed that the FCC was losing most of its cases in the D.C. Circuit. However, an analysis by Trauth and Huffman showed that while this was untrue, the FCC did lose the most visible cases, those dealing with constitutional issues.[54] Trauth and Huffman showed the problem to be a confrontation of two philosophies endorsed by the Reagan presidency. One was the appointment of judges to the D.C. Circuit who reflected the ideals of judicial restraint, namely a reverence for the Constitution, a deference to democratically elected lawmakers, and a preference for uniformity and predictability in the law.

At the same time, the chair of the FCC, Mark Fowler, was pursuing an "activist" agenda of deregulation. This agenda favored the "marketplace model" of regulation favored by the Reagan administration, which represented a major departure from the "trusteeship model" of regulation that the Commission had used since its inception.[55] The Bush administration adopted and advanced these conflicting philosophies, which pitted the conservative court of appeals against the deregulatory efforts of the FCC.

5.2.2   U.S. Supreme Court

The Supreme Court is empowered to review decisions from the U.S. court of appeals. In broadcast cases, the Court has sided with the FCC.

The Communications Act also provides that decisions of the court of appeals are subject to review by the U.S. Supreme Court upon issuance of a discretionary writ of certiorari. Refusing to issue the writ enables the Supreme Court to decline to review some cases. Most FCC cases are now decided by the Court of Appeals for the District of Columbia Circuit. The court of appeals, the more experienced of the two courts in broadcast matters, has tended to overturn the FCC; the Supreme Court, less schooled in broadcast issues, has supported the Commission.[56]

5.3   PRESIDENT

During wartime the president is authorized to establish priorities for use of the airwaves. The president also assigns frequencies for federal government use and nominates FCC commissioners.

Section 305 of the Communications Act authorizes the president of the United States to assign all radio frequencies used by the federal government. Since a major portion of the electromagnetic spectrum is assigned to the federal government, including the military, this is a major responsibility.

---

[54] Denise M. Trauth and John L. Huffman, "A Case Study of a Difference in Perspectives: The DC Circuit Court of Appeals and the FCC," 33 *J. Broadcasting & Electronic Media* 269 (1989).

[55] *Id.*

[56] Erwin G. Krasnow, Lawrence D. Longley, and Herbert A. Terry, *The Politics of Broadcast Regulation*, 3rd ed. (New York: St. Martin's, 1982) 63.

5.3.1 Wartime Powers

During wartime the president is authorized to establish priorities for the use of the airwaves.

In the event of a general war or attack upon the nation, Section 606 of the Communications Act empowers the president to direct or establish priorities for essential communications with any commercial or governmental carrier and to prevent obstruction of telecommunications. The president may also suspend or amend rules and regulations; close stations and facilities; and authorize U.S. government use and control of radio communications during war, a presidentially declared threat of war, public peril, disaster, or national emergency, or a need to preserve the neutrality of the country.[57]

During wartime, the National Security Council is directed to provide the president with policy direction in the execution of duties under Section 606 of the Communications Act. In addition, the director of the Office of Science and Technology Policy is empowered to direct the war power functions of the president under Section 606.[58]

In nonwartime emergencies, the director of the Office of Science and Technology Policy is expected to establish a Joint Telecommunications Resources Board to assist in exercising the emergency functions.

5.3.2 Appointing FCC Commissioners

The president is able to influence communications policy by appointing FCC commissioners who will support presidential programs.

The president also wields power over broadcast regulation by appointing members of the FCC and selecting the chairperson. Although only a majority of the commissioners can be from a given political party, the president still enjoys wide latitude in selecting individuals who hold similar political and policy beliefs. Since appointments to the FCC are closely watched by the entire telecommunications industry, the president rarely appoints a commissioner if the industry is politically opposed to the nomination.[59]

The selection of the chairperson is especially significant, since this person is expected to move the Commission in the direction advocated by the president. Loyalty and devotion to administration goals are expected of the chairperson, especially when reappointment is possible. The president also nominates an individual to head the United States Information Agency (USIA), which operates the Voice of America, Radio Free Europe, and Radio Liberty, all of which engage in informational broadcasting on an international basis. Since the end of the cold war in Eastern

---

[57] 47 U.S.C. § 606.

[58] *Id.*

[59] Krasnow, Longley, and Terry, *Politics,* 68.

Europe, the need for some of the propaganda services such as Radio Free Europe has been questioned.

5.3.3   Influence on Cabinet-Level Offices

The president can influence certain communications policies through cabinet-level offices, such as the Department of State.

The influence of the president is also evident through certain cabinet-level offices. Of particular note is the Department of State, which represents the United States in communications disputes with neighboring countries. The Department of State conducts negotiations with countries such as Cuba, which has long violated international agreements by transmitting excessive power on AM broadcast frequencies, resulting in interference for American stations in the southern states.

The Department of State also plays a role in dealing with the international allocation of frequencies. A United Nations organization, the International Telecommunications Union (ITU), coordinates international treaties and multilateral agreements to allocate the broadcast spectrum to various countries to prevent interference. The ITU does not have regulatory authority, so its actions are effective only to the extent that individual nations are willing to abide by its conditions. Still, the ITU has dealt with radio since 1906. At a 1906 conference the Union assigned call letters to all nations of the world, assigning the letters *K, N,* and *W* to the United States.[60] In the 1930s the ITU also allocated the frequencies from 540 to 1600 kilocycles to AM broadcasting.

Spectrum space is allocated at meetings of the World Administrative Radio Conference (WARC), which the ITU holds periodically. The Department of State, the FCC, and the NTIA (EMG 5.6) represent the United States at WARC conferences. Prior to such meetings, the FCC seeks public input on topics of importance to U.S. communication interests. The Department of State officially represents the United States at WARC meetings. If an international conference, such as WARC, agrees on a treaty, the State Department presents the treaty to the president for ratification with the advice and consent of the Senate.

A WARC meeting in 1979 was called to revise radio regulations adopted in 1949. The meeting sought to address the concerns of more than 70 new countries that had gained independence and wanted a share of the spectrum. The conference nearly doubled the size of the AM frequency band, although many of the new frequencies are shared with other services. The conference also agreed to retain the segment of the ultra-high-frequency band (UHF) used for television, although it is also shared with other services.

---

[60] Under Section 303 of the Communications Act the FCC assigns call letters to American nongovernmental stations. American broadcasting stations use call signs beginning with *W* if located east of the Mississippi, and *K* if located west.

President Reagan supported establishment of Radio Marti, a U.S. propaganda service broadcasting to Cuba. TV Marti was put into service during the Bush administration, and President Clinton has continued support of the service.

5.3.4 Personal Agenda

Some presidents bring to office certain communications issues they want addressed. They can use their power directly or indirectly to influence the issues.

Each president also brings to office some agenda for the broadcast industry. For example, President Carter expressed concern about the sexual content of television, although he did not pursue the issue. Richard Nixon battled with the press and used his power to cut funding for public broadcasting after he thought it was too critical of his administration.

Ronald Reagan left a major imprint on the broadcasting industry. Deregulation was a hallmark of his presidency, and he selected FCC commissioners who eliminated many rules and regulations. Beyond that, Reagan challenged the Fairness Doctrine and urged the FCC to abolish it. As we shall see in Chapter 11, his efforts were successful, and he fought off congressional attempts to revive the doctrine.

5.4 CONGRESS

Congress can modify the Communications Act. In addition, Congress controls the FCC's budget, and the Senate approves those nominated to be FCC commissioners.

Since the foundation of broadcast regulation is the Communications Act, Congress maintains a major influence on regulation through the act. As we have seen, Congress wrote not only the Radio Act of 1927 but also the Communications Act of 1934.

5.4.1 Legislation

Congress, through its legislative power, can pass laws that impact the electronic media.

Because Congress created the Communications Act, it also has the power to amend it. Many attempts have been made to modify the act, and attempts, both successful and unsuccessful, occur on a regular basis (EMG 3.2.3). After the FCC abolished the Fairness Doctrine in 1987, Congress made several attempts to codify the doctrine, and may well do so again. In 1978 and 1979, a major congressional effort to rewrite the Communications Act and deregulate broadcasting, telephone, and cable also failed.

Other efforts have been more successful. Congress has twice passed legislation impacting the cable industry. In 1984, Congress passed a comprehensive regulatory plan for cable as part of a Cable Communications Policy Act. The 1984 plan shifted most franchising authority to local governments and away from the FCC. As we will see in subsequent chapters, the cable act failed to provide for problems related to rate increases and a lack of competition, so Congress reregulated cable in 1992.

5.4.2 Appropriation

Congress appropriates the funds that allow government agencies to operate, and congressional representatives use the budget process to gain favor for pet projects.

Congress is assigned authority to determine the budget of government agencies it controls, including the FCC. This enables Congress to control the total amount of money allotted to the FCC for its work, and also allows Congress to influence the goals for which funds are used. In the highly political atmosphere of Capitol Hill, this gives Congress an important trump card in FCC decision making. In 1993, FCC funding problems developed as the FCC experienced a major increase in workload when it had to implement reregulation of cable following passage of the 1992 cable act (EMG 7.2.2.4). Both Congress and the Clinton administration were faced with finding funds for the FCC.

If an influential legislator backs a proposed project, it may be funded. On the other hand, an FCC project that is unpopular with a key representative may not be funded. Both Senate and House subcommittees hold annual budget hearings to examine FCC budget requests, and individual lawmakers may influence proposals through other means.

Congress also works in conjunction with other governmental agencies to ensure that specific needs are met. When seeking a license, applicants are required to submit an environmental assessment pertaining to transmitting towers and satellite earth stations. The goal is to determine if any adverse environmental effects stem from the tower or earth station. In some instances, the results of the environmental assessment are dealt with by the Environmental Protection Agency, while in other cases the FCC will deal with the problem. The Federal Aviation Administration (FAA) also is brought into the picture. The FCC is directed to work with the FAA to resolve problems that might adversely affect the public welfare. Transmitting towers may be planned for airport flight paths and a failure to properly light a tower may pose a hazard to air traffic.

5.4.3 Confirmation

The Senate has discretionary confirmation power over presidential appointments, including those to independent regulatory agencies.

The fact that the appointment and reappointment of FCC commissioners must be approved by the Senate Commerce Committee also gives Congress important status in the conduct of the FCC. The president usually consults key senators from a nominee's home state and political party to seek support for a nominee. Influential senators can block a nomination, or push it through approval. Further, when the Senate Commerce Committee holds hearings on nominees, senators have the opportunity to make their own pet projects known and can exact concessions from nominees who might threaten them.[61]

A vivid example of the power of Congress over the FCC occurred in the latter days of the Reagan presidency. Since President Reagan had urged the FCC to abolish the Fairness Doctrine, many members of Congress were offended when the FCC carried out his wish. In retribution, key leaders of the Senate Commerce Committee refused to hold hearings for nominees to the FCC who were filling vacant positions. As a result, the FCC was forced to operate with three commissioners, rather than five, well into the Bush presidency. With only three commissioners the president had less leeway in forging political strength to push his packages through the FCC, and the Commission tended to defer action on important issues.

5.4.4 Investigation

Congress can appoint special committees to investigate the FCC or issues on which the Commission may have to act.

Congress also appoints special committees to investigate the functioning of the FCC and other agencies in relation to certain regulatory problems. Since the public is so aware of concerns in radio, television, and cable, FCC handling of these industries has led to an especially large number of special committees, and has developed reputations for individual members of Congress who have headed the committees.

A variety of issues may be heard by the FCC, but eye-catching topics such as violence on TV, children's television, and political advertising, a topic close to the heart of elected officials, are favorites of lawmakers.

5.5 EQUAL EMPLOYMENT OPPORTUNITY COMMISSION

The Equal Employment Opportunity Commission enforces federal discrimination laws. The FCC requires stations and cable operators to maintain EEO programs relating to hiring and nondiscrimination in the workplace. The FCC reviews broadcast compliance with EEO requirements as a part of license application and license renewal.

The Equal Employment Opportunity Commission (EEOC) is the federal agency created by the Civil Rights Act of 1964 that administers equal opportunity laws. In 1969, the FCC incorporated Equal Employment Opportunity (EEO) requirements into its rules for broadcast licensees (EMG 8.1.6.3), and later extended the EEO requirement to cable (EMG 8.3.6).

The FCC expects more of licensees and cable operators in terms of EEO requirements than the federal government expects of most other private employers.

---

[61] Krasnow, Longley, and Terry, *Politics*, 106.

Licensees and cable systems must do more than just avoid discrimination. FCC rules also require them to take specific, positive steps to ensure affirmative action for women and minorities.

To ensure that stations and cablecasters do not discriminate, the FCC expects them to maintain an EEO policy that prohibits discrimination based on race, color, sex, religion, or national origin. The policy must indicate the positive steps taken to recruit, hire, and promote women and minorities. Specifics of the FCC's EEO policies will be discussed in EMG 8.1.6.3.

The FCC relies on the EEOC to provide information on discrimination complaints filed with the EEOC against broadcasters and cablecasters. The Commission reviews EEO records on a periodic basis, most notably examining the records of broadcasters when an application for a license is filed, and at license renewal. Adherence to EEO policies is used by the FCC in judging whether a station is operating in the public interest. In recent years, the FCC has fined a number of stations and/or given them short-term license renewals for EEO violations. Civil rights groups have actively scrutinized station adherence to EEO standards and have filed petitions with the FCC to deny renewals when they believe EEO programs are not followed.

5.6   NATIONAL TELECOMMUNICATIONS AND INFORMATION ADMINISTRATION

> The National Telecommunications and Information Administration advises the president on telecommunications matters and promotes presidential policy to the FCC, Congress, and the public.

The National Telecommunications and Information Administration (NTIA) was established in 1978 as a part of the Department of Commerce. The goal of the NTIA is to advise the president on telecommunications policies and to lobby the FCC, Congress, and the public on acceptance of executive branch policy and viewpoints. The NTIA also coordinates the use of the electromagnetic spectrum by federal agencies and departments.

The NTIA adopts a broad view of "telecommunications" and examines such items as data communications, telephone service, radio and television broadcasting, air and sea radar, radio navigation, and emergency warning systems.

The work of the NTIA is divided among five offices. These include:

1. Office of Policy Analysis and Development, which generates domestic and federal communications policy, for instance, deregulation of the various industries and minority ownership;
2. Office of International Affairs, which examines the international competitiveness of U.S. telecommunications;
3. Office of Spectrum Management, which considers domestic issues regarding the use of the radio frequency spectrum;

4. Office of Telecommunications Applications, which promotes the development of educational and public telecommunications services—in particular, funding of public radio and television facilities; and
5. Institute for Telecommunications Sciences, the research arm of NTIA.

The NTIA is not especially visible to the public, particularly in its role of advising the president. However, the NTIA has become more visible when pushing the telecommunications policy of the president. President Bush, for instance, opposed congressional efforts in 1992 to reregulate the cable industry. During the proceedings, the NTIA was accused of providing Congress with figures supplied by the cable industry that showed that reregulation would cause cable rates to go up.[62]

5.7 CITIZEN GROUPS

Citizen groups influence regulation by filing petitions with the FCC and fighting broadcast cases in court. Groups also pressure broadcast stations and cable systems to bring about change at the local level.

Since virtually everyone watches TV or listens to radio, members of the public have played a greater role in pressuring the electronic media than less visible means of communication. The bulk of citizen group activity in broadcast cases has occurred since 1966, and the impetus for citizen group activity can be traced to one significant case.

5.7.1 Petitions to Deny License Renewal

In 1966, a citizen group's victory gave nonbroadcasters the right to intervene in license renewal hearings.

Until 1966, only those who demonstrated an economic stake in an FCC broadcast license proceeding could participate in the case. But in March 1966, the U.S. Court of Appeals, District of Columbia Circuit, ruled that the Office of Communications of the United Church of Christ could challenge the license renewal of WLBT-TV, Jackson, Mississippi, on the grounds that the station discriminated against black viewers (EMG 8.1.3.1). More importantly, the court gave responsible community groups, including "civic associations, professional societies, unions, churches, and educational institutions or associations" the right to challenge license renewal applications.[63] Citizen groups had discovered a significant method of bringing pressure on a broadcast licensee.

From the late 1960s until the mid-1970s, citizen groups seized the initiative and filed record numbers of petitions to deny license renewal. In 1970, for exam-

---

[62] Harry A. Jessell, "Cable Bill Battle Hits Home," *Broadcasting,* 21 Sept. 1992, at 46–47.
[63] Office of Communications of the United Church of Christ v. FCC, 359 F.2d 994, 1002 (D.C. Cir. 1966).

ple, 15 petitions to deny were filed with the FCC, but in 1975, 94 petitions were filed. After that, the number of petitions to deny slowed.

Even though the majority of petitions to deny did not succeed, citizen groups nevertheless found that the petitions sometimes brought concessions from the FCC, such as a requirement that stations serve subgroups within a station's coverage area. The broadcast industry usually put such requirements into practice, so the overall result of a challenge was sometimes beneficial.

5.7.2   Negotiated Settlements

Citizen groups sometimes found they could achieve their goals by filing legal suits and negotiating for settlements.

A more important lesson learned by the citizen groups was that petitions to deny could pave the way for negotiations with broadcasters that avoided protracted legal proceedings. A 1969 case against KTAL-TV, Texarkana, Texas, opened the door to this practice. Several black groups in Texarkana and the United Church of Christ negotiated an agreement with KTAL in which they withdrew a petition to deny in return for agreement by the station to resolve differences over hiring practices and programming issues (EMG 8.1.3.2). The FCC endorsed the use of negotiations and a number of groups adopted the tactic.

Another area where a citizen group worked out an agreement involved the proposed change of a radio station's format. The conflict arose when classical music station WEFM-FM, Chicago, was sold (EMG 13.2.5). The new owner planned to change the station's format to rock music. A citizen group filed a petition to deny the sale, but withdrew its petition when the new owner made a monetary donation to improve the service of other classical music stations in Chicago.[64]

5.7.3   Petitions to Enforce FCC Policies

Another citizen group tactic was to bring suits against the FCC in an effort to gain favorable implementation of FCC rules.

Not all citizen groups seek to challenge license renewals. A number of groups try to pressure the FCC to enforce specific rules or policies the groups believe are being violated. The Fairness Doctrine was such a policy. In 1967, a single individual, John F. Banzhaf III, relied on the doctrine after WCBS-TV in New York refused to give him reply time to rebut cigarette commercials. The FCC ruled that anticigarette public service announcements had to be aired to provide a reply to the commercials. The court of appeals upheld the ruling.[65] As Chapter 11 explains, the FCC moved away from its anticigarette ruling, and in 1970 Congress banned the advertising of cigarettes or small cigars on radio or television.

---

[64] *See* Zenith Radio Corp., 38 F.C.C.2d 838 (1972), and Citizens Comm. to Save WEFM v. FCC, 506 F.2d 246 (D.C. Cir. 1974).

[65] Banzhaf v. FCC, 405 F.2d 1082 (D.C. Cir. 1968).

In 1969, the National Citizens Committee for Broadcasting (NCCB), the United Church of Christ, and others filed friend of the court briefs in the famous *Red Lion* Fairness Doctrine case (EMG 11.5.1). Finally, in 1984, a local group, the Syracuse Peace Council, led the fight against editorials supporting development of a nuclear power plant in upstate New York. The group won the right to reply to the editorials, but the case eventually played a major role in the FCC's elimination of the Fairness Doctrine (EMG 11.6.1).

Citizen groups sometimes win at one level only to lose at another. In 1971, for instance, a group called the Business Executives' Move for Vietnam Peace failed to convince the FCC that WTOP-AM, Washington, D.C., should allow them to buy advertising time to speak out against the conduct of the Vietnam War. The U.S. Court of Appeals, D.C. Circuit, ruled in their favor, but, as noted in Chapter 11, the U.S. Supreme Court overturned the decision, saying that broadcasters are not required to sell such "editorial advertisements" if their general policy is to refuse such advertising.[66]

5.7.4 Changing Philosophies

The earliest citizen groups exemplified liberal orientations, but more recent groups have sprung from conservative backgrounds.

During the 1970s, citizen groups tended to represent liberal philosophies. The movement reached its peak during that decade with the formation of such well-known groups as Action for Children's Television (ACT), the National Black Media Coalition, the Media Access Project, and others.

In the 1980s and 1990s the impact of liberal citizen groups has declined and been replaced by conservative and/or religious oriented groups, such as Accuracy in Media (AIM).[67] These groups are often well funded and have large, national memberships. One such group, the Coalition for Better TV, claimed the support of numerous other interest groups, including Jerry Falwell's Moral Majority. In 1981, the group announced plans to monitor network TV for profanity, sexual content, and excessive violence. The goal was to identify advertisers of the most disapproved shows and to boycott them for one year. However, the boycott was not carried out.

5.8 SELF-REGULATION

Industry guidelines once played a strong part in the self-regulation of radio and TV stations. Now, broadcast stations and cable systems look out for themselves rather than rely on efforts by lobbying groups.

One of the tactics business groups have used to limit or prevent regulation by the government is to resort to industry self-regulation. However, sometimes the

---

[66] Decision combined with and reported in CBS v. Democratic Nat'l Comm., 412 U.S. 94 (1973).
[67] Krasnow, Longley, and Terry, *Politics,* 60.

efforts fail. The radio broadcasting industry is a prime example of such an effort, since Secretary of Commerce Herbert Hoover urged the broadcasters to solve their own problems in the early 1920s. But the radio broadcasters could not solve the signal interference problems of that day, so Congress stepped in and implemented regulation of radio broadcasting. Even though regulation is now firmly in place, broadcasters and cablecasters sometimes turn to self-regulation to prevent more stringent regulation by Congress or the FCC.

5.8.1 Codes of the National Association of Broadcasters

For many years the National Association of Broadcasters administered radio and television codes that presented guidelines for programming and advertising.

For decades radio and television stations forestalled additional regulation by the government by adhering to advertising and programming codes implemented by the National Association of Broadcasters (NAB). The NAB's Radio Code, adopted in 1929, and the Television Code, adopted in 1952, were voluntary in the sense that stations did not have to belong to the NAB or specifically subscribe to the codes. Nevertheless, the Congress and the FCC allowed the broadcast industry to use these codes as industry guidelines for good practice. Further, the FCC refrained from establishing rules in areas covered by the codes.

The advertising division included provisions covering limits on commercialization, medical product advertising, contests and premiums, and other offers. The program standards dealt with education and culture, news, children, controversial public issues, religion, and politics.

Both the radio and TV codes were dissolved in 1982 when it appeared the Justice Department would hold that commercial time limits in the TV code violated antitrust laws. The abolition of the codes paralleled another change. The networks had long operated departments of standards and practices, which housed their censors. The censors decided which program content, including commercials, would be appropriate to run on the network. As a result, the networks acted as filters by screening commercials and program concepts that, in turn, were usually followed by the affiliated stations. Financial belt-tightening by the networks decreased much of the network censoring and left the policing of advertising and program content to the stations themselves.

5.8.2 Violence on Television

Renewed efforts to reduce violence on television has led the cable industry to mount an antiviolence campaign.

Cablecasters made a self-regulatory move in 1993 by agreeing to reduce the amount of violence on cable networks,[68] in response to mounting congressional

---

[68] "Cable Promises to Curb Violence," *Broadcasting*, 1 Feb. 1993, at 33.

pressure to curb TV violence. The cable plan urges each cable network to draft a plan to limit violence, and includes a joint meeting with the broadcasting networks to discuss the problem. Broadcast network executives also said they would curb violence in their programs.[69] Both the major cable networks and television networks also bowed to pressure and announced that they would carry announcements warning of violent content in their programs.

DISCUSSION QUESTIONS

1. If the FTC finds that a broadcast station has engaged in deceptive advertising, is there any way the FCC can use that information against a station? If so, how?
2. What justifies holding broadcast stations to tougher Equal Employment Opportunity standards than most other businesses?
3. Explain instances where a local citizen group might bring influence against a broadcast station or cable system.
4. To what extent is Congress likely to achieve its goals if it conducts a hearing or investigation of a broadcast/cable issue rather than pass a new law?
5. Is the value of the NTIA primarily to the president or to the American people? Explain.

SUGGESTED READINGS

Baughman, James L. *Television's Guardians: The FCC and the Politics of Programming, 1958–1967.* Knoxville: U of Tennessee P, 1985.

Gartner, Michael. *Advertising and the First Amendment.* New York: Priority, 1989.

Krasnow, Erwin G., Lawrence D. Longley, and Herbert A. Terry. *The Politics of Broadcast Regulation.* 3rd ed. New York: St. Martin's, 1982.

Pennybacker, John H. " 'Activitism' v. 'Restraint': The DC Circuit, the FCC and the Supreme Court." *Journal of Broadcasting* 28 (1984): 153.

Trauth, Denise M., and John L. Huffman. "A Case Study of a Difference in Perspectives: The DC Circuit Court of Appeals and the FCC." *Journal of Broadcasting & Electronic Media* 33 (1989): 269.

United States Congress. House. Committee on Energy and Commerce. *Children's Television Act of 1989.* Washington, DC: GPO, 1989.

---

[69] "TV Industry to Senate: Self-Regulation, Not Legislation, the Answer to Violence," *Broadcasting & Cable,* 24 May 1993, at 14.

Chapter 6

REGULATED ELECTRONIC MASS MEDIA SERVICES

Section 303 of the Communications Act of 1934 directs that the Federal Communications Commission classify stations, assign bands of frequencies to the classes, and prescribe the nature of their services. The Commission, in turn, has established a Table of Frequency Allocations that assigns and classifies all frequencies from 9 kHz to 300 GHz.[1] Within this wide range, the Commission has set aside frequency bands for various types of services—radio navigation (use of radio to determine position), maritime mobile (ship-to-shore or ship-to-ship communication), aeronautical fixed (aircraft navigation, safety, and flight preparation transmissions), standard frequency (transmission of specified frequencies for scientific and technical purposes), radio astronomy, space research, amateur, satellite communication, and many others. The services that offer programming intended for reception by the general public (or some significant portion thereof) occupy a relatively small portion of the radio frequencies. However, because of their intensive use, the Commission has been forced to try to impose order on these important frequency bands. These are *traffic* matters; that is, the law directs the Commission to take such action in order to minimize interference, to utilize the electromagnetic spectrum efficiently, and to comply with international agreements.

The Commission must also regulate a relatively new concept of mass communication: delivery by wire-based media. Historically, wired media were used for common carrier purposes—communications facilities for hire on a point-to-point basis. The first small community antenna television systems in the late 1940s and early 1950s were harbingers of dramatic change. We are now in the midst of that change, and the rate of change appears to be accelerating. Regulators must deal with, for example, cable operators who own television program production and

---

[1] 47 C.F.R. § 2.106.

distribution facilities and who want to get into the telephone business. They must also deal with telephone companies who want to get into the television program production and distribution business. And they must deal with all kinds of companies who want to get into interactive communication, a hybrid that combines elements of both mass and point-to-point communication. Further, as this paragraph is being written, the U.S. Congress is considering legislation for creation of an *information superhighway,* a nationwide communications connector that would enhance the creation and combining of new technologies and communications services and would be available to businesses and individuals.

So in this chapter, we survey not only the Commission's methods for ordering the radio frequencies, we also look at mass communication and related services that use wire. First we review some basics of electromagnetic energy so we can understand just why the FCC does what it does in these traffic matters. Then we look at, in turn, full-power radio broadcasting, full-power television broadcasting, low-power broadcast stations, omnidirectional microwave services, direct broadcast satellite, cable television, satellite master antenna television systems, video dialtone, and auxiliary and related services.

6.1   RADIO WAVES

A radio transmitter uses alternating current to cause a transmitting antenna to radiate radio waves that, as a form of electromagnetic energy, travel at constant velocity and are characterized by frequency and wavelength, which vary inversely.

You can easily observe simple wave action. Drop a pebble into a still pool, and you see ripples spread from the splash. The ripples consist of wavelets—water-level patterns that alternate between crests and troughs—that travel at constant speed. The ripples spread their energy over ever wider areas, losing form until they no longer exist.

Similar wave action conveys and diffuses sound. A vibrating object generates sound waves. Sound waves consist of alternating patterns of condensation and rarefaction of air molecules that move eardrums (or microphone diaphragms) back and forth. Sound waves, too, travel at a constant speed. And they lose form as they spread farther from their source until the sound can no longer be heard.

Like sound, electromagnetic energy also originates from a source, radiates in waves at a constant speed, and spreads itself ever thinner as it travels further from its source.[2] While there are many natural sources of electromagnetic energy—for example, the sun, the stars, and lightning—we are interested in that created by people, particularly for communication purposes.

---

[2] For a more detailed explanation of electromagnetic energy and generation, modulation, and detection of radio waves, see F. Leslie Smith, *Perspectives on Radio and Television: Telecommunication in the United States* (New York: Harper, 1990) 234–244.

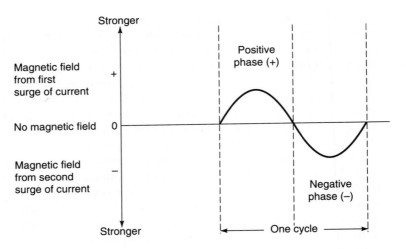

FIGURE 6.1   Phases in alternating current

People use transmitters to communicate "over the air." A transmitter produces a form of electromagnetic energy called *radio energy* or *radio waves.*[3] It does so by feeding an electric current into a transmitting antenna. The current *oscillates*; that is, it alternates direction of flow, first in one direction, then the other. Each change in direction is a half-cycle. As shown in Figure 6.1, two successive half-cycles (a positive phase and a negative phase) make one complete oscillation or *cycle*. This is *alternating current* (AC), a form of electricity that includes normal household current. But while the AC in your home flows at a rate of 60 cycles per second, the lowest rate for radio transmission is 9,000 cycles per second.

In the transmitting antenna, the electric current creates coexistent electrical and magnetic fields of force around the antenna. The direction in which the current flows determines the direction toward which these fields' lines of force point, that is, their *polarity*. When the alternating current in the antenna reverses direction, it creates new electrical and magnetic fields around the antenna. These new fields, opposite in polarity, push the old fields away from the antenna (Figure 6.2). The alternating current again reverses direction, and the whole process starts over again.

Since newly created fields push previous fields away from the antenna, they continually radiate outward. Two successive sets of electrical and magnetic fields of force—the *positive phase* and the *negative phase,* according to their respective polarity—constitute one radio wave. The distance from any point on a wave (say, the beginning of the positive phase) to that same point on the next wave is the *wavelength.*

---

[3] A reminder: *radio* in this context is generic; it refers to all uses of radiated electromagnetic energy to transmit information and so includes such media as television, microwave relay, and satellite communication as well as radio broadcasting.

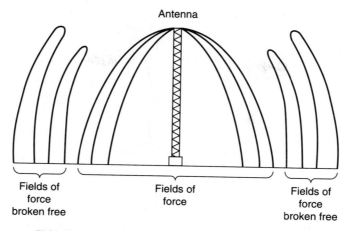

FIGURE 6.2   Lines of force radiating from antenna

The strength or *amplitude* (Figure 6.3) of the alternating current in the transmitting antenna determines the strength of the radiated waves. The amplitude of the waves, in turn, determines the strength of the signal you get in your receiver. Radio and other electromagnetic waves travel at a *velocity* (speed) of 300,000,000 meters (186,000 miles) per second in a vacuum (they travel somewhat slower in the earth's atmosphere). Those figures probably sound familiar to you as the speed of light, and indeed visible light constitutes one form of electromagnetic energy. The number of waves a source generates each second is called *frequency*. Since velocity is constant, frequency varies inversely with wavelength. Thus, as illustrated by the width of the wavelength in Figure 6.4, the longer the wavelength, the lower the frequency; and vice versa.

If you were to arrange all forms of electromagnetic energy in order of frequency, from highest to lowest, you would have what physicists call the *electromagnetic spectrum*. Figure 6.5 shows where the radio frequencies fit into the spectrum.

FIGURE 6.3   Amplitude and wavelength

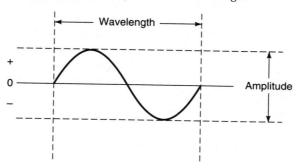

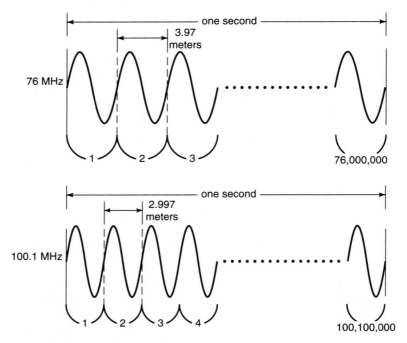

FIGURE 6.4   Frequency and wavelength

6.1.1   Propagation

In the medium frequencies, propagation is primarily through ground waves and sky waves; in the very high and ultra high frequencies, propagation is primarily through direct waves. As radio waves travel, they attenuate until they become so weak that they cannot be detected by receivers; all other factors being equal, the higher their frequency, the sooner radio waves attenuate.

As frequency and wavelength vary, so does *propagation*, the manner in which waves travel, the paths they take. In the medium frequency (MF) band, where the AM broadcast service is located, radio energy travels most efficiently by ground wave and sky wave propagation. As shown in Figure 6.6, a *ground wave* follows the curvature of the earth with minimal fading for as far as it reaches.[4] The higher the transmitting frequency, however, the more subject ground waves are to *attenuation* (loss of amplitude or strength) from being conducted by the soil, and the less useful they become. So ground wave signals from AM radio stations with higher frequencies (such as 1590 kHz) do not get out as far as those from stations with lower frequencies (such as 550 kHz), all other things being equal.

---

[4] Typically 10–70 miles, depending on frequency, power, and soil conditions. *Fading* is a periodic gradual loss-then-regaining of the transmitted signal.

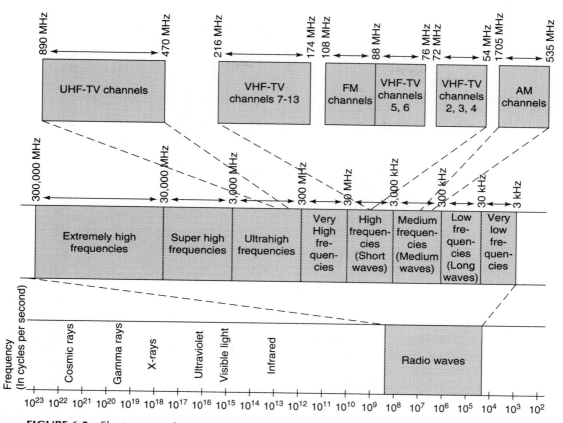

FIGURE 6.5   Electromagnetic spectrum

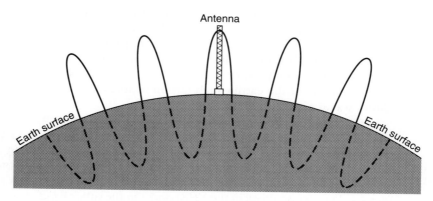

FIGURE 6.6   Ground wave propagation

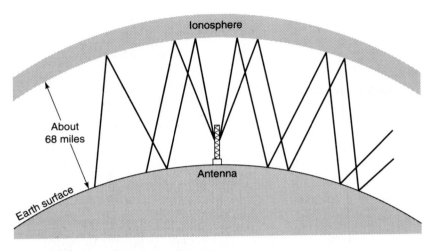

FIGURE 6.7 Sky wave propagation

A *sky wave* radiates away from the earth, as illustrated in Figure 6.7. During the day, most sky waves keep traveling and are lost to this world. At night, changes in the ionosphere bend these sky waves back to earth, and they may strike ground hundreds of miles from the transmitter, a phenomenon called *skipping*. They can bounce between earth and ionosphere several times. While sky waves achieve spectacular distances, they do fade; they create unpredictable coverage patterns, and, of course, they are useful primarily at night.

The very high frequency (VHF) band contains FM radio and television channels 2 to 13; the ultra high frequency (UHF) band, television channels 14 to 69. In these bands, radio energy travels most efficiently by *direct wave* propagation. The waves themselves are very short as compared with MF waves, and radio direct waves behave much like visible light. They travel in straight lines, may be blocked by physical objects, may be reflected, and are subject to bending. To a large extent, direct wave propagation is line-of-sight.[5] Good reception requires a straight line between transmitting and receiving antennae; as illustrated in Figure 6.8, the horizon (curvature of the earth), high terrain features, and tall structures all can block direct waves and cause poor or no reception.

Higher frequencies (shorter wavelengths) result in proportionately less coverage, all other things being equal. So direct wave propagation in VHF and UHF does not cover nearly the distance that ground and sky waves cover in MF. Higher frequency TV and FM radio channels do not have the coverage potential of lower channels. And stations in the entire UHF television band operate at a distinct coverage disadvantage to those in the VHF band. On the other hand, direct wave propagation makes for very predictable coverage patterns. These higher frequency bands

---

[5] In reality, FM and TV station signals do spread somewhat beyond line of sight.

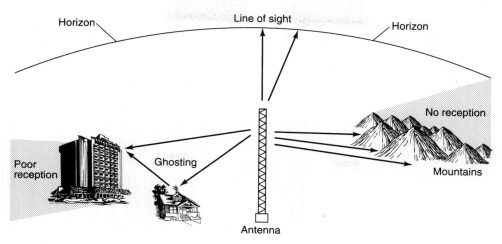

FIGURE 6.8   Direct wave propagation

also accommodate wider channels and a greater number of channels than does the MF band.

6.1.2   Transmission and Reception

Broadcast station equipment performs three basic functions: (1) production of audio and video signals; (2) generation of the station's carrier; and (3) modulation of the carrier to carry audio and video information. A receiving set picks up the transmitted modulated signal and recovers audio and video.

A microphone converts sound patterns into corresponding electrical patterns called audio. A television camera lens focuses light reflected from a scene onto a video pickup;[6] the video pickup converts the light patterns into corresponding electronic patterns, dots of energy divided into 525 horizontal lines (sometimes called "scan lines"), and as the electrons leave the pickup one line at a time, they become the video signal.[7] Meanwhile, the transmitter has created an alternating electrical current of constant amplitude and frequency. This current alternates at the station's assigned transmission frequency and is called the *carrier, carrier frequency*, or *carrier signal*. The audio and video signals feed into the transmitter, and there they are used to *modulate* (change) the carrier signal so that it carries the

---

[6] Until the late 1980s, video pickups in television cameras were vacuum tubes; since that time, however, most cameras have been manufactured to use a solid-state video pickup called a *charge-couple device*.

[7] Audio and video recordings simply store data that represent the patterns of these signals; the recordings can then be played back at will to recreate the audio and video signals.

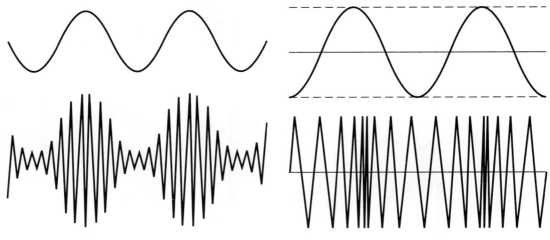

FIGURE 6.9   Amplitude modulation   **FIGURE 6.10**   Frequency modulation

information contained in the audio and video signals. As shown in Figures 6.9 and 6.10, the carrier's amplitude is modulated in AM radio and its frequency is modulated in FM radio. In television, video is amplitude modulated, and audio is frequency modulated. The modulated carrier goes to the antenna and creates radio waves.

These waves strike a receiving antenna and induce a small electrical signal, a weak reproduction of the modulated carrier frequency. In the receiving set, a tuner circuit blocks all frequencies except those to which the set is tuned. After amplification and further processing, the audio signal is recovered and fed to the speaker, and the video signal is recovered and fed to the picture tube. The speaker turns the electrical audio signal back into sound. The picture tube directs each electron of the video signal to a phosphor;[8] the electron hits the phosphor and causes it to glow briefly. Thus, the picture reconstructs the original light pattern, dot-by-dot, line-by-line, in such rapid succession that we see the result as a whole moving picture.

6.1.3   Interference

Interference—the mutual action of two sets of radio waves—takes the form of static and station interference; common forms of station interference are co-channel, adjacent channel, and second-adjacent channel.

As shown in Figure 6.11, *natural static* results from atmospheric disturbances, such as lightning. *Induced static* originates from electrical machines and devices—the faulty ignition of a nearby automobile, a vacuum cleaner or food mixer running in another room, a faulty starter in a fluorescent light fixture. These sources generate electromagnetic waves—static signals—that attach

---

[8] A *phosphor* is a substance that lights up when struck by radiation.

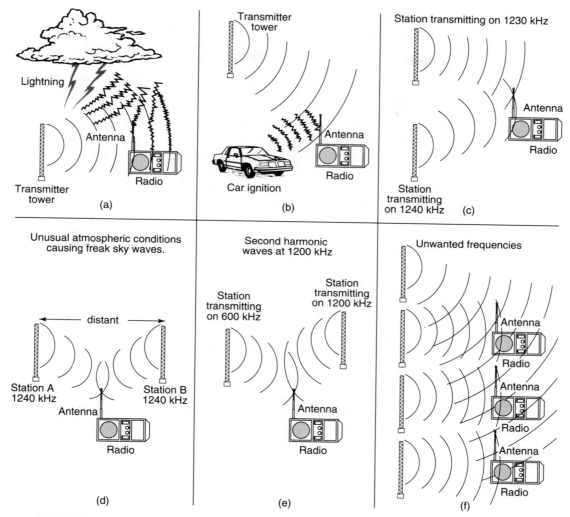

FIGURE 6.11 Forms of interference

themselves to the positive and negative peaks of a radio wave. In FM the frequency of the radio wave contains the program information, so FM receivers simply clip off the peaks and eliminate the static, leaving the program information intact. In AM the amplitude—the positive and negative peaks themselves—carries the program information; a receiver that clipped static would also clip some of the program information.

Station interference involves signals of two or more stations. You tune to one station, but receive one or more other stations on the same setting at the same time. Interference weakens or distorts the signals. Two common types of station interference are adjacent channel and co-channel interference. In *adjacent channel interference*, you tune to a frequency—say, 1230 kHz on the AM radio band—and pick up not only the nearby station operating on it but also a strong station operating on the next frequency, 1220 or 1240 kHz. In *second-adjacent channel interference* you would pick up an interfering signal from a station two frequencies away, 1210 or 1250 kHz. *Co-channel interference* involves two stations on the same frequency.

FM radio, primarily because of the design of the receiver, is not nearly as subject to any of these types of interference. However, as the number of FM stations increased during the 1980s (EMG 6.2.2.6), the various types of station interference did begin to show up as a problem, particularly in population centers with a large number of FM stations. Such interference often takes the form of two stations "flip-flopping"—first you hear one, and then you hear the other.

Early in the history of broadcasting, it became apparent that a system was needed to prevent massive interference among broadcast stations. Sky waves, particularly, caused problems; they were unpredictable and, as noted in the previous section, could skip long distances. So systems were developed for classifying and assigning broadcast stations. These systems are explained in the following sections.

6.2 FULL-POWER RADIO BROADCASTING

In a notice titled "Amendment of the Commission's Rules with Regard to the Establishment of Regulation of New Digital Audio Radio Services,"[9] the FCC proposed to open a brand new radio broadcasting service: satellite digital audio radio. Various factions of the radio business argue, however, over the form digital audio radio (DAR; also called digital audio broadcasting, DAB) should take, whether it should be transmitted from satellites or from terrestrial-based towers, whether it should be in the existing radio bands or in a brand new frequency band. Until those arguments are settled and the long complicated process of standard-setting accomplished, we must be satisfied with the two domestic aural-only services currently authorized by the FCC. One is the oldest broadcast service, AM radio. The other is the younger (and more recently successful) radio service, FM radio. The Commission also licenses nongovernment international broadcasting stations. These three services—AM radio, FM radio, and international broadcasting—are the subjects of this section.

6.2.1 AM Broadcasting

The AM broadcasting band is 535–1705 kHz divided into 117 channels. The FCC classifies both channels and stations.

---

[9] 7 F.C.C.R. 7776, 1992.

In the AM broadcasting[10] band, stations transmit on carrier frequencies spaced at 10 kHz intervals. Their sidebands[11] extend 5 kHz above and below those center frequencies, so the first AM station frequency is at 540 kHz, but a station using that frequency actually transmits a band of frequencies, 535–545 kHz.[12] Thus we can say that the AM "channel" is 10 kHz wide.

Obviously, with over 5,000 AM stations authorized and only 117 channels, most of those channels are used by more than one station. The method by which the FCC achieves multiple use of AM frequencies involves two related classifications—stations and channels.

6.2.1.1 Service Areas and Protection

The FCC classifies AM stations in terms of service area (primary, intermittent, secondary) and protection.

The FCC's definition of service area involves two concepts, the geographic area covered and the type of radio wave that serves that area. The *primary service area* is that served by a station's ground wave; in that area, the signal is not subject to objectionable interference or fading. The *intermittent coverage area* is also served by a station's ground wave, but it is beyond the primary area and so is subject to some interference and fading. The *secondary coverage area* is that served by a station's sky wave; in that area, the signal may be subject to some fading.[13] In the FCC's AM station classification scheme, the concept of service area is tied to that of signal protection. A station is *protected* when FCC rules specify that its signal be free of interference from other stations transmitting on the same and adjacent frequencies. In order to protect the signal, these other stations must use restrictive operational modes—transmit with relatively low power; reduce power at night (to reduce sky wave propagation); operate only in the daytime (to eliminate sky wave propagation); use a directional antenna array (to focus its signal away from the other stations); or employ some combination of these measures. As shown in Figure 6.12 and explained in the following paragraphs, a station's classification determines whether its signal is protected in each of its service areas.

6.2.1.2 AM Channel and Station Classification

AM radio stations classified A, B, and D operate on clear channels; B and D operate on regional channels; C on local channels; and B in the expanded band.

As shown in Figure 6.13, 60 of the 117 AM channels are designated clear channels.[14] As implied by the name, these channels are "clear" of objectionable

---

[10] Until 1978, the FCC's official name for AM radio was "standard broadcasting."

[11] *Sidebands* are the frequencies immediately above and below the center frequency. They are created when the transmitter modulates the carrier frequency, and they contain the information that actually constitutes the programming—the audio and, in the case of a TV signal, the video.

[12] 47 C.F.R. § 73.14.

[13] *Id.*

[14] 47 C.F.R. § 73.25.

Channel Classes		Station Classes	Service Areas		
			Primary	Intermittent	Secondary
		A	Protected	Protected	Protected
Regional		B	Protected	May be materially limited or destroyed due to interference from other stations	
Clear		D	Protected	May be obtained depending on station assignments, but if operated at night, may be limited by interference	If operated at night may be generally prevented by interference
	Local	C	Protected		

FIGURE 6.12 AM channels and station classes and service areas
SOURCE: 47 C.F.R. §§ 73.21, 73.182

Channel Classification			Frequencies (kHz)	Station Classification	
				Dominant	Secondary
Clear (60)	U.S. Clears (36)		640, 650, 660, 670, 680, 700, 710, 720, 750, 760, 770, 780, 810, 820, 830, 840, 850, 870, 880, 890, 1020, 1030, 1040, 1080, 1100, 1110, 1120, 1160, 1170, 1180, 1200, 1210, 1500, 1510, 1520, 1530	A	B, D
	Clears shared by U.S. and foreign countries (8)	with Canada (2)	1070, 1130	None	B, D
		with Mexico (5)	1000, 1060, 1090, 1140, 1190		
		with Cuba (1)	1560		
	Foreign clears (16)	Canada (7)	540, 690, 740, 860, 990, 1010, 1580	None	D
		Mexico (6)	730, 800, 900, 1050, 1220, 1570		
		Canada & Mexico (2)	940, 1000		
		Bahamas (1)	1540		
Regional (41)			550, 560, 570, 580, 590, 600, 610, 620, 630, 790, 910, 920, 930, 950, 960, 970, 980, 1150, 1250, 1260, 1270, 1280, 1290, 1300, 1310, 1320, 1330, 1350, 1360, 1370, 1380, 1390, 1410, 1420, 1430, 1440, 1460, 1470, 1480, 1590, 1600	B, D	
Local (6)			1230, 1240, 1340, 1400, 1450, 1490 (These frequencies are classified as regional for Alaska, Hawaii, Puerto Rico, and the Virgin Islands.)	C	

FIGURE 6.13 AM channel and station classification

interference, allowing the signals of selected stations to reach long distances. Three classes of stations operate on clear channels.

- Class A stations.[15] These are the most powerful; they are the clear-channel *dominant* stations. A Class A station provides primary and secondary service over an extended area and at relatively long distances from its transmitter. Its primary service area is protected from objectionable interference by stations on both the same and adjacent channels; its secondary service area is protected from interference on the same channel. A Class A station operates with 50 kilowatts (kW) of power (the highest power allowed to AM radio broadcasting stations in the United States) and unlimited time, which means that it may broadcast 24 hours a day.[16] By international agreement, the FCC may license dominant stations to operate on 36 of the 60 clear channels.

Broadcast stations operating on a clear channel classified other than A are *secondary* stations. These include Class B stations and Class D stations. The FCC may license such stations on all clear channels, including the 13 on which other North American countries have preference (that is, may operate dominant stations), so long as they operate to protect (EMG 6.2.1.1) the dominant stations on those channels.

- Class B stations.[17] A Class B station is an unlimited time station that normally provides service only over a primary service area, but its exact service area depends on geographical location, power, and frequency. A Class B station operating on a clear channel must provide protection to the Class A station(s) on that channel. It should be located so that it both provides and receives a specified degree of ground wave protection with respect to other Class B stations. The FCC authorizes few Class B stations to operate with less than 0.25 kW (250 watts) and none with more than the maximum 50 kW.

- Class D stations.[18] A Class D station receives no nighttime protection and may have to suffer some interference in its service area from the Class A and Class B stations on its frequency. Further, it must transmit so as to protect the nighttime signal of all Class A and Class B stations that operate on the same frequency. In doing so, it may be required to use one or more of the operating modes described at the end of EMG 6.2.1.1. The power allowed a Class D station is determined by formulas contained in the FCC rules and by the specific protection it must give other stations.

---

[15] 47 C.F.R. § 73.21(a)(1). The power specification is for the 48 contiguous states; Class A station power and protection is different for Alaska.

[16] 47 C.F.R. § 73.1710.

[17] 47 C.F.R. § 73.21(a)(2).

[18] 47 C.F.R. § 73.21(a)(3).

Forty-one frequencies are regional channels.[19] A regional channel is one on which Class B and Class D stations may operate, each of which normally provides service to a city[20] and its contiguous rural area. Class B stations protect each other; Class D stations protect Class B stations.

Six frequencies are local channels. A local channel is one on which a number of stations may operate, each of which provides service to a community and its contiguous suburban and rural areas.

- Class C stations.[21] Any station that operates on a local channel is, by definition, a Class C station, and Class C stations operate on no other class of channel. A Class C station provides service only over a primary service area. The signal of a Class C station receives daytime (ground wave) protection only. However, some Class C stations, in order to avoid interfering with other stations, must reduce their primary service areas through use of a directional antenna array. The FCC licenses no Class C station to operate with less than 250 watts[22] and none to operate with more than 1 kW.

By international agreement in 1979, the upper end of the AM broadcasting band was extended to include the frequencies 1605–1705 kHz.[23] This expanded band was not opened to U.S. broadcasters right away. But in 1991 the Commission took the unprecedented step of announcing that applications for new stations in the band would *not* be accepted. Instead, it adopted measures encouraging voluntary migration to the 10 new frequencies by those *existing* stations whose migration would achieve the greatest reduction of interference in the original (535–1605 kHz) band. Stations moving to the expanded band would be Class B; operate full time with 10 kW daytime power, 1 kW nighttime power, and nondirectional antennas; and have extended geographical spacing between stations transmitting on the same frequency.

6.2.1.3 *Applications for Stations*
Each time an applicant wishes to build a new station or increase power on an existing one, the application must demonstrate that the proposed new signal will not interfere (beyond FCC limits) with existing signals.

New stations require a frequency search. The prospective applicant hires a consulting engineer to study existing AM radio assignments, measure the strength of their signals in the area of the proposed station, and recommend a frequency for which to apply.

---

[19] 47 C.F.R. § 73.26.

[20] The wording of 47 C.F.R. § 73.21(b) is "a principal center of population."

[21] 47 C.F.R. § 73.21(c)(1).

[22] When the minimum power was raised to 250 watts, stations operating with 100 watts were allowed to continue to do so.

[23] FCC Public Notice 25215 of Jan. 15, 1980.

The FCC first opened the expanded band for stations in 1993. "Until further notice,"[24] applicants for that band cannot propose a new station; they apply to move an existing station from the original AM band and to operate that station in a certain specified manner (EMG 6.2.1.6.2). The FCC selects from among competing applicants based on the amount that interference would be reduced by the proposed moves.[25]

6.2.1.4 AM Stereo
The FCC delayed 11 years before selecting an AM stereo standard.

The FCC authorized AM stereo broadcasting in 1982.[26] Competing firms proposed a number of different systems for AM stereo. Most were incompatible; that is, a stereo signal transmitted with one system could not be received on a receiver that utilized another system. The Commission opted to allow marketplace forces to determine the industry standard; that is, whichever system was installed by the most stations and utilized by the greatest number of receiver manufacturers would become the standard.

For a number of reasons, however, AM stereo did not catch on among either broadcasters or listeners. No national standard emerged, and AM stereo did not help AM broadcasters to stem the erosion of their listening audience (EMG 6.2.1.6). After 10 years, Congress forced the issue. The Telecommunications Authorization Act of 1992 required that the FCC select a standard. Of those AM stations that had installed stereo equipment, the greatest number had invested in Motorola's C-Quam system. Additionally, C-Quam circuitry was built into most AM-stereo-capable auto radios. So in 1993 the FCC designated the Motorola C-Quam system as the national standard.[27]

6.2.1.5 AM Carrier Services
FCC rules allow AM radio stations to transmit subaudible signals on their carriers.

Subaudible means that the signal cannot be heard on the ordinary consumer radio receiver, and the station may use it to offer services in addition to its broadcast programming.[28] A utility company, for example, might pay a radio station to transmit a signal in connection with utility load management.[29] A station that broad-

---

[24] 47 C.F.R. § 73.30.

[25] The Commission awards these channels on an allotment basis that works as follows. All applications must be submitted at the same time. The FCC examines the applications and determines the *improvement factor* (the calculation for which is set forth in 47 C.F.R. § 73.35) for each. The station with the highest improvement factor gets the highest priority for an allotment; that with the next highest improvement factor gets the next highest priority, and so on until all the allotments are filled.

[26] AM Stereophonic Broadcasting, 47 Fed. Reg. 13,152 (Mar. 29, 1982).

[27] Amendment of the Commission's Rules to Establish a Single AM Radio Stereophonic Transmitting Equipment Standard, 58 Fed. Reg. 66,300 (December 20, 1993).

[28] 47 C.F.R. § 73.1570.

[29] A utility company—say, an electric company—usually offers rate breaks to its customers who participate in a load management program. The company installs a special receiver in the participating cus-

casts such a signal must not degrade or disrupt its own program signal or that of any other station. The service is regulated according to the specific use to which it is put—common carrier (available for others to use; licensee does not control content), private carrier (available for specific others to use; licensee does not control content), or broadcasting (licensee controls content and intends it to be received by the general public).[30]

6.2.1.6 1991 AM Rules

To revitalize an ailing AM broadcast service, the FCC in 1991 adopted a strategy of rule and policy changes to reduce congestion and interference in the AM band. The strategy involved three elements: technical standards, migration, and consolidation.

Broadcasting developed about 1920, and the form in which it developed was AM radio. The FCC began licensing both TV and FM stations in 1941, but these media were not widely adopted by the public until the 1950s and the 1960s. So in effect, for 30 years AM radio was the only broadcast medium for the majority of the public.

After World War II, however, channel congestion and interference increased dramatically in the AM band. The incidence of static and other incidental radio frequency emissions in the urban environment grew with the variety and number of new electrical and electronic devices being introduced. Adjacent channel and second-adjacent channel interference grew with the plethora of new stations signing on.

Radio receiver manufacturers responded to the station interference by designing and manufacturing receivers so they picked up less than the full AM channel—which, in turn, resulted in a decline in fidelity. The listening audience gradually tuned away from AM to stations on the FM band, which offered higher technical quality, better aural fidelity, and stereophonic reproduction. Receiver manufacturers, noting this shift in audience preference, focused efforts on FM. They ceased research to improve AM receivers and made AM radio circuitry as cheaply as possible even on the most sophisticated AM-FM receivers. In many cases the quality of sound from an AM receiver was little better than that from a telephone—suitable for conversation but not for music. As a result, FM stations co-opted the successful popular music formats. AM stations responded by programming formats such as news, talk, and nostalgia, which did not require good audio response.

---

tomer's home or business. (The receiver is special because it consists of circuitry that can pick up a subaudible tone from an AM station but *not* the station's regular program channel; it does not even look like a radio.) During periods of peak load (that is, whenever the most electricity is being used in the company's service area), the company transmits the subaudible tone using the AM station's carrier. The special receivers pick up the signal and turn off the customers' appliances. When the peak load subsides, the company transmits another subaudible tone that signals the receivers to turn the appliances back on.

[30] 47 C.F.R. § 73.127.

Some saw the FCC's 1982 authorization of AM stereo (EMG 6.2.1.4) as a chance to compete effectively with FM. Continued audience erosion, however, meant that AM licensees had less money for such speculative technical enhancements and so were reluctant to invest in a particular stereo system, especially since a system other than the one chosen might develop into the standard, rendering their investment worthless. Stereophonic reproduction did not particularly enhance the formats that had become AM's programming niche, and most AM licensees saw little reason to invest in a stereo system.

AM radio, once a vital service, could not compete in the marketplace. By the early 1990s, FM had 77 percent of all radio listening,[31] and about two-thirds of all AM stations were losing money.[32]

The FCC, however, was not ready to write off AM. It launched a program to transform and revitalize the AM broadcast service by the year 2000. In a series of actions from 1986 through 1990, the Commission identified and worked toward easing what it believed to be the most pressing problems. In a 1991 Report and Order[33] the FCC adopted a comprehensive strategy aimed at reducing congestion and interference on the AM band. This strategy consisted of three elements that resulted in numerous rule and policy changes.

6.2.1.6.1 Technical Standards
Technical standards were revised to reduce primary service area interference.

These rule changes were designed to work on a long-range basis. In adopting them, the FCC increased protection from stations on adjacent channels, adopted more accurate methodology for measuring nighttime coverage and interference, and required that some stations, when requesting changes in facilities, reduce interference by 10 percent. The Commission decided not to require manufacturers to build better receivers. But it did take note of existing efforts to develop a better AM receiver, said that it would publish a list of receivers that met its voluntary model standards, and would otherwise promote development of receivers with higher audio fidelity.

6.2.1.6.2 Migration
Interfering stations were encouraged to move to the 10 new channels in the 1605–1705 kHz segment of the AM band.

The problem was, of course, that most existing radio receivers had been built before the opening of the expanded band (EMG 6.2.1.2).[34] With fewer listeners even able to pick them up, stations on the new channels would be at a competitive

---

[31] "Radio Weekly Reach on AM-FM Stations," *Broadcasting*, 10 Dec. 1990, at 52.

[32] Peter Viles, "59% of Radio Stations Lost Money in '91," *Broadcasting*, 6 July 1992, at 6.

[33] AM Technical Standards, 6 F.C.C.R. 6273 (1991).

[34] FCC officials met with U.S. receiver manufacturers in 1988 to urge an early start on production of sets capable of receiving signals in the new band. "RIO [*sic*] is stage for AM spectrum conference," *Broadcasting*, 23 May 1988, at 55.

disadvantage to stations in the original band—at least until enough full-band radios were sold. So the FCC encouraged migration by giving certain attractive technical advantages to expanded-band stations. The FCC did this by defining two models of AM station operations: Model I parameters for expanded-band stations and Model II parameters for stations in the original band. Model I parameters would include those described in EMG 6.2.1.2—Class B status operating full time, 10 kW daytime power, 1 kW nighttime power, nondirectional antennas, and extended geographical spacing between stations transmitting on the same frequency—plus AM stereo and technical quality competitive with FM. Model II parameters would *aim* toward full-time operation, competitive technical quality, wide daytime coverage, and night-time coverage at least 15 percent of that for daytime. But in reality, Model II station operation would have to reflect the realities of the original band—dense station population coupled with wide variations in spacing, power, antenna patterns, and interference protection.

The Commission also built in a transition period of five years for migrating stations. During that time, a station would be allowed to operate on both the original and the expanded-band frequencies, and duopoly and national ownership rules (EMG 7.1.3.3.2 and 7.1.3.3.3) would be waived.

6.2.1.6.3 *Consolidation*
The FCC provided incentives for stations causing interference to be closed down.

The third element in the FCC's strategy to reduce congestion and interference in the AM band involved nontechnical rule changes. Interfering stations that voluntarily gave up their licenses would receive certificates allowing them to defer payment of capital gains taxes. Further, the Commission relaxed its multiple ownership rules for licensees proposing changes in facilities that would result in a significant reduction of interference; a licensee who had already reached local ownership limits, for example, would be allowed to buy another AM station—one operating on or near a frequency plagued by interference—for the purpose of putting it off the air (which would thus reduce the interference).

6.2.2   FM Broadcasting

The FM broadcasting band is 88–108 MHz divided into 100 channels.

FM broadcasting uses the band of frequencies 88–108 MHz. It contains 100 channels,[35] each 200 kHz wide. The FCC refers to FM channels by channel number as in television. As shown in Table 6.1, the first FM channel is 201; the last, 300. But stations identify themselves to the public by center frequency, similar to AM radio. The first FM frequency is 88.1, and the last is 107.9.[36] Commercial stations may

[35] Exceptions: As explained later in this chapter, FCC rules provide for one additional FM channel at 87.9 MHz, channel 200, for certain noncommercial educational FM stations. 47 C.F.R. § 73.512(a)(1).
[36] 47 C.F.R. § 73.201.

TABLE 6.1   FM Broadcast Channels/Frequencies

Channels Reserved for Noncommercial Educational Stations									
201	202	203	204	205	206	207	208	209	210
88.1	88.3	88.5	88.7	88.9	89.1	89.3	89.5	89.7	89.9
211	212	213	214	215	216	217	218	219	220
90.1	90.3	90.5	90.7	90.9	91.1	91.3	91.5	91.7	91.9

Channels in the Table of Allocations									
221	222	223	224	225	226	227	228	229	230
92.1	92.3	92.5	92.7	92.9	93.1	93.3	93.5	93.7	93.9
231	232	233	234	235	236	237	238	239	240
94.1	94.3	94.5	94.7	94.9	95.1	95.3	95.5	95.7	95.9
241	242	243	244	245	246	247	248	249	250
96.1	96.3	96.5	96.7	96.9	97.1	97.3	97.5	97.7	97.9
251	252	253	254	255	256	257	258	259	260
98.1	98.3	98.5	98.7	98.9	99.1	99.3	99.5	99.7	99.9
261	262	263	264	265	266	267	268	269	270
100.1	100.3	100.5	100.7	100.9	101.1	101.3	101.5	101.7	101.9
271	272	273	274	275	276	277	278	279	280
102.1	102.3	102.5	102.7	102.9	103.1	103.3	103.5	103.7	103.9
281	282	283	284	285	286	287	288	289	290
104.1	104.3	104.5	104.7	104.9	105.1	105.3	105.5	105.7	105.9
291	292	293	294	295	296	297	298	299	300
106.1	106.3	106.5	106.7	106.9	107.1	107.3	107.5	107.7	107.9

operate only on the last 80 channels in the FM band. The first 20 are reserved for noncommercial educational stations.

6.2.2.1 FM Station Zones

For purposes of assigning FM stations, the Commission has divided the country into three zones designated I, I-A, and II.

As shown in Figure 6.14, Zone I includes all or parts of 18 northeastern states and the District of Columbia. Zone I-A consists of Puerto Rico, the Virgin Islands, and the southern four-fifths of California (below the 40th parallel). Zone II consists of the rest of the country, including Alaska and Hawaii.[37]

6.2.2.2 Station Classifications

Stations are assigned to zone by classification: A, B1, B, C3, C2, C1, or C.

FM stations with the strongest signals, those classified in the C series, may operate only in Zone II. The next strongest stations, those in the B series, operate in

[37] 47 C.F.R. §§ 73.205, 73.505.

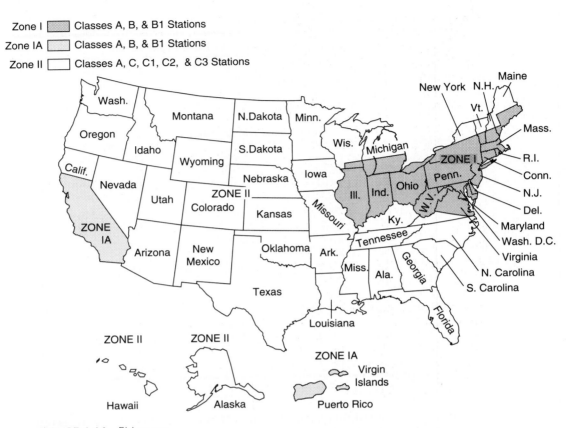

Zone I ▨ Classes A, B, & B1 Stations
Zone IA ▨ Classes A, B, & B1 Stations
Zone II ☐ Classes A, C, C1, C2, & C3 Stations

FIGURE 6.14   FM zones

Zones I and IA. The weakest stations, those classified A, operate in any of the three zones.

The relationship of zones to station classes is shown in Table 6.2. Two of the terms in that table need some explanation: *contour* refers to the distance from the transmitting antenna the signal reaches with a specified strength; *height above average terrain* (HAAT) is exactly what it seems: the height of the transmitting antenna above the average level of the terrain in the area. The figures in the table are actually representative rather than hard and fast specifications; FCC rules provide formulas that applicants use to figure exact facilities, so within each class individual stations vary by HAAT, power, and distance.[38] The rules also provide specifics on minimum distance separations for stations on same and adjacent channels.[39]

---

[38] The figures (and the formulas) differ for FM stations in Puerto Rico and the Virgin Islands.
[39] 47 C.F.R. §§ 73.207, 73.213.

TABLE 6.2   FM Zones and Station Classes

Zones	Station Classes	Minimum Power (kW)	Maximum Power (kW)	HAAT* (meters)	Class Contour in Distance (km)
I IA II	A	0.1	6	100	28
I IA	B1	>6.0†	25	100	39
I IA	B	>25.0	50	100	52
II	C3	>6.0	25	100	39
II	C2	>25.0	50	150	52
II	C1	>50.0	100	299	72
II	C	100.0	100	600	92

SOURCE: 47 C.F.R. §§ 73.210, 73.211
*HAAT = Height above average terrain.
†> = Greater than.

6.2.2.3   Table of Allotments
An FCC table allots commercial FM channels to specific communities.

Should you wish to build a new FM station, you go to the FM table of allotments,[40] look up your city, choose an unused channel assigned to that city, and apply for it. If there are no vacant channels, you either find a community that does have vacant FM channels or petition the FCC to amend the table to move one into your city. In the latter case, you usually have to hire a consulting engineer to perform much the same functions as in AM radio and to ensure that your application adheres to FCC rules concerning minimum mileage separations between channels to protect from co-channel and adjacent channel interference.

6.2.2.4   Noncommercial Educational FM (NCE-FM)
FM channels 201–220 are reserved for noncommercial educational stations.

These 20 channels are often referred to as the *reserved portion* of the FM band. A station that operates on one of these channels is by definition noncommercial educational. A nonprofit educational organization *may* operate a noncommercial station on one of the commercial channels, 221–300.[41] Most, however, choose one of the reserved channels if available. These first 20 channels are not included in the FCC's table of allotments, and noncommercial FM stations are assigned on an application-demand basis, much like AM.

6.2.2.4.1   NCE-FM Station Classification
Low-power noncommercial educational FM stations are Class D.

---

[40] 47 C.F.R. § 73.202.

[41] In this case the licensee must comply with all requirements pertaining to station classification and frequency allocation that apply to commercial stations. 47 C.F.R. § 73.513.

Noncommercial educational FM (NCE-FM) stations carry the same classifications as commercial stations[42] with one exception: a station that operates with no more than 10 watts transmitter power output is a Class D station.

By the mid-1970s about half of all educational FM stations were of this low-power variety. As these stations continued to proliferate, they occupied frequency space that could have been used by other educational stations that wished to go to higher power. Congestion of the reserved portion of the band had become critical in some areas. As a result, the FCC in 1978 adopted rules for 10-watt stations. Under these rules, the Commission ceased accepting applications for new 10-watt stations. Existing Class D stations were directed either to raise power or to move. And the choices for moving were, in the order of Commission preference as stated in the rules, (1) to a vacant commercial channel (where the Class D stations have secondary status; that is, would have to operate so as to protect the signals of the commercial stations), (2) to Channel 200 (87.9 MHz), or (3) to secondary status on a noncommercial channel. These rules are still in effect.[43]

6.2.2.4.2 NCE-FM Interference and Protection
FCC rules require that noncommercial educational FM stations operate so as to protect the signals of TV stations transmitting on channel 6.

The VHF frequency allocation is such that the reserved portion of the FM band and the audio signal for TV channel 6 abut each other. Since TV audio is frequency modulated (FM), this explains why, if you live in a community that has a TV station operating on channel 6, you can tune your FM radio all the way to the lower end of the dial and pick up the channel 6 audio signal.[44] Channel 6 TV stations, however, have in the past suffered technically from this proximity. They complained that the transmissions of some NCE-FM stations interfered with their TV signal. In response, the FCC in 1985 adopted technical standards and procedures[45] for NCE-FM stations designed to reduce interference with TV channel 6.[46]

---

[42] 47 C.F.R. § 73.506.

[43] 47 C.F.R. § 73.512. There are certain exceptions for stations in Alaska and for stations near the Canadian or Mexican border.

[44] This applies to over-the-air receivers; that is, those *not* hooked up to a cable system.

[45] Noncommercial FM stations (TV Channel 6 Protection), 57 Rad. Reg. 2d (P&F) 107 (1985).

[46] 47 C.F.R. § 73.525. NCE-FM stations must operate to protect signals in two specific situations. The first is in Alaska. From 1955 to 1982, the FCC had allocated use of the 76–100 MHz frequency band in Alaska to government and nongovernment fixed-operations radio. In 1982, the FCC reallocated that band to VHF-TV channels 5 and 6 and FM radio channels 201–260 (88–100 MHz). Alaskan Radio and Television Allocations, 90 F.C.C.2d 507 (1982). However, some nongovernment fixed operations (mainly radio common carriers) that were authorized before 1982 continued to operate in the 76–108 MHz band. Therefore Commission rules, 47 C.F.R. §§ 73.220(b), 73.501(b), and 73.603(b), require that Alaskan stations using TV channels 5 or 6 or any FM radio channel accept interference from, but cause no harmful interference to, those remaining nongovernmental fixed operations.

The second is in New York City. FCC rule, 47 C.F.R. § 73.220(a), protects a channel in New York City from objectionable interference. The channel is 206 (89.1 MHz), a station the United Nations operates with power of 20 kW ERP and antenna height of 500 feet.

6.2.2.5   *FM Stereo and Subcarrier Services*

The FCC has provided for multiplex transmission by FM broadcast stations, designating a standard for stereophonic broadcasting and permitting nonbroadcast subcarrier transmissions as Subsidiary Communications Services.

As noted earlier, the FM channel is 200 kHz wide, 20 times wider than the distance between AM carrier frequencies. That width provides the space for FM radio to be a medium of high fidelity, capable of transmitting and reproducing most of the pitches that most of us can hear, from a low of 50 Hz to a high of 15,000 Hz.

The width of the FM channel also provides space for stereophonic reproduction. The FCC selected an FM stereo system for the industry standard in 1961.[47] The selected FM stereophonic system uses multiplex transmission. The word *multiplex* refers to the sending of two or more signals simultaneously over the same channel. In an FM channel, the carrier (the center frequency of the channel) and its sidebands contain the main program information. However, another frequency within the channel may be generated and modulated so as to contain additional information, so long as its sidebands do not overlap those of the main carrier. This is called a *subcarrier*, and the information that provides for stereophonic reproduction in FM is carried in a subcarrier.

The multiplex stereo technique is designed to be *compatible*. This means that when an FM station transmits in stereo, a stereo receiver (which has the circuitry to detect the stereo subcarrier) picks up the programming in stereo, while a monaural receiver (which does not have the stereo subcarrier detection circuitry) receives only the main program channel (which is the left and right stereo channels combined into one).

Multiplex technology has the potential, of course, to transmit other types of information, even content completely unrelated to the transmitting station's main program channel. FCC rules provide for such nonbroadcast uses of FM subcarriers and give them the name *Subsidiary Communications Services* (SCS).[48] An FM licensee may utilize subcarrier transmissions for SCS without prior FCC authorization. Regular FM receivers pick up the station's broadcast signal, but only receivers with the proper circuitry can pick up the SCS signal.

The most frequent use of SCS is to provide "functional music," background music for department stores, shopping malls, and the like.[49] The FCC suggests other uses: specialized foreign-language programs, radio reading services for the sight-impaired, utility load management (EMG 6.2.1.5), market and financial data and news, paging and calling services, traffic control switching, bilingual TV audio, point-to-point or point-to-multipoint messages. Generally, a station provides such

---

[47] 47 C.F.R. § 73.322. The Commission revised this rule in 1986 to allow for other systems of stereophonic broadcasting.

[48] 47 C.F.R. § 73.295 for commercial stations; 47 C.F.R. § 73.593 for noncommercial stations.

[49] Remember: A station's SCS transmission is programmed separately from its broadcast channel. The background music you hear in a shopping mall is specially prepared to be background music for shopping; it is *not* the broadcast programming of an easy listening station with the commercials blanked out. In fact, it may be coming from a subcarrier of your favorite hard rock station.

subcarrier services to make money. Many noncommercial stations use their subcarriers to provide reading services, but they may also use them to earn a profit (as long as the reading service remains on a nonprofit basis). As with AM carrier services (EMG 6.2.1.5), an SCS is regulated in accord with its use—broadcast, common carrier, or private carrier.

6.2.2.6   Docket 80-90

FCC actions with regard to stereophonic transmission and AM-FM program duplication may have contributed to the eventual success of commercial FM; its docket 80-90 may have had a negative impact on the income of FM stations.

The FCC moved FM into its present frequency band in 1945. AM radio was at its height, and three years later the public began to discover TV. Audiences did not find FM attractive. The receivers were expensive and did not sound much better than AM receivers. In many cases FM programming was exactly the same as AM; AM-FM licensees would duplicate AM programming on the FM station. Audiences were content with AM radio and fascinated with television. Advertisers put their money in AM and TV. FM stations lost money almost without exception. From 1949 through 1952, over 350 FM station owners voluntarily returned licenses to the FCC.

The FCC took several regulatory actions to encourage the new aural medium. In 1961 it authorized FM stations to broadcast stereophonically (EMG 6.2.2.5). Two years later, the Commission adopted an FM nonduplication rule. This rule required licensees of AM-FM combinations in all but the smallest cities to program the FM stations separately from AM most of the time.[50] Such stations had to look for formats—preferably formats that did not duplicate those already in the market and that would show off FM's technical advantages.

FM stations were thus in exactly the right position when, in the late 1960s, rock music had begun to evolve and divide into increasingly esoteric forms, and rock fans discovered stereophonic reproduction. FM stations programmed these new forms of rock as well as other formats that took advantage of FM's high fidelity and stereophonic reproduction capability. By 1970, FM stations successfully competed for shares with AM stations in some large markets. In 1979, FM passed AM in overall market shares and, in succeeding years, increased its lead.

So successful was FM that the FCC decided to make room for more FM radio stations. In 1980 the FCC proposed changes in FM; the proposal became known by its FCC file number, "docket 80-90." In 1983 the Commission approved most docket 80-90 changes, primarily modification of station and channel classifications.[51] In 1989 the FCC authorized yet another class of FM station. These actions resulted in the station classification system described in EMG 6.2.2.2. They also allowed the addition of hundreds of new FM stations to a radio marketplace that already had many stations.

---

[50] Subsequently modified, then eliminated in AM-FM Program Duplication, 103 F.C.C.2d 922 (1986).
[51] Commercial FM Broadcast Assignments, 94 F.C.C.2d 1019 (1983).

TABLE 6.3   International Broadcasting
Frequencies in kilohertz (kHz)

	Region 3 only:
5,950–6,200	7,100–7,300
9,500–9,775	11,700–11,975
15,100–15,450	17,700–17,900
21,450–21,750	25,600–26,100

SOURCE: 47 C.F.R. § 73.702(f).

When the national economy turned sour in the early 1990s, the downside of docket 80-90 was revealed. Companies reduced advertising expenditures, which meant that revenues dropped for advertising-supported media. FM radio was no exception. With nearly 5,000 stations on the air, a lot of FM broadcasters were sharing a lot less ad revenue. In 1991, over 55 percent of all FM stations responding to a survey by the National Association of Broadcasters reported losing money. Critics laid part of the blame directly at the door of docket 80-90.[52]

6.2.3   International Broadcasting

U.S. international broadcasting stations use amplitude modulation to transmit radio programming intended for direct reception by the general public in foreign countries. Most stations use multiple frequencies because of multiple target countries and because of seasonal changes in propagation characteristics.

The FCC has allocated to the international broadcasting service eight different frequency bands (one of which is to be used only for transmissions to one region) between 5,950 and 26,100 kHz (Table 6.3). Carrier frequencies occur every 5 kHz.[53]

Both the federal government and private organizations operate international broadcasting stations. Only the nongovernment stations are licensed by and subject to the rules of the FCC.[54] Section 73.788 of the FCC rules requires that a licensee of an international broadcast station

render only an international broadcast service which will reflect the culture of this country and which will promote international goodwill, understanding, and cooperation. Any program solely intended for and directed to an audience in the continental United States does not meet the requirements for this service.

Propagation characteristics change with the seasons, and a station usually wishes to broadcast different programs simultaneously to different parts of the

---

[52] *See, e.g.,* Don West, "DeSales Street," *Broadcasting,* 13 Apr. 1992, at 16.
[53] 47 C.F.R. § 73.702(f)(3).
[54] *Id.*

world, so the Commission has set up the international broadcast service somewhat different from the domestic services. The Commission divides the world into 74 geographical zones and the year into four seasons.[55] A station's license specifies the zones or the areas of reception within those zones (such as a country or a part of a country) to which the station may transmit. The license does not specify frequencies.

Six months prior to the start of each season, the licensee submits to the FCC an application for that season to request (1) the frequency or frequencies desired for transmission to each zone or area authorized; (2) the specific hours it wishes to transmit to those zones or areas on each frequency, and (3) the power, antenna gain, and antenna bearing (direction) it desires to use. After processing all such applications, the Commission then notifies each licensee as to what (of the request) it actually gets; that is, the FCC tells the applicant how to operate the station during the season. FCC rules allow the licensee to request a change from the original proposal or authorization.[56]

International broadcasting stations operate with not less than 50 kW power.[57] All use directional antennas oriented toward the zones or areas they serve.[58] The Commission normally grants one frequency for use at any one time for any one program transmission. However, an international broadcasting station may engage in multiple operation; that is, the station may broadcast on one frequency over two or more transmitters simultaneously.[59] Also, when the station transmits a program intended for reception in more than one zone or area, the Commission may authorize use of additional frequencies. In fact, the Commission, "on a showing of good cause,"[60] may even authorize a licensee to use more than one frequency to transmit a program at any one time to a single zone or area.

6.3 FULL-POWER TELEVISION BROADCASTING

Full-power television broadcasting is the senior electronic visual mass medium in the United States. U.S. television broadcasting was first authorized for transmission to the general public in 1941, operating only on VHF channels. The United States' entry into World War II, however, resulted in a diversion of materials and manufacturing capacity to support military operations. As a result, widespread adoption and growth among consumers was delayed until 1947. The FCC opened the UHF television band in 1952, approved the present system of color television in 1953, and over the years made a number of technical improvements and enhancements to the

---

[55] Seasons change at 0100 G.M.T. on the first Sunday of the first month of each season: March season (March–May); May season (May–September); September season (September–November); November season (November–March).

[56] 47 C.F.R. § 73.702.

[57] 47 C.F.R. § 73.751.

[58] 47 C.F.R. § 73.753.

[59] 47 C.F.R. §§ 73.701(d), 73.702(g), note 3.

[60] 47 C.F.R. § 73.702(h).

existing NTSC[61] television system.[62] In this section, we look at the following aspects of television broadcasting: its portion of the radio frequencies, the table of allocations, transmission, and subsidiary services.

6.3.1   Television Broadcast Channels

The television broadcasting service consists of 68 6-MHz channels numbered 2–69 in the VHF and UHF frequency bands.

Television's 68 channels are spread across four bands of frequencies. Three bands are in the very high frequency (VHF) range—54–72 MHz contains channels 2 to 4; 76–88 MHz, channels 5 and 6;[63] and 174–216 MHz, channels 8 to 13. The fourth band consists of ultra high frequencies (UHF), 470–806 MHz, and contains channels 14 to 69.[64] Effective in 1983, the Commission reallocated UHF channels 70 to 83 (806–890 MHz), previously in the television broadcast band, to land mobile use.[65] The Commission has also adopted a plan for land mobile radio to share with television broadcasting UHF channels 14 to 20 (470–512 MHz) in 13 urbanized areas; these channels are not available for broadcast use until further action by the Commission.[66]

6.3.2   TV Table of Allocations

An FCC table, which may be amended, allots specific television channels to specific communities; about one-third of the allotments are reserved for noncommercial educational licensees.

The TV table assigns approximately 2,000 channels to nearly 900 communities. As in FM, if you wish to move an existing channel, you must petition to amend the table of allocations.[67] Again, you would need a consulting engineer to find a channel and to ensure that the selection adheres to FCC rules concerning minimum

[61] The National Television System Committee recommended the present technical standards to the FCC.

[62] As this section is being written the FCC prepares to consider a radical change in the nature of television—the switch to digital television transmission. Digital broadcast transmission was originally presented as a means to achieve high-definition television and other picture improvements, but the actual possibilities and implications of over-the-air digital transmission to the home go far beyond being simply a better way to do what is now being done. It is also far beyond the scope of extended discussion for the present context!

[63] See Note 46 for an explanation of TV channels 5 and 6 in Alaska.

[64] Channel 37 has been reserved exclusively for the radio astronomy service. In Hawaii, the frequencies in channel 17, 488–494 MHz, have been allocated for nonbroadcast use; therefore channel 17 is not assigned to Hawaii. 47 C.F.R. § 73.603(c) and (d).

[65] UHF Television Reception Improvements, 90 F.C.C.2d 1121 (1982). Land mobile radio is used by state and local public safety agencies (such as police and fire departments) and by all kinds of small and large businesses that need two-way communication with their on-the-move motor cars, vans, and trucks.

[66] 47 C.F.R. § 73.682(a)(15).

[67] 47 C.F.R. § 73.607.

mileage separations between channels to protect from co-channel and adjacent channel interference. These minimum mileage requirements are complex in nature and vary by channel and by geographical region.[68]

6.3.3   TV Power and Antenna Height

A television station operates with a video transmitter and an audio transmitter. ERP and antenna height vary by channel and by zone.

The visual signal is amplitude modulated (the color signal is added as a subcarrier on the picture carrier);[69] the aural, frequency modulated. The terms *visual power* and *aural power* refer to the strength in watts of the two signals. Television antennas have a multiplier effect. A video transmitter may put a 10,000-watt signal into the transmitting antenna, but the antenna radiates a signal that is the equivalent of the output of a higher-powered transmitter. This is due to the construction of the antenna. If the antenna is constructed with a multiplier factor of, say, 17, then the effective radiated power (ERP)—as opposed to the actual power of the transmitter—is $17 \times 10,000 = 170,000$ watts.

FCC rules specify that television stations operate with a visual ERP of no less than 100 watts but contain no maximum limits for visual ERP and no minimum or maximum heights for antennas. Instead, a series of equations is provided to determine maximum ERP as a function of antenna height. As antenna height increases, power must decrease.[70] The ERP of the aural transmission must not exceed 20 percent of the peak radiated power of the visual signal.[71]

Noncommercial educational and subscription television (STV) stations must adhere to the same technical standards as commercial stations. However, before beginning operation, an STV applicant must seek FCC approval of the station's system of scrambling the signal at the transmitter, decoding the signal at the set, and other aspects of the STV system.[72]

6.3.4   Multichannel TV Sound and Subcarrier and VBI Services

FCC rules allow a TV station to use its audio signal for stereo and other MTS applications and for SCS and to use its vertical blanking interval for telecommunications services and for coded captions.

---

[68] 47 C.F.R. §§ 73.610, 73.611.

[69] 47 C.F.R. § 73.682.

[70] 47 C.F.R. § 73.614.

[71] 47 C.F.R. § 73.682(a)(15).

[72] 47 C.F.R. § 73.644(a). While about 30 full-power stations transmitted as STVs during the late 1970s and early 1980s, the spread of cable TV service (which included the availability of premium channels) eventually put them all out of business. As of this writing, the only functioning STV operations are low-power television stations.

The FCC acted on stereophonic reproduction for television in 1984.[73] In adopting rules,[74] the Commission left open the potential for further technological advances by allowing the use of any stereo system so long as it is compatible with existing monaural receivers. And while the rules do not designate any one system as the national standard, they do provide protection for the frequency used by the pilot subcarrier of one particular system, that recommended by the Broadcast Television Systems Committee, a manufacturers' group.[75]

We have used the term *stereo,* but the FCC rule making used the more encompassing term *multichannel television sound* (MTS) and provided not only for stereo but also for *second audio program* (SAP) channels. A TV station may use such a channel to transmit, for example, a Spanish-language version of its main audio channel; an individual who has an appropriately equipped TV receiver is able to switch back and forth between the main sound channel (carrying the regular English-language program audio) and the SAP channel (carrying the Spanish version of the program audio).

A TV station may also offer Subsidiary Communications Services (EMG 6.2.2.5) through subcarriers on its audio channel[76] and the equivalent of SCS on its video channel. The latter is referred to in the FCC rules as *telecommunication services* and makes use of the vertical blanking interval (VBI)[77] of the video signal.[78] Commission rules suggest some possible telecommunications services: teletext (Box 6.1), paging, computer software, bulk data distribution, aural messages. A station may operate VBI services on a broadcast, point-to-point, or common carrier basis; if operated as a common carrier, the operation is subject to common carrier regulation. A station may lease out its VBI for others to provide service, but the station must still maintain control of content and is responsible for ensuring that the service's technical operation conforms to FCC regulations.

FCC rules specify that closed captioning (Box 6.2) is to be carried on a portion of the VBI.[79] TV stations do not have to transmit closed captions. But FCC rules

---

[73] Subcarrier Frequencies in the Aural Baseband of Television Transmitters, 49 Fed. Reg. 18,100 (Apr. 27, 1984).

[74] 47 C.F.R. § 73.669.

[75] The pilot subcarrier allows receivers to recognize that transmissions are in stereo and to switch into the stereophonic reception mode. *Protection* in this case means that the rules prohibit the use of 15,734 Hz in the television channel for any purpose other than the pilot subcarrier for the BTSC system. The FCC thus both (1) permits use of other stereo systems and (2) ensures that when these other systems are transmitting stereo audio signals, BTSC-type receivers do not detect them (since the signals would probably not be received as stereo by BTSC-type receivers).

[76] 47 C.F.R. § 73.667.

[77] The vertical blanking interval is the "black bar" you see when the picture on your television set rolls. The lines that compose the VBI contain various types of ancillary information needed for the television signal but also have room to carry other types of content. The FCC has designated lines 10–18 and 20 for such uses. 47 C.F.R. § 73.682(23).

[78] 47 C.F.R. § 73.646.

[79] Line 21 of fields 1 and 2. The signals on fields 1 and 2 are to be two distinct data streams, for example to supply captions in different languages or at different reading levels. Stations may use line 21 to carry additional text that may or may not be caption-related; however, captioning takes priority to non-caption-related text services (generally called *extended data services*). 47 C.F.R. § 73.682(22).

BOX 6.1   So What Is Teletext?

In teletext, pages of information are encoded onto the vertical blanking interval (VBI) in a repeating cycle, one after another, with no pause. If you wish to see these teletext pages, you must have a television receiver equipped with decoding circuitry. Let us say you are watching the evening news from a television station that, in addition to its regular programming, offers a teletext service. You see a story on the newscast that interests you and decide to check the teletext version. You punch the teletext button on your remote control, and the picture from the station's newscast is replaced by the opening page of the teletext service. That opening page contains an index, and you note that the story you wish to check starts on page 73. You punch 73 into the remote. When that page comes up in the transmission cycle (which takes, at most, a matter of seconds), the decoder "grabs" and uses a frame-store device to hold and display the page on the receiver screen. That page remains on the screen until you punch in another order.

FCC rules allow the content of a teletext transmission to be completely unrelated to the content of the broadcast channel onto whose VBI the teletext is encoded. For example, when you switch from that newscast to the station's teletext service, you may find that the station has leased it out to a direct mail sales organization, and the content is not news and information but advertising for gold chains and cubic zirconia.

BOX 6.2   Okay Then, So What Is Closed Captioning?

Closed captioning serves primarily the hearing impaired and those who understand little or no English. In closed captioning, the dialogue of a TV program is typed onto short strips or captions; these captions are then encoded into the VBI. If you are watching a TV program on a receiver equipped with closed-caption decoding circuitry, you can elect either to watch the program as transmitted (no captions) or the program with the captions inserted into the picture.

implementing the Television Decoder Circuitry Act of 1990[80] require that all TV receivers manufactured for sale in the United States after July 1, 1993, be capable of receiving and displaying coded captions.

---

[80] Pub. L. No. 101-431.

6.4 LOW-POWER BROADCASTING SERVICES

The FCC has authorized a number of types of stations that broadcast to the general public using very low power levels. Three of the most evident are low-power television stations, translator stations, and booster stations.

6.4.1 Low-Power Television

Low-power television stations operate with 10 or 1,000 watts as secondary stations on regular TV channels. They have fewer restrictions and requirements than full-power TV stations.

In March 1982, the FCC opened yet another TV broadcast service, Low-Power Television Broadcasting (LPTV).[81] In doing so, the Commission made possible the creation of hundreds of low-power ministations. Persons and groups with limited capital could put on the air stations that would have limited coverage areas but freedom to program to whatever extent the licensees wished and financial resources allowed.

An LPTV station has few of the programming restrictions that apply to a full-service station. It may originate programming—live, recorded, or microwave- or satellite-relayed. On the other hand, the LPTV station does not have to originate any programming; it may rebroadcast the signal of another TV station (with permission of the originating station, of course). Further, the LPTV station may operate on a total subscription basis.[82]

The procedure for a person wishing to put a new LPTV station on the air is similar to that for a new AM station: have a consulting engineer do a channel search, and once a channel has been found, make application, demonstrating that the proposed station would not cause interference. As explained in EMG 8.2.1, however, the FCC uses a lottery to actually award new LPTV licenses.

An LPTV station may operate on any available channel. An LPTV station on a VHF channel may use a transmitter with a maximum power of 10 watts; on UHF, 1,000 watts.[83] Its signal reaches about 2 to 10 miles, depending on channel, antenna height, antenna array, and terrain factors. It has "secondary status"; it must neither interfere with nor receive interference from any existing LPTV, TV translator, or full-service television station. An LPTV that happens to operate on a channel listed in the table of allocations must vacate if someone proposes to operate a full-power station on that channel. If an existing full-power station changes facilities and the change results in interference involving a proposed or existing LPTV station, the LPTV must adjust to eliminate the interference.[84] An LPTV station that shares a UHF

---

[81] Low Power Television Broadcasting, 47 Fed. Reg. 21,468 (May 18, 1982).

[82] 47 C.F.R. § 73.731(g).

[83] There is, however, no limit on ERP other than what is necessary to avoid interference. 47 C.F.R. § 74.735.

[84] 47 C.F.R. § 74.703. The FCC protects full-service stations to at least their Grade B contours. 47 C.F.R. § 74.705.

channel with land mobile users must protect those stations.[85] And it must protect any existing cable television system that would suffer interference at the headend or the output channels where the system uses a converter.[86]

6.4.2   Translator and Booster Stations

FM and television translator and booster stations operate at low power and receive, amplify, and rebroadcast the signal of a full-power primary station.

These stations usually operate unattended. Translators rebroadcast on a different channel from the primary station[87] (hence, "translator"); boosters, on the same channel. Translator and booster stations provide service to areas that are unable to receive signals directly because of distance from the primary station or intervening terrain barriers. Both provide service to areas unable to receive signals directly.[88]

A translator may be licensed to the people who live in its coverage area or to a local government. If the translator lies within the coverage area of the primary, it may be licensed to a broadcast licensee.[89] Under rule 74.763(d), a translator should not transmit when signals of its primary station are not being transmitted.

A translator may originate only public service announcements (PSAs), emergency warnings of imminent danger, and solicitations for or acknowledgment of its own financial support. The PSAs and financial support messages may be no longer than 30 seconds, at intervals no less than one hour. The warning messages may be no longer nor more frequent than necessary to protect life and property.[90] A TV translator, however, may convert to an LPTV station simply by notifying the FCC.[91] It may then originate programming, so long as it conforms to LPTV requirements, one of which calls for an operator to be on duty during origination.

A broadcast booster station, on the other hand, is licensed to,[92] and may be located only within the predicted coverage area[93] of, the primary station. The booster's purpose is to boost the primary's signal in areas where that signal should be picked up over the air but in reality can be received poorly or not at all. A booster may originate no programming for its audience,[94] and FCC rules contain no provision for a TV booster station to convert to an LPTV station.

---

[85] 47 C.F.R. § 74.709.
[86] 47 C.F.R. § 74.703.
[87] The repeated full-power station.
[88] 47 C.F.R. §§ 74.731 and 74.1231.
[89] 47 C.F.R. §§ 74.732 and 74.1232(d).
[90] 47 C.F.R. §§ 74.731 and 74.1231(f) and (g).
[91] 47 C.F.R. § 74.731.
[92] 47 C.F.R. § 74.732(g).
[93] In the technical language used in the rule, the "predicted Grade B contour."
[94] 47 C.F.R. § 74.731.

6.5 OMNIDIRECTIONAL MICROWAVE SYSTEMS

Omnidirectional microwave services consist of 6-MHz channels in the microwave frequencies and include the Instructional Television Fixed Service, the Multipoint Distribution Service, some channels in the Operational Fixed Service, and wireless cable.

For the most part, stations operating in these services transmit omnidirectionally (in all directions)[95] with radiated power of no more than 2,000 watts. They provide one-way transmission from a stationary transmitter to multiple receiving facilities located at fixed points. In other words, they send out TV programming using the microwave frequencies. Their coverage is determined by line of sight; even a leafy tree branch or foliage can block the signal from a receiving antenna. The frequencies used by three of these services are shown in Table 6.4.

6.5.1 Instructional Television Fixed Service

The Instructional Television Fixed Service (ITFS) consists of five groups of four channels each, intended for the transmission of instructional TV material for use by schools. Excess channel capacity may be used for other purposes.

The FCC licenses ITFS stations to accredited educational institutions and to nonprofit organizations that provide instructional TV material to accredited institutions.[96] A typical application would take the form of a county school district with a central TV origination facility that transmits video instruction or supplementary material to schools all over the county. Some educational institutions allow one or more of their channels to be carried by cable systems. The rules also allow the "excess capacity" of ITFS channels to be used for almost any purpose at all, including revenue-producing lease of the channels to private parties (such as wireless cable systems; EMG 6.5.3).

6.5.2 Multipoint Distribution Service

The multipoint distribution service consists of 13 channels.

The multipoint distribution service (MDS) originally contained only two 6-MHz channels. Operators of MDS stations were licensed as common carriers and therefore could originate no programming of their own. The idea was that they would provide facilities for others, primarily businesses who needed to transmit material to a number of different reception points. The channels had the bandwidth necessary for business, scientific, and industrial uses such as data processing.

---

[95] FCC rules do contain provisions for directional transmission.
[96] 47 C.F.R. § 74.931.

TABLE 6.4   ITFS and MDS (Wireless Cable) Channels (in MHz)

Original MDS Channels

Channel 1   2150–2156
Channel 2   2156–2166

A Group[†]	B Group[†]	C Group[†]	D Group[†]
A1 2500–2506	B1 2506–2512	C1 2548–2554	D1 2554–2560
A2 2512–2518	B2 2518–2524	C2 2560–2566	D2 2566–2572
A3 2524–2530	B3 2530–2536	C3 2572–2578	D3 2578–2584
A4 2536–2542	B4 2542–2548	C4 2584–2590	D4 2590–2596

E Group[‡]	F Group[†]	G Group[†]	H Group[§]
E1 2596–2602	F1 2602–2608	G1 2644–2650	H1 2650–2656
E2 2608–2614	F2 2614–2620	G2 2656–2662	H2 2662–2668
E3 2620–2626	F3 2626–2632	G3 2668–2674	H3 2674–2680
E4 2632–2638	F4 2638–2644	G4 2680–2686	

SOURCE: 47 C.F.R. §§ 74.902, 21.901.
[†] ITFS channels.
[‡] Reallocated from ITFS to MMDS; existing ITFS licensees operating on these channels allowed to remain.
[§] Reallocated from OFS.

However, MDS channels were used more and more for transmission of video entertainment for consumers. Because of this, demand for channels increased, and the FCC reallocated to MDS the ITFS E and F bands (four channels each) in 1983[97] and the operational fixed service (OFS) H band (three channels) in 1991.[98] In 1987 the Commission gave MDS licensees the option of electing *non–common carrier status*, which would allow parties both to operate and to program MDS stations.[99] The push for these moves came from the budding wireless cable business.

6.5.3   Multichannel Television/Wireless Cable

Multichannel television (also called "wireless cable") systems distribute a subscription program service to consumers using a combination of channels from the MDS, OFS, and ITFS services.

The origins of multichannel television go back to the 1970s, before cable television was universally available in medium and large markets. At that time, entrepreneurs began to lease individual MDS channels to distribute pay entertainment services such as Home Box Office to areas where pay cable was not available. They

---

[97] Instructional Television Fixed Service, Multipoint Distribution Service, and Private Operational Fixed Microwave Service, 9 F.C.C.2d 1203 (1983). Since these eight channels came in two bands of four, they were known as the *multichannel multipoint distribution service.*
[98] Second Report and Order, 6 F.C.C.R. 6792 (1991).
[99] Multipoint Distribution Service, 2 F.C.C.R. 4251 (1987).

transmitted programming on one or two MDS channels for reception by apartment complexes, hotels, and other multiunit dwellings.

In 1977 new technology reduced the price of MDS transmitting and receiving antennas, and MDS programmers offered their service to private homes. They enjoyed a measure of success. But they saw that once the cities had awarded cable franchises and been wired for cable television, they could not compete. After all, cable television was a multichannel medium, and the MDS programmers had at best only a couple of channels with which to work. However, if they could get access to a group of 6-MHz channels in the microwave frequencies, they could offer a multichannel service to compete with cable. And since they would not have to get a franchise (which also meant they would not have to pay franchise fees, operate access channels, or carry unprofitable "public-service" services) nor lay cable (which represents a huge capital investment for cable systems), they could charge less for their service and still make a profit.

They turned their attention to the channels of the ITFS,[100] most of which were unused in most markets. The FCC was petitioned to reallocate ITFS channels to MDS. As an interim measure to make more channels available to program distributors, the FCC amended its rules for the operational fixed service (OFS) in 1981[101] to use certain OFS channels in the delivery of pay-TV programming to multiunit dwellings. FCC rules were subsequently revised again to permit use of OFS channels for home service and, as described in the preceding two sections, to reallocate channels to MDS and to allow ITFS licensees to lease out their unused capacity. So now with this collection of channels from various sources, the entrepreneurs who programmed and marketed them were true *multichannel television operators* (often shortened to *multichannel operators*).

In 1983 a number of firms announced plans for multichannel television systems to compete with cable operators in some of the nation's cities. In the meantime, multichannel operators started using the term *wireless cable*, an oxymoron intended to imply that, with respect to content, theirs was a "cablelike" service. When complaints arose in the late 1980s concerning the virtual monopoly that cable systems had in most markets, the FCC recognized wireless cable as a service and further liberalized rules in an attempt to enhance its potential as a competitor to cable. The Commission even provided for direct licensing of some ITFS channels to wireless cable operators.[102]

6.5.4 Local Multipoint Distribution Service

In 1992, the FCC opened yet another multichannel service, the Local Multipoint Distribution Service (LMDS).[103] LMDS, operating in the 28-GHz band, offers its services through strategically placed transmitter/receiver units similar to cellular tele-

---

[100] ITFS then had 28 channels—four each in seven bands lettered sequentially A through G. See Table 6.4.

[101] Until then, OFS had been used primarily by cities and oil companies.

[102] First Report and Order, 5 F.C.C.R. 6410 (1990); and Second Report and Order, 6 F.C.C.R. 6791 (1991).

[103] Local Multipoint Distribution Service, 8 F.C.C.R. 557 (1992).

phone. Special technology allows an LMDS operator to offer up to 98 one-way video channels or a mix of one-way and two-way services including video-on-demand, interactive TV and high-definition TV, high-speed data, personal communications, telephone, and educational services. The FCC licenses two operators in each of 489 cellular service areas nationwide, and CellularVision, the firm that developed LMDS, franchises the system to operators.

6.6   DIRECT BROADCAST SATELLITE

Interim FCC rules define the direct broadcast satellite service as a radio communi- cation service in which signals transmitted or retransmitted by space stations are intended for direct reception by the general public. Uplink transmitters would op- erate in the 17.3–17.8 GHz range; for the downlink, the satellite would transmit in the 11.7–12.5 GHz range.

During the late 1970s, increasing numbers of television programmers used sat- ellite relay to deliver their product. These were "wholesalers" (primarily cable TV networks) who sent their programming by satellite to "retailers" (primarily cable systems)[104] who, in turn, made the programming available to the public. The satel- lite signals were *not* intended for reception by the general public; nonetheless, in- creasing numbers of individuals bought satellite receiving equipment and picked up programming directly from the satellite. This was the beginning of the medium known variously as TVRO (television receive-only), home satellite, and the "back- yard dish industry." Eventually most of the signals were encrypted, and legisla- tion[105] provided for the packaging, marketing, and retailing of these essentially "wholesale" signals to backyard dish owners.

In the meantime, some companies believed that the use of satellite receiving dishes by private citizens had the potential for profit. The idea was proposed for a new satellite service that would be designed specifically for direct reception by the general public: *direct broadcast satellite* (DBS). The FCC adopted the DBS rules in 1982.[106] This was to be something new; it was *not* the same as TVRO. Direct broad- cast satellites would operate with high power (around 120 watts for each channel, which is high power for a satellite) and utilize the Ku frequency band rather than the lower-frequency and lower-power (25–30 watts was typical) C band of most

---

[104] Cable television programmers were particularly aggressive in making use of this new networking medium, satellite relay, for program delivery. Public broadcast networks also pioneered the use of satellite. Broadcast networks and program syndicators eventually followed.

[105] The Satellite Home Viewer Act of 1988, Pub. L. No. 100-667, amended the Copyright Act, title 17 of the U.S. Code, by creating a new statutory license for certain secondary transmissions of "supersta- tion" and network station signals made by satellite carriers to satellite home dish owners.

[106] Direct Broadcast Satellite Service, 90 F.C.C.2d 676 (1982); and 47 C.F.R. § 100.1 et seq. The term *space station* that appears in the presummary to this section is the term used by the FCC.

existing satellites (from which TVRO owners picked up signals).[107] The audience would use small (about 18-inch) antennas to receive the satellite signals.

The Commission wanted to see how the DBS service would develop, what it would actually be, before adopting permanent rules. Thus, the 1982 rules were labeled *interim*. Within a year or so, the Commission had received 14 applications for interim service. It accepted 8 for filing. These initial applicants proposed to offer a variety of service through DBS: direct broadcast; pay television; advertiser-supported program service; availability for retransmission by broadcasters, by cable systems, and by LPTV stations; teletext; leased-channels system; high-definition television; and audio services.[108] None, however, carried through. As cable service increased penetration and expanded programming during the 1980s, the view became prevalent that consumers would not see a need for nor invest in DBS. By the end of the decade Europe had launched its first direct broadcast satellite. NHK, Japan's national network, also had a high-power system operating. The United States, however, was still waiting. Only two U.S. companies appeared to have both the will and the means to launch direct broadcast satellites: United States Satellite Broadcasting, controlled by Hubbard Broadcasting (a pioneer group owner of radio and TV stations), and DirecTv, planned by Hughes Communications (a division of General Motors). They planned to have their satellites launched and running sometime in 1994.

6.7 CABLE TELEVISION

Cable television systems first developed during the late 1940s and early 1950s. This was a period during which there were very few television stations but increasing numbers of people who wanted to watch TV and bought their first receiving sets. The early cable ventures were called "community antenna television systems," and their only service was to bring television broadcast signals to small and isolated communities where stations could not be picked up directly off the air. The numbers of both stations and systems grew during the 1960s and 1970s. As more TV broadcast signals became available in more areas, the community antenna systems developed other services in an effort to continue to attract customers, and in the process of doing so they evolved into today's cable television systems.

At first examination, it would seem that because they do not transmit over the air, cable systems would be exempt from government regulation. That, however, is not the case. In this section, we examine the following areas of cable television

---

[107] 47 C.F.R. § 100.21. Satellite communication service developed using frequencies in the 4–6 GHz range (the C band) and later added those in the 12–14 GHz range (the Ku band). The transmissions of Ku-band satellites, because they use higher frequencies, are more directional than those of C-band satellites.

[108] "Good News, Bad News in DBS Spacerush," *Broadcasting*, 20 July 1981, at 23; "Teletext, DBS Top FCC Agenda," *Broadcasting*, 26 Oct. 1981, at 25.

systems: the means by which they deliver their signals, the frequency spectrum they use, and the dual state-federal nature of regulation.

6.7.1   Cable Television Signal Delivery

Cable television delivers its service by use of a broadband conductor installed in public right-of-way.

Broadband means that the wire, by which cable systems deliver their service directly to each subscriber's receiver, can carry a wide range of frequencies. Coaxial cable, which for years was the only conductor used in cable systems, is literally coaxial—a conductor and a metal sheath share the same axis. The center conductor, which carries the signals, is a single strand of copper or copper-covered aluminum; the sheath, which prevents signal leakage, is aluminum. The center conductor is inside the sheath, separated from it by a spacer such as plastic foam. A black plastic outer sheath covers the cable. The coaxial configuration allows the cable to carry more frequencies than could the unsheathed conductor by itself. For example, a telephone wire can carry a frequency range of about 400 to 2,800 Hz, a total of 2,400 Hz. Coaxial cable, using current analog technology, can carry a frequency range of some 54 to 400 MHz, a total of 346 MHz (enough capacity for 50 to 54 television channels). Many cable operators are installing optical fiber as a replacement for coaxial cable in some parts of their systems. Optical fiber has several times the carrying capacity of coaxial cable. And development of digital compression technology could multiply that capacity to 500 or more channels. Cable operators view this expanded capacity as the means to provide video-on-demand (VOD)[109] service or near-video-on-demand (NVOD)[110] service.

Many systems also have one-way addressability, allowing the cable operator to send a signal "downstream" so that it goes to one subscriber or one group of subscribers and to no others. The most common use of one-way addressability is for pay-per-view (PPV) service. In a system with advanced one-way addressability, when a subscriber changes service (say, adding a tier or dropping two pay services) or even drops service, the operator can make the changes or cancel the service from the headend without dispatching an installer. Two-way addressability would allow a subscriber to send a signal "upstream" to the headend and ultimately to any other point on the system (such as another subscriber). This would allow cable

---

[109] The cable system would send to your home programming (say, a currently popular movie) that you choose to see at the time you want to see it.

[110] The cable system would devote a number of channels entirely to continuous repeat plays of the same program (perhaps a currently popular movie). As an example, the starting times for a 120-minute movie could be staggered over four channels (say, 301 to 304) as follows:

Channel 301:	1:00		3:00		5:00		7:00		9:00 ...	
Channel 302:		1:30		3:30		5:30		7:30		9:30 ...
Channel 303:		2:00		4:00		6:00		8:00		10:00 ...
Channel 304:		2:30		4:30		6:30		8:30		10:30 ...

Such scheduling would mean that no subscriber would have to wait more than 30 minutes to see any program being offered.

systems to offer interactive services (including telephone) complete with sophisticated video. That, however, requires a switched network, a technical capability that telephone companies have and that most cable companies viewed as prohibitively expensive to build themselves.[111] One way to achieve this interactive capability would be to combine the resources of the telephone companies and the cable systems, which is precisely what began to occur in 1993.[112]

The signal origination point for a cable system is the headend.[113] Located at the headend are receiving antennas (for broadcast signals, microwave, and satellite) and various devices that process signals and put them on cable channels, such as distribution amplifiers, interference filters, multiplex equipment, and switching gear. A trunk line carries the signals from the headend to individual neighborhoods. A bridger transfers the signals to feeder lines for carriage through neighborhoods. Taps transfer the signals to drop lines that go to individual subscribers' homes. The conduction medium, coaxial cable or optical fiber,[114] is placed in public right-of-way either mounted on existing utility poles or threaded through underground conduits. In-line repeater amplifiers keep the signals boosted throughout the length of the system.

6.7.2 Cable System Spectrum

Cable television channels numbered 14 and higher do not use the same frequencies as correspondingly numbered TV broadcast frequencies.

---

[111] The means by which a subscriber presently orders a PPV event on most cable systems is tied in with the local telephone system; a telephone call is made to the system to place the order. Two-way addressability would allow *impulse ordering;* that is, the subscriber could order (and be billed for) a PPV event simply by pushing a button on the cable remote control. Similarly, it would allow impulse VOD.

[112] In some cases cable operators combined with telephone companies to construct systems; in other cases cable operators utilized telephone-company-constructed facilities; in yet others telephone companies decided to go into the cable business and cable operators decided to go into the telephone business. *See, e.g.,* Rich Brown, "Comcast Demonstrates New Phone Service," *Broadcasting,* 14 Sept. 1992, at 11; Rich Brown, "Twain Meet Over Video Dialtone," *Broadcasting,* 23 Nov. 1992, at 14; Harry A. Jessell, "Bell Atlantic Takes Early Lead," *Broadcasting,* 4 Jan. 1993, at 45; Randy Sukow and Rich Brown, "Time Warner Unveils 'Full Service' TV," *Broadcasting,* Feb. 1993, at 6; RB, "US West Answers Video Dialtone Call," *Broadcasting,* 8 Feb. 1993, at 4; Rich Brown, "Southwestern Bell Makes First RBOC Cable Entry for $650 Million," *Broadcasting,* 15 Feb. 1993, at 3; HAJ, "The Telcos Are Coming," *Broadcasting,* 1 Mar. 1993, at 10; Joe Flint, "Telcos Closing in on Video," *Broadcasting,* 1 Mar. 1993, at 6; Sean Scully, "Telco's N.J. Video System Will Be Fiber Optic," *Broadcasting,* 3 May 1993, at 61. Some proposed telco-cable cooperative ventures were subsequently canceled. *See, e.g.,* Mark Berniker, "Going Their Own Way into Video," *Broadcasting & Cable,* 2 May 1994, at 36.

[113] The headend is the facility to which all signals—direct off-the-air, microwave-relay, satellite, local origination—intended for distribution to subscribers go for processing and for transmission (that is, being sent down the system on specific channels). The distribution medium—coaxial cable or optical fiber—that carries the signal through the franchise area and to subscribers originates at the headend as the trunk line.

[114] Present technology is at the "optical-to-the-neighborhood" level: signals go by optical fiber to a node serving about 500 homes and by coaxial cable the rest of the way. Equipment to downconvert the frequencies carried by optical fiber is currently too expensive to put into each subscriber's home.

Cable television systems offer an average of about 35 channels. Some in big markets offer more; some in smaller markets, fewer. The types of signals they carry include local television broadcast stations, locally originated programming, and satellite-delivered national program services. Cable channels 2 to 13 use the same part of the spectrum on a cable system as broadcast channels 2 to 13 do "over the air." But the spectrum used by cable channels above 13 differs from that used by correspondingly numbered broadcast channels.[115] This means that a television receiver connected to a cable system will receive only cable channels 2 to 13 unless it is used with a converter or is a cable-ready receiver.[116]

If a subscriber has ordered only the basic service tier,[117] the drop line may connect directly to the television receiver, particularly if the receiver is cable-ready. Otherwise the drop line may connect to a converter, and a short length of cable then connects the converter to the receiver. For non-cable-ready receivers, the converter processes cable channels 14 and above so that the receiver will accept and display them. For subscribers who have ordered a level of service above basic, the converter unscrambles and passes those premium channels and additional tiers for which the subscriber pays; other premium channels and extra-pay tiers are blocked or seen as scrambled.[118] For this service, the subscriber usually pays an installation fee when first hooked up, a deposit for the converter, and a monthly fee thereafter.

6.7.3 Federal and State Regulation

Cable systems are franchised by local governments, not licensed by the federal government. Nonetheless, FCC regulations define and apply to cable systems.

Since a cable system does not use over-the-air radio frequencies to transmit its service, it does not need a license from the federal government to operate. However, it does need a *franchise* from the government of the locale into whose right-

---

[115] Despite the metal sheath, some signal leakage does occur from coaxial cable. FCC rules prevent cable system use of the frequency bands 108–137 MHz and 225–400 MHz unless the system is in compliance with certain standards limiting the strength of leaked signals. Otherwise signal leakage from the cable system would interfere with transmission in the aeronautical radiocommunication service.

[116] *Cable-ready* means that the receiver's tuner will receive cable channels numbered 14 and above without a converter and that the cable itself can be connected to the set without an adapter. (A non-cable-ready set has a twin-lead antenna connection, and a 300-ohm/75-ohm adapter must be used so the cable input can be attached.) A cable-ready receiver often cannot be used except through a connection to a cable system; that is, it will not work with an external antenna to pick up over-the-air signals.

[117] Discussed in EMG 10.3.1. For right now, we may define the basic service tier as all local TV broadcast signals that the system carries plus all franchise-required signals (such as public, educational, and governmental access channels). The basic service tier is the lowest level of service, the least that someone can pay for and still be considered a cable subscriber.

[118] Some cable systems use equipment placed outside the subscriber's home, at the tap, to limit access to premium channels and extra-pay tiers; systems with sophisticated technology can control this equipment from the headend.

of-way the cable operator will lay the system's cable. Typically, this is a city council or a county commission.[119] Some state legislatures have enacted laws governing city and county franchise agreements. Further, as discussed in EMG 3.2.3, Congress has asserted authority over cable television and defined the legal relationship between a franchising authority and cable systems that operate within its jurisdiction. Congress has also charged the Federal Communications Commission with carrying out the intent of federal law with respect to cable television. As a result, the federal government has exclusive jurisdiction over certain areas of cable operation (such as signal carriage), while local governments have jurisdiction over other matters (such as provision of access channels).

Section 602 of the Communications Act of 1934, as amended, defines a cable system as

> a facility consisting of a set of closed transmission paths [that is, cable channels] and associated signal ... equipment that is designated to provide cable service which includes video programming and which is provided to multiple subscribers within a community. . . .[120]

Cable service is defined as

> (A) The one-way transmission to subscribers of (i) video programming, or (ii) other programming service, and (B) subscriber interaction, if any, which is required for the selection of such video programming or other programming service.[121]

Video programming is "programming provided by, or generally considered comparable to programming provided by, a television station,"[122] and *other programming service* is anything else "that a cable operator makes available to all subscribers generally"[123]—perhaps a cable audio service or an electronic text service.

The Commission has written most of its cable television rules in terms of the *system community unit*. Paragraph (dd) of section 76.5 defines community unit as what most people think of as a cable system—"a cable television system, or portion of a ... system that operates ... within a separate and distinct community," which can include unincorporated areas. Other FCC rules deal with franchising, system operation and administration, types of signals carried, technical and equipment requirements, system ownership restrictions, and subscriber rates and service.

---

[119] Cities and counties are legally created by the states within whose boundaries they lie, and city and county ordinances must comply with state laws. Therefore, the term *state regulation* is used in this section to refer to the power of the local franchising authority.

[120] 47 C.F.R. § 522(7).

[121] 47 C.F.R. § 522(6).

[122] 47 C.F.R. § 522(19).

[123] 47 U.S.C. § 533(13).

6.8   SMATV SYSTEMS

SMATV systems are cable-system-like facilities that operate on private property.

FCC rules list a number of types of facilities that the Commission specifically excludes from being cable systems. One of these is a satellite master antenna television system. The abbreviation for such a system is SMATV, usually pronounced "*smat*-vee."

A SMATV system is set up and operates very much like a cable system. It uses coaxial cable to provide programming of both local TV broadcast stations and satellite-delivered cable services to subscribers. The difference, however, is that the subscribers are inevitably residents of an apartment building or complex, a condominium, or some other such commonly owned multiple-unit dwelling. Thus, while a cable system puts its cable in the public right-of-way, a SMATV system puts its cable entirely on the private property of the multiple-unit dwelling. Since SMATV systems do not use public right-of-way, they do not have to have a franchise.

6.9   VIDEO DIALTONE

The FCC's video dialtone concept allows telephone companies to deliver—on a common carrier basis—video created, owned, and offered by others.

The Commission approved the video dialtone concept in 1992, allowing telephone companies to offer video delivery services within their own service areas.[124] Under this concept, the telephone companies may construct and offer facilities through which video programmers can deliver informational and entertainment programming to customers.

Even before the video dialtone ruling, telephone companies were replacing their standard telephone wires with optical fiber. This gave them a conduction medium that was broadband enough to carry many video signals at once. The necessity for "fiber-to-the-neighborhood,"[125] however, meant that the line going into the customer home would be, for the time being, regular copper telephone wire. Copper wire was (and had been for years!) adequate for POTS ("plain ol' telephone service"). The problem for video dialtone service, of course, was getting those 6-MHz video signals from the utility pole to the customer's television receiver. Until the early 1990s, copper telephone wire had been able to pass no more than a low-resolution slow-scan video picture at best. By 1994, however, rapid advances in digital compression technology had overcome that particular bottleneck, and a full television channel, as required by the video dialtone concept, could be compressed enough for transmission over copper wire into a customer's home. Inside the video-

---

[124] Telephone Company—Cable Television Cross-Ownership Rules, 7 F.C.C.R. 5781 (1992).
[125] See note 114.

dialtone customer home, the copper wire connects to a highly sophisticated converter/decompresser box with two-way capability.

The telephone system is, by definition, switched and addressable, features that make possible the following scenario. You, as a customer, could use a video dialtone system similar to the way you use a video rental store. Two major differences would be that, with video dialtone, you would not have to leave home, and the desired video would never be "out," so you could view it right away. It would be true impulse video-on-demand.[126] In this video rental store analogy, the programmer offers videos through the telephone company's video dialtone system rather than on shelves in a store. Using the converter's remote control, you (1) call up a menu of video offerings through video dialtone, (2) order from that menu a program—say, a recently released feature film—just by pushing a button on the remote, (3) have the movie start immediately (and chances are good that you would be able to stop, still frame, slow down, speed up, and repeat segments of the movie, just as though watching it on a videocassette recorder), and (4) receive a charge for the movie on your regular telephone bill. Once you have paid your bill, the telephone company retains some of the video charge for the services it has rendered and sends the remainder on to the video programmer. As discussed in some detail in Chapter 8, a video dialtone programmer does not need a franchise to operate, and the telephone company that provides video dialtone facilities is regulated as a common carrier.

6.10 AUXILIARY AND RELATED ELECTRONIC MEDIA

FCC rules provide for services related to the regular broadcast and cable television services. These include experimental stations, auxiliary stations, low-power auxiliary stations, the cable antenna relay service, and a group of low-power radio-broadcasting-like station types. This section is provided to make you aware of the existence of these other services and stations and to explain their relationship to the "main" regulated electronic media that are the focus of this volume.

6.10.1 Experimental Broadcast Stations

The FCC licenses experimental broadcast stations to carry on development and research in television, radio, and other types of telecommunications services intended for reception by the general public.

These stations serve as testing platforms in the development and advancement of new broadcasting technology, equipment, systems, or services.[127] They transmit

---

[126] See note 111.

[127] 47 C.F.R. § 74.101. Regular broadcast stations can also get authorization to carry out research and experimentation; however, for development work that is extensive or requires other than normal modes of transmission, an experimental station is needed.

only when necessary to the research for which they have been licensed, and they may offer no regular schedule of programming.[128] Experimental broadcast stations may be licensed to operate on any frequency allocated to the broadcast services or various categories of auxiliary stations.[129] They are licensed for one year,[130] and the FCC grants only one license to a person unless it can be demonstrated that a particular project requires additional stations.[131]

6.10.2 Broadcast Auxiliary Stations

The FCC licenses auxiliary stations to relay programs and associated material for broadcast stations. The categories consist of remote and TV pickup; aural and TV broadcast STL; aural inter city, TV relay, and TV translator relay; and aural and TV microwave booster stations.

These stations use frequencies in the microwave range. In general terms, a broadcaster would use auxiliary-station types as follows: a pickup station for communication between the studio and the away-from-studio origination point on a remote,[132] an STL to get the signal from the studio to the station's distant transmitter, a relay station to transmit program material to another station or to a translator station, and a booster station as an intermediate link to relay the signals of one of the other auxiliary stations. These are set forth in Table 6.5.

The FCC allows broadcasters to use these auxiliary services on a temporary basis without first having to get licenses. The broadcaster need only address an informal request to the Commission. Such operation should be on a temporary basis; if the station were to use these frequencies regularly, it would have to get a license. Further, such operation is on a secondary, noninterference basis; a station with a license in the auxiliary service would have priority for a frequency in that service over a station operating on a temporary basis.

6.10.3 Low-Power Auxiliary Stations

Devices authorized as low-power auxiliary stations are intended for uses such as wireless microphones, cue and control communications, and synchronization of TV camera signals.

---

[128] 47 C.F.R. § 74.182.

[129] 47 C.F.R. § 74.103. Experimental stations may not, of course, operate so as to interfere with other stations.

[130] 47 C.F.R. § 74.15.

[131] 47 C.F.R. § 74.134.

[132] A *remote* is a broadcast that originates away from the studio. Whether a radio broadcast from the opening of a new shopping center or a TV report live from the scene of a breaking news event, the signal that originates at the remote site must be routed back to the studio for broadcast. Pickup stations provide the means for terrestrial (that is, not using satellite) studio-remote communication in such situations.

TABLE 6.5 Types and Uses of Broadcast Auxiliary Stations

Aural Broadcast Auxiliary Stations	Television Broadcast Auxiliary Stations
Remote pickup. Transmits material and associated cues, orders, and instructions between the studio and locations away from the studio for radio stations	TV pickup. Transmits TV program material and related communications from scenes of events occurring at points removed from TV broadcast station studios to TV broadcast or low-power TV stations.
Aural broadcast STL.* Transmits program material from studio to transmitter of radio stations.	TV broadcast STL.* Transmits visual program material between studio and transmitter of TV stations.
Aural broadcast ICR.† Transmits program material and related communications between radio stations.	TV relay. Transmits visual program material between TV stations or from a remote pickup receiver site of a single station.
An aural broadcast ICR may also be used to transmit program material between an FM station and an FM translator station.	TV translator relay. Relays programs and signals of a TV broadcast station to television translator stations.
Aural broadcast microwave booster station. Retransmits the signals of an aural broadcast STL or ICR station.	TV microwave booster. Retransmits the signals of a TV pickup, TV STL, TV relay, or TV translator relay station.

SOURCES: 47 C.F.R. §§ 74.431, 74.501, 74.531, 74.601, 74.631.
*STL = Studio-transmitter link
†ICR = Inter city relay

The most common examples of low-power auxiliary stations are wireless microphones that performers and other participants wear during production. The FCC has also authorized use of such stations to transmit cues and orders to production personnel and participants, send comments, interviews, and reports from the scene of a remote broadcast, and to provide synchronizing signals to portable, hand-held wireless TV cameras.[133] FCC rules limit transmission to approximately 100 meters. The rules also restrict the granting of licenses in this service to licensees of broadcast stations, networks, and cable TV system operators that originate their own programming; to licensees in the multipoint distribution service; and to motion picture and television producers.[134]

6.10.4 Cable Antenna Relay Services

Cable operators use microwave systems in the cable antenna relay service (CARS)[135] to transmit signals from one place to another in preparation for distribution to the public.

Such signals can include those of television (video and audio), AM radio, FM radio, ITFS, and cablecasting. The FCC licenses stations in CARS only to cable televi-

---

[133] 47 C.F.R. § 74.831.
[134] 47 C.F.R. § 74.832.
[135] 47 C.F.R. §§ 78.1–78.11.

sion operators and to cooperative enterprises owned by cable television operators. CARS stations have license terms of five years,[136] and they operate in the 12.70–13.20 GHz range.[137]

CARS includes the following types of stations: local distribution service (LDS) stations, cable television relay service studio to headend link (SHL) stations, and cable television relay service (pickup) stations. Typically, uses for each of these station categories are:

- LDS stations: Relay signals from a local transmission point to one or more receiving points, from which the signals are distributed to subscribers. For example, a cable operator serving a large franchise area might build a single headend, then use LDS stations to transmit the signals to hubs located in various parts of the area, from which radiate the cables that carry signals to subscriber homes. An LDS station may operate within one cable system or among several cable systems.
- SHL stations: Relay television program material and related communications (such as technical instructions) from a cable television studio to the headend of a cable system.
- Pickup stations: Used as mobile transmitter by cable operators to cablecast a remote (that is, production away from the studio).[138]

6.10.5 Wired Radio Stations

Other types of radio services authorized by the FCC to serve the general public (or some specific segment of that public) include travelers' information stations, tunnel radio systems, and carrier current systems. Most operate with some type of wire antenna.

Travelers' information stations are considered part of the local government radio service. Eligibility for authorization to operate a travelers' information station is limited to states, territories, possessions, cities, counties, towns, or similar governmental entities, including park districts and other types of districts and authorities.[139] FCC rules specify that a traveler's information station (TIS) is to transmit only noncommercial voice information pertaining to traffic and road conditions, traffic hazard and travel advisories, directions, availability of lodging, rest stops, and service stations, and descriptions of local points of interest. TIS announcements may not identify the commercial name of any business establishment. However, when those announcements pertain to departures, arrivals, and parking areas at air, train, or bus terminals, the station may give the trade name of the carriers—the airline, the bus line, and so on.

---

[136] 47 C.F.R. § 78.29.
[137] 47 C.F.R. § 78.18.
[138] 47 C.F.R. § 78.5.
[139] 47 C.F.R. §§ 90.17 and 90.242. School districts may *not* operate TIS stations.

Until 1991, traveler's information stations were limited to operating on just two frequencies. Those frequencies were 530 and 1610 kHz, the extreme ends of the AM radio band. When the FCC opened the AM expanded band, however, it also allowed traveler's information stations to apply for operation on any AM frequency so long as they did not interfere with full-power AM stations operating on the same or adjacent frequencies.[140] Traveler's information stations transmit with either of two types of antennas: (1) a conventional radiating antenna similar to that used by full-power stations, in which case they are limited to 10 watts of power; or (2) a cable antenna[141]—a length of wire no longer than 3.0 kilometers—in which case they are limited to 50 watts of power. Normally, a TIS uses a single transmitter. However if an applicant can show need, the FCC will authorize a system of stations, each with a separate transmitter, to cover large areas.

An application for a TIS station must be accompanied by statements that certain types of interference, so far as the applicant can determine, will not occur. Other technical information must also accompany the application. The FCC reserves the right to suspend, modify, or withdraw a TIS authorization, without a hearing if necessary, to resolve interference problems, implement agreements with foreign countries, or in other circumstances warranting such action.[142] License terms for TIS stations are five years.[143]

Just as the name implies, tunnel radio systems operate within a tunnel, mine, or similar structure.[144] They may transmit on any frequency (usually AM), and their signals must not go beyond the confines of the tunnel itself. They do not need FCC licenses to operate. When you travel by automobile and listen to the radio, the radio signal will fade out as you enter a tunnel. In some cases entrepreneurs have taken advantage of this. They install in the tunnel a long line[145] that radiates special advertising-supported radio programming, and they post signs advising you of the frequency to which to tune to get their programming.

A carrier current system transmits radio energy through use of a special line[146] or over the electric power lines. A carrier current system using electric power lines can be designed so that either (1) the lines radiate the radio frequency signals, and the signals are picked up "over the air,"[147] or (2) the lines carry the signals by conduction, and the signals are received by direct connection to the lines.[148] Car-

---

[140] 6 F.C.C.R. 6273 (1991).

[141] Such antennas are often referred to as "leaky" cables because they conduct a modulated current but also radiate a signal.

[142] 47 C.F.R. § 90.242.

[143] 47 C.F.R. § 90.149.

[144] 47 C.F.R. § 15.211.

[145] The FCC calls this an *intentional radiator*, a device that intentionally generates and emits radio frequency energy by radiation or induction. 47 C.F.R. § 15.3.

[146] Again, a "leaky" coaxial cable. 47 C.F.R. § 15.221.

[147] Again, an intentional radiator.

[148] This is an example of what the FCC calls an *unintentional radiator*, a device that intentionally generates radio frequency energy for use *within the device*, or that sends radio frequency signals by conduction to associated equipment by way of connecting wiring but is *not* intended to emit RF energy by radiation or induction. 47 C.F.R. § 15.3.

rier current systems do not need FCC licenses to operate. You will sometimes hear carrier current referred to as *wired wireless* or *campus-limited*, and colleges have installed carrier current stations to supply campus-originated radio programming to the dormitories. They usually transmit on AM radio frequencies.

DISCUSSION QUESTIONS

1. The FCC's 1991 rule making aimed at rescuing AM radio was discussed in this chapter. What were the primary regulatory mistakes—of omission and commission—that made such a rescue necessary in the first place? What *should* the FCC have done or been doing all along to keep AM a strong, viable medium? What regulatory mistakes do you see being made with FM?

2. Radio spectrum positions are scarce. Nonbroadcast spectrum users such as public safety and industry complain about radio-frequency congestion, particularly in large population centers. There have been suggestions that a national broadband network—cable or optical fiber crisscrossing the country and connected to every home and business—would obviate the need for over-the-air transmission and thus allow the release of the broadcast spectrum for other uses. What other advantages would accrue from such a plan? What are the disadvantages? If this were to come about, how should government policy deal with existing TV broadcast licensees?

3. Digital compression technology works with over-the-air channels as well as on wired channels. What impact do you see that having on full-power TV stations, LPTV stations, and wireless cable systems? What are the regulatory implications?

4. What do you see as the implications of the telephone companies getting into the video delivery business? Frame your answer from at least three points of view: the consumer, the regulators (primarily Congress and the FCC), and competing media. Who would the competing media be? The telephone companies want to be able to control content as well as deliver it. What are the implications of that?

5. What do you think are the motivations for the owner of an apartment complex putting in a SMATV system? Why not just allow the local cable franchisee to offer service to tenants?

SUGGESTED READINGS

Baldwin, Thomas E., and D. Stevens McVoy. *Cable Communication*. 2d ed. Englewood Cliffs, NJ: Prentice, 1988.

Bartlett, Eugene R. *Cable Television Technology and Operations: HDTV & NTSC Systems.* New York: McGraw, 1990.

Brody, E. W. *Communication Tomorrow: New Audiences, New Technologies, New Media.* New York: Praeger, 1990.

Crandall, Robert W. *After the Breakup: U.S. Telecommunications in a More Competitive Era.* Washington, DC: Brookings, 1991.

De Sonne, Marcia L. *Spectrum of New Broadcast/Media Technologies: Technological Developments Impacting Broadcasting Markets, Businesses, and Operations*. Washington, DC: National Association of Broadcasters, 1990.

Hakanen, Ernest A. "Digital Audio Broadcasting." *Telecommunications Policy* 15 (Dec. 1991): 491–496.

Harris, Charon J. "Advanced Television and the Federal Communications Commission." *Federal Communications Law Journal* 44 (May 1992): 491.

Huff, W. A. Kelly. "FCC Standard-Setting with Regard to FM Stereo and AM Stereo." *Journalism Quarterly* 68 (autumn 1991): 483–490.

Huff, W. A. Kelly. "NRSC AM Radio Improvement." *Feedback* 34(3) (summer 1993): 15–20.

Johnson, Leland L. *Direct Broadcast Satellites: A Competitive Alternative to Cable Television?* Santa Monica, CA: Rand, 1991.

Klopfenstein, Bruce C., and David Sedman. "Technical Standards and the Marketplace: The Case of AM Stereo." *Journal of Broadcasting and Electronic Media* 34 (spring 1990): 171–194.

Moeller, Phillip. "The Age of Convergence." *American Journalism Review* (Jan./Feb. 1994): 22–28.

Mothersole, Peter L. *Broadcast Data Systems: Teletext and RDS.* London: Butterworth, 1990.

Noll, A. Michael. *Introduction to Telephones & Telephone Systems.* Boston: Artech, 1991.

Rau, Michael. "Allocating Spectrum by Market Forces." *Catholic University Law Review* 35 (spring 1986): 737.

Slater, Jim. *Modern Television Systems: To HDTV and Beyond.* London: Pitman, 1991.

White, Ward. "Home Satellite Dish Industry: A Brief Study of Growth and Development." *Howard Law Journal* 34 (1991): 243.

Yates, Robert K. *Fiber Optics and CATV Business Strategy.* Norwood, MA: Artech, 1990.

Chapter 7

FACILITY OWNERSHIP

In the United States, the government does not normally determine whether an individual may start a retail business. By way of illustration, let us say that you wish to open a fast-food outlet: The Hometown Independent Hamburger Company. Certainly, in order to get this business up and running you will have to deal with and meet the requirements of various levels of government. You may wish to incorporate; you will have to obtain a building permit to construct or remodel; you will have to demonstrate that your business complies with certain codes and standards, ranging from health, safety, and the environment to electrical wiring, zoning, and parking spaces. But no level of government will prevent you from opening your burger store just because, say, there are already three fast-food outlets on the same block, or because you already own another burger establishment in town, or because your customers will use public streets and sidewalks to reach your store.

Where the proposed retail business, however, is an electronic media outlet, the final determination often *does* lie with the government. Let us say that you decide the fast-food business will be too greasy for your taste, so you opt instead to start a radio station: WHIR, Hometown Independent Radio Company. Or a television station: WHIT, Hometown Independent Television Company. Or a cable system: Hometown Independent Cable Company. In any of these situations, you could very well find yourself dealing with government-imposed ownership requirements, hurdles that you have to overcome and showings that you have to make in order to acquire your station or cable system.

In this chapter, we examine these restrictions and hurdles. The focus is on ownership of electronic media outlets—patterns of, qualifications for, and limitations on. In part 7.1, we look at these aspects in the context of broadcast licensees; in part 7.2, of cable operators. In part 7.3, we review regulatory requirements and limitations on ownership in other electronic mass media.

7.1 BROADCAST LICENSEES

A broadcaster may own a broadcast station business but holds only a renewable license to use the frequencies on which the station transmits.

In broadcasting, the licensee is the person or corporate entity entrusted with operation of the station by the FCC. While the licensee may own the physical plant—land, building, equipment, transmitter—the frequencies on which the station operates are borrowed, terms of the loan being operation in the public interest and adherence to all applicable sections of the Communications Act and FCC rules. A licensee must sign a waiver disclaiming ownership of frequencies.[1] The license itself is temporary, and the radio licensee must reapply every seven years; the television licensee, every five years.[2] Therefore, when the words *owner* and *ownership* appear in reference to a licensee, they apply only to the physical plant. However, if the distinction between the two words is understood, we can use *owner* synonymously with *licensee.*

7.1.1 Patterns of Station Ownership

A station may be owned by one person, a partnership, a group of persons, or a corporation. Ownership combinations include single, single with AM-FM combination, duopoly, group, co-owned, cross-media, media conglomerate, and conglomerate owners. Nonprofit organizations operate most noncommercial stations in the reserved channels, although some transmit on nonreserved channels, and some operate commercial stations.

Quite often the official owner is a corporate entity. Even if one individual is sole owner, that owner may incorporate for tax or other purposes. Corporate ownership can be complicated. For example, the corporation that holds a broadcast station license may, in turn, be a wholly owned subsidiary of another corporation that, in turn, is owned by five or six other publicly held (their shares are traded on a stock exchange) corporations.

Deregulation in the late 1970s and 1980s encouraged the use of creative financing to build and acquire stations and brought new concepts of ownership to broadcasting. The *limited partnership*, for example, consists of two entities:

1. a *general partner* who puts up relatively little money, assumes all liability, and runs the business, and
2. *limited partners,* who invest heavily and usually assume no liability, take no part in directing or setting policy for the business, and reap tax, profit, resale, and other benefits.

---

[1] 47 U.S.C. § 304.
[2] 47 U.S.C. § 307(c).

In the radio-TV business, an owner whose sole or main business is one broadcast station is called a *single owner*. A *group owner* has two or more stations in different cities. An owner with AM and FM radio stations in the same city is a *single owner with an AM-FM combination*, even when the stations program independently. An owner with multiple stations in the same service in the same city (for example, two FM stations) is a *duopoly* owner (EMG 7.1.3.3.1–7.1.3.3.2).

An individual or company may own broadcast stations along with other media—a newspaper, a cable television firm, a magazine, or some combination of these. Broadcasting mixed with other media is *cross-media ownership* or *cross ownership*. A broadcast station and another medium in the same town are said to be *co-located*. When media holdings are large, extensive, and national or international in scope, the ownership is often called a *media conglomerate*. Broadcasting mixed with other types of business—say, a trucking line, an airline, a kitchen appliance firm, and a tire company—is *conglomerate ownership*.

Most noncommercial educational (often called *public*) broadcasting stations are owned by nonprofit organizations. Beyond this broad generalization, it is difficult to categorize types of ownership. Public television stations tend to be owned by state educational broadcasting commissions, by colleges and universities, by broad-based nonprofit community corporations, and by school boards and systems. A few noncommercial TV stations are owned by other types of licensees, such as religious organizations. Public radio station ownership is even more diverse. In addition to state commissions, universities, community corporations, and school boards, public radio stations are licensed to organizations such as churches, religious groups, seminaries, high schools, college student government associations, cities, counties, and boys' clubs. In addition to public stations, there are noncommercial educational stations owned by religious groups. Churches, evangelical associations, seminaries, and other such organizations operate many radio stations.

Most educational noncommercial stations operate on reserved FM and TV channels.[3] Some licensees, though, operate noncommercial broadcast stations in the AM band. For example, Ohio University operates noncommercial WOUB, Athens, Ohio, at 1340 kHz. Moody Bible Institute operates both WMBI, Chicago, 1110 kHz, and WDLM, East Moline, Illinois, 960 kHz. Some nonprofit institutions also operate commercial stations, for example, University of Missouri's KOMU-TV, channel 8, Columbia, Missouri, and University of Florida's WRUF, 850 kHz, and WRUF-FM, 103.7 MHz.

7.1.2   Licensee Qualifications

In order to be considered for a broadcast license, an applicant must (1) have had no previous broadcast license revoked by a court for violating antitrust laws, (2) file a written formal application, and (3) submit FCC-required information on citizen-

---

[3] The FCC has reserved certain FM radio and TV channels for use only by noncommercial educational licensees; see EMG 6.2.2.4. There are no channels in the AM radio band reserved specifically for noncommercial educational operation.

ship, character, financial, technical, and "other" qualifications. The FCC must find that the public interest would be served before it grants a license.

The U.S. Congress and the FCC have set up two general types of restrictions on ownership of broadcast stations—one concerning who qualifies for a license; the other, how many licenses one licensee may hold. In this section we discuss the who; in the next, the how many.

In writing the Communications Act, Congress made clear that not just everyone would be allowed to operate a broadcast station in the United States. The legislators wrote into the act certain requirements, and only applicants that met those requirements would be licensed as broadcasters. For example, Section 313(b) of the act prohibits the grant of a license to an applicant who has had a previous broadcast license revoked by a court for violating antitrust laws.[4] Section 308(a) requires a prospective licensee to file a formal written application.

But in writing the Communications Act, Congress also created the FCC. And with respect to qualifications for a broadcast license, the act made clear that the *specifics* were to be provided by the Commission. In Section 309(a), Congress directed that the FCC was to grant a license only after determining the grant would serve the public interest, convenience, and necessity. And in Section 319(a), Congress required that applicants supply the FCC with any information it may require concerning "citizenship, character, . . . financial, technical, and other" qualifications. Therefore, an important key to understanding licensee qualifications is how the FCC interprets each of these statutory[5] requirements.

7.1.2.1   Citizenship

A broadcast licensee must be a U.S. citizen or an ownership entity controlled by U.S. citizens.

With respect to citizenship, the Commission grants licenses only to U.S. citizens and their companies. Box 7.1 lists types of parties that the FCC has determined do *not* meet their citizenship standard.

In 1991, the trade press reported interest in raising the percentage of ownership that foreign investors could hold in U.S. broadcast stations. Proponents argued that raising the limits would encourage foreign investors, which in turn would generate an infusion of capital, boost prices of stations, and reduce the foreign-trade imbalance. Opponents pointed out that such a move could result in foreign interests controlling U.S. broadcast media, and they buttressed their argument with the fact that U.S. assets were already being sold to the highest foreign bidders, citing the

---

[4] The purpose of antitrust law is to protect trade from monopoly. *See, e.g.,* EMG 14.3.5 and 14.4 for a discussion of antitrust laws and the networks.

[5] A *statute* is a law passed by the lawmaking branch of government. At the national level, that lawmaking branch is the Congress, and the provisions of the laws that Congress passes are said to be *statutory.* So in this case, a statutory requirement is one that is spelled out in the basic law of interstate communication, the Communications Act.

BOX 7.1   FCC-Defined "Noncitizens"

The Federal Communications Commission has determined that entities in the following categories are not U.S. citizens for purposes of licensing:

1. Foreign governments
2. Aliens
3. Representatives of aliens or foreign governments
4. Corporations organized under foreign laws
5. Corporations with aliens as directors
6. Corporations of which 20 percent or more of the stock is owned or voted by
   a. aliens,
   b. foreign governments,
   c. representatives of aliens or foreign governments, or
   d. corporations organized under foreign laws.
7. Corporations controlled by other corporations that have
   a. aliens as officers,
   b. aliens occupying 25 percent or more of the director positions on the boards, or
   c. at least 25 percent of their stock owned or voted by
      (1) aliens,
      (2) foreign governments,
      (3) representatives of foreign governments, or
      (4) corporations organized under foreign laws.

---

recent sales of media conglomerate MCA, Inc., CBS Records, Rockefeller Center, and the Pebble Beach golf club.[6]

7.1.2.2 *Character*

A broadcast licensee must *not* have a bad record with respect to relevant laws. Where there has been misconduct, the FCC considers the nature of both the misconduct and the responsible party, and in some cases, makes this consideration even when the misconduct was the fault of the licensee's parent company (if the licensee is a wholly owned subsidiary of that parent) or if the misconduct occurred at another of the licensee's stations (if the applicant is a group owner).

The Commission has interpreted the character requirement to mean the *absence* of a bad record resulting from violations of relevant laws. In line with that interpretation, any of the items listed in Box 7.2 could be grounds to deny an application for initial grant (or renewal) of a broadcast station license.

---

[6] "Foreign Ownership: Salvation or Selling Out," *Broadcasting,* 15 July 1991, at 36.

BOX 7.2   FCC-Defined Evidence of Poor Character

- Violations of the Communications Act or the Commission's rules
- Evidence of fraud or misrepresentation in programming or in dealing with the FCC
- Convictions of fraud before another government agency
- Criminal convictions involving fraud, deceit, dishonesty, or false statements*
- Convictions for violations of antitrust laws
- Any felony convictions†

---

* Policy Regarding Character Qualifications in Broadcast Licensing, 102 F.C.C.2d 1179 (1986), reconsideration granted in part, denied in part, 1 F.C.C.R. 421 (1986), appeal dismissed sub nom. National Association for Better Broadcasting v. FCC, No. 86-1179 (D.C. Cir., June 11, 1987).
† Policy Regarding Character Qualifications in Broadcast Licensing, 5 F.C.C.R. 3252 (1990).

These things do not automatically disqualify an applicant. The FCC considers how, when, and by whom the misconduct was performed—whether done willfully, whether part of a pattern of misconduct, how recently it took place, its seriousness, the nature of participation by managers and owners, and efforts made to remedy the problem. The Commission also considers the applicant's record of compliance with FCC rules and regulations.

This character policy applies to all license applicants—real persons, partnerships, and corporations. The actual ownership of an applicant, however, can be complicated, and this, in turn, complicates the matter of character determination. The FCC has attempted to sort through and set policy in two such situations. One involves an applicant that is wholly owned by another company (the *parent* company). What if the applicant (the subsidiary) has a good record, but the parent has had some legal problems? Should the FCC take into account the transgressions of the parent company when considering the applicant?

Largely as a result of the *RKO* and *Mid-Florida* cases (Box 7.3), the Commission has said that it will consider the character of the parent company only if

1. the parent has been involved in misconduct before the FCC, *or*
2. a shareholder, officer, or employee of the parent is involved in the day-to-day operation of the applicant.

The other complication for character determination involves group ownership. What if one station in the group has been guilty of misconduct as defined by FCC policy? Should the Commission take that into account in dealing with the applica-

---

BOX 7.3   Loosening and Tightening the Character Qualifications: *RKO*, *Mid-Florida*, and *Williamsburg*

In 1981, as part of a highly complex proceeding involving character qualifications, a federal appeals court upheld an FCC decision not to renew RKO General's license for channel 7 in Boston. The court ruled that RKO had withheld evidence in its renewal application concerning wrongdoings of its parent company—bribing officials in foreign countries, violation of federal rules on political contributions, continuous billing overcharges, attempts at illegal financial activities, and falsification of records.*

Also in 1981, the FCC approved a settlement among a group of competing applicants for Orlando's channel 9.† This case, initiated 13 years earlier, involved among other issues character qualifications. One of the officers of the original licensee corporation had been indicted on charges of violating laws relating to organized illegal gambling.

In 1986, citing these two cases to illustrate "the epic length and complexity which proceedings involving character issues may assume,"‡ the FCC adopted a policy that, according to critics, could have been interpreted to allow almost any kind of behavior short of direct violations of the Communications Act (Box 7.2, first four items). Flaws in this policy became apparent just four years later when Gregory Knop, principal of Radio Station WKSP, Kingstree, SC, was convicted of drug trafficking.§ The FCC subsequently rewrote its policy to take into account felony convictions, some misdemeanors, and antitrust violations when considering character in broadcast licensing proceedings (Box 7.2, last two items).

---

* RKO v. FCC, 670 F.2d 215 (1981). In 1987, an FCC administrative law judge (ALJ) denied license renewal for all 14 of RKO's remaining stations, citing fraudulent billing practices and misrepresentation. Had this decision prevailed, RKO would have lost millions of dollars invested in its stations. The next year, however, the Commission finessed the ALJ's decision by ruling that RKO could sell its stations, albeit not at full market value. This ruling failed to resolve the issue of RKO's qualifications as a licensee but—rightly or wrongly—did allow RKO to recover some of its investment.

† Mid-Florida Television Corp., 87 F.C.C.2d 203 (1981).

‡ Policy Regarding Character Qualifications in Broadcast Licensing, 102 F.C.C.2d 1179 (1986).

§ Williamsburg County Broadcasting Corp., 5 F.C.C.R. 3034 (1990).

tion of another station in the group? After all, they both have the same owner. Here, the Commission has said that misconduct on the part of another, commonly owned station will be considered only if that misconduct is of such nature that it casts doubt on the qualifications of the owner to hold *any* license at all.

7.1.2.3   Financial Ability

Applicants must certify to the FCC that they have enough money available to build the station and to operate it for three months without relying on advertising revenues.

Like almost any new business, a commercial broadcast station does not make much money when it first signs on the air. The new station is not well known, has no track record as an advertising vehicle, and therefore usually does not bring in many advertising dollars. Often, station expenses exceed income during a station's first few months of operation; without a financial pad on which to fall back, the station could go broke and sign off the air before it reaches the financial break-even point. In an attempt to prevent such an occurrence, the FCC has adopted a "three-month" certification requirement; the applicant certifies to the Commission that it has enough capital to build the station and then operate it for three months.[7] This does not mean the applicant must possess the entire amount as cash in hand. Most applicants actually obtain a line of credit[8] to cover construction and operation costs. The Commission staff checks some financial certifications to determine if the applicants have told the truth; for most applicants, these checks are done on a random basis. However, applicants with many applications pending before the FCC are always checked.[9]

7.1.2.4   Technical

Applicants must make showings to the FCC concerning technical plans, rule compliance, and operation.

The Commission does not require the applicant to demonstrate personal technical ability. The applicant may hire other persons to search for a frequency, write equipment specifications, put together and test transmitter and studio gear, and operate and maintain the various machines and black boxes used to produce and transmit programming. But the applicant does have to show plans for equipment and staff that demonstrate adequate technical preparation. And the applicant must show compliance with the Commission's technical rules. An applicant for an AM broadcast facility must also show that the proposed assignment of frequency "will tend to effect a fair, efficient, and equitable distribution of radio service among the several states and communities,"[10] that international agreements are not violated,

---

[7] Financial Qualification Standards for Aural Broadcast Applicants, 69 F.C.C.2d 407 (1978); and Financial Qualifications Standard for Broadcast Television Applicants, 72 F.C.C.2d 784 (1979).

[8] A line of credit is the maximum amount of credit a lender or lenders will give.

[9] Financial Qualifications of Broadcast Permit Applicants, 62 Rad. Reg. 2d (P & F) 638 (1987).

[10] 47 C.F.R. § 74.24(a).

that the daytime signal will cover the community of license, that no more than 300 persons or 1 percent of the population (whichever is more) live within a mile or so of the transmitter,[11] and that interference with existing stations will be minimal.[12]

7.1.2.5 *Other Qualifications*

Applicants must provide the FCC with plans for public-issue programming; show their compliance with ownership limitations; and, if applying for reserved channels, show that they will provide a noncommercial educational service. FM or TV antenna farms must be shared.

The Commission has not defined the "other" category in a specific section. However, there are qualifications scattered throughout the rules that do not seem to derive directly from the citizenship, character, financial, or technical statutory requirements and thus fit in this catch-all "other" category.

One of these qualifications has to do with programming. An applicant must determine issues that face the community the station will serve, then program to respond to at least some of those issues.[13] However, the FCC's application, Form 301, requires only that the applicant "attach as an exhibit a brief description of the planned programming services relating to the issue of public concerns facing the proposed service area." At one time, the FCC required a detailed presentation of programming plans as one means to determine whether the public interest would be served by granting the applicant a license (a result of the Blue Book, EMG 9.3). As discussed in EMG 9.6.3, however, the Commission eliminated most such reporting on programming during its 1980s deregulation period. One of the few remnants is this requirement that new-station applicants provide a description of public issue programming, which, in turn, stems from the remnants of the FCC's requirement for ascertainment.

A second "other" qualification deals with ownership. FCC rules place certain limitations on station ownership (EMG 7.1.3.3), and an applicant must show that the proposed station does not exceed these limitations.

A third qualification focuses on applicants for noncommercial educational reserved FM and TV channels. Such applicants must show that they are nonprofit educational organizations. Educational FM applicants must also show that they will use the stations for the advancement of an educational program (in the broad sense).[14] Educational TV applicants must show that they will use the stations primarily to serve educational needs of the community, for the advancement of educa-

---

[11] The signal in this area (which, in terms of signal strength, is the one volt per meter contour) is usually so strong that residents pick it up, no matter what station they try to listen to. So the FCC wants the transmitter located to put as few persons as possible in this area.

[12] The applicant must show that the signal of the proposed AM radio station will not overlap that of other stations on the same and adjacent channels beyond certain specified minimums. 47 C.F.R. § 73.37.

[13] For a discussion of ascertainment, see EMG 10.1.2.1.

[14] 47 C.F.R. § 73.503(a).

tional programs, and to furnish a nonprofit and noncommercial television broadcast service.[15]

A fourth "other" qualification deals with placement of transmitting antennas. The FCC encourages FM and TV stations that serve a given community to group their transmitting antennas together at a common site into an antenna "farm." In fact, FCC rules prohibit granting or renewing a license for an FM or TV broadcasting station to anyone who owns or controls the only good site for such a farm and refuses to allow other stations to use it. The Commission reasons that such a refusal would unduly limit competition among stations or even the number of stations.[16]

7.1.3   Station Ownership Limitations

Historically, the purpose of the FCC's ownership rules has been diversification.

Having looked at the first general type of restriction on broadcast station ownership, who qualifies for a license, we now examine the second general type of restriction—rules that limit the number of stations one licensee may own. There are six of these rules (EMG 7.1.3.3), some local in scope and some national. Some of the rules date back to the 1930s. The rules were derived from the libertarian assumption that a community and its citizens are best served when they have access to as many competing voices, reflecting varying opinions and different views, as possible. The purpose of the rules was diversification—to prevent broadcast stations from being owned by relatively few individuals and corporations. The Commission reasoned that such monopoly would prevent maximum competition in broadcasting and reduce the numbers of origins and outlets reflecting different views, opinions, and ideas. Also, it would raise the number of absentee owners unfamiliar with the needs and interests of the communities to which their stations are licensed.

7.1.3.1   Exceptions and Relaxations

Despite the FCC's ownership rules, control of many strong stations is still concentrated because the rules are prospective, may be waived, and have been relaxed.

Even after the Commission's ownership rules had been in effect for years, the strongest stations in large and medium-sized markets were often licensed to group owners. And some broadcast stations remained under common ownership with other media outlets (such as newspapers) in the same community. These ownership concentrations continued at least in part because most of the FCC's ownership rules apply prospectively, not retroactively. This means that when the Commission adopts a new ownership rule, the licensee who already owns media outlets in a combination forbidden by the rule does not have to comply with it. The licensee must obey the rule in any future sales or acquisitions but does not have to divest

---

[15] 47 C.F.R. § 73.621(a).
[16] 47 C.F.R. §§ 73.239, 73.635.

(that is, sell off or otherwise get rid of holdings) to comply. Thus, the rule's prospective nature "grandfathers in" existing combinations. For example, years after the one-to-a-market (EMG 7.1.3.3.4) and newspaper/broadcast cross-ownership (EMG 7.1.3.3.6) rules went into effect, radio station WGN, WGN-TV, and the *Chicago Tribune* remained under common ownership; they were an existing combination that had been grandfathered in when the rules went into effect.

The Commission also has the power to waive any of its own rules when petitioned by an applicant. In the petition, the applicant must show that the public would be better served by the waiver of the rule than by adherence to the rule. If the showing is convincing, the Commission may grant the waiver. Through use of the waiver mechanism, some licensees have been able to retain and even acquire station-ownership combinations otherwise forbidden by the FCC's rules.

Further, the deregulation movement (EMG 9.6.3) affected ownership limitations, fostering a trend to liberalize and relax all ownership rules. In 1979 and 1984, the Commission did away with certain types of ownership restrictions that applied to large markets and regional concentrations and raised national ownership limits (EMG 7.1.3.3.3). In 1988, the Commission loosened the duopoly (EMG 7.1.3.3.2) and one-to-a-market (EMG 7.1.3.3.4) rules. In early 1991, an influential staff proposal urged the FCC to eliminate or relax most of its ownership rules. The report cited increased competition from newer, multichannel media such as cable, and said that broadcasters, if they were to survive and compete effectively, would have to be able to own large numbers of stations nationally or more than one station locally.[17]

In 1992, the Commission used the poor financial health of the radio industry as grounds to gut the duopoly and national multiple ownership rules for radio stations. Deregulation had allowed the number of stations to increase, and many companies had bought stations by taking out large loans; the 1990s recession, however, dried up advertising revenues, licensees could not meet payments on their debt loads, and stations began to fail. By 1992, out of some 10,800 commercial radio stations, more than 100 had shut down just in the previous year, a number were in bankruptcy, and hundreds were restructuring debts. The relaxed rules allowed financially successful licensees to buy more radio stations. Subsequently, the Commission also relaxed the national multiple ownership rules for television stations.

7.1.3.2 *Attribution*

The FCC has defined the type and extent of investment and control that is subject to its ownership rules; such ownership is said to be *attributable*. Corporate licensees are covered in that the rules apply to partnerships, direct ownership interests, and voting stock of 5 percent or more (10 percent or more for passive investors). However, if one party holds more than 50 percent of the stock of a licensee, the Commission does not consider that the other stockholders have control. A *local marketing agreement* is an arrangement reached between stations to share programming or commercial time-sales functions; the FCC equates LMAs with ownership and applies ownership rules to these agreements.

---

[17] Office of Plans and Policy Working Paper #26. *Broadcast Television in a Multichannel Marketplace*, DA 91-817, 6 F.C.C.R. 3993 (1991).

The ownership rules state that the Commission will not grant a license to any party that "directly or indirectly owns, operates or controls" one of the forbidden combinations. This brings up the question of *attribution:* What "counts" as ownership or control? For example, how little stock in a licensee can one party own and still be considered an owner for purposes of the multiple-ownership rules?

The rules, as published in the *Code of Federal Regulations,* define in some detail ownership and control that is attributable (that is, that "counts"). Besides owners and investors, the rules also apply to officers and directors of broadcast stations, cable systems, and daily newspapers. The FCC considers such persons to have "cognizable interest" in the outlets with which they are associated. There are even explanatory notes that detail how the rules apply to ownership situations involving investment companies, insurance companies, banks, holding companies, trusts, nonvoting stock, and limited partnerships.

"Passive investors" include institutions that hold ownership interest in broadcast licensees primarily as an investment; they do not necessarily seek to control the licensee or set its policies. Such institutions often include investment companies, insurance companies, banks, holding companies, and trusts. Passive investors also include parties that hold certain forms of equity (part ownership) that provide for investment without control—for example, nonvoting stock and limited partnerships. In 1992, the FCC proposed raising the attributable interest threshold for regular (that is, not passive) investors to 10 percent and for passive investors to 20 percent.

An example will demonstrate how these rules apply. Two outlets (say, two broadcast stations, or a TV station and a cable system) *do* share common ownership and *are* subject to the ownership rules if one party

1. has at least 5 percent of the stock in the corporate owner of each, *or*
2. has at least 1 percent of the stock in one and manages the other, *or*
3. sits on the board of one and holds a corporate office in the other.

On the other hand, the outlets do *not* share common ownership, even if one party has stock in both corporate owners,

1. when that party's share in at least one of the corporations totals less than 5 percent, *or*
2. if another party in at least one of the corporations holds more than 50 percent of the voting stock.

The economic recession of the 1990s brought on yet an additional complication in the determination of applicability. As scores of radio stations failed financially and went dark (EMG 7.1.3.1), increasing numbers of survivors entered into varying forms of local marketing agreements. A fairly typical local marketing agreement (LMA) might consist of one station in a market handling advertising sales (and sometimes programming) for another, often financially weaker, station in the same market; the first shares revenues with the second. In another common LMA variation, two stations enter into a time brokerage contract; one buys large blocks of time from the other, supplies the programming to fill the time, and sells the advertising availabilities (places for commercials) within it.[18]

In local marketing agreements, the handling station gains advantages in selling advertising on multiple outlets (against, of course, one less competitor), and the handled station is able to cut expenses, receive an income, and avoid bankruptcy or going off the air. In some of these arrangements, one station handles two or more stations in a market. LMAs do raise questions in connection with the multiple-ownership rule, since they sometimes appear to give one party control of multiple stations in a market. And, in fact, the FCC has equated time-brokerage LMAs with ownership in their local-limit ownership rules.

7.1.3.3   *Rules*

Six rules restrict broadcast ownership: radio contour overlap (duopoly), television contour overlap (duopoly), national multiple ownership ("12-20-20"), one-to-a-market, newspaper/broadcast cross-ownership, and TV-cable.

The first five come from the FCC's multiple ownership regulation, Section 73.3555;[19] the sixth, from Section 613 of the Communications Act.[20] The multiple ownership and cable cross-ownership rules also contain notes that define terms and explain how the various provisions apply in certain situations.

(In the following discussion of these rules, you will find the term *service*. That term refers to an FCC-defined and -regulated use of the radio frequencies. In these rules we are concerned with three broadcast services—AM radio, FM radio, and broadcast television.)

7.1.3.3.1   *Radio Contour Overlap (Duopoly)*

In a community with 14 or fewer commercial radio stations, one party may own 3 stations (no more than 2 in one service) but may not own more than 50 percent of the total number of stations in the market. In a community with 15 or more commercial radio stations, one party may own 4 stations (no more than 2 in each service); but in acquiring stations, the total audience share of all stations that would be owned by the acquiring party may not exceed 25 percent. Time brokerage agreements count as ownership.

That is a complicated rule. First, what is a contour? The full term is *blanketing contour*, and it is the FCC's technical definition for the area that a station's signal

---

[18] 47 C.F.R. § 73.3555. *Time brokerage* as a practice dates back at least to the 1930s. In its classic form, the broker buys the time blocks at a discounted rate, sells availabilities to advertisers at a higher rate, and pockets the difference. The broker can be an individual, a company, anyone. Under an LMA, of course, the broker is another radio station.

[19] 47 C.F.R. § 73.3555.

[20] 47 U.S.C. § 533(a)(1). The applicable FCC rule is in 47 C.F.R. § 76.501. A 1994 bill introduced in the Senate would direct the FCC to review all broadcast ownership rules and eliminate those not necessary to achieving the goal of media diversity. Kim McAvoy, "Senate Opens Superhighway Lane for Broadcasters," *Broadcasting & Cable*, 7 Feb. 1994, at 6.

TABLE 7.1   Local Limits on Radio Station Ownership

| Number of Stations in the Market | Number of Stations Permitted under Common Ownership | | | Other Limitations |
	Total	(AMs: No More Than . . .)	(FMs: No More Than . . .)	
14 or fewer	3	(2)	(2)	May own no more than half the stations in the market.
15 or more	4	(2)	(2)	May control stations with combined share of no more than 25 percent at acquisition.

covers. Second, how do all those numbers sort out? Table 7.1 should help to explain the relationship of the number of stations in a market to the number of AM and FM stations allowed under common ownership in that market. We'll also use some examples.

To illustrate how this rule works, let us set up a scenario and look at the implications of the formula in three situations. The scenario involves four commercial AM radio stations in a particular market. Three have financial problems, and their licensees are anxious to cut their losses. The fourth is making money, and the licensee may be interested in some kind of deal with the other three.

For the first situation, we make these four the only stations in a small market. Here, the rule would allow the successful licensee to acquire control of (through purchase, investment, or a time brokerage agreement) just one of the other three. With the acquisition of this one other station, the licensee would control two stations, half the number in the four-station market. Since the rule prohibits common control of more than half the stations in the market, the licensee would be allowed to purchase no more stations in this four-station market.

For the second situation, we add two more commercial radio stations to the market, say two FMs. In this six-station market, the rule would allow the money-making licensee to acquire two stations. That would bring the number under common ownership to three (the maximum allowed by the rule) and to 50 percent of the total number of stations in the market (again, the maximum allowed by the rule). But the licensee could still buy only one of the three available AM stations. With this acquisition, the licensee would control two AM stations, and the rule limits ownership to no more than two AMs or two FMs. The only way the licensee could acquire that allowable third station would be to convince the owner of one of the FMs to sell.

Finally, let us put our scenario in a market served by 34 commercial radio stations. In addition to the three AMs, there are also two FMs available for sale. Our licensee is, of course, still limited to acquisition of no more than one of the AMs. But, since the cap on commonly controlled stations in that market is 4, the rule *might* allow acquisition of one AM and two FMs. Why "might"? Because the audience-share limit also applies. So we look at ratings and discover that the licensee's existing AM commands a 10 share in the market, that the two FMs get shares of 6 and 8, and the three AMs get 3, 3, and 4. If the licensee acquires the two FMs, that puts total share for the three stations at 24; additional acquisition of any AM would put the licensee over the 25-share limit and would, therefore, be prohibited under the local ownership rule. However, *the 25-share limit applies only at the time of the acquisition.* The licensee may, for example, acquire the two FMs, then—through effective programming and promotion—increase the combined share of the three stations (the original AM and the two acquired FMs) above 25 without having to divest (that is, sell off) one or more of the stations.

7.1.3.3.2 Television Contour Overlap (Duopoly)
One party may own no more than one TV station in a community.

For years, the FCC had in place a rule to prevent duopoly in the ownership of radio and TV stations. In broadcasting, *duopoly* refers to control of two or more stations in the same service in the same community by one party, and Commission concern with duopoly dates back to at least 1938.[21] With limited numbers of broadcast frequencies available in any specific locale, it seemed logical to the policymakers of an earlier day that control of broadcast stations in a community should *not* be concentrated (EMG 7.1.3). As means to that end, the FCC adopted a duopoly rule. This rule prohibited common ownership of multiple stations in a service—AM, FM, or TV—if their signals overlapped. More recent appointees to the Commission, however, worried less about the public's right to hear varying points of view than about the licensees' right to operate stations as profitable businesses, free from governmental restriction. The result was the 1992 rule changes (EMG 7.1.3.1), one of which modified the duopoly rule for radio by expanding local ownership limits.

Under the duopoly rule for television stations, one party may still *not* own two or more television stations if their signals overlap. And for radio, one party may not own stations in the same service (AM or FM)—*beyond the local limits outlined in EMG 7.1.3.3.1*—if their signals overlap.[22]

7.1.3.3.3 National Multiple Ownership ("12-20-20")
Nationwide, one party may hold attributable interest in

1. no more than 52 stations—12 TV, 20 AM, and 20 FM;
2. an additional 3 AM and 3 FM stations (total of 23 each) as long as the additional stations are controlled (more than half owned) by small businesses or racial minorities;
3. an additional 2 TV stations (total of 14) as long as the additional stations are controlled by racial minorities;

---

[21] *See, e.g.,* Genessee Broadcasting Corp., 5 F.C.C. 183 (1938).

[22] The specification for "signal" varies with the services—5 millivolts per meter (5.0 mV/m) ground wave contour for AM; 3.16 mV/m contour for FM; Grade B contour for television. These all refer to a certain strength of the signal as defined in the FCC rules.

4. TV stations whose collective market areas encompass no more than 25 percent of the nation's households (even if the number of stations owned is fewer than 12);

5. minority-controlled TV stations whose collective market areas encompass no more than 30 percent of the nation's households (even if the number of stations owned is fewer than 14).

In computing the 25/30 percent limit, UHF television stations are credited with only half the homes in their market areas.

The FCC imposed numerical limitations on station ownership first for FM in 1940,[23] then for TV in 1941.[24] In 1953, the Commission adopted a rule limiting one party to owning no more than 7 stations in each service—TV, AM, and FM.[25] Thirty-two years later, the FCC raised the limits to 12 and added a few complications. In 1992, the Commission raised the limits for AM and FM radio to 20 stations in each service. That brought the national-limit formula to 12-20-20.

This so-called 12-20-20 rule can be confusing because its limits are actually both more and less than 12-20-20. With respect to the *more*, consider a radio station group owner with controlling interest (more than 50 percent of the stock) in 40 radio stations—20 AMs and 20 FMs. That group owner has reached the limit and cannot acquire controlling interest in even one more radio station without first getting rid of one of the currently owned stations. That group owner may, however, acquire attributable but not controlling interest (that is, less than 50 percent of the stock) in as many as 6 additional stations—3 AMs and 3 FMs—as long as those stations are controlled by small businesses or by racial minorities. Similarly, a TV group owner that already holds controlling interest in 12 television stations may acquire attributable but not controlling interest in as many as 2 additional TV stations, as long as those stations are controlled by racial minorities. The FCC included these higher limits in the rule to encourage the entry of new minority and small business entities into broadcasting, as well as the expansion of existing minority and small broadcasting organizations.[26] So the 12-20-20 limit can actually go as high as 14-23-23.

In certain situations, however, a group owner may be limited to *fewer* than 12 television stations. Consider, for example, a group-owner company that has controlling interest in VHF television stations serving New York, Los Angeles, Chicago, Philadelphia, San Francisco, Boston, and Miami. As shown in the "All Stations VHF" columns of Table 7.2, these seven markets account for just under 25 percent of all TV households in the country. Because of the 25 percent of national households limitation, that group owner could not acquire controlling interest in another TV

---

[23] 5 Fed. Reg. 2382, 2384 (June 26, 1940).

[24] 6 Fed. Reg. 2282, 2284 (May 6, 1941).

[25] Multiple Ownership of AM, FM and TV Stations, 18 F.C.C. 288 (1953).

[26] Revision of Radio Rules and Policies, 57 Fed. Reg. 42,701 (1992). The rule defines *small business* as a firm with revenues of less than $500,000 a year and total assets worth less than $1 million. It defines *minority* as "Black, Hispanic, American Indian, Alaska Native, Asian and Pacific Islander." 47 C.F.R. § 3555(e)(3).

TABLE 7.2   Percentage of TV Households Attributed to Seven Markets Under 47 C.F.R. § 73.3555 with Varying Station Types

Market Name	All Stations VHF		Some Stations UHF	
	Type	%U.S. TV HH	Type	%U.S. TV HH
New York	VHF	7.35	UHF	3.68
Los Angeles	VHF	5.32	UHF	2.66
Chicago	VHF	3.27	UHF	1.64
Philadelphia	VHF	2.87	VHF	2.87
San Francisco	VHF	2.41	VHF	2.41
Boston	VHF	2.32	VHF	2.32
Miami	VHF	1.40	VHF	1.40
TOTALS		24.94		16.98

SOURCE: Arbitron.

station (except, perhaps, in a very small market), despite the fact that the group consists of "only" seven TV stations. However, it could acquire attributable but not controlling interest in additional TV stations controlled by racial minorities. How many additional stations? Up to 7, as long as the collective market areas of all stations in which the group owner holds attributable interest encompass no more than—and notice the new, higher figure here—*30* percent of the nation's TV households.

We are almost finished with this complicated national ownership rule, but we need to consider one final factor. Let us look again at that seven-large-market group owner. But this time, let us make the stations in New York, Los Angeles, and Chicago operate on UHF channels. That means the group owner may take advantage of the rule's UHF "50 percent discount" for those three markets. With that discount, the seven markets are credited with only 16.98 percent of total U.S. households (the "Some Stations UHF" column of Table 7.2), and under the rule the group owner may acquire additional TV stations. The UHF signal does not reach as far as a comparable VHF signal, and the FCC included this UHF discount as one attempt to make up for the physical disparity between the transmissions of VHF stations and those of UHF stations.[27]

7.1.3.3.4   One-to-a-Market

A party that owns a radio station in a community may own no more than one television station in that community. However, the FCC has indicated willingness to waive this restriction in certain situations.

In 1970, the FCC revised the multiple-ownership rules[28] to add the one-to-a-market limit (now found in Section 3555(d) of the FCC's rules). If the signal of either the radio (AM 2.0 mV/m contour; FM 1.0 mV/m contour) or the TV (Grade A

---

[27] Multiple Ownership of AM, FM and Television Broadcast Stations, 50 Fed. Reg. 4666 (1985).
[28] Multiple Ownership of Standard, FM, and TV Broadcast Stations, 22 F.C.C. 306.

contour) station covers the entire community of license of the other station, then one party may not own or control both stations.

Originally, the rule would have also prohibited formation of new AM-FM combinations in the same market. However, at the time the one-to-a-market rule was under consideration, AM stations were still dominant, and stand-alone[29] FM stations generally lost money. That being the case, the FCC recognized that FM radio probably still needed the economic shelter and protection afforded by co-ownership. Therefore, upon reconsideration,[30] the Commission dropped the proscriptive AM-FM ban in 1971.

In 1989, the one-to-a-market rule was weakened by an expansion of the waiver policy. The Commission did this by adding to the multiple-ownership rules a note that practically invited applications for waivers of the one-to-a-market restriction. The note stated that the FCC would "look favorably" on waiver applications that met either of two standards. In one, the Commission would approve a single party acquiring both a radio station and a television station in the same community

1. if that community were one of the 25 largest markets, and
2. if, after the acquisition, there were in the community at least 30 "separately owned, operated and controlled broadcast stations" (counting all television stations in the ADI and all radio stations in the metro area).[31]

The second situation in which the FCC would favorably consider waiving the one-to-a-market rule involves "failed" stations. The Commission might, for example, approve the waiver application for a television licensee who wished to acquire an AM radio station that had not been operated for a number of months or that was in bankruptcy proceedings.

7.1.3.3.5 TV Station/Cable Cross-Ownership
One party may not own or control both a cable television system and a television station in the same community.

This prohibition is found in Section 613 of the Communications Act[32] and Section 76.501 of the FCC's rules. Specifically this rule prohibits common ownership

---

[29] A *stand-alone* FM was one not co-owned with an AM station in the same city.

[30] Multiple Ownership Rules, 28 F.C.C.2d 662 (1971).

[31] The Area of Dominant Influence (ADI) is the definition of a market as applied by the Arbitron Ratings Company. Arbitron has divided the United States into ADIs based on central cities and their television stations. Each county is assigned to one of these areas as determined by the predominance of television viewing in that county; if, for example, most people in a county view stations in Houston most of the time, that county is assigned to the Houston ADI. The metro area includes only those ADI counties that comprise and are close to the central city. City-based radio stations usually judge competitive success on the basis of their performance in the metro area.

[32] 47 U.S.C. § 533(a).

if the television station's Grade B contour[33] overlaps any part of the cable system's service area (the geographic area within which the system serves subscribers).

The Commission adopted the TV/cable cross-ownership rule in 1970,[34] long before Congress wrote it into law. The rule was retroactive; it ordered divestiture to break up existing prohibited combinations and forbade formation of such combinations in the future. Subsequently, the Commission amended the rule[35] to require divestiture only in cases where the television station

1. was a full-service broadcast station (which excluded satellite stations that simply rebroadcast another station's programming and originated none of its own),
2. put a signal over the entire community, and
3. was the only station in town that met the other two criteria.

Divestiture was to have been completed by August 10, 1977.

In 1984, the Commission further modified the rule to require divestiture only in "egregious" (glaringly bad) situations.[36] The FCC interpreted egregious to mean one party owning both the only cable system and the only commercial broadcast station in town. Of the remaining TV/cable combinations that had existed at the time of the original 1970 ruling, 13 were nonegregious (the broadcast station was not the only commercial station in town) and 5 were egregious. The FCC voted to grandfather in the 13 nonegregious cases. Later that year, President Ronald Reagan signed into law the Cable Communications Policy Act, which added the TV/cable prohibition to the Communications Act and contained a provision that made ungrandfathered combinations illegal.[37] Accordingly, the FCC ordered divestiture within three years for the 5 egregious combinations and dismissed a 1980 petition for elimination of the TV/cable cross-ownership rule.

7.1.3.3.6 *Newspaper/Broadcast Cross-Ownership*
One party may not own or control both a broadcast station and a daily newspaper in the same community.

The FCC's rule lists three elements that define this prohibited ownership combination. First, the station's signal (AM 2.0 mV/m; FM 1.0 mV/m; TV Grade A contour) encompasses the entire community in which the newspaper is published; second, the newspaper is published at least four days a week, using the English language; and third, the newspaper is published daily and circulates to the general public in the community. A college newspaper does not count.

---

[33] See note 22.

[34] CATV, 23 F.C.C.2d 816 (1970).

[35] Cable Television Systems, et al., 55 F.C.C.2d 540 (1975), *reconsideration denied,* 58 F.C.C.2d 596 (1976).

[36] CATV Cross Ownership, 56 Rad. Reg. 2d (P & F) 87.

[37] 47 U.S.C. § 613(a).

The Commission showed concern over newspaper/broadcast combinations as early as the 1940s.[38] One of the grounds for denial of renewal in the 1969 *WHDH* case was that the Boston station was owned by the Boston *Herald-Traveler*.[39] In 1970, the Commission began rule-making proceedings to eliminate newspaper/broadcast combinations. The Commission cited studies showing the dominant role of television stations and daily newspapers as sources of news and suggested that the proposed regulations would serve "the purpose of promoting competition among the mass media involved and maximizing diversification of service sources and viewpoints."[40] The Commission also expressed concern about disruption of service the divestiture might cause and asked for public comment; this expression of concern would figure prominently in an eventual Supreme Court decision on the matter. In 1975, the Commission finally adopted regulations to deal with newspaper/broadcast combinations. They banned formation of new combinations. They also required divestiture,[41] but only in "the most egregious cases," those where the newspaper/broadcast ownership combination monopolized the marketplace of ideas. This boiled down to 18 small markets where the same party owned both the only newspaper and either the only television station or the only broadcast station of any kind.[42] The Commission subsequently waived the divestiture requirement for 2 of these ownership combinations. But the others had until January 1, 1980, to divest either the station or the newspaper. Petitioned for reconsideration, the FCC reaffirmed the rules in all material respects.[43]

Various parties appealed the regulations in the U.S. Court of Appeals for the District of Columbia. Broadcast and newspaper interests argued that the rules were too strict. The National Citizens Committee for Broadcasting, a public interest group, and the U.S. Justice Department contended that the rules did not go far enough, that the Commission should have requested divestiture in all newspaper/broadcast cross-ownerships. In its decision, the court affirmed the prospective ban. However, it vacated the limited divestiture requirement. The court said that both the FCC's own divestiture policy and the Communications Act required the Commission to adopt a divestiture requirement for *all* newspaper/broadcast cross-ownerships and that waivers should be granted only in those cases where such cross-ownerships are clearly in the public interest.[44]

Broadcasting and newspaper interests appealed the decision to the U.S. Supreme Court. In *FCC* v. *National Citizens Committee for Broadcasting* (1978),[45] the high court affirmed the appeals court judgment upholding the FCC's rule but reversed that concerning divestiture. As to the latter, the Court said that the Com-

---

[38] Mansfield Journal Co. v. FCC, 180 F.2d 28 (1950).

[39] WHDH, Inc., 16 F.C.C.2d 1 (1969).

[40] Multiple Ownership of Standard, FM & TV Broadcast Stations, 22 F.C.C.2d 339, at 346 (1970).

[41] In 47 C.F.R. § 73.3555(e), the FCC stated that it would not renew the license of any station that was part of one of the forbidden newspaper/broadcast combinations beyond Jan. 1, 1980.

[42] Multiple Ownership, 50 F.C.C.2d 1046 (1975).

[43] Multiple Ownership, 53 F.C.C.2d 589 (1975).

[44] National Citizens Comm. for Broadcasting v. FCC, 555 F.2d 938 (1977).

[45] 436 U.S. 775.

mission, in its 1975 order, had adequately explained that diversification was not its only concern and had noted that a sweeping divestiture order might cause serious economic and stability problems among newspaper/broadcast owners, leading to a lessening of service to the stations' communities and, thus, harming the public interest. So the rules were upheld; most preexisting newspaper/broadcast combinations could remain, new ones could not be formed, and the 16 remaining "egregious" combinations *would* have to divest.

7.1.3.4   *Educational Licensees Exempted*
Numerical limitations on ownership do not apply to noncommercial educational licensees.

Section 73.3555(f) specifically exempts educational licenses. So, for example, North Texas Public Broadcasting operates two television stations in the Dallas–Fort Worth market, KERA, channel 13, and KDTN, channel 2. The Mississippi Authority for Educational Television operates eight television transmitters across its state.[46]

7.2   CABLE OPERATORS

A cable system must have a periodically renewable franchise from local government in order to place its cable in the public right-of-way.

Unlike a broadcast station, which uses the radio frequencies, a cable system does not distribute its signal by use of a scarce natural resource in the public domain. Instead, it builds, maintains, and uses its own physical conduit, the cable. In order to connect the system headend to the subscribers, however, the cable must be placed in the public right-of-way. The *local governmental authority*, typically a city council or a county commission within whose boundaries a right-of-way lies, controls access to that right-of-way. The city council or county commission is also the *franchising authority* because it will not allow a would-be cable operator to build a system without first receiving an application for, and granting at its discretion, a *cable franchise*.[47]

7.2.1   Patterns of Cable System Ownership

The entity that holds the franchise for cable service in a locale is the cable *operator*. An operator that holds franchises in (often many) different areas is a *multiple system operator* (MSO).

---

[46] 47 C.F.R. §§ 0.181–0.186, 0.381–0.387.

[47] 47 U.S.C. §§ 602(9), 621(a)(1). Operators of wireless cable systems (EMG 6.5.3) and satellite master antenna television systems (EMG 6.8), on the other hand, do *not* use the public rights-of-way and so do *not* need a franchise to operate.

Most cable systems are franchised to MSOs. There are some exceptions. Individual franchisees operate some systems, primarily in small towns and rural areas. A few local governments operate their own cable systems (although the majority of cable operators oppose municipal ownership). Some schools, colleges, and other institutions operate cable systems. For the most part, however, the typical cable operator is private and corporate and is an MSO.

7.2.2 Cable System Ownership Limitations

Legal limitations affect the following aspects of cable system ownership: common ownership with certain other media in the same market, subscribers reached, number of cable systems, and cable program services.

Before Congress acted, the FCC had in place rules that affected some aspects of cable system ownership. The two cable acts, however, wrote most of those FCC prohibitions and other ownership restrictions into Section 613 of the Communications Act.[48]

7.2.2.1 TV Station/Cable Cross-Ownership

One party may not own or control both a cable television system and a television station in the same community.

During the 1970s and 1980s, the FCC adopted as rules three restrictions on system ownership. One was the TV/cable rule that, as noted in EMG 7.1.3.3.5, was subsequently written into law by the Cable Communications Policy Act of 1984 and prevented common ownership of a TV station and a cable system in the same community.

7.2.2.2 Telephone/Cable Cross-Ownership

A party that owns a telephone company in a community may provide delivery facilities that others can use to transmit video programming in that same community, but it cannot own or control the programming transmitted on those facilities. It may own cable systems in communities that it does not serve as a telephone company.

The second of those FCC restrictions was the telco/cable cross-ownership rule. A company could not operate both a telephone system and a cable system in the same area. Telephone poles are usually placed in the public right-of-way, so many cable companies rent space from the local telephone company (telco) for trunk and feeder lines (EMG 6.7.1). If allowed to compete with other entities for a cable franchise, the telephone company could set a high pole-use fee, placing its competi-

---

[48] 47 U.S.C. § 533.

tors at a disadvantage. Congress wrote the telco/cable cross-ownership rule, too, into law with passage of the Cable Communications Policy Act of 1984.[49]

The act does, however, allow common ownership of a telephone company and a cable system in FCC-defined rural areas.[50] It also allows a telephone common carrier to seek a waiver of the telco/cable rule in areas where low population density would not provide enough economic support for an independent cable company to exist. The FCC interprets this to mean fewer than 30 homes per mile of cable.[51] And the act allows a telephone company to own a cable system so long as the system is *either*

1. leased back to a franchised cable operator *or*
2. outside the telephone company's local service area.

By the late 1980s, many cable operators were being criticized for poor service and large increases in subscriber fees. Persons in Congress and the executive branch urged that telephone companies be allowed to get into the cable business. The argument was that telephone companies could provide that which was lacking in most markets—competition for the local franchised cable system and, therefore, incentive to improve service and moderate rate increases. The telephone companies themselves wanted to get into the business, but cable operators wanted the telco/cable cross-ownership ban to stay in place. Several of the "information superhighway" bills in Congress (EMG 6, opening section) would allow telephone companies to enter the cable business in their service territories and, conversely, cable operators (among others) to offer local telephone service. And in 1993, a U.S. district court judge ruled that the telco/cable cross-ownership ban violated the First Amendment rights of telephone companies; the ruling, however, applied only to the plaintiff, Bell Atlantic.[52]

7.2.2.3 *Network/Cable Cross-Ownership*

A party that owns a national broadcast TV network may own cable systems that collectively serve no more than 10 percent of homes passed nationwide and no more than 50 percent of homes passed in any single market.

---

[49] The FCC has also adopted rules specifically to protect against potential pole-attachment abuses by the telephone companies. *See, e.g.,* 47 C.F.R. §§ 1.1402, 1.1403, 1.1404, and 63.57.

[50] 47 C.F.R. § 63.58.

[51] 47 C.F.R. § 63.56(b)(2).

[52] Chesapeake & Potomac Tel. Co. v. United States, 830 F. Supp. 909. For capsule descriptions of ownership provisions in the information superhighway legislation, see, for example, Kim McAvoy, "Ups and Downs on the Infohighway," *Broadcasting & Cable*, 7 Mar. 1994, at 5.

   In addition to the Cable Act, another barrier came from the judicial branch. The 1982 modified final judgment issued by Judge Harold Greene in his supervision of the breakup of AT&T prevented the several Bell operating companies from providing "information services," a term that included cable-television service. Judge Greene lifted that ban in 1991. United States v. Western Elec. Co., 767 F. Supp. 308 (D.C. 1991), *appeal docketed* No. 91-5263 (D.C. Cir. Aug. 30, 1991) (stay lifted on Oct. 7, 1991), *application for review denied*, American Newspaper Publishers Ass'n v. United States, 60 U.S.L.W. (Oct. 30, 1991).

The third of those FCC restrictions on cable system ownership was the network/cable cross-ownership rule, which banned broadcast TV networks from owning cable systems.[53] Congress did *not* write this rule into law, and in 1992 the FCC changed the rule.[54] Under the new rule, a broadcast TV network may own cable systems within certain percentage limitations.

Those network/cable-system percentage limitations are based on the concept of "homes passed," the number of household units that *could* have cable service. Consider, for example, two houses, side by side. The local cable system's feeder line goes right by both houses, so the residents of both houses could get cable service if they wanted. One house in fact does subscribe to cable service, but the other does not. So while only one house is a cable subscriber, both are "homes passed."

The network/cable-system percentage limitations apply at national and local levels. Under the FCC's rule, the owner of a broadcast television network may own cable systems that serve no more than 10 percent of all homes passed in the United States and no more than 50 percent of homes passed in any given market. The local market limitation, however, is waived where the network-owned system competes with another cable system serving the same area. The FCC also said that it would review this 10/50 percentage limitation in 1995 to determine if it is still necessary.

7.2.2.4 *MMDS and SMATV/Cable Cross-Ownership*

One party may not own a cable system and, in the same community, acquire a multichannel multipoint distribution service or a satellite master antenna service.

By the time Congress passed the 1992 cable act, nearly 56 million households, over 60 percent of households with television, subscribed to cable television. And the numbers showed no signs of decreasing. As a result of such growth, the cable television business had become a dominant, nationwide medium.[55]

During the 1980s and early 1990s, various components of the cable business combined through mergers and acquisitions. Large MSOs bought up independent cable systems and smaller MSOs, concentrating ownership of cable systems into fewer and fewer hands; this was horizontal integration. At the same time, the MSOs also acquired, in whole or in part, many of the cable networks that supplied their systems with satellite-delivered program services; this was vertical integration. As a result, said critics, cable operators had the incentive and ability to favor their affiliated programmers. This made it more difficult for non-cable-affiliated programmers to be carried on cable systems. It worked the other way, too; vertically integrated program suppliers had the incentive and ability to favor their affiliated cable opera-

---

[53] 47 C.F.R. § 76.501.

[54] Common Ownership of Cable Television Systems and National Television Networks, 7 F.C.C.R. 6156.

[55] U.S. Congress, Conference Committee, *Conference Report: Cable Television Consumer Protection and Competition Act of 1992*, 102d Cong., 2d Sess.; S. 12 (Washington, DC: GPO, 1992) 55–56.

tors over nonaffiliated cable operators and over other multichannel video retailers such as wireless cable[56] and direct broadcast satellites.

With such concentration, continued this line of criticism, new programmers and competitors to cable (those other multichannel video retailers) had an extra hard time entering and succeeding in the marketplace. The net result was a reduction in the number of media voices available to consumers and, since cable systems had no competition in most communities, artificially high rates for cable subscribers.

These criticisms came from various groups—non-cable-affiliated programmers and cable-system competitors (such as wireless cable firms); broadcasters, motion picture producers, and other such competing businesses; consumer groups; the cable subscribers themselves. They made themselves heard in the halls of Congress, and the result was a series of provisions in the 1992 cable act to curb concentration and encourage competition. One of these amended Section 613 of the Communications Act[57] to prevent a cable operator from "buying out" local competitors. It forbids the operator of a cable system in a community from acquiring a multichannel multipoint distribution service (MMDS)[58] or a satellite master antenna television system (SMATV)[59] in any part of the cable system's franchise area. Existing cable/MMDS and cable/SMATV combinations, however, are "grandfathered in." Further, the FCC may waive this restriction where necessary to ensure that all residents can have programming.

7.2.2.5 *Franchising and Competition Reduction*

A franchising authority may, in some cases, refuse to grant a franchise to an applicant if the grant would reduce competition.

This was another result of congressional concern with competition (or the lack thereof) in the cable business. The 1992 cable act makes clear that a franchising authority may refuse to grant an application for a cable franchise in situations that would result in reduced competition in cable service within the jurisdiction (of the franchising authority). According to Section 613(d), the franchising authority may deny the franchise because of

(1) . . . ownership or control of a cable system in the jurisdiction; or (2) in circumstances in which the State or franchising authority determines that the acquisition of such a cable system may eliminate or reduce competition in the delivery of cable service in such circumstances.[60]

---

[56] An omnidirectional microwave service that offers cablelike service for subscribers; EMG 6.5.3.

[57] 47 U.S.C. § 533(a)(2).

[58] Multiple channels in the microwave frequencies assigned to one licensee, usually used to offer wireless cable service; EMG 6.5.2.

[59] In essence, a cable system that operates on private property—that is, the system's wiring is not laid in public rights-of-way so it does not need a franchise; EMG 6.8.

[60] 47 U.S.C. § 533(d).

7.2.2.6 *Limitations on Subscribers and Owned Programming*

Nationwide, one party may hold attributable interest in cable systems that account for

1. no more than 30 percent of all homes passed; and
2. an additional 5 percent (total of 35 percent) of all homes passed, provided that the additional percentage is passed by systems that are controlled by racial minorities.

A cable system with 75 or fewer channels may carry national program services in which the cable operator has attributable interest

1. to total no more than 40 percent of the total number of channels on the system; and
2. an additional 2 channels or 5 percent if those additional services are controlled by racial minorities.

Homes passed refers to the total number of homes that *could* subscribe to a cable system. For example, if 60,000 homes in a particular community are hooked up to the cable system and another 15,000 could be hooked up if their residents so desired, that cable system would be said to have 60,000 subscribers out of 75,000 homes passed. *Attributable interest* has the same meaning for cable systems and programmers as for broadcast stations (EMG 7.1.3.2). So of all homes in the United States that could subscribe to cable, one person or company may own in whole or in part cable systems that account for no more than 30 percent, plus another 5 percent if the additional homes are served by cable systems in which racial minorities hold the controlling interest. And a cable operator may program no more than 40 percent of a system's channels with program services owned in whole or in part by the operator, plus another 2 channels or 5 percent (whichever is greater) if racial minorities hold controlling interest in the additional services. Operator-owned local and regional channels do not count toward the limits, and the restriction does not apply to systems with more than 75 channels.[61]

The first limitation addresses *horizontal concentration*, the total number of homes a cable operator can reach. The second deals with *vertical integration*, ownership of both programming and distribution. If not controlled, both could lead to near-monopoly situations. Congress was concerned with the possibility that a cable operator could control the flow of information to a majority of homes in the United States, determining the content of that information and obstructing the formation of effective competition. Those concerns were reflected in the Cable Television Consumer Protection and Competition Act of 1992,[62] which directed the FCC to for-

---

[61] Congress addressed other aspects of vertical integration in section 12 of the 1992 cable act, which added a new section 616 to the Communications Act. In response, the FCC adopted rules designed to prevent cable operators and other multichannel video programming distributors (which includes wireless cable, direct broadcast satellites, and other such services) from coercing program services into granting ownership interests or exclusive distribution rights in exchange for program carriage agreements. Cable Act of 1992—Program Distribution and Carriage Agreements, 58 Fed. Reg. 60, 390, Nov. 16, 1993.

[62] Pub. L. No. 102–385, 106 Stat. 1460, § 11.

mulate limitations. The Commission adopted the rules summarized above in 1993.[63]

A district court judge, however, ruled that national subscriber limits were unconstitutional. "The First Amendment," said the judge, "protects the right of every citizen to reach the minds of any willing listeners and, thus, the opportunity to win their attention."[64] A government regulation that limits the number of subscribers that one cable operator may serve, on the other hand, leaves that operator with "no intra-medium means of speaking to the rest of its potential audience."[65] As a result of that ruling, the FCC put a stay[66] on the effective date of its national subscriber limits pending appeal.

7.3   LICENSEES IN OTHER SERVICES

In Chapter 6, we discussed other regulated media, in addition to broadcast stations and cable systems, that can be used to distribute programming to large numbers of persons. Our survey of legal restrictions and requirements on ownership would not be complete without a review of those that apply to these other media—low-power television (LPTV) stations, the instructional television fixed service (ITFS; EMG 6.5.1), wireless cable, the multipoint distribution service (MDS; EMG 6.5.2), and direct broadcast satellite (DBS; EMG 6.6).

7.3.1   Low-Power Television Station Ownership

FCC rules place no limit on the number of LPTV licenses one party may hold.

The rules allow almost anyone to hold LPTV licenses, including networks, licensees of existing stations, and cable operators.[67] However, as discussed in EMG 8.2.1, the FCC uses a lottery system to award LPTV licenses, and its rules do limit the number of applications that one party may submit for each lottery.

7.3.2   Instructional Television Fixed Service Licensees

An ITFS licensee must be educational in nature, may operate multiple transmitters at one location, and is limited to four channels in a single area.

---

[63] Cable Act of 1992—Program Distribution and Carriage Agreements, 58 Fed. Reg. 60, 390, Nov. 16, 1993.

[64] Daniels Cablevision, Inc. v. United States, 835 F. Supp. 1 (1993).

[65] *Id.*

[66] *Stay* is a legal term meaning to stop or hold off. Here, the FCC adopted national subscriber rules but held off enforcing them until, on appeal, final judicial determination could be made concerning constitutionality.

[67] 47 C.F.R. § 73.732.

The FCC's rules for the instructional television fixed service severely limit the types of applicants that qualify for licenses. Applicants must meet all requirements of the Communications Act. Additionally, the rules make clear that the FCC will license an ITFS station only to the following types of applicants:

1. an accredited institution engaged in the formal education of enrolled students, or
2. a governmental organization engaged in the formal education of enrolled students, or
3. a nonprofit organization whose purposes
   a. are educational and
   b. include providing educational and instructional television material to the groups named in (1) and (2), and that is
   c. otherwise qualified under the statutory provisions.[68]

The Commission places no limit on the number of stations that may be operated by one licensee so long as they are justified in the initial application,[69] and they allow a licensee to operate multiple transmitters at one location. But the rules do limit a licensee to no more than four channels for use in a single area of operation.[70]

7.3.3 Wireless Cable Operators

A wireless cable operator may, in some limited cases, receive a license for as many as eight unused ITFS channels.

There are, however, a number of regulatory barriers that must be overcome.[71] These are discussed in the context of the licensing process in EMG 8.2.2.

7.3.4 Multipoint Distribution Service Licensees

MDS licensees may use more than one channel, may not be co-owned with a cable system, and must choose to operate as a common carrier or a non–common carrier.

In EMG 6.5.2 we noted that MDS originally had only 2 channels but that the total was raised to 13. The whole point of increasing the number of channels in the service was so that one entity could acquire several licenses in order to market a multichannel offering in competition with cable TV. So unlike the situation in television broadcasting, one MDS licensee may have four or more transmitters in a given area.

---

[68] 47 C.F.R. § 74.932.
[69] 47 C.F.R. §§ 74.902, 74.931.
[70] 47 C.F.R. § 74.902(d).
[71] 47 C.F.R. § 74.990.

The ban against MDS co-ownership with a cable system derives from the MMDS and SMATV/cable cross-ownership law (EMG 7.2.2.4). The FCC allows MDS licensees to operate either as non–common carriers or common carriers. If operated on a *common carrier basis*, the station will transmit subscriber-supplied information to points designated by the subscriber. In other words, the licensee does not control programming but may only lease out facilities to others. If operated on a *non–common carrier basis*, the station's transmissions may consist of any or all of the following:

1. information originated by persons other than the licensee;
2. licensee-manipulated information supplied by persons other than the licensee;
3. information originated by the licensee.[72]

This allows the MDS/MMDS licensee to lease channels to others, or to originate programming, or to do both.

7.3.5 Direct Broadcast Satellite Licensees

The FCC has said a DBS licensee will be classified according to the type of service provided by the satellite.

Applicants in the direct broadcast satellite (DBS) service must meet basically the same citizenship requirements as those in the broadcast services.[73] In its 1982 order adopting interim rules for direct broadcast satellites (EMG 6.6), the Commission announced that it would regulate DBS systems according to the service proposed on their applications. For example, a DBS operator that runs and controls the content of a direct-to-home programming service resembles a broadcast licensee. Such a service must adhere to requirements of Title III[74] of the Communications Act, the section that applies specifically to broadcasting.[75] A DBS operator that functions as a common carrier must offer satellite transmission services indiscriminately to the public in conformity with a tariff filed under Title II[76] (common carrier requirements) of the Communications Act. A DBS operator that runs some channels as a broadcaster and others as a common carrier is subject to either broadcast or common carrier regulation, according to the specific channels involved.

---

[72] 47 C.F.R. § 21.903.

[73] 47 C.F.R. § 100.11.

[74] Sections numbered in the 300s; these apply to broadcast stations.

[75] If the DBS operator provides programming on a subscription basis, the Commission normally classifies the service as broadcasting (unless it determines otherwise).

[76] Sections numbered in the 200s; these all apply to common carriers.

7.3.6 SMATV Operators

A SMATV operator usually either has a contract with, or is, the owner of the multi-unit dwelling to which the system provides service. Some regulation does impact SMATV ownership.

Usually resident fees for SMATV service are included in the rent or condominium service fee. They may or may not be identified as such on the monthly bill. Sometimes the resident may receive a separate bill for SMATV service. If the SMATV operator is a contractor—an entrepreneur who runs the system but has no other connection with the ownership or management of the dwelling—there is usually some type of fee-split arrangement; part of the resident fee will go to the operator, and part will go to the owner.

Despite the fact that a SMATV system needs no license or franchise, there is regulatory impact on ownership. It is affected by the MMDS and SMATV/cable cross ownership law (EMG 7.2.2.4) and may be affected by any FCC rule making concerning ownership of video programming (EMG 7.2.2.4).

7.3.7 Video Dialtone Ownership

A telephone company may have no cognizable interest in the programmers that use its facilities or the video programming that it carries in its service area. However, it may provide financing for the programmers.

"Cognizable" is defined as "5 percent or more."[77] Therefore, a telephone company may actually hold up to 5 percent equity in both the programmers and the programming. It may not buy a cable system in its service area for the specific purpose of providing video dialtone service. It may, however, buy a cable system and lease it to a franchised cable operator.

DISCUSSION QUESTIONS

1. What companies own the broadcast stations and cable systems that serve your home? In what other business interests, media or otherwise, are these owners involved? Start your search with the current *Broadcasting & Cable Yearbook* (Washington, DC: Bowker, annual) and *Television & Cable Factbook* (Washington, DC: Television Factbook, annual). A reference librarian can help you locate the annual reports of publicly traded companies.

2. Some have argued that citizens of foreign countries should be allowed to own controlling interest in broadcast stations. They say that this would bring needed foreign investment capital into the business. What additional "pro" arguments can you think of? Why would this *not* be a good idea?

---

[77] 47 C.F.R. § 63.54(e).

3. You read in this chapter that for years the broadcast ownership rules aimed at fostering maximum competition in broadcasting; at increasing the numbers of origins and outlets reflecting different views, opinions, and ideas; and at keeping to a minimum the number of absentee owners unfamiliar with the needs and interests of the communities to which their stations are licensed. Are those aims still valid? Why, or why not?

4. How have the deregulatory efforts of the 1980s and 1990s affected the aims mentioned in question 3? Why; what has changed?

5. What disadvantages for the public, short-range and long-range, could result from the FCC's rule change to allow local radio duopoly ownership?

6. Why not allow monopolies in broadcasting and cable? Why should there be any worry at all about diversity of ownership so long as those who hold the licenses and franchises play your favorite music, schedule your favorite sitcoms and soap operas, and carry MTV? After all, the government could mandate carriage of differing political views for those who care about "that kind of stuff."

SUGGESTED READINGS

Bagdikian, Ben H. *The Media Monopoly.* 3rd ed. Boston: Beacon, 1990.

Barsamian, David, ed. *Stenographers to Power: Media and Propaganda.* Monroe: Common Courage, 1992.

Bates, Benjamin J. "Deregulation and Station Trafficking." *Journal of Broadcasting and Electronic Media* 33 (summer 1989): 317–333.

Bates, Benjamin J. "Breaking the Logjam: The Impact of Cable on Local Market Competition." *Journal of Media Economics* 4 (3) (1993): 47–57.

Brennan, Timothy J. "Vertical Integration, Monopoly, and the First Amendment." *Journal of Media Economics* 3 (1) (spring 1990): 57–76.

Chan-Olmsted, Sylvia, and Barry R. Litman. "Antitrust and Horizontal Mergers in the Cable Industry." *Journal of Media Economics* 1 (2) (fall 1988): 3–28.

Compaine, Benjamin M., ed. *Who Owns the Media? Concentration of Ownership in the Mass Communications Industry.* 2d ed. White Plains, NY: Knowledge Industry, 1982.

DeJong, Allard Sicco, and Benjamin J. Bates. "Channel Diversity in Cable Television." *Journal of Broadcasting and Electronic Media* 35 (spring 1991): 159–166.

Hilliard, Robert L., and Robert G. Picard. "Plurality, Diversity, and Television-Newspaper Crossownership." *Journal of Media Economics* 2 (spring 1989): 785–792.

Howard, Herbert H. "A Critique of the Fowler FCC's 1984–85 Multiple Ownership Rule." *Hastings Journal of Communications and Entertainment: COMM/ENT* 10 (summer 1988): 555–569.

Howard, Herbert H. "Group and Cross-Media Ownership of TV Stations: A 1989 Update." *Journalism Quarterly* 66 (winter 1989): 785–792.

Kleiman, Howard. "Content Diversity and the FCC's Minority and Licensing Policies." *Journal of Broadcasting and Electronic Media* 35 (fall 1991): 411–429.

Levin, Stanford L., and John B. Meisel. "Cable Television and Competition: Theory, Evidence, and Policy." *Telecommunications Policy* 15 (Dec. 1991): 519–528.

McChesney, Robert W. "The Battle for the U.S. Airwaves, 1928–1935." *Journal of Communication* 40 (autumn 1990): 29–57.

McGregor, Michael A. "Cable/Newspaper Cross-Ownership: Pre-empting Local Regulatory Options." *Communications and the Law* 10(5) (Oct. 1988): 19–27.

McGregor, Michael A. "Connections among Deleted Underbrush Policies, FCC Character Standards, and State Criminal Law." *Journal of Broadcasting and Electronic Media* 34 (1990): 153–170.

Parsons, Patrick R. "In the Wake of Preferred: Waiting for Godot." *Mass Comm Review* 16 (1&2) (1989): 26–37.

Turow, Joseph. *Media Systems in Society: Understanding Industries, Strategies, and Power.* New York: Longman, 1992.

Chapter

8

PERMISSION TO OPERATE

The key to ownership for most electronic mass communication outlets is the government warrant or authorization that allows them to operate; that is, to *use* the medium by which they distribute programming to their audiences. An outlet such as a radio or television broadcast station, a wireless cable system, or a direct broadcast satellite distributes its programming "over the air." It uses equipment that generates, modulates, and transmits electromagnetic energy, and to do so the outlet needs a *license* from the Federal Communications Commission. A cable system distributes its programming in the form of electromagnetic energy, too, but confines that energy to a physical conductor (that is, *not* over the air) and so needs no FCC license. However, the cable system does need to "lay" the conductor, miles of coaxial cable or optical fiber, in order to deliver programming to its subscribers. It lays the cable in the public right-of-way, and in order to do that the system needs a *franchise* from the local government within whose boundaries lies the needed right-of-way.

The award of permission to operate is discretionary; that is, the granter may, for cause, refuse to grant the authorization. Further, once granted the authorization may be taken away or, its term being finite and subject to periodic review, not renewed. So not only is it important to *get* the authorization initially, it is also important to *keep* it. Without this permission to operate one is literally not in the program distribution business.

That is the subject of this chapter: getting and keeping permission to operate. We look at licensing for, first, full-power broadcast stations, then other wireless electronic mass media; at franchising for cable systems; at permission to operate for two other wired electronic mass media, satellite master antenna television and video dialtone; and at special employment rules for program packagers.

192

8.1   BROADCAST STATION LICENSING

Since the license is the vehicle that allows a broadcaster to be a broadcaster, naturally broadcasters are very concerned about the license. Their major concerns usually center around six aspects: the process of getting the license in the first place; additional licensing procedures they may face; intervention of the public in the licensing process; comparative hearings; the periodic necessity to apply for renewal of the license; and the possibility of losing the license.

8.1.1   Initial Licensing of Broadcast Stations

The major steps in getting a license for a new broadcast station include the would-be licensee filing an application for a construction permit (CP) and giving certain notice, the FCC staff processing the application (at which point any of several problems can occur), the FCC granting the CP, the applicant constructing the station, and the FCC granting the license.

The model set forth in the above summary—the major steps—is the one we shall follow to study the initial licensing process. Along the way, we shall also investigate those "problems" to which the summary alludes.

8.1.1.1   *Application.*
Section 308(a) of the Communications Act prohibits the FCC from granting any kind of authorization—construction permit, station license, modification of license, or renewal of license—without first having received written application. Section 319 requires that a party wanting to put a new broadcast station on the air have a construction permit (CP) from the FCC before even starting to build the station.[1] Therefore, the would-be new-station operator, once an available channel has been found, must file an application for a construction permit and remit the appropriate application fee.[2] The application requires information concerning the qualifications of the applicant (EMG 7.1.2) and technical aspects of the station. It also calls for information on program proposals. And here the applicant must be able to demonstrate a knowledge of the issues facing the prospective community of license and a commitment to program responsively to those issues. This requirement varies according to type of station.

The application must include certification that no one connected with the applicant (such as partners or directors) has been convicted for trafficking or possession of drugs.[3] If the completed station will employ five or more persons, the applicant's planned equal employment opportunity program (EMG 8.1.6.3) must be

---

[1] See Box 8.4 later in this chapter for a listing of some of the pertinent application forms.
[2] Under 47 U.S.C. § 158, the FCC must charge a fee not only for applications for broadcast station construction permits but for all applications of any kind in every service.
[3] 47 C.F.R. § 1.2002. Under Section 5301 of the Anti-Drug Abuse Act of 1988, persons convicted of drug trafficking or possession may be denied "federal benefits," the definition for which encompasses a license from the FCC. 21 U.S.C. § 862.

filed.[4] And the applicant may have to submit an Environmental Assessment if construction of the station would impact the area with respect to certain concerns.[5] These concerns include wilderness areas, wildlife preserves, endangered species, historic locales and structures, Native American religious sites, surface features (such as filling in a wetlands area), high intensity lights in residential areas, and radio frequency radiation.

8.1.1.2 *Application Notices.*

The application, when it goes to the Commission, must contain certification that a notice has been run in the local newspaper. The notice makes public the fact that a station has been proposed for the community and provides FCC-specified information such as the name of the applicant and the requested channel and power.[6] The applicant also sets up a public inspection file (EMG 8.1.6.4). The file must contain copies of the completed application for construction permit, any other applications the applicant has sent to the Commission, and all associated exhibits, letters, documents, amendments, citizen agreements, and other material.[7] These requirements are designed to give local citizens notice of the application and opportunity to examine it and to file comments, objections, or petitions to deny with the Commission.

Also at this time, applicants in certain specified situations must consult with several sensitive radio installations. For example, the National Radio Astronomy Observatory at Green Bank, West Virginia, must be notified of plans for any station proposed in specified areas of western Virginia or eastern West Virginia. This gives the Green Bank facility and the Naval Radio Research Observatory, Sugar Grove, West Virginia, opportunity to determine and comment on whether the proposed station would interfere with their work.[8]

8.1.1.3 *Staff Processing.*

At the FCC, the CP application is received, dated, and forwarded to the Mass Media Bureau. There, the staff examines it. If the application is substantially complete, it is accepted for filing and assigned a file number. If the staff finds a few things missing, the applicant is directed to supply the missing information. If not substantially complete, the application is returned. An application that does not comply with FCC requirements and contains no request for waiver of those requirements is said to be *defective*. An application is also defective if the applicant fails to respond to staff requests for additional material. Defective applications are not accepted for filing or, if already accepted, are dismissed.[9]

The staff also examines each application to determine whether the applicant must obtain Federal Aviation Administration (FAA) approval of the proposed antenna. FCC standards for antenna structures developed in conjunction with the FAA

---

[4] FCC Form 386A.
[5] 47 C.F.R. § 1.1307.
[6] 47 C.F.R. § 73.3580
[7] 47 C.F.R §§ 73.3526, 73.3527.
[8] 47 C.F.R. § 73.1030.
[9] 47 C.F.R. § 73.3566.

are spelled out in Section 17.7 of the Commission's rules. Those rules specify that the applicant must submit a form to the FAA for an antenna structure that is a "hazard to air navigation"—that is, over 200 feet high or near or on an airport. The FCC staff prescribes antenna tower painting and lighting specifications.

As required by Section 309(b) of the Communications Act, the Commission publishes "at regular intervals" a public notice of all accepted applications and amendments to applications.[10] This allows interested parties to file competing applications (EMG 8.1.1.4.2) and petitions to deny (EMG 8.1.1.4.1). The public notice also announces a cutoff date beyond which the FCC will no longer accept such filings.

8.1.1.4 Application Problems

Grant of a construction permit may be delayed or blocked by a petition to deny, a competing application, an informal objection, or a hearing on motion by the FCC itself.

The application may be perfect. However, problems such as these could still arise.

8.1.1.4.1 Petition to Deny.

Section 309(d) of the Communications Act directs the Commission to wait at least 30 days after issuance of its public notice before granting the construction permit. This allows "any party in interest" to file a petition to deny application. Such a petition must show that the petitioner is, in fact, "a party in interest," must show *prima facie*[11] allegations that grant of the application would be inconsistent with the public interest, and must be accompanied by affidavits of persons with personal knowledge of the matter. A copy of the petition goes to the applicant. The applicant may then file an opposition, and the petitioner may reply.[12] The Commission, which must act on the petition to deny before acting on the original application, has two choices in the matter. It may deny the petition, stating reasons for its denial. Or if it finds that the petition raises serious issues, doubts, or questions of fact as to whether grant of the application would serve the public interest, the Commission may designate the matter for hearing. However, it must be emphasized here that the FCC interprets Sections 309(e) and (f) of the Communications Act to require hearings only when the petition to deny cites *specifics* that throw the matter of the grant into question[13]—for example, an ongoing police investigation of the applicant on suspicion of some criminal activity. A petitioner's vague charge that the applicant is simply not worthy would normally not trigger a hearing.

---

[10] 47 C.F.R. § 73.3564.

[11] *Prima facie* is a Latin phrase that, as used here, means "on the face of it" and refers to a fact that will be considered true unless disproved by contrary evidence.

[12] 47 C.F.R. § 73.3584.

[13] In other words, the FCC normally designates the matter for hearing only if the petition reveals "a substantial and material question of fact." Hale v. FCC, 425 F.2d 556 (1970).

8.1.1.4.2 Competing Applications.   Parties that wish to apply for the same frequency or channel must also file applications within the 30-day period following the FCC's public notice.[14] If the FCC finds such applications in good order and accepts them for filing, that means there are now multiple applications for the same facility. The applications are said to be *mutually exclusive,* and the FCC designates the matter for hearing to compare and to determine which application should be granted. The comparative hearing is discussed later in this chapter.

8.1.1.4.3 Informal Objections.   The Commission also provides the informal objection as a means to affect the licensing process. Anyone may file; there is no specified form, no requirement for extra copies, and no time limit. An informal objection can be a letter. The objector must sign the letter but can send it any time before the Commission takes action.[15]

8.1.1.4.4 Hearings on Motion by the Commission.   Even without petitions to deny or competing applications, the Commission could still designate the matter of the application for hearing. Section 309(e) of the Communications Act orders the Commission to hold a hearing any time it has reason to believe that the public interest might not be served by the grant. Evidence for such belief could come from the FCC staff's own examination of the application and the applicant, from an informal objection, or, of course, from a petition to deny.[16]

8.1.1.5 Grant.   The Mass Media Bureau staff refers to the five-member Commission for consideration certain classes of applications: those recommended for hearing; those involving novel questions of policy; and those on which the Mass Media Bureau wants instruction. For routine applications, the staff itself may make the grant for the CP.[17] However, first the staff must make the following determinations: (1) there are no mutually exclusive applications; (2) the applicant meets all qualifications; (3) the applicant does not violate law or FCC rules or policies; and (4) a grant would serve the public interest.[18]

Even in the case of mutually exclusive applications, the five-member FCC *may* still make a grant before the hearing. It may grant the CP to one of the competing applicants or to a group composed of two or more of the applicants. To do so, the Commission must first determine that certain conditions exist, including that the public interest would be better served by making the grant immediately than by waiting until after the hearing. And the recipient must understand that the grant may be withdrawn after the hearing if the decision favors another applicant. Such prehearing grants, however, almost never happen. They are not routine procedure and are used only in comparative renewal situations (EMG 8.1.7.2).

---

[14] 47 C.F.R. §§ 73.3571–73.3573.

[15] 47 C.F.R. § 73.3587.

[16] 47 C.F.R. § 73.3593.

[17] 47 C.F.R. § 73.3561, 73.3562.

[18] 47 C.F.R. § 73.3591.

8.1.1.6 *Construction*

Upon grant of a construction permit, the FCC allows 24 months for completion of a television station, 18 months for all other types of stations.[19]

Additionally, the applicant—now a permittee—has 30 days from grant of the CP within which to submit an ownership report (EMG 8.1.6.1). If the permittee does not complete the station in time, the CP is automatically forfeited.[20] However, the Commission does allow a permittee to apply for an extension of the CP, good for another six months, and even a CP to replace an expired CP.[21]

In addition to allowing the permittee to build the station, the CP also covers permission to conduct equipment and programming tests. For both tests, the permittee must first notify the FCC in Washington. The equipment tests[22] provide opportunity to ensure that everything works as it should and to check that all equipment complies with pertinent rules, engineering standards, and terms of the CP. The station may then run program tests, provided that the permittee applies for a station license within 10 days[23] (at which time it must file another Ownership Report). The station may continue program tests under the CP until the Commission acts on the application.[24] If the license is granted, of course, the station continues to program.

8.1.1.7 *License.*   Section 319(c) of the Communications Act directs the Commission to determine "that all terms, conditions, and obligations set forth in the application and construction permit have been fully met" and that nothing has come up since issuance of the CP that would "make the operation of such station against the public interest. . . ." Having made that determination, the Commission may then issue the station license.

8.1.2 Subsequent Licensing of Broadcast Stations

Additional licensing procedures are required for the broadcaster to do any of the following: operate booster and auxiliary transmitters, change facilities, renew a license that is about to expire, or change control of the station.

Most broadcasters face most of these situations, all of which require that the broadcaster again deal with licensing procedures of one kind or another.

8.1.2.1 *Operation of Auxiliary and Booster Transmitters.*   In addition to their broadcast transmitters, most licensees also operate other types of transmit-

---

[19] 47 C.F.R. § 73.3598.

[20] 47 C.F.R. § 73.3599.

[21] 47 C.F.R. § 73.3564.

[22] 47 C.F.R. § 73.1610.

[23] Stations that use directional antenna systems must file an application for license requesting program test authority.

[24] 47 C.F.R. § 73.1620.

ters that they use to support their broadcast operations. Most are used internally; that is, to get a signal from one place to another as part of the process of putting together station programming. These are auxiliary broadcast stations (EMG 6.10.2). Some TV and FM broadcasters use additional transmitters externally. They simulcast[25] on both the station's main transmitter and one or more booster stations (EMG 6.4.2) to fill in "blank spots" in their coverage areas. Auxiliary and booster stations must be licensed by the FCC. And although the processes involved in initial licensing and renewal are not nearly as complicated as those for a broadcast station, they do constitute another licensing chore for the broadcaster. Booster station licensing is discussed in EMG 8.2.1.

8.1.2.2   *Change of Facilities.*

The licensee must go through much the same process just described to do major modifications of existing facilities—for example, to change power, time of operation, frequency, location, antenna array, or transmitting equipment.[26] Application is made,[27] notice is required, problems may arise, a CP may be granted—all similar to construction of a brand new station.

Commission rules do, however, provide for limited operation with facilities at settings other than those specified in the license or even in FCC rules. The mechanism for this is the *short-term authorization* (STA).[28] The variation must be justified, of course, but normally a licensee need only notify the FCC 10 days in advance or, in the event of unforeseen equipment damage or failure, within 24 hours. The STA lasts for 180 days (90 days for equipment problems) with the possibility of extensions.

8.1.2.3   *Renewal.*

The renewal process is discussed in detail later in this chapter. As we shall see, getting a license renewed successfully involves much more than simply filling out forms truthfully and submitting them on time.

8.1.2.4   *Transfer.*

The licensee must secure prior FCC permission to sell the station or otherwise assign or transfer control of the license or the CP to another party.[29] Section 310(d) of the Communications Act requires that the FCC first pass on a prospective transferee or assignee, so the application for assignment of license[30] calls for about the same information as the application for a new station.

---

[25] *Simulcast* means to broadcast the same programming on two different stations or two different transmitters.

[26] 47 C.F.R. § 73.3530. Minor changes can be accomplished without opening up the application for challenges.

[27] FCC Form 301.

[28] 47 C.F.R. § 73.1635.

[29] 47 C.F.R. § 73.3540.

[30] FCC Form 314. When the transfer of control involves a corporate shift or realignment with no real change in who actually controls the licensee, FCC Form 316 ("Short Form") is used. However, if control goes from one group of stockholders or partners to another, Form 314 must be used. The distinction is important because the short-form applications are not subject to petitions to deny, nor do they require the divestiture of grandfathered ownership combinations. For this reason, some companies go to great lengths to characterize their transfers as "short form."

Also like new-station applicants, transfer applicants must submit plans for their equal employment opportunity programs.

8.1.2.4.1   *Tax Certificate Policy*
A licensee who sells a station to a minority-controlled company is eligible for a tax break.

As we discussed in Chapter 2, the theoretical basis for freedom of expression includes the concept of a marketplace of ideas, a free interchange of opinions, ideas, concepts, and information, all of which clamor for hearing and acceptance. The United States, however, has changed markedly from the rural, agrarian, sparsely populated society in which the First Amendment to the Constitution was written. Today, conditions are such that, without regulation of some type, the marketplace could become dominated by certain interests and ideas. Over the years, government at various levels has taken on the task of protecting the marketplace by regulating so as to prevent monopoly control. The FCC is no exception. The Commission has long regulated to promote diversity of ownership and control. Most of the ownership rules discussed in Chapter 7 derive at least in part from this aim. One of the FCC's concerns over diversity has focused on the comparative lack of minority ownership in the electronic media; without such ownership, went this line of reasoning, the viewpoints of African Americans, Hispanics, and other racial or ethnic minorities would not be adequately represented in the electronic segment of the marketplace of ideas. As a result, the Commission adopted procedures to encourage the sale of existing broadcast stations to minorities. Two of these were the minority preference in comparative hearing situations and the distress sale policy, discussed below in EMG 8.1.4 and 8.1.7.1 respectively. A third was the tax certificate policy.

Under a provision of the Internal Revenue Code,[31] the Commission is empowered to grant tax certificates to increase ownership by minorities.[32] The certificate permits the seller to defer paying capital gains taxes on the sale if proceeds from the transaction are reinvested in certain media properties within two years of sale. The minority purchaser may not resell the property for one year unless the buyer is another minority, the rationale being that the tax certificate program serves the public interest—which, in this case, means diversification of media ownership—only if the station remains under minority control. The FCC also encourages investment in minority firms; a party who sells media properties to a nonminority buyer is eligible for a certificate to defer gains on that sale *if* the party invests the returns from the sale in a minority-controlled start-up[33] company. The tax certificate program also applies when cable systems are involved.

---

[31] 26 U.S.C. § 1071(a).

[32] Public Notice, FCC 76-337, 59 F.C.C.2d 91 (1976); Public Notice, FCC 78-322, 68 F.C.C.2d 979 (1978); Public Notice, FCC 78-725, 43 Fed. Reg. 47,612, Oct. 16, 1978; Policy Statement, General Docket 82-797, FCC 82-523, 92 F.C.C.2d 849 (1983); Report and Order, General Docket 82-797, FCC 84-647 (1985).

[33] *Start-up* means that the organization has just been formed—in this case, formed specifically for the purpose of going into the radio-TV business.

8.1.3 Participation in the Broadcast Licensing Process by Nonapplicants

> The 1966 WLBT case established the right of the public to participate in the licensing process, giving citizen groups leverage in dealing with broadcast licensees. Not all citizen group allegations, however, warrant a hearing, and licensees do not have to negotiate with such groups and may not surrender to others their responsibility to determine how to serve the public interest.

The Communications Act clearly states that the FCC must determine that the public interest would be served before awarding a license. Yet, until 1966, the public—you—had almost no say in the licensing process. The FCC asserted that only other licensees alleging electrical interference or economic injury could intervene in a station's license renewal proceedings; individual citizens—members of the community the station was licensed to serve—could not. The WLBT cases changed that.

8.1.3.1 *WLBT Cases.*
The origins of these cases date from 1955 when the Commission received complaints concerning racial discrimination by television station WLBT in Jackson, Mississippi. The complaints alleged that the station cut network programming that dealt with racial integration and aired programs urging continuation of racial segregation without presenting the other side of the issue. The Commission, however, routinely renewed WLBT's license.

In 1964, the FCC received a petition from the Office of Communication of the United Church of Christ (UCC), a local church, and two Mississippi residents. They asked to intervene (that is, present evidence and arguments) in renewal proceedings for the television station. The petitioners said the station had failed to serve the general public because it broadcast a disproportionate amount of commercials and entertainment and did not give a fair and balanced presentation of controversial issues, especially those concerning black citizens, who composed almost 45 percent of the population within WLBT's service area. The Commission contended that the petitioners had no standing, and so it held no hearing on the matter. However, it did grant WLBT a short-term renewal (EMG 4.1.7.7); full license terms at that time were three years, and the FCC renewed WLBT's license for only one year.

UCC appealed. In *Office of Communication of the United Church of Christ* v. *FCC* (1966),[34] the appeals court reversed the Commission's decision and ruled that the public—in this case, as represented by the petitioners (now appellants)—could intervene in renewal proceedings.[35] As usual in such situations, the court remanded (sent back) the case to the Commission for correction of the adjudi-

---

[34] 359 F.2d 994.

[35] The 1966 decision in the WLBT case set the prerequisite for standing as an intervener—"responsible spokesman for representative groups having significant roots in the community." Later decisions have given individual members of a station's audience such standing. *See, e.g.,* Joseph v. FCC, 404 F.2d 207 (1968); Hale v. FCC, 425 F.2d 556 (1970); Harrea Broadcasters, Inc. 52 F.C.C.2d 998 (1975).

cated defect in its proceedings—that is, the lack of hearings and participation by the public.

So the FCC held hearings on WLBT's renewal application, listened to testimony from the UCC group, and gave the station a full three-year license term, saying UCC had failed to prove its case. The church again appealed. This time, in *Office of Communication of the United Church of Christ* v. *FCC* (1969),[36] the court ordered the Commission to vacate (throw out) the renewal and to open the channel for new applicants. The court ruled that public interveners do not bear the burden of proof. Rather, said the court, interveners present evidence, and the Commission must investigate, gather facts, and, if it finds cause to believe a violation has occurred, prosecute or regulate. As a result of the WLBT cases, members of the community now have a mechanism by which they can affect programming of a broadcast station, by which they can ensure that the station serves the interests of the community.

8.1.3.2 KTAL Case.

Some groups have used the petition to deny as a means to convince broadcasters to negotiate, as the KTAL case illustrates. Although licensed to Texarkana, KTAL-TV identified with, had its main studios in, and aimed most programming efforts at the larger city of Shreveport, Louisiana, 70 miles away. The Office of Communication of the United Church of Christ worked with 12 local organizations and filed a petition to deny renewal of KTAL's license. The licensee and the groups negotiated and agreed upon a policy statement whereby KTAL would improve Texarkana local service. The groups withdrew the petition. The FCC approved the agreement as being in the public interest and renewed KTAL's license in 1969.[37] Citizen groups have since successfully negotiated, not only in renewals, but also in matters involving sales of stations to new owners, changes of entertainment formats, and responsiveness to local needs.

On the other hand, not all attempts to intervene have succeeded. Two residents of Salt Lake City, Utah, challenged the license renewal of KSL, an AM station in that city, objecting that the station had violated the Fairness Doctrine (which was still in effect at the time) and constituted one part of a local monopolistic media concentration (the Mormon church controlled KSL, a Salt Lake City newspaper, and a number of other local media outlets). The FCC refused to grant a hearing, and a federal court upheld the refusal.[38] The court ruled that the citizens' allegations did not suffice to show issues of fact substantial enough to require a hearing.[39] Additionally, the Commission has stated that a licensee does not have to negotiate or enter into agreements with citizen groups. Further, it is the licensee alone who has the responsibility to determine how to serve the public interest; no agreement may take that responsibility away from the licensee.[40]

---

[36] 425 F.2d 543.

[37] KCMC, Inc., 19 F.C.C.2d 109 (1969).

[38] Hale v. FCC, 425 F.2d 556 (1970).

[39] But, of course, it is possible that hearing proceedings themselves would have yielded substantial issues of fact!

[40] Citizen Agreements, 57 F.C.C.2d 42 (1975).

8.1.4   Comparative Broadcast Licensing Proceedings

Despite a judicially sanctioned legal provision allowing use of random selection procedures, the FCC holds hearings and uses its *comparative criteria* to select licensees from among mutually exclusive applications for full-power broadcast facilities. Over the years, court rulings and FCC actions have changed those criteria.

Earlier in this chapter we mentioned the comparative hearing. Two or more parties apply for the same frequency or channel, all meet the basic requirements for licensing, so the FCC designates the matter for hearing to compare applications and award the license. The comparative hearing is an adversary situation in which each applicant attempts to point out its own fine qualities and the negative qualities of all other applicants. After the hearing concludes and the record closes, based on all evidence submitted, the administrative law judge (ALJ) in charge of the hearing renders an initial decision. The decision is a written document that selects one applicant to receive the license and explains why that particular applicant was chosen. The decision, of course, is subject to appeal and review as described in EMG 4.1.5.

In 1965, the Commission adopted a *Policy Statement on Comparative Hearings*.[41] The statement established two primary objectives of such hearings—best practicable service to the public and diversification of control of mass media. Then it listed seven criteria on which applicants were to be judged and described how the Commission used and weighed each in comparative proceedings.[42] It explained that the Commission does not have to use these criteria, but they would help to achieve consistency and clarity and to eliminate extraneous time-consuming elements from the hearing process. After some adding and subtracting as a result of court rulings and Commission action,[43] the list of criteria was as follows:

1. diversification of control of the media of mass communication;
2. integration of ownership into management (factors considered include full-time participation in station operation by owners, local residence and past participation in civic affairs, minority ownership, daytimer status, female ownership, and past broadcast experience);
3. proposed program service;
4. past broadcast record (as an owner or owner/participant);
5. efficient use of frequency;
6. other factors;

---

[41] 1 F.C.C.2d 393.

[42] A footnote to the statement makes clear that the criteria do not apply to situations in which the licensee of an existing station has filed for renewal and other applicants have filed in attempts to get the station's channel. However, as we shall see, the statement has indeed been used for exactly such situations!

[43] For example, the Commission eliminated one of its original criteria, character, and subsequently treated it only as a basic qualification issue (EMG 7.1.2.2), and consideration of ethnic or racial minorities was added as a factor in the ownership integration criterion after the court ruling in TV 9, Inc. v. FCC, 495 F.2d 929 (1973); *cert. denied*, 419 U.S. 986 (1974).

7. use of auxiliary power equipment (so that, for example, if the electric utility company's line to a station goes down, the station can generate its own power and continue to operate).

In making a choice in comparative proceedings, the ALJ attempts to weigh each applicant's showing on each of the criteria designated as issues in the hearing, giving each factor the relative value suggested in the 1965 *Policy Statement.* Some examples illustrate: All other things being equal, the ALJ will prefer applicants who control no other medium of mass communication, especially broadcast stations, to those who do; applicants who will run proposed stations themselves to those who will be absentee owners and hire others to operate them; applicants who have lived in the community of (prospective) license to nonresident applicants; and applicants whose proposed station will make more efficient use of frequencies than those of other applicants. All other things being equal, applicants in a comparative hearing who have unusually poor records of previous station ownership are at a clear disadvantage.

In these examples we have used the phrase "all other things being equal." The problem is that "all other things" are rarely equal. One applicant, for example, will be superior in some areas, another in other areas, and the FCC must weigh all factors before making a decision. Some have suggested that the FCC should abandon comparative criteria and use instead a lottery or even an auction to select a licensee from among qualified competing applicants.

In 1982, the U.S. Congress provided the FCC with means to eliminate much of the trouble that devolves from mutually exclusive applications. It amended Section 309 of the Communications Act to allow the Commission to use random selection to grant the license or CP.[44] The Commission has to determine that all applicants meet basic requirements to hold a license. If two or more applicants qualify, the Commission can use random selection procedures—in effect, a lottery—to determine which applicant receives the grant. The law also directs the Commission to devise means to ensure that the random selection procedures are weighted to give preference to applicants who would increase diversification of ownership in broadcasting, especially members of minority groups (EMG 8.1.2.4.1).

The FCC moved to use a lottery process to select among applicants for contested channels in the case of LPTV and TV translator stations.[45] However, for full-power broadcast stations, the Commission said that it would use a lottery only as a tiebreaker in comparative proceedings.[46] In other words, mutually exclusive applications for full-power broadcast facilities would go all the way through the hearing stage, then—if the ALJ applied the comparative criteria and found two or more

---

[44] Pub. L. No. 97-259, 98 Stat. 1087. Congress had first written random selection procedures into the law in 1981. 95 Stat. 736. However, the Commission was unable to devise the required weighting procedures and so voted not to implement random selection. Lottery Selection among Applicants, 89 F.C.C.2d 257 (1982). Congress subsequently passed the 1982 law and corrected the problems.

[45] Lottery Selection among Applicants, 93 F.C.C.2d 952 (1983).

[46] Lottery Selection among Applicants, 57 Rad. Reg. 2d (P&F) 427 (1984).

applicants equally qualified—the award of the license would be determined using random selection procedures. The procedures would *not* be weighted in favor of minority applicants. This could be done, said the FCC, because it would use lottery tiebreakers under the general public interest authority granted by the Communications Act, not under the 1982 amendment to Section 309.

But the Commission was wrong. A 1988 appeals court decision[47] held that the FCC could not hold preferenceless lotteries. The FCC, said the court, had exceeded its authority; such preferences must be accorded in *any* license selection procedures that come within the broad meaning of the term *system of random selection.*

The question remained: Should the Commission use lotteries to *replace* completely the comparative hearing process in the selection of licensees for contested AM, FM, and TV facilities? In 1990, the FCC decided that such replacement would not serve the public interest.[48] The potential efficiency gains from use of lotteries, said the Commission, would be outweighed by a possible reduction in licensee quality. The Commission would, instead, direct its efforts toward improving the efficiency and integrity of the traditional comparative hearing process. In 1994, however, the FCC announced that it was putting a freeze on comparative proceedings, a result of the court decision in *Bechtel* v. *FCC* (1993).[49] The court had ruled that the integration of ownership into management, one of the principal criteria used in evaluating applicants for new broadcast facilities, was arbitrary and capricious and therefore unlawful, and the Commission would process no more comparative proceedings until it decided what to do next. Meanwhile, in 1993, Congress passed legislation authorizing the *auction* of certain frequencies (EMG 8.2.4). This was a first; and while none of the regular AM, FM, or TV frequencies were involved, some viewed this law as a precedent that could eventually affect the manner in which broadcast licensees are selected.

8.1.5   Broadcast License Renewal Procedures

Radio stations must apply for renewal of license every seven years; television stations, every five years.

---

[47] Telecommunications Research and Action Ctr. v. FCC, 836 F.2d 1349 (1988). This case actually developed out of Commission rules by which tiebreaker lotteries would be used in the award of licenses for the instructional television fixed service without the media diversity and minority ownership preferences mandated by Section 309.

[48] Random Selection of Broadcast Applicants, 5 F.C.C.R. 4002 (1990).

[49] 10 F.3d 875. The Bechtel appeal aimed specifically at the FCC's policy of awarding comparative credit to an applicant who, if granted a broadcast license, would participate in the day-to-day management of the station. The FCC's freeze announcement is reported in "Washington Watch," *Broadcasting & Cable,* 3 Jan. 1994, at 53. The FCC had already made changes designed to streamline its procedures, speed up the appeals process, and encourage settlements among competing applicants. Comparative Hearing Process, 6 F.C.C.R. 157 (1990); and Comparative Hearing Process (Reconsideration), 6 F.C.C.R. 3403 (1991). It had also opened proceedings to review the criteria themselves. Reexamination of the Policy Statement on Comparative Broadcast Hearings, 7 F.C.C.R. 2664 (1992), and 8 F.C.C.R. 5475 (1993).

Those maximum terms are set in Section 307(c) of the Communications Act. Near the end of a term, a licensee who wishes to renew for another term must file application, and the FCC may grant renewal only if it first finds that such grant would serve the public interest. However, the FCC's Mass Media Bureau must process renewal applications for 2,500–3,000 full-power broadcast stations each year (plus those for translator, booster, ITFS, auxiliary, and cable antenna relay stations) and cannot possibly investigate each applicant. So, in fact, renewal is granted routinely. Generally, only the following situations will trigger renewal problems: obvious misrepresentations, inconsistencies, or missing information on the application; citizen complaints in the station's file; informal objections; petitions to deny; or applications from other parties to use the station's frequency (discussed in the next section).

All radio licenses in a given state expire at 3:00 A.M., local time, on the first day of a particular month every seven years; all television licenses, every five years. The Commission has set expiration dates so that the broadcast station licenses of a different state or group of states expire every other month (starting with February).[50]

8.1.5.1 *Filing*

At renewal time the FCC requires of the licensee several items—information on EEO, contracts, and for TV applicants, children's programming—in addition to the renewal application.

A station must file for renewal no later than four months prior to the expiration date.[51] In completing the renewal application form,[52] a TV applicant must respond to, among other things, several requirements of the Children's' Television Act of 1991. The form asks whether the licensee has complied with the act's commercial limits (EMG 13.3.1),[53] and it calls for an attachment showing compliance with the act's programming requirements (EMG 10.1.2.2.1).

The renewal application, accompanied by the station's Broadcast Equal Employment Opportunity Program Report[54] and the filing fee, is sent to the FCC's Gettysburg, Pennsylvania offices.[55] Additionally, the station must have on file with the FCC copies of all contracts as described in EMG 8.1.6.2 (below) and, if it has five or more employees, a current Broadcast Station Annual Employment Report.[56]

8.1.5.2 *Other Renewal Duties.*   Other renewal duties include insertion of certain materials in the station's public inspection file and broadcast of prefiling and postfiling announcements. Those "certain materials" that go into the file include a statement that the prefiling announcements were broadcast, a statement that the

---

[50] 47 C.F.R. § 73.1020.

[51] 47 C.F.R. § 73.3500.

[52] FCC Form 303-S.

[53] If the response is negative, the applicant must list and explain those programs that exceeded the limit.

[54] FCC Form 396.

[55] Transfer of Certain Application Processing Functions, 58 Fed. Reg. 19,771, Apr. 16, 1993.

[56] FCC Form 395B.

postfiling announcements have been scheduled, and one copy of the completed application form and the accompanying reports and attachments sent to the Commission for renewal. The announcements are discussed more fully immediately below; the file, in EMG 8.1.6.4.

8.1.5.3   *Renewal Notices*

The license renewal process requires the licensee to use the station to make prefiling and postfiling announcements to the public.

The local notification procedures for renewal differ somewhat from those of most other applications, described earlier in this chapter. The renewal notice must begin six months before the expiration date of the station license (which is two months before the renewal application is filed), and the station must broadcast the notice on the first and sixteenth days of each month at specified times. The Commission also specifies exact wording. In the month that the licensee submits the renewal application, the required wording changes, and the station must carry this announcement for three months. So there are actually two forms of the renewal notice—the prefiling announcement and the postfiling announcement. One says that the application will be filed; the other, that it has been filed. Otherwise, both carry essentially the same message: that renewal time approaches, that members of the community may examine the renewal application, and that members of the community may file with the FCC petitions and comments concerning the application and the station's performance in meeting the public interest.[57]

8.1.6   Additional Broadcast Station Regulatory Requirements

Licensees have certain ongoing FCC responsibilities.

We have finished with our discussion of license renewal procedures per se. FCC requirements, however, are a fact of operational life for broadcast licensees not just at license renewal time but all year round every year. They can affect the regulatory status of a station; a licensee that is derelict in fulfilling these requirements risks trouble with the FCC—a warning, a forfeiture, perhaps even problems at license renewal time. We would, therefore, be remiss if we did not discuss these ongoing requirements in a comprehensive review of broadcast station licensing such as this.

Many of these requirements are technical in nature. Certainly keeping equipment operating within prescribed parameters, staying on frequency, and maintaining the required station logs and technical records[58] are essential. But given decent equipment and conscientious supervision and training of a reliable operational staff, these requirements *should be* fairly routine. There are other requirements, how-

---

[57] 47 C.F.R. § 73.3580.
[58] *See, e.g.,* 47 C.F.R. §§ 73.1800, 73.1820, and 73.1835.

ever, that involve certain aspects connected with the business of being a broadcaster, and they usually require the direct attention of the licensee or of high-level station management employees. These include the filing of reports and contracts, adhering to a program of equal employment opportunity, and maintaining a public inspection file. (Not addressed in this section is that group of requirements that many feel to be most important of all: programming. Regulatory requirements and restrictions on programming are the sole subject of five entire chapters—9, 10, 11, 12, and 13.)

8.1.6.1 *Reports*

A licensee must report to the FCC on employment and ownership annually.

The Commission requires each licensee with five or more employees to file on or before May 31 of each year an Employment Report.[59] The licensee must also file an Ownership Report[60] once a year. This is due on the annual anniversary date of the once-every-five-years or once-every-seven-years renewal date. However, for any given year, if there have been no changes since the last Ownership Report was filed, the licensee does not have to file a new one. The Commission will accept instead certification that the licensee has reviewed the existing report and that the report is accurate.[61]

8.1.6.2 *Contracts*

A licensee who enters into or changes certain types of agreements or contracts must file a copy with the FCC within 30 days. Certain other contracts must be retained at the station.

These include network affiliation contracts, almost any documents having to do with ownership or control of the station, management consultant contracts, and any management contracts that provide for someone to share both profits and losses of the station. The licensee keeps certain other contracts at the station ready for inspection upon request by the Commission—time brokerage contracts involving radio stations whose signals overlap, contracts in which the station has leased out use of the information-carrying functions of its subcarrier or vertical blanking interval to others (EMG 6.2.1.5, 6.2.2.5, and 6.3.4), contracts with chief operators,[62] and time sales contracts with any advertiser who buys four or more hours per day

---

[59] FCC Form 395B. 47 C.F.R. § 73.3612.

[60] FCC Form 323; 323E for noncommercial stations.

[61] 47 C.F.R. § 73.3615. Of course, as explained earlier in this chapter, any change of ownership that also involves transfer of control of the station (gain or loss of 50 percent or more of the ownership shares) requires prior FCC approval.

For years, the FCC also required annual filing of a form on which licensees reported income and expenditures in various categories and the resulting profit or loss. The Commission then used the data to compile annual financial statistics for the trade. However, in 1982 the FCC eliminated the annual financial report.

[62] The licensee of each AM, FM, or TV broadcast station must designate a person holding a commercial radio operator license or permit to serve as the station's chief operator. This individual is responsible

(except for programs such as athletic contests, musical programs, and other long-form special events).[63]

8.1.6.3   *Equal Employment Opportunity Program*

Broadcast licensees must establish a positive and ongoing program for equal employment opportunity. That program is proposed when first applying for a license, its implementation is reported at license renewal time, and its results are submitted annually. The FCC evaluates each station's EEO effort at license renewal time; stations found deficient are subject to additional investigation. The FCC also conducts a midterm review of each TV station's employment practices.

As mentioned in EMG 5.5, the FCC has adopted requirements for equal employment opportunity. These requirments, set forth in FCC rule 73.2080, state in part:

> Equal opportunity in employment shall be afforded by *all licensees or permittees* of commercially or noncommercially operated AM, FM, TV, or international broadcast stations . . . to all qualified persons, and no person shall be discriminated against in employment by such stations because of race, color, religion, national origin, or sex.[64]

In 1992 those requirements were locked into law with an amendment that directed the Commission not to revise rule 73.2080 or the forms used to report pertinent employment data except as directed by Congress.[65] Licensees are expected to comply through both avoidance of discrimination and affirmative action to ensure equal employment opportunity (EEO). Each station must establish and put into effect a positive, continuing program to afford minorities and women equal opportunity in all areas of employment. The Commission defines minorities as "Blacks not of Hispanic origin, Asians or Pacific Islanders, American Indians or Alaskan Natives, and Hispanics."[66] The areas of employment with which the FCC is concerned include recruitment, selection, training, placement, promotion, pay, working conditions, demotion, layoff, and termination. The goals of the program are set forth in Box 8.1.

Additionally, as we briefly discussed previously in this chapter, licensees or prospective licensees must submit certain documents to the Commission in which they (1) describe what type of EEO program they plan, (2) explain how they have implemented that plan, and (3) report the actual employment statistics that have resulted from the plan. One of these documents is the Broadcast Equal Employment Opportunity Model Program Report.[67] The FCC requires that initial and transfer

---

for certain FCC-required inspections, calibrations, measurements, and technical records. 47 C.F.R. § 73.1870.

[63] 47 C.F.R. § 73.3613.

[64] 47 C.F.R. § 73.2080. Italics added.

[65] 47 U.S.C. § 334(a).

[66] EEO Rules for Broadcasters, 2 F.C.C.R. 3967 (1987).

[67] FCC Form 396A.

BOX 8.1   Equal Employment Opportunity Program

Under the terms of its program, a station shall:

1. define the responsibility of each level of management to ensure a positive application and vigorous enforcement of its policy of equal opportunity, and establish a procedure to review and control managerial and supervisory performance;
2. inform its employees and recognized employee organizations of the positive equal employment opportunity policy and program and enlist their cooperation;
3. communicate its equal employment opportunity policy and program and its employment needs to sources of qualified applicants without regard to race, color, religion, national origin, or sex, and solicit their recruitment assistance on a continuing basis;
4. conduct a continuing program to exclude all unlawful forms of prejudice or discrimination based upon race, color, religion, national origin, or sex from its personnel policies and practices and working conditions; and
5. conduct a continuing review of job structure and employment practices and adopt positive recruitment, job design, and other measures needed to ensure genuine equality of opportunity to participate fully in all organizational units, occupations, and levels of responsibility.

SOURCE: 47 C.F.R. § 73.2080(b).

---

applicants use this form to set forth the EEO program they plan if their application for license is granted.

At license renewal time, all licensees must submit a Broadcast Equal Employment Opportunity Program Report.[68] A renewal applicant whose station has fewer than five full-time employees need complete only those parts of the form that require identification of the station and licensee and certification that the contents of the form are true. Applicants with five or more full-time employees, however, use this form to report *specifically* how the EEO program requirements listed in Box 8.2 have been carried out. The form asks who is the EEO-responsible officer in the station, the means by which the station's policy was disseminated, where and how the station recruited women and minorities, what were the statistics on hiring and promotion over a specific 12-month period,[69] the availability of women and minori-

---

[68] FCC Form 396.

[69] The station may not satisfy EEO requirements by hiring women only in secretarial positions and minorities only in custodial and other menial positions. Form 396 requires specific information about the total positions filled and the percentage filled with women and minorities in the "upper four" job

---

BOX 8.2   EEO Program Requirements

A broadcast station's equal employment opportunity program should reasonably address itself to the specific areas set forth below, to the extent possible, and to the extent that they are appropriate in terms of the station's size, location, and so forth:

1. disseminate its equal opportunity program to job applicants and employees;
2. use minority organizations, organizations for women, media, educational institutions, and other potential sources of minority and female applicants, to supply referrals whenever job vacancies are available in its operation;
3. evaluate its employment profile and job turnover against the availability of minorities and women in its recruitment area;
4. undertake to offer promotions of qualified minorities and women in a nondiscriminatory fashion to positions of greater responsibility;
5. analyze its efforts to recruit, hire, and promote minorities and women and address any difficulties encountered in implementing its equal employment opportunity program.

SOURCE: 47 C.F.R. § 73.2080(c).

---

ties in the local labor force,[70] and whether there were complaints against the station alleging discriminatory employment practices.

Every year licensees with five or more full-time employees must file a Broadcast Station Annual Employment Report.[71] Licensees must use this form to report the ways in which their EEO programs have worked out in actual practice. They fill in two separate tables, one for full-time employees and one for part-time employees; this is to prevent the hiring of women and minorities only as part-time employees. In each table they state the number of persons in each of several job categories and, within each category, the number that were male, female, and each of the FCC's minority categories. A group broadcaster must ensure not only that each of the group's owned stations has filed an employment report but also that a report has been submitted for headquarters employees whose duties involve operational management of the stations.

---

categories—officials and managers, sales personnel, technicians, and "professionals." Professional positions are those that require either a college degree or enough experience to provide a comparable background. They include positions such as on-air personnel, reporters, writers, producers, directors, artists, accountants, programmers, and film buyers.

[70] All licensees with five or more employees must file EEO program information on women. However, licensees in markets where minorities constitute less than 5 percent of the labor force do not have to file such information for minorities.

[71] FCC Form 395B.

The FCC reviews a station's EEO effort at license renewal time using a two-step approach. The first step consists of an initial evaluation based on all available information concerning the station's EEO record. Such information consists of the station's Broadcast Equal Employment Opportunity Program Report, any EEO complaints filed against the station, the composition of the station's workforce as compared with the area labor force, and any other pertinent data. If the station has an acceptable EEO record, no further analysis takes place. If not, the second step is taken. The station is subjected to an investigation of the EEO areas in which it appears to be deficient. This investigation will involve requests that the licensee submit additional information on those areas. For a station that is not in compliance with FCC EEO requirements, the Commission may impose a variety of remedies. These include admonishment ("the raised eyebrow," EMG 4.1.7.1), reporting conditions,[72] short-term renewal, forfeiture, and for particularly egregious cases, designation for hearing.[73]

A comparison of station workforce to area labor force is used as the primary vehicle by which to identify stations that require further investigation. A station with an employment profile that falls outside of the FCC's processing guidelines[74] will be sure to trigger the second phase. However, in its primary statement on the process, *EEO Rules for Broadcasters,* 2 F.C.C.R. 3967 (1987), the Commission emphasized that each station's *overall* record is fully examined regardless of its profile and even if the profile is within the FCC's processing guidelines. The ultimate assessment of EEO compliance is not determined solely on the basis of quantitative tests of minority and female employment. There must be positive and continuing effort, and licensees are not to regard the processing guidelines as quotas or "safe harbors."

TV stations actually have yet another review of EEO efforts. This one was written into law by the 1992 cable act, Section 22(f) of which amended the Communications Act[75] to require that the FCC conduct a "midterm review." The Commission reviews each TV station's employment practices halfway through its license term for advisory purposes. Where the review reveals problems that could affect the next license renewal if uncorrected, the Commission so informs the licensee; a poor review by itself does not hurt the station's chance for renewal.[76]

---

[72] This sanction usually consists of requiring the station to submit three successive annual reports detailing the steps it has taken to bring its EEO program into compliance.

[73] EEO Rules for Broadcasters; Beaumont Branch of the NAACP and the Nat'l Black Media Coalition v. FCC, 854 F.2d 501, at 506 (1988); Bilingual Bicultural Coalition on Mass Media v. FCC, 595 F.2d 621 (1978).

[74] The Commission has provided its staff with processing guidelines by which the percentages of women and minorities among a station's employees are compared with those in the area's labor force. The staff of a station with 5 to 10 full-time employees should include women and minority-group members at a ratio of at least 50 percent of their availability in the labor force overall; in the upper four job categories (note 69), at least 25 percent. For a station with 10 or more employees, those ratios should be at least 50 percent both for the total staff and for the upper four job categories. Public Notice No. 80-61, released February 13, 1980.

[75] 47 U.S.C. § 334(b).

[76] Implementation of Section 22 of the Cable Television Consumer Protection and Competition Act of 1992; Equal Employment Opportunities, 8 F.C.C.R. 5389 (1993).

8.1.6.4 Public Inspection File.   The FCC requires that each broadcast station maintain a public inspection file at the station for any member of the community to request and examine.[77] The required contents of the file are listed in Box 8.3.

The FCC requires licensees to maintain the public inspection file so that members of the community can participate in the license renewal process. The records, reports, and letters in the file provide the facts. The booklet, *The Public and Broadcasting—A Procedural Manual,*[78] tells how to use these facts in dealing with the FCC. It describes how to file complaints, to participate in application proceedings (including informal objections and petitions to deny), to participate in a hearing proceeding, to petition for rule making, and to find needed information.[79]

A member of the community may inspect the public file during regular business hours without an appointment (although, for the convenience of all concerned, one should probably be made). A licensee usually maintains the file at the station. FCC rules, however, allow the file to be located at any other publicly accessible place, such as a public registry for documents or an attorney's office. Copies may be requested of anything in the file; the station may charge reasonable costs of reproduction and has seven days to get the copies ready (longer, if the city of license contains no reproduction facilities). The station does not, however, have to honor mail requests for copies.

8.1.6.5 Regulatory Fees
Broadcasters and other regulated media must pay a yearly regulatory fee.

In 1993, the administration of President Bill Clinton proposed a budget designed to reduce the federal deficit.[80] One of the revenue-generating measures included in the bill as passed by Congress was a requirement that communications businesses regulated by the FCC pay for the cost of that regulation. Estimates were that these annual regulatory fees would bring in some $82 million a year. The fee that a full-power broadcaster pays is determined by service (AM or FM radio; VHF or UHF television) and market size. The federal fee schedule also includes low-power TV stations, TV translator stations, TV booster stations, broadcast auxiliary stations, cable systems, cable antenna relay stations, telephone services (cellular, personal communications service, local, long-distance, and competitive access provider), satellite receive-only earth stations, and satellites.

8.1.7 Loss of Broadcast License

Three avenues/situations that can lead to loss of license include (1) violations of law or regulation, (2) a strike application, and (3) a petition to deny renewal. A

---

[77] 47 C.F.R. § 73.3526.

[78] 49 F.C.C.2d 1 (1974).

[79] The Public and Broadcasting—A Procedure Manual, 49 F.C.C.2d 1.

[80] Budget Reconciliation Act, FY 1994, Pub. L. No. 103-66, 107 Stat. 312 (1993). The FCC started rule-making procedures to implement these fees in 1994. 1994 F.C.C. online Archives NRMC4017.TXT (FCC proposes to implement a new Section 9 of the Communications Act—assessment and collection of regulatory fees).

BOX 8.3   Public Inspection File Contents

All stations must include the following:

1. Copies of various documents the station has filed with the FCC such as
   a. Applications (for example, the current application for renewal of license) and all documents related to, or required to accompany, those applications
   b. Citizen agreements, any to which the station is party
2. Ownership reports, all since 1965
3. Political file, the contents of which are discussed in EMG 12.6
4. Employment Reports, all
5. The Public and Broadcasting—A Procedural Manual, an FCC publication
6. Written comments and suggestions from the public concerning station operation*
7. Quarterly programs/issues list (a result of the ascertainment process, EMG 10.1.2.1)†
8. Statement of compliance with requirement (EMG 8.1.5.2) for prefiling and postfiling announcements (if a renewal applicant)

Commercial TV stations (only) must include the following:

9. Records to back up the licensee's certification (on the license renewal application) that the station has complied with the commercial limitations on children's programming (EMG 13.3.1), updated on an annual or quarterly basis
10. Records to show how the station served the educational and informational needs of children as described in EMG 10.1.2.2.1

Commercial radio stations (only) must include the following:

9. Time brokerage contracts to which the station is a party (EMG 8.1.6.2), either as the brokering station or the brokered station

Noncommercial stations (only) must include the following:

9. Records to show compliance with programming requirements of the Children's Television Act of 1991
10. List of donors who supported specific programs

SOURCE: 47 C.F.R. § 73.3526.

---

* Specific requirements for inclusions and arrangement are in 47 C.F.R. § 73.1202.
† Noncommercial educational FM radio stations that are Class D or whose programming is wholly educational are exempt from this requirement.

licensee may avoid a hearing by selling the station to a minority at a distress-sale price.

In EMG 4.1.7.8 and 4.1.7.9 we discussed the FCC's two most severe sanctions for erring broadcasters. One is denial of renewal; the other, revocation. In that section we also discussed the role and frequency of violations of law and regulation as factors in loss of license. In this section we focus on the competing application and the petition to deny—two other factors that sometimes serve as the means by which those violations of law and regulation come to light. But first, we deal with an escape mechanism, the distress sale.

8.1.7.1   *Distress Sales.*

Normally, once the FCC has designated the license of a station for hearing, the broadcaster may not sell the station to avoid losing the license through nonrenewal or revocation. The rationale behind this restriction is that, if the allegations of wrongdoing (whatever they may be) are true, the licensee should *not* be allowed to benefit in any way—certainly not by being allowed to continue to operate the station, but also not by profiting from sale of the station. However, there is an exception to this general rule: the distress sale. The Commission set forth the concept of distress sales in 1978 with the adoption of a *Statement of Policy on Minority Ownership of Broadcast Facilities;*[81] that is, a licensee faced with a renewal or revocation hearing could sell the station to an applicant with significant minority interest. Two years later the FCC defined distress-sale price as 75 percent of fair market value.[82] This policy both allows an allegedly errant licensee to get off the hook and works toward the FCC's goal of increasing minority ownership in broadcasting.

The FCC's policy of minority preference, as manifest in the distress-sale policy and the comparative hearing criteria (EMG 8.1.4), was challenged in court twice, the result of FCC decisions in two unrelated cases. The appeals court ruled on both in 1989. In one decision, a three-judge panel said that the use of minority criteria in comparative hearings was constitutional.[83] In the other decision, a different panel of the same court ruled that the distress-sale policy was *not* constitutional, that it "unduly burdens . . . an innocent nonminority, and is not reasonably related to the interests it seeks to vindicate."[84] Some legal experts suggested that the second opinion, should it ultimately prevail, might also mean the end of the FCC's tax certificate program (EMG 8.1.2.4.1).[85] At this point, then, the judicial verdict on the FCC's policies aimed at helping minorities gain access to broadcast ownership was split. Both cases went to the U.S. Supreme Court, and in the consolidated decision, *Metro Broadcasting* v. *FCC,*[86] the high court ruled that neither the minority preference in comparative hearings nor the minority distress-sale policy violated the equal protection clause of the Fifth Amendment of the U.S. Constitution. Both served impor-

---

[81] 68 F.C.C.2d 1689.

[82] Grayson Enterprises, Inc., 77 F.C.C.2d 152 (1980).

[83] Winter Park Communications v. FCC, 873 F.2d 347 (1989).

[84] Shurberg Broadcasting v. FCC, 876 F.2d 902 (1989).

[85] "Distress Sales Unconstitutional, Says Court," *Broadcasting,* 3 Apr. 1989, at 32.

[86] 497 U.S. 547 (1990).

tant governmental objectives within the power of Congress and were substantially related to the achievement of those objectives. Further, neither policy imposed undue burdens on nonminorities; nonminority applicants could have no legitimate expectation that their applications would be granted without consideration of public interest factors. The interest in enhancing diversity of broadcast programming was an important governmental objective.

8.1.7.2 Petitions to Deny and Competing Renewal Applications

In challenges of applications to renew license, the FCC limits payments in negotiated settlements and awards a *renewal expectancy* to deserving incumbents.

Occasionally, one or more parties will challenge the incumbent licensee at renewal time. In some cases, the challenger petitions the FCC to deny renewal of the license[87]—perhaps a citizen group dissatisfied with the way the station has served the public interest, as in the KTAL case (EMG 8.1.3.2). In other cases, the challenger files as a competitor for the license. This, too, could be a citizen group, but it could also be individuals hoping to get the license and run their own station as a business. In either situation, the charge is often that the incumbent licensee has not done well in serving the public. If the FCC judges the petition to deny, it may designate the matter for hearing; the Communications Act requires a hearing for all competing applications.

8.1.7.2.1 Payment to Challengers.
The incumbent, meanwhile, may attempt to negotiate with the challenger. If the negotiation is successful and the challenger agrees to withdraw, they seek FCC approval of the settlement. Conditions of the settlement have often required the incumbent to pay the challenger. This gave rise to charges by licensees that most such challenges amount to blackmail. Competing applications filed for this purpose were labeled *strike applications*. Petitions to deny were often said to be used primarily to extort huge amounts of money and concessions from the applicant. Broadcasters saw this as a very real problem and, since such an extortion represented an abuse of process, the FCC took steps to remedy the situation. In 1989, the Commission revised its rules to curb such practices,[88] labeling them "abuses" of the renewal process. The Commission limited payments and said that it would scrutinize such settlements to ensure that they were in the public interest.

8.1.7.2.2 Renewal Expectancy.
If the matter goes to hearing, the FCC listens to both sides. And in a *comparative renewal* hearing, the challenger would appear to have the advantage. The incumbent is almost always bound to have made some mistakes in running the station, and the challenger will be sure to bring those to light; the challenger, on the other hand, having had no station, will have made no mistakes. No matter how good the incumbent's record in serving the public interest, the challenger could promise more. And the challenger's application would

---

[87] The petition to deny is not limited to full-power AM, FM, and TV broadcast stations; it can be used in all licensing situations, from low-power television to direct broadcast satellite.
[88] Broadcast Renewal Applications, 4 F.C.C.R. 4780 (1989).

certainly be structured to look better than the incumbent's in any weighing of comparative criteria (EMG 8.1.4).

A 1982 appeals court decision,[89] however, helped to tilt the process more toward the incumbent. That decision affirmed the Commission's policy of granting a *renewal expectancy* to deserving incumbents.[90] An incumbent earns a renewal expectancy by demonstrating "meritorious" service to the public—usually a substantial record with respect to ascertainment, programming to meet the problems, needs, and interests of the community, and programming to meet the informational and educational needs of children. The expectancy outweighs any comparative advantage the challenger might have as a result of comparative criteria; the better the incumbent's record, the greater the expectancy to which the incumbent is entitled.

In its 1989 rules revision,[91] the FCC further tilted the process toward the incumbent by reducing both the opportunity to settle and the amount of money involved. Under the revised rules an incumbent may make *no* payment if a challenger withdraws a strike application before the initial decision in a comparative hearing. The incumbent *may* make a payment for settlement after the initial decision, but even then, the Commission limits such payments to "legitimate and prudent expenses." These restrictions are designed to reduce the chances that a competitor will file an application just for the purpose of extorting large sums of money[92] (EMG 8.1.7.2.1) and to prevent such competitors from pressuring incumbents to settle early in the comparative proceedings.

Under the changed rules, competing applicants can no longer presume that they can acquire the incumbent's transmitter site (should the incumbent lose), a presumption that previously allowed challengers to avoid completing the engineering portion of their applications and to avoid having to find a new transmitter site. And the FCC revised its construction permit application to require more detailed financial, ownership, and management-ownership integration information. On the previous form, applicants had only to check a box indicating they were "financially qualified"; on the revised form, they have to estimate the cost of building and operating the station and list their sources of funding. This applies to all applications, yet its primary purpose is to deter the submission of competing applications aimed at extortion.

8.2   LICENSING OF OTHER WIRELESS MASS MEDIA

Some of the other wireless media go through licensing procedures very similar to those described for full-power broadcast stations. Others are quite different, and what is different about them is usually that the procedures are much simpler. Some licensing procedures are shared by almost all; for example, the requirement to consult with certain sensitive radio installations (EMG 8.1.1.2) and the possibility of having to submit an Environmental Assessment (EMG 8.1.1.1). Each service has its own application forms as illustrated by Box 8.4, and their license terms vary as

---

[89] Central Fla. Enter. v. FCC, 683 F.2d 503 (1982).

[90] Cowles Broadcasting, Inc., 86 F.C.C.2d 993 (1981).

[91] See note 88.

[92] Rather than for the purpose of obtaining a license and operating a station.

BOX 8.4 FCC Application Forms: A Sampler

The following titles illustrate the variety of application forms used by the Federal Communications Commission. These are just a few of the forms used for just a few of the various services regulated by the FCC.

CP APPLICATION

301	Commercial Broadcast Station
340	Noncommercial Educational Broadcast Station
309	International or Experimental Broadcast Station
346	Low-Power TV, TV Translator, or TV Booster Station
349	FM Translator or FM Booster Station
330	Instructional Television Fixed Service (Authorization, but license needed also)
494	Microwave Radio Station (MDS and MMDS; no separate license needed, but Form 494-A must be filed to certify completion of construction)

LICENSE APPLICATION

302	Broadcast Station
302-FM	FM Broadcast Station
310	International, Experimental Television, Experimental [over-the-air] Facsimile, or Developmental Broadcast Station
347	Low-Power TV, TV Translator, or TV Booster Station
350	FM Translator or FM Booster Station
313	Auxiliary Radio Broadcast
327	Cable Television Relay Service (Applies for authorization [no separate CP needed] and renewal)
330-L	Instructional Television Fixed Service

LICENSE RENEWAL

303-S	Commercial and Noncommercial AM, FM, or TV Broadcast Station
311	International or Experimental Broadcast Station
348	Translator [TV and FM] or Low-Power Television Station
313-R	Auxiliary Broadcast Station (short-form)
330-R	Instructional Television Fixed Station and Response Station and Low-Power Relay Station
405-A	Specified Services (including MDS and MMDS)

BOX 8.5   License Terms for LPTV, Translator, Booster, Auxiliary, and Experimental Stations

LPTV and TV Translator Stations: 5 years, on a staggered schedule similar to that for full-power TV stations.

FM Translator Stations: 7 years, on a staggered schedule similar to that for full-power FM stations.

TV and FM Boosters Stations: Concurrent with the term of the primary station's license.

Auxiliary Broadcast Stations: By type of licensee—

  Broadcast station: Concurrent with the term of the broadcast station's license.

  Radio and cable networks, Cable TV operators, Motion picture producers, TV program producers: Concurrent with the term of area broadcast licenses.

  TV networks: 5 years from date of grant.

Cable Television Relay Stations: 5 years from date of grant.

Experimental Broadcast Stations: 1 year.

Instructional Television Fixed Stations: 5 years from date of grant.

Multipoint Distribution Stations: 10 years (expiration date is May 1 of the expiration year).

SOURCE: 47 C.F.R. § 21.45, 74.15, 78.29.

---

illustrated in Box 8.5. We shall look at low-power television, translator, and booster stations; the omnidirectional microwave services; and direct broadcast satellites. Finally, we look at new means of awarding licenses in the nonbroadcast spectrum, the pioneer's preference, and the auction.

8.2.1   LPTV, Translator, and Booster Station Licensing

LPTV and TV translator station licensees are usually chosen with a lottery. The license terms of LPTV, translator, and booster stations parallel those of full-power TV and radio stations.

The licensing process for low-power television (LPTV) stations (EMG 6.4.1) and for translator and booster stations (EMG 6.4.2) is very similar to that of full-power broadcast stations. The major exception involves mutually exclusive applications for LPTV and television translator stations. In such situations the FCC uses random selection procedures—a lottery—to pick the licensee.[93]

---

[93] 47 C.F.R. § 1.1601.

The lottery begins with the Commission issuing a public notice that announces the opening of a national "window," a filing period during which interested parties may submit applications.[94] The filing period lasts for five days, and no one party may submit more than five applications for new LPTV and TV translator stations in a single filing period.[95] After receiving the applications, the Commission issues another public notice announcing the specifics of the public lottery, describing each applicant's preferences[96] and selection probabilities, and assigning each applicant a block of numbers.[97] Once the lottery is held, the Commission issues yet another public notice announcing the winner of the lottery as a tentative selectee; then if the FCC determines that the public interest would be served, the selectee is awarded a construction permit.[98] The FCC accepts applications for TV booster stations at any time. If there are mutually exclusive applications, the licensee is selected by a lottery. Mutually exclusive applications for FM translator and FM booster stations, however, require comparative hearings.

With respect to license renewals, LPTV stations that originate programming must broadcast prefiling and postfiling announcements as close to the schedule required of full-power TV stations as possible. LPTV stations that do no local origination, and TV and FM translator stations and booster stations, must give notice of their filing in a local newspaper.[99] None has to maintain a public inspection file, but LPTV stations must file annual employment reports,[100] are subject to equal employment opportunity requirements,[101] and must file network affiliation contracts with the FCC.[102]

8.2.2 Licensing of Omnidirectional Microwave Stations

The FCC selects from among mutually exclusive applications in the ITFS using comparative criteria and in the MDS/MMDS using a lottery. Wireless cable operators must make certain showings to be licensed to use ITFS channels. A licensee of an MDS/MMDS station must choose to operate as a common carrier or a non–common carrier and has some requirements that differ from those of a broadcast station licensee.

---

[94] Low Power Television and Translator Service, 102 F.C.C.2d 195 (1984); 47 C.F.R. § 73.3572.
[95] 47 C.F.R. § 73.3564(d).
[96] The legal mandate for minority preferences in lottery selection procedures was discussed in EMG 8.1.4.
[97] These are the numbers that will represent the applicant in the drawing: the greater the preference given the applicant, the more numbers that applicant receives, and the greater the chance that a number representing that applicant will be selected in the drawing.
[98] 47 C.F.R. § 73.3572. In other words, the Commission first holds the lottery, then examines the application to determine if the selectee is qualified to be a licensee.
[99] 47 C.F.R. § 73.3580(d) and (g).
[100] 47 C.F.R. § 73.3612.
[101] 47 C.F.R. § 73.2080.
[102] 47 C.F.R. § 73.3613.

As we noted in EMG 7.3.2, the FCC licenses ITFS stations only to certain types of educational institutions. In deciding among mutually exclusive applications for ITFS channels, the FCC uses comparative criteria. Among those criteria are elements such as local ownership, number of channels requested, and number of programming hours proposed. As a tiebreaker, the FCC considers the number of students for whom ITFS programming would constitute all or part of formal class material.

When the applicant for an unused ITFS channel is a wireless cable operator, that fact must be stated in a cover letter attached to the completed application form.[103] The applicant must also make the following showings:

1. there will still remain, if the license is awarded, at least eight other ITFS channels available for future use by instructional licensees;
2. the applicant already has a license or lease rights for (or is about to get a license for) at least four MDS/MMDS channels;[104] and
3. no other MDS/MMDS channels are available.

In the event of competing applications from a qualified applicant who would operate the channels as ITFS facilities, the ITFS applicant would be awarded the contested channel(s).[105]

In applying for an MDS/MMDS station, an applicant must submit a statement indicating whether the proposed station will operate on a common carrier basis or a non–common carrier basis (EMG 7.3.4).[106] A common carrier applicant must make clear any possible relationship with a program originator. Licensees are selected from among mutually exclusive applications using a lottery.[107]

MDS/MMDS licensees have a number of requirements similar to those of broadcast licensees. For example, applications must make certain public interest showings;[108] reflect possession of the necessary qualifications—legal, financial, and "otherwise"; and demonstrate that the applied-for frequencies are available.[109] A Licensee Qualification Report[110] must be filed annually,[111] certain records must be made available to the public, and the station must establish and follow an EEO program.[112] There are, however, a few requirements that do not exactly parallel those

---

[103] 47 C.F.R. § 74.991.

[104] This demonstrates that the applicant already has access to additional channels on which the wireless cable service will be based. The applicant may apply for the MDS/MMDS channels simultaneously with the ITFS channels, but if the MDS/MMDS application is refused, the ITFS channels will not be granted either.

[105] 47 C.F.R. § 74.990.

[106] 47 C.F.R. § 21.900.

[107] 47 C.F.R. § 21.33.

[108] 47 C.F.R. § 21.13.

[109] 47 C.F.R. § 21.900.

[110] FCC Form 430.

[111] 47 C.F.R. § 21.11.

[112] 47 U.S.C. § 554 (especially paragraph (h)(1)), and 47 C.F.R. § 21.307.

of broadcast licensees. For example, a renewal applicant may file one "blanket" application to cover a commonly owned group of stations.[113] The rules contain procedures that prevent trafficking in licenses.[114] The rules also make special provision to allow licensees to render free services to any agency of the U.S. government in connection with preparations for the national defense; a station that does this is to file a report every six months.[115] And licensees are to make an annual report to the Commission, a copy of which goes in the public inspection file, on subscribers, programming, and operation.[116]

8.2.3 Licensing of Direct Broadcast Satellites

As we noted in EMG 6.6, the present rules for the direct broadcast satellite (DBS) service are interim in nature, so applications are for *interim* DBS systems. An application must include a description of applicant plans for the type of service (for example, advertising-supported or subscription, open or encrypted), technology, and "all other pertinent information."[117] Once filed, the FCC allows 45 days for comment and petitions; then, after staff review, makes a determination as to whether the public interest would be served by an authorization.[118]

Once an authorization has been granted, the permittee must proceed "with diligence." Arrangements for construction must be completed within a year, and the satellite station must be in operation within six years (unless the FCC grants an extension).[119] Federal law and FCC regulation place EEO requirements on a DBS licensee.[120] DBS license terms are five years.[121]

8.2.4 Pioneer's Preference and Auctions

An innovator comes up with an idea for a new over-the-air communications service. The next move is for the innovator to request a change in the FCC's rules that would allocate the frequencies that could be used by the proposed new service. If the FCC allocates the frequencies, normally anyone—not just the innovator—can apply for them. The innovator, the party who invested time and money to develop the proposed service in the first place, may thus face a mutually exclusive applica-

---

[113] 47 C.F.R. § 21.11.

[114] For example, transfer of ownership is prohibited until completion of construction, and a licensee who wishes to sell an MDS or MMDS station that has been owned less than a year may be required to show that the proposed sale is not for the purpose of a profitable sale (rather than for the public interest). 47 C.F.R. § 21.39.

[115] 47 C.F.R. § 21.301.

[116] 47 C.F.R. § 21.911.

[117] 47 C.F.R. § 100.13.

[118] 47 C.F.R. § 100.15.

[119] 47 C.F.R. § 100.19.

[120] 47 U.S.C. § 554 (especially (h)(1)), and 47 C.F.R. § 100.51.

[121] 47 C.F.R. §§ 90.149 and 100.17.

tion situation, competing for frequencies with anyone else who wants to offer the service. Under rules adopted in 1991, however, innovators of new products and services petition for a *pioneer's preference*. If granted, the pioneer's preference states that the petitioner's application for a construction permit or license will *not* be subject to mutually exclusive applications. The purpose of these rules, the FCC said, was to "foster the development of new services and improve existing services by reducing for innovators the delays and risks associated with the current FCC allocation and licensing processes."[122] The FCC granted CellularVision, for example, a pioneer's preference[123] for its role in developing the local multipoint distribution service (EMG 6.5.4).

In 1993, Congress passed a budget bill that provided for the auctioning of spectrum space.[124] The frequencies involved, 200 MHz that were formerly under government control, had recently been released for use by commercial, for-profit operators. The law contains provisions to ensure that small businesses, rural telephone companies, and businesses owned by women and minorities get their share of licenses under the auctions. None of the frequencies involved the regular AM, FM, or TV broadcasting services,[125] but as we mentioned in EMG 8.1.4, there was concern over the precedent that appeared to have been set.

8.3   CABLE SYSTEM FRANCHISING

With respect to cable systems, a *franchise* is an authorization to construct a cable system using public right-of-way and easements.[126] It is granted by a *franchising authority*, which is "any government entity empowered by Federal, State, or local law to grant a franchise,"[127] typically a city council or, in unincorporated areas, a county commission. Federal law forbids a cable operator from providing service without a franchise.[128] So a franchise is as vital to a cable system as a license is to a broadcast station. We shall look at six aspects of cable franchising: initial franchising, franchise modification, franchise renewal, sale of the cable system, rates and rate-setting, and additional requirements. As you read these sections, it may help to

---

[122] Preference to Applicants Proposing an Allocation for New Services, 6 F.C.C.R. 3488 (1991).

[123] Suite 12 Group Petition for Pioneer's Preference, 8 F.C.C.R. 557 (1993).

[124] Budget Reconciliation Act, FY 1994, Pub. L. No. 103-66, 107 Stat. 312 (1993). The FCC adopted rules for spectrum auctions to cover new and emerging personal communication services, including telephones, pagers, and mobile computers. 1993 F.C.C. online Archives NRMC-4016.TXT (FCC adopts rules to implement competitive bidding to award spectrum licenses.).

[125] Interactive video and data services (IVDS; a form of over-the-air interactive TV) would, however, use some of this spectrum. The lottery to award the first round of licenses in that service was exempt and would proceed as scheduled because it had been set up before the law was passed. Future IVDS licenses, however, would have to be auctioned. Harry A. Jessell, "Washington Watch," *Broadcasting & Cable*, 16 Aug. 1993, at 23.

[126] 47 U.S.C. § 522(9); and 47 U.S.C. § 541(a).

[127] 47 U.S.C. § 522(10).

[128] 47 U.S.C. § 541(b). A cable system operated by a local government within its own boundaries, however, does not need a franchise. 47 U.S.C. § 541(f).

keep in mind the historical setting and developments, discussed in some detail in EMG 3.2.3, that led to the adoption of federal regulations for a locally franchised service.

8.3.1 Initial Franchising

Cable systems are franchised by local governments. However, federal law prohibits exclusive franchises and spells out what the franchising authority may require and regulate as terms of the franchise. A franchisee may not redline in building the system. The operator of a new cable system must file a registration statement with the FCC.

As we mentioned above, most franchising authorities are cities or counties. A number of states have passed laws that impact cable franchising—for example, to ensure consistency of service across jurisdictions.[129] But a state also may go one step further and decide to handle franchising duties directly for the various jurisdictions within its boundaries; in this case the state, not the cities and the counties, is the franchising authority. However, for the remainder of EMG 8.3, we shall use the term *city* or *franchising authority* to represent all situations.

The initial franchises in most areas of the United States have already been awarded. Franchising authorities now typically deal with franchise renewals and, in a few cases, with applicants wishing to provide competing cable service in an area already served by an existing cable system.[130] Nonetheless, a knowledge of the initial franchise process is helpful in understanding the overall nature of cable regulation.

This process starts when a city wishing to establish cable television service for its citizens advertises a *request for proposal* (RFP). The RFP invites prospective franchisees to submit applications. These applications describe the system the applicant would build—number and types of channels, tiers, and services; subscriber fees; programming; facilities; ownership; financial support. The city compares the various applications; it may pay a consultant to help in this task, analyzing each proposal to determine which offers the best combination of services balanced with the most realistic financial projection. In a public proceeding, the city council chooses the best proposal and awards the franchise. After the award, there may be negotiation on specific terms of the franchise.

A large city may be divided into several areas, each separately franchised. Federal law, however, prohibits the granting of exclusive franchises. If a city refuses to allow an applicant to operate an additional cable system in an area already

---

[129] *Jurisdiction* is the geographical area within which a governmental body or official has the right and the power to operate. A city government has jurisdiction within its corporate boundaries; a county government has jurisdiction in the unincorporated areas within its boundaries. So in this case, the state would enact laws to ensure that its counties and cities are all doing somewhat the same thing in their franchising efforts.

[130] The cable business has given this latter situation the somewhat semantically loaded name *overbuild*.

franchised to a cable operator, the applicant may appeal to the federal court system.[131]

Federal law allows the franchising authority to require the would-be operator to provide a number of different elements in exchange for award of the franchise. These include:

1. assurance that the operator has financial, technical, or legal qualifications to provide cable service;[132]
2. adherence to a schedule for completion of construction;
3. adherence to customer-service requirements (which may exceed those established by the FCC [EMG 8.3.6]);[133]
4. payment of a franchise fee not to exceed 5 percent of the system's gross revenues per year;[134]
5. specified facilities and equipment;[135]
6. channels for public, educational, and governmental (PEG) access use;[136]
7. assurance that the operator will provide adequate support for PEG channels;[137]
8. agreement that some cable services will be carried only under certain conditions or not at all "if such cable services are obscene or are otherwise unprotected by the Constitution of the United States";[138] and
9. (a) 30 days' advance written notice of changes in channels or video program services (a requirement found to be unconstitutional by a federal district court judge)[139] and (b) written notice advising subscribers of the location of the franchising-authority office taking comments on programming and channel changes.[140]

A cable system is not to be regulated as a common carrier or a utility.[141] However, a system that offers a *service* that, if offered by a common carrier, would be subject to regulation may be required to file an informational tariff (EMG 8.4.2) for that service. Further, a cable operator who, in addition to cable systems, also owns other communications facilities, whether offered on a common carrier or a private contract basis, can be regulated as the owner of those other facilities.[142]

---

[131] 47 U.S.C. § 541(a).

[132] 47 U.S.C. § 541(a).

[133] 47 U.S.C. § 552(a).

[134] 47 U.S.C. § 542(a).

[135] 47 U.S.C. § 544(b).

[136] 47 U.S.C. § 531.

[137] 47 U.S.C. § 541(a).

[138] 47 U.S.C. § 544(d).

[139] Daniels Cablevision, Inc. v. United States, 835 F.Supp 1 (1993), at 9.

[140] 47 U.S.C. § 544(h).

[141] 47 U.S.C. § 541(c).

[142] The information tariff would specify rates, terms, and conditions for the provision of the service, including whether it is offered to all subscribers generally. 47 U.S.C. § 541(d).

Once the franchise has been awarded, the franchisee may begin building the system. The law *requires* that the franchising authority ensure that the franchisee, in building the system, does not fail to extend it into low-income districts,[143] a cable operator practice called "redlining."[144] But the city must allow a reasonable amount of time for service to reach all homes in the franchise area.[145]

The cable system is authorized to begin operation only after it has filed a *registration statement* with the FCC. This is not an FCC form; it is simply a statement that identifies the system, operator, and service area; specifies the date on which the system provided service to 50 subscribers; and tells what television broadcast signals the system carries.[146] The FCC, in turn, publishes a public notice of the filing of the registration statement.[147]

8.3.2 Franchise Modification

A cable operator may request from the franchising authority a modification of the original franchise agreement.

To obtain a modification of an equipment or facilities requirement, the operator must demonstrate that compliance would be "commercially impracticable"[148] and, because of that, the requested modification is appropriate. To change services required by the franchise, the operator must demonstrate that the mix, quality, and level of services required by the franchise would be maintained after change. If the franchising authority turns down the request for modification, the operator may appeal the decision in court. However, if a franchise-required service is no longer available, or if its price has increased and the operator has not been allowed to raise rates to compensate, the operator may with 30 days' notice move or even delete it. The operator may not modify franchise-required access channels but may move among channels and tiers any service not subject to rate regulation.

8.3.3 Franchise Renewal

The renewal process can be started as early as three years before the existing franchise expires by either the franchising authority or the cable operator. The major steps in the process consist of a public proceeding, submission of a renewal

---

[143] 47 U.S.C. § 541(a).

[144] Also called "cream-skimming"; in the past some cable companies failed to provide service to low-income neighborhoods, believing that such neighborhoods yield significantly lesser percentages of subscribing homes and higher percentages of service piracy and equipment theft than "better" neighborhoods.

[145] 47 U.S.C. § 541(a).

[146] 47 C.F.R. § 76.12.

[147] 47 C.F.R. § 76.17.

[148] According to the law, a requirement is "commercially impracticable" (which, assumedly, means the operator would lose money on it) "as a result of a change in conditions which is beyond the control of the operator and the nonoccurrence of which was a basic assumption on which the requirement was fixed." 47 U.S.C. § 545(f).

proposal by the operator, and a decision by the franchising authority. A decision to deny is considered preliminary, and a final decision is rendered after an administrative proceeding.

Three years before the existing franchise expires, a six-month period begins during which the cable operator may request that renewal proceedings be started,[149] or the franchising authority may start them on its own initiative. The proceedings themselves are held for the purpose of allowing the public to comment on the operator's performance and the community's cable needs for the future. Upon conclusion of these initial proceedings, the cable operator may submit a proposal for renewal of the franchise. The franchising authority then has the choice either to renew the franchise or issue a preliminary assessment that the franchise should not be renewed. If the latter, an administrative proceeding may be requested by the cable operator or commenced by the franchising authority on its own initiative.[150] The purpose of the proceeding, in which both the franchising authority and the cable operator participate, is to consider the following factors:

1. Has the operator substantially complied with terms of the existing franchise and the law?
2. Has the quality of the operator's service (other than programming) been reasonable in light of community needs?
3. Can the operator provide the facilities and services in the renewal proposal?
4. Will the proposal meet future cable-related community needs?

Upon conclusion of the proceeding, the franchising authority issues a decision either granting or denying the renewal proposal. A denial must be based on the above four factors, and the operator may appeal the decision in court.[151]

If the renewal is denied, all appeals fail, the operator is faced with sale of the system, and there are no provisions in the franchise concerning price, the law requires that the transaction be at "fair market value."[152] The law also provides for the revocation of an existing franchise.[153] In such cases (and in the absence of franchise provisions on price), the sale is to be "at an equitable price."[154]

8.3.4 Sale of the Cable System

Newly constructed or purchased cable systems may not be sold for three years. Otherwise, a franchising authority has 120 days to act on a request to sell a system.

---

[149] The franchising authority must start the proceeding within six months after the cable operator submits the request.

[150] The decision and the commencement of the hearing must all take place within four months of the time the cable operator submits the proposal for renewal.

[151] 47 U.S.C. § 546.

[152] 47 U.S.C. § 547(a).

[153] 47 U.S.C. § 546(i).

[154] 47 U.S.C. § 547(b).

The FCC may waive the three-year antitrafficking provision if the franchising authority approves the sale and if the Commission finds that the public interest would be served. For sales or transfers proposed after that initial three-year period, if the franchising authority has failed to act on the request by the end of the 120 days, the request is deemed granted.[155]

8.3.5   Rates and Rate Setting

A cable system is exempt from subscriber rate regulation if the franchising authority chooses not to regulate or if the system faces effective competition. Otherwise the system is regulated under FCC formulas. Rates for a system's basic service tier, equipment, and installation are regulated by FCC-certified franchising authorities or, in the absence of certification, the FCC itself. Rates for additional tiers above basic service are regulated by the FCC on request from subscribers or local governments. The FCC also has the authority to regulate charges for leased-access channels.

The Cable Television Consumer Protection and Competition Act of 1992[156] put the FCC in the business of regulating the rates that cable systems charge[157] for subscriber service and for use of leased-access channels (EMG 10.3.4). By direction of that law, the Commission has adopted regulations dealing with rates, terms, and dispute settlement procedures for use of leased-access channels. It has also adopted an extensive and complicated set of regulations dealing with subscriber rates.[158]

Cable systems derive over 90 percent of gross revenue from subscriber fees. So for cable operators the setting of the rate they may charge subscribers is a serious matter. They challenged the rate-setting provisions of the 1992 cable act in court, but in 1993 a federal judge ruled the law constitutional.[159] Under this law, a cable system is free to set rates without first getting approval if the local franchising authority chooses not to regulate cable service or if the cable system faces *effective competition.* The law says effective competition exists when the cable system operates in either of the following two contexts:

1. serves less than 30 percent of the households in the franchise area, or
2. competes with at least one other multichannel provider that is
   a. available to at least 50 percent of the area's households *and*
   b. subscribed to by over 15 percent.

A *multichannel provider* is a business that makes multiple channels of video programming available to subscribers or customers, for example another cable system,

---

[155] Unless the franchising authority and the requesting party agree on an extension. 47 U.S.C. § 537.

[156] Pub. L. No. 102-385, 106 Stat. 1460, §§ 3, 9, 10.

[157] 47 U.S.C. § 543.

[158] 47 C.F.R. §§ 76.900–76.985; 1993 F.C.C. online Archives NRCB 4006.TXT (FCC orders further rate reductions while preserving incentives for cable operators to invest in new services); and 1993 F.C.C. online Archives NRCB 4009.TXT (Frequently asked questions regarding cable television regulations).

[159] Daniels Cablevision v. United States, 835 F.Supp 1 (1993).

a wireless cable system, a direct broadcast satellite service, or a TV receive-only satellite program distributor.

However, if the local franchising authority does choose to regulate cable service and the cable system does not face effective competition, cable rates are regulated by the franchising authority or directly by the FCC itself using, in either case, regulatory guidelines developed by the Commission.

The rates that are regulated are those for the basic service tier, installation, and monthly equipment rates. The law defines *basic service tier* as consisting of, at a minimum, all broadcast TV signals the system carries (except for satellite-delivered superstations) and franchise-required access channels. The FCC has established two methods, benchmark and cost of service, by which rates may be regulated. The rules for the *benchmark* method are based on rates at systems subject to competition; regulated systems whose charges are above the benchmark must lower their rates. The aim is to ensure that subscribers to systems which do *not* face effective competition pay rates no higher than subscribers to systems that *are* subject to effective competition.[160]

Under the *cost-of-service* method, a system operator may charge a higher rate by showing that the cable system's expenses are unusually high. Similar to the pricing policies the FCC has applied for years to the telephone business, cost-of-service allows a system operator to charge subscribers at a rate that equals the cost to the operator of providing regulated services, including operating expenses, plus a rate of return of 11.25 percent after taxes.

For a franchising authority to regulate rates, it must be certified by the FCC. The law spells out the procedure for certification, for disapproval of certification, for FCC review of authority-set rates, and for revocation of jurisdiction. In the event of disapproval or revocation, the FCC regulates the system's rates directly until the franchising authority is certified.

The law also provides for regulation of what it labels *cable programming services*. These are "second-tiers" or "extend-basic" tiers, usually a group of non-premium channels that are available for an extra charge (in addition to the rate for basic service). Only the FCC regulates these rates, and it does so only if requested. Subscribers as well as local and state authorities may request such regulation if they find the rates to be "unreasonable." Again, in response to the law, the FCC has established complex formulas by which to regulate the rates for such services. Under the Cable Act, rates for pay-per-view and pay-per-channel (à la carte pricing) programming are not regulated either by the franchising authority or the FCC.

Other provisions of the law aim at closing possible loopholes. The FCC, for example, is required to publish annual statistical reports on rates. It has also developed regulations to prevent evasions of rate regulation (such as through retiering). Rates are to be uniform throughout a system, and rate discrimination among subscribers

---

[160] For systems whose rates were over the benchmark, the Commission rolled back rates 10 percent in April 1993, then another 7 percent in February 1994. 1993 F.C.C. online Archives NRCB 4006.TXT (The administrative burden of rate regulations is reduced for cable systems with 1,000 or fewer subscribers).

may be prohibited, but systems are free to offer discounts to senior citizens and other economically disadvantaged groups.[161] Two specific billing practices are made illegal: the *negative option* (subscribers automatically get an optional extra-charge service unless they ask not to receive it) and *buy-through* (basic-service subscribers have to subscribe also to extended basic before they can get a premium channel).[162]

8.3.6 Additional Cable System Regulatory Requirements

Each year, the operator of a cable system must file a financial report and a report on EEO performance. The operator must also ensure that the system maintains a public inspection file, meets FCC standards with respect to customer service, notifies subscribers of purchase rights on in-home cable wiring, provides protection for subscribers against exposure to certain types of programming, and follows certain procedures to ensure the privacy of subscribers.

The primary purpose of the annual financial report is to provide the information needed to regulate subscriber rates.[163] Congress wrote EEO for cable into law,[164] and FCC regulations spell out program requirements.[165] The law requires that a cable operator file an EEO report for each employment location that has more than five full-time employees. The rules make clear that such locations include not only each cable system but also every "headquarters office"[166]—for example, facilities (such as regional legislative affairs offices and central billing and accounting departments) that supervise or support groups of cable systems but are not attached to any single system. The law lists 15 job categories on which a system must report, and the FCC issues a Certificate of Compliance to each system whose annual EEO report indicates that it is in compliance. Additionally, the FCC has established a schedule whereby it investigates each system's EEO compliance every five years; in those years during which a system is due for investigation it must submit a supplementary information sheet on its EEO efforts.[167]

Cable operators must make available for public inspection annual employment reports[168] and the political file.[169] All employment reports for five years must be available both at the operator's central office and at every location with more than

---

[161] Federal, state, or local governments may also require cable systems to install equipment for the hearing impaired.

[162] The prohibition against buy-through does not apply to a cable system whose technology prevents it from offering premium channels on a per-channel basis to basic-only subscribers. This exemption ends when the system technology is modified so that the technological limitation is eliminated or in the year 2002, whichever comes first.

[163] 47 U.S.C. § 543(g).

[164] 47 U.S.C. § 554.

[165] 47 C.F.R. § 76.75.

[166] 47 C.F.R. § 76.71.

[167] 47 C.F.R. § 76.77.

[168] 47 C.F.R. § 76.79.

[169] 47 C.F.R. § 76.305.

five employees. The political file requirements for cable systems parallel those for broadcast stations (EMG 12.6). These political file requirements apply only to candidate requests for time on local origination programming—programming created and controlled by the system operator—*not* to programming on any access, network, or broadcast channels the system carries.[170]

As called for by law,[171] the FCC has established minimum requirements for cable system office hours, telephone operator availability, acceptable response times for service calls, billing, and refunds. The Commission has also determined that an operator must notify a subscriber who voluntarily drops cable service that system-installed home wiring[172] may be purchased at "replacement cost." If the subscriber declines, the operator must remove the wiring in 30 days or it becomes the property of the former subscriber.[173]

An operator must make available to subscribers by sale or by lease a device that permits obscene or indecent programming to be blocked. Additionally, under the 1992 cable act, an operator who planned to unblock and allow all subscribers to receive a premium channel[174] that programs movies rated X, NC-17, or R was required to notify subscribers at least 30 days in advance and advise them that the channel will be blocked on request.[175] As we noted in EMG 8.3.1., however, a federal district court judge's 1993 ruling found that requirement to be unconstitutional.[176]

Each year, the cable operator must provide every subscriber with a separate, written notice describing (1) exactly what "personally identifiable information"[177] the system collects on the subscriber, (2) what is to be done with it, (3) how long the system keeps the information, (4) how the subscriber may examine it, and (5) legal limitations on its collection and the rights of subscribers to enforce those limitations. The operator may not disclose such information to others without prior consent from the subscriber and must destroy it once it has served the purpose for which it was collected. Anyone wronged by the act of a cable operator in violation of the privacy restrictions may bring civil action in a federal district court.[178]

8.3.7   Other Legal Elements Affecting Cable Systems

The Communications Act (as amended by the 1992 cable act) directs the FCC to adopt and update rules to ensure that special functions of new TV receivers and

---

[170] The regulation uses the term *origination cablecasting.*
[171] 47 U.S.C. § 552.
[172] 47 U.S.C. § 544(i).
[173] 47 C.F.R. § 76.802.
[174] Cable systems sometimes do this on a temporary basis to entice subscribers to *upgrade* by adding the services.
[175] 47 U.S.C. § 544(d).
[176] *See* note 139.
[177] These limitations do not cover aggregate data that do not identify particular persons.
[178] 47 U.S.C. § 551.

videocassette recorders (VCRs) are not rendered obsolete by changes in cable scrambling systems. The Commission is to deal especially with the meaning of "cable ready" and "cable compatible," with the use of converter boxes, and with the promotion of alternative sources through which subscribers may acquire converter boxes and remote controls. Insofar as scrambling and encryption efforts affect receivers and VCRs, the FCC is to determine circumstances when such efforts are appropriate.[179]

Some provisions have been written into law specifically to help the cable operator conduct business. For example, Congress has made piracy of signals from cable systems illegal and punishable by fine and imprisonment.[180] And a cable operator may indicate to subscribers just how much of their total bill is due to certain forms of government regulation. Each monthly subscriber bill may list the amount of that bill that goes (1) to pay the franchise fee, (2) to support access channels, and (3) to pay any fee or assessment charged by any governmental authority on the transaction between the operator and the subscriber (such as a sales tax).[181] However, the operator must pass through to subscribers any reduction in its franchise fee.[182]

8.4 PERMISSION TO OPERATE FOR OTHER WIRED SYSTEMS

Neither a satellite master antenna television system nor video dialtone service needs a franchise to operate.

The advantages of this are many. It eliminates franchise fees, PEG and leased access channels, must-carry, cable rate regulation, public inspection files, political programming requirements, and so on and so on. Regulation does, however, affect some aspects of the right to operate for both media.

8.4.1 Operational Qualifications of a SMATV System

A satellite master antenna television system[183] may not use or cross public right-of-way. If it serves two or more multiunit dwellings, they must all be under common ownership. Otherwise, the system is legally a cable system and needs a franchise to operate.

---

[179] 47 U.S.C. § 544A.

[180] 47 U.S.C. § 553. A person who is not a cable television subscriber but who has cable service (perhaps through a clandestine feed off a subscribing neighbor's tap) without knowledge of the cable operator is said to be *pirating* service.

[181] 47 U.S.C. § 542(c).

[182] 47 U.S.C. § 542(e).

[183] EMG 6.8.

Section 602(7) of the Communications Act says that a "cable system" is *not*, among other things,

> a facility that serves only subscribers in 1 or more multiple unit dwellings under common ownership, control, or management, unless such facility or facilities uses any public right-of-way. . . .[184]

A satellite master antenna television (SMATV) system does share at least one regulatory requirement with cable systems. If more than five employees work on a system, it must comply with EEO provisions specified by the Communications Act.[185]

Several cases and decisions have helped to delineate the boundary between cable and SMATV systems. One of these clarified that "use" of a public right-of-way includes even situations in which a system's cable lies only partly within the right-of-way and in which a system only transmits signals *across* a public right-of-way by use of microwave. In such cases, the system would have to get a franchise.[186]

The phrase *multiple unit dwellings* is also significant. A delivery system that provides cable service to multiple detached single-family homes within a planned-development community is a cable system, not a SMATV, even if the system makes no use of the public right-of-way.[187]

A 1993 U.S. Supreme Court decision upheld the "under common ownership" part of the definition. Earlier, an appeals court had ruled that the law, which exempted from municipal regulation some SMATV systems (those serving commonly owned buildings) but not others (those serving groups of buildings not commonly owned), violated the equal protection clause of the Fifth Amendment. The Supreme Court, however, overturned that decision, ruling unanimously that a SMATV system that serves separately owned buildings—even if it does not use or cross public rights-of-way—must acquire a municipal franchise.[188]

8.4.2   Video Dialtone Operational Parameters

The video dialtone basic platform service is regulated under common carrier law; in order to offer such service, a telephone company must file a tariff and apply for authorization to supply the service.

Under Section 203 of the Communications Act of 1934, as amended, a common carrier must

---

[184] 47 U.S.C. § 522(7)(B).

[185] 47 U.S.C. § 554, especially paragraph (h)(1).

[186] Rollins Cablevue, Inc. v. Saienni Enter., 633 F. Supp. 1315 (1986). Apparently, however, the use of infrared links to transmit signals across a public right-of-way would not require a franchise. Channel One Sys. v. Connecticut Dep't of Pub. Util. Control, 689 F. Supp. 188 (1986).

[187] Massachusetts Community Antenna Television Comm'n, 2 F.C.C.R. 7321 (1987).

[188] FCC v. Beach Communications, 61 U.S.L.W. 4526 (1993).

file with the Commission . . . schedules showing all charges . . . and showing the classifications, practices, and regulations affecting such
charges. Such schedules shall . . . be posted and kept open for public
inspection. . . .[189]

This filing is called a *tariff*, and it states exactly what a particular communications
service will be, the terms under which it is to be offered, and its cost. Under Section
214, a common carrier must obtain from the FCC "a certificate that the . . . public
convenience and necessity require"[190] addition of equipment or services before
actually adding them. A telephone company wishing to offer video dialtone service
must, therefore, both apply for a certificate and file a tariff.

In its filings for video dialtone service, the telco applicant will ask for permission to provide within its local service area a common carrier transmission service
that programmer-customers may use to provide video programming to subscribers.
This transmission service is the *basic platform service*, and it must be made available on a non-discriminatory, equal access basis to all video programmers who wish
to use it. The system must have enough capacity that it can be used by video programmers who wish to offer multiple channels.

As discussed in EMG 7.3.7, telephone companies that provide video dialtone
service may have no cognizable interest in its programmers. Additionally, they may
not

(i) determine how video programming is presented for sale to consumers;
including decisions concerning the bundling or "tiering," or the price, terms,
and conditions of programming offered to consumers, or (ii) otherwise
have a cognizable interest in, or exercise control over, video programming
provided directly to subscribers within their telephone service areas.[191]

They *are* allowed to offer capabilities designed to enhance and facilitate use of the
basic platform service. These include such services as video gateways (such as
menus, help screens, menu-creation and search capabilities), video manipulation
(such as program storage, time shifting, replay), and interactive capability. Also
available will be ancillary services such as billing and collection, order processing,
installation of in-home wiring, and equipment.

8.5   EEO RULES FOR MULTICHANNEL
PROGRAM PACKAGERS

Although multichannel program packagers need no license or franchise, they must
still adhere to FCC EEO rules.

---

[189] 47 U.S.C. § 203.
[190] 47 U.S.C. § 214.
[191] 47 C.F.R. § 63.54(d)(2).

Multichannel program packagers take existing programming and resell it over some type of common carrier or third-party distribution system. An example would be a company that uses video dialtone or leases channels on a direct broadcast satellite to retail a group of programming services. Such packagers, since they use channels operated by others, do not need a government-granted "permit to operate." Nonetheless, in 1993 the FCC extended EEO rules that had been adopted for cable to television (EMG 8.3.6) to cover these multichannel program packagers also.[192] The rules do not apply to packagers who deal with only a single channel or who offer multiple connected channels.[193] The rules exempt the operators (in our example, the telephone company or the DBS licensee) as long as they have no control over the content or packaging of the program.

DISCUSSION QUESTIONS

1. Why are broadcast stations licensed by the federal government while cable systems are franchised by state or local governments? What do you think is the rationale for this difference?

2. Why should members of a community have any say in the licensing process of a broadcast station that serves that community? Sure, there is all that stuff about the public interest and the frequencies being scarce natural resources in the public domain, but those frequencies would not be worth a hill of beans to the community without that station operating on them. And after all, it was the licensee who took the risk, put up the money, did all the legwork, fought with government bureaucrats, and did all the other things necessary to get that community service called a "station" up and running. What right has some "citizen group" to intervene in, say, license renewal proceedings?

3. Why does the FCC seem to put so much emphasis on employment of women and members of racial and ethnic minority groups by electronic media outlets? What do you think are the legal reasons? Are these policies justified in moral terms? Do book publishers, outdoor advertising companies, direct mail firms, and other mass media businesses have the same legal requirements on employment as the regulated electronic media? Do these other media have the same moral responsibility? Explain and defend your answers.

4. Why does the FCC seem to put so much emphasis on increasing ownership of electronic media outlets by members of racial and ethnic minority groups? What do you think are the legal reasons? Are these policies justified in moral terms? If, as stated in the text, minority owners might increase viewpoint diversity, could the same be said for females? With respect to comparative hearings, is ownership diversity really more important than past experience? Defend your answers.

5. How would you solve the FCC's dilemma concerning mutually exclusive applications? Would you continue to conduct time-consuming hearings with all the motions, appeals,

---

[192] 8 F.C.C.R. 5389.

[193] Such as a premium cable programmer that offers a "multiplex" service—the same movie carried continually on two or more different channels, each with a different starting time (say, 30 minutes apart) so as to offer subscribers near-video-on-demand. A packager can offer up to six connected channels before coming under the rules.

and other delay tactics that can so lengthen such proceedings? Would you opt for lottery selection? What about an auction, with the license going to the highest bidder? Or would you urge that Congress pass legislation for yet another option, your own idea? If so, what is your idea? No matter what solution you pick, explain how it would serve the public interest and ensure that the best party finally got the license.

6. Commercial broadcast stations earn the majority of their revenues from sale of advertising time. Cable systems earn the majority of their revenues from sale of service to subscribers. In the 1992 cable act, Congress made the FCC responsible for regulating subscriber rates. Tell why Congress should or should not also make the FCC responsible for regulating rates for advertising time sales. Or is the FCC already in the ad rate regulation business? Check EMG 12.3 before you answer that one!

SUGGESTED READINGS

Bartlett, Eugene R. *Cable Television Technology and Operations: HDTV & NTSC Systems.* New York: McGraw, 1990.

Copple, Robert F. "Cable Television and the Allocation of Regulatory Power: A Study of Governmental Demarcation and Roles." *Federal Communications Law Journal* 44 (Dec. 1991): 1.

Fenneran, William B., and Richard E. Wiley, eds. *The Cable Television Consumer Protection and Competition Act of 1992: What Does It Mean?* Englewood Cliffs, NJ: Prentice, 1993.

Fife, Marilyn D. "A Critical Assessment of Equal Employment Opportunity Policy in U.S. Telecommunication Industries." *Mass Comm Review* 15 (2&3) (1988): 3–9.

Gleason, Timothy W. "Killing 'Gnats with a Sledgehammer'? Case Study: Fairness Doctrine and a Broadcast License Denial." *Journalism Quarterly* 68 (winter 1991): 805–813.

Hazlett, Thomas W. "Private Monopoly and the Public Interest: An Economic Analysis of the Cable Television Franchise." *University of Pennsylvania Law Review* 134 (July 1986): 1335.

Hazlett, Thomas W. "The Policy of Exclusive Franchising in Cable Television." *Journal of Broadcasting and Electronic Media* 31 (1987): 1–20.

Johnson, Leland L. *Direct Broadcast Satellites: A Competitive Alternative to Cable Television?* Santa Monica, CA: Rand, 1991.

Kleiman, Howard. "Content Diversity and the FCC's Minority and Gender Licensing Policies." *Journal of Broadcasting and Electronic Media* 35 (1991): 411–429.

McGann, Anthony F., and J. Thomas Russell. "Hostile Takeovers in Broadcasting." *Journal of Media Economics* 1 (2) (fall 1988): 29–40.

Pennybacker, John H. "The Character Standard: Will It Survive RKO?" *Journal of Broadcasting and Electronic Media* 29 (1985): 161–174.

Phipps, Steven P. "Unlicensed Broadcasting in the US: The Official Policy of the FCC." *Journal of Broadcasting and Electronic Media* 34 (spring 1990): 137–152.

Phipps, Steven P. "Unlicensed Broadcasting and the Federal Radio Commission: The 1930 George W. Fellowes Challenge." *Journalism Quarterly* 68 (winter 1991): 823–828.

Quinlan, Sterling Red. *The Hundred Million Dollar Lunch.* Chicago: O'Hara, 1974.

Schroepfer, Terrence J. "Allocating Spectrum Through the Use of Auctions." *Hastings Journal of Communications and Entertainment Law: COMM/ENT* 14 (fall 1991): 35–45.

Schroepfer, Terrence J. "Fee-Based Incentives and the Efficient Use of Spectrum," *Federal Communications Law Journal* 44 (May 1992): 411.

Sewell, Stephen F. "Assignments and Transfers of Control of FCC Authorizations under Section 310(d) of the Communications Act of 1934." *Federal Communications Law Journal* 43 (July 1991): 277.

Smith, Kim. "Why Ascertainment Failed." *Communications and the Law* 11 (2) (June 1989): 49–60.

Spitzer, Matthew L. "The Constitutionality of Licensing Broadcasters." *New York University Law Review* 64 (Nov. 1989): 990.

Spitzer, Matthew L. "Justifying Minority Preferences in Broadcasting." *Southern California Law Review* 64 (Jan. 1991): 293.

Veraldi, Lorna, and Stuart A. Shorenstein. "Gender Preferences." *Federal Communications Law Journal* 45 (Apr. 1993): 219.

Yates, Robert K. *Fiber Optics and CATV Business Strategy*. Norwood, MA: Artech, 1990.

Chapter
9
PUBLIC INTEREST

The Communications Act of 1934 compels the Federal Communications Commission to "encourage the larger and more effective use of radio in the public interest."[1] The phrase "public interest," often combined with "convenience" and "necessity," appears 11 times in the act. The precise meaning of the phrase has long been the subject of considerable debate. Both the FRC and FCC have issued policy statements aimed at clarifying public interest requirements, and numerous court cases have dealt with the issue as well. Despite this, the public interest standard has become the basis for FCC rules, policy decisions, and evaluations of the performance of radio and television stations. Furthermore, the public interest standard provides justification for various forms of content regulation that might otherwise constitute a violation of broadcasters' freedom of speech. In this chapter we will trace the history of the public interest standard, discuss relevant FCC decisions and policy statements, and review court decisions in which the public interest was a principal issue. We conclude with a summary of policy changes adopted since 1978 as the FCC revised its enforcement of the public interest standard and effectively deregulated the electronic media.

9.1   ORIGINS OF THE PUBLIC INTEREST STANDARD

Since it was first applied to broadcasting in the Radio Act of 1927, the public interest standard has evolved into the fundamental basis on which the FCC regulates the electronic media. It is considered the "touchstone" of the FCC's authority to regu-

---

[1] 47 U.S.C.A. § 303(a)(g).

late.[2] It is the basis on which rules and regulations are promulgated and the standard by which all licensing decision are made.

The phrase "public interest" is not unique to broadcasting. It was possibly first used with respect to regulation of public utilities. On the national level, the phrase goes back to the 1876 Supreme Court decision in *Munn* v. *Illinois*,[3] and Congress first "suggested" the phrase in the Transportation Act of 1920.[4]

Congress may have intentionally applied the broad standard to broadcasting because the Radio Act of 1912 had so completely failed to establish any regulatory authority (EMG 3.1.2). The 1927 act specifically granted the Federal Radio Commission authority to regulate radio. But beyond that it codified the public interest standard, ensuring a broadly based, flexible regulatory framework. This gave the FRC the authority to make policy as issues evolved, without having to wait for Congress to pass new legislation. The Communications Act of 1934 granted the same authority to the FCC.

The courts and the FCC have established that the radio spectrum is in the public domain. Licensees of radio and television stations, MMDS, DBS, and other facilities never *own* frequencies, they merely *borrow* them from the public. The notion that the airwaves belong to the people is the basic premise of what is called the *trustee model*. Licensees act as trustees for the public as they operate broadcast facilities in the public interest, convenience, and necessity.

9.1.1 The 1928 Statement

The FRC served early notice that the public interest standard would be applied to programming content as well as technical matters.

The Federal Radio Commission attempted the first comprehensive interpretation of the public interest standard in 1928.[5] The statement dealt mostly with the technical task of interference reduction, but there were two significant references to programming content. First, the Commission stated that broadcasters should not use their stations for their own private matters, an issue to figure prominently in the *KFKB* case just two years later (EMG 9.2.1). Second, the statement contained the notion that the interests of the audience take precedence over those of licensees. This notion would later reappear in major FCC policies and court decisions including the *Mayflower* doctrine (EMG 11.1.1), the Fairness Doctrine (EMG 11.1.2), and the *Red Lion* decision (EMG 11.5.1).

9.1.2 *Great Lakes* Decision

A major factor in the *Great Lakes* decision was the FRC's determination of which station would best serve the public interest.

---

[2] Pottsville Broadcasting v. FCC, 309 U.S. 134 (1940).
[3] 94 U.S. 113 (1876).
[4] Darrel Holt, "The Origin of 'Public Interest' in Broadcasting," 1 *Educ. Broadcasting Rev.* 15 (1967).
[5] 2 FRC Ann. Rep. 166 (1928).

BOX 9.1   FRC Public Interest Guidelines: The *Great Lakes* Decision

In its *Great Lakes* decision the FRC offered broadcasters the following guidelines concerning what would and would not be considered to be in the public interest:

1. A station should provide well-rounded programming that meets the needs, tastes, and desires of the community it serves.
2. Programming practices would be considered at renewal time in determining whether a station has met public interest requirements.
3. When two stations seek the same frequencies, the station with the longest record of continuous service has the advantage. If there is a substantial difference between the programming service of the two, the station with superior programming will have the advantage.
4. The Commission reasserted its opposition to programming for private interests, referring to stations which do so as "propaganda stations."*

---

* Great Lakes Broadcasting Company, 3 FRC Ann. Rep. 32 (1929).

One year after the 1928 statement the FRC attempted to further delineate the meaning of the "public interest." The Great Lakes case focused on a conflict among three Chicago area stations requesting technical modifications. In its decision, the FRC established programming content as a definite criterion of the public interest standard.[6] As shown in Box 9.1, the Commission attempted to offer specific guidelines for broadcasters. Interestingly, in what could be interpreted as a precursor to what later became the Fairness Doctrine, the Commission also stated that when important issues are discussed, the public interest requires opposing viewpoints to be broadcast.

In *Great Lakes Broadcasting* v. *FRC*, a U.S. court of appeals upheld the Radio Commission's treatment of programming as a primary criterion of the public interest standard.[7] In fact, the court's decision was partially based on the FRC's evaluation of the programming service rendered by WENR, one of the stations involved:

We base this opinion upon a consideration of the excellent service heretofore rendered to the public by WENR, and its programs for public instruction and entertainment, and the popularity of the station; also its ability by means of its 50,000 watt transmitter to cover a large area; and the assured financial responsibility behind it. . . . Under these circumstances, it is contrary to justice, and against the public convenience, interest, and necessity

---

[6] Great Lakes Broadcasting Co., 3 FRC Ann. Rep. 32 (1929).
[7] Great Lakes Broadcasting Co. v. FRC, 37 F.2d 993 (1930).

to apportion operating time in the proportion of two-sevenths to WENR and five-sevenths to WLS.[8]

The *Great Lakes* decision, because it contains the seeds of concepts that would later germinate into significant regulatory policies, could be considered the most important decision of the Federal Radio Commission. In addition to establishing programming content as a criterion of the public interest, the decision included notions forming the basis for ascertainment requirements (EMG 10.1.2.1) and the Fairness Doctrine (EMG 11.1.2).

The public interest standard served as the basis for two later court decisions involving technical matters. In *Reading Broadcasting* v. *FRC*, the Radio Commission had denied an application for a Reading, Pennsylvania, station to increase power and change frequency to 620 kilocycles. The modifications would have resulted in interference with stations WTMJ in Milwaukee and WLBZ in Maine. The FRC, taking each station's overall service into account, concluded that the modifications were not in the public interest and denied the application. An appeals court upheld the Commission's decision, calling the public interest standard the "paramount consideration."[9]

In *Journal Company* v. *FRC* the court reversed an FRC decision that had allowed two stations in different cities to switch operating frequencies to 620 kilocycles. The switch caused one station substantial interference and reduction in coverage area. The appeals court cited two primary reasons for reversing the FRC. First, the Radio Commission had failed to notify the injured station of the modification or offer it a hearing on the matter. Second, the court ruled that "where a broadcasting station has been constructed and maintained in good faith, it is in the interest of the public and common justice to the station that its status should not be injuriously affected, except for compelling reasons."[10]

9.1.3 *FRC* v. *Nelson Brothers*

In the *Nelson Brothers* case the U.S. Supreme Court upheld the FRC's authority to regulate programming on the basis of the public interest standard.

The Supreme Court rendered its first opinion involving the public interest standard in 1933. An FRC decision to grant full-time operating authority to one station had effectively revoked the license of two others. WJKS in Gary, Indiana, wanted to broadcast on 560 kilocycles. WIBO, owned by Nelson Brothers Bond & Mortgage, and WPCC, owned by a church, were already sharing time on that frequency.

The FRC granted the modification and terminated the licenses of WIBO and WPCC. WIBO was a commercial operation and full time affiliate of the NBC net-

---

[8] *Id.* at 995 (1930).
[9] Reading Broadcasting Co. v. FRC, 48 F.2d 458 (1931).
[10] Journal Co. v. FRC, 48 F.2d 461 (1931).

work, which was carried on other stations reaching the Gary market. WPCC's programming, which was entirely religious, was also duplicated by area stations.

WJKS's programming included safety programs for steel workers, children's programs, discussions with civic leaders, and programs designed to meet the needs of Hungarian, Polish, Russian, and other foreign audience members.[11] In a decision based primarily on a comparative analysis of programming, the FRC granted full-time operation to WJKS. A U.S. court of appeals overruled the FRC, holding that the decision was arbitrary and capricious.[12] The FRC then appealed the case to the U.S. Supreme Court.

The Supreme Court affirmed the FRC's allocation of the frequency to WJKS.[13] The Court held that the FRC was entitled to evaluate and consider programming services provided by the various stations:

> In granting licenses the Commission is required to act "as public convenience, interest, or necessity requires.". . . In the instant case the Commission was entitled to consider the advantages enjoyed by the people of Illinois under the assignments to that State, the services rendered by the respective stations, the reasonable demands of the people of Indiana, and the special requirements of radio service at Gary.[14]

9.2 JUDICIAL AFFIRMATION OF PROGRAM REVIEW

The courts have consistently upheld the authority of the FRC and FCC to exercise broad regulatory powers under the public interest standard.

The *Great Lakes* and *Nelson Brothers* decisions established precedent for the courts to uphold the FRC's authority to consider programming in evaluating public interest performance. Most cases throughout the 1920s dealt primarily with technical issues. Indeed, even the *Great Lakes* case focused on disputes over assignments of transmitter power, frequency, and hours of operation. So, what if a case focused *only* on matters related to programming? Would the Radio Commission use the public interest rationale to deny service or even revoke a station's license *solely* on the basis of programming practices?

Several points of law would seem to discourage, if not prohibit, such a decision. The First Amendment protects against abridgment of free speech. Moreover, Section 29 of the Radio Act of 1927 specified that the FRC would not have the "power of censorship" and could make no regulation that would hinder "the right

---

[11] The FRC was also attempting to equalize the number of stations allocated among various designated geographical zones. Indiana happened to be in a zone that was under quota, while Illinois was over quota.

[12] Nelson Bros. Bond & Mortgage Co. v. FRC, 62 F.2d 854 (1932).

[13] FRC v. Nelson Bros. Bond & Mortgage Co., 289 U.S. 266 (1933).

[14] *Id.* at 284.

of free speech by means of radio communications. . . ."[15] Six significant cases—the *KFKB*, *Trinity*, *NBC*, *Pottsville*, *Sanders*, and *WOKO* cases—settled any doubt regarding the matter.

9.2.1 *KFKB Broadcasting v. FRC*

In the *KFKB* case the court held that the FRC's consideration of a station's programming in making license renewal decisions does not amount to censorship.

This case is commonly referred to as the "Brinkley Case." During the 1920s, radio attracted a number of individuals that broadcast historian Erik Barnouw labeled "faddists, medicine men and messiahs."[16] Perhaps the most remarkable was John Brinkley. Brinkley had purchased bogus medical degrees from diploma mills in St. Louis and Kansas City and obtained a license to practice medicine in Kansas. Through reciprocity agreements, he successfully sought licenses in several other states as well. In 1917, "Doc" Brinkley moved to the small community of Milford, Kansas. He soon gained fame for performing a so-called goat gland operation that was touted as a cure for male impotence. The operation was performed by surgically inserting tissue from the testes of goats into the scrotum of patients suffering from either impotence or enlargement of the prostate. The procedure was sheer medical quackery, but it apparently offered enough of a mental boost to "cure" some psychologically based cases of impotence. Regardless of its medical merit, the operation provided Brinkley with sufficient wealth and fame to obtain a broadcast license. In 1923 he began essentially to practice medicine over the radio.

Brinkley's KFKB was licensed to operate on 1050 kHz at 1000 (later 5000) watts. Powerful for its time, the signal reached several states. KFKB offered a variety of programming, including fundamentalist religion, guitar and banjo ensembles, cowboy singers, and accordionists.[17]

It was the "Medical Question Box," a program aired in three half-hour segments, that got Brinkley into trouble with the FRC. The program featured Brinkley reading letters in which listeners described symptoms of various ailments. Having never seen the patient, Brinkley would render a diagnosis and recommend purchase of one or more of his own prescriptions from his own pharmaceutical supply house. Since the prescriptions were identified by number, other listeners with similar symptoms would place orders as well. Box 9.2 contains examples of letters to Brinkley and his over-the-air diagnoses.[18]

By 1925 the American Medical Association had labeled the goat gland operation a fraud and states began to rescind Brinkley's medical licenses. Then, in 1930, the Federal Radio Commission denied KFKB's license renewal. The FRC said that

[15] Section 29 was reenacted as section 326 of the Communications Act of 1934.
[16] Erik Barnouw, *A Tower in Babel* (New York: Oxford U P, 1966) 168, Vol. 1 of *A History of Broadcasting in the United States.*
[17] *Id.* at 170.
[18] KFKB v. FRC, 47 F.2d at 671 (1931).

BOX 9.2   "The Medical Question Box": Examples of Brinkley's "Diagnoses"

The following diagnoses, published in the court's decision, are typical of those Brinkley would make. Notice that he makes a diagnosis, then suggests multiple prescriptions. Brinkley was also not shy about questioning previous medical treatment and offering his own diagnosis without ever having seen the patient.

Here's one from Tillie. She says she had an operation, had some trouble 10 years ago. I think the operation was unnecessary, and it isn't very good sense to have an ovary removed with the expectation of motherhood resulting therefrom. My advice to you is to use Women's Tonic No. 50, 67, and 61. This combination will do for you what you desire if any combinations will, after three months persistent use.

Sunflower State, from Dresden, Kansas. Probably has gall stones. No, I don't mean that, I mean kidney stones. My advice to you is to put him on Prescription No. 80 and 50 for men, also 64. I think that he will be a whole lot better. Also drink a lot of water.

Brinkley's practice of diagnosing patients whom he had not seen contravened the public health and safety and, therefore, the public interest. Further, he operated KFKB solely for his own private interests. The Commission held that while a licensee may expect some compensation for programming efforts, the interest of the public must remain paramount.[19]

Brinkley appealed, contending that the FRC's denial of renewal based on programming constituted censorship and, therefore, violated Section 29 of the Radio Act. The appeals court disagreed and upheld the FRC's authority to consider programming in deciding whether renewal of a station's license is in the public interest. The court held that the FRC had "exercised its undoubted right to take note of appellant's past conduct, which is not censorship."[20]

9.2.2   *Trinity Methodist Church* v. *FRC*

In the *Trinity* decision the court ruled that the First and Fifth Amendments do not prohibit the FRC from denying license renewal purely on the basis of programming concerns.

---

[19] The notion that it is the interest of the listening public, and not the broadcaster, that is paramount became a major holding of the Supreme Court in the 1969 *Red Lion* decision (see EMG 11.5.1).

[20] KFKB Broadcasting Ass'n v. FRC, 47 F.2d 670. The court's decision failed to end Brinkley's medical or broadcasting career. For an extended treatment of Brinkley's endeavors, see Gerald Carson, *The Roguish World of Dr. Brinkley* (New York: Holt, 1960).

This case is commonly called the "Shuler case." Reverend Shuler was, at his worst, never considered a threat to public safety as was Brinkley. Because his case focused squarely on speech—things Shuler said over the radio—the case even more strongly established programming as a major criterion of the public interest standard.

Reverend Robert Shuler used his pulpit and radio station KGEF to attack what he perceived as civic problems in the city of Los Angeles.[21] KGEF transmitted with 1,000 watts at 1300 kHz on a share-time basis with another station. It was a non-profit, noncommercial operation sustained by contributions solicited by Shuler. Shuler was the actual owner-operator, but the station was licensed to his church, Trinity Methodist. Religious programs constituted the majority of the schedule, and Shuler himself preached sermons and hosted weeknight programs called the *Bob Shuler Question Hour* and *Bob Shuler's Civic Talks*. It was these two programs that brought on the controversy.

Shuler attracted large audiences, estimated as high as 600,000 listeners, and he took advantage of the forum to mount attacks on various individuals and organizations in Los Angeles.[22] He routinely broadcast allegations of wrongdoing on the part of the police chief and the entire police department, prominent businessmen, judges, and the city bar association. Shuler's attacks supposedly led to the resignation or decision not to seek re-election of a mayor, a district attorney, and a city prosecutor. He eventually incurred the wrath of many of Los Angeles's most powerful leaders. By the time Shuler applied for renewal in 1930, the Commission had received complaints about his broadcasts. The question before the FRC was clear. Given Shuler's attacks over the airwaves, would the public interest be served by renewing his license?

The renewal hearing, held in January of 1931, was anything but typical. The FRC normally held hearings in Washington, D.C., utilizing its own legal staff to present cases against licensees. This hearing, however, was in Los Angeles. A local businessman, George Lyon, was allowed to handle the case for the FRC, and a former city prosecutor that Shuler had forced to resign actually served as legal counsel for Shuler. The hearing examiner recommended renewal, but after oral arguments were heard by the full Commission the FRC ruled that renewal would not be in the public interest. The station was forced off the air on November 13, 1931.

The FRC based its decision on the grounds that

1. Shuler had used the station to attack a religious organization, namely the Roman Catholic Church,
2. Shuler's broadcasts were perceived as sensational rather than instructive, and

---

[21] The Robert Shuler discussed in this section should not be confused with the Reverend Robert Schuler, a television evangelist based in California.

[22] Charley Orbison, "Fighting Bob Shuler: Early Radio Crusader," 21 *J. of Broadcasting* 462 (1977).

3. Shuler had twice been convicted of attempting to obstruct justice through his broadcasts.[23]

On appeal, Shuler's approach differed from that of Doc Brinkley. Brinkley's appeal had been based on statutory grounds—the anticensorship provision of Section 29 of the 1927 act. Shuler, on the other hand, based his appeal on constitutional grounds. Shuler contended that the FRC decision, based as it was on past programming, violated his First Amendment right to free speech. He also argued that his Fifth Amendment rights were violated because the decision deprived him of his property (the radio station) without due process of law.

In rejecting Shuler's First Amendment arguments the appeals court even more firmly established a public interest standard.[24] The court held that since the airwaves are channels of interstate commerce, Congress may exercise its regulatory power subject only to limitations imposed by the Constitution itself. The Radio Act of 1927, passed by Congress, specified that the FRC must determine if the public interest would be served before awarding, renewing, or modifying any station license. To do so the FRC, when considering whether renewal of a license will serve the public interest, must examine the licensee's past programming. The court listed various offenses the FRC had charged Shuler with and concluded that denial of renewal did not constitute a violation of free speech. The court reasoned that Shuler could still indulge in character assassinations of public officials:

> He may just as freely as ever criticize religious practices of which he does not approve. He may even indulge private malice or personal slander—subject, of course, to be required to answer for abuse thereof—but he may not, as we think, demand, of right, the continued use of an instrumentality of commerce (radio) for such purposes.[25]

Shuler's Fifth Amendment arguments were rejected on the basis of the public trustee model (EMG 7.1). The court held that the frequency never *belonged* to Shuler in the first place. Instead, he merely had permission from the government to *use* it. The court added that due process had been served, since Shuler was notified of the hearing and of the issues involved and was given opportunity to demonstrate why the license should be renewed.

Shuler lost on both counts, and the court upheld the FRC's authority to deny license renewal solely on the basis of programming content. Together, the Shuler and Brinkley cases offered strong judicial affirmation that the public interest standard authorized the FRC to regulate programming matters.

---

[23] The Orbison research cited above concluded, after examination of the FRC decision and the hearing transcript, that most of the FRC's grounds for denial were either irrelevant or not supported by the record.

[24] Trinity Methodist Church, South v. FRC, 62 F.2d 850 (1932).

[25] *Id.* at 852.

9.2.3   *FCC v. Pottsville Broadcasting*

> In the *Pottsville* case the U.S. Supreme Court declared that the public interest standard was the *touchstone* of authority for the Federal Communications Commission. The Court made it clear that the FCC, in making decisions regarding the licensing of stations, must consider the public interest, convenience, and necessity.

In May 1936, the Pottsville Broadcasting Company sought a construction permit to put a station on the air in Pottsville, Pennsylvania. The FCC denied the petition on two grounds. First, the respondent was perceived to be financially disqualified, and second, the applicant did not sufficiently represent the public interest of the community.

When Pottsville appealed the decision, the court remanded the case for reconsideration because the FCC's public interest concerns were based on an erroneous interpretation of Pennsylvania law. In the meantime, the FCC had received two additional applications for the available frequency. The Commission announced that it would award a license only after comparing the public interest potential of all three stations, but a U.S. court of appeals ordered the Commission to first consider the remanded Pottsville application.[26]

The FCC appealed and the Supreme Court ruled that just because a legal error was committed, the appeals court had no authority to grant priority status to Pottsville. But more importantly, the Court strongly upheld the public interest doctrine, calling it the touchstone of authority for the Federal Communications Commission. The Court said, "The Commission's authority at all times is to measure applications by the standard of public interest, convenience, or necessity."[27] The standard would apply whether deciding to renew a license or issue it in the first place.

9.2.4   *FCC v. Sanders Brothers Radio*

> In the *Sanders* case the Supreme Court offered a more narrow interpretation of the public interest standard.

In 1936, a Dubuque, Iowa, newspaper applied for a construction permit for a new radio station. An existing station—WKBB, owned by Sanders Brothers Radio—petitioned the FCC to deny the license on the basis of three arguments:

1. there was insufficient advertising revenue to support an additional station in Dubuque;
2. adequate service to the area was already being rendered by WKBB; and
3. grant of the additional service would not serve the public interest.

The FCC granted the license anyway, after concluding that the public interest would be served by an additional station. A U.S Court of Appeals overruled the FCC,

[26] Pottsville Broadcasting v. FCC, 98 F.2d 288 (1940).
[27] FCC v. Pottsville Broadcasting, 309 U.S. 134 (1940).

holding that since the issue of economic injury to the existing station was not considered by the Commission, the decision was arbitrary and capricious.[28]

The Supreme Court overturned the lower court, holding that the public interest standard did not force the FCC to consider economic injury to existing stations when considering an application for a broadcast facility.[29] The Court went on to suggest that programming and business matters were off limits to the FCC:

> [T]he Act does not essay to regulate the business of the licensee. The Commission is given no supervisory control of the programs, of business management, or of policy. In short, the broadcasting field is open to anyone, provided there be an available frequency over which he can broadcast without interference to others, if he shows competency, the adequacy of his equipment, and the financial ability to make good use of the assigned channel.[30]

The Court did say that an important element of the public interest is the ability of the licensee to render the best practicable service to the community, and that the purpose of the Communications Act is to protect the public, not the licensee. But as long as the actual signal of one broadcaster is not interfering with competitors, it is up to each to survive or succumb according to the ability to make programs attractive to the public.

The *Sanders Brothers* decision is interesting in that it appears to contradict the Brinkley, Shuler, and *Pottsville* decisions. The Court had seemingly reduced the role of the FCC back to that of a traffic cop functioning primarily to prevent technical interference. The decision also includes notions of marketplace regulation (or deregulation) that would gain prominence some 40 years later.

The decision certainly indicated a shift to a more narrow interpretation of FCC powers under the public interest standard. After all, the Court said the Commission had no supervisory control over programs, business matters, or station policies. But if such a shift did occur it was abruptly reversed in the *NBC* case, decided just three years later.

9.2.5 *NBC* v. *United States*

In the *NBC* case the Supreme Court offered a compelling endorsement of broad FCC powers under the public interest standard.[31]

During the late 1920s and 1930s, the major networks dominated the radio industry. The FCC became increasingly concerned as the networks gained control of large shares of advertising revenues and dominated prime time schedules. Indus-

---

[28] Sanders Bros. Radio Station v. FCC, 106 F.2d 321 (1939).
[29] FCC v. Sanders Bros. Radio Station, 309 U.S. 470 (1940).
[30] *Id.* at 475 (1940).
[31] NBC v. United States, 319 U.S. 190 (1943).

try experts and a majority of FCC commissioners believed that new rules were necessary to curtail the networks' influence. So, in 1943, the FCC passed the "Chain Broadcasting Regulations," designed to limit the power that networks exerted over local affiliates.[32] The rules focused on network ownership of stations and contractual arrangements that restricted affiliates' choices regarding which network programs to carry.

NBC and CBS challenged the rules on the basis of three principal arguments:

1. The FCC was supposed to function primarily as a traffic cop and acted outside the powers conferred upon it by Congress in passing the chain broadcasting rules.
2. The standard of public interest was unconstitutionally vague.
3. The chain broadcasting rules violated the networks' First Amendment rights.

Once again, the high court was asked to rule on critical regulatory questions. Does the public interest standard authorize the FCC to regulate nontechnical matters? Does the FCC exceed its authority in using programming as a major criterion of public interest? Does the regulation of programming content violate broadcasters' First Amendment rights?

The Supreme Court, with Justice Frankfurter delivering the opinion, upheld the chain broadcasting regulations. The 1934 act, the Court said, does not restrict the FCC to mere supervision of traffic. The Commission must also determine the composition of that traffic. Frankfurter used language from the 1934 act and the argument that radio frequencies are a scarce resource to justify a broad public interest standard:

> The "public interest" to be served under the Communications Act is thus the interest of the listening public in the "larger and more effective use of radio." The facilities of radio are limited and therefore precious; they cannot be left to wasteful use without detriment to the public interest.[33]

Frankfurter then quoted from the chain broadcasting rules:

> With the number of radio channels limited by natural factors, the public interest demands that those who are entrusted with the available channels shall make the fullest and most effective use of them. If a licensee enters into a contract with a network organization which limits his ability to make the best use of the radio facility assigned him, he is not serving the public interest.[34]

---

[32] FCC Order No. 37, Docket No. 5060 (1941).
[33] 319 U.S. at 216 (1943).
[34] 319 U.S. at 218 (1943).

The Supreme Court also rejected the claim that the public interest doctrine is unconstitutionally vague, but Frankfurter offered only a brief quote from a previous decision to explain the Court's position. He wrote:

> It was a mistaken assumption that this is a mere general reference to public welfare without any standard to guide determinations. The purpose of the act, the requirement it imposes, and the context of the provision in question show the contrary.[35]

The Court then returned to the scarcity notion to reject the network's First Amendment claims. Frankfurter argued that, unlike other modes of expression, radio is not available to all, and some who wish to use it must be denied.

Does this denial amount to an abridgement of First Amendment rights? No, said Frankfurter:

> The right of free speech does not include, however, the right to use the facilities of radio without a license. The licensing system established by Congress in the Communications Act of 1934 was a proper exercise of its power over commerce. The standard it provided for the licensing of stations was the "public interest, convenience, and necessity." Denial of a station license on that ground, if valid under the Act, is not a denial of free speech.[36]

The significance of the *NBC* case, summarized in Box 9.3, is difficult to overstate. It would be over 25 years before the Supreme Court would again issue a decision directly addressing the public interest standard and the FCC's authority to regulate electronic media.

Justice Murphy's dissent in the *NBC* case presented a perspective that has recently gained attention. Murphy warned of the potential for radio to become a weapon of authority, misrepresentation, and even oppression instead of a means of entertainment and enlightenment. This perspective is now referred to as the "impact" or "pervasiveness" rationale used to justify differential treatment of electronic and print media regarding matters of content regulation.

By the mid-1940s the public interest standard was firmly entrenched. But some legal and industry experts disagree with the interpretation of the public interest standard in the *NBC* decision. They suggest that Congress never intended government intervention into programming matters. W. T. Mayton, an Emory Law School professor, asserts that the *NBC* decision was more the result of progressive attitudes favoring social change than of an accurate interpretation of the Communications Act. Mayton argues that a "New Deal" philosophy of active government prevailed at the time of the decision and that Justice Frankfurter and the FCC, influenced by this

---

[35] The quote was taken from New York Central Sec. Corp. v. United States, 287 U.S. 12 (1932).
[36] 319 U.S. at 227 (1943).

BOX 9.3 The Significance of *NBC* v. *United States*

The *NBC* case endures as the most powerful and sweeping statement ever made by the U.S. Supreme Court in support of a broadly based regulatory authority of the FCC. In this one decision the Court:

1. affirmed the right of the FCC to exercise broad powers over the broadcasting industry;
2. affirmed that the public interest standard is the touchstone of FCC authority to exercise broad regulatory powers;
3. held that the public interest standard is not unconstitutionally vague;
4. offered a scarcity rationale—the notion that regulation is necessary because the airwaves are limited—as justification for the public interest standard and for content regulation; and,
5. ruled that regulations that may result in license revocation or nonrenewal do not violate broadcasters' First Amendment rights.

---

philosophy, misinterpreted the act.[37] For support, Mayton cites the Court's more narrow decision in *FCC* v. *Sanders Radio*.

9.2.6 *WOKO* v. *FCC*

The *WOKO* case demonstrated that the powers of the FCC under the public interest standard are limited and cannot be exercised arbitrarily or capriciously.

A review of license revocations and denial of renewals over the years reveals that misrepresentation to the FCC or concealment of information is considered a major violation of the public interest standard (EMG 4.1.7.9).[38] A case involving a New York radio station provides an early example of the FCC's disdain for concealment of information. More importantly, it offers indication of the limits of the FCC's authority under the public interest standard. In 1942, station WOKO in Albany, New York, applied for license renewal. The station had moved to Albany in 1931 after owner Harold Smith convinced the local newspaper to buy shares to help solve the station's ongoing financial problems. Smith also obtained a CBS affiliation through negotiations with CBS executive Sam Pickard, a former member of the Fed-

---

[37] W. T. Mayton, "The Illegitimacy of the Public Interest Standard at the FCC," 38 *Emory L.J.* 715 (1989). *See also* T. W. Hazlett, "The Rationality of U.S. Regulation of the Broadcast Spectrum," 33 *J. of Law & Econ.* 133 (1990) and M. Sophos, "The Public Interest, Convenience, and Necessity: A Dead Standard in the Era of Broadcast Deregulation," 10 *Pace L. Rev.* 661 (1990).

[38] *See* Frederic A. Weiss, David Ostroff, and Charles E. Clift III, "Station License Revocations and Denials of Renewal, 1970–78," 24 *J. Broadcasting* 69 (1980).

eral Radio Commission. During the negotiations, Pickard suggested he be given stock in the station, but requested that his ownership be kept secret to avoid the embarrassment of having CBS associates learn about the arrangement. Smith agreed and did not disclose the fact to the FRC.

By the mid-1930s, FCC license renewal forms required greater detail concerning stockholders, so Smith was eventually forced to inform the Commission of Pickard's ownership. Upon receiving WOKO's renewal application in 1942, the Commission decided to deny renewal when it was determined that the station had previously concealed the fact that Pickard was an owner.

In considering WOKO's appeal the court focused on whether the FCC had rightfully exercised its power granted under the Communications Act.[39] First, the court acknowledged that the public interest standard provided the Commission broad powers, but warned that the FCC could not act without constraint:

> The broad scope of authority, or standard of action, established by the Communications Act is that the public interest, convenience, and necessity must be served. Within that framework the administrative agent is free to exercise its expert judgment; it cannot act unconstitutionally, for neither could its principal, the Congress, and the stream cannot rise higher than its source; it must proceed within the scope of authority granted it, that is to say . . . it cannot act arbitrarily or capriciously.[40]

The court ruled that license nonrenewal should be based on compelling reasons that have direct bearing on the public interest. Although a station license may be revoked for false statements, failure to reveal minority ownership in the WOKO case did not constitute a compelling reason for nonrenewal. Furthermore, the FCC failed to weigh adequately all elements regarding the public interest involved in the nonrenewal of WOKO's license. The court reversed the FCC's decision, concluding that license revocation would deprive the community of WOKO's service when there was no reason to believe the station would not operate in the public interest.[41]

9.3   BLUE BOOK

In the Blue Book the FCC offered programming guidelines designed to help broadcasters meet public interest obligations. The Commission stated that broadcasters should avoid advertising excesses and devote airtime to discussion of public issues, nonsponsored programming, and local live programming.

---

[39] WOKO, Inc. v. FCC, 153 F.2d at 627 (1946).
[40] *Id.* at 628.
[41] WOKO, Inc. v. FCC, 153 F.2d 623 (1946).

By the mid-1940s it was clear to the FCC that the networks were as dominant a force as ever in the broadcasting industry. It was also clear that licensees were uncertain regarding how to best meet public interest requirements. So, in 1946 the Commission issued a policy statement titled *Public Service Responsibility of Broadcast Licensees*. Released in the form of a memo, the statement was called the Blue Book because of its blue cover.

The Blue Book was an attempt by the Commission to clarify its position on the public interest standard by offering programming guidelines. The FCC wanted to help broadcasters understand what was expected of them at renewal time.

The first part of the Blue Book was a rather detailed attempt by the Commission to justify inclusion of programming performance as a criterion of the public interest standard. But the most notable section of the Blue Book was a list of four public interest factors that the Commission said would receive particular attention in licensing decisions. The first three factors were actually types of programming the Commission considered to be in the public interest. First, stations should carry *sustaining or nonsponsored programs*. The Commission stated that airing sustaining programs helps to maintain overall program balance, provides time for programs serving minority interests and for nonprofit organizations, and provides time for certain types of programs inappropriate for sponsorship.

Second, stations should carry *local live programs*. The Commission acknowledged that network and transcribed programming and news received from wire services could be aired. But airing such programs to the extent that local programming is confined to unpopular time segments would be considered a violation of the public interest.

The third factor was *programming devoted to the discussion of public issues*. Again, the Commission urged stations to carry such programming during popular listening hours.

The final public interest factor was the *elimination of advertising excesses*. The Blue Book warned broadcasters against excesses that were incompatible with their public responsibilities but suggested that adoption of specific guidelines was a matter better left to self-regulation.[42]

License renewal forms were revised to make them compatible with the Blue Book. The new forms required stations to indicate proposed programming and to provide a detailed programming analysis for a one-week period selected at random by the FCC. The FCC also provided uniform definitions of programming types in an attempt to reduce confusion over terms used in programming records.

Not surprisingly, the Blue Book was not warmly received. Broadcasters feared it signaled increased FCC intrusion into programming practices. These concerns were mostly short lived, however. In 1951, the license of station WBAL in Baltimore was renewed despite the fact that the FCC had concluded that WBAL had compiled quite an unsatisfactory programming record. The station's programming had contained an excess of commercials and devoted an insufficient amount of time

---

[42] Public Service Responsibility of Broadcast Licensees, FCC Memorandum issued March 7, 1946.

to local issues and sustaining programs. Two commissioners strongly dissented, claiming that WBAL's programming was clearly not in the public interest and that the licensee had no vested interest or property right to the frequency.[43]

9.4   1960 PROGRAMMING POLICY STATEMENT

The FCC instituted a new requirement in 1960. To meet the public interest standard, stations would have to ascertain the needs and interests of the community and show how their programming met those needs.

The FCC held a series of hearings in the late 1950s to determine broadcasters' perceptions of problems associated with fulfilling public interest obligations. The hearings convinced the Commission that additional clarification of the public interest standard was necessary. So, in 1960, the FCC once again attempted to delineate broadcasters' public interest programming responsibilities. The document's official name was *Report and Statement of Policy re: Commission en banc Programming Inquiry*. It is generally referred to by its more popular title, the "1960 Programming Policy Statement." As in the Blue Book, the Commission began the 1960 statement with a discussion of court decisions and other interpretations of the public interest standard that had called for broad FCC regulatory powers:

> In view of the fact that a broadcaster is required to program his station in the public interest, convenience, and necessity, it follows that despite the limitations of the First Amendment and Section 326 of the Act, that his freedom to program is not absolute. The Commission does not conceive that it is barred by the Constitution or by statute from exercising any responsibility with respect to programming. . . . The licensee, is, in effect, a "trustee" in the sense that his license to operate his station imposes upon him a non-delegable duty to serve the public interest in the community he had chosen to represent as a broadcaster.[44]

The Commission dropped its insistence on sustaining programs, but otherwise the programming factors emphasized in the 1960 Programming Policy Statement were similar to those of the Blue Book. The Commission identified the following as the major elements of programming necessary to meet public interest needs and desires: opportunity for local self-expression, the development and use of local talent, programs for children, religious programs, educational programs, public affairs programs, editorialization by licensees, political broadcasts, agricultural programs,

---

[43] Applications of Hearst Radio, Inc. (WBAL), 15 F.C.C. 1149 (1951).

[44] Report and Statement of Policy re: Commission en banc Programming Inquiry, 44 F.C.C. at 2311–2314 (1960).

news programs, weather and market reports, sports, service to minority groups, and entertainment programming.

The Commission was careful to point out that the list of elements did not constitute a rigid formula for station programming practices. Just how the various elements would be incorporated into a station's programming was left to the discretion of the licensee.

The 1960 Programming Policy Statement offered a significant new development regarding the public interest standard. In order to assure that stations operate in the public interest, applications for new stations, renewals, and modifications were revised to require licensees to indicate:

1. measures taken to actually determine the tastes, needs, and desires of the community, and
2. ways in which the licensee proposed to meet those needs and desires.

Thus, the 1960 Programming Policy Statement gave birth to the FCC's *ascertainment requirements.*[45] More formal requirements were instituted in 1971.[46] In fact, the Commission stated that the principal ingredient of the licensee's obligation to operate in the public interest would be the "diligent, positive, and continuing effort" to discover and fulfill the broadcast needs and interests of the community.[47] Ascertainment requirements would be a major component of license renewal until they were repealed in the 1980s (EMG 9.6.3).

9.5   ATTEMPTS AT PROGRAMMING LIMITATIONS

The FCC has regulations placing a variety of restrictions on programming. Many restrictions were lifted in the 1980s, but significant ones remain.

As evidenced in the Brinkley and Shuler cases, the FRC demonstrated early on that certain programming practices would not be tolerated. Armed with a public interest standard authorizing broad discretion in regulating the airwaves, the FCC has promulgated a number of policies restricting programming in one way or another. Programming requirements and restrictions are discussed in detail in other chapters. The following brief summary is intended as an illustration of governmental restrictions on programming under the public interest standard.

The Chain Broadcasting Rules were among the first that affected programming. Since then, the FCC has adopted prime-time access rules that limit network programming to three of the four prime-time viewing hours and financial interest and syndication rules that restricted networks' ability to have financial interest in and

---

[45] Ascertainment procedures upheld in Henry v. FCC, 302 F.2d 191 (1962).
[46] Primer on Ascertainment of Community Problems by Broadcast Applicants, 27 F.C.C.2d 650 (1971).
[47] *Id.*

syndicate programs.[48] Section 315 of the Communications Act places considerable restrictions on political broadcasts and political advertising, and Section 312 requires stations to allow candidates for federal office to advertise on their stations.

The personal attack rules impose procedures to be followed when an individual is attacked during any issue-oriented programming. Those procedures include a requirement that the individual be given airtime to respond to the attack. The FCC has both prohibited and encouraged editorialization, and until its repeal in 1987, the Fairness Doctrine forced broadcasters to air programs dealing with issues of public concern and make sure that overall coverage of issues was balanced.

The courts have established that indecent programming is protected by the First Amendment. Despite this, the broadcast of indecent or profane language is prohibited under federal law[49] and licensees have been fined as much as $500,000 for airing programming the FCC considered to be indecent.[50]

Section 317 of the Communications Act requires sponsorship identification of advertising and there are restrictions on the amount and types of advertising allowed in children's programming.[51] Congress has banned public broadcasters from editorializing[52] and prohibited airing any information on lotteries except those officially endorsed and run by the states. The FCC also has a policy prohibiting the broadcast of hoaxes.[53] Until 1980, the FCC banned all low power television operators from providing any programming service at all.[54]

Past and present regulations have also placed restrictions on cable programmers. These include the must carry and nonduplication rules (EMG 10.3.2, 13.4.1). And cable is the only mass medium for which rules require operators to provide public access to their facilities.

9.6 REINTERPRETATION OF THE PUBLIC INTEREST STANDARD: DEREGULATION OF RADIO AND TELEVISION

The 1980s marked a radical change in interpretation of the public interest standard. The "public interest" was used to justify elimination of many regulations, and the trustee model was challenged by a new marketplace philosophy.

In the late 1970s the FCC announced plans to eliminate several key regulatory policies affecting radio. The announcement was only the beginning of a dramatic

[48] Competition and Responsibility in Network Television Broadcasting, 23 F.C.C.2d 382 (1970). Amended in 50 F.C.C.2d 829 (1975). In 1993 the FCC eliminated the financial interest rules and announced a two-year moratorium on syndication restrictions. *See* 8 F.C.C.R. 3282 (1993).
[49] 18 U.S.C.A. § 1464.
[50] H. A. Jessell, "Infinity Fined $500,000 for Stern," *Broadcasting & Cable*, 16 August 1993, at 6, 15.
[51] Children's Television Act of 1990, Pub. L. No. 101-437, 1990 H.R. 1677, 104 Stat. 996 (1990).
[52] FCC v. League of Women Voters of Cal., 468 U.S. 364 (1984).
[53] 7 F.C.C.R. 4106 (1992).
[54] 82 F.C.C.2d 47 (1980).

series of deregulatory moves in which the Commission ultimately repealed scores of policies affecting many aspects of radio and television station operations. A few of the discarded policies, including the formal ascertainment requirements discussed above, had previously been identified by the FCC as critical to a licensee's public interest performance.

A number of factors account for the dramatic change. Clearly, the FCC was aware of congressional attempts to rewrite the Communications Act of 1934. Some of the proposed rewrites included deregulatory measures, mostly affecting radio. Of course, it is also clear that FCC commissioners, especially FCC chair Mark Fowler, advocated deregulation. With the FCC seriously questioning the need for content regulation, it is not surprising that many policies were ultimately abolished. Of course, the influence of the executive branch on telecommunication policy during this era should not be underestimated. The Carter and Reagan administrations effectively deregulated a number of industries in the 1970s and 1980s.

9.6.1 Marketplace Philosophy

> Proponents of the marketplace philosophy advocate elimination of FCC restrictions on programming content. Under the marketplace philosophy, the question of whether a station's programming serves the public interest is determined *not* by the FCC but by its survival in the marketplace.

The official beginning of radio and television deregulation may be traced back to September 27, 1979. On that date the FCC issued its "Notice of Inquiry and Proposed Rulemaking in the Matter of Deregulation of Radio."[55]

The notice provided a new economic perspective on telecommunications regulation called the *marketplace philosophy*. The FCC acknowledged that adoption of the economic, marketplace model and proposed rule changes would denote a clear departure from previous regulatory policy. Though not explicitly acknowledged, the new model also signaled a dramatic shift in interpretation of the public interest standard.

The Commission justified the shift in philosophy on the basis of three major changes in the radio industry:

1. competition had increased substantially, especially in larger markets;
2. radio was no longer the dominant mass medium it had been before television; and,
3. increased diversity of American society had resulted in a change in the American community, and radio had responded to that change by becoming more specialized.

The FCC also announced criteria of good performance that sounded much like an economics lecture. First, the goods or services supplied should correspond to

---

[55] 73 F.C.C.2d 457 (1979).

what the public wants. Second, these goods and services should be provided at the lowest possible cost. Marketplace regulation would shift the determination of public interest to the public:

> Consumers, by their choice of purchases, determine which producers (providers) will succeed. Moreover, not only does the competition among producers for consumers lead to the production of goods and services that consumers want most, the same competitive process forces producers continually to seek less costly ways of providing those goods and services. As a result, parties operating freely in a competitive market environment will determine and fulfill consumer wants, and do so efficiently. [56]

The Commission also stated that regulation is necessary only when the marketplace clearly fails to protect the public interest—not where there is only a *potential* for failure. But the Commission did not specify what precisely constitutes a marketplace failure. Were the Brinkley and Shuler cases examples of marketplace failure? In both cases the stations attracted large audiences and survived very well in the marketplace. Would this mean that Brinkley and Shuler would have satisfied marketplace criteria for renewal? Certainly the marketplace approach would require a different analysis of these and other cases.

As explained in Box 9.4, the scarcity rationale was also reevaluated. The Commission claimed that scarcity would be defined differently than it had been in the early days of radio, since virtually all goods and services are scarce, not just radio waves.

A discussion of the marketplace rationale was presented in a law journal article by then FCC chair Mark Fowler and Daniel Brenner. [57] Fowler and Brenner criticized what they called the "vague" public interest standard and advocated elimination of the trustee model. Instead of government defining public interest and specifying how to meet it, they suggested that the marketplace, the listeners and viewers, should define the public interest. They concluded that given advances in electronic media technology, the scarcity rationale was simply no longer viable. The only real scarce resource, they argued, was advertising dollars, not megahertz.

Fowler and Brenner's arguments signaled another dramatic change in FCC policy. The public interest standard, they argued, violated broadcasters' First Amendment rights. The FCC and courts had previously held that First Amendment rights of listeners and viewers were most important. [58] Fowler and Brenner disagreed, saying the rights of speakers (including broadcasters) must be protected.

---

[56] Notice of Inquiry and Proposed Rulemaking in the Matter of Deregulation of Radio, 73 F.C.C.2d at 492 (1979).

[57] Mark S. Fowler and Daniel L. Brenner, "A Marketplace Approach to Broadcast Regulation," 60 *Texas L. Rev. 207 (1982).*

[58] Red Lion Broadcasting Co. v. FCC, 395 U.S. 367 (1969).

BOX 9.4   Marketplace Philosophy and the Scarcity Rationale

The FCC's deregulation of radio and acceptance of the marketplace philosophy was accompanied by a new interpretation of the scarcity rationale. Two types of scarcity were delineated.

1. *Supply or technological scarcity* exists when the number of frequencies available for allocation is limited.
2. *Demand scarcity* exists when the number of persons desiring frequencies exceeds the number available.

By 1980 the FCC, obviously moving away from previous emphasis on technological scarcity, suggested that in radio broadcasting, demand is related to the amount of profit a particular frequency or station could be expected to generate. Demand scarcity, therefore, is based on economic rather than technological factors.

To increase the market value of a station, the licensee must program according to consumer demands. This allows the marketplace to regulate programming decisions such as how many commercials to air each hour and provides an economic, rather than a regulatory, inducement to serve the public interest. The need for government regulation is negated because consumers—not the governmental regulations—require licensees to operate in the public interest.*

---

* 73 F.C.C.2d 457 (1979).

The Commission demonstrated this shift in First Amendment perspective in 1983 when it announced the repeal of a number of policies affecting programming:

> [P]olicies cautioning broadcasters not to engage in certain programming practices or establishing rigid guidelines in relation to such programming raise fundamental questions concerning the constitutional rights of broadcast licensees, and therefore cannot be retained in the absence of a clear and compelling showing that the public interest demands their retention.[59]

Then, in abolishing the Fairness Doctrine in 1987, the Commission denounced the assertion that the rights of listeners and viewers were more important than those of broadcasters and argued that broadcasters should be afforded the same First Amendment protection as the print media.[60] Fowler and Brenner called for

---

[59] Elimination of Unnecessary Broadcast Regulations, 54 Rad. Reg. 2d (P&F) 1043 (1983).
[60] Syracuse Peace Council v. FCC, 867 F.2d 654 (1989).

elimination of all content and business regulation and suggested that licenses should be revoked only in extreme cases.

Clearly, not all ideas expressed by Fowler and Brenner were accepted by the FCC and converted into policy. But the marketplace philosophy, at least in part, provided the rationale for the deregulation of the broadcast industry.

9.6.2 Court Challenges to Marketplace Regulation

The courts have upheld the FCC's authority to repeal regulatory policies under the marketplace philosophy.

The most significant court challenge to marketplace regulation occurred in 1981 when the FCC refused to get involved in the regulation of radio station formats. A citizen group had petitioned the Commission to stop the sale of one of Chicago's two classical music stations. The proposed buyer intended to convert the station to a rock format. The FCC insisted that the public interest would best be served if marketplace forces and competition among broadcasters determined the makeup of station formats. The U.S. Supreme Court upheld the Commission's policy in *FCC* v. *WNCN Listener's Guild*. The Court endorsed the FCC's reliance on marketplace forces to regulate format changes rather than action on behalf of dissatisfied listeners. The Court concluded that "marketplace regulation was a constitutionally protected means of implementing the public interest standard of the act."[61]

In *WOLD* v. *FCC* a Commission decision regarding satellite communications was challenged. The FCC had decided to allow the sale of a few transponders for domestic satellites (domsats) on a non–common carrier basis (EMG 7.3.4). The appeals court upheld the decision, emphasizing the need for broad FCC authority in an industry as dynamic and rapidly changing as satellite communications. Then the court offered a strong endorsement of marketplace regulation, saying, "the public interest touchstone of the Communications Act, beyond question, permits the FCC to allow the marketplace to substitute for direct Commission regulation in appropriate circumstances."[62]

In *TRAC* v. *FCC* the court upheld a number of FCC deregulatory moves.[63] The FCC had repealed policies prohibiting deceptive commercials, the use of a station to promote nonbroadcast business interests, and failure to adhere to sales contracts. The court said that the public interest standard is best left to the discretion of the FCC, which "may rely on marketplace forces to control broadcast abuse if the Commission reasonably finds that a marketplace approach offers the best means of controlling the abuse."[64] The court concluded that the FCC had provided a rational explanation for reliance on marketplace forces.

---

[61] FCC v. WNCN Listener's Guild, 450 U.S. 582 (1981).
[62] WOLD Communications v. FCC, 735 F.2d 1465 (1984).
[63] Telecommunications Research and Action Ctr. v. FCC (TRAC I), 800 F.2d 1181 (1986).
[64] *Id.* at 1185.

9.6.3 Summary of Deregulatory Policy Changes

A significant number of FCC restrictions and requirements imposed on broadcasters have been eliminated. Some policy changes directly affect the manner in which the FCC determines whether stations have met public interest obligations.

The FCC followed through on its promise to deregulate radio in 1981.[65] Three years later, similar revisions were made in policies affecting television.[66] As the decade continued, more regulations were eliminated. The following sections provide a comprehensive summary of policy changes adopted since 1980. The major policy changes are outlined in Box 9.5.

1. *Elimination of Nonentertainment Programming Guidelines*—Previous policy required television stations to air 5 percent local programming, 5 percent public affairs, and a total of 10 percent nonentertainment programming. AM and FM stations were required to air a minimum of 8 percent and 6 percent nonentertainment programming respectively.[67] All percentage guidelines were eliminated.

2. *Elimination of Formal Ascertainment Requirements*—Since the 1960 Policy Statement each station was required to ascertain the needs and interests of the local community and show how its programming would meet those needs.[68] As stated previously, the requirements were made substantially more demanding in the 1970s.[69] At that time licensees were required to complete five basic tasks:

   a. Prepare composite studies summarizing ethnic breakdown, economic and governmental activities, and other distinctive elements of the community.

   b. Conduct interviews with leaders from community interest groups. Each significant interest group had to be contacted or the ascertainment (and possibly the station's license renewal) would be considered defective. The name and organization of each person interviewed had to be recorded. The composition studies were to be used to guide selection of interviewees.

   c. Conduct random surveys of the general public to determine community needs and interests.

   d. Use the information collected in the interviews and surveys to compile a list of community problems.

---

[65] Deregulation of Radio, 84 F.C.C.2d 968 (1981).

[66] Revision of Programming and Commercialization Policies, Ascertainment Requirements, and Program Log Requirements for Commercial Television Stations, 98 F.C.C.2d 1076 (1984).

[67] 43 F.C.C.2d 638 (1973).

[68] One study concluded the actual annual cost of ascertainment to be almost $7,000, and an informal NAB survey found the range of costs to be from $2,500 to $9,000 (cited in 98 F.C.C.2d 1076).

[69] *See* 27 F.C.C.2d 650 (1971), and 57 F.C.C.2d 418 (1975).

BOX 9.5   Summary of Major Deregulatory Policy Changes Since 1980

The following policy changes affect both radio and television stations.

1. Minimum nonentertainment programming time guidelines have been eliminated.
2. Ascertainment requirements have been greatly relaxed.
3. Restrictions on commercials have been eliminated.
4. Stations are no longer required to keep program logs.
5. Ownership limits—including limits on the total number of stations and on stations within a single market—have been significantly relaxed.
6. The three-year antitrafficking rule has been eliminated.
7. The long-form license renewal application has been eliminated.
8. License renewal periods have been extended.
9. The Fairness Doctrine has been eliminated.
10. The problems/programs list has been eliminated.
11. A large number of what the FCC calls "underbrush" policies have been eliminated.

---

e. Specify programming aired in response to particular community problems. The programming could not be limited to announcements and news stories.

All information was to be maintained in the station's public file.[70]

The FCC eliminated all formal ascertainment requirements.[71] Stations must still identify local needs and provide appropriate programming (EMG 10.1.2.1), but it is up to the licensee how ascertainment will be achieved.[72]

3. *Elimination of Limits on Commercials*—Television stations had been limited to 16 commercial minutes per hour, and restrictions were also placed on the length and type of commercials that could be aired.[73] The Commission has eliminated all restrictions on length, number, or type of commercials. However, in 1993 the FCC initiated proceedings to determine whether the public interest would be served by

---

[70] *See also* Ascertainment of Community Problems, 27 F.C.C.2d 650 (1971) and In the Matter of Ascertainment of Community Problems by Renewal Applicants, 57 F.C.C.2d 418 (1975); *reconsideration granted in part*, 61 F.C.C.2d 1 (1976). FCC ascertainment procedures were upheld in Henry v. FCC, 302 F.2d 191 (1962).

[71] 98 F.C.C.2d 1076 (1984).

[72] Formal ascertainment requirements had already been eliminated for commercial radio (*see* Second Report and Order in BC Docket 79-219, 49 Fed. Reg. 19,019, May 4, 1984), and for television stations in small markets (*see* 86 F.C.C.2d 798 (1981)).

[73] 43 F.C.C.2d 638 (1973). *See also* 8 F.C.C.R. 7277 (1993).

reestablishing commercial limits for television stations. The Commission's action was based, in part, on concern over the proliferation of program-length commercials.

4. *Elimination of Program Log Requirements*—Previous policy required stations to maintain detailed programming records known in the industry as program logs. Logs had to be kept for at least two years and made available upon demand for public and FCC inspection. The logs were required to indicate the type, time, and source of all programs run, the time, placement, and length of all commercials, the amount of public service programs aired, and other information.[74] After deregulation, stations were no longer required to keep program logs on file for public or FCC inspection.

5. *Elimination of the 7-7-7 Rule*—Longstanding policy had restricted ownership to seven AM, seven FM and seven television stations. No more than five of the seven television stations could be VHF. These restrictions, as well as ones limiting the number of a particular type of facility one owner may operate in a given market have been significantly relaxed (EMG 7.1.3.3).[75]

6. *Elimination of the Anti-Trafficking Rule*—Previous policy required station owners to hold licenses for at least three years. The new policy eliminated the three-year rule and permitted "market forces" to govern most sale transactions.[76]

7. *Elimination of Long Forms for License Renewal*—Previous policy required commercial television stations to complete a 21-page renewal application which asked for detailed information regarding nonentertainment and children's programming, public service announcements, and ascertainment procedures. Forms for noncommercial stations were 15 pages. Radio renewal forms were only two pages but required a substantial amount of information. The FCC instituted a simplified renewal process consisting of five review components (EMG 8.1.5).[77]

8. *Extension of License Renewal Period*—The license renewal terms were extended from three to five years for television, and from three to seven years for radio.

---

[74] *See* Amendment of Program Logging Rules for Television Broadcast Stations, 5 F.C.C.2d 185 (1966), and Program Logs, 44 F.C.C.2d 845 (1974).

[75] Amendment of the Commission's Rules Relating to Multiple Ownership of AM, FM, and Television Broadcast Stations, 100 F.C.C.2d 17 (1984).

[76] In the Matter of Amendment of Section 73.3597 of the Commission's Rules (Applications for Voluntary Assignments or Transfers of Control), 55 Rad. Reg. 2d (P&F) 1081 (1982). *See also* 99 F.C.C.2d 971 (1985), and 4 F.C.C.R. 1710 (1989).

[77] Revision of Application for Renewal of License of Commercial and Noncommercial AM, FM, and Television Licensees, 49 Rad. Reg. 2d (P&F) 740 (1981); *reconsideration denied*, 50 Rad. Reg. 2d (P&F) 704 (1981).

9. *Abolition of the Fairness Doctrine*—In 1974, the FCC stated that adherence to the Fairness Doctrine was the most important factor of license renewal.[78] Thirteen years later, it abolished the Fairness Doctrine (EMG 11.6).[79]

10. *Elimination of the "Problems/Programs" List*—Previous policy required that stations' public files contain a list of no more than ten significant problems and needs of the community served by the station in the preceding year. Stations were required to describe programs aired to meet the needs. At first the FCC revised the policy to require an annual "issues/programs" list, also to be placed in the public file. The list was to contain full, narrative descriptions of 5 to 10 issues to which the station gave particular attention during the preceding three months and a description of how each issue was treated. Program descriptions would include the date, time, and duration of the broadcasts.[80] The FCC later required stations to submit the information quarterly as opposed to annually (EMG 10.1.2.1).

11. *Elimination of "Underbrush" Regulations*—Underbrush regulations were accumulated rules, policies, doctrines, and interpretive statements which, the FCC contended, unnecessarily restricted broadcasters and wasted Commission resources.

    The FCC, in its progression of underbrush policy statements from 1983 to 1986, offered the following justifications for elimination of the regulations:

    a. The policies are unwarranted and unnecessary.
    b. Prohibiting certain types of programming practices stifles creativity and discourages the development of innovative programming.
    c. Broadcasters were unlikely to engage in program abuses related to underbrush policies for reasons other than FCC restrictions. Alternative remedies are available through other agencies and through civil and criminal actions. Advertisers and the general public also serve to discourage abuses.
    d. Some of the regulations were outside the Commission's expertise.
    e. Many of the regulations targeted activities that are susceptible to regulation by marketplace forces.
    f. Some of the regulations may have been in violation of broadcasters' First Amendment rights.

    The first underbrush announcement was issued in 1983. The FCC eliminated prohibitions against the use of inaccurate or exaggerated

---

[78] Handling of Public Issues Under the Fairness Doctrine and the Public Interest Standards of the Communications Act (1974 Fairness Report), 48 F.C.C.2d 1 (1974).
[79] Syracuse Peace Council v FCC, 2 F.C.C.R. 5043 (1987).
[80] 98 F.C.C.2d 1076 (1984).

coverage maps, and *hypoing*, which is deliberately engageing in excessive promotional activities during ratings periods.[81]

The second announcement eliminated prohibitions against:

a. broadcast of astrological information;

b. advertisement of alcoholic beverages in states where it is prohibited by law;

c. station placement of harassing phone calls and broadcasts that result in such calls;

d. contractual agreements between broadcasters and music format service companies;

e. repeated, continuous playing of a single record, and

f. use of sirens, horns, and other sound effects in commercials and promotional announcements.

The same announcement eliminated a requirement to announce when polls are conducted in a non-scientific manner and a policy encouraging broadcast of foreign language programs.[82] Restrictions on announcements and advertisements of horse racing events were eliminated in 1984.[83]

In January 1985 the Commission eliminated policies forbidding contests and promotions which could adversely affect the public, and a ban on scare announcements or headlines which could mislead or frighten the public.[84] One week later, more underbrush policies were repealed. This time the Commission eliminated policies or rules prohibiting:

a. distortion of audience ratings;

b. station personnel conflicts of interest, including selection of sports announcers;

c. promotion of non-broadcast business interests of a licensee;

d. misleading concert promotion announcements;

e. failure to adhere to sales contracts; and

f. false, misleading, and deceptive commercials.[85]

One year later the Commission eliminated policies prohibiting stations from engaging in fraudulent billing practices, network clipping (cutting off the first or last few seconds of a network program in order to squeeze in extra local commercials),[86] and combined advertising rates for AM-FM and television-radio combinations. Policies prohibiting stations from engaging in joint sales practices were also eliminated.[87]

---

[81] 54 Rad. Reg. 2d (P&F) 705 (1983).

[82] 54 Rad. Reg. 2d (P&F) 1043 (1983).

[83] 56 Rad. Reg. 2d (P&F) 976 (1984).

[84] 57 Rad. Reg. 2d (P&F) 939 (1985).

[85] Elimination of Unnecessary Broadcast Regulation, 57 Rad. Reg. 2d (P&F) 913 (1985).

[86] Telecommunications Research and Action Center issued a petition to reconsider elimination of the fraudulent billing and the network clipping policies. The FCC responded to the petition but sustained the policy changes. *See* 63 Rad. Reg. 2d (P&F) 21 (1987).

[87] 60 Rad. Reg. 2d (P&F) 1184 (1986).

12. *Elimination of Technical Regulations*—The FCC has also eliminated scores of polices related to technical matters. For example, in one 1989 statement the Commission repealed rules or policies that:

   a. required frequent calibration of transmission line meters to make sure television stations operate at the authorized power;

   b. required "color burst" signals to be omitted during black and white programs to avoid interference,[88]

   c. restricted stations' signal radiation patterns (This policy was also designed to reduce visual signal interference and provide more accurate measurement of signal patterns);

   d. delineated methods of safe equipment installation and safety specifications; and

   e. prohibited any television station from broadcasting one video and a completely different audio signal.[89]

Other examples of technical policies either relaxed or eliminated by the Commission include television standards for maximum vertical and horizontal blanking intervals, a ban on rebroadcast of personal radio service material (CB and general mobile radio services), signal quality requirements for FM and AM stereo transmission, and restrictions on call letter assignments. The Commission has significantly relaxed restrictions on transmitter power and hours of operation of AM daytime stations, and *simulcasting*, the duplication of AM programming on co-owned FM stations, is no longer prohibited.

9.6.4   Court Challenges to Deregulation

The courts have, for the most part, upheld the FCC's deregulation of radio and television.

Several significant court cases have involved challenges to specific aspects of deregulation. The shortened renewal procedures and the elimination of program log and ascertainment requirements have been of particular concern to opponents of deregulation. They argue that deregulation makes it impossible to determine whether a station is meeting its public interest responsibilities.

In *Black Citizens for a Fair Media* v. *FCC,* a citizen group challenged the new renewal procedures.[90] They claimed the shortened renewal form violated the FCC's statutory mandate to determine that the public interest, convenience, and necessity would be served by granting a license. The petitioners claimed that it would be impossible to know whether a licensee has operated in the public interest without

---

[88] The color burst is a "synchronizing signal" that, when transmitted, allows the television set to decode the color information and produce proper colors on the screen.

[89] Technical and Operational Regulations of Part 73, Subpart E, Television Broadcast Stations, 4 F.C.C.R. 2004 (1989).

[90] Black Citizens for a Fair Media v. FCC, 719 F.2d 407 (1983); cert. *denied* 467 U.S. 1255 (1984).

determining the station's amount of non-entertainment programming. The new, shortened renewal form does not ask stations to provide this information.

A U.S. Court of Appeals upheld the simplified renewal process, holding that the Communications Act did not *require* the FCC to ask program-related questions. The court noted that the Commission had previously eliminated non-entertainment percentage guidelines, leaving licensees only a general obligation to offer programs responsive to local issues.

The court concluded that the Commission could make public interest determinations using the simplified procedures. The court reasoned that the FCC is given broad discretion in determining the public interest and that the FCC's reliance on public participation (through the public file and complaints) is not unreasonable.

The United Church of Christ (UCC) twice challenged the FCC's new policies affecting radio. In the first case, *Office of Communication of the United Church of Christ* v. *FCC* (or UCC III) the court essentially upheld the deregulation of radio. More specifically, the court upheld the elimination of formal ascertainment, minimum nonentertainment programming guidelines, and commercial limits.[91] The one exception pertained to program logs. The court held that the requirements for the new programs/problems (later called the issues/programs) list had not been adequately explained, particularly since the Commission planned to rely heavily on the public to determine which stations failed to meet their public interest obligations.

In response to the court, the FCC revised the policy, requiring the issues/programs list to be prepared quarterly as opposed to annually, and dropping the 10-issue maximum. But UCC challenged the new policy as well. This time the court focused on whether the revised policy might pose a threat to enforcement of the public interest standard.[92] The court was especially concerned about the ability of third parties, at renewal time, to file a petition to deny renewal:

> The FCC has stated that it now relies on petitions to deny in enforcing the statutorily mandated public interest requirement of the Communications Act. Yet, the Commission's revised issues list fails to provide an adequate basis for a prima facie showing in a petition to deny.[93]

The court also suggested that the FCC had not adequately considered a suggested alternative logging procedure which conceivably would have provided more significant information. Convinced that the FCC's revisions to the requirement were only cosmetic, the court once again remanded the issue to the Commission.

---

[91] Office of Communication of United Church of Christ v. FCC, 707 F.2d 1413 (1983). (This case is sometimes referred to as "UCC III." It was obviously not the first case involving this organization to reach the courts.)

[92] Office of Communication of the United Church of Christ v. FCC, 779 F.2d 702 (1985). (This case is sometimes referred to as "UCC IV.")

[93] *Id.* at 714.

This time the FCC made revisions which would ultimately stand up to court scrutiny[94] By 1988 the FCC had applied the new policy to all television licensees.[95]

In *Action for Children's Television* v. *FCC,* two aspects of television deregulation were challenged. First, ACT challenged the repeal of long-standing guidelines on commercials in children's programming, which were eliminated in 1984 along with all quantitative commercial guidelines.[96] Second, ACT claimed that the FCC had failed to justify elimination of the program log requirement.

The court upheld the revision of program log requirements, but ruled that the Commission had failed to explain adequately the elimination of commercial guidelines for children's programming.[97] The court appeared to suggest that the Commission had overlooked specific guidelines for children when commercial limits were eliminated:

> Only when [the] NAB specifically requested clarification as to the 1984 Report's scope did the Commission come forward and indicate that the general deregulation of television commercialization extended to children's television as well. Even in response to that call for clarification, the Commission deigned to fashion only two sentences (and two moderately pertinent footnotes), explaining in the most cursory fashion that deregulation of children's television commercialization was "consistent" with the general de-emphasis of qualitative guidelines and that commercials help support children's television.[98]

Since the FCC had previously based its regulation of children's programming on the premise that the marketplace functions inadequately when children are in the audience, the court found it unacceptable that the FCC would suddenly embrace what had been an unthinkable conclusion that the market actually did operate to restrain the commercial content of children's television.

In response to the court's remand the FCC solicited comments on the matter of commercialization of children's programming.[99] The Commission never established new restrictions because in 1990 Congress passed a children's television bill which included restrictions on advertising in children's programs.[100] In 1991 the FCC issued a policy statement implementing the new restrictions.[101]

---

[94] Deregulation of Radio, 104 F.C.C.2d 505 (1986).

[95] 3 F.C.C.R. 1032 (1988).

[96] 98 F.C.C.2d 1076 (1984).

[97] Action for Children's Television v. FCC, 821 F.2d 741 (1987).

[98] *Id.* at 745.

[99] Revision of Programming and Commercialization Policies, Ascertainment Requirements, and Program Log Requirements for Commercial Television Stations, 2 F.C.C.R. 6822 (1987).

[100] Children's Television Act of 1990, Pub. L. No. 101-437, 1990 H.R. 1677, 104 Stat. 996 (1990). *See also,* 5 F.C.C.R. 7199 (1990).

[101] Policies and Rules Concerning Children's Television Programming; Revision of Programming and Commercialization Policies, Ascertainment Requirements, and Program Log Requirements for Commercial Television Stations, 6 F.C.C.R. 2111 (1991). *Reconsideration granted in part and denied in part,* 6 F.C.C.R. 5093 (1991); *further modification,* 6 F.C.C.R. 5529 (1991).

The FCC's elimination of "underbrush" polices was challenged in *Telecommunications Research and Action Center* v. *FCC* (TRAC I).[102] Specifically, TRAC objected to elimination of prohibitions against ratings distortion, station personnel conflicts of interest, promotions of nonbroadcast business interests, misleading concert promotions, failure to adhere to sales contracts, and the broadcast of false, misleading, and deceptive commercials.

The Court of Appeals concluded that the FCC had provided rational explanations for eliminating the policies. The court was satisfied with the FCC's conclusion that marketplace forces were a more appropriate and efficient means of regulation. The court also deferred judgment of the public interest standard to the FCC: "It has also been repeatedly emphasized that the Commission's judgment regarding how the public interest is best served is entitled to substantial judicial defense."[103]

A U.S. Court of Appeals upheld the Commissions antitrafficking rule in 1990. The Office of Communication of the United Church of Christ argued that the Communications Act required the FCC to restrict station trafficking and that the profit motive in the trafficking of stations would conflict with the public interest standard. Both arguments were rejected. The court ruled that since there was no evidence of a decline in programming quality since elimination of the three-year rule, there was no evidence of a threat to the public interest.[104] The court also held that repealing the rule did not conflict with the Communications Act: "The Act itself contains no prohibition of trafficking, let alone a three-year rule, and we decline petitioners' invitation to amend the statute judiciously so as to include one."[105]

9.7 PUBLIC INTEREST STANDARD TODAY

Despite deregulation and the emergence of the marketplace philosophy, the public interest standard remains the fundamental basis of FCC authority to regulate the electronic media.

The emergence of the marketplace model and elimination of a considerable amount of content regulation does not mean that the public interest standard has been repealed. This would require a major revision of the Communications Act. In fact, the FCC and courts have justified marketplace regulation and deregulatory policy changes on the basis of better serving the public interest. Given a Democratic president for the first time in 12 years and significant turnover on the FCC in the early 1990s, a number of questions seem relevant:

1. How will the regulatory authority vested in the FCC under the public interest standard be used?

---

[102] Telecommunication Research and Action Center v. FCC, 800 F.2d 1181 (1986).
[103] *Id.* at 1184.
[104] Office of Communication of the United Church of Christ v. FCC, 911 F.2d 813 (1990).
[105] *Id.* at 817.

2. Will increased reliance on marketplace forces result in elimination of additional regulations?

3. Can the marketplace—the demands of viewers and listeners—effectively enforce a public interest standard?

Other critical regulatory issues facing the electronic media as we approach the next century include the viability of the scarcity rationale, the extent to which pervasiveness or impact rationales used by Congress and the FCC will be accepted by the courts, and whether the courts will move toward greater protection for the First Amendment rights of broadcasters as opposed to those of listeners and viewers.

DISCUSSION QUESTIONS

1. From the perspective of regulatory policy, why might the *Great Lakes* decision be considered the most important decision of the FRC?

2. Both Doc Brinkley and Reverend Shuler had large listening audiences. Does this mean that their stations should have met the public interest standard? Why or why not? Did the marketplace function effectively in these cases?

3. Compare and contrast the arguments made by the defendants in the Brinkley and Shuler cases.

4. In what way did the Supreme Court decision in the *Sanders Brothers* case offer a more narrow interpretation of the public interest standard? How does the Court's position in *Sanders* compare to the regulatory position of the FCC today?

5. Explain the significance of the *NBC* case regarding the public interest standard and the authority of the FCC to regulate programming.

6. Why might the Blue Book and 1960 Programming Statement be considered infringements on the First Amendment rights of licensees?

7. Discuss the relationship between the public interest standard, deregulation, and the marketplace philosophy.

8. How has the FCC's approach to the First Amendment changed over the last 15 years? In what ways might this affect regulatory policy in the next century?

9. Analyze the reasons given by the FCC for the elimination of underbrush policies. Are the reasons valid? Does the elimination of so many policies conflict with the public interest standard?

10. Which policy changes occurring under deregulation have had the most impact on the electronic media? Why? Which of the changes are beneficial to the industry and the listening and viewing audience, and which are not?

11. Assess the interpretations of the FCC and the courts with respect to deregulation and the public interest. Is the public interest standard still the "touchstone" of regulatory authority? Given deregulation and the marketplace philosophy, has the public interest standard been significantly watered-down?

SUGGESTED READINGS

Bates, Benjamin J. "Deregulation and Station Trafficking." *Journal of Broadcasting and Electronic Media* 33 (1989): 317.

Baughman, James L. *Television's Guardians: The FCC and the Politics of Programming.* Knoxville: U of Tennessee P, 1985.

Besen, Stanley M., et al. *Misregulating Television: Network Dominance and the FCC.* Chicago: U of Chicago P, 1984.

Brotman, Stuart N. ed. *The Telecommunications Deregulation Source Book.* Boston: Artech, 1987.

Holt, Darrel. "The Origin of 'Public Interest' in Broadcasting." *Educational Broadcasting Review* 1 (1967): 15.

Kahn, Frank J., ed. *Documents of American Broadcasting.* 4th ed. Englewood Cliffs, NJ: Prentice, 1984.

Kim, Haeryon. "Theorizing Deregulation: An Exploration of the Utility of the 'Broadcast Policy-Making System' Model." *Journal of Broadcasting and Electronic Media* 36 (1992): 153.

Le Duc, Don R. *Beyond Broadcasting: Patterns in Policy and Law.* White Plains, NY: Longman, 1987.

McGregor, Michael A. "Connections among Deleted Underbrush Policies, FCC Character Standards, and State Criminal Law." *Journal of Broadcasting and Electronic Media* 34 (1990): 153.

Middleton Kent R., and Bill F. Chamberlin. *The Law of Public Communication,* 3rd ed. White Plains, NY: Longman, 1994.

Powe, Lucas A. *American Broadcasting and the First Amendment.* Berkeley: U of California P, 1987.

Spitzer, Matthew L. "The Licensing of Broadcasters." *New York University Law Review* 64 (1989): 990.

Whitney, Jack W., and Gregg P. Skall. *The Broadcaster's Survival Guide: A Handbook of FCC Rules and Regulations for Radio and TV Stations.* New York: Scripps, 1988.

Chapter

10

PROGRAMMING REQUIREMENTS

Congress has used the rationale of scarcity, discussed in Chapters 2 and 9, to regulate what may, must, and must not be said in broadcast programming. This has made broadcasting the most regulated of mass media.

Other mass media use wireless, over-the-air transmission to deliver programming to consumers. Still other mass media use wired delivery but also use wireless technology as an integral part of their overall system.[1] In both cases, Congress has applied content regulation.

Actually, laws and rules spell out very few specific do's and don'ts for programming, and most of those specifics affect broadcast content only peripherally. On the other hand, regulation under the vague and broad "public interest" standard has, over the years, had serious and long-range effects on broadcast programming; this is discussed at length in Chapter 9.

In this chapter we examine programming requirements. These requirements consist of laws, rules, and policies that prescribe material that must appear in the programming—announcements, identification requirements, even the amount of programming. We look at requirements first for the full-power broadcast media, second for other wireless mass media, and finally for cable and other wired media. Programming *restrictions*—regulation that limits or places conditions on programming material—are discussed in Chapter 13.

---

[1] Cable systems, for example, rely extensively on terrestrial microwave to transmit signals from one place to another in preparation for distribution to the public. EMG 6.10.4. Telephone companies use microwave and satellite relay for internal signal delivery.

10.1 PROGRAMMING REQUIREMENTS FOR BROADCAST STATIONS

For purposes of presentation and explanation, we divide programming requirements into six areas—required communications; community service communications; political and issue communications; emergency communications; repeated communications; and subsidiary communications. As we shall see in succeeding sections, there are requirements in some of these same areas for other media, too.

10.1.1 Required Communications

The Communications Act and the Federal Communications Commission require that certain types of material be broadcast in certain ways. These requirements affect the following aspects of station operation: overall operating schedule of the station; radio nonduplication; station identification; sponsorship identification; contest terms; commercial separation; identification of recorded material; required local notices.

10.1.1.1 *Schedules of Operation*
FCC rules specify minimum operating schedules for broadcast stations.

A basic requirement concerns total amount of programming. The FCC prescribes maximum and minimum operating schedules for most types of stations. Maximum schedules specify the total number of hours a station is *authorized* to transmit—that is, how long a broadcast station *may* stay on the air—each day. But the minimum schedules specify how long a station *has to* transmit programming—that is, how long it *must* stay on the air—each day.

Minimum operating schedules are spelled out in FCC rule 73.1740. Every day of the week except Sunday, commercial AM and FM radio stations must operate at least two-thirds of the total hours authorized during each of two time periods: (1) 6 A.M. to 6 P.M. and (2) 6 P.M. to midnight, local time. Two types of stations need comply with the minimum only during the 6-to-6 period: AM Class D stations[2] authorized for nighttime operations and, of course, AM daytimer stations.[3]

Educational FM stations must operate at least five hours a day, at least six days a week, and at least 36 hours per week. A station licensed to an educational institution does not have to operate when school is normally out—Saturdays, Sundays, and official school vacation or recess periods. However, a station that meets or even exceeds these minimums may still find itself forced to operate on a share-time basis. If another party files application for a license to operate on the same frequency, the FCC expects the station licensee and the applicant to reach some kind of agreement on a share-time arrangement; otherwise the Commission will designate the matter for hearing, usually an unbearably heavy expense for an educational licensee or

---

[2] AM station classifications are explained in EMG 6.2.1.2.
[3] 47 C.F.R. § 73.1740.

applicant. To avoid such a share-time situation, an educational FM station must operate at least 12 hours each day of the year.[4]

Noncommercial educational AM and TV stations have no required minimums. However, the FCC reserves the right to take into consideration at license renewal time their hours of actual operation.[5] The implication, of course, is that the FCC could designate the renewal for hearing and question whether the station's operating schedule had made efficient use of the channel.

A commercial TV station over three years old must operate at least 28 hours each week and at least 2 hours each day of the week. During its first 36 months of operation, however, the station has lower minimums. From initial sign-on to 18 months, the station need operate only 12 hours per week; months 19 through 24, 16 hours per week; months 25 through 30, 20 hours per week; and months 30 through 36, 24 hours per week. During this first three years, the station must operate at least 2 hours daily but only for five days a week.[6]

10.1.1.2   *Radio Nonduplication*

Two radio stations that are commonly owned or controlled in the same service whose signals overlap must program separately from each other at least 75 percent of the time.

The situations that trigger this rule are explained in Box 10.1. A station in such a situation may broadcast programming that duplicates that of the other station no more than 25 percent of the total hours in its average broadcast week.[7]

10.1.1.3   *Station Identification*

A broadcast station must officially identify itself periodically.

Sections 303(o) and (p) of the Communications Act allow the FCC to assign call letters to stations and to require "to be published such call letters and other such announcements and data as in the judgment of the Commission may be required for the efficient operation of radio stations. . . ." The FCC does assign call letters and does require stations to use them at particular times and in particular ways.

FCC rule 73.1201 calls for a broadcast station to identify itself when it signs on, when it signs off, and each hour at a "natural break" in programming as close to the hour as possible. A TV station may identify itself by either audio or video.

An official station identification (ID) announcement consists of the station's call letters immediately followed by the community specified in its license as the station's location. However, the station may insert between call letters and city the

---

[4] 47 C.F.R. § 73.561.
[5] 47 C.F.R. § 73.1740(b).
[6] 47 C.F.R. § 73.1740(a)(2).
[7] 47 C.F.R. § 73.3556. *Duplicate,* in this context, means the broadcast of identical programming within any 24-hour period. The rule is actually worded in terms of this prohibition; it is otherwise construed in this section in terms of meaning and consequence to the licensee.

BOX 10.1   Radio Nonduplication

Two radio stations must program separately from each other at least 75 percent of the time when the following conditions exist:

1. the two stations are under common ownership, or one has a time brokerage agreement with the other (EMG 7.1.3.2); *and*
2. both stations are AM, or both are FM; *and*
3. the two stations' signals (FCC defined contours; EMG 7.1.3.3.1) overlap; *and*
4. the overlap area constitutes more than half the total service area of either station.

SOURCE: 47 C.F.R. § 73.3556.

---

name of the licensee, the station's frequency or channel number, or both. Also, the station may add the names of other communities after that of the city of license.[8]

During simultaneous programming, two co-owned AM radio stations assigned to the same city—one in the 535–1605 kHz band and the other in the 1605–1705 kHz band[9]—can give joint station identifications. This rule provides for the overlap period inherent in the FCC's policy of encouraging AM stations to migrate to the expanded band.[10]

In a satellite station[11] operation, the originating station may make identification announcements for the satellite during periods when its signal is being simultaneously rebroadcast by the satellite. An identification announcement for a TV satellite must include the satellite's channel number; that for a radio satellite, its frequency.

A subscription television (STV) station must make ID announcements just before and just after encoded[12] programming, but it does not have to make any such announcements during encoded programming. If and when the station does any nonencoded[13] programming, it must make station identification announcements just like any other television station.

Rule 73.787(a) requires an international station to identify itself when it signs on, when it signs off, and on the hour. This rule does not contain the "natural

---

[8] 47 C.F.R. § 73.1201(b).

[9] The expanded AM band (1605–1705 kHz) and the FCC's migration policy are explained in EMG 6.2.1.6.2.

[10] As implied in EMG 6.2.1.6.2, the typical migration pattern will include a period during which the migrating licensee operates both the original station in the 535–1605 kHz AM band and the new station in the expanded (1605–1705 kHz) AM band.

[11] This term does *not* refer to a space satellite. This type of satellite station rebroadcasts the signal of another station. The satellite usually serves areas in which direct reception of the originating station is unsatisfactory due to distance or intervening terrain factors.

[12] *Encoded* here means scrambled for all receivers but those of STV subscribers.

[13] The signal is received unscrambled by all television sets.

break" leeway allowed to domestic stations; presumably an international station must arrange programming so that a break for station identification occurs precisely on the hour. An international broadcast station must ensure that its station IDs, as well as its program announcements and all "oral continuity," are "made with international significance." Such announcements must be "designed for the foreign . . . countries for which the service is primarily intended."[14]

10.1.1.4 *Sponsorship Identification*

Section 317 of the Communications Act requires identification of sponsors. Exemptions include the broadcast of free recordings, classified advertising programs, and motion pictures produced originally for theatrical release.

The FCC augments this legal requirement in rule 73.1212. The sponsorship identification requirement consists of several elements. A *sponsor* is (1) any party other than the licensee or cable operator (or their employees) who (2) furnishes or pays for (3) a program or program element and who (4) expects some sort of plug. The *program* may be any length. The *program element* may also be any length and in any number of forms, such as tape, film, script, music, scenery, props, or talent. *Payment* is "money, service, or other valuable consideration."[15] A *plug* is "identification of a person, product, service, trademark, or brand name beyond identification reasonably related to the use of such service or property"[16] on the program. A station or cable system that runs such a program or program element must ensure an announcement is made that reveals both the fact of sponsorship and the identification of the sponsor.

The key element is the plug. If the "service or property" comes in exchange for a plug, then the sponsorship identification rule applies. This pertains even if the station or cable channel is noncommercial. With respect to commercials, mention of the sponsor's trade name or product meets the requirement, "when it is clear that the mention . . . constitutes a sponsorship identification."[17] However, stations may not air "teaser"[18] announcements.[19]

On the other hand, if the other party furnishes the service or property for free or at nominal cost and receives no plug, sponsorship identification is not required. For example, record companies and distributors routinely supply new releases free to many popular music radio stations. They may send video versions to music-for-

---

[14] 47 C.F.R. § 73.787(b).

[15] 47 C.F.R. § 73.1212(a).

[16] 47 C.F.R. § 73.1212(a)(2).

[17] 47 C.F.R. §§ 73.1212(g) and 76.221(f).

[18] A teaser attempts to whet the curiosity of the public concerning some upcoming event. One example would be a newspaper and billboard campaign featuring a cartoon of a large chicken accompanied by the words, "The Chicken is coming! The Chicken is coming!" A month of this is followed by another campaign—"The Chicken is here! Chicken King is here!" announcing the opening of a new outlet for a franchised fried chicken chain. Broadcast stations could not air that The-Chicken-is-coming! campaign because the ads contain no identification of product or sponsor.

[19] Teaser Announcements, 40 F.C.C. 60 (1959); and Teaser Announcements, 27 Fed. Reg. 5274, June 5, 1962.

mat TV stations. They hope the station will play them, thus giving the records the exposure they need to convince the public to buy and to create a "hit" or a "million seller." Station programmers, however, use their own judgment as to which, of the many releases they receive, get played. The programmers, the stations, and the licensees are under no obligation for the records received, not even an obligation to play them on the air. And so they have no obligation to reveal the donors of the records they use.[20]

10.1.1.4.1 Third Parties.   The Commission's rule specifies that the required announcement must identify the true identity of the sponsor or donor. In some cases, an agent may make the arrangements for the program on behalf of a third party. The licensee, when aware of such, should ensure that the announcement reveals the identity of the third party, rather than the agent.

10.1.1.4.2 Sponsorship Identification in Political and Issue Programs.   As we discuss in Chapter 12, political programs are subject to the requirements of Section 317 of the Communications Act. EMG 12.4 explains the sponsorship identification requirements for a station that airs a political program for which it receives "any film, record, transcription, talent, script, or other material or service of any kind . . . either directly or indirectly."[21]

10.1.1.4.3 Kickbacks.   An FCC policy[22] requires an announcement when performers have "kicked back" a portion of their pay to appear on a program. Some producers may demand kickbacks of various types—for union contract fees; for additional production expenses (such as extra musicians needed for the performer's song or act); for the difference between the single and the group union contract fee (for group appearances). In such cases, there must be at least an audio announcement that the performer or the performer's agent paid to have the performer appear on the program.

10.1.1.4.4 Exclusions and Waivers.   Sections 317 and 508 of the Communications Act both exclude from the sponsorship identification requirement arrangements where the element of the plug is missing.[23] A common example is that explained above, the provision of recordings to broadcast stations.

Additionally, the Communications Act allows the FCC to waive sponsorship identification requirements whenever the Commission finds, in the words of Section 317(d), "that the public interest, convenience, or necessity does not require the broadcasting of such an announcement." FCC rule 73.1212 specifies two such waivers for broadcast licensees and cable operators that originate programming—

---

[20] Applicability of Sponsorship Identification Rules, 40 F.C.C. 141 (1963), at 144.

[21] 47 C.F.R. § 73.1212(d).

[22] Performers' Fees, 23 F.C.C.2d 588 (1970).

[23] This same exclusion applies to Section 507 of the Communications Act, the section that deals with plugola and payola. *See* EMG 13.2.1.

"want ad" (that is, classified advertising) programs and feature motion picture films. To qualify for the waiver, the want ads must come from individuals, not businesses (of any kind). Further, the station must make a daily list of each advertiser's name, address, and telephone number and make that list available "to members of the public who have a legitimate interest in obtaining the information contained in the list."[24]

For a feature film to qualify for the waiver, it must have been produced originally for showing in motion picture theaters. This means that made-for-TV movies are fully subject to the sponsorship identification requirement. One reason for the theatrical feature film waiver is that such a movie may contain material that would have been considered plugs, had the film been prepared originally for television, and the plug is not disclosed as such (thus, technically violating Section 507 of the Communications Act[25]).

10.1.1.4.5 Interpretations. The FCC has provided interpretations of the sponsorship identification rules in two public notices, *Applicability of Sponsorship Identification Rules,* May 6, 1963,[26] and a 1975 modification.[27] The volumes of the FCC *Reports* and *Record* contain further interpretations. For example, in 1991 the FCC warned that a public service announcement (PSA) that is paid for by governmental, nonprofit, or other entities must clearly (1) identify the sponsor of the message and (2) state that the PSA is a paid announcement.[28]

10.1.1.5 Contest Terms

On-air promotion and advertising of broadcaster-conducted contests must reveal material terms.

A major concern of the FCC is that stations not broadcast contests that are deceptive. To achieve this goal FCC rule 73.1216 states:

A licensee that broadcasts or advertises information about a contest it conducts shall fully and accurately disclose the material terms of the contest, and shall conduct the contest substantially as announced or advertised. No contest description shall be false, misleading or deceptive with respect to any material term.

A number of items constitute the material terms of a contest. They include the following information: (1) how to enter or participate; (2) eligibility requirements; (3) entry deadline dates; (4) whether prizes can be won; (5) when prizes can be won; (6) the extent, nature, and value of prizes; (6) time and means of selecting

[24] 47 C.F.R. §§ 73.1212(g)(2) and 76.221(f)(2).
[25] EMG 13.2.1.
[26] 40 F.C.C. 141.
[27] Amendment of the Commission's "Sponsorship Identification" Rules, 52 F.C.C.2d 701 (1975).
[28] Sponsorship Identification Requirements Applicable to Paid-For Public Service Messages, 6 F.C.C.R. 5861 (1991).

winners; and (7) tiebreaking procedures.[29] Stations conducting a contest are expected to disclose the material terms of the contest. They should be presented whenever the station attempts to state the terms or conditions of the contest, but need not be a part of brief promotional announcements that don't attempt to explain all details of the contest. Stations often prepare printed explanations of the material terms that can be presented to people who want the full terms of the contest.

10.1.1.6 Commercial Separation

Separating material must be placed between commercials and content in children's programming.

As part of its rules on children's programming (EMG 10.1.2.2), the Commission has ordered that commercial material be "separated from a children's program to which it is related by intervening and unrelated program material."[30] And that intervening material may not be commercials. The FCC, along with many parents, hopes this break helps the child to "shift gears" mentally and realize that the commercials are not a part of the surrounding program.

10.1.1.7 Mechanical Reproduction

A broadcast of recorded material must be identified as such if (1) the audience might believe it to be live or (2) it purposely attempts to simulate a live broadcast.

FCC rule 78.1208 requires a broadcast station, when it airs two types of program material, to notify the audience if the material is mechanically reproduced—that is, a playback of a tape, a film, or a disc recording. The first type is that in which the element of time has special significance. This includes broadcast of a speech, a news event, a special event, or any event that, when not identified as recorded, would make the audience think that it occurs as they see or hear it. The second type of recorded program material that requires a mechanical reproduction announcement is that in which an affirmative effort is made to create the impression that it is live.

The station must announce material as taped, filmed, or recorded at the beginning of the program. The announcement must consist of clear language, phrased in terms the public can understand. A television station may make the announcement aurally or visually.

The station does not have to make such an announcement before any program in which the element of time has no special significance. Nonetheless, the licensee must not try to create the impression that the program is live. Further, the station need not make the announcement for taped, filmed, or recorded commercials, promos, or public service announcements.

---

[29] 47 C.F.R. § 73.1216(b).
[30] 6 F.C.C.R. 5093 (1991).

10.1.1.8 *Renewal-Notice Announcements.*   Yet another category of communications required by regulation consists of the notices that a broadcast station must air during the six months prior to expiration of its license. FCC rule 73.3580 contains requirements for these prefiling and postfiling announcements, and they are discussed in EMG 8.1.5.3.

10.1.2 Community Service Communications

It is not enough just to identify advertisers and repeat station call letters. Such "mechanical" requirements, while definitely serving some public interest ends, do not respond to the main thrust of operation in the public interest. Congress and the FCC have made clear that stations are to serve their communities of license by finding out the needs of those communities—and "needs" in this context does *not* mean more David Letterman or *The Simpsons* or *Beverly Hills 90210*—then devising programming to respond to those needs. Two community service programming requirements are those involving ascertainment and the special needs of children.

10.1.2.1 *Programming in Response to Ascertained Issues*

A licensee must ascertain community issues and provide "significant treatment" of them in station programming.

One highly important requirement is that the licensee find out what issues face the communities in the station's service area and then program in response to those issues. These elements form the basis of the issues/programs list that must be put into the public inspection file (EMG 8.1.6.4). The process of determining those issues is called *ascertainment*. In the 1970s[31] the FCC spelled out specific procedures that stations were to follow in performing their ascertainment chores. In 1984, the Commission completed a process of eliminating these procedures for all broadcast stations.[32] However, *the requirement to ascertain, and to program in response to, community issues remained.* The Commission made this very clear in its 1984 order:

> Our action here does not constitute a retreat from our concern with the programming performance of . . . station licensees. [W]e are . . . retaining the obligation of licensees to provide programming that responds to issues of concern to the community. The quarterly issues/programs list will provide the public and the Commission with the information needed to monitor licensees' performance under this new regulatory scheme. . . .[33]

---

[31] Ascertainment of Community Problems, 27 F.C.C.2d 650 (1971); and Ascertainment of Community Problems by Renewal Applicants, 57 F.C.C.2d 418, 441 (1975), *reconsideration granted in part,* 61 F.C.C.2d 1 (1976).

[32] Revision of Programming and Commercialization Policies, Ascertainment Requirements, and Program Log Requirements, 98 F.C.C.2d 1076 (1984).

[33] 98 F.C.C.2d at 1077.

The most important point here is that all licensees must provide some issue-responsive programming. The FCC will generally defer to licensee discretion on how the issues are ascertained. Nonetheless, station licensees who do *not* establish and use systematic procedures to determine community issues—who "ascertain" only by talking to friends, acquaintances, and fellow business leaders at the country club and at chamber of commerce meetings and *not* with leaders and representatives from organized labor, significant minority communities, and other constituent groups in their community of license—these licensees open themselves to challenge at license renewal time.

10.1.2.2   *Programming for Children*

The Children's Television Act of 1990 requires television station licensees to present programming that meets the needs of children.

As noted in one review of research,[34] the relationship between children and television is of special interest for at least two reasons. First, young children watch a lot of television. And second, a continuing concern over the nature of symbolic messages available to young people has existed for years, dating at least from the time of Plato. So it is not surprising that broadcast regulators, spurred certainly by public pressure (and perhaps by an ever-increasing accumulation of social science research results that pointed toward the probability of linkages between television viewing and personal behavior), have attempted to encourage the availability of positive children's television programming.

In a 1974 Children's Television Report and Policy Statement, the FCC urged licensees to increase programming on both weekends and weekdays that would educate as well as entertain children. Further, the FCC said children's programming would now be evaluated at license renewal.[35] Subsequent examinations of program practices by the FCC revealed that the report did not increase the amount of educational or informational children's TV programming. In 1979 the Commission initiated a rule-making procedure to develop options for children's programming that ranged from establishing mandatory programming requirements to increasing the number of nonbroadcast video outlets providing programs for children.[36]

The FCC proceeding was completed in 1983.[37] It noted the amount and variety of children's programming in existence, and rejected mandatory children's programming requirements for TV stations. The Commission said that it would be impossible to require mandatory quotas for children's programs because quotas would infringe on constitutionally protected licensee discretion. However, the Commission did state that licensees were obligated, at license renewal, to show attention to the needs of children in the audience, but indicated that licensees

---

[34] George Comstock, Steven Chaffee, Natan Katzman, Maxwell McCombs, and Donald Roberts, *Television and Human Behavior* (New York: Columbia UP, 1978) 173.

[35] Children's Television Report and Policy Statement, 50 F.C.C.2d 1; *aff'd on reconsideration* 55 F.C.C.2d 691 (1975).

[36] Children's Television Programming and Advertising Practices, 75 F.C.C.2d 138 (1979).

[37] Children's Television Programming and Advertising Practices, 96 F.C.C.2d 634 (1983).

could cite alternative sources of programming available to children, such as public broadcasting or cable. Such alternatives could be used to show that adequate outlets for children's programming already existed, thus alleviating the need for increased children's programming by a TV station. On appeal, the court in *Action for Children's Television v. FCC*[38] agreed with the Commission that alternative program sources could be considered in measuring the need for children's television. However, the court did not feel the FCC was eliminating the obligation of licensees to present programs for children.

While the FCC decision not to impose program requirements was under review, another case emerged. In *Washington Association for Television and Children v. FCC*,[39] a citizen group sought to deny license renewals of TV stations that did not carry regularly scheduled weekday children's programming. The suit maintained that such failure violated the FCC's policy on children's programming. However, the court of appeals ruled that the policy did not require regularly scheduled children's programming.

The Children's Television Act (CTA) of 1990 impacted licensee procedures by placing restrictions on advertising (EMG 13.3.1) and additional requirements on license renewal and ascertainment. To a large extent, however, its aim was at programming, and it added requirements that stations must program for children. In writing the CTA, Congress said that television station licensees and cable operators should provide programming "that serves the special needs of children." In addition, the programming must "take into consideration characteristics of the child audience."[40] The general thrust of the CTA applies to noncommercial educational stations as well as commercial stations.[41]

10.1.2.2.1   Requirements.   FCC regulation of children's programming based on the 1990 act has proved almost as vague as the legislation itself. The FCC requires television stations "to serve the educational and informational needs of children"[42] in their communities through both overall programming and programming particularly targeted to children. The FCC defines children as persons 16 years or younger. It defines children's programming as programming that aids in the "positive development of . . . the child's intellectual/cognitive or social/emotional needs"[43] in any way.

In addition to a station's own children's programming, the FCC also allows the licensee to claim credit for:

Any special nonbroadcast efforts which enhance the value of children's educational and informational television programming, and any special ef-

---

[38] 756 F.2d 899 (1985).
[39] 712 F.2d 677 (1983).
[40] Pub. L. No. 101-437, Title I, 101, 104 Stat. 996.
[41] 47 C.F.R. § 73.520.
[42] 47 C.F.R. §§ 73.520 and 73.671.
[43] 47 C.F.R. §§ 73.520 and 73.671.

fort to produce or support educational and informational television programming by another station in the licensee's marketplace. . . .[44]

However, nonbroadcast efforts must be related to children's television programming. They cannot be unrelated community-based activities, such as sponsoring a Little League team or a Brownie troop.[45]

Significantly, there are no hard-edged minimum criteria that television stations must meet—no number or length of children's programs demanded, no specific allocation of programs to segments of the child audience. Instead, the FCC has chosen to allow maximum flexibility in meeting the requirements. For example, programming that truly responds to "the special needs of children" may be any length from a half-minute public service announcement to a full-length program. The Commission wished to avoid providing safe harbors—guidelines on number and length of programs that a station could follow to avoid license-renewal problems—because broadcasters might regard them as minimums.[46]

10.1.2.2.2 "Permissive" Guidelines.   The Commission has, however, established what it called "permissive" guidelines to help a licensee determine the educational and informational needs of the children in its community. The FCC encourages the use of these guidelines but does not require them. The suggested FCC guidelines are as follows:

1. circumstances within the community,
2. other programming of the station (that is, programming *not* aimed specifically at children),
3. programming aired on other broadcast stations, and
4. other programs for children available in the broadcaster's community of license.[47]

However, according to a study by the Center for Media Education, the rules proved so broad that licensees initially cited programs from *Leave It to Beaver* to *Bucky O'Hare and the Toad Wars* as fulfilling FCC requirements. The study said, "Broadcasters appear to have seized upon the second part of the [FCC's] definition. . . . 'Pro-social' has become a term among broadcasters that allows them to describe anything in terms that sound vaguely beneficial."[48] In response to the

---

[44] 47 C.F.R. §§ 73.520, 73.671.

[45] Unless, of course, the station plans programming based around and on the team and the troop—programming that aids in the positive development of the intellectual, cognitive, social, or emotional needs of children.

[46] Children's Television Programming, 6 F.C.C.R. 5093 (1991).

[47] Children's Television Programming, 6 F.C.C.R. 2111 (1991).

[48] Quoted in Joe Flint, "Study Slams Broadcasters' Kids Act Compliance," *Broadcasting,* 5 Oct. 1992, 40–41.

study, the FCC launched an inquiry into how to modify its children's programming rules. The Commission's aim was to determine more precisely what broadcasters must do to comply with the Children's Television Act of 1990.[49]

10.1.3 Political and Issue Communications

Section 315 of the Communications Act requires station licensees to grant equal opportunity on their stations to political candidates. Section 312(a)(7) requires "reasonable access" for candidates for federal office. FCC rules 73.1920, 73.1930, and 76.209 require reply time in the event a station airs an editorial endorsing or condemning a political candidate or a personal attack on an individual during a discussion of a controversial issue. These elements of law and regulation are fully discussed in Chapters 11 and 12 but are mentioned here because each entails programming that a licensee must air.

10.1.4 Emergency Communications

Broadcast stations have certain programming obligations in connection with emergency preparedness.

Sections 1 and 4(o) of the Communications Act tie creation of the FCC in with the national defense and charge the Commission with use of radio and wire communications to promote "safety of life and property."[50] In response, the FCC has created rules and procedures concerning broadcast of communications relating to emergencies. Such communications involve Emergency Broadcast System (EBS) tests and emergency information. Under the FCC's rules, all stations, whether or not EBS volunteers, are required to broadcast certain material.

10.1.4.1 Emergency Broadcast System. FCC rules 73.901–73.962 deal with the Emergency Broadcast System. EBS, based on broadcast stations, serves as an emergency communications system for the 50 states, the District of Columbia, Puerto Rico, the Virgin Islands, and Guam. EBS design calls for the system to activate within minutes, primarily for the president of the United States in time of war or national crisis. The national EBS is activated only upon White House request, which is called an Emergency Action Notification (EAN). As shown in Table 10.1, the major news services and many of the national commercial radio and television networks carry the notification to the stations. The system can also operate at state and local levels, and stations may cooperate with officials at those levels on a voluntary basis in emergencies involving a threat to life or property.

---

[49] Policies and Rules Concerning Children's Television Programming Policies Revision of Programming for Television Broadcast Stations, 8 F.C.C.R. 1841 (1993).

[50] 47 U.S.C. §§ 151 and 154(o).

TABLE 10.1   EBS Participants

Radio and Television Networks	Cable Networks and Program Suppliers
ABC Radio and ABC-TV	Cable News Network
Associated Press Radio	Cinemax
CBS Radio and CBS-TV	Disney Channel
Mutual Broadcasting System (Westwood)	Entertainment and Sports Programming Network
MUZAK	(ESPN)
NBC Radio (Westwood)	Family Channel
NBC-TV	Home Box Office
National Public Radio	Movie Channel
Public Broadcasting Service	MTV
Satellite Music Network (ABC)	Nashville Network
United Press International Audio	Nickelodeon
Unistar	Showtime
	VH-1
	Weather Channel
News Services	**Common Carriers**
Associated Press (AP)	American Telephone and Telegraph (AT&T)
United Press International (UPI)	

SOURCE: 47 C.F.R. § 73.912

10.1.4.1.1 Voluntary Nature.   Networks, stations, and other nongovernment communications services volunteer to participate in EBS activities. When an EAN is sent out, all stations cease commercial activity. EBS stations remain on the air to broadcast authorized announcements; all others shut down until the White House terminates the state of emergency.

10.1.4.1.2 Required Tests.   All broadcast stations (except LPTV and 10-watt noncommercial stations), whether or not EBS volunteers, must maintain equipment to receive EANs by monitoring specified stations. All stations must also conduct random and unscheduled on-the-air tests once a week between 8:30 A.M. and local sunset. The test consists of a standard Test Script and an Attention Signal, composed of two specific tones emitted simultaneously by an encoder device.[51]

The Commission warns that stations are not to add background music to, render a musical version of, or otherwise alter the EBS Test Script. The Attention Signal may not be recorded (Box 10.2), but the Test Script may be. Automated radio stations must have on duty at all times an operator who can interrupt the automation system and run the normal EBS test.[52]

---

[51] However, activation of the Emergency Broadcast System at state or local level by a broadcast station or coordinated tests of EBS operational procedures for an entire state or Operational (Local) Area may be conducted in lieu of the weekly transmission tests of the attention signal and the test script. 47 C.F.R. § 73.961(d).

[52] Automated Programming Systems, 72 F.C.C.2d 788; and False or Deceptive Emergency Warnings, 69 Rad. Reg. 2d (P & F) 274 (1991); see Table 10.1.

BOX 10.2   Don't Mess with EBS

Following is the text of a public notice issued by the FCC in 1991:

FCC Emphasizes Importance of Emergency Broadcast System

Recently the Commission fined the licensee of radio station KSHE(FM), Crestwood, MO, $ 25,000 for broadcasting a false emergency alert that the United States was under nuclear attack. The Commission noted that broadcasting false or deceptive emergency warnings is a serious violation of a licensee's fundamental obligation to serve the public interest. In addition, it stated that KSHE's use of tones popularly mistaken for the Emergency Broadcast System (EBS) Attention Signal tones, undermined the integrity of the EBS. It also conflicted with the clear intent of the Commission's EBS rules which are designed to deal with true national, state or local emergencies.

The Commission is warning broadcasters not to alter the weekly EBS test or air any musical rendition or alteration of the test script as outlined in the EBS Checklist. This would undermine the serious nature of the system. The FCC noted that use of prerecorded (taped) EBS encoder tones is not in compliance with Sections 73.940 or 73.906. The EBS encoder should be used to generate the tones. . . .

SOURCE: FCC Public Notice, May 15, 1991, 69 Rad. Reg. 2d (P & F) 274.

10.1.4.1.3 Modernization Proposed.   In 1992 the FCC proposed a new emergency alerting system to replace the current EBS.[53] The new system would provide an operational structure by which all system participants would work together on a voluntary, organized basis during emergency situations. The Commission also asked for recommendations for a new device to upgrade existing EBS alerting equipment. This device would be designed to improve the efficiency by which broadcast stations disseminate emergency information to the public.

10.1.4.2 Emergency Information.   Stations may also provide emergency information at the local level. FCC rule 73.1250 allows stations to follow certain normally forbidden practices, "furthering the safety of life and property"[54] in situations ranging from hurricanes and tidal waves to changes in school bus schedules. If responsible public officials so request, a station may, at its discretion, transmit emergency point-to-point messages to request or dispatch aid and assist in rescue operations. An AM station may use full daytime facilities at night under the following conditions: "when necessary to the safety of life and property, in dangerous condi-

---

[53] Rules Regarding the Emergency Broadcast System, 7 F.C.C.R. 6903 (1992).
[54] 47 C.F.R. § 1250(a).

tions of general nature, . . . on a noncommercial basis,"[55] and when no other station providing such information puts a clear nighttime signal into the area.[56]

Television stations may transmit emergency information either by picture and sound or by picture only (except in official EBS operation, where stations must transmit such information by both sound and picture). Otherwise a station must confine itself to its normal, licensed mode of operation.

A national EBS activation takes precedence over local or state emergency operation. And the FCC may stop any such emergency operation "if required in the public interest."[57]

10.1.5   Repeated Communications

Section 705 of the Communications Act[58] prohibits unauthorized use of radio, television, or wire communication. No one may divulge or make public such communication, when it is intended for reception by another person, unless the sender so authorizes. Sections 2510 and 2511 of the U.S. Criminal Code make willful or attempted interception of wire or oral communications a crime and provide penalties for violators. The Federal Communications Commission has adopted rules that further regulate use of communications created by others. In this case *repeated* means broadcast of program material that originated elsewhere than the transmitting station. Included in this concept are broadcasts of telephone conversations, recorded material, and signals from other stations.

10.1.5.1   *Broadcast of Telephone Conversations*

A person called by telephone whose voice is to be broadcast must be so notified before the broadcast or before the start of recording for the broadcast, whichever comes first.

Neither law nor FCC regulation requires that a station broadcast any telephone conversations. However, a station that chooses to do so does have an obligation to communicate that intention to the person who is to be broadcast. If a station plans to use someone's telephone comments on the air, it must so notify the person before the comments are made. FCC rule 73.1206 requires that a licensee notify the person at the other end of the telephone line of intent to broadcast the conversation before broadcasting it live or recording it for later broadcast.

10.1.5.1.1   *Surprise Calls.*   Legally, a radio announcer should not make a surprise telephone call to an individual for use on the air. The telephone rings, the

---

[55] 47 C.F.R. § 1250(f).

[56] After cessation of the emergency, any station that broadcast point-to-point messages and any AM station that used daytime facilities during nighttime hours must notify the FCC in writing to explain the nature of the emergency and the broadcast. Additionally, the AM station must certify that it operated on a noncommercial basis and that no other adequate broadcast service existed.

[57] 47 C.F.R. § 1250(d).

[58] 47 U.S.C. § 605.

individual answers "Hello," and the conversation has already begun without the required notification. Nor may the notification come during or after the conversation, even when the station records the conversation for later broadcast.

10.1.5.1.2 Exception.   The telephone warning rule does allow one exception. The licensee does not have to give notification in a situation where the other person already knows (or may be presumed to know) from the circumstances of the conversation that the station will broadcast it. However, the Commission has limited this exception to just two rather specific situations. First, the other person has some association with the station (as, for example, a reporter or stringer who calls in a story). Or, second, the other person originates the call and the call obviously comes in connection with a program on which the station customarily broadcasts telephone conversations (as when a listener telephones a call-in talk show).

10.1.5.2 Rebroadcasts

A broadcast station that retransmits the signal of another station must usually have permission unless the other station is a radio amateur or citizens band station.

FCC rule 73.1207 deals with rebroadcasting. *Rebroadcast* means that a broadcast station receives and retransmits material transmitted by another station. Retransmission may be simultaneous or subsequent to reception. The material can be a complete program, a part of a program, or any transmission. The station from which the material is received may be a broadcast station or any other type of station. On the other hand, the concept of rebroadcast does not include transmission of programming from point of origin to a broadcast station (as with networking and broadcast "remotes") by use of common carrier, even when the common carrier includes radio (for example, microwave or satellite relay). Nor does it include use of remote pickup broadcast stations (EMG 6.10.2) as a program relay (as when getting the signal from a remote to the studio by radio instead of telephone lines).

Again, neither law nor FCC rules require that one broadcast station retransmit the signal of another.[59] However, as with broadcast of telephone conversations, a station that chooses to rebroadcast usually has an obligation involving communication; in most cases, the Commission requires that the rebroadcasting station first get permission from the originating station. We can divide the rule into areas based on the type of station being rebroadcast—domestic broadcast stations (that is, licensed in the United States), foreign broadcast stations, U.S. government stations, and nonbroadcast stations.

10.1.5.2.1 Domestic Broadcast Stations.   One broadcast station must get permission to rebroadcast another. The rebroadcasting station must have written consent of the originating station. It must keep that consent and make it available if the FCC calls for it. This requirement applies only to the rebroadcast of U.S. broadcast stations.

---

[59] Except in some very specific situations.

A station that wishes to retransmit an FM station's nonbroadcast subcarrier transmissions (subsidiary communications service, EMG 6.2.2.5) must also obtain prior permission from the originating station. On the other hand, written consent is not needed for Emergency Broadcasting System (EBS) rebroadcasts. Under FCC rules, a station that originates emergency communications under a detailed EBS Operational Plan has granted authority to other participating stations to rebroadcast its signal.

FCC rule 73.788(d) governs retransmission requirements for nongovernment international broadcasting stations in the United States. An international station may transmit the program of a domestic broadcast station with certain provisions. First, of course, the international station must get written permission from the originating station. Second, sponsorship or advertising matter in the rebroadcast program must adhere to the rule for international stations (EMG 6.2.3), requiring that content "reflect the culture" of the United States and promote goodwill. Third, "when station identifications are made, only the call letter and frequency designation of the international station is given on its assigned frequency." And fourth, an international station may not carry the programming of another international station unless the two stations are both owned by the same licensee and are, in fact, part of the same transmission service (that is, the two stations are used in a complementary fashion to overcome distance and atmospheric factors and achieve continuity of service).[60]

10.1.5.2.2   Foreign Broadcast Stations.   For the most part, rule 73.1207(b)(4) allows a domestic station to rebroadcast the signal of a foreign broadcasting station without consent of the originating station. Exceptions include stations in those countries with which the United States has an agreement that states otherwise. For example, a U.S. station should obtain consent to rebroadcast programs from Canada and most Latin American countries and give call letters and location of the originating station during the rebroadcast. Otherwise, a U.S. station may rebroadcast material from a foreign domestic station or from a foreign international broadcast station (such as Radio Peking, BBC World Service, Radio Moscow) with impunity.

10.1.5.2.3   U.S. Government Stations.   The Voice of America (VOA) and Armed Forces Radio and Television Service (AFRTS) do not generally clear their programming for domestic distribution. A U.S. domestic broadcast station may rebroadcast VOA or AFRTS only by special arrangement among the parties concerned.

A station may, without specific authorization, rebroadcast time signals originated by the Naval Observatory and the National Bureau of Standards and messages by the National Weather Service. Rule 73.1207(d) does specify some requirements for their use. Among them are the following: all require identification as to origin; the time signals must be rebroadcast without delay or advertising; the weather messages must be rebroadcast within one hour of receipt and associated advertising must not convey the impression of government endorsement of the advertised items.

---

[60] 47 C.F.R. § 73.788(d).

10.1.5.2.4 Nonbroadcast Stations. A broadcast station may rebroadcast the transmissions of a nonbroadcast (for example, point-to-point) station. If the nonbroadcast station is privately owned (except for stations in the amateur or citizens band services), the broadcaster must first get permission from the nonbroadcast licensee. If the nonbroadcast station is a common carrier station, the broadcaster must get prior permission from both the originator of the message and the licensee of the station. If the nonbroadcast station is a federal government station, the broadcaster must first get permission from the government agency that originates the message.

Under a 1972 FCC policy statement,[61] a broadcast station may monitor police, fire, and Federal Aviation Authority radio transmissions for news tips. But it may use the contents in news and other programs only if officials of the monitored public safety agencies first grant authorization; otherwise the broadcaster violates Section 705 of the Communications Act.

Section 705 of the Communications Act specifically exempts amateur radio ("ham") transmissions from the nondisclosure requirement. FCC rule 73.1207(c)(3) allows a broadcast station to rebroadcast amateur and citizens band transmissions, either live or delayed, with or without approval of the operators involved. However, the broadcasters may *not* use ham or CB radio to perform routine work for the station—weather and traffic reports and the like. For such uses, the station must use broadcast auxiliary facilities (EMG 6.10.2). On the other hand, the broadcaster may use amateur and CB facilities in emergency situations that involve human safety or immediate threat to property.

Further, a broadcast station may pick up and rebroadcast amateur transmissions that originate in a foreign country. For example, suppose a particular country has suffered war, famine, or natural disaster and a broadcaster monitors a radio amateur conversation originating from that country describing conditions there. The station may broadcast that description. However, unless the United States has a third-party agreement with the country, only licensed amateurs may talk with one another; the broadcaster may not become directly involved in the amateur transmission. The broadcaster cannot use the amateur station in the role of reporter or translator in order to convey, directly or indirectly, questions or subjects on which the broadcaster wants comment. And the FCC requests that the broadcaster provide it with date and nature of transmission anytime a transmission from a radio amateur in another country is broadcast.[62]

10.1.6 Subsidiary Communications

Transmissions using aural subcarriers, the television vertical blanking interval, and similar subsidiary signals are exempt from most programming requirements imposed on the main broadcast signal.

[61] Broadcast of FAA Communications, 37 Fed. Reg. 3567 (Feb. 17, 1972).
[62] *Id.*

The concept of additional signals, subsidiary to the main broadcast signal, was introduced in EMG 6.2.1.5, 6.2.2.5, and 6.3.4. In our present discussion, we are concerned with those that are required to be transmitted. Most of the required subsidiary signals are technical in nature—the television color burst and the signal for FM stereophonic transmission, for example—and therefore not appropriate for discussion within the context of this volume. The more obvious content-oriented subsidiary signals include AM carrier services, aural subcarrier services, and the TV vertical blanking interval services. These are discussed in Chapter 6 and, as implied in that discussion, are *not* required—for example, no AM station has to transmit a signal for utility load management, and no TV station has to transmit a teletext service. Assuming that a station does choose to offer one of these subsidiary communications services, however, it would be relevant to inquire (1) whether the requirements imposed on the main broadcast channel also apply to these subsidiary channels and (2) what, if any, special requirements there are for these subsidiary channels.

The answer to the first question is, "Not really." In most cases, material transmitted on subcarrier services does not require announcements for station identification,[63] mechanical reproduction, or sponsorship identification. Aural subcarrier services are also exempt from requirements of the personal attack and political editorial rules and the Zapple doctrine (EMG 11.3.1–11.3.3. and 12.1.3.1), and of political broadcasting (equal opportunities [EMG 12.1] and reasonable access [EMG 12.5]).[64]

FCC rules declare VBI services, too, exempt from political broadcasting and similar requirements. However, a 1986 appeals court decision[65] held that the FCC had erred in concluding that teletext was not broadcasting and therefore not subject to the political-candidate equal opportunities requirements of Section 315 of the Communications Act. The act defines broadcasting as dissemination of radio communications intended for reception by the general public, and teletext was intended for the general public. Further, reasoned the court, teletext clearly falls within the act's definition in Section 3 of "radio communication" as "transmission by radio of writing, signs, signals, pictures, and sounds of all kinds."[66] Therefore, since teletext is broadcasting, and broadcasting is subject to Section 315, then so is teletext. The court did agree with the Commission, however, that teletext is not subject to Section 312, the federal-candidate access provision (EMG 12.5).

As for special programming requirements, FCC rule 73.593 comes close. It requires a noncommercial educational FM station to ensure that profit-making uses of its subcarrier do not harm any existing or potential reading service for the blind or are otherwise inconsistent with its public broadcasting responsibilities.

---

[63] In footnote 18 of Subsidiary Communications Authorizations, 48 Fed. Reg. 28,445, 28,449, June 22, 1983, however, the FCC says that station identification is required for FM subcarrier operations that take place when the station does not transmit broadcast programming.

[64] The FCC exempted FM subcarrier services from the Fairness Doctrine and the political broadcasting requirements in WFTL Broadcasting Co., 45 F.C.C.2d 1152, at 1153–1154 (1974), and Greater Washington Educational Telecommunications Ass'n, Inc., 48 F.C.C.2d 948 (1974).

[65] Telecommunications Research and Action Center v. FCC, 801 F.2d 501 (1986), *cert. denied*, 482 U.S. 919 (1987).

[66] 47 U.S.C. § 153(b).

10.2 PROGRAMMING REQUIREMENTS FOR OTHER WIRELESS MASS MEDIA

In this section we discuss the program requirements for wireless mass media other than full-service broadcast stations. These other media include the following: low-power television, translator and booster stations, instructional television fixed service, multichannel multipoint distribution service, and direct broadcast satellite.

10.2.1 Programming Requirements for Low-Power Television Stations

> The more an LPTV station resembles a full-power TV station in facilities and programming, the more it must fulfill the programming requirements of a full-power TV station.

As explained in EMG 6.4.1, stations that operate in the low-power television (LPTV) service have fewer requirements than do full-service television stations. The primary programming requirement is that an LPTV station must operate as a broadcast station, that is, transmit programming intended for reception by the general public.

10.2.1.1 *LPTV Schedules of Operation.*

According to FCC rules, an LPTV station has no minimum number of hours that it must operate (rule 74.731[i]), does not have to operate on a regular schedule (rule 74.763[a]), and may cease operation entirely for 30 days (rule 74.763[b]). In the latter case, the licensee must notify the FCC (1) that the station is off the air (no later than the tenth day of the cessation) and (2) when it is back on the air. If the cessation runs longer than 30 days, the licensee must file an informal request for additional time no later than the thirtieth day.

10.2.1.2 *LPTV Station Identification.*

Rule 74.783 contains station identification requirements for LPTV stations. An LPTV that does locally originated programming must follow rule 73.1201, the station ID guidelines for full-service stations (EMG 10.1.1.3). An LPTV that does not originate local programming (for example, an automated station that broadcasts only material received by satellite or microwave) must transmit its call sign once per hour in international Morse code at a speed of no more than 20 words per minute. Such transmission may be automated.

10.2.1.3 *LPTV Political and Issue Communications.*

In its LPTV order,[67] the FCC addressed application of political and issue communication requirements. Obligations under the personal attack rule and the requirements of Section 315 of the Communications Act apply to LPTV stations on a sliding scale; that is, the obli-

---

[67] Low Power Television Broadcasting, 47 Fed. Reg. 21,468 (May 18, 1982).

gations vary with the individual low-power station's capacity to originate local programming. For example, a station with no local production equipment—perhaps an automated operation that simply transmits programming as it comes off a satellite—would not have to (because it would not be able to) deal with local issues or allow candidates and victims of personal attack to respond. An LPTV that uses cameras and other production gear to originate its own programming would be fully subject to such requirements. The "reasonable access" requirement of Section 312(a)(7) of the Communications Act applies to an LPTV station so long as the candidates provide program material that is compatible with the station's origination equipment.

10.2.1.4 LPTV and the Emergency Broadcast System.

An LPTV that originates local programming is expected to participate in EBS tests. However, it does not have to have the encoding device needed to produce the two-tone signal (EMG 10.1.4.1.2).

10.2.1.5 LPTV Rebroadcasts.

Rule 74.784 deals with rebroadcasts. To rebroadcast another station's signal, an LPTV must get prior consent from the other station. The LPTV station must also notify the FCC of the call letters of the originating station and certify that written consent to rebroadcast has been obtained. An LPTV that originates local programming and, during this local programming, retransmits the signal of another station must follow rule 73.1207, the rebroadcast guidelines for full-service stations (EMG 10.1.5.2).

10.2.1.6 Other LPTV Programming Requirements.

Rule 74.780 lists full-service broadcast rules that also apply to LPTV. In addition to those discussed above, these rules include the following:

73.653	Operation of television aural and visual transmitters.
73.1212	Sponsorship identification (EMG 10.1.1.4).
73.1208	Broadcast of recorded material (EMG 10.1.1.7).
73.3580(d)	Local notice of renewal (EMG 8.1.5.3). Applies only to LPTV stations that originate their own programming.
73.1206	Broadcast of telephone conversations (EMG 10.1.5.1).

10.2.2 Programming Requirements for Translator and Booster Stations

Translator and booster stations have station identification requirements. A translator must obtain rebroadcast permission from its primary station.

Rule 74.763(a) says that a TV translator need operate on no regular schedule. It may also go dark for 30 days, as described in EMG 10.2.1.1. However, it is expected to provide service to the extent within its control and to avoid unwarranted interruption.

Rules 74.783 and 74.1283 spell out station identification requirements for TV translators and for FM translators and boosters, respectively. An FM booster's ID is always made by its primary station, and the primary fulfills the station identification requirement for its booster by giving its own (the primary's) station ID.

TV and FM translator stations have two options. First, the translator may arrange to have its station identification made by its primary station. Under this option, the translator's ID consists of its call letters and its location. The FM primary gives the translator ID once during each of three periods—7–9 A.M., 12:55–1:05 P.M., and 4–6 P.M. The TV primary station is to identify the translator twice during the periods 7–9 A.M. and 3–5 P.M. A TV or FM primary station that signs on later than the 7–9 A.M. period must give the translator ID as soon as possible. If the TV primary gives its translator's ID visually, the ID must be "easily readable"; if aurally, "clearly understandable."

The second station identification option for a translator station is to give its ID once an hour in international Morse code. This procedure is described in EMG 10.2.1.2, above.

Rules 74.784 and 74.1284 are the rebroadcast requirements for TV and FM translators, respectively. A translator must have prior permission as described in EMG 10.1.5.2 to retransmit its primary station. The TV rule limits a translator to simultaneous retransmission (that is, no delay broadcasts).

In its order authorizing the low-power television service,[68] the FCC noted that a translator is expected to carry the EBS tests originated by its primary station (EMG 10.1.4.2). Rule 74.780 applies the TV broadcast regulations discussed in EMG 10.2.1.6 to TV translators.

10.2.3   Programming Requirements for Instructional Television Fixed Service Stations and Wireless Cable Operators

> The primary content of ITFS transmission is to be instructional. An ITFS licensee that wishes to use excess channel capacity for other purposes must transmit at least an FCC-specified minimum of instructional programming. A wireless cable operator licensed to use ITFS channels must make available to instructional programmers an FCC-specified minimum of transmission time.

FCC Rule 74.931 is specific as to type of programming that a licensee in the instructional television fixed service (ITFS) is to transmit. That rule makes clear that ITFS stations are licensed primarily to "transmit formal educational programming offered for credit to enrolled students of accredited schools."[69] The programming may be instructional and cultural; the schools may be grade schools, colleges, or universities, public or private.[70]

---

[68] *Id.*

[69] 47 C.F.R. § 74.931.

[70] Medical service courses offered by hospitals to their staffs or to medical students as training for state or national licenses or certifications qualify as instructional programming.

The exception to this educational-only programming requirement, of course, is that "excess" ITFS channel capacity may be used for other purposes[71] such as lease-out to a wireless cable operator (EMG 6.5.3). An ITFS licensee that elects to do this must meet another programming requirement. This requirement consists of minimum hours of programming and "preservation" for ITFS material and is summarized in Box 10.3.

A similar requirement affects wireless cable operators licensed to use ITFS channels. They must be prepared to share those channels with educational institutions or entities (that is, educators). FCC rules require such an operator to grant educators access up to 40 hours a week per ITFS channel.[72] An educator who wishes to take advantage of this provision must apply to the FCC and must provide the wireless cable licensee with the planned schedule of programming at least four months in advance of transmission.[73]

Rule 74.963 says that an ITFS station need operate on no regular schedule. The station may operate as much as 24 hours a day, seven days a week, unless its license specifies otherwise. However, it may not radiate unmodulated carrier or unnecessary transmissions for extended periods, except for tests and adjustments.

Rule 74.982 specifies that an ITFS station must identify itself (give its call sign) both visually and aurally when it signs on, when it signs off, and each hour on the hour. The station may defer the on-the-hour ID if it would break the continuity of the content (for example, a demonstration or a lecture); in such cases, the station should identify itself at the first normal break in programming.

Rule 74.984 deals with retransmissions by an ITFS station. Consent of the originating station must be obtained. Wireless cable operators must secure permission from a local TV station that has opted for retransmission consent status (discussed in EMG 10.3.3 below) to carry the station's signal. For many operators, however, this requirement is moot. A wireless cable system has a limited number of channels compared with, say, a cable or SMATV system. Since wireless cable opera-

---

[71] 47 C.F.R. § 74.931 also establishes other categories of uses to which ITFS stations *may* be put. These include the following:

1. Instructional- and institutional-related material including:
   - In-service training and instruction in special skills and safety programs
   - Extension of professional training
   - Material informing persons and groups engaged in professional and technical activities of current developments in their particular fields
   - Material directly related to the administrative activities of the licensee (such as the holding of conferences with personnel, distribution of reports and assignments, and exchange of data and statistics)
   - Other similar endeavors
2. Interconnection with (for purposes of feeding, receiving, or exchanging educational material) other ITFS stations, commercial and noncommercial educational television broadcast stations, closed-circuit educational television systems, and cable systems.

[72] Within the first three years of operation on the ITFS channels, the wireless cable operator must also share with the educator the cost of up to five receive sites per channel. Thereafter, no such cost-sharing is required so long as there are enough other available ITFS frequencies for the educator to build and operate a system.

[73] 47 C.F.R. § 74.992.

BOX 10.3   ITFS Programming Minimums for "Excess Capacity" Usage

1. If the ITFS entity is in its first two years of operation, the licensee must, on each channel, *program* ITFS (that is, instructional) material at least 12 hours a week and up to four hours a day.
2. If the ITFS entity has been operating longer than two years, the licensee must, on each channel,
   a. *Preserve* at least 40 hours a week for ITFS programming. The preservation
      (1) *Must* include at least 6 hours per weekday (Monday through Friday), excluding holidays and vacation days.
      (2) *May* consist of either
         (a) Airtime strictly reserved for ITFS use and not used for non-ITFS programming, or
         (b) Time used for non-ITFS programming but subject to ready recapture by the licensee for ITFS use with no economic or operational detriment of the licensee.
   b. *Program* ITFS material at least 20 hours per week and at least 3 hours per weekday, excluding holidays and vacation days.
3. Only ITFS programming and preserved airtime scheduled between 8 A.M. and 10 P.M., Monday through Saturday, will qualify to meet these requirements.

SOURCE: 47 C.F.R. § 74.932.

---

tors have no must-carry obligations (discussed in EMG 10.3.2 below), they usually opt to carry no local TV broadcast signals. After all, their subscribers can pick them up off the air. Instead, wireless cable system channels are devoted to satellite-delivered services such as USA, MTV, CNN, ESPN, and HBO.

10.2.4   Direct Broadcast Satellite Programming Requirements

Congress has put educational and political programming responsibilities on DBS licensees.

In its 1982 order authorizing direct broadcast satellites (DBS),[74] the Federal Communications Commission announced a policy of minimum regulation during the early phase of the new service. The exact uses to which DBS would be put—the nature of its service—could not be predicted. Therefore, said the Commission, during the initial phase of DBS development, minimal regulation would encourage innovation and experimentation.

---

[74] Direct Broadcast Satellites, 90 F.C.C.2d 676.

Ten years later—and in the face of what appeared to be imminent launch of at least two DBS services (EMG 6.6), Congress imposed regulation.[75] It added a new Section 335 to the Communications Act, directing the FCC to take certain actions. As a result, the Commission opened a rule-making proceeding[76] with the following aims:

1. Require that a DBS licensee reserve 4 to 7 percent of satellite channel capacity "exclusively for noncommercial programming of an educational or informational nature."[77] During times when that capacity is not being used for such programming, however, the licensee would be able to use it for other purposes. In 1993, however, a federal district court judge ruled that the law requiring the FCC to make this channel-capacity set-aside was unconstitutional. There was, he said, no evidence "that educational television is in short supply in the homes of DBS subscribers, nor is there any reason to conclude that [the law] . . . quell[s] anti-competitive DBS provider practices."[78] There being no compelling regulatory purpose for the set-aside, the law was therefore an unjustifed First Amendment burden on DBS service providers.

2. Place "public interest or other requirements for providing video programming"[79] on DBS licensees. These requirements would make DBS licensees, at a minimum, subject to the following sections of the Communications Act:
   a. 312(a)(7) requiring reasonable access by candidates for elective federal office (EMG 12.5) and
   b. 315 requiring equal opportunities for candidates for elective office (EMG 12.1).

3. Examine the possibilities for "localism"[80] through DBS—that is, the manner and methods by which DBS might serve and respond to local needs and interests.

Like wireless cable systems, direct broadcast satellite programmers must secure permission from a TV station that has opted for retransmission consent status (discussed in EMG 10.3.3 below) to carry the station's signal. Reports of programming plans for the two DBS services projected to start in 1994, however, do not include carriage of any local TV stations.[81]

---

[75] Cable Television Consumer Protection and Competition Act of 1992, Pub. L. No. 102-385, 106 Stat. 1460, at 1501.
[76] Direct Broadcast Satellite Public Service Obligations, 58 Fed. Reg. 12,917.
[77] 47 U.S.C. § 335(b)(1).
[78] Daniels Cablevision, Inc. v. United States, 835 F. Supp. 1 (1993), at 8.
[79] 47 U.S.C. § 335(a).
[80] 47 U.S.C. § 335(a).
[81] Rich Brown, "DBS Services Ready Their Lineups," *Broadcasting & Cable*, 14 Feb. 1994, at 16.

10.3   CABLE SYSTEM PROGRAMMING REQUIREMENTS

Six legal programming requirements that affect cable operators are the basic service tier, must carry, retransmission consent, leased channels, emergency information, access channels, and origination cablecasting.

Congress's first comprehensive cable legislation, the Cable Communications Policy Act of 1984,[82] added a few requirements to the business of cable system operation. But for the most part its effect was *de*regulatory. A cable operator could, for example, set rates and adjust program services relatively free of governmental restrictions or requirements. The Cable Television Consumer Protection Act of 1992,[83] however, *re*regulated cable—reregulated it, some would say, with a vengeance. Irrespective of the rationale and motivations (discussed in EMG 3.2.3) for that reregulation, the net result of the 1984 and 1992 acts was that federal law now impacted almost every area of cable operation, including that of programming. As a result, there are several substantial programming requirements—things a cable operator has to include on a system's lineup of services. These requirements have to do with the basic service tier, must-carry, retransmission consent, leased access, emergency information, access channels, and origination cablecasting. Each is discussed in a separate subsection below; court challenges to such requirements are discussed in a final subsection.

As you read the narrative and the informational boxes in this section, you will come across the term *activated channels*. That term as used in the Communications Act refers to

[Cable system] channels engineered at the headend . . . for provision of services generally available to residential subscribers . . ., regardless of whether [those] services are actually provided. . . .[84]

In other words, activated channels are those the cable operator uses (or could use immediately if desired) for delivery of programming to home subscribers.

10.3.1   Basic Service Tier

A cable operator must establish a basic service tier, it must be entry-level service for cable subscribers, and it must contain all broadcast TV signals the system carries and all franchise-required channels.

The focus of Section 623 is on rate regulation. As we pointed out in EMG 8.3.5, however, one part of that section[85] requires cable operators to offer a *basic service*

---

[82] 98 Stat. 2779 (1984).
[83] 106 Stat. 1460 (1992).
[84] 47 U.S.C. § 522(1).
[85] 47 U.S.C. § 543(b)(7).

tier. This is *not* necessarily the same thing as a "basic tier" that operators had, until implementation of the 1992 law, been free to create and market as they wished. For the legally mandated basic service tier, there are exact specifications of what is to be put on it and the role it is to play in the subscriber package. The public must be able to subscribe to the basic service tier by itself, and subscription to it *must* be a prerequisite to access to any other tier of service. This tier must consist of, at a minimum, all broadcast TV signals the system carries[86] and all franchise-required access channels. The cable operator may add other signals and services to the basic service tier.[87]

10.3.2 Must-Carry

A cable system has to carry as part of its basic service tier the signals of local commercial TV stations that have opted for must-carry status, qualified noncommercial educational TV stations, and qualified LPTV stations; the precise number varies with the number of channels on the system.

Among the most complicated programming requirements of the 1992 cable act is must-carry. In this statutory version of must-carry, cable systems have to carry the signals of local commercial TV stations,[88] qualified noncommercial educational TV stations, and qualified LPTV stations,[89] and as indicated in the previous section, they must be carried on the basic service tier. The rule's numerical and mechanical requirements for full-power TV stations are outlined in Table 10.2, for LPTV stations in Table 10.3. The law defines "local commercial television station" and "qualified noncommercial educational television station" as summarized in Box 10.4, and "qualified low power station" as summarized in Box 10.5. Some of the must-carry "dilemmas" are explained in Box 10.6.

In order to get must-carry status, a commercial television station must declare itself on a triennial basis as explained below. All noncommercial stations are automatically must-carry. Many LPTV stations, however, are not eligible for must-carry status.[90]

---

[86] "All broadcast TV signals" includes all local and distant TV broadcast signals the system carries (except satellite-delivered superstations) and all must-carry signals and retransmission-consent signals (below). As we shall see in the next section, these two categories overlap.

[87] If the cable system is not subject to effective competition (EMG 8.3.5), the subscriber rate for this basic service tier would be regulated by the franchising authority or the FCC. The cable operator could add to this tier video programming signals and services over and above the required minimum; these added channels would be subject to the same rate regulation as the required signals.

[88] This includes stations that devote most or all of their programming to direct marketing. Implementation of Section 4(g) of the Cable Television Consumer Protection and Competition Act of 1992 Home Shopping Station Issues, 8 F.C.C.R. 5231 (1993).

[89] 47 U.S.C. §§ 534(a), and 535(a).

[90] An LPTV gets must-carry status: (1) only if the LPTV is "qualified" (Box 10.5) and (2) only on a cable system whose franchise area is outside the 160 largest Metropolitan Statistical Areas (MSAs) and which cannot find enough full-power local commercial stations to meet its must-carry minimum. Relatively few LPTV stations fit this profile. So in a large number of cases, an LPTV station will *not* be carried on the local cable system unless the cable operator has the inclination and the channel capacity to do so.

TABLE 10.2 Cable System Must-Carry Requirements: Local Full-Power TV Stations

Usable Activated Channels	Number of Must-Carry Commercial TV Stations	Number of Must-Carry Noncommercial TV Stations
12 or fewer	3*	1[†,‡]
13–36	One-third of activated channels	At least 1; no more than 3[‡]
37 or more	One-third of activated channels	All that request carriage except those that duplicate others[‡]

SOURCE: 47 U.S.C. §§ 534(b) and 535(b)–(d).

*A system with 12 or fewer channels and 300 or fewer subscribers does not have to meet this minimum so long as it does not delete any already-carried TV broadcast signal.

[†]A system with 12 or fewer channels does not have to delete any programming that was provided as of March 29, 1990, to make room for a noncommercial station. The first channel that becomes available, however, must be used to add a noncommercial station.

[‡]A cable system must continue to carry any noncommercial educational television station that it carried on March 29, 1990, subject to waiver from the operator and the station. An operator who must add noncommercial stations may put them on unused PEG channels, if the franchise authority agrees.

TABLE 10.3 Cable System Must-Carry Requirements: Local Low-Power TV Stations*

Usable Activated Channels	Number of Must-Carry Low-Power TV Stations
35 or fewer	1
36 or more	2[†]

SOURCE: 47 U.S.C. § 534(c)

*Required only of cable systems whose franchise areas are outside the 160 largest Metropolitan Statistical Areas and cannot find enough full-power local commercial stations to meet their must-carry minimum.

[†]With approval of the franchising authority, one of these may be put on an unused PEG channel.

The cable operator has to put a must-carry signal on a specific channel as agreed to by the station.[91] The operator may not charge the station either to carry

[91] For carriage of full-power local commercial television stations, 47 U.S.C. § 534(b)(6) specifies channel positioning as follows:

Each signal carried in fulfillment of the carriage obligations of a cable operator under this section shall be carried on the cable system channel number on which the ... station is broadcast over the air, or on the channel on which it was carried on July 19, 1985 [the date of the appeals court's *Quincy* decision declaring the FCC's must-carry rules unconstitutional, note 113], or on the channel on which it was carried on January 1, 1992, at the election of the station, or on such other channel number as is mutually agreed upon by the station and the cable operator. ...

The language in 47 U.S.C. § 535(g)(5) is the same for carriage of qualified local noncommercial educational television stations, except that the phrase, "or on the channel on which it was carried on January 1, 1992" is eliminated.

BOX 10.4   Definitions of Full-Power TV Stations Eligible for Must-Carry

Local commercial station

A. A full power commercial TV station in the same market as the cable system that does not choose retransmission-consent status (EMG 10.3.3).

B. Does *not* include LPTVs, TV translators, passive repeaters, any station that does not deliver a signal of specified strength to the headend,* distant-signal stations.[†]

Qualified noncommercial educational television station

A. Either
   1. licensed by the FCC as a noncommercial educational television station and owned and operated by a public agency, nonprofit foundation, corporation, or association and is qualified to receive CPB community service grants; or
   2. owned and operated by a municipality and transmits mostly noncommercial programming for educational purposes.

B. *Does* include
   1. noncommercial educational television station translators with at least 5 watts of power that serve the franchise area;
   2. full-service television stations or translators that are licensed to a channel reserved for noncommercial educational use;
   3. other stations and translators that the FCC determines qualify.

Qualified local noncommercial educational television station

A. A qualified noncommercial educational television station that
   1. lies within 50 miles of the cable system's headend, or
   2. puts a Grade B service contour over the cable system's headend.

---

* Unless the station agrees to pay costs of getting a good signal to the headend.
[†] Unless the station agrees to pay the copyright royalty fee (EMG 15.3.11) and any other expenses that are caused from its carriage.

SOURCE: 47 U.S.C. §§ 534(h)(1), 535(1)–(2); and 47 C.F.R. § 73.3555(d)(3)(1).

BOX 10.5   Definition of LPTV Stations Eligible for Must-Carry

To be eligible for must-carry status, an LPTV station must:

1. operate at least the minimum number of hours required of full-power TV stations (EMG 10.1.1.1);
2. meet FCC requirements with respect to political candidates (Chapter 12), children's programming (EMG 10.1.2.2), and equal employment opportunities (EMG 8.1.6.3);
3. provide local news and informational programming that full-power stations do not meet (because they are located at a distance from the LPTV's community of license);
4. comply with FCC requirements to minimize interference;
5. be located no more than 35 miles from, and deliver a good over-the-air signal to, the cable headend; and
6. be licensed to a community that lies outside the 160 largest MSAs and whose population is no more than 35,000.

SOURCE: 47 U.S.C. § 534(c).

---

the signal or to put it on a specific channel.[92] The signal must be carried "without material degradation"[93] as defined by the FCC. If the operator plans to delete or reposition the signal, it must notify in writing no less than 30 days in advance (1) the station and, for noncommercial stations, (2) the system's subscribers. The operator may not delete or reposition a commercial station while a ratings survey is going on in the market.[94] A TV licensee who wishes to complain about station carriage or channel placement files the complaint first with the cable operator (who has 30 days to respond) and, if agreement is not reached between those two parties, then with the FCC.[95]

A cable operator has to put *all* of a must-carry station's signal on the system. "All" includes the station's entire broadcast-day program schedule, its regular TV broadcast picture and audio, any closed captioning, and, where technically possible, program-related material in the vertical blanking interval (VBI) or in aural subcarriers (EMG 6.3.4).[96] "All" does not include, however, programming the FCC requires deleted, such as under the syndicated exclusivity (EMG 13.4.2) and network

---

[92] The law does specify exceptions having to do with signal delivery, distant signals, and existing agreements. 47 U.S.C. §§ 534(b)(10), and 535(i).

[93] 47 U.S.C. §§ 534(b)(4)(A), and 535(g)(2).

[94] 47 U.S.C. §§ 534(b)(9), and 535(g)(3).

[95] 47 U.S.C. §§ 534(d), and 535(j).

[96] For noncommercial stations, this category would include program-related signals needed for receipt of programming by handicapped persons or for educational or language purposes.

BOX 10.6   Must-Carry Dilemmas

What happens if . . . ?

The number of local commercial stations is greater than the number of channels required for must-carry?

> In such cases, if the operator decides to carry a station affiliated with a network, it must carry the affiliate of that network that is closest to its headend.*

Two or more stations eligible for must-carry on a particular system carry the same programming† most of the broadcast day? This could be, for example, two affiliates of the same network.

> The operator need carry only one such station. If the operator elects to carry more than one such station, all "count" toward meeting the must-carry requirements.‡

Two or more public stations program substantially the same?

> An operator with 37 or more channels whose must-carry requirement includes 3 public stations need carry only one of those stations.§ In some cases, two or more public stations affiliated with the same state network may be eligible for must-carry. If their programming is substantially the same, an operator with 13–36 channels need carry only one such station.‖

There is no local public station?

> A system with 36 or fewer channels must import the signal of a public station.

---

* The law actually requires carriage of the affiliate "whose city of license reference point, as defined in [47 U.S.C. § 75.53 as of January 1, 1991] . . . is closest to the principal headend of the cable system." 47 U.S.C. § 534(b)(2)(B).
† The law uses the term *substantially duplicates.* 47 U.S.C. § 534(b)(5).
‡ 47 U.S.C. § 534(b)(5).
§ 47 U.S.C. § 535(e).
‖ 47 U.S.C. § 535(b)(3)(C).

nonduplication (EMG 13.4.1) rules.[97] The operator can choose whether to carry other VBI and subcarrier services[98] and broadcast signal enhancements that are unneeded by cable subscribers.[99]

10.3.3 Retransmission Consent

A commercial TV broadcast licensee chooses either must-carry or retransmission consent on a three-year cycle. The latter choice means that multichannel video programmers must obtain licensee permission to carry the station signal.

Under Section 325(b) of the Communications Act, as amended, commercial TV broadcasters have the opportunity every three years[100] to choose between two options with respect to cable carriage: must-carry or retransmission consent.

A broadcaster who opts for the latter is announcing, in effect, "No one may carry my signal and sell it to subscribers without getting my permission to do so." The need to get permission under retransmission-consent stations holds true for any *multichannel video programming distributor*. This is a category that, according to Section 602(11) of the Communications Act of 1934, as amended:

> means a person such as, but not limited to, a cable operator, a multichannel multipoint distribution service, a direct broadcast satellite service, or a television receive-only satellite program distributor, who makes available for purchase, by subscribers or customers, multiple channels of video programming.

In most cases, a broadcaster's motivation behind opting for retransmission consent is to negotiate with cable and other multichannel systems for compensation in return for permission to carry the station's signal.[101] (Noncommercial stations and

---

[97] In such cases, the cable operator is allowed to provide substitute programming. A local noncommercial station whose signal is carried on a cable system may not assert network nonduplication rights. 47 U.S.C. § 535(g).

[98] For example, teletext and other subscription or advertising-supported services.

[99] Such as ghost-canceling, an enhancement TV stations add to cut doubling of images or shadowlike images in their received signals. 47 U.S.C. §§ 534(b)(3), and 535(g)(1).

[100] The initial choice was October 5, 1992.

[101] The licensee of a TV station that usually commands large audiences—a network affiliate, for example, or a successful, big-city independent station—might feel that cable systems *need* to carry the station (in order to satisfy existing subscribers and to attract new ones) and would therefore opt for retransmission consent. A licensee whose station draws relatively small audiences—a new station, a station with specialized (such as non-English) programming, or a second or third independent in a market—might opt for must-carry.

Neither option guarantees carriage for a station. The problem with retransmission consent is obvious: it is entirely possible that a cable operator might say, "Thanks, but no thanks." With respect to must-carry, there might be too many signals. For example, a system with a limited number of activated channels that is located between two large markets—say, Los Angeles and San Diego—might

LPTV stations do not have the retransmission consent option, nor do stations that were superstations as of May 1, 1991.)

The broadcaster does not have to make a blanket choice for all systems in the station's coverage area; the station may opt for must-carry on some systems and retransmission consent on others. However, where two or more multichannel systems have overlapping service areas—say, two rival cable systems in one franchise area or SMATV and wireless cable operations in a cable system's franchise area—the broadcaster must make the same choice for all.

10.3.4   Leased Channels

A cable operator with a system of more than 35 channels must allow third parties to lease and program some of its channel capacity; the precise number of channels varies with the number of channels on the system. One-third of that channel capacity may be set aside for programming from minority or educational sources.

Section 612 of the Communications Act, as amended, requires designation of channel capacity "for commercial use by persons unaffiliated with the operator. . . ."[102] Commercial use is defined as "provision of video programming, whether or not for profit."[103] The common name for these channels is *leased access.*

The exact channel capacity that must be so designated varies with the number of activated channels as indicated in Box 10.7. When this section was added to the Communications Act in 1984, cable operators did not have to delete services they were currently providing to comply with this requirement. For example, a system that provided subscriber services on all 40 of its activated channels on that date did not have to remove four of them in order to achieve the minimum 10 percent available for leasing. However, as channel capacity subsequently became available—say, through expansion of the number of channels or by voluntarily dropping one or more of the existing program services—the law required that it be made available for commercial use.

A party wishing to use leased-access channel capacity does *not* have to lease an entire channel 24 hours a day for weeks on end. A direct-sales firm, for example, might wish to air its 30-minute infomercial 10 times across two weeks; it would lease from the cable system only those 10 half hours. The 1992 cable act amended

---

have such a large number of stations eligible for must-carry that it can pick and choose to fulfill its must-carry obligation.

Since the retransmission consent provision was added to law by the 1992 cable act, the first round of negotiations took place in 1993. The large multiple system operators held tough, and very few broadcasters were able to negotiate direct cash payments solely for carriage of their signals. For a summary description of the types of deals for which broadcasters settled in that first round, *see* Joe Flint, "Stations Stay for No Pay," *Broadcasting & Cable,* 11 Oct. 1993, at 6.

[102] 47 U.S.C. § 522(b).

[103] 47 U.S.C. § 522(b)(5).

BOX 10.7   Cable System Leased-Access Channel Requirements

A cable system with activated channels as indicated must designate the following percentages for commercial use:

Fewer than 36 activated channels—Designate none, unless required by a franchise that was in effect on October 30, 1984, the date of enactment of legislation requiring these channels.

From 36 through 54 activated channels—Subtract (from the total number of activated channels) those channels required or prohibited by federal law or regulation, then designate 10 percent of the remainder.

From 55 through 100 activated channels—Subtract those channels required or prohibited by federal law or regulation, then designate 15 percent of the remainder.

Over 100 activated channels—Designate 15 percent.

SOURCE: 47 U.S.C. § 532(b)(1).

---

this section to allow cable operators to enforce a "written and published"[104] policy prohibiting sexually objectionable material[105] from leased access channels; it also made cable operators liable for transmission of such material over leased access.[106] Under the 1984 act, they had neither the power to prohibit nor the liability.

The cable operator may utilize such channel capacity to provide other services until such time as someone requests it for commercial use. If the operator fails to make it available or insists on unreasonable terms or prices, the aggrieved party may take the matter to court or petition the FCC.

The 1992 cable act added a new use for leased-access capacity. Cable operators may use up to one-third of that capacity for programming by a "qualified minority programming source" or a "qualified educational programming source."[107] Carriage of such programming does not substitute for the must-carry requirement to carry qualified noncommercial educational television stations.

---

[104] 47 U.S.C. § 522(h).

[105] The wording of 47 U.S.C. § 522(h) is: "Any cable service [that] . . . in the judgment of the franchising authority is obscene, or is in conflict with the community standards in that it is lewd, lascivious, filthy, or indecent or otherwise unprotected by the Constitution. . . ."

[106] 47 U.S.C. § 558.

[107] 47 U.S.C. § 522(i)(1). That paragraph goes on to exclude programming provided over a cable system on July 1, 1990. Paragraph (2) of that section defines *qualified minority programming source* as one that "devotes substantially all of its programming to coverage of minority viewpoints, or to programming directed at members of minority groups, and which is over 50 percent minority-owned. . . ."

Paragraph (3) defines *qualified educational programming source* as one that "devotes substantially all of its programming to educational or instructional programming that promotes public understanding of mathematics, the sciences, the humanities, and the arts and has a documented annual expenditure on programming exceeding $15,000,000. . . ."

10.3.5 Emergency Information

Cable subscribers must get the same EBS information when viewing cable channels as they would get if tuned to a broadcast station.

Cable operators did not have a congressionally mandated role in emergency information before 1992. Now they do and must comply with FCC standards to ensure subscriber access to emergency information.[108]

10.3.6 Access Channels

The franchising authority may require a cable operator to designate channel capacity for public, educational, or governmental use.

This power is granted the franchising authority (EMG 8.3.1) under Section 611 of the Communications Act of 1934, as amended. The franchising authority may also require rules and procedures for use of the channel capacity so designated. The defining term is *access channels;* the community has access to them, which means the community may program them. Public access programming is material that groups or individual members of the community provide. In addition to the public, local government and educational and other institutions can also use access channels. Because of such uses, access channels are often called *PEG channels*—public, education, government.

PEG uses have first priority on access channels. However, when not being used for transmission of PEG material, the system operator may use the access channels for other purposes. Section 611 calls for the franchising authority to adopt rules that spell out when the operator may, and must cease to, use PEG-designated channel capacity for other purposes.

The franchising authority may include a requirement for designated PEG channel capacity in both the request for proposal (for a new operator) and as part of an existing operator's franchise renewal. Franchise or franchise renewal agreements that call for PEG channel capacity are enforceable, *even when the operator has proposed such channels voluntarily* (that is, the franchising authority did not require them)!

The franchising authority may also require a cable operator to designate channel capacity on an institutional network[109] for educational or governmental use. Terms and procedures parallel those for PEG-designated cable channels.

Just as with leased-access channels, cable operators now have the power to prohibit sexually objectionable material from PEG channels.[110] And just as with

---

[108] 47 U.S.C. § 544(g).

[109] A cable operator constructs or operates an institutional network as a communications network that is generally available only to subscribers who are not residential subscribers. Business subscribers, for example, might use an institutional network for high-speed transfer and dissemination of data information.

[110] As per Section 10(c) of the Cable Consumer Protection and Competition Act of 1992, the FCC added a new Section 76.202 to its rules enabling cable operators to prohibit the use of PEG channels for

leased-access channels, they are also legally liable for transmission of obscene material.[111] Neither was true under the 1984 law.

10.3.7 Origination Cablecasting

Origination cablecasting is subject to many of the same programming requirements as broadcasting.

FCC rule 76.5(w) defines *origination cablecasting* as "programming (exclusive of broadcast signals) carried on a cable television system over one or more channels and subject to exclusive control of the cable operator." Origination cablecasting refers only to programming the system operator controls; that is, the operator chooses to present the programming and exercises direct control over its content.

Three broadcast programming requirements pertain also to origination cablecasting.[112] Rule 76.221 applies all requirements for sponsorship identification (EMG 10.1.1.4). Rule 76.205 applies requirements discussed in Chapter 12 involving use by candidates for public office, including equal opportunity requests, prohibition against censorship, exclusion of certain types of programming, regulation of charges, ban on candidate discrimination, keeping of records, the seven-day rule, and candidate qualifications. Rule 76.209 applies the personal attack and political editorial (EMG 11.3.1 and 11.3.2) rules to origination cablecasting.

10.3.8 Court Challenges of Cable Programming Requirements

In federal district court decisions, statutory requirements for a basic tier, must-carry, retransmission consent, leased channels, and access channels were found to be constitutional.

Cable television interests entered court challenges against these requirements, contending that such laws interfere with the First Amendment right of operators to program their cable channels as they wish.

The federal courts had already twice declared FCC-created must-carry *rules* (which required cable systems to carry the signals of local full-power broadcast TV

---

programming obscene material, sexually explicit conduct, or material soliciting or promoting unlawful conduct. The rule also allows a cable operator to allow any access user (or any access manager or administrator who has agreed to assume the responsibility of certifying) to certify that its programming does not contain, and that reasonable efforts will be used to ensure that live programming does not contain, such material.

[111] 47 U.S.C. § 558.

[112] Several of the programming restrictions on broadcasting also apply to origination cablecasting. These are discussed in Chapter 13.

stations) to be unconstitutional.[113] So within days of the 1992 cable act being signed into law, two lawsuits were filed challenging its must-carry provision. Four months later the U.S. District Court for Washington, D.C., rejected on a 2-1 vote the plaintiff's contention that must-carry is unconstitutional on First Amendment grounds.[114] The court said that operators have economic incentives to refuse carriage of broadcast signals. A cable system's refusal to carry a broadcast station, reasoned the court, results in decreased audience for the station. And when stations lose audience, cable systems gain both viewers and advertising dollars.

The other requirements were heard in a second case. The requirement for a basic service tier was part of the rate regulation provisions of the 1992 cable act, provisions, wrote the judge in that case, that are "wholly unrelated to content";[115] the First Amendment was not involved. Retransmission consent was valid because Congress has constitutional authority to provide creative artists with copyright protection; broadcasters are creative artists, and retransmission consent constitutes copyright protection despite being written into the cable act rather than the Copyright Act. The PEG and leased access provisions were valid because their purpose was to enable "a broad range of speakers to reach a television audience that otherwise would never hear them [which] . . . is an appropriate goal and legitimate exercise of federal legislative power."[116]

Appeals, however, were inevitable.[117] So as of the date the final manuscript for this book went to the publisher, the last word on the ability of these requirements to withstand constitutional muster was yet to be written.

10.4   PROGRAMMING REQUIREMENTS FOR SMATV SYSTEMS AND VIDEO DIALTONE SERVICES

> Both SMATV operators and video dialtone programmers may have to deal with retransmission consent.

A SMATV operator may put on its channels the signals of TV stations that have must-carry status for cable systems in the same area. Unlike a cable system, the SMATV system does not have to carry such signals; but if it does elect to carry them it may do so without permission from the stations. A TV station that opts for retrans-

---

[113] Quincy Cable TV v. FCC, 768 F.2d 1434, *cert. denied sub nom.* National Ass'n of Broadcasters v. Quincy Cable TV, 476 U.S. 1169 (1986); Century Communications Corp. v. FCC, 835 F.2d 292 (1987), *cert. denied sub nom.* Office of Communication of United Church of Christ v. FCC, 486 U.S. 1032 (1988).

[114] Turner Broadcasting v. FCC, 819 F. Supp. 32 (1993).

[115] Daniels Cablevision, Inc. v. United States, 835 F. Supp. 1 (1993), at 7.

[116] *Id.*, at 6.

[117] Harry A. Jessell, ed., "Washington Watch: As Expected, the Cable Industry Filed an Injunction Requesting a Stay of the Must-Carry Rules," *Broadcasting & Cable*, 2 May 1993, at 52; and Harry A. Jessell, "Court Upholds Heart of Cable Act," *Broadcasting & Cable*, 20 Sept. 1993, at 10.

mission consent is a different matter; if the SMATV system elects to carry the signal of such a station, the system operator must get permission to do so.[118]

Apparently the same would hold true for video dialtone programmers. The issue of retransmission consent would be moot, of course, to the telephone company that provides the video dialtone service, since FCC rules forbid telco control of programming (EMG 8.4.2). But the video programmers that use the service, despite not being mentioned as a specific category in the law defining "multichannel video programming distributor,"[119] probably would have to get permission to carry the signal of a station that has opted for retransmission consent.

DISCUSSION QUESTIONS

1. How can Congress and the FCC make all these requirements—things that electronic mass media *have* to program—in the light of the First Amendment to the U.S. Constitution? And why do the courts let them get away with it? Station identification, for example: What would happen if Congress attempted to prescribe identification requirements for print media? (Or has that happened already? Just what are the requirements for second class mailing privileges?)

2. Go down the list of requirements in this chapter and, for each one, ask yourself why and what if. Start at the top with required minimum schedules of operation for broadcast stations. Why have such a requirement? Make an argument for its elimination. If it were eliminated, what (if anything) would be different—better and worse? Now do that same mind exercise with the other requirements—station identification, sponsorship identification, and so on. (If you come up with some really good arguments, type them up as the basis of a petition for rule making and send it to the FCC. Your instructor will give you 10 points extra credit if the Commission adopts the rule you propose!)

3. What other programming requirements would you place on the various electronic mass media? What other types of content that is not already required? Why? Justify your choice in terms of (a) the Communications Act and (b) the First Amendment to the U.S. Constitution.

4. Full-power broadcast stations, low-power broadcast stations, translator stations, booster stations, wireless cable, direct broadcast satellite—they are all over-the-air media aiming at large audiences. What are the differences among them with respect to programming requirements, and why should there be any difference?

5. If you have your TV set hooked up to an antenna, you can pick up full-power commercial TV broadcast stations for free. If you have your TV set hooked up to a cable system, you may be able to pick up those same stations, but if they have opted for retransmission consent, you will also eventually wind up paying for them. After all, the cable operator is certainly going to pass along to you any charges (prorated, of course, among all other subscribers) that the station levies for carriage. Is that fair? What about from the cable system's point of view? What about from the TV station's point of view?

6. What do you think of the programming requirements of the Children's Television Act? Do the ends justify the means? If so, should these same types of requirements be applied to

---

[118] 47 U.S.C. § 325(b)(1).
[119] 47 U.S.C. § 522(12).

radio, motion pictures, comic books, direct mail, magazines, newspapers, and books? Why, or why not?

SUGGESTED READINGS

Atkin, David, and Robert LaRose. "Cable Access: Market Concerns Amidst the Marketplace of Ideas." *Journalism Quarterly* 68 (autumn 1991): 354–362.

Banks, Mark J., and Sara E. Titus. "The Promise and Performance of Low Power Television." *Journal of Media Economics* 3 (2) (fall 1990): 15–25.

Brenner, Daniel L. *Cable Television and Other Nonbroadcast Video: Law and Policy.* New York: Boardman, continuing.

Einhorn, Michael A., ed. *Price Caps and Incentive Regulation in Telecommunications.* Boston: Kluwer, 1991.

Engleman, Ralph. "The Origins of Public Access Cable Television: 1966–1972." *Journalism Monographs* 123 (Oct. 1990).

Gershon, Richard A. "Pay Cable Television: A Regulatory History." *Communications and the Law* 12 (2) (June 1990): 3–26.

Krueger, Elizabeth, and Kimberly Corrigan. "Broadcasters' Understanding of Political Broadcast Regulation." *Journal of Broadcasting and Electronic Media* 35 (summer 1991): 289–304.

Lampert, Donna N. "Cable Television: Does Leased Access Mean Least Access?" *Federal Communications Law Journal* (Mar. 1992): 245.

Limburg, Val E. "The Decline of Broadcast Ethics: *U.S. v. NAB.*" *Journal of Mass Media Ethics* 4 (1989): 214–231.

Palumbo, Michael J. "Has the Marketplace Failed the Children: The Children's Television Act of 1990." *Seton Hall Legislative Journal* 15 (1990): 345.

Porter, Gregory S., and Mark J. Banks. "Cable Access as a Public Forum." *Journalism Quarterly* 65 (spring 1988): 39–45.

Setzer, Florence. *Broadcast Television in a Multichannel Marketplace.* Washington, DC: Office of Plans and Policy, Federal Communications Commission, 1991.

Stone, Alan. *Public Service Liberalism: Telecommunications and Transitions in Public Policy.* Princeton: Princeton UP, 1991.

Versfelt, David S. "Constitutional Considerations of the Children's Television Act of 1988: Why the President's Veto Was Warranted." *Hastings Journal of Communications and Entertainment: COMM/ENT* 11 (summer 1989): 625–664.

Chapter 11

FAIRNESS

The concept of fairness in radio and television programming dates back to the early days of broadcast regulation, and no aspect of regulation has been more controversial. Proponents have maintained that public ownership of the airwaves and the scarcity of usable frequencies for broadcasting require licensees to treat controversial issues in a balanced manner. However, critics of the Fairness Doctrine argued that the doctrine had a chilling effect by discouraging broadcasters from airing controversial items. In 1987 the FCC eliminated most provisions of the doctrine. To understand what still remains, it is necessary to understand what preceded it.

11.1 DEVELOPMENT OF THE FAIRNESS DOCTRINE

The Fairness Doctrine grew out of the notion that the granting of a broadcast license left the licensee with an obligation to present all sides of controversial issues.

Soon after the Radio Act of 1927 was enacted, efforts were made to include fairness language in the legislation regulating broadcasting.[1] But early attempts failed, either because Congress killed the legislation or the president vetoed it.

One of the initial statements concerning fairness in broadcasting came in 1929 in the FRC's *Great Lakes Broadcasting* case:

In so far as a program consists of discussion of public questions, public interest requires ample play for the free and fair competition of opposing

---

[1] For a discussion of pre-1959 fairness developments, *see* Thomas J. Houser, "The Fairness Doctrine—an Historical Perspective," 47 *Notre Dame Lawyer* 550 (1972).

views and the Commission believes that the principle applies to all discussion of issues of public importance.[2]

Even though the Fairness Doctrine was not to be made law for two decades, *Great Lakes* did enunciate the importance of a balanced presentation of public issues. This notion of fairness played a part in three other early cases, *Trinity Methodist Church*,[3] *KFKB Broadcasting*,[4] and *Chicago Federation of Labor*.[5] These cases, which were discussed in Chapter 9, do not directly make a case for fairness but do reflect the FRC position that broadcast licensees should use their facilities to benefit the public. The concern for fairness was also evident in 1938 when the FCC refused to grant a license to a station that planned to use its facilities to present a fundamentalist view of the Bible. The FCC said that a station devoted to one purpose could not serve the general public.[6] The Commission then voiced a belief that would be echoed in subsequent FCC and court opinions. Noting the scarcity of frequencies, the FCC concluded "that the interests of the listening public are paramount to the interests of the individual applicant in determining whether public interest would best be served by granting an application."[7] The FCC said a one-sided presentation would be unacceptable.

11.1.1   The *Mayflower* Decision

In the *Mayflower* decision the FCC ruled that stations could not use their facilities to advocate their own opinions.

Despite the acknowledgment of the need for fairness in programs dealing with public issues, the Commission for many years was not inclined to permit stations to air their opinions about controversial topics. That position was most clear in 1941 when the FCC questioned the license renewal of a Boston radio station, WAAB, which was engaged in editorializing about political candidates and other topics of controversy. After a competing company, Mayflower Broadcasting Corporation, applied for the channel, WAAB agreed to stop editorializing to get its license renewed. The FCC, in a ruling known as the *Mayflower* decision, said that a truly free radio could not be used to advocate the causes of the licensee. "In brief," said the Commission, "the broadcaster cannot be an advocate."[8]

Not only had WAAB used its facilities to advocate station opinion, it had also failed to present the public with contrasting viewpoints. The Commission observed:

---

[2] 3 FRC *Ann. Rep.* 32 (1929).
[3] Trinity Methodist Church, South v. FRC, 62 F.2d 850, *cert. denied*, 284 U.S. 685 (1932).
[4] KFKB Broadcasting v. FRC, 47 F.2d 670 (1931).
[5] Chicago Fed'n of Labor v. FRC, 41 F.2d 879 (1929).
[6] Young People's Ass'n for Propagation of the Gospel, 6 F.C.C. 178 (1938).
[7] *Id.* at 181.
[8] Mayflower Broadcasting Corp., 8 F.C.C. 333, at 340 (1941).

Freedom of speech on radio must be broad enough to provide full and equal opportunity for the presentation of all sides of public issues. Indeed, as one licensed to operate in a public domain the licensee has assumed the obligation of presenting all sides of important public questions, fairly objectively and without bias. The public interest—not the private—is paramount.[9]

The *Mayflower* case not only established that stations could not editorialize but continued the path toward development of the Fairness Doctrine. Four years later another case addressed the need for a station to program important public issues. The case involved WHKC, Columbus, Ohio.[10] Several labor groups had petitioned against renewal of the station's license because the station refused to sell time to groups it disagreed with for discussing controversial topics or soliciting memberships.

WHKC worked out an agreement with the labor groups to change the station policies, and the petition was dropped. In reviewing the agreement, the FCC noted that each station has a duty to be sensitive to problems of public concern, and to make sufficient time available, on a nondiscriminatory basis.

A year after the WHKC case the FCC issued its Blue Book, in which it reviewed program requirements of licensees (EMG 9.3). In it, the FCC identified four programming requirements relevant to serving the public interest. One of the four was broadcasting programs that discussed public issues. The Commission said a vigorous presentation of a viewpoint was important in a democracy and stressed that "the public interest clearly requires that an adequate amount of time be made available for the discussion of public issues. . . ."[11]

Several months after releasing the Blue Book, the FCC ruled on another significant fairness case, *Robert Harold Scott.*[12] Scott, an atheist, asked the FCC to revoke the licenses of three California radio stations that refused to provide him time to broadcast his views. He argued that the stations carried religious programs that directly and indirectly attacked atheism.

The FCC felt Scott's complaint was too broad, since it involved three stations, and refused to revoke the licenses. However, it did make several important statements on the fairness concept it was developing. First, the Commission stated that a licensee had a duty to make time available for the presentation of opposing views on current controversial issues of public importance. Second, the FCC said that time should be made available for ideas that "have a high degree of unpopularity."[13] And third, the Commission said that an idea or organization could become a controversial issue of public importance deserving broadcast time if it was attacked by others.

---

[9] *Id.*
[10] United Broadcasting Co., 10 F.C.C. 515 (1945).
[11] Public Service Responsibility of Broadcast Licensees, FCC Memorandum issued March 7, 1946, at 40.
[12] 11 F.C.C. 372 (1946).
[13] *Id.* at 376.

11.1.2   Birth of the Fairness Doctrine

> In 1949 the FCC established the Fairness Doctrine and also gave stations the right to editorialize.

Dissatisfaction with the FCC's ruling against licensee editorializing had simmered ever since the *Mayflower* ruling in 1940. Individual citizens, broadcast licensees, and the National Association of Broadcasters opposed the ruling as a limitation on free speech, and repeatedly asked the FCC to clarify what the decision meant. Finally, the Commission was forced to review its position. In 1948 it held hearings on its ban on editorializing, and in 1949 the FCC issued a report titled *In the Matter of Editorializing by Broadcast Licensees* (Report on Editorializing).[14] The report was the birth of the Fairness Doctrine and it gave broadcasters a twofold obligation: (1) to provide a reasonable amount of time for the presentation of public issues and (2) to provide reasonable opportunities for contrasting views on controversial issues of public importance.

The Commission commented that the public interest required licensees to devote a reasonable percentage of their broadcast time to the discussion of public issues of interest to the community.

> And we have recognized, with respect to such programs, the paramount right of the public in a free society to be informed and to have presented to it for acceptance or rejection the different attitudes and viewpoints concerning these vital and often controversial issues which are held by the various groups which make up the community. It is the right of the public to be informed, rather than any right on the part of the Government, any broadcast licensee or any individual member of the public to broadcast his own particular views on any matter, which is the foundation stone of the American system of broadcasting.[15]

Thus, the FCC made official the fairness obligation that had been developing for two decades. Licensees were now obligated to adhere to the twofold requirement of the Fairness Doctrine. This has been known as the general Fairness Doctrine, which is distinct and separate from more specific fairness requirements such as personal attacks and political endorsements, which are discussed later in this chapter.

In establishing the Fairness Doctrine the FCC also made another significant move. It reversed the *Mayflower* decision and gave stations the right to editorialize.

In 1960, the Commission more clearly embraced editorializing. In a report describing licensee programming obligations, editorializing was identified as one of

---

[14] 13 F.C.C. 1246 (1949).
[15] *Id.* at 1249.

FRANK AND ERNEST   by Bob Thaves

YESTERDAY THE MANAGEMENT OF THIS STATION WISHED YOU A GOOD MORNING. HERE IS MISTER PRESTON COSGROVE WITH AN OPPOSING VIEW....

© 1979 by NEA. Inc. T.M. Reg. U.S. Pat. Off.   THAVES 11-23

SOURCE: Reprinted by permission of NEA, Inc.

14 elements "usually necessary to meet the public interest, needs and desires of the community in which the station is located."[16]

Cable systems, like broadcast stations, were required to adhere to the Fairness Doctrine, although the cable rules applied only to local origination cablecasting, meaning the nonbroadcast programming carried by the cable system over which it has exclusive control.[17] Programming received from satellite-delivered services is not considered to be locally originated.

11.1.3   Fairness Included in the Communications Act?

In 1959 Congress amended the Communications Act with language that many believed included the Fairness Doctrine in the Communications Act. In 1986 the D.C. Court of Appeals concluded that Congress had not made fairness a binding statutory obligation.

An ongoing complaint about the Fairness Doctrine had been that the FCC, a government agency, created it and administered its own notion of fairness. This led to demands to amend the Communications Act with fairness requirements. Some feel that Congress codified the doctrine in 1959 when it amended Section 315 of the Communications Act to exempt news programming from the equal-time rule.[18]

---

[16] Report and Statement of Policy Re: Commission en Banc Programming Enquiry, 44 F.C.C. 2303 (1960). The position that stations should editorialize was reversed in the 1980s when the FCC deregulated radio and television (EMG 9.6).

[17] 47 C.F.R. § 76.5(w).

[18] Steven J. Simmons, *The Fairness Doctrine and the Media* (Berkeley: U of California P, 1978), reviewed the legislative history of the 1959 amendments and on page 47 concludes that "Congress gave statutory recognition and approval to the doctrine." Dwight L. Teeter, Jr. and Don R. Le Duc, *Law of Mass Communications*, 7th ed. (Westbury, NY: Foundation, 1992), on page 392 say that Congress never bothered to codify the doctrine on a formal basis.

The circumstances that led to the congressional action began with an FCC decision in the Lar Daly case.[19] Daly, who was challenging the incumbent mayor of Chicago, Richard Daley, asked for equal time on a Chicago TV station after the station showed the mayor receiving the president of Argentina.[20] The FCC decision that Daly was entitled to equal time presented a problem. If broadcast news departments could not show officeholders doing legitimate duties during an election campaign without having to provide time to challengers, stations might stop covering political candidates during campaign periods. This was not a pleasing possibility for incumbent members of Congress. As a result, Congress passed legislation that exempted certain types of news programs from equal time requirements (EMG 12.1). Congress said:

> Nothing in the foregoing sentence shall be construed as relieving broadcasters, in connection with the presentation of newscasts, news interviews, news documentaries and on-the-spot coverage of news events, from the obligation imposed upon them under this Act to operate in the public interest and to afford reasonable opportunity for the discussion of conflicting views on issues of public importance.[21]

In 1986 the U.S. court of appeals was asked to review an FCC decision in the so-called TRAC case. TRAC is an abbreviation for Telecommunications Research and Action Center, the public interest group that brought the case. In the decision, the Commission refused to apply the political broadcasting rules or the Fairness Doctrine to teletext. The court upheld the Commission's authority to exempt teletext from the Fairness Doctrine. In doing so, the court had to consider the argument that the 1959 congressional statement had codified the Fairness Doctrine, an action that prevented the Commission from altering the fairness obligation. The court concluded:

> We do not believe that language adopted in 1959 made the fairness doctrine a binding statutory obligation; rather, it ratified the Commission's longstanding position that the public interest standard authorizes the fairness doctrine.[22]

The court said the words used by Congress were meant to preserve an administrative construction, specifically, the public interest mandate.[23] In 1992, the Eighth Circuit Court of Appeals also concluded that Congress did not intend to codify the

---

[19] Columbia Broadcasting Sys., 26 F.C.C. 715 (1959).

[20] Daley's son, who had the same name, served as mayor of Chicago in the early 1990s.

[21] Pub. L. No. 86-274, 73 Stat. 557 (1959).

[22] Telecommunications Research and Action Ctr. v. FCC, 801 F.2d 501, at 517 (1986), *reh'g denied*, 806 F.2d 1115, *cert. denied* 482 U.S. 919 (1987)(TRAC).

[23] In the denial of rehearing, two judges dissented, arguing that the Fairness Doctrine had been codified. However, Judge Bork wrote a separate opinion to challenge the dissent. He said, "Had Congress affirmatively intended to make the fairness doctrine a statutory command, it surely would have employed a

Fairness Doctrine,[24] further reinforcing the belief that Congress had not included the doctrine in the Communications Act. As we will see later in this chapter, the TRAC ruling left the door open for the FCC to repeal the Fairness Doctrine.

11.2 ADMINISTERING THE FAIRNESS DOCTRINE

The FCC's administration of the Fairness Doctrine was controversial. The Commission was slow to provide stations with guidance in implementing the general doctrine and often relied on case-by-case developments for interpretation.

The first of the two fairness requirements, devoting a reasonable amount of time to public issues, has largely been ignored by the FCC.[25] The second requirement, to present contrasting views on controversial issues, had provided the bulk of difficulty and controversy. This requirement had generated three problems: (1) defining a "reasonable opportunity" for contrasting views; (2) determining when an issue is "controversial," and (3) deciding which issues are Fairness Doctrine issues.

11.2.1 Reasonable Opportunities

Each station was expected to provide a reasonable opportunity for conflicting viewpoints once a controversial issue had been presented. It was not sufficient for another media outlet to present the opposing viewpoint; the originating station or system must present the opposing viewpoint.[26]

Under the general Fairness Doctrine, the balance of viewpoints was not required in individual programs, but in the station's overall programming. Once a station aired a public issue of controversy it could safely argue that opposing viewpoints had been presented in overall programming if confronted with a demand for reply time. The Commission gave stations a large amount of scheduling freedom, and primarily expected them to demonstrate a reasonable, good-faith effort to present opposing viewpoints. However, as we will see later in this chapter, there is less leeway when the station presents a personal attack or political endorsement.

Indicators of reasonable coverage included the total amount of time presented on each side, frequency of presentation of viewpoints, and scheduling of presentations of viewpoints on the issue. The FCC stated that no mathematical ratio, such as 3-to-1 or 4-to-1, be used to measure the total amount of time allocated to contrasting viewpoints.

---

more direct and less offhanded approach than . . . a disclaimer within a proviso to the 1959 amendment to the Communications Act of 1934." 806 F.2d 1116.

[24] *Arkansas AFL-CIO v. FCC*, 980 F.2d 1190 (1992).

[25] See Bill F. Chamberlin, "The FCC and the First Principle of the Fairness Doctrine: A History of Neglect and Distortion," 31 *Fed. Comm. L. J.* 407 (1979).

[26] Handling of Public Issues Under the Fairness Doctrine (1974 Fairness Report), 48 F.C.C.2d 1, at 11 (1974).

When frequency of presentation was considered, the goal was to avoid an imbalance of one side compared with the other. As stated in the 1974 Fairness Report:

> This imbalance might be a reflection of the total amount of time afforded to each side, of the frequency with which each side is presented, of the size of the listening audience during the various broadcasts, or of a combination of factors.[27]

The Commission was clear about providing reasonable opportunity in scheduling of presentations. The Commission stated, "It is patently unreasonable for a licensee consistently to present one side in prime time and to relegate the contrasting viewpoints to periods outside prime time."[28] Thus, if a TV station aired an editorial in the early evening news, it would have been unfair to offer a reply late at night.

The rules have also been specific when a controversial issue has been presented in a sponsored program. The *Cullman* doctrine[29] specified that if a licensee presented one side of a controversial issue in a sponsored program, it must present contrasting viewpoints, even when there is no sponsor willing to pay to present the other side.

11.2.2   Controversial Issues

The 1949 *Report on Editorializing* did not define the terms *controversial* or *public issue*. In response to pleas for guidance, the FCC issued a so-called Fairness Primer in 1964.[30] The primer was a compilation of fairness cases that did provide licensees with some guidance. Still, it was up to the licensee to judge the impact an issue was likely to have on the community.

In the 1974 *Fairness Report,* the FCC issued three guidelines in deciding whether an issue was of public importance: how much media coverage it had received, how much attention it had received from public officials and community leaders, and "a subjective evaluation of the impact that the issue is likely to have on the community at large."[31] Media coverage alone was not sufficient to define public importance; instead, the third test, assessing public impact, was considered most important.

Public issues were not confined to any specific type of programming. They could be raised in programming ranging from newscasts to documentaries to entertainment shows. One place where public issues had been believed especially evident was in ballot issues. The FCC had required stations to provide an opportu-

---

[27] *Id.* at 17.

[28] *Id.*

[29] Cullman Broadcasting Co., 40 F.C.C. 576 (1963).

[30] Applicability of the Fairness Doctrine in the Handling of Controversial Issues of Public Importance, 40 F.C.C. 598 (1964).

[31] 48 F.C.C.2d 1, at 12.

nity for contrasting views when covering bond proposals, initiatives, recall efforts, and referenda. However, the FCC eliminated the requirement regarding ballot issues in 1992. The case involved a complaint that KARK-TV, Little Rock, Arkansas, did not properly present the views of those opposed to a ballot issue proposing the alteration of interest rates for consumer credit and loans. The FCC held that the ballot issue requirement was drawn from the Fairness Doctrine, which had been repealed in 1987.[32] A court of appeals decision upheld the FCC's repeal, saying that it is within the discretion of the FCC to change its interpretation of what "operation in the public interest" entails.[33]

Another part of the "controversy" issue was which controversial issues a station had to cover. This was another issue the FCC was long in addressing. In the 1974 *Fairness Report*, the FCC said the obligation to cover important issues was one of the most basic requirements of the Fairness Doctrine but gave stations discretion in choosing which issues and news items they presented.

A year later, the Commission changed positions in the *Patsy Mink* case. Mink, a member of Congress, contacted a number of broadcast stations asking them to air a tape containing her opinions on pending strip mining legislation. The requests went to stations that had aired a program prepared by the U.S. Chamber of Commerce. Congress was planning strip mining legislation that Mink supported. Mink said her tape would provide views in contrast to the Chamber's broadcast. However, WHAR in Clarksburg, West Virginia, refused Mink's request, saying it had not broadcast the Chamber's program or any programming on strip mining.[34]

Representative Mink, supported by the Media Access Project, a media reform group, complained to the FCC, arguing that WHAR should be required to carry the program. They said that strip mining was of extraordinary importance to WHAR's listeners and the Clarksburg area had the highest percentage of strip-mining land in West Virginia. The FCC agreed with Mink and Media Access that the issue was so important to WHAR's service area that the station was required to provide coverage. The FCC stressed that it had no intention of "intruding on licensees' day-to-day editorial decision making," but nevertheless found WHAR in violation of the Fairness Doctrine.[35]

11.2.3   Which Issues Require Contrasting Viewpoints?

The most controversial aspect of the general Fairness Doctrine has been deciding which issues, once carried by a station, are so controversial and of such public importance that the station must present opposing viewpoints.

[32] Arkansas AFL-CIO and the Committee Against Amendment 1 against Television Station KARK-TV, 7 F.C.C.2d 541 (1992).

[33] 980 F.2d 1190 (1992). The majority opinion also concluded that Congress did not intend to codify the Fairness Doctrine when it amended the Communications Act. In a follow-up ruling, *reh'g en banc*, 11 F.3d 1430 (1993), the full court affirmed that the FCC need not apply the Fairness Doctrine to election issues.

[34] Representative Patsy Mink, 59 F.C.C.2d 987, at 996 (1976).

[35] *Id.* at 994.

A complaint to the FCC about a fairness violation required two steps under the general doctrine. First, what issue was raised in the broadcast, and second, was the issue truly controversial and of public importance?[36] While seemingly simple, this problem caused the FCC considerable difficulty.

In one case NBC news aired a news series on the problem of air traffic safety and congestion, and in doing so mentioned the presence of private pilots. The Aircraft Owners and Pilots Association complained that the mention of private pilots made that a second issue. The FCC Broadcast Bureau agreed and said NBC would have to program pro–private pilot viewpoints. However, the full commission disagreed, saying the thrust of the program dealt with the issue of congestion at airports.[37]

A different conclusion was reached when another media reform group, Accuracy in Media, Inc. (AIM), filed a complaint against a Public Broadcasting Service program that examined the functioning of the U.S. legal system, including the courts and prisons. The program included reference to the trials of several black activists. AIM said the discussion of the trials made them a fairness issue. PBS said the issue was how well the law enforcement system was working. The FCC disagreed with both parties, saying the program raised two subissues—whether the prisons could rehabilitate criminals and whether blacks received justice in the United States.[38]

These two cases illustrate the problem that stations faced in determining whether an issue was really controversial and of public importance. The FCC gave little guidance to stations, and former FCC commissioner Benjamin Hooks indicated how nebulous the FCC standards were. Determining whether an issue was controversial and of public importance was "almost like pornography: I may not be able to define it, but I know it when I see it."[39]

11.3   FAIRNESS AND ACCESS TO THE MEDIA

The general Fairness Doctrine promoted the dissemination of viewpoints by allowing the licensee to control response to public issues. The personal attack and political editorial rules specifically provided reply opportunities on important matters.

Individuals and groups have long argued that they should have a mandatory right of access to appear on broadcast stations to present their views on topics they felt were important. When the Fairness Doctrine was adopted in 1949, it did not give any individual or group a right of access to radio and TV stations. Instead, the concept favored the presentation of public issues so that people could benefit from

---

[36] Ford Rowan, *Broadcast Fairness—Doctrine, Practice, Prospects* (New York: Longman, 1984) 100.
[37] National Broadcasting Co., 25 F.C.C.2d 737 (1970).
[38] Accuracy in Media, Inc., 39 F.C.C.2d 416 (1973), *aff'd on other grounds,* 521 F.2d 288 (1975). PBS was found to have provided balance on these issues in its overall programming.
[39] Simmons 179.

learning about important topics. Licensees had the discretion to present balanced viewpoints or to decide if they would be presented. As a result, licensees could air controversial issues in newscasts or editorials without having to allow anyone outside the station to appear on the station.

In 1967, the FCC changed the rules when it provided access rights to individuals who were subjected to a so-called personal attack and to candidates whose opponents had been endorsed in a station's political editorial. Whereas most of the Fairness Doctrine has been general in nature, these rules are very specific.

11.3.1 Personal Attack Rule

A personal attack on a specified person or group requires a right of reply on the station's or cablecaster's facilities.

The personal attack rule states that if a station broadcasts an attack on the honesty, character, integrity, or like personal qualities of an identified person or group during the presentation of views on a controversial issue of public importance, the following actions must be taken within one week of the attack. The station must:

1. notify the person or group who is attacked of the date, time, and identification of the broadcast;
2. send the person or group a tape, script, or if neither is available, a reasonable summary of the broadcast; and
3. offer a reasonable opportunity to respond on the station. The reply requirement does not stipulate equal time, as does Section 315, and the person or group receiving time does not have to pay for it.

The personal attack rule has several exceptions. It does not apply to (1) foreign groups or individuals, (2) legally qualified political candidates, their spokespeople, or people associated with their campaigns, or (3) attacks in bona fide news broadcasts. However, station editorials are included within the scope of the rule.[40]

Let us consider an illustration. A radio station broadcasts an editorial in which it accuses the head of the city council of wasting taxpayer money and being self-serving in plans to hire a full-time public relations associate to promote city council activities. Would this constitute a personal attack?

Yes, the hiring of a public relations employee by a public agency could be a controversial item. A specific person is the object of the editorial, and the broadcast questions the integrity or like personal qualities of this individual. Since the station initiated the attack, it would now be obligated to notify the head of the city council of the editorial, to provide a script or tape of the attack (either should be available), and to offer a reasonable opportunity to reply on the station. In this instance, the FCC requires that the object of the attack be given access to the station's facilities.

---

[40] 47 C.F.R. § 73.123.

11.3.2 Political Editorial Rule

If a station or cable system editorializes for or against a candidate for office, a right of reply is required.

Broadcast stations have always been viewed as an important means of communication for informing the public about people who seek political office. The political editorial rules allow licensees to use their facilities to air their opinions about candidates. The rules state that when a station editorializes for or against a legally qualified candidate for political office it must do the following:

1. provide notification of the date and time of the editorial,
2. furnish a script or tape of the editorial, and
3. offer reasonable reply time on the station. If the editorial is broadcast within 72 hours before the election, notification and offer of reply time must be sufficiently in advance to permit a reasonable response. Editorials aired more than 72 hours before the election require notification within 24 hours.

Who is notified and offered reply time depends on the nature of the editorial. If a candidate is *endorsed* in the editorial, all other legally qualified candidates for the office in question must be notified and offered reply time. However, the station would be wise to insist that representatives rather than the candidates themselves, present the reply. The reason is that doing so would invoke equal time rules under Section 315, since a candidate for office would now appear on the air. The candidate would not appear in the endorsement, since the message would be presented by the licensee or a spokesperson for the station. Thus, to have the opposing candidate(s) appear in the replies would trigger the "equal opportunities" of Section 315. To avoid this problem, stations can offer reply time to representatives of the opposing candidate(s).

If a candidate is *opposed* in an editorial, the station must notify and offer reply opportunity to the candidate who is opposed. Once again, the station can satisfy the rules by allowing a candidate's representative to present the response rather than putting the candidate on the air and triggering equal time requirements.

Here is another illustration. A television station runs an editorial in its evening newscast three days prior to an election in which the station manager appears on the air to endorse candidate B for mayor. Candidates A and C are also in the race. Obviously, this would be an editorial endorsement. The station would be obligated to notify candidates A and C within 24 hours of the editorial and would have to offer a reasonable reply opportunity to representatives of the two candidates.

Studies of editorial practices show that no more than 10 percent of stations have ever engaged in political editorializing. Licensees may shun political editorials because they don't want to risk running afoul of FCC rules, but it is more likely that stations do not wish to give up the free time that political editorials and replies would entail.

11.3.3 Quasi-Equal Opportunities

In 1970, the FCC established a corollary to the Fairness Doctrine known variously as the "Zapple doctrine" and the "quasi-equal opportunities" doctrine. While a part of the Fairness Doctrine, the Zapple doctrine actually applies only to supporters of political candidates. As we will see in further detail in Chapter 12, the doctrine requires a station selling time to supporters of a candidate during a campaign period to afford comparable time to the supporters of an opponent.

11.4 ADVERTISING

> Product advertising has generally been kept free of fairness rules, but when consumers sought to buy time to promote their ideas about social issues, the Fairness Doctrine was applied.

In only one instance has the Fairness Doctrine been applied to the advertising of a commercial product, but the FCC subsequently backed away from that decision. As noted in Chapter 5, the application came in 1967 when John Banzhaf asked the FCC to require a station carrying commercials for cigarettes to carry free public service messages about the dangers of smoking.[41] The Commission ruled that cigarette advertising needed to be balanced with health warnings but stressed that cigarette advertising was a "unique situation." As a result, the cigarette ruling was not applied to other product advertising. Eventually, Congress passed the Public Health Cigarette Smoking Act of 1969, which completely banned cigarette advertising from the airwaves after 1971.

After the Banzhaf ruling, public interest groups tried to get the FCC to extend the Fairness Doctrine to commercials for a high octane gasoline, arguing that the gasolines presented an air pollution concern similar to that for smoking. In *Friends of the Earth* the FCC refused to extend the Fairness Doctrine to such products,[42] but the court of appeals overturned the decision. It concluded that advertisements for large cars and high-test gasoline posed health problems just as in the case of cigarette commercials.[43] Eventually, the FCC reconsidered the case and again refused to extend the Fairness Doctrine to product commercials.[44] In a 1974 review of the doctrine the Commission addressed the application of the Fairness Doctrine to advertising. It concluded the cigarette advertising decision was a mistake, and said it would not extend the doctrine to product commercials, even if the product was controversial.[45] Obviously, the FCC feared opening a door where so many

---

[41] WCBS-TV: Applicability of the Fairness Doctrine to Cigarette Advertising, 8 F.C.C.2d 381, *stay and reconsideration denied*, 9 F.C.C.2d 921 (1967), *aff'd sub nom. Banzhaf v. FCC*, 405 F.2d 1082 (D.C. Cir. 1968), *cert. denied*, 396 U.S. 842 (1969).

[42] Friends of the Earth, 24 F.C.C.2d 743 (1970).

[43] Friends of the Earth v. FCC, 449 F.2d 1164 (1971).

[44] In re Neckritz, 37 F.C.C.2d 528 (1972).

[45] Handling of Public Issues Under the Fairness Doctrine, 48 F.C.C.2d 1 (1974).

products could be construed to be controversial that stations would be inundated with fairness requests.

But, even though the FCC would not apply the Fairness Doctrine to product commercials, the Commission said it would apply it to commercials devoted to the discussion of public issues in an "obvious and meaningful way."[46] This led to so-called *editorial* or *advocacy* advertisements that were designed for use by groups or individuals who wished to advertise their views on controversial issues. The goal was not to advertise a product but to present ideas about issues. Often editorial ads took the form of countercommercials that sought to oppose other viewpoints. An example occurred in the early 1970s when a number of fairness complaints were filed against Army and Marine public service messages that included recruitment pitches.[47] An example of such an announcement said:

> Announcer: Are you a young man who likes a challenge and who likes to do his best at anything he does? Well, if you are * * * the United States Army needs you. Life in the Army demands the very best you have * * * and in return the Army offers you educational opportunities * * * travel * * * good pay * * * and most important * * * the opportunity to make a really worthwhile contribution to the security of your country. For all the facts * * * visit your local Army recruiter. Your future * * * your decision * * * choose Army.[48]

Opponents of the Vietnam War argued that such announcements presented one side of a controversial issue, since they stressed the benefits of enlistment, without mentioning draft deferments. They maintained the announcements had to be assessed in terms of the war, since recruits would probably be stationed in Vietnam. To express their viewpoint, the activists asked stations to run countercommercials that balanced the recruitment ads. Here is an example:

> * * * Christina spends her time trying to forget, but can't. For every draftee that goes off to war, there is a Christina left behind—sometimes for good. * * * There are legal alternatives to military service. You may be entitled to one of a number of deferments provided by law. For information write this address. * * *[49]

The activists filed a fairness complaint after stations would not run the countercommercials. However, the FCC agreed that stations did not have to run the ads. The Commission did not view the recruitment ads as being pro-war, but framed

---

[46] *Id.*

[47] *See* Donald Jelinek, 24 F.C.C.2d 156 (1970), and Albert Kramer, 24 F.C.C.2d 171 (1970), *aff'd sub nom.* Green v. FCC, 447 F.2d 323 (D.C. Cir. 1971); Alan Neckritz, 24 F.C.C.2d 175 (1970), *aff'd*, 446 F.2d 501 (1971).

[48] Green v. FCC, 447 F.2d 323 (1971).

[49] *Id.* at 325.

its analysis in terms of the government's right to raise an army. It concluded that even though the war and the draft were controversial issues, the recruitment messages were not automatically tied to those issues.

Stations that carried editorial ads had an obligation to present an opposing viewpoint even though the ideas in the ad were not those of the station. As we shall see in the following section, the Supreme Court was eventually asked to decide whether broadcast stations had to accept editorial advertisements.

11.5 CONSTITUTIONALITY OF THE FAIRNESS DOCTRINE

Doubt as to whether the FCC could enforce the Fairness Doctrine without violating the First Amendment led to a crucial court challenge.

The FCC created and administered the Fairness Doctrine, a fact that left doubt as to whether the Commission could enforce the doctrine without violating the First Amendment. A test of the doctrine's constitutionality finally came in the *Red Lion* case that began in 1964.

11.5.1 *Red Lion* Decision

In *Red Lion*, the Supreme Court reviewed the constitutionality of the Fairness Doctrine and extended the reach of viewpoint access.

Radio station WGCB of Red Lion, Pennsylvania, broadcast a program by the Reverend Billy James Hargis in which he discussed a book by Fred J. Cook called *Goldwater—Extremist on the Right*. Hargis leveled a number of charges, including that Cook was associated with a Communist-affiliated publication, and Cook asked for free time to reply. The station refused. The FCC ruled in favor of Cook and ordered the station to provide free reply time.

Red Lion appealed the decision, but a court of appeals ruled that the Fairness Doctrine was not unconstitutionally vague and required the station to provide free response time. Red Lion appealed to the U.S. Supreme Court and the decision was combined with a case brought by the Radio Television News Directors Association (RTNDA). RTNDA had sought to have both the personal attack rule and the Fairness Doctrine held in violation of the First Amendment. A court of appeals struck down both the personal attack rule and the Fairness Doctrine. In 1969, the Supreme Court ruled on the combined cases. In doing so, it not only reviewed the constitutionality of the Fairness Doctrine but took the opportunity to address the status of broadcasting and the First Amendment.

The central issue before the Court was whether Congress had the power to impose affirmative duties on broadcasters, such as those required in the Fairness Doctrine and its personal attack rule, that would require them to air content they preferred not to air. The Court concluded that broadcasters had a duty to provide adequate coverage of controversial issues. Such coverage, according to the Court, must be fair in that it accurately reflects the opposing views.

The Court then turned to the constitutional issue. Broadcasters had argued that the First Amendment protected their right to use their frequencies to broadcast what they chose, and to exclude those they did not want to use a frequency. The Supreme Court pointed to the scarcity of frequencies in dismissing the argument. "When there are substantially more individuals who want to broadcast than there are frequencies to allocate," said the Court, "it is idle to posit an unabridgeable First Amendment right to broadcast comparable to the right of every individual to speak, write or publish."[50] In other words, broadcasting is unique; it has a scarcity of frequencies that requires First Amendment treatment different from speaking or publishing. All who want to broadcast can hope to do so, but limited frequencies mean some can receive licenses and others cannot. However, the Court also placed a restriction on those who do obtain licenses—they cannot monopolize a radio frequency to the exclusion of others who wish to speak:

> There is nothing in the First Amendment which prevents the Government from requiring a licensee to share his frequency with others and to conduct himself as a proxy or fiduciary with obligations to present those views and voices which are representative of his community and which would otherwise, by necessity be barred from the airwaves. . . . Because of the scarcity of frequencies, the Government is permitted to put restraints on licensees in favor of others whose views should be expressed on this unique medium. But the people as a whole retain their interest in free speech by radio and their collective right to have the medium function consistently with the ends and purposes of the First Amendment. It is the right of the viewers and listeners, not the right of the broadcasters, which is paramount.[51]

Thus, the *Red Lion* decision presented a new view of the First Amendment status of broadcasters, one that favored access for ideas. The Court believed that broadcasters were entitled to First Amendment protection, but the scarcity of frequencies permitted the government to elevate the First Amendment status of viewers and listeners above that of broadcasters. The Court said:

> It is the right of the public to receive suitable access to social, political, aesthetic, moral and other ideas and experiences which is crucial here.[52]

Even though the *Red Lion* opinion strongly favored the public's right of access to the broadcast media, subsequent actions by the FCC and the Supreme Court

---

[50] Red Lion Broadcasting Co. v. FCC, 395 U.S. 367, at 388.
[51] *Id.* at 389–390.
[52] *Id.* at 390.

itself were less supportive of access. Another Supreme Court decision illustrates the shift of opinion.

11.5.2 *Columbia Broadcasting System* Decision

In an application of the Fairness Doctrine to editorial advertising, the Supreme Court rejected the idea of an unqualified right of access.

Several years after *Red Lion*, the Supreme Court was asked to approve a general right of access to broadcast stations. In *Columbia Broadcasting System, Inc.* v. *Democratic National Committee*[53] the Court rejected the idea.

The question arose when a group opposed to U.S. conduct of the Vietnam War sought to buy commercial time on Washington, D.C., radio station WTOP-AM after the station denied them free time under the Fairness Doctrine. The radio station said its overall programming had presented fair treatment of the war issue and that it was not obligated to give free reply time. The station refused to sell advertising time, citing a policy of refusing ads for controversial topics. At the same time, the Democratic National Committee wanted to buy commercial time to solicit funds for the party. Both groups asked the FCC to require broadcasters to accept their commercials, but the FCC refused, and the Supreme Court upheld the FCC.

The Court reiterated that licensees are public trustees with a duty to adhere to fairness standards. However, the Court changed its focus on access when it addressed the question of broadcasters' rights.

The Court said that Congress intended for broadcasters to develop the widest journalistic freedom as long as they met their public trustee obligations. Enlarging the right of access by allowing groups to buy editorial advertising time, according to the Court, would enlarge the government's role in violation of the First Amendment. Approving editorial ads would require the FCC to oversee too much of the day-to-day operations of stations in determining whether a particular individual or group had been given sufficient opportunity to present its viewpoint and whether a particular viewpoint had been sufficiently aired. Further, the Court believed, the marketplace would be heavily weighted in favor of the wealthy and the time set aside for editorial advertising could be monopolized by those of one political persuasion. Against this background, the Supreme Court decided that stations should not be required to carry editorial advertising to achieve fairness.

Justice Douglas, who concurred with the decision, argued that broadcasters should have the same First Amendment rights as the print media. He said that scarcity also existed in the print media, and maintained that fairness controls were a mistake that encroached on the First Amendment. The latter view was one that the FCC ultimately adopted in seeking to abolish the Fairness Doctrine.

---

[53] 412 U.S. 94 (1973).

11.6   FAIRNESS DOCTRINE REPEALED

As early as 1981 the FCC took steps to repeal the Fairness Doctrine. After much legal maneuvering, the doctrine was repealed in 1987, although the personal attack and political editorial rules remained intact.

For years opponents of the Fairness Doctrine had argued for its repeal, but it was not until the mid-1980s that action began in earnest. On August 4, 1987, the Commission voted to repeal the Fairness Doctrine, but left several provisions intact: the personal attack and political editorializing rules.

Impetus for the repeal came from the deregulatory position taken by President Reagan and his appointees to the Commission. In a 1985 Fairness Report,[54] the FCC decided the doctrine was no longer needed. The Commission argued that the scarcity argument was no longer valid and that enough outlets now existed to expose the public to controversial issues of public importance. Second, the Commission maintained that the doctrine so inhibited broadcasters from airing controversial items that the amount of controversial programming and the number of diverse views reaching the public was reduced rather than enhanced. Congress refused to repeal the doctrine and instead ordered a two-year study of fairness enforcement policies.

Repeal of the Fairness Doctrine was complicated by the belief that the doctrine seemed to have been written into law with an amendment to Section 315 of the Communications Act (EMG 11.1.3). Two court decisions by the U.S. court of appeals gave the FCC authority to act. The first case, *Telecommunications Research and Action Center* v. *FCC*,[55] held that the Fairness Doctrine had not been incorporated into the Communications Act in a 1959 amendment, thus enabling the FCC to repeal it (EMG 11.1.3).

11.6.1   *Meredith* Case

Meredith Corporation v. *FCC* provided a vehicle by which the FCC could ask the federal courts to declare the Fairness Doctrine unconstitutional.

The second case, *Meredith Corporation* v. *FCC*,[56] was an appeal of a Commission decision that Meredith Corporation's Syracuse television station, WTVH, had violated the Fairness Doctrine. The station had aired a number of editorials endorsing a proposed nuclear power plant as a good investment for the people of New York State. A group called the Syracuse Peace Council asked for reply time, but the station refused. The FCC ruled in favor of the Peace Council.

---

[54] Inquiry into Section 73:1910 of the Commission's Rules and Regulations Concerning the General Fairness Obligations of Broadcast Licensees, 102 F.C.C.2d 143 (1985).

[55] 801 F.2d 501 (1986).

[56] 809 F.2d 863 (1987).

Meredith took the case to the U.S. Court of Appeals, a circumstance that worked to the advantage of the FCC. Since Congress would not let the FCC drop its enforcement of the doctrine, an appeal of an FCC Fairness Doctrine violation decision to the federal courts gave the Commission an opportunity to have the doctrine ruled unconstitutional.

Meredith argued that the FCC's 1985 Fairness Report called for repeal of the doctrine. In light of the Commission's own doubts about the doctrine, the court remanded the case to the FCC, ordering the Commission to determine whether continuation of the doctrine was constitutional or contrary to the public interest.

Congress realized that the doctrine was in jeopardy and passed a bill to add a fairness clause to the Communications Act. However, President Reagan vetoed the bill and Congress was unable to override the veto.

11.6.2 FCC Repeal of the Fairness Doctrine

Meanwhile, the Commission sought comments on the doctrine as the Court had ordered. On August 4, 1987, the FCC announced that the doctrine was not constitutional and did not serve the public interest. The outcome was repeal of the doctrine, with the exception of the personal attack and political editorializing rules. These two rules remain in effect for both broadcasting and cable. An obligation to provide balanced coverage of ballot issues also survived but was subsequently abandoned by the FCC,[57] a decision upheld by an appeals court.

In its opinion, the Commission returned to earlier arguments. First, it held that the doctrine actually inhibited broadcasters from covering controversial issues of public importance. The Commission wrote:

> In sum, the fairness doctrine in operation disserves both the public's right to diverse sources of information and the broadcaster's interest in free expression. Its chilling effect thwarts its intended purpose, and it results in excessive and unnecessary government intervention into the editorial processes of broadcast journalists. We hold, therefore, that under the constitutional standard established by *Red Lion* and its progeny, the fairness doctrine contravenes the First Amendment and its enforcement is no longer in the public interest.[58]

The Commission also refuted the scarcity argument, saying that the concept was irrelevant and that what was important was that both the electronic press and the printed press should enjoy the same First Amendment protection, a parity the decision created.[59] Finally, the Commission stated that its action served to eliminate

---

[57] Arkansas AFL-CIO v. KARK-TV, 7 F.C.C.R. 541 (1992).

[58] Syracuse Peace Council, 2 F.C.C.R. 5043, at 5052 (1987); *reconsideration denied*, 3 F.C.C.R. 2035 (1987).

[59] 2 F.C.C.R. 5043, at 97.

government interference in the marketplace of ideas, a clear reference to its own deregulatory policies.

A review of the FCC's decision by the court of appeals upheld repeal of the Fairness Doctrine.[60] Many members of Congress were unhappy with the repeal and legislation was passed in 1987 to make the Fairness Doctrine law. President Reagan vetoed that legislation and since then no major push has been made to reinstitute the doctrine, though supporters of it still promise to do so.

Efforts to revive the Fairness Doctrine continued through 1993 but did not succeed. By late 1993 and early 1994 legislators had turned their attention to questions of televised violence and the so-called information superhighway. As a result, efforts to revive the Fairness Doctrine took a back seat.

DISCUSSION QUESTIONS

1. Why should broadcast stations be required to adhere to fairness rules when newspapers and magazines have no such requirements?

2. Do the political editorializing rules encourage or discourage stations from endorsing or opposing political candidates on the air? Explain your answer.

3. What factors in the personal attack rules might cause stations to avoid such broadcasts?

4. An organization has run national advertising on broadcasting and cable that has taken a pro-life position, that is, praising the decision to have children, even when circumstances are difficult, and the joys of raising them. If the Fairness Doctrine required an opposing viewpoint, what might the announcements say?

5. Should fairness rules apply to product advertising? Explain.

6. How might government rules enforcing fairness when programming controversial issues actually inhibit the coverage of such topics?

7. Who do you think benefits most from enforcement of the Fairness Doctrine: the public, interest groups, politicians? Explain.

8. Compare the view of the First Amendment and broadcasting in the *Red Lion* decision with that used in the Brinkley and Shuler decisions discussed in Chapter 9.

SUGGESTED READINGS

Brennen, Timothy. "The Fairness Doctrine as Public Policy." *Journal of Broadcasting & Electronic Media* 33 (fall 1989): 419.

Chamberlin, Bill F. "The FCC and the First Principle of the Fairness Doctrine: A History of Neglect and Distortion." *Federal Communications Law Journal* 31 (1979): 361.

Friendly, Fred W. *The Good Guys, the Bad Guys and the First Amendment: Free Speech vs. Fairness in Broadcasting.* New York: Random, 1976.

Geller, Henry. *The Fairness Doctrine in Broadcasting.* Santa Monica, CA: Rand, 1973.

Houser, Thomas J. "The Fairness Doctrine—an Historical Perspective." *Notre Dame Lawyer* 47 (1972): 550.

---

[60] Syracuse Peace Council v. FCC, 867 F.2d 654 (1989), *cert. denied*, 110 S. Ct. 717 (1990).

Rowan, Ford. *Broadcast Fairness—Doctrine, Practice, Prospects*. New York: Longman, 1984.

Shapiro, Andrew O. *Media Access—Your Right to Express Your Views on Radio and Television*. Boston: Little, 1976.

Simmons, Steven J. *The Fairness Doctrine and the Media*. Berkeley: U of California P, 1978.

Sullivan, John Paul. "Editorials and Controversy: The Broadcaster's Dilemma." *George Washington Law Review* 32 (1946): 719.

Chapter

12

POLITICAL PROGRAMMING

This chapter will cover that portion of content regulation pertaining to political broadcasting. Congress has not sought to ban political speech but instead has enacted specific laws to ensure "reasonable opportunities" for all political candidates to the broadcast media and access rights to enable federal political candidates to gain airtime. These requirements are unique to broadcasting and cable; the print media, which are not licensed by the government, have no similar stipulations. As we examine the laws governing political speech, consider who benefits most from the regulations: politicians or the public.

12.1 SECTION 315

In its broadest form, Section 315 is the equal opportunity law for political broadcasting. It requires a broadcasting station or cable system to provide equal opportunities to all candidates for a given office once it permits a legally qualified candidate for that office to use its facilities.

Section 315 of the Communications Act contains the equal opportunities rules that are frequently and incorrectly known as the equal time rules. Congress wrote Section 315 into the Radio Act of 1927, transferred it to the Communications Act of 1934, and substantially altered it in 1959. Section 315 states:

If any licensee shall permit any person who is a legally qualified candidate for any public office to use a broadcasting station, he shall afford equal opportunities to all other such candidates for that office in use of such broadcasting station.[1]

Section 315 applies not only to full-power broadcast stations, but to low-power TV stations (LPTV),[2] and to cable TV.[3] The FCC requires cable operators who offer access on their nonbroadcast channels to legally qualified candidates for public office to provide equal opportunities to all other candidates seeking that same office.[4] A cable operator is not required to inform candidates about their opponent's cablecast but within one week of the opponent's cablecast must provide equal opportunities if requested by a legally qualified candidate.[5]

Here is how equal opportunity works: If station WXXX sells Mary Jones time to campaign for mayor, other legally qualified candidates for mayor must also be allowed to purchase time on the station. WXXX could have decided not to sell time to candidates for mayor, but once the station sold time to one candidate for that office, it was obligated to provide equal opportunities to all other legally qualified candidates for that office. As we will see later, stations cannot refuse political advertising requests by federal candidates.

As the FCC points out, the correct phrase when referring to the rights of political candidates is "equal opportunity," not "equal time."[6] If candidate A chooses to place spots in prime time on TV and candidate B prefers to place spots in the early evening news, the candidates have "equal opportunity" to appear on the station, but not "equal time." The spots for candidate B probably won't be seen or heard by as many people as the spots for candidate A. On the other hand, if candidate B also wants spots in prime time, the station cannot discriminate against candidate B and must try to fit the spots into the primetime schedule. Even though the spots for both candidates might be in prime time, they need not be on the same day of the week, the same time of day, or in the same programs. To provide equal opportunities, "All a station need do is to make available periods of approximately equal audience potential to competing candidates to the extent that this is possible."[7] Since the terms *equal opportunity* and *equal time* are often used interchangeably, we have in the present chapter sometimes used the term *equal time*. Unless otherwise indicated, we mean "equal opportunities."

The FCC's implementation of Section 315 sometimes seems contradictory. On the one hand, licensees are not required to provide time to every state, county, and local candidate, but on the other hand, the Commission expects stations to offer reasonable amounts of time to such candidates based on the licensee's judgment of

---

[1] 47 U.S.C. § 315(a).

[2] 47 C.F.R. § 74.780.

[3] 47 C.F.R. § 73.1940, § 76.5, and § 76.205.

[4] 47 C.F.R. § 76.5(v).

[5] 47 C.F.R. § 76.205(e).

[6] The Law of Political Broadcasting and Cablecasting: A Political Primer (1984 Political Primer), 100 F.C.C.2d 1476 (1984).

[7] 100 F.C.C.2d, at 1505.

BOX 12.1   Equal Opportunity Stipulations

1. Section 315 applies to both broadcast stations and cable TV.
2. Only legally qualified candidates have a right to equal opportunities.
3. Candidates seeking the same office must have the opportunity to appear before the same size audience.
4. Stations and cable systems are not required to provide access to local and state candidates but must provide access to candidates for federal office.
5. Equal opportunities apply only to the same office and same election.

---

the importance of the races and the amount of public interest in them.[8] A station can limit the sale of time to certain nonfederal races, and need not accept a particular length of paid announcement that a candidate wishes to use or need not sell time many months in advance of an election.[9]

Equal opportunities applies only to the same office and same election.[10] If a licensee provides free time to one candidate, other qualified candidates for that office must be given free time if they request it. However, the FCC has ruled that a candidate is not entitled to free time if an organization supporting an opposing candidate makes a large purchase of time on behalf of the opponent.[11] A station is not required to notify a legally qualified candidate when an opponent has been given time. The candidate is expected to request the time, and the request must be made within seven days of the broadcast activating Section 315.[12] The fact that a candidate has little chance of winning, which might be the case with a fringe party or independent candidate, has no bearing on equal opportunities. If Section 315 applies, a station or system cannot deny equal opportunities to a legally qualified candidate. A summary of the major equal opportunity stipulations appears in Box 12.1.

12.1.1   Use of Facilities

A candidate "uses" the facilities of a station or system by actually appearing in a political message that is controlled, approved, or sponsored by the candidate or the candidate's authorized committee once the candidate is legally qualified.

Section 315 states that a "use" of a station's facilities requires the station to provide a "use" for all opposing candidates as well. What is a *use*? In order for the

---

[8] 100 F.C.C.2d, at 1525–1526.
[9] W. Roy Smith, 18 F.C.C.2d 747 (1969).
[10] Sam Morris, 4 Rad. Reg. (P & F) 885 (1984).
[11] Carter/Mondale Reelection Comm., 81 F.C.C.2d 409 (1980).
[12] 47 C.F.R. § 73.1940(e).

appearance to be considered a use, the candidate must appear personally, by voice on radio, or by voice, picture, or both on TV. As long as the candidate is recognized by members of the public, the appearance is considered a use.[13] Even though the candidate may only speak or appear in a tag at the end of a commercial, the rules apply to the entire spot if the candidate is recognizable. In the case of a political program, the candidate's appearance must be significant to the total program and must be of "substantial length."[14]

As of 1992, the FCC expanded the use concept by specifying that a use applies only to an appearance by a candidate that is controlled, approved, or sponsored by the candidate or the candidate's authorized committee after the candidate becomes legally qualified.[15] This stipulation was added to the FCC rules because of two concerns by candidates. The first concern was with political spots put together by a group supporting a political candidate, spots that might include an appearance by the candidate, but which were not "controlled, approved, or sponsored" by the candidate. Such groups, usually independent political committees (EMG 12.7), often support a candidate with television spots that include campaign footage of the candidate. Previously, these spots constituted a use even though the candidate had nothing to do with them. Under the 1992 provisions, the control, approval, or sponsorship by the candidate must be established in order for a spot or program to qualify as a use.

The rise of negative advertising posed a particular problem since candidates sometimes found their picture or other depiction appearing in spots opposing them, even though they had no control over the spot. Such spots are not considered uses, since they are not under the control, approval, or sponsorship of the candidate.

The second concern was with candidate appearances in old musical recordings, movies, and television programs that were produced long before the candidate ever thought of running, and over which the performer had little or no control, in terms of content. The issue was first addressed in 1972 when comedian Pat Paulsen appeared on a television program called "The Mouse Factory" and said he was running for president. Many thought he was joking, but Paulsen denied it, and the FCC declared him to be a legally qualified candidate for the Republican Party's nomination for president because he was legally qualified to appear on the New Hampshire ballot. Even though Paulsen appeared in a strictly entertainment-oriented context, his appearance was construed to be a use requiring equal opportunities.[16] As a result, he could no longer appear on entertainment-oriented television shows without giving rise to equal time requirements.

The issue arose again during Ronald Reagan's campaigns for president when TV stations had to stop running his old movies and portions of *Death Valley Days* in which he appeared as a host. Reagan's appearance was considered to be

---

[13] 100 F.C.C.2d 1476, at 1489.

[14] *Id.*, at 1493.

[15] Codification of the Commission's Political Programming Policies, 7 F.C.C.R. 4611, 4613 (1992).

[16] Pat Paulsen, 33 F.C.C.2d 197 (1972); *aff'd sub nom.* Paulsen v. FCC, 491 F.2d 887 (9th Cir. 1974).

a use even though the appearance had nothing to do with his candidacy.[17] As a result of the Paulsen and Reagan cases, the FCC held that if an actor became a legally qualified candidate for public office, that person's appearances on telecasts of his or her movies were considered uses as long as the actor was identifiable.[18] However, the 1992 ruling changes that position. Only if the candidate's appearance in a program is controlled, approved, or sponsored by the candidate or the candidate's authorized committee is the appearance a use. Syndicated reruns of television shows and old movies can be shown, since they would be under the control of the station.

The FCC has also had to consider whether appearances by other individuals on broadcast programs were uses once the individuals became political candidates. A number of situations can constitute uses. For example, a congressional representative's broadcast report to constituents is a use after the representative becomes a legally qualified candidate for reelection.[19] A minister's appearance on a religious program is a use. If the minister does not pay for the time, opponents are entitled to free time. However, if the church congregation or board of trustees pays for the program with the goal of advancing the candidacy of the minister, opponents must pay to appear on the air.[20] An advertiser who regularly presents his or her own commercials on a station creates a use after becoming a legally qualified candidate. Since the advertiser pays for the time, opponents would also have to pay to appear on the air.[21] Finally, a presidential candidate's appearance on a network variety show is a use.[22] In 1992, presidential candidate Bill Clinton gained considerable publicity when he played his saxophone on the *Arsenio Hall* show.

The question of use has also arisen regarding radio or television employees who become candidates for office. The general rule is that a broadcast performer's appearances on the air in the course of regular duties, such as announcing, singing, acting, or newscasting, are uses, as long as the performer is identified or identifiable on the air.[23] However, the Commission has ruled that the political opponent of a radio disc jockey would be entitled only to the amount of time in which the disc jockey's voice was heard—not to the time used for playing records. If the announcer's voice is neither identified or identifiable to the public, the on-air appearance is not a use.[24]

Newscasting presents some special considerations. Where the newscaster is identified by name or is seen on the air, the appearance constitutes a use. If a radio

[17] Adrian Weiss (Ronald Reagan films), 58 F.C.C.2d 342 (1976), *review denied,* 58 F.C.C.2d 1389 (1976).

[18] 100 F.C.C.2d 1476, at 1491.

[19] Clinton D. McKinnon, 40 F.C.C. 291 (1957); Hon. Joseph S. Clark, 40 F.C.C. 325 (1962).

[20] Rev. Billy Robinson, 23 F.C.C.2d 117 (1970).

[21] Georgia Assoc. of Broadcasters, 40 F.C.C. 343 (1963); *see also,* KKTV, 40 F.C.C. 282 (1957) and Joseph V. Gartlan, Jr., 32 F.C.C.2d 609 (1971).

[22] Lar Daly, 40 F.C.C.2d 314 (1960).

[23] Kenneth E. Spengler, 40 F.C.C. 279 (1956); KGUN, 40 F.C.C. 293 (1958).

[24] WENR, 17 F.C.C.2d 613 (1969); KYSN Broadcasting Co., 17 F.C.C.2d 164 (1969).

newscaster is identified by name up to the date of candidacy, but not thereafter, his or her newscasts are uses, provided the person's voice is identifiable.[25]

The U.S. Court of Appeals for the District of Columbia has ruled that when a journalist who is running for office appears on the air, the appearance constitutes a use.[26] The question arose when William Branch, a reporter for a Sacramento television station, ran for town council. Branch wanted to keep his job, but the station said it would not provide the airtime required to meet the equal opportunity requirements of his opponents. When the court said Branch's reporting amounted to a use, the station asked Branch to take an unpaid leave for the duration of the campaign.

In some instances where on-air employees of stations have become candidates for public office, the stations have sought waivers or partial waivers of the equal opportunity rights from opposing candidates. These waivers include agreements by which an opposing candidate will settle for a number of free spots and/or programs rather than the total amount of time to which the opponent might be entitled each week if the station employee holds a prominent position. Opposing candidates need not accept such waivers, and where they do, they often require the station employee to make no reference to his or her candidacy during regular broadcasts.[27]

Another question about a use is: How long must an on-air appearance last to be considered a use? The present position is that a fleeting appearance is not a use.[28] The question was raised when the National Urban Coalition asked the FCC to rule on a two-minute public service television announcement including 120 people, many of them leading political, sports, and entertainment personalities, all singing the song "Let the Sun Shine In." No one's name was mentioned and no voices were separately identified. After the spot was completed, one of the persons appearing in it became a candidate for public office. In the spot the candidate was visible in two scenes—one for 4.2 seconds in a long-range shot of 100 persons, and the other for 2.8 seconds in a medium shot of about six people, in which the lower half of the candidate's face was visible. The FCC said the spot was not a use because the candidate was not readily identifiable.[29]

In the early 1990s the FCC was faced with a challenge to its exclusive jurisdiction to determine the lawfulness of political advertising charges under the lowest unit charge rule (EMG 12.3). The issue arose when political candidates in Georgia and Alabama sued broadcast stations for charging rates allegedly in excess of those permitted under Section 315. The question was whether state courts could exercise jurisdiction over broadcast advertising rates or whether the authority was lim-

---

[25] *See* Public Notice: Newscaster Candidacy, 40 F.C.C. 433 (1965); *see also* WBAX, 17 F.C.C.2d 316 (1969) and RKO General, Inc., 25 F.C.C.2d 117 (1970).

[26] Branch v. FCC, 824 F.2d 37 (1987), *cert. denied,* 485 U.S. 959 (1988).

[27] 100 F.C.C.2d 1476, at 1491.

[28] *Id.* at 1492.

[29] National Urban Coalition, 23 F.C.C.2d 123 (1970).

BOX 12.2   Items Exempted from the Use Concept

1. Bona fide newscasts
2. Bona fide news interviews
3. Bona fide news documentaries
4. On-the-spot coverage of bona fide news events
5. Debates and news conferences

---

ited to federal law. After assessing public reaction, the FCC upheld the position that federal law preempts state causes of action in deciding the lowest unit charge.[30]

12.1.2   Exemptions to a Use

Five types of appearances are not considered uses in terms of Section 315: newscasts, news interviews, documentaries, spot news, and candidate debates.

In 1959, Congress amended Section 315 by specifying four types of broadcasts that are not considered uses, and are thus exempt from the equal opportunities provision. They are summarized in Box 12.2 and include the following.

1. *Bona fide newscasts,* including but not limited to interviews with political candidates during newscasts,[31] are exempt. Regularly scheduled news shows including the *Today Show, Good Morning America,* and *This Week with David Brinkley* are bona fide newscasts. Over the years, the FCC has also included less traditional types of programs in the scope of bona fide newscasts. It ruled that a weekly religious news program, which included interviews with ministers who were candidates for public office, was a bona fide newscast since it dealt with current religious news.[32] In addition, *Entertainment Tonight* and *Entertainment This Week* have been accepted as bona fide news programs. The FCC said the news exemption to Section 315 hinges on "whether the program reports news of some area of current events," not on the subject matter covered.[33]

The FCC has refused to apply the news exemption when the newscaster is a legally qualified candidate. In deciding the question, the Commission said news-

---

[30] Order of Reconsideration: Exclusive Jurisdiction with Respect to Potential Violations of the Lowest Unit Charge, 7 F.C.C.R. 4132 (1992).

[31] 47 C.F.R. § 76.205(a)(1).

[32] Telegram to Reverend Donald L. Lanier, Oct. 26, 1972. *See* F.C.C.2d 1476, at 1495.

[33] Request for Declaratory Ruling by Paramount Pictures Corp., 3 F.C.C.R. 254 (1988).

casts were not exempt appearances when the news director, who presented the news, was a candidate for public office.[34]

2. *Bona fide news interviews* are exempt as long as they are regularly scheduled, and the broadcaster controls and produces the program content, format, and participants.[35] Interview programs such as *Meet the Press,* the *Larry King Show*, and *Face the Nation* are examples of bona fide news interview shows. The *Donahue* program has also been found to be exempt because the program is able to offer comprehensive treatment of newsworthy topics.[36] The FCC also exempted a *Governor's Radio Press Conference* in which news reporters phoned the governor in his office, asking him questions he answered over the air. The program was regularly scheduled, was under the control of the participating stations, and was not designed to enhance the candidacy of the governor.[37]

A "Governor's Forum," however, was not granted an exemption. In the program, members of the public submitted questions to the governor. The governor's staff selected the questions to be answered on the air, the governor recorded answers to the questions, and his staff sometimes edited the recordings before sending them to participating stations. The FCC said the program was not solely under the control of the stations.[38] The FCC has also refused to exempt one-time special interviews,[39] and a proposed news interview program titled *Know Your Congressman* that was to begin 11 weeks before the primary election.[40] The program was believed to be scheduled too close to the election.

3. *Bona fide news documentaries* are exempt, but only if the candidate's appearance is incidental to the presentation of another topic that is the focus of the documentary.[41] For example, a candidate for mayor who is leading a fight against drug use in the community could appear in a documentary about the drug problem. Since the program is about drug use and not about the candidate, the candidate's appearance would be incidental to that subject.

4. *On-the-spot coverage of bona fide news events* is not a use.[42] On-the-spot coverage of political conventions,[43] reports by major officeholders

---

[34] Public Notice: Use of Station by Newscaster Candidate, 40 F.C.C. 433 (1965).

[35] 47 C.F.R. § 76.205(a)(2).

[36] Multimedia Entertainment, Inc., 56 Rad. Reg. 2d (P & F) 143 (1984).

[37] Hon. Michael V. DiSalle, 40 F.C.C. at 348–349.

[38] 40 F.C.C. 348 (1962).

[39] Station KFDX-TV, 40 F.C.C. 347 (1962).

[40] WIIC-TV, 33 F.C.C.2d 629 (1972).

[41] 47 C.F.R. § 76.205(a)(3).

[42] 47 C.F.R. § 76.205(a)(4).

[43] 100 F.C.C.2d 1476, at 1500.

on crucial events,[44] awards ceremonies,[45] public announcement of a candidacy,[46] and similar items are legitimate news events that can be reported without creating a use.

12.1.2.1 Debates
Debates may be aired on broadcast stations or cable channels without being considered a use, although certain rules must be followed.

The broadcast of a debate between political candidates or of a candidate's press conference is considered on-the-spot coverage of a bona fide news event and is also exempt from Section 315. But that has not always been the case.

The first debate to be televised was the famous 1960 presidential confrontation between Senator John F. Kennedy, the Democratic candidate, and Vice President Richard M. Nixon, the Republican candidate. At that time, debates were subject to Section 315 requirements, but Congress temporarily suspended the equal opportunity rules, depriving all other candidates for president of equal time. The reason for the congressional action was to allow the debates to be broadcast without requiring Kennedy and Nixon to purchase time for the debates. As is typical, a number of "minor party" candidates were in the race. The networks would not have carried the debates without charge, and they likely would have been forced to carry them for free if they had been obligated to include all of the candidates.

The next time debates were scheduled was in 1976 when President Ford and Jimmy Carter planned to debate. Again, there was a question about how to deal with the equal opportunity rules. In September 1975, the FCC voted to alter the rules.[47] In handing down the so-called Aspen Rule,[48] the Commission decided that live broadcasting of candidates' *entire* news conferences, press conferences, and debates would be considered bona fide on-the-spot news events and exempt from the equal time rules. To qualify as bona fide news events, debates had to be initiated by a nonbroadcast entity, could not be held in a TV studio, and had to be broadcast in their entirety. The League of Women Voters sponsored the Ford-Carter debates as the nonbroadcast entity and also initiated debates between President Reagan and Walter Mondale during the 1984 campaign.

---

[44] Telegram to ABC, CBS, and NBC, 40 F.C.C. 276 (1956); *see also* Republican National Committee, 40 F.C.C. 408 (1964); *aff'd per curiam, sub nom.* Goldwater v. FCC and U.S.A., Case No. 18963 (D.C. Cir. 1964); *cert denied*, 379 U.S. 893 (1964).

[45] National Broadcasting Co., Inc., 37 F.C.C.2d 678 (1972). During ceremonies preceding a World Series game, a legally qualified candidate for public office was to give an award to baseball star Jackie Robinson.

[46] Complaints of Republican National Committee, Socialist Labor Party, Communist Party, U.S.A., 37 F.C.C.2d 799 (1972). The complaints stemmed from a broadcast by Senator George McGovern, Democratic presidential nominee, to announce a replacement for his choice of vice presidential candidate.

[47] Aspen Institute, 55 F.C.C.2d 697 (1975), *aff'd sub nom.* Chisholm v. FCC, 538 F.2d 349 (D.C. Cir.), *cert. denied*, 97 S. Ct. 247 (1976).

[48] The FCC acted in response to a petition by the Aspen Institute for Humanistic Studies.

In 1983, the FCC further modified the debate rules by holding that broadcasters could also sponsor political debates with the debates qualifying as on-the-spot coverage of bona fide news.[49] However, there are some stipulations that the broadcast of a debate must fulfill if it is to avoid being considered a use. First, the event must be broadcast live or on a delayed basis currently enough so that the news value is still topical. Second, the broadcaster or cablecaster must use good faith judgment in assessing the newsworthiness of the event, so that the broadcast informs the public and does not favor a particular candidate. Broadcasters and cablecasters who sponsor debates are also permitted to restrict debates to the most significant candidates, and if they delay the broadcast, they can edit out some elements as long as they make good faith judgments that neither favor nor disfavor a candidate. Candidate "forums" or "town meetings," where only one candidate appears, are not considered debates.[50]

In the late 1980s, the FCC extended the debate exemption to debates sponsored by political parties and political candidates. In 1988, the FCC exempted a televised debate sponsored by Michael Dukakis and Richard Gephardt, both candidates for the Democratic Party presidential nomination.[51] In 1989, a minor party candidate complained to the FCC after the FCC ruled that debates between presidential candidates Dukakis and George Bush were exempt from the equal opportunities requirement even though the two major political parties sponsored the debates. The Commission said the news value of a debate and not its sponsor is the primary factor in determining whether a debate is exempt as spot news.[52]

There have been other challenges to the revised rules. Senator Edward Kennedy complained to the FCC when then president Jimmy Carter attacked him in a press conference. Kennedy wanted time to respond to the attack, but the networks refused to give it to him. The FCC upheld the networks on the grounds that the press conference was carried live. Further, the networks had previously covered a Kennedy press conference. On appeal, the U.S. Court of Appeals for the D.C. Circuit sided with the FCC, saying the intent of Congress was to rely on the discretion of journalists.[53]

The D.C. Circuit also upheld an FCC decision that minor-party candidates for president and vice president can be excluded from televised debates. The challenge came from Sonia Johnson, a Citizens Party nominee who was not allowed to participate in a presidential debate between the Republican and Democratic candidates in 1984. Johnson received less than 1 percent of the vote in the election and finished fifth. The court said the Commission had not exceeded its authority in determining

---

[49] Henry Geller, 95 F.C.C.2d 1236 (1983). Geller was a driving force behind the Aspen Institute, which petitioned the FCC to revise the portion of Section 315 dealing with spot news coverage.

[50] Chicago Educational Television Ass'n (WTTW), 58 F.C.C.2d 922 (1976); Station WCLV (FM), 59 F.C.C.2d 1376 (1976).

[51] Request for Declaratory Ruling, WCVB-TV, 63 Rad. Reg. 2d (P & F) 665 (1987).

[52] In re Fulani, 65 Rad. Reg. 2d (P & F) 644 (1988).

[53] Kennedy for President Comm., 77 F.C.C.2d 971, *review denied*, 77 F.C.C.2d 971, *aff'd*, Kennedy for President Comm. v. FCC, 636 F.2d 432 (1980).

that debates between legally qualified candidates are spot news items exempt from Section 315 requirements. Citing the U.S. Supreme Court in *CBS* v. *Democratic National Committee* (EMG 11.5.2), the court said no one has a First Amendment right of access to the broadcast medium. The court concluded that Section 315 of the Communications Act "ensures that all candidates from all points of the political spectrum will be able to utilize the media" and that no candidate can monopolize political debate.[54]

12.1.3   Legally Qualified Candidates

The stipulations of Section 315 apply only to candidates who are legally qualified. To be legally qualified a candidate must publicly announce his or her candidacy, qualify for the office, and either qualify for a place on the ballot or be eligible to be a write-in candidate.

Publicly announcing candidacy for office may be as simple as stating publicly the intention to seek election or nomination to a given office. Many candidates hold public press conferences for this purpose. Filing the required papers to qualify for a place on the ballot may also constitute a public announcement. However, candidates are not legally qualified simply because people expect them to run or because supporters are raising funds for a campaign. In 1967, Eugene McCarthy, who had announced his bid for the Democratic presidential nomination, requested equal time after Lyndon Johnson appeared on TV and was asked about his reelection plans. The FCC turned down McCarthy's request, since Johnson had not publicly announced his intention to run even though McCarthy expected Johnson to be his opponent.[55]

The second stipulation in becoming legally qualified is that the candidate must be qualified under the appropriate local, state, or federal law to hold the office he or she intends to seek. At a minimum, this means being a U.S. citizen and residing in the geographic area the office represents; but other requirements may apply. In all instances, the candidate must prove that he or she is a legally qualified candidate in order to gain the equal opportunity rights.[56]

The third stipulation for becoming a legally qualified candidate involves meeting one of two conditions. (The qualifications for being a legally qualified candidate are summarized in Box 12.3.) The candidate must either qualify for a place on the ballot or be eligible to be a candidate on a write-in basis. Qualifying for a place on the ballot means satisfying the first two requirements; in other words, meeting the public announcement requirement and the legal requirements for the office. Making the commitment to seek election as a write-in candidate requires a good faith effort to achieve nomination or election. A mere announcement that a person is a

---

[54] Johnson v. FCC, 829 F.2d 157 (1987).
[55] Sen. Eugene J. McCarthy, 11 F.C.C.2d 511 (1968), *aff'd*, 390 F.2d 471 (1968).
[56] 100 F.C.C.2d 1476, at 1482.

BOX 12.3

A candidate is legally qualified if he or she:

1. publicly announces his/her intention to run for office;
2. meets the requirements for office;
3. qualifies for a place on the ballot or seeks office as a write-in candidate.

---

write-in candidate is not sufficient to qualify that individual for equal opportunities.[57] A write-in candidate must make a "substantial showing" that he or she is a bona fide candidate by following such typical campaign procedures as establishing a campaign headquarters, making campaign appearances, and sending out literature.[58] Moreover, a write-in candidate must make a public commitment to seek election by the write-in method.[59]

An additional rule applies to candidates for president and vice president. Such individuals are considered legally qualified for nomination or election only in the states in which they qualify under the usual standards. But if a candidate qualifies in any 10 or more states, the candidate will be considered legally qualified in all states, territories, and the District of Columbia, even though he or she might not have qualified in the remaining states.[60]

It is important to note that the equal opportunities rule applies only to legally qualified candidates for the *same* office or position. As a result, during primary elections, Section 315 applies only to intraparty contests. Thus, in the primaries, it is Democrat versus Democrat and Republican versus Republican. Republican and Democratic candidates for the same office become opponents only after their political parties have selected them as their candidates for office. As a result, the interparty competition takes place during general elections when Democrats confront Republicans. Thus, the benefits of Section 315 are restricted "to candidates of the same class or character as the candidate or candidates who may have been permitted to use a broadcasting station in the first place."[61]

It is also significant that Section 315 applies only to a candidate seeking public office. The FCC refused to invoke the equal opportunities rule when an individual sought the position of county Republican committeeman, which is a party position, not a public office.[62]

---

[57] 47 C.F.R. § 73.1940.
[58] *Id., See also* Socialist Workers Party, 26 F.C.C.2d 244 (1970).
[59] Amendment of Part 73 of the Commission's Rules, 60 F.C.C.2d 615 (1976).
[60] 47 C.F.R. § 1940(2)(ii).
[61] Kay v. FCC, 443 F.2d 638, 645 (D.C. Cir. 1970).
[62] Lester Posner, 15 F.C.C.2d 807 (1968).

12.1.3.1 The "Zapple Doctrine." In 1970, the FCC established a qualification to Section 315 that has come to be known as "quasi-equal opportunities" or the Zapple doctrine (named after the person who brought the issue before the Commission). The Zapple doctrine is actually a part of the Fairness Doctrine that is applied to one aspect of political activity and is one of the few remaining aspects of the now-defunct Fairness Doctrine (EMG 11.3.3).

Whereas Section 315's equal opportunity provision applies to a use by an actual candidate, the Zapple doctrine applies to supporters of political candidates. Specifically, it states that if stations sell time during an election campaign to supporters or representatives of a candidate who urge the candidate's election, discuss campaign issues, or criticize an opponent, then the station must afford comparable time to the spokesperson of an opponent.[63] Suppose that Mary Smith is running for mayor. A group of her supporters buys time to support her platform and to attack the positions taken by her opponent, John Doe. Under the Zapple doctrine, the station must offer an opportunity for a reply by a representative of John Doe, not John Doe himself.

There are restrictions to the Zapple doctrine. First, it applies only to major political parties, not to minor or fringe candidates.[64] Second, it applies only to formal campaign periods when there are legally qualified candidates.[65] When the general Fairness Doctrine was in effect, political discussion outside of campaign periods was covered by its provisions. Third, it does not apply to appearances of candidate supporters on bona fide news programming that is exempt from Section 315 requirements.[66] Finally, stations are not required to supply free time to the opposing side when the initial side paid for its time. The FCC did not discuss the Zapple rule when it abolished the Fairness Doctrine, so it presumably remains in effect.

12.2 PROHIBITION AGAINST CENSORSHIP

Section 315 stipulates that broadcast stations and cable systems are prohibited from censoring the content of political messages.

The no-censorship provision was designed to ensure that stations treat candidates fairly. Nevertheless, for many years broadcasters worried about what would happen when a station carried a political message—one Section 315 required the station to carry—in which a candidate made libelous comments about an opponent. Was the station to be responsible for the libelous remarks because it had broadcast the message, or was the candidate who made the remarks responsible?

---

[63] Letter to Nicholas Zapple, 23 F.C.C.2d 707, 19 Rad. Reg. 2d (P & F) 421 (1970); *reaff'd in re:* Complaint of Committee for the Fair Broadcasting of Controversial Issues, 25 F.C.C.2d 283 (1970).
[64] First Fairness Report, 36 F.C.C.2d 47–50 (1972).
[65] 100 F.C.C.2d 1476, at 1535.
[66] *Id.*

A test of the issue came in 1959 when WDAY-TV in Fargo, North Dakota, aired a campaign message in which a candidate stated that the North Dakota Farmers' Union was Communist controlled. A $100,000 lawsuit was filed against the station. When the case reached the U.S. Supreme Court, the Court affirmed that a licensee was barred from censoring the comments of a political candidate under Section 315. Further, the Court ruled that Section 315 preempted state defamation law and protected the broadcaster from liability for statements made by a political candidate during a broadcast.[67] As a result, a station may not refuse to broadcast a candidate's message on the grounds that it contains libelous remarks. To do so would be censorship.[68]

Clearly, this position favors the marketplace of ideas; it emphasizes the importance of stations airing, and the public hearing, whatever a candidate might have to say. The prohibition on censorship is applied strictly. A candidate's message cannot even be censored when it deals with matters other than candidacy.[69] Stations and systems also may not require candidates to submit scripts or tapes for prior review of items such as "accuracy," "taste," or "libelousness."[70] Such review could form the basis for possible censorship. However, scripts or tapes can be requested in advance to determine if the candidate will appear in the spot so as to make it a use, to ascertain proper sponsorship identification in the case of a paid message, or to determine if a spot is of the correct length. These considerations help a station comply with the law and would not involve censorship.

One issue where the question of censorship has arisen is airing political messages that might incite racial violence. In 1972, J. B. Stoner, a candidate for the Democratic nomination for senator from Georgia, made the following remarks in radio spots:

> I am J. B. Stoner. I am the only candidate for U.S. senator who is for the white people. I am the only candidate who is against integration. All the other candidates are race mixers, to one degree or another. I say we must repeal Gambrell's civil rights law. Gambrell's law takes jobs from whites and gives those jobs to the niggers. The main reason why niggers want integration is because the niggers want our white women. I am for law and order with the knowledge that you cannot have law and order and niggers too. Vote white. This time vote your convictions by voting white racist J. B Stoner into the runoff election for U.S. senator. Thank you.[71]

Stoner's radio spots created an uproar and several groups asked the FCC to require stations to stop broadcasting them, saying they had created racial tension.

---

[67] Farmers Educ. and Co-op Union v. WDAY 260 U.S. 525 (1959).

[68] Port Huron Broadcasting Co., 12 F.C.C. 1069 (1948); WDSU Broadcasting Corp., 16 F.C.C. 345 (1951).

[69] WMCA, Inc. 40 F.C.C. 241 (1952).

[70] 100 F.C.C.2d 1476, at 1511–1512.

[71] Atlanta NAACP, 36 F.C.C.2d 636 (1972).

The FCC refused to ban the spots as long there did not seem to be a "clear and present danger of imminent violence which might warrant interfering with speech which does not contain any direct incitement to violence."[72]

In the 1980 presidential campaign, another problem arose when a candidate for the Citizens Party used a creative effort to draw attention to his campaign. The radio spot began:

MAN'S VOICE: Bullshit!

WOMAN'S VOICE: What?

MAN'S VOICE: Carter, Reagan, and Anderson. It's all bullshit! Bullshit!

CANDIDATE: Too bad people have to use such strong language, but isn't that what you think too? That's why we started an entirely new political party, the Citizens Party.[73]

The FCC received many complaints and demands to ban the spots but again made clear that no censorship was possible unless the spots generated a clear and present danger to society.

In 1983 the FCC was concerned when *Hustler* magazine publisher Larry Flynt said he would use clips of X-rated film in television spots promoting his presidential candidacy. Congressional legislation was introduced to allow broadcasters to refuse to air pornographic political ads despite the no-censorship provision. The FCC announced that it would not apply the no-censorship provision to obscene or indecent political spots.[74] The issue was defused when Flynt did not run.

During the 1992 political campaign, another concern arose when a candidate for U.S. Senate ran graphic antiabortion ads that included scenes of dead fetuses. Broadcasters again were in a dilemma. If they didn't show the spots, they risked violating the political broadcast rules. If they did run them, they risked being sued.

The FCC reviewed the spots to see if the content constituted indecency as described in Chapter 13. The Commission concluded the spots were not indecent and could not be banned. However, the FCC did say that TV stations could run a disclaimer warning viewers that the spot might contain scenes that could be disturbing to children.[75]

12.3   LOWEST UNIT CHARGE

Section 315 prohibits stations and systems from charging candidates more than the lowest unit charge for each class and period of time. The goal of this rule is to prohibit sales practices that discriminate against candidates and in favor of commercial advertisers.

---

[72] *Id.* 635, 637.

[73] Barry Has a Word For It," *Newsweek,* 27 October 1980, at 40.

[74] 100 F.C.C.2d 1476, at 1513.

[75] Letter to Vincent A. Pepper and Irving Gastfreund, 7 F.C.C.R. 5599, 5600 (1992).

Not only does Section 315 provide equal opportunities for legally qualified candidates, it also stipulates how much a station can charge them to use its facilities. This rule, called the *lowest unit charge,* applies only to uses by legally qualified candidates and is in effect during two periods of the campaign:[76]

- during the 45 days preceding the date of a primary or primary runoff election; and,
- during the 60 days preceding the date of a general or special election.

During these preelection periods, a broadcaster or cablecaster must sell time at the "lowest unit charge" for the same class and amount of time for the same period. Charges for time sold during other time periods cannot exceed "the charges made for comparable use of such station by other users. . . ."[77] The lowest unit charge applies equally to broadcasting and cable. Congress added the lowest unit charge rule in 1972 as part of a plan "to give candidates for public office greater access to the media and . . . to halt the spiraling cost of campaigning for public office.[78] In adopting the requirement, Congress said it intended to place candidates on a par with a broadcast station's most-favored advertiser.[79]

The political broadcasting rules, including the lowest unit charge, summarized in Box 12.4, has long been a source of confusion for stations, systems, and candidates. The media have expressed concern about their obligations while candidates have been uncertain of their rights. Of particular concern has been equal application of complicated advertising rate schedules. Candidates are to be told of all advertising discounts used to arrive at the lowest unit charge. This is to include discounts

1. for the same "class" (the rate categories most stations have, such as fixed-position spots, preemptible spots, run-of-schedule spots, and discount packages);
2. for the "amount of time" (meaning the length of time purchased, e.g., 30 seconds, 60 seconds, 1 hour); and
3. for the "same period" (the time of the broadcast day, such as prime time, early fringe, etc. for TV, morning drive for radio, plus other time designations such as Class A, Class B, etc.).

Only candidates or their authorized campaign committees are entitled to the lowest unit charge. Groups formed to support a candidate are not entitled to the rate.[80]

---

[76] 47 U.S.C. § 315(b).

[77] 47 U.S.C. § 325(b)(2).

[78] S. Rep. No. 96, 92d Cong., 1st Sess. (1971), reprinted in 1972 U.S.C.C.A.N. 1773, 1774.

[79] S. Rep. No. 96, 1780.

[80] 100 F.C.C.2d at 1530.

BOX 12.4   Criteria for Determining if Political Advertising Qualifies for the Lowest Unit Charge

1. The advertising must qualify as a "use" of the station or cable system by a candidate.
2. The "use" must occur within 45 days before a primary or primary runoff election or 60 days prior to a general or special election.
3. Only candidates or their authorized campaign committees qualify for the lowest unit charge.

To better illustrate the lowest unit charge, imagine that a radio station sells a single fixed-position, 60-second spot in morning drive time to its regular advertisers for $50. However, if advertisers use a frequency discount, which lowers the price because a greater number of spots is purchased, the price is $40 each for 100 such spots or $4,000 total cost. A legally qualified political candidate seeking the lowest unit charge is entitled to pay $40 for a single fixed-position spot in drive time, even though the $40 charge stems from a discount rate for 100 spots. If the candidate wanted to buy spots in other rate categories, such as daytime or afternoon drive, he or she would be entitled to the lowest unit charge for those time periods.

The FCC "audited" 30 broadcast stations in 1990 to measure compliance with the political broadcasting rules and found a number of lowest-unit-charge violations.[81] The FCC fined two stations, KRON-TV, San Francisco, and KDFW-TV, Dallas–Fort Worth, $25,000 each for violations, and issued revised political broadcasting rules. One of the bigger conflicts with the lowest unit charge has come from the preemptible sales category. A preemptible commercial is one that may be moved, or preempted, from its position if another advertiser wants the slot and is willing to pay a higher rate. Political candidates often want a fixed position; they do not want their spots being moved by the station or system, but they also want the lowest unit rate, which is usually not for a fixed position or nonpreemptible spot. As a compromise, the FCC now permits broadcasters and cablecasters to sell only to candidates a special discounted class of nonpreemptible time.[82]

To inform candidates of lowest unit charge options, stations must give candidates a written disclosure statement when they ask about advertising rates. The statement must identify all available classes of time, the lowest unit charge for each class, and privileges associated with each class.[83]

Broadcasters complain that they lose money during political campaigns because they have to sell candidates time at the lowest unit charge rather than the higher fees they could charge commercial customers. Nevertheless, the lowest unit

---

[81] Report on Political Programming Audit, 68 Rad. Reg. 2d (P & F) 113 (1990).
[82] Clarification of the Commission's Political Programming Policies, 7 F.C.C.R., 4615 (1992).
[83] *Id.* at 4619.

charge rule helps candidates save campaign funds, and since members of Congress face reelection every two years, they have a vested interest in the rule. A Senate campaign reform bill in 1993 gave broadcasters even more cause for concern, since it threatened to set advertising rates even lower than the lowest unit charge in some situations.

As noted above, the lowest unit charge applies only to a "use" 45 days before a primary or primary runoff election or 60 days preceding a general or special election. What policies apply to political advertising rates when the lowest unit charge does not apply? If a legally qualified candidate buys time in periods outside the lowest unit 45- or 60-day time frames, the charges made for a use of a station may not exceed those made for "comparable use" of the station by advertisers. To put it simply, a station selling time outside the lowest unit charge dates can charge a political candidate as much as it charges other advertisers for "comparable use" of the station.[84]

12.4 SPONSORSHIP IDENTIFICATION REQUIREMENTS

All paid political messages must include a statement identifying the sponsor of the message.

To make certain that the public has no problem in distinguishing political messages from other broadcast messages, the FCC imposes specific sponsorship identification requirements. This stipulation stems from Section 317 of the Communications Act, which requires that stations broadcast sponsorship identification announcements (EMG 10.1.1.4). The FCC requires that a sponsorship identification announcement be made at the beginning and conclusion of any program using political material. But if the program is five minutes or less, including spot announcements, only one announcement is required. The announcement may be at the beginning or conclusion of the program or announcement.[85]

The sponsorship identification must be specific. The FCC requires that stations announce (1) that the broadcast was sponsored (with the phrase "paid for" or the phrase "sponsored by") and (2) announce the true identify of the person or entity paying for the announcement.[86] Thus, the sponsorship identification announcement could state "Paid for by the Committee to Elect Mary Smith."

The increased use of shorter political advertisements, such as 10- or 15-second spots, has brought a change in the technique that TV stations and cablecasters can use to include the sponsorship identification in spot announcements. Sponsorship identification on TV may use video identification only, but must use letters equal to or greater than 4 percent of the vertical picture height and must air for at least four

---

[84] 100 F.C.C.2d 1476, at 1519.
[85] 47 C.F.R. § 73.1212.
[86] *Id.*

seconds.[87] Radio stations, of course, have no choice but to make an audio identification announcement.

You may hear political identification spots that identify the chairperson or other officer of a candidate's campaign committee. FCC rules do not require such identification, but state laws often do. In addition, the Federal Election Commission requires that candidates for federal elective office identify whether their announcements are paid for by the candidate or by a bona fide campaign committee.[88]

12.5   SECTION 312 AND ACCESS

In Section 312 of the Communications Act, Congress requires broadcast stations, but not cable systems, to sell or give time to legally qualified candidates for federal elective office.

Not only does Congress believe that political candidates should have equal opportunities to use the airwaves, but in 1971 it passed legislation to give candidates for federal elective office even greater access to the broadcast media. The result was Section 312 of the Communications Act, which requires stations to give reasonable access to legally qualified candidates for federal elective office.[89] As we noted before, a station can choose not to sell time to candidates for state or local office. But Section 312 gives broadcasters no choice; they must provide access to a candidate for federal office on the threat of license revocation.[90]

The FCC has elected to avoid formal rules defining "reasonable access" and relies on the reasonable, good faith judgment of its licensees to provide it. Nevertheless, the FCC has set forth guidelines to measure a licensee's judgment in providing reasonable access.[91] These guidelines state that: (1) reasonable access must be provided to legally qualified federal candidates either on a paid or free basis; (2) reasonable access must be provided at least during the 45 days before a primary and 60 days before a general or special election (whether access should be provided before these periods or before a convention or nonprimary caucus is determined by the Commission on a case-by-case basis); (3) both commercial and noncommercial stations must observe the access rules, but cable television systems are exempt from Section 312;[92] (4) commercial stations and noncommercial stations that utilize spot time for underwriting announcements must make spot announce-

---

[87] Codification of the Commission's Political Programming Policies, 7 F.C.C.R. 1616 (1992).

[88] Joint Agency Guidelines for Broadcast Licensees, 69 F.C.C.2d 1129 (1978).

[89] 47 U.S.C. § 312(a)(7).

[90] Section 312(a)(7) states: "The Commission may revoke any station license or construction permit . . . for willful or repeated failure to allow reasonable access to or to permit purchase of reasonable amounts of time for the use of a broadcasting station by a legally qualified candidate for federal elective office on behalf of his candidacy."

[91] *See* Report and Order, 68 F.C.C.2d 1079 (1978), updated in Codification of the Commission's Political Programming Policies, 7 F.C.C.R. 687 (1991).

[92] Codification of the Commission's Political Programming Policies, 7 F.C.C.R. 4612 (1992).

ments available to federal candidates in prime time, but broadcasters can refuse to sell political advertising to federal candidates during news programs;[93] (5) access time must be sold on the basis of the lowest unit charge; and finally, (6) stations cannot censor the content of political material.

The significance of the "reasonable access" law can be measured against the fact that candidates spent an estimated $240–$275 million on local spot advertising in 1992, and $55 million on network advertising. A sizable proportion of that amount was spent by presidential candidates and candidates for other federal offices. Certainly, Section 312 requirements do favor Congress, leading to the observation that members of Congress decided to combat the rising costs of federal election campaigns by imposing requirements designed to reduce their own campaign costs at the expense of the government-regulated broadcast industry.[94] On the other hand, Section 312 rules help keep campaign costs down and give less wealthy candidates an opportunity to seek federal office.

Nevertheless, Section 312 has presented novel problems. One arose in 1979 when the Carter/Mondale Presidential Committee asked the three major networks to sell it 30 minutes of prime time to show a documentary of President Jimmy Carter's first term. Walter Mondale was vice president. The request came 11 months before the presidential election, just after Carter announced he was seeking reelection.

The networks refused the request, stating it was too early to sell time to a reelection campaign. Even though an FCC license is not needed to operate a network, the networks are nevertheless bound by Section 315 through their owned and operated stations. The FCC and the U.S. court of appeals ruled that the refusal violated the reasonable access requirement of Section 312. On appeal, the Supreme Court affirmed the lower court. The networks argued that neither the First Amendment nor the Communications Act requires broadcasters to accept paid editorial advertisements. The high court disagreed, stating that reasonable access law constitutes a proper balancing of the First Amendment rights of candidates, the public, and broadcasters.[95]

Another case that developed at the same time questioned whether Section 312 requires that candidates be given free time when opponents are sold time. The case, *Kennedy for President* v. *FCC*,[96] involved a request by Senator Edward Kennedy that he be given free time in response to network coverage of President Carter, Kennedy's opponent in the 1980 Democratic primary. The networks had broadcast a Carter speech and a press conference and had offered to sell Kennedy time. How-

---

[93] Because state and local candidates have no right of access to broadcast facilities, stations may ban the sale of advertisements in news programs to federal candidates, despite the other provisions of Section 312. The Commission bases this decision on the belief that Section 312 was not intended to provide candidate access to specific programming. 7 F.C.C.R. 678, at 682.

[94] Dwight L. Teeter, Jr., and Don R. Le Duc, *Law of Mass Communications,* 7th ed. (Westbury, NY: Foundation, 1992) 391.

[95] Carter/Mondale Presidential Comm., Inc., 44 F.C.C.2d 631, *reconsideration denied,* 74 F.C.C.2d 657 (1979), *aff'd sub nom.* CBS v. FCC, 629 F.2d 1 (D.C. Cir. 1980), *aff'd,* 453 U.S. 367.

[96] 636 F.2d 432 (1980).

ever, Kennedy argued that the *Carter/Mondale* decision meant that the networks had to honor his request for free time. An appeals court rejected Kennedy's request, stating that Section 312 did not create a right to use a station's facilities without charge. Broadcasters, said the court, can satisfy their obligation under Section 312 by giving free time or by selling the candidate time under the rate structure described in Section 315.[97]

Yet another problem arose in 1992 when a federal candidate asked WAGA-TV, Atlanta, Georgia, to air the candidate's 30-minute political program "Abortion in America: The Real Story." WAGA refused to run the program outside the hours the FCC had specified as acceptable for broadcasting indecent material (see EMG 13.1.1.3.3), because the program included graphic scenes supposedly showing aborted fetuses. Station officials argued that such material constituted indecent content and offered to provide the candidate with price and availability information in the safe harbor period.

The next chapter will include the FCC's handling of the indecency argument, a decision that was not made at the time the complaint was filed against WAGA-TV. The Commission did state that until it provided definitive guidance on the question of indecency, a licensee could reasonably conclude that Section 312 does not require it to air material that it reasonably and in good faith believes is indecent during hours outside the safe harbor. In the meantime, the Commission asked for public comment on the issues raised by the decision.

12.6 POLITICAL FILE

The FCC requires broadcasters and cablecasters to keep records of all requests for airtime made by or on behalf of candidates for public office.

The Commission's rules require stations and cable systems to maintain, and permit public inspection of, all requests for broadcast time made by or on behalf of candidates for public office.[98] The file is to include all requests for airtime made by or on behalf of candidates for public office, as well as an indication of whether or not the candidate was sold time, and if so, the charges for the time. If free time is provided, that is also to be documented. All records in the political file are to be maintained for two years. Each station or cable system is expected to permit public inspection of the political file.

12.7 INDEPENDENT POLITICAL COMMITTEES

Independent political committees, sometimes called political action committees or PACs, are committees authorized to raise or spend money on behalf of a candidate.

---

[97] *Id.* at 436.
[98] *See* 47 C.F.R. § 773.1940(d) for the broadcasting rule; 47 C.F.R. § 76.207 for the cable rule.

Independent political committees have been active since 1980 purchasing spot advertisements supporting or opposing the election of legally qualified candidates, but the political advertising rules do not apply to them in the same way as they do to candidates or their authorized committees.

First of all, the FCC has ruled that stations and cable systems are not required to sell time to independent political committees. Section 312 requires broadcast stations to sell time to federal candidates but the requirement does not extend to other candidates or groups.[99]

As you will recall from our discussion of uses (EMG 12.1.1), a political spot showing a legally qualified candidate was previously considered a use even if an independent committee paid for it. Thus, an independent committee could pay for a spot that supported or opposed a candidate, a spot showing the candidate, and the spot constituted a use even though the candidate had nothing to do with it. That practice was changed in 1992 to limit a use to a spot "controlled, approved or sponsored" by the candidate.

Independent political committees also do not qualify for the lowest unit charge. The Commission has stipulated that the lowest unit charge applies only to uses, which are appearances on the air by a candidate personally.[100]

12.8   OPPOSITION TO SECTIONS 315 AND 312

Opponents of Sections 315 and 312 have argued for repeal or revision of the rules governing political broadcasting.

Opposition to the political broadcasting rules has existed for some time. In 1975, the American Bar Association's House of Delegates urged repeal or revision of the rule. The major broadcasting networks have long opposed the rule, as have some members of Congress and the FCC. Opponents of the rule generally believed that broadcast stations would air more political programming and cover the political campaigns more thoroughly if they were not restricted by the equal time rules. Stations also argue that they lose money during elections, because they must move out regular advertisers paying higher rates to fit in political spots at the lowest unit charge.

In 1975, Senator William Proxmire introduced a bill that would have made candidates for president and vice president exempt from equal time rules. In 1981, the deregulation-minded FCC urged Congress to repeal both Sections 315 and 312 of the Communications Act. The Commission position was that the rules inhibited coverage of political events, and that marketplace forces would lead to better coverage.[101] Congress refused to honor the request.

---

[99] 7 F.C.C.R., at 682.

[100] 100 F.C.C.2d at 1514.

[101] FCC Report No. 5068, Setting Forth Proposals for Amending the Communications Act (Sept. 17, 1981).

Since 1981, the FCC has continued to emphasize deregulation and marketplace competition, but with no major push to delete the equal time rules. As Teeter and LeDuc observed, members of Congress are not likely ever to voluntarily release broadcasting from the constraints of federal programming regulations so long as they can continue to gain such political advantage from the "equal opportunities," "lowest advertising rate," and "reasonable access" provisions of the Communications Act of 1934.[102]

DISCUSSION QUESTIONS

1. Why are Sections 312 and 315 applied to the electronic media during political campaigns when print media have no similar requirements?
2. Several dozen "minor party" candidates qualify and run for president each election but are excluded from debates. How can this be justified?
3. Compare the sponsorship rules for presenting broadcast debates that existed between 1975 and 1983 with those that have existed since 1983.
4. During what two time periods must the lowest unit charge be utilized? Why is the lowest unit charge not used throughout a political campaign?
5. What rule applies to supporters or spokespersons of candidates who speak on behalf of a candidate during a campaign? How does the rule work?
6. Should stations and cable systems be allowed to ban any type of content in political ads? If so, what type of content?
7. How can we justify exempting bona fide news material from the equal opportunity rules when incumbent candidates have a greater opportunity of making news than challengers?
8. How does maintenance of a political file by a broadcaster or cable operator serve the public?
9. Identify the factors in determining the lowest unit rate. Which factors might pose problems in adhering to the rule?
10. Critics of the equal opportunities rule charge that the rule is no longer needed. What do you think?
11. Why is Section 312 applied only to broadcast stations and not to cable systems?

SUGGESTED READING

Engle, Eric. "FCC Regulation of Political Broadcasting: A Critical Legal Studies Perspective." *Communications and the Law* 14 (Sept. 1992): 3.

"Equal Time Equals Unequal Treatment to Newscaster Candidates," *Loyola Entertainment Law Journal* 9 (1989): 283.

"An Informed Electorate: Requiring Broadcasters to Provide Free Airtime to Candidates for Political Office." *Boston University Law Review* 72 (Jan. 1992): 143.

---

[102] Teeter and LeDuc, 391–392.

Kassman, M. "The Defamation You Can't Refuse: Section 315's Prohibition on Censoring Political Broadcasters." *Hastings Journal of Communications and Entertainment*: 13 (fall 1990): 1.

"Law of Political Broadcasting & Cablecasting: A Political Primer." 100 FCC2d 1476 (1984).

Leibowitz, Matthew L., and John M. Spencer. *Broadcasting & the Law: Political Handbook.* Miami: Miami Broadcasting & Law, 1988.

Minow, Newton. *Equal Time: The Private Broadcaster and the Public Interest.* New York: Atheneum, 1964.

National Association of Broadcasters. *Political Broadcast Catechism*, 12th ed. Washington, DC: NAB, 1988.

"Reclaiming a Public Resource: The Constitutionality of Requiring Broadcasters to Provide Free Television Time to Candidates for Federal Office." *New York University Review of Law & Social Change* 18 (1990–91): 213.

Chapter 13

PROGRAMMING RESTRICTIONS

In Chapter 10, we looked at programming requirements, elements that law and regulation required be included in the content transmitted by electonic mass media. In Chapters 11 and 12, we have seen restrictions and obligations placed on the electronic media to stimulate fairness and provide equity in political programming. These laws and doctrines did not forbid speech but imposed affirmative obligations on stations to provide fairness and equality for political messages. Congress, the courts, and the FCC have also placed restrictions on electronic media content, restrictions that often do restrict speech. These are restrictions that would never be tolerated by publishers in the print media, but factors unique to broadcast communication have been used to justify regulation. As you read this chapter, consider the validity of banning these forms of speech from the airwaves.

13.1 OFFENSIVE LANGUAGE

The unique characteristics of broadcasting—its pervasiveness, its entry into the home, its accessibility to children, and the scarcity of frequencies—have been used to justify regulation of offensive content.

Nowhere is the lack of First Amendment parity between radio-TV and other communications more obvious than when dealing with offensive program content. Broadcast stations are subject to rigid restrictions that other media do not face. The reason for the extensive prohibition of offensive content goes back to the uniqueness of radio and television broadcasting identified in the early days of broadcast regulation; its pervasiveness, its entry into the home, its accessibility to children, and the scarcity of frequencies. These factors have regularly been cited in placing restraints on the broadcasting of offensive material.

13.1.1 Background of Regulation

Section 326 of the Communications Act prohibits the censorship of broadcast content, but Section 1464 of the U.S. Code prohibits the broadcasting of obscene, indecent, or profane language. The FCC has elected to enforce Section 1464, bringing actions after broadcast.

Not only has offensive content been extensively regulated, but for many years the broadcast industry was faced with a conflict of two statutes. On the one hand, Section 326 of the Communications Act, which was put into place in 1927 (EMG 3.1.3.1), specifically prohibited the FCC from exercising the power of censorship over radio communications or interference with the right of free speech by means of radio communication. On the other hand, Congress in 1948 incorporated prohibitions in Section 1464 of the U.S. Criminal Code that forbid the broadcasting of "obscene, indecent, or profane language."[1] Violators are subject to a fine of up to $10,000, or two years in jail, or both for violating the criminal code.[2] The Communications Act also empowers the FCC to impose fines, grant short-term license renewals, and in severe cases, revoke licenses for violations. Not until the late 1970s did the Supreme Court specifically address the broadcasting of questionable material.[3] In the meantime, licensees were faced with restrictions against three types of content identified in Section 1464, profanity, obscenity, and indecency.

In the past, the FCC was faced with two approaches to Section 1464. First, it could leave interpretation of the statute to the Department of Justice. If doing so led to a conviction of a licensee, the FCC would decide how the conviction would apply to renewal of license. The other approach to the statute has been to assume that the Commission is also obligated to enforce it by preventing the broadcasting of obscene and indecent programs. The latter approach is the one chosen by the Commission.

13.1.1.1 Profanity

The regulation of profane language on radio and television is rarely an issue.

Profanity is the form of statutorily forbidden language that elicits the fewest complaints or that least bothers the FCC, the one for which the FCC was first to set standards, and the one least likely to get a broadcaster in trouble. Profanity is the use of irreverent or irreligious words, words such as *hell, damn,* and *God damn it.*

---

[1] 47 U.S.C. §§ 312(a)(6); 503 (b)(1)(D).
[2] 18 U.S.C. §§ 307, 308, 1468. While the financial penalty under Section 1464 remains $10,000, the FCC's base fine for a finding of indecency is $12,500.
[3] FCC v. Pacifica Found., 438 U.S. 726 (1978).

"The following program has been edited for television. Violence has been taken out to make room for more sex."

SOURCE: Reprinted with special permission of King Features Syndicate.

The FCC has taken the position that the intention of the speaker is the determining factor in judging profanity. Cases are not considered unless there is evidence that the speaker intended to utter words "importing an imprecation of divine vengeance or implying divine condemnation, so used as to constitute a public nuisance."[4] This means that unless a speaker so repeatedly uses profanity to invoke a curse as to cause public nuisance, the FCC will not bring action. The result is that the conversational uses of profanity by broadcast announcers and performers is not considered seriously offensive.

13.1.1.2   Obscenity

In *Miller* v. *California* the Supreme Court said that for a work to be considered obscene it must meet three tests: (1) an average person, applying contemporary community standards, must find that the work, taken as a whole, appeals to purient interests; (2) the work must describe, in a patently offensive way, sexual conduct as defined by an applicable state law; and (3) the work must lack serious literary, artistic, political, scientific value. The broadcasting of obscene material is always illegal.

In the eyes of the law, obscenity is a much more serious misdeed than profanity, so serious that the broadcasting of obscenity is always illegal. The test of obscenity is a difficult one and is based on the U.S. Supreme Court's 1973 ruling in *Miller* v. *California.*[5] The standard involves three parts, all of which must be met if a broadcast is to be ruled obscene and thus not protected by the Constitution. The three parts are:

---

[4] *The FCC and Broadcasting* (Washington, DC: FCC Pamphlet, 1974).
[5] 413 U.S. 15 (1973).

1. Would the average person, applying contemporary community standards, find that the work, taken as a whole, appeals to prurient interest?
2. Does the program depict or describe, in a patently offensive way, sexual conduct as defined by state law?
3. Does the broadcast lack serious literary, artistic, political, or scientific value?

Obscene material has been denied First Amendment protection because it is so offensive to contemporary moral standards.[6]

13.1.1.3   Indecency

While obscenity standards generally developed in the print media, the FCC displayed a reluctance to become involved in obscenity determinations in cases involving broadcast stations. Instead, the Commission pursued the concept of indecency and eventually won Supreme Court support for it.

The FCC's reaction to the broadcasting of objectionable language has been complicated. On the one hand, broadcasters sometimes aired questionable material that did not meet the tests established in *Miller* or earlier definitions of obscenity. On the other hand, Section 1464 of the Criminal Code, as we have seen, empowered the FCC to take action against profanity, indecency, or obscenity. Thus, while the definition of obscenity, which applies to all media, was carved out in the print media, the FCC looked to an alternate standard to judge broadcasts that were objectionable but not obscene.

A first glimpse at the broadcasting precedents came in the early 1960s when a South Carolina disc jockey named Charlie Walker was found guilty of broadcasting offensive language. Walker was convicted under Section 1464 for telling off-color and indecent jokes on the air. The FCC eventually refused to renew the license of the station that carried Walker's remarks but based its decision on an alleged attempt by the station to mislead the FCC with false evidence. When the court of appeals affirmed the refusal, it emphasized the attempt to mislead the FCC.[7] As a result, neither case addressed the question of obscenity as it applied to broadcasting.

The next FCC action was brought in 1964 against the Pacifica Foundation, a noncommercial licensee whose radio stations specialized in unorthodox programming.[8] Pacifica presented alternative programming, programs that offered diversity to the public. At the same time, content outside the mainstream ran head-on into content concerns.

The case was generated from complaints about an on-air discussion by several homosexuals regarding their beliefs and concerns, and the reading of several poems and a novel by their authors. Those filing complaints said the programs were so

---

[6] Roth v. United States, 354 U.S. 476 (1957).
[7] Robinson v. FCC, 334 F.2d 534 (1964).
[8] Pacifica Found., 36 F.C.C. 147 (1964).

offensive that the station's license should not be renewed. The FCC decided to renew the license of the station, even though it was obvious that some listeners had been offended. The Commission said the programs were not patently offensive, and noted that the dramatic works were presented by serious and notable writers. Further, the licensee had edited out some passages of the material, and had broadcast all but one of the programs late at night. The FCC said that those who were offended did not have the right to rule such programming off the air through the Commission's licensing power. To do so would allow "only the wholly inoffensive, the bland, [to] gain access to the radio microphone or TV camera."[9]

A third case developed in 1970 when the FCC fined Philadelphia station WUHY-FM $100 after it aired an interview with Jerry Garcia, leader of the music group the Grateful Dead. Garcia used a number of "patently offensive" words during the course of an interview about ecology and interpersonal relations. The FCC said the remarks were indecent, not obscene, and defined indecency as follows:

> we believe the statutory term, "indecent" should be applicable, and that in the broadcast field, the standard for its applicability should be that the material broadcast is (a) patently offensive by contemporary community standards, and (b) utterly without social value.[10]

A fourth case arose in 1973 when radio stations were broadcasting what was called "topless radio," call-in talk shows in which listeners talked about sexual problems and concerns on the air. It is interesting to note that these discussions were often done in a pandering manner, with the program hosts making fun of the sexual concerns. The FCC publicly expressed displeasure at the programs and imposed a fine of $2,000 against WGLD-FM, Oak Park, Illinois.[11] Among the language that was evaluated was the following:

> Female Listener: . . . of course I had a few hangups at first about—in regard to this, but you know what we did—I have a craving for peanut butter all that (sic) time so I used to spread this on my husband's privates and after a while, I mean, I didn't even need the peanut butter anymore.
> Announcer: (Laughs) Peanut butter, huh?
> Listener: Right. Oh, we can try anything—you know—any of these women have called and they have, you know, hangups about this, I mean they should try their favorite—you know like—us . . .
> Announcer: Whipped cream, marshmallow . . ."

The FCC held that the material violated both the indecency and obscenity clauses of Section 1464. The Commission acknowledged that sex was not to be totally forbidden as a program topic and that licensees had a right to present pro-

---

[9] *Id.* at 149.
[10] WHUY-FM Eastern Educ. Radio, 24 F.C.C.2d 408 (1970).
[11] Sonderling Broadcasting Corp. (WGLD-FM), 27 Rad. Reg. 2d (P&F) 285 (1973).

gramming that might offend some listeners. Nevertheless, the Commission fined WGLD $2,000, and it invited a court test of its decision.

Rather than fight the FCC, WGLD paid the fine, but two citizen groups appealed it on the grounds that the public had been deprived of listening alternatives. When the case was heard by the U.S. court of appeals, the FCC noted the presence of children in the audience during the program and warned of the pervasive, intrusive nature of radio. The court agreed that the Commission had a right to determine that a program is obscene without infringing on the public's right to listening alternatives as long as the program is presented during daytime hours.[12] Thus, the Commission received judicial support of its efforts to regulate broadcasts of offensive language but the court did not rule on the FCC's interpretation of indecency.

13.1.1.3.1 *Pacifica Decision*

A decision involving WBAI-FM, New York, gave the FCC a chance to solidify the indecency concept. The Supreme Court upheld the FCC's action and in so doing validated the FCC's definition of indecency.

In 1975, another case came before the FCC, one that produced a definition of indecency. The case occurred when the Pacifica station in New York City, WBAI-FM, played a monologue titled "Filthy Words" by comedian George Carlin. In the recording, Carlin repeatedly used "the seven words you can't say on the public airwaves." The monologue was broadcast in the middle of the afternoon and WBAI preceded it with a disclaimer that acknowledged that the language was sensitive and might be offensive to some listeners. The station justified playing the recording by identifying it as a satire on contemporary language. One listener, a man who heard the broadcast while riding in his automobile with his son, complained to the FCC.

The FCC ruled that the content of the broadcast was not so much obscene as "indecent," because it involved language that described sexual and excretory activities and organs in a patently offensive manner. The FCC called the words that Carlin had used repeatedly during his 12-minute monologue, "obnoxious, gutter language."[13] The Commission noted that time of day was a factor in its definition of indecency, since children were undoubtedly in the audience. Finally, the Commission distinguished indecent language from obscene language by stating that indecent language does not appeal to a prurient interest. The FCC did not penalize WBAI but it warned that further complaints about indecent language could lead to sanctions.

The Commission based its decision on four reasons. First, children have access to radios and in many cases are unsupervised by parents. Second, radio receivers are found in the home, a place where people's private interest is entitled to extra deference. Third, unconsenting adults may tune in a station with no warning that offensive matter will be or is being broadcast. Finally, the FCC cited the shortage of

---

[12] Illinois Citizens Comm. for Broadcasting v. FCC, 515 F.2d 397 (1974).
[13] Pacifica Found. Inc., 56 F.C.C.2d 94, at 98 (1975).

spectrum space as a factor justifying its decision, a key factor in distinguishing broadcasting from other media.[14]

Although the FCC used the *Pacifica* decision to prohibit broadcasting of the "seven dirty words," it did not want to completely limit use of the words. As a result, use of the words was limited to times when children were less likely to be in the audience (which the FCC defined as between 10 P.M. and 6 A.M.). According to the Commission, this was an attempt to "channel" listening behavior, to limit it to times when children would not be in the audience, rather than to prohibit it.[15]

The U.S. court of appeals overturned the FCC; however, in *FCC v. Pacifica Foundation*,[16] the Supreme Court reversed the court of appeals and held that the FCC was justified in taking its action. The Court acknowledged that the words were not obscene but concluded that the FCC had the authority to find them patently offensive and "indecent" and thus in violation of Section 1464 of the U.S. Code. The Supreme Court held that Section 326 of the Communications Act, the no-censorship provision, had not been violated.[17] Section 326, the Court noted, bars editing program content in advance, but it stated that the FCC possesses the power to review content after broadcast.

The Supreme Court did not totally strip away First Amendment protection from indecent speech but noted that context and content are critical variables in determining First Amendment protection. In terms of the Carlin material, the content was found to be "vulgar," "offensive," and "shocking," thus supporting regulation.[18] The context also supported regulation. Referring to the scarcity of frequencies, the pervasiveness of broadcasting, and the ability of broadcasts to invade the home, the Court held that restriction of the words was warranted. Nevertheless, the Supreme Court warned that the decision was to be narrowly construed because of the variables concerning broadcasting; variables such as the accessibility of the programs by children, the context of the broadcast, and whether the material was transmitted by radio, television, or cable.[19]

As is clear from the 5-4 vote of the Court, the justices were not unanimous in upholding the ruling. Justice Stewart, writing for all four dissenting justices, said the FCC did not have the authority to regulate the "seven dirty words," since they were not obscene. Yet, the majority of the justices agreed with the FCC and upheld its action.[20]

13.1.1.3.2 Shock Radio

"Shock jocks" presented the next problem with indecency when they began airing innuendo and double entendre to avoid the seven filthy words.

---

[14] *Id.* at 97.

[15] *Id.* at 98.

[16] 438 U.S. 726 (1978). The "Filthy Words" are *shit, piss, fuck, cunt, cocksucker, motherfucker,* and *tits.*

[17] *Id.* at 738.

[18] *Id.* at 748.

[19] *Id.* at 751.

[20] *Id.* at 762–777.

Following the *Pacifica* decision, a period of relative calm existed in the effort to control the broadcasting of offensive language. For more than 10 years, the FCC restricted its action to policing the ban on the "seven dirty words," and no broadcasters were punished for airing indecent language during this period. For broadcasters, the rules were quite clear: avoid the "seven dirty words" if you do not want to get into trouble with the FCC. But the ban on the dirty words did not prevent broadcasters from airing content that was still considered offensive, even though the "seven dirty words" were not used. So-called shock jocks began to appear on radio stations in some of the major cities, and their blend of irreverent humor and innuendo had again caught the attention of the FCC. Letters of complaint flooded the FCC and listeners complained to their congressional representatives.

In April 1987, the Commission again addressed the issue of inappropriate language. The programs of three radio stations were examined as examples of "Raunch Radio." Infinity Broadcasting, the licensee that broadcast Howard Stern, was cited for more than incidental use of sexually oriented language, sexual innuendo, and double entendre.[21] A Santa Barbara, California, station licensed to the Regents of the University of California was identified as having played sexually explicit lyrics in recorded music that the FCC found to be indecent ("Makin Bacon," by the Pork Dukes),[22] and the Pacifica station in Los Angeles was cited for airing excerpts of the play *The Jerker*, which depicted a homosexual dying of AIDS.[23] The Commission noted extensive use of patently offensive language referring to sexual and excretory organs and functions in the broadcast and held it to be indecent.

The Commission issued warnings to the three stations and the radio industry that the term *indecency* would now mean more than the repetitive use of Carlin's "seven dirty words." In the future, the Commission said it would apply the generic definition of indecency developed in *Pacifica*:

> A description or depiction of sexual or excretory activities or organs in a manner patently offensive by contemporary community standards for the broadcast media.[24]

The FCC warned that the *context* of broadcasts would be important in determining if indecency existed. This meant that the manner in which the words or depictions were aired would be critical. Were the words or depictions isolated or fleeting, did the program have "merit," and were children likely to be in the audience?[25] The question of context was tested when a listener complained to the FCC about a National Public Radio news program that included portions of a conversation between an alleged mobster and an associate that had been tape-recorded and used in court. The words *fuck* and *fucking* were used in the conversation a number

---

[21] Infinity Broadcasting Corp., 2 F.C.C.R. 2705 (1987).

[22] Regents of the Univ. of Cal., 2 F.C.C.R. 2703 (1987).

[23] Pacifica Found., Inc. 2 F.C.C.R. 2698 (1987).

[24] Infinity Broadcasting Corp. (Reconsideration Order), 3 F.C.C.R. 932 (1987).

[25] New Indecency Enforcement Standards to be Applied to All Broadcast and Amateur Radio Licenses, 2 F.C.C.R. 2726 (1987).

TABLE 13.1   Variations of the Safe Harbor Rule

Indecency Could Not Be Aired	Safe Harbor Hours	Duration
6 A.M.–10 P.M.	10 P.M.–6 A.M.	1978–1987
6 A.M.–midnight	midnight–6 A.M.	1987–1988
Total Ban	None	1988–1989
6 A.M.–8 P.M.	8 P.M.–6 A.M.	1989–1992
6 A.M.–midnight	midnight–6 A.M.	1992–1993
6 A.M.–8 P.M.	8 P.M.–6 A.M.	1993–

of times. The FCC concluded that since the words appeared in a legitimate news context, the broadcast was not patently offensive and therefore not indecent. The listener took the case to the U.S. court of appeals, but the court held that listeners generally do not have standing to appeal indecency complaints beyond the FCC. The Supreme Court let the decision stand.[26]

13.1.1.3.3 Safe Harbor.   Not only did the new criteria broaden the concept of indecency, but the FCC once again addressed the times during which the indecency prohibitions of Section 1464 would apply. This so-called safe harbor has been subject to varying political pressures and variations as noted in Table 13.1. As you will recall, the FCC in the 1978 *Pacifica* decision indicated that it felt stations needed to be cautious of children being in the audience until 10 P.M. In November 1987, the FCC imposed a 6 A.M. to 12 midnight ban on the broadcast of indecent material. This provided for a "safe harbor" for indecent material from 12 midnight to 6 A.M., a time when children were not likely to be in the audience.[27] However, in *Action for Children's Television* v. *FCC*[28] the U.S. court of appeals threw out the Commission's new time limitation, saying that the FCC had not channeled indecent material in a proper manner. The court said a reasonable safe harbor for indecent material was constitutionally mandated. In addition, the court said that the FCC had not shown that children would be listening to radio or watching television between 10 P.M. and midnight. Further, the court argued that the Commission was restricting indecency to protect children age 12 and under by using data on viewing patterns of children age 12 and over. As a result, the court asked the Commission to provide data on the number of children actually listening to indecent programs as opposed to those simply listening to radio.[29] The court sent the issue back to the FCC for study.

Meanwhile, Congress got into the act and in September 1988 banned indecent material 24 hours a day.[30] The FCC instituted plans to implement the Congressional ban,[31] but both sides of the issue believed that the Supreme Court might support

---

[26] Branton v. FCC, 1993 U.S. App. Lexis 12801, cert. *denied*, 1994 U.S. Lexis 3143.

[27] Infinity Broadcasting Corp., 3 F.C.C.R. 937, note 47 (1987).

[28] 852 F.2d 1332 (1988) (ACT I).

[29] *Id.* at 1343.

[30] Pub. L. No. 100-459, Sec. 608, 102 Stat. 2228 (1988).

[31] Enforcement of Prohibitions against Broadcasting Obscenity and Indecency, 4 F.C.C.R. 457 (1988).

their position when it ruled on a case involving "dial-a-porn," recorded porno-graphic messages available to telephone callers at a modest charge. *Sable Com-muniations* v. *FCC* stemmed from a 1988 measure in which Congress had made it illegal to provide obscene or indecent commercial telephone messages in interstate commerce.[32] The Supreme Court upheld the ban on obscene telephone communi-cations but struck down a complete prohibition on indecent telephone communi-cation. The Court said that sexual expression that is indecent but not obscene is protected by the First Amendment. It conceded, however:

> The government may ... regulate the content of constitutionally pro-tected speech in order to promote a compelling interest if it chooses the least restrictive means to further the articulated interest.[33]

In 1989, the U.S. Court of Appeals for the District of Columbia stayed imple-mentation of the 24-hour ban and again sent the issue back to the FCC.[34] The court stressed that speech identified as indecent but not obscene is constitutionally pro-tected and may be regulated "only with due respect for the high value our Constitu-tion places on freedom and choice in what the people say and hear."[35] Thus, curtail-ment of the "safe harbor" time slots intruded on constitutionally protected expression interests.

After soliciting public comments on the total ban, the FCC in 1990 issued a report on indecency.[36] The Commission concluded that the 24-hour ban on inde-cent broadcasts was in agreement with the constitutional position taken by the Supreme Court in *Sable*. The FCC said it was likely that significant numbers of chil-dren ages 17 and under listen to radio and view television at all times without active parental supervision. As a result, the Commission concluded, only a total ban on indecent content would accomplish the government's interest in protecting children from broadcast indecency.[37]

The Commission also commented on the merit of a questionable item. The issue was whether an objectionable item would be excused from the definition of indecency if it had merit. The Commission said that merit is one of many variables in the context of a work, one that should not be given greater weight than other variables. As a result, the merit of a work has no bearing on a finding of indecency.[38]

In 1992, the FCC announced a ban on indecent material broadcast between the hours of 6 A.M. and 10 P.M. on public broadcast stations that go off the air at or before 12 midnight, and on all other broadcasting stations between 6 A.M. and 12 midnight. The Commission reaffirmed its concern that significant numbers of chil-dren ages 17 and under listen to radio during the 6 A.M. to 12 midnight period. The

[32] 492 U.S. 115 (1989).
[33] *Id.* at 126.
[34] Action for Children's Television (ACT II), 932 F.2d 1504 (1991), *cert. denied*, 117 L. Ed. 2d 507 (1992).
[35] *Id.* at 1508.
[36] Enforcement of Prohibitions against Broadcast Indecency in 18 USC § 1464, 5 F.C.C.R. 5297 (1990).
[37] *Id.* at 5309.
[38] 3 F.C.C.R. 930, at 932.

BOX 13.1   KGB-FM, San Diego: "Sit On My Face"

Male Chorus:

Sit on my face and tell me that you love me. I'll sit on your face and tell you I
love you, too. I love to hear you moralize when I'm between your thighs. You
blow me away. Sit on my face and let my lips embrace you. I'll sit on your face
and then I'll love you (?) truly. Life can be fine, if we both sixty-nine, if we sit
on faces (?) the ultimate places to play, (?) We'll be blown away.

SOURCE: 7 F.C.C.R. 3208 (1990).

Commission said it would permit broadcasters to submit marketwide data to demonstrate that no appreciable child audience existed during the hours in question.[39]
In 1993 a U.S. court of appeals said the FCC position was unconstitutional because
it did not adequately justify the 6 A.M. to midnight ban.[40]

The FCC has resorted to issuing fines against stations found to be guilty of
indecency. For example, the FCC fined WIOD-AM, Miami, $10,000 for playing such
songs as "Walk with an Erection" and "Penis Envy" during midday.[41] The FCC also
fined KGB-FM, San Diego, $25,000 for morning drive time broadcasts of the songs
"Candy Wrapper" and "Sit On My Face"[42] (see Box 13.1). As this book goes to
press, WLUP-FM, Chicago, has indecency charges pending for segments of programs
dealing with penis size.[43]

The FCC apparently bases the amount of the fine on the severity of the indecency. The material in Box 13.2 warranted only a modest fine although the base
fine for broadcasting indecent material is $12,500. Nevertheless, the FCC has flexed
its muscle by levying a series of fines totaling $1,284,750 against Infinity Broadcasting, which syndicates the *Howard Stern Show* and various stations that carry it.
Neither Infinity nor the stations that carry the program have paid; all are appealing
the fines in the courts.[44]

As you will note, all the cases cited here have dealt with charges of indecent
radio programming. However, in 1988, the FCC did charge a Kansas City TV station,
KZKC, with indecency for broadcasting the movie *Private Lessons* during prime
time. The movie, which depicts an older woman introducing a young boy to sex,
had not been edited for broadcast, a fact the station acknowledged. The FCC fined
the station $2,000.[45]

---

[39] Enforcement of Prohibitions against Broadcasting Indecency, F.C.C. 92-445, 57 Fed. Reg. 46,132
(1992).

[40] Action For Children's Television v. FCC, 1993 U.S. App. Lexis 30125.

[41] WIOD, Inc., 6 F.C.C.R. 3704 (1992).

[42] KGB-FM, 7 F.C.C.R. 3207 (1992).

[43] Evergreen Media Corp., 6 F.C.C.R. 3708 (1991).

[44] Harry A. Jessell, "Infinity Fined $5,000 for Stern," *Broadcasting & Cable*, 16 Aug. 1993, at 6.

[45] Kansas City Television, Ltd., 4 F.C.C.R. 6706 (1989).

BOX 13.2   Radio Station WYBB-FM, Folly Beach, SC: "Crap"

WYBB was fined $3,750 for the following broadcast at 9 A.M. by two announcers:

VOICE 1: (Unintelligible) Maybe it's nine.

VOICE 2: I don't know and who really gives a crap?

VOICE 1: Oh Oh.

VOICE 2: Yes, we can say crap.

VOICE 1: Yes?

VOICE 2: Crap, crap, crap, crap, crap, crap.

VOICE 1: That's right, just can't say shit.

VOICE 2: Oh, then we won't.

VOICE 1: That's right.

SOURCE: 7 F.C.C.R. 1595–1596 (1992).

The efforts of the FCC to single out broadcasting for special indecency limitations has not been without criticism. The Supreme Court's narrow 5-4 ruling in *Pacifica* indicates the division on the high court. Justice Brennan criticized the majority for approving censorship of radio communication solely because the words were offensive, and he accused the Court of imposing its notions of propriety upon the American people. Yet, the ruling established the right of the FCC to regulate indecency, a legal concept applied only to broadcasting. Moreover, the efforts by the FCC to define indecency have been described by one observer this way: "The FCC has reinforced the medium's unique status as the least constitutionally protected element of the press."[46]

13.1.1.4 *Obscenity/Indecency on Cable*

Obscenity is banned on cable, and several states have attempted to enact laws regulating indecent content.

The growth of cable has led to concerns about offensive content in that medium, and history has shown two patterns. When Congress wrote the cable act of 1984, most franchising authority was taken from the FCC and given to state or local authorities. The 1984 cable act banned the transmission of obscenity over cable, gave state and local franchise authorities power to prohibit obscene programming in franchise agreements, and required systems to offer subscribers "lock boxes" for sale or lease so that the viewing of a given channel could be restricted.

---

[46] Donald E. Lively, *Essential Principles of Communications Law* (New York: Praeger, 1992) 270.

Since the FCC has had no power to restrict cable content under the 1984 cable act, a number of states attempted to regulate indecent material on cable. One major effort occurred in Utah, where the state legislature passed a cable indecency act that made it a public nuisance for cable systems to present indecent material. The Utah law had defined indecent material as "the visual or verbal disposition or description of human sexual or excretory organs or functions, . . . exposure of genital, pubic area, buttocks, or the showing of any portion of the female breast below the nipple." The Utah statute allowed the showing of such material only from midnight to 7 A.M., and provided fines up to $1,000 for first offenders and $10,000 for repeat offenders.

A district court ruled that the Utah statute was overly broad and disagreed that the Supreme Court's approval of broadcast indecency limitations in *Pacifica* justified state regulation. In distinguishing cable from broadcasting, the court said that cable viewing requires the payment of fees and the act of subscribing. It noted that lock boxes are available to restrict undesired programs, and viewers receive program guides about the nature and content of programs. The court of appeals affirmed the decision, as did the Supreme Court.[47]

Another attempt at regulation occurred when the city of Miami, Florida, passed an ordinance that banned the transmission of obscene or indecent material by wire or cable. The ordinance used the three-pronged test in *Miller* v. *California* to determine whether material was obscene. Indecent material was defined as a depiction of a human or excretory organ or function which the average person, applying contemporary community standards, would find to be patently offensive.

A district judge said the ordinance was too broad. The court held that the *Pacifica* decision, which was cited as the leading case restricting indecency, is not the precedent since it was a narrow application. *Miller*, said the court, is the precedent since it limits regulation to obscenity. Thus, the attempts of the ordinance to regulate indecency exceeded the limits established in *Miller* and were unconstitutional.[48] The U.S. court of appeals affirmed the decision.

13.1.1.4.1 Cable Act of 1992
The cable act of 1992 placed cable and the regulation of cable indecency under the FCC.

Under the 1992 cable act, the FCC adopted rules against indecency.[49] In establishing the rules, the FCC relied on the Supreme Court's decision in *Sable Communications* v. *FCC*[50] (EMG 13.1.1.3.3), which permitted government regulation of indecent material if a compelling government interest exists. The Commission found such a compelling government interest with cable—to reduce children's ex-

---

[47] Community Television of Utah v. Wilkinson, 611 F. Supp. 1099 (D. Utah 1985), *aff'd*, 800 F.2d 989 (10th Cir. 1986), *aff'd*, 107 S. Ct. 1559 (1987).
[48] Cruz v. Ferre, 9 Media L. Rep. 2050 (S.D. Fla. 1983).
[49] 47 U.S.C. §§ 532(h) and 10(a)).
[50] 492 U.S. 115 (1989).

posure to indecent materials on cable leased access channels.[51] The Commission specifies that cablecasters must block access to a channel with indecent programs unless the subscriber supplies the operator with a written request for the programming. The subscriber must be 18 years of age to receive indecent content. Channels have to be blocked only while indecent programming is being shown.

Cable operators have some flexibility in dealing with programming on commercial leased access channels. The new FCC rules permit a cable system to require certification from the program provider that the programming is not obscene or indecent and need not be blocked. If a program provider will not provide certification, the cablecaster can refuse to let the provider use the system's facilities.[52]

In the case of live programming, the FCC permits programmers to certify that they will exercise "reasonable efforts to insure that no obscene programming or indecent programming on a nonblocked channel will be present." This applies to the transmission of obscene material on both leased and PEG channels as discussed in Chapter 10.

In a challenge to the application of the indecency rules, the court in *Alliance for Community Media* v. *FCC* invalidated the cable indecency rules. The rules were not completely dismissed; instead the court ordered that they be reheard.[53]

13.2 PROGRAM REGULATIONS

The obligation to broadcast in the public interest involves a responsibility not to broadcast a variety of material. Restrictions exist, or have existed, regarding the broadcasting of payola, lotteries, some contests, hoaxes, radio format changes, drug lyrics, news distortion, and television violence.

Many aspects of electronic media program content have been restricted to halt practices seen as harmful to the public. Some of these restrictions date back to the early days of radio broadcasting and others are fairly new. In some cases, the program restrictions have experienced deregulatory pressures that have altered their impact. In all cases, these program regulations are based on the theory that licensees operate on the public airwaves, and that the government can impose restrictions on behalf of the public interest.

13.2.1 Payola and Plugola

Payola is an illegal practice in the radio industry, while plugola is considered on a case-by-case basis. Payola, under-the-table payments to disc jockeys for playing

---

[51] Implementation of Section 10 of the Cable Consumer Protection and Competition Act of 1992: Indecent Programming and Other Types of Materials of Cable Access Channels, MM Docket No. 92-258, FCC 93-72, 58 Fed. Reg. 7990 (February 11, 1993).
[52] 47 U.S.C. §§ 532(h), 10(b).
[53] 1993 U.S. App. Lexis 30126.

certain records, is contrasted with plugola, the gratuitous on-air reference to a product or service.

In 1959, the radio industry suffered a major scandal when some disc jockeys took under-the-counter payments from record companies for playing records that music companies wanted promoted. The problem was that the payments were not revealed to the audience, leading to concerns about public deception. This practice is known as *payola*, and both Congress and the FCC took steps to stop it. While the practice has slowed, it has not stopped, and laws and regulations adopted in the wake of the 1959 payola scandal remain in force and require station employees to avoid payola. Payola may not be as widespread as it was in the 1950s but the FCC continues to detect payola activities.[54]

The Communications Act (Sections 317 and 507) defines payola as the unreported payment of something of value to a station employee for the on-air promotion of an event, services, or goods (EMG 10.1.1.4). In its most common form, payola involves accepting payment from record promoters or distributors in return for playing a record; but it can also involve accepting free tickets or vacation trips in return for promoting the product or service on the air. In either instance, a station employee is compensated by an outside source and the station is not. Further, the public is misled, since the source of the payment is not disclosed.

The two sections of the Communications Act have different goals. Section 507 is directed at those people who make unreported payments of a valuable consideration and at those who accept them.[55] Such people are expected to report the fact to station licensees before the matter is broadcast. Violations of Section 507 are punishable by a fine of up to $10,000, imprisonment for up to a year, or both.

As noted in EMG 10.1.1.4, Section 317's rule on sponsorship identification requires licensees to announce that the item in the program is paid for and to disclose the identity of the person furnishing the money or other valuable consideration.[56] Of course, the FCC may levy penalties against a station for violations.

The specialization of radio formats has been recognized in payola regulations. Stations whose formats make them susceptible to payola—popular music stations being the primary example—are expected to employ a higher degree of diligence in making certain that their employees comply with the requirements.

Plugola is a variation of payola. Plugola is the apparent gratuitous mention of a commercial product in an entertainment program. The FCC does not have specific regulations regarding plugola, but has chosen to deal with problems on a case-by-case basis.[57]

---

[54] Commission Warns Licensees about Payola and Undisclosed Promotion, 64 Rad. Reg. 2d (P&F) 1338 (1988).

[55] 47 U.S.C. § 507.

[56] 47 U.S.C. § 317.

[57] FCC Docket No. 14,119, 35 Fed. Reg. 7982 (1970).

Whether the concern is payola or plugola, a "valuable consideration" must be presented in return for the broadcast of a product endorsement or similar presentation in order for the act to constitute wrongdoing. Gifts of modest value do not constitute payola or plugola.

13.2.2 Lotteries

For many years, the U.S. Criminal Code prohibited stations from broadcasting a lottery. To be considered a lottery, broadcast information had to include three things: prize, chance, and consideration. Lottery laws are no longer enforced by the FCC, but may be subject to state regulation. State-run lotteries were exempted from the lottery prohibition.

Section 1304 of the U.S. Code prohibits the broadcasting of any advertisement or information concerning a lottery.[58] In recent years, the term lottery has been most commonly associated with money-making giveaway contests approved by the various states, and, as we shall see, Section 1304 does have bearing on state sponsored lotteries and its abolute ban has been eliminated. However, the earliest concern with lotteries was the widespread use of contests in promoting stations and advertised products. The FCC was concerned that the very act of listening to or viewing a station might constitute the consideration (that is, the price) required to win a chance at a prize in a broadcast giveaway. As a result, broadcast lotteries were made illegal.

According to FCC rules, a giveaway constitutes a lottery if three elements are present. These elements are:

1. *Prize*. Is a prize, something of value, offered to participants?
2. *Chance*. Is the winner selected by chance, such as a random drawing, rather than by a test of the participant's skill or other factors within his or her control? Is the amount of the prize determined by chance?
3. *Consideration*. Must the contestant spend money or substantial time or effort to qualify for the prize?

Under FCC rules, if all three elements existed in a giveaway, the broadcaster could not air any information either as an advertisement, a station contest, or even in a public service announcement about the giveaway. Further, it made no difference whether the lottery was to benefit a nonprofit or commercial enterprise.

Let us use a simple example. Suppose that a grocery store wanted to advertise a $500 shopping spree. With each purchase, contestants could guess the correct number of pennies in a large glass container. The winner would be drawn from the entrants guessing the correct number and would win the shopping spree. Does this material constitute a lottery?

---

[58] 18 U.S.C. § 1304.

The answer is yes. A prize, the shopping spree, would be awarded. Consideration would exist, since participants would have to make a purchase to enter. The element of chance also would exist, since the winner would be drawn from the entrants who guessed the correct number of pennies. All three elements would exist, making the contest a lottery.

The promotion could easily be made legal by removing the consideration—the requirement that only those making a purchase can enter. If anyone going to the store could fill out an entry blank without a purchase, only two elements would exist and the contest would not be a lottery. The time spent going to the store and the gasoline used getting there would likely be considered too incidental to constitute consideration.

As of 1990, the Commission amended its lottery rules to conform to the Charity Games Advertising Clarification Act of 1988.[59] As a result, broadcasters can now advertise lotteries conducted by (1) nonprofit organizations; (2) governmental organizations; and (3) commercial entities, as long as the lottery is clearly occasional and not the primary purpose of the commercial organization. This enables stations to broadcast material about such games of chance as bingo that previously could not be broadcast. Broadcasting information about certain Indian gaming activities is also legal.[60] However, ads for gaming activities, such as casino gambling, are illegal, although a U.S. district court has held that ban to be unconstitutional.[61] Fishing contests are specifically exempted from the federal prohibitions on broadcasting lotteries but only if the contest is not conducted for profit or personal gain. The proceeds from such contests must be used to pay the costs of the contest and not be used to establish civic, philanthropic, or charitable funds.[62]

There is a major stipulation to the rules allowing the broadcasting of lottery information. The rules apply *only* if the lottery is not prohibited by the state in which it is conducted. Congress left states the authority to regulate the broadcasting of lotteries, and many states retain laws similar to those the FCC previously enforced. As a result, licensees are advised to check the laws of their state before broadcasting advertisements that constitute a lottery.

13.2.2.1   *State-Sponsored Lotteries*
Even though Section 1304 prohibited the broadcasting of lotteries, Congress amended the U.S. Code to exempt state-conducted lotteries.

In 1976, Congress enacted Section 1307(a), which exempted broadcasts concerning state-conducted lotteries when the broadcast was in the state conducting

---

[59] Pub. L. No. 100-625, 100 Stat. 3205 (1988), codified at 18 U.S.C.A. § 1307.

[60] Indian Gaming Regulatory Act, Pub. L. No. 100-497, Sec. 21, 102 Stat. 2457 (1988). The activity must be (1) on Indian lands; (2) owned by an Indian tribe or grandfathered to them; (3) permitted by law in the state where held; and (4) games played against the house must include a compact to permit such games and all requirements of the compact must be met.

[61] "Court Overrules FCC; Allows Gaming Ads," *Broadcasting & Cable*, 19 Apr. 1993, at 18.

[62] 18 U.S.C. § 1305 (1982).

the lottery or in an adjacent state that also conducted a lottery.[63] In 1988, Congress further expanded the Section 1307 exception to Section 1304. It held that advertisements for state-conducted lotteries could be broadcast on behalf of the home state, if the state had a state-run lottery, or in any other state having a state-operated lottery.[64]

The U.S. Supreme Court had also been called on to decide a question concerning state-conducted lotteries. The issue was whether stations could broadcast news information about state lotteries, such as winning numbers and prize lists, when the lottery was conducted in another state. The question arose when the FCC refused to allow a New York station to broadcast the winning number in either the New Jersey or New Hampshire lottery. A U.S. court of appeals overruled the Commission,[65] and the Supreme Court agreed that lottery information could be broadcast as news in any state, with or without a lottery.[66]

Whether stations in states without lotteries could broadcast commercials for lotteries in neighboring states became an issue when a North Carolina radio station wanted to air spots for the Virginia lottery. Station WMTK-FM, Moycock, North Carolina, is located near the Virginia border and more than 90 percent of its listeners are from Virginia. North Carolina does not have a state lottery but Virginia does. The station went to court and challenged the "neighboring state" rule, and a lower court ruled in favor of the station. The court assessed the restriction under the four-factor test for commercial speech set forth in *Central Hudson Gas & Electric Corp.* v. *Public Service Commission of New York.*[67] The factors are (1) whether speech concerns lawful activity and is not misleading and (2) whether the asserted governmental interest is substantial; and if so, (3) whether the regulation directly advances the asserted interest and (4) whether the regulation is more extensive than necessary to serve the interest.

A court of appeals affirmed the ruling but on appeal, the U.S. Supreme Court in *United States* v. *Edge Broadcasting Co.* upheld the rule prohibiting stations in states without lotteries from carrying commercials for lotteries in neighboring states. In weighing the *Central Hudson* test the Supreme Court concluded that the lottery rules regulate commercial speech in a manner consistent with the First Amendment. On the first factor, the Court said the statutes are constitutional, and in terms of the second factor, governmental interest, the Court said the government has a substantial interest in supporting the policy of nonlottery states and not interfering in the policy of lottery states. The third factor, whether the regulation advances the government's interest, was really answered by the fourth factor. The Court concluded that Congress did not favor lottery or nonlottery states but instead chose to support nonlottery states' antigambling policies. The court wrote:

---

[63] 18 U.S.C. § 1307(a).
[64] § 1307(a)(1)(B).
[65] *See* New Jersey State Lottery Comm'n. v. United States, 519 F.2d 1398 (3d Cir. 1975).
[66] New Jersey State Lottery Comm'n. v. United States, 420 U.S. 371 (1975).
[67] 447 U.S. 557 (1980).

The activity underlying the relevant advertising—gambling—implicates no constitutionally protected right; rather, it falls into a category of "vice" activity that could be, and frequently has been, banned altogether.[68]

Justice Stevens, who dissented, saw things differently. "The United States has selected the most intrusive, and dangerous form of regulation possible," he said, "a ban on truthful information regarding a lawful activity imposed for the purpose of manipulating, through ignorance, the consumer choices of some of its citizens."[69]

13.2.3 Contests

Lotteries and contests are quite similar. A lottery differs from a simple contest in that a lottery contains the three elements of prize, chance, and consideration. However, a contest may contain only one or two of these elements. The FCC expects licensees to avoid contests that are deceptive or misleading. To avoid deception, stations are expected to disclose the material terms of contests.

As noted in EMG 10.1.1.5, FCC regulations require full disclosure of licensee-conducted contests. Misleading contests, however, represent another problem. The concern here is that the station might misrepresent the terms of the contest or overstate the amount that can be won. In this regard, the Commission has imposed sanctions against stations for changing the terms of a contest once it had begun. For example, a Seattle station ran a contest and said listeners could enter as often as they wished. One listener who wanted to be certain about the entry rule consulted station employees and was told she could submit duplicate entries. The listener submitted more than 800 entries. When the station tried to change the rules to prohibit duplicate entries, the listener complained to the FCC. The Commission said the station violated FCC rules by not fully and accurately disclosing the material terms of the contest.[70]

In another situation, the FCC fined a station for failing to conduct a contest as announced. The station promoted a "Missing Key Caper" in which it said the winner would receive $1,000 and the lease of an automobile for a year. The winner of the contest received the money, but complained to the FCC when he failed to receive the car. The station said it had an agreement with an auto dealership that promised to provide the car to promote its business. When the dealership changed hands, the new owner refused to honor the agreement and the station said it was not obligated to provide the car. The FCC disagreed and said the station was obligated to conduct the contest as announced.[71]

---

[68] 1993 U.S. LEXIS 4402, 61 U.S.L.W. 4759, at 4762.
[69] 61 U.S.L.W. 4759, at 4765.
[70] KSEA-FM, 5 F.C.C.R. 7105 (1990).
[71] WRJT-FM, 6 F.C.C.R. 7385 (1991).

Rigged contests, those where the outcome has been predetermined, are prohibited by Section 509 of the Communications Act. Again, the concern is with deception of the public.

13.2.4   Hoaxes

The FCC prohibits the broadcasting of hoaxes that might alarm the public.

The growth of competition among radio stations led to a new programming restriction in 1992, a prohibition against the broadcasting of certain hoaxes. The Commission adopted the rule after several high-profile hoaxes were broadcast between 1989 and 1992. The Commission felt the hoaxes alarmed the public and led to needless diversion of public safety and law enforcement resources.

Several of the hoaxes illustrate the programming that led to the ban. In 1990, KROQ-FM, Pasadena, California, broadcast a morning-drive segment titled "Confess Your Crime." Hosts Kevin Ryder and Gene Baxter took a call from a man claiming to have killed his girlfriend. The caller was actually Doug Roberts, an Arizona disc jockey who was a friend of Ryder and Baxter, and who was later hired by KROQ. Not only did police investigate the alleged crime, but the story was also featured on the NBC television show *Unsolved Mysteries*. Up to that time, the perpetrators of the hoax concealed it, but viewers of the TV show noticed similarities in the voice of the caller and Roberts, who was now working for KROQ.[72] The FCC sent a letter to the station admonishing it for airing the hoax.

Another hoax was broadcast in 1991 by KSHE-FM, St. Louis, Missouri. In this incident, the morning show host broadcast a false nuclear attack warning that included sound effects of a bomb explosion. The deejay said listeners had been calling his show and saying the United States should "nuke Iraq," and he was concerned about how lightly listeners were taking the idea of nuclear war. The FCC fined KSHE $25,000.[73]

In another hoax, WALE-AM, Providence, Rhode Island, broadcast a report that a talk show host had been shot outside the station while on a cigarette break. Police heard the broadcast and rushed emergency crews to the station.[74] The FCC sent the licensee a letter admonishing the station for airing the hoax, despite prompt disciplinary and remedial action.

In response to these and other hoaxes, the FCC adopted a rule that prohibits a broadcaster from "knowingly broadcasting false information concerning either a crime or a catastrophe if it is foreseeable that the broadcast will cause substantial public harm, and broadcast of the information does in fact directly cause such harm."[75] Violators of the broadcast hoax rule can be fined up to $25,000 for each day a station continues the hoax, with a maximum fine of $250,000.

---

[72] KROQ-FM, 6 F.C.C.R. 7262 (1991).
[73] KSHE-FM, 6 F.C.C.R. 2289 (1991).
[74] WALE-FM, 7 F.C.C.R. 2345 (1992).
[75] Amendment of Part 73 Regarding Broadcast of Hoaxes, 7 F.C.C.R. 4106 (1992).

13.2.5 Radio Format Changes

Just as activists pushed for programs to serve children, other groups sought to prevent the change of radio formats that serve specific audiences.

One of the areas where citizen groups focused attention in the 1970s was on the sale of radio stations and the subsequent change of format. The sale of stations often meant a loss of classical or jazz music that occurred when the new owners would change to new formats, thus disappointing existing, loyal listeners, and listener groups were sometimes formed to oppose such changes. However, the FCC was not sympathetic to the calls for regulation of radio formats, leading to a decade-long battle in the courts.

Historically, the FCC maintained that it had no power to intervene in program selections of licensees. Specifically, the FCC was reluctant to regulate *entertainment* formats; stations that had made public-interest programming commitments were still expected to live up to those commitments. Thus, a radio station could change its programming format from country music to rock music without FCC permission. In 1970, during the height of citizen group activity, the first case testing format changes reached the U.S. court of appeals, and the court held that the FCC must hold hearings on format changes if the change threatened the preferences of a segment of the audience.[76]

That case was followed by another in which the Zenith Radio Corporation planned to sell its Chicago station, WEFM. GCC Communications, the buyer of the station, planned to change the format from classical to rock music. A Citizens Committee to Save WEFM asked the FCC to hold a hearing to determine if the change in format was in the public interest (EMG 5.7.2).

The FCC refused to hold hearings on the format change and the case was appealed. The D.C. Circuit Court of Appeals ruled against the FCC and required the Commission to consider whether format changes were in the public interest. The court said the Commission must determine if a format is unique, and if so, how changing it would affect the community.[77]

The FCC responded to the ruling by issuing a policy statement in which it said that format regulation was unnecessary. The Commission said the government should not intervene in programming, and that marketplace forces were the best judge of formats.[78]

A group called the WNCN Listeners Guild challenged the policy statement and the court of appeals again overruled the FCC. The court said the statement violated the Communications Act and said the Commission's use of marketplace forces to create diversity in programming did not adequately reflect the public interest stan-

---

[76] Citizens Comm. to Preserve the Present Programming on WGKA-AM and FM v. FCC, 436 F.2d 270 (1970).

[77] Citizens Comm. to Save WEFM v. FCC, 506 F.2d 246 (1974) (en banc).

[78] Changes in the Entertainment Formats of Broadcast Stations, 60 F.C.C.2d 858 (1976), *reconsideration denied*, 66 F.C.C.2d 78 (1977).

dard.[79] On appeal, the Supreme Court reversed the D.C. Circuit. The high court said the policy statement was consistent with the Communications Act, and that the FCC was not required to review entertainment programming to decide if licensees operate in the public interest.[80] Thus, the FCC was not required to consider proposed format changes when deciding whether to act on a transfer of license.

13.2.6 Drug Lyrics

Around 1970, the FCC began to get complaints about radio stations playing records that involved drug lyrics. Its reaction to the situation was another instance of "raised eyebrow" regulation. The Commission refused to ban records with drug lyrics but ordered stations to be aware of the content of record lyrics.

Concerned that the songs were promoting and glorifying the use of illegal drugs such as marijuana and LSD, the Commission in 1971 issued a public notice in which it told licensees that they were to make reasonable efforts before broadcast to ascertain the meaning of songs containing drug-oriented lyrics.[81] Five weeks later FCC staffers released a list of 22 songs that were identified as having drug-oriented lyrics.

The release of the notice and the list of records caused confusion among licensees, since some stations felt the FCC wanted them to discontinue playing records with drug lyrics completely, and other stations believed the listed songs were clearly banned by the Commission. Since the FCC really intended the list of records to be examples of songs with drug lyrics, the FCC issued a subsequent memorandum to clear the air.[82]

The memorandum repudiated the list of 22 songs and stated that the evaluation of which records to play was "solely for the licensee." But, at the same time, the Commission said a station could jeopardize its license by failing to exercise licensee responsibility regarding the playing of records with drug lyrics. Songs with incidental references to drugs or those that warn against the dangers of drugs would not be problems, but stations were to establish procedures to screen songs that might promote drug usage. The FCC did not say that stations could not play records with drug lyrics, but they were to take steps that would enable them to make reasonable judgments. To help make decisions, the FCC urged that one or more staff members have a reasonably current understanding of slang or "street" references to popular drug terminology.

In *Yale Broadcasting* v. *FCC*,[83] Yale argued that the Commission's drug lyrics policy imposed an unconstitutional burden on the broadcaster's freedom of speech and asked that the policy be thrown out. The U.S. Court of Appeals, District of

[79] WNCN Listeners Guild v. FCC, 610 F.2d 838 (1979).
[80] FCC v. WNCN Listeners Guild, 450 U.S. 582 (1981).
[81] Licensee Responsibility to Review Records Before Their Broadcast, 28 F.C.C.2d 409 (1971).
[82] Memorandum Opinion and Order, 31 F.C.C.2d 377 (1971).
[83] 478 F.2d 594 (1973), *cert. denied*, 414 U.S. 914.

Columbia, upheld the FCC's position on drug lyrics and the Supreme Court refused to hear the case. The court of appeals stated its position as follows:

> Supposedly, a radio licensee is performing a public service—that is the raison d'etre of the license. If the licensee does not have specific knowledge of what it is broadcasting, how can it claim to be operating in the public interest? Far from constituting any threat to freedom of speech of the licensee, we conclude that for the Commission to have been less insistent on licensees discharging their obligations would have verged on an evasion of the Commission's own responsibilities.[84]

13.2.7 News Distortion

Concerns about the rigging, staging, or distorting of news led to concerns about misleading the public. Still, the FCC has been reluctant to take action. The FCC has expressed concern about news staging, and about news distortion by slanting the news or altering events.

The FCC policy on news staging and distortion has developed over the years on a case-by-case basis. The Commission has rarely punished broadcasters for distorting or staging news, but has stated its disdain for the practice. In a 1969 documentary titled "Hunger in America," CBS showed a child it said was suffering from malnutrition, when it was actually suffering from another illness. The Commission stated that "rigging or slanting the news is a most heinous act against the public interest—indeed, there is no act more harmful to the public's ability to handle its affairs.[85] Still, involving the Commission in questions of news accuracy raises First Amendment questions.

The FCC has provided some guidelines. In a case involving the coverage of demonstrators outside the 1968 Democratic political convention, the FCC observed that news staging involves "a purportedly significant 'event' which did not in fact occur but rather is 'acted out' at the behest of news personnel."[86] Such an event could mislead the public and cause the Commission to intervene.

There are several forms of news distortion. One is where the news is produced and directed by broadcast journalists. This was the case in 1967 when a Chicago television station arranged for a pot party so the station's news staff could film it. In analyzing the event, the FCC stated that some cases of news staging are obvious:

> For example, the licensee's newsmen should not, upon arriving late at a riot, ask one of the rioters to throw another brick through a store window for its cameras. . . . If the window is already broken, it is staging a news event—one which did not in fact occur, but is acted out at the request of

---

[84] 478 F.2d at 599 (1973).
[85] Hunger in America, 20 F.C.C.2d 151 (1969).
[86] Democratic Nat'l Convention Television Coverage, 16 F.C.C.2d 657 (1969).

the news personnel; the licensee could fairly present such a film only with the full disclosure of its nature.[87]

In more recent rulings, however, the Commission said it will permit such practices unless they affect the basic accuracy of the events being reported.[87]

News staging also occurs in "pseudoevents" that are in fact staged but are treated as news. Events such as television press conferences, political town meetings, and other media events are planned and carefully orchestrated. This staging is not a major concern of the FCC.[89] The Commission has said that distortion must involve a significant event and has refused to consider "window dressing" concerning the *manner* of news presentation.[90] As long as the essential facts of the news stories are broadcast in an accurate manner, presentational devices are not a factor.

Distortion can also occur through news editing. Routine editing of video- or audiotape to fit a newscast is not intentional distortion. By the same token, planning questions, establishing camera angles, and plotting lighting are not believed to intentionally misrepresent news events.

Deliberate distortion may arise in two contexts. One is when a station instructs the news staff to slant the news. For instance, the FCC refused to renew the licenses of three radio stations when the licensees ordered news personnel at the stations to favor certain political candidates.[91] Distortion may also occur when events are intentionally altered. A California physician complained to the FCC when he was identified in a *60 Minutes* broadcast about insurance fraud. After being given access to videotape outtakes from the program, he complained that CBS had staged an interview in which an employee of a medical clinic admitted engaging in fraud. The FCC said the distortion was not significant, and a court of appeals agreed.[92] In general, the FCC is concerned about the potential for serious deception of the public, but the public is also viewed as having enough knowledge to protect itself from potentially distorting news devices.

13.2.8 Television Violence

The ongoing concern with violent content has led to attempts to restrict such programming by bringing lawsuits in the courts.

Just as attempts are made to protect children in terms of programming aimed at them, attempts have also been made to protect children from violent content in adult-oriented dramatic fare. The FCC has been reluctant to tamper with television violence, so the courts became an alternate source of relief. One lawsuit was brought after a real-life incident was allegedly copied from a made-for-TV movie.

---

[87] WBBM-TV, 18 F.C.C.2d 132–133 (1969).
[87] WPIX, Inc., 68 F.C.C.2d 386 (1978). *See also* Oscar B. White, 87 F.C.C.2d 954 (1981).
[89] Hon. Harley O. Staggers, 25 Rad. Reg. 2d (P&F) 413 (1972).
[90] 18 F.C.C.2d 132.
[91] Star Stations of Ind., 51 F.C.C.2d 95 (1975).
[92] Galloway v. FCC, 778 F.2d 16 (1985).

The incident occurred in 1974 after NBC broadcast a drama called "Born Innocent." The story included scenes in which inmates of a detention facility for juvenile offenders raped a young woman with a plunger. Several days later, a nine-year-old was attacked in a similar manner by four older children using a soft drink bottle.

The parents of the girl sued NBC for negligence in showing the attack in the movie. They maintained that the rape scene caused the assailants to imitate the act and asked for $11 million in damages. The lawsuit posed a major threat to broadcasters, since it raised the possibility that they could be held liable for behavior imitating scenes from television.

NBC successfully argued at the trial level that the case should not hinge on negligence because television dramatic material is protected by the First Amendment. This forced the opposing counsel to prove that NBC had waived its First Amendment rights by intending that violence follow its presentation of the drama.[93]

A second case concerned the generalized effects of television violence. The 1977 case involved the trial of a 16-year-old Florida boy, Ronnie Zamora, who was charged with killing an elderly woman. Zamora's defense counsel brought lawsuits against the three major networks for a total of $25 million dollars. He argued that Zamora had watched so much TV violence that he was "subliminally intoxicated" by the murders he had seen depicted on television. The trial judge rejected the claims and Zamora was found guilty of murder.[94]

From a programming and creative viewpoint, producers and programmers have always argued that the First Amendment protects their creative activity, even though violent content seems to be used to attract an audience. That position conflicts with the belief of certain members of Congress and social scientists that violent content can be linked to violent behavior, particularly in some children.

13.3   CHILDREN'S PROGRAMMING

Concern has been expressed about programs and advertisements aimed at children. The FCC has generally given the licensee latitude to deal with such problems but has instituted limits on commercials in cable and television programs.

As noted in our discussion of indecent programming, the presence of children in the broadcast audience has led to concerns about programming practices that impact children. In terms of programs aimed specifically at children, the concerns are about both program content and advertising. The FCC response to these concerns has generally been to defer to licensee discretion when programming to children. As a result, citizen groups have brought a number of actions challenging the nature of children's programming.

---

[93] Olivia N. v. NBC, 126 Cal. App. 3d 488, 178 Cal. Rptr. (Cal. Ct. App. 1st Dist., 1981).
[94] Zamora v. CBS, 480 F. Supp. 199 (1979).

13.3.1 Commercial Limits

A major concern has been the number of commercials aired during children's programs. Broadcasters and advertisers have generally supported more commercial minutes per hour than groups concerned with children's programming.

When the FCC deregulated TV, it did away with commercial time limits for television advertising but let the guidelines for children's programming stand. These guidelines limited commercials in children's programming to 9½ minutes of commercial time per hour on weekends, and 12 minutes per hour on weekdays.[95] The deregulation was extended to children's programming when the FCC subsequently issued a statement eliminating all commercial time limits, including those for children's TV programming.[96]

Action for Children's Television challenged the elimination of the time limits, arguing that the FCC had not adequately justified the elimination. The Court of Appeals for the District of Columbia sent the decision back to the Commission for failing to justify the deletion.[97]

At the same time, the National Association of Better Broadcasting (NABB) appealed an FCC ruling that the producers of program-length commercials need not be identified.[98] The citizen group argued that Los Angeles television station KCOP did not tell the audience that *He Man and Masters of the Universe* was a sponsored program. The program was aired on the basis of barter syndication, a practice by which the Mattel Toy Company, manufacturer of the toy line on which the program was based, and Group W Productions, who produced the program, made the program available to the TV station in exchange for two minutes of advertising time during the station's children's programming. NABB argued that Mattel and Group W should be identified under Section 317 of the Communications Act, which requires broadcasters to identify anyone who pays for a commercial or a program with services, money, or something else of value (EMG 10.1.1.4). NABB said the producers of *He Man* should be identified, since the companies gave something of value—the program.

The FCC ruled that KCOP did not have to announce that Mattel and Group W had provided the station with the cartoon. The Commission said children were adequately protected from deceptive messages both by the sponsorship identification requirements in Section 317 of the Communications Act and the 1974 Children's Program Policy Statement, which required distinctions between programming content and commercial material.

The court of appeals disagreed. It said that the prevalence of barter in children's programming required the FCC to create a policy to determine when swap-

[95] Children's Television Report and Policy Statement, 50 F.C.C.2d 1 (1974), *reconsideration denied*, 55 F.C.C.2d 691 (1975).
[96] Revision of Programming and Commercialization Policies, 98 F.C.C.2d 1076 (1984), *reconsideration denied*, 100 F.C.C.2d 358 (1986).
[97] Action for Children's Television, 821 F.2d 741 (1978).
[98] *See* Action for Children's Television, 58 Rad. Reg. 2d (P&F) 61; and Children's Programming (Profit Sharing Arrangements), 58 Rad. Reg. 2d (P&F) 90.

ping a program for advertising time did not amount to sponsorship of the program that required identification.[99]

In 1988, Congress passed legislation ordering the FCC to set standards for advertising aimed at children, but the president vetoed it. Two years later, Congress passed the Children's Television Act of 1990, which included limitations on advertising aimed at children[100] (EMG 10.1.2.2). This time the legislation was allowed to become law. The law limits advertising aimed at children to 12 minutes per hour on weekdays and 10½ minutes per hour on weekends. The commercial limits apply to cable operators as well as television broadcasters, and pertain to programs "originally produced and broadcast primarily for an audience of children 12 years old and under."[101] Thus programs aimed at teenage audiences, and those originally produced for a general audience that are significantly viewed by children, are excluded from the commercial limits. Since the law went into effect, the FCC has concluded that several stations violated the rules.

While not specifically addressing commercial limits, the FCC has prohibited "host selling," where program hosts, characters, or personalities endorse products. It has ordered a clear separation between programming and advertising on children's programming to blunt the growth of "program length commercials."[102]

13.3.2   Programming Requirements

Advocates of children's programming argue that broadcasters air programs to entertain but do little to educate or inform. FCC efforts to increase informational programs have been weak.

In a 1974 Children's Television Report and Policy Statement, the FCC urged licensees to increase programming that would educate as well as entertain children. Further, the FCC said children's programming would now be evaluated at license renewal.[103] Subsequent examinations of program practices by the FCC revealed that the report did not increase the amount of educational or informational children's TV programming. In 1979 the Commission initiated a rule-making procedure to develop options for children's programming.

The Commission said that it could not require mandatory quotas for children's programs because quotas would infringe on constitutionally protected licensee discretion. However, the Commission did state that licensees were obligated, at license renewal, to show attention to the needs of children in the audience, but indicated that licensees could cite alternative sources of programming available to children, such as public broadcasting and cable. As noted in Chapter 10, the FCC

---

[99] National Ass'n for Better Broadcasting v. FCC, 830 F.2d 270 (1987).

[100] Pub. L. No. 101-473; 104 Stat. 997 (October 18, 1990); Policies and Rules Concerning Children's Television Programming, 5 F.C.C.R. 7199 (1990).

[101] 5 F.C.C.R. 7199.

[102] *Id.* at 7201.

[103] Children's Television Report and Policy Statement, 50 F.C.C.2d 1; *aff'd on reconsideration,* 55 F.C.C.2d 691 (1975).

policy was challenged in the courts before Congress finally settled the issue. The Children's Television Act of 1990 requires licensees to carry programs for children but gives them considerable discretion in doing so (EMG 10.1.2.2).

13.3.3 Program Content

In addition to the concern about whether children's programs are actually broadcast, viewers have regularly raised questions about the content of children's programs, especially concerns about violence in programs. The FCC has been asked to restrict violence in children's programming but has not done so.

In a 1975 report, the FCC said that industry self-regulation was preferable to rigid government standards when evaluating sexual or violence-oriented program material. The Commission argued that to regulate content would raise constitutional questions about intrusion into program content and would require highly subjective judgments.[104]

In an effort to establish some standards, the chair of the FCC brought together the heads of the networks and the National Association of Broadcasters, the voluntary industry organization that established codes and standards for broadcasters. The outgrowth of this interaction was a 1975 amendment to the NAB Television Code that established the "family viewing hour." Under the concept, programs of a violent or sexually oriented nature were banned before 9 P.M. (8 P.M. Central). In addition, the policy recommended the use of viewer advisories when an occasional unsuitable program was aired during the family viewing hour, and urged broadcasters to notify the public in advance of programs that would have unsuitable content.

The "family viewing policy" is an interesting example of the "raised eyebrow" approach to regulation. The FCC expressed concern with unsuitable content, but stimulated self-regulation as a solution. Nevertheless, the policy was challenged in *Writers Guild of America* v. *FCC*[105] as being illegal government practice. The issues were never formally resolved, but the family viewing hour was abandoned and is no longer enforced.

13.4 CABLE TELEVISION CONTENT RESTRICTION

Regulation of cable content developed when broadcasters sought protection against the cable practice of importing into local markets the same programs stations were airing, and to which stations had purchased exclusive broadcast rights.

In 1965 the FCC imposed nonduplication rules on cable systems to prohibit them from carrying distant station programs that duplicated local programming.[106]

---

[104] Report on the Broadcast of Violent, Indecent, and Obscene Material, 51 F.C.C.2d 418 (1975).
[105] 609 F.2d 355 (1979), *cert. denied*, 449 U.S. 824 (1980).
[106] First Report and Order in Docket Nos. 14,895 and 15,233, 38 F.C.C. 683 (1965).

The rules prohibited cable systems from duplicating local programming during a 15-day period before and after local broadcast. The rules were instituted to deal with what was believed to be a problem of "unfair and unequal competition" between broadcast stations and cable systems. These rules provided nonduplication protection for both network and syndicated programs. The original 1965 rules covered only microwave cable systems, but in 1966 the FCC expanded the rules to all cable systems. [107]

The 1966 ruling required all cable systems to notify the Commission before carrying any distant signal. For some time the Commission attempted to review each instance where a distant signal was imported into one of the top 100 local television markets, with a goal of retaining "a healthy maintenance of television broadcast service in the area." [108] However, the system was cumbersome, and in 1972 the FCC developed a new policy that reduced the nonduplication protection. Henceforth, cable systems were required to refrain only from simultaneous duplication. [109] Thus, the FCC was engaged in a policy that on the one hand protected local television stations and television program sources while on the other hand permitted the growth of cable, which often duplicated the programs shown on local stations.

13.4.1   Network Exclusivity

> The network nonduplication rules are designed to prevent systems from violating the exclusive rights television stations have to show network programs in their markets. The network nonduplication rules prohibit a cable system from carrying the network programming of a distant TV broadcast affiliate if a local affiliate carries that same programming.

If a television station is affiliated with CBS, the station does not want cable to bring in the signal of another CBS affiliate from another city and make it available to its subscribers. To do so dilutes the station's share of audience for CBS programs, and more importantly, defeats exclusivity agreements between CBS and its affiliates. Thus, the network exclusivity rules prohibit cable systems from duplicating the network's programs on a local station.

The nonduplication rules protect TV stations in two levels. In the 100 largest (by population) television markets, stations are protected from duplicated cable programming from systems located within a 35-mile radius of the station that carry the station and have 1,000 or more subscribers. In smaller (100-plus) markets the rule is the same but the protection covers a 55-mile radius.

The nonduplication rules protect local affiliates only from "distant signals" outside the 35- or 55-mile zones, but the rule offers total protection from duplication inside the zones. Prior to 1990, nonduplication applied only to programs dupli-

---

[107] Second Report and Order in Docket Nos. 14,895, 15,233, and 15,971, 2 F.C.C.2d 725 (1966), *aff'd,* Black Hills Video Corp. v. FCC, 399 F.2d (1968).

[108] 2 F.C.C.2d 725, at 804.

[109] Cable Television Report and Order, 36 F.C.C.2d 143 (1972).

cated at the same time they were carried on local stations. In other words, a cable system importing *Roseanne* via a distant signal could not show it at the same time the local affiliate carried it. That rule remains in effect, and as of 1990, the FCC has extended nonduplication protection to programs offered by an affiliate at any time.[110] Thus, a cable system cannot duplicate a local station's program by moving it to another time slot. To avoid duplicating a local program, cable systems can carry a substitute,[111] "black out" the imported signal, or carry the local station's program on both the assigned channel and that of the "distant" signal.

13.4.2 Syndication Exclusivity

A syndicated television program is one distributed to television stations without using a television network. The syndex rules allow a local TV broadcast station to prohibit a cable system from carrying the syndicated programming of a distant TV broadcast station if the local station carries that same programming.

A syndicated television program is one distributed to television stations without using a television network. Reruns of *Cheers* or episodes of *Jeopardy!* that appear on local TV stations are examples of syndicated programs. The syndicated exclusivity rule, or "syndex" as it is often called, permits the distributor of a syndicated program to negotiate with a local television station to provide the station with exclusive rights to show the program in its market. Once a station obtains exclusive rights to a syndicated program, the syndex rules allow the station to forbid any cable system to import the program into the local market from a distant station. The rules defining distant signals, discussed above, also apply to syndex.

The syndex rules have been impacted by decisions from the courts and from Congress. As we will see in Chapter 15 (EMG 15.3.11), the Supreme Court has ruled that cable systems do not violate copyright law, thus enabling them to pick up signals aired by TV stations and retransmit them to other locations.[112] However, in 1976, Congress, as part of the Copyright Revision Act, established a compulsory copyright licensing system requiring cable systems to pay a set fee for importing distant TV signals into local TV markets. As a result, the FCC in 1980 decided the syndicated exclusivity rules were no longer needed.[113]

Broadcasters petitioned the FCC to reinstate syndex, but the FCC refused to overturn its decision.[114] However, in 1987 the Commission bowed to pressure and instituted a review of the 1980 decision to eliminate syndex. In 1988 it reestablished the syndicated exclusivity rules. The Commission based its reversal on the enormous audience and revenue growth that cable had experienced since 1980.

---

[110] Amendment of Parts 73 and 76 of the Commission's Rules Relating to Program Exclusivity in the Cable and Broadcast Industries, 3 F.C.C.R. 5299 (1988); *on reh'g*, 4 F.C.C.R. 1711 (1989).

[111] § 47 C.F.R., 76.67(d).

[112] *See* Fortnightly Corp. v. United Artists, 392 U.S. 390 (1968), and Teleprompter Corp. v. CBS, 415 U.S. 394 (1974).

[113] CATV Syndicated Program Exclusivity Rules, 79 F.C.C.2d 663 (1980).

[114] Syndicated Program Exclusivity and Sports Telecasts, 56 Rad. Reg. 2d (P&F) 625 (1984).

The FCC believed that the lack of syndicated exclusivity was harming television stations and might also affect the supply of syndicated programs.[115]

In 1989 the court of appeals upheld the syndex rules in *United Video* v. *FCC.*[116] The court agreed with the Commission that duplication of programming makes the programs less valuable, and noted that exclusivity is a key to programming success for both broadcast and cable TV.[117] As a result, the court concluded that the Commission's action was neither arbitrary nor capricious.

Congress also included a provision in the Satellite Home Viewer Act that ordered the FCC to add the syndicated exclusivity rules to satellite carriers where possible. However, the FCC concluded that it was not economically or technically feasible to extend the syndex rules to satellite carriers. The Commission said the small number of satellite subscribers would prohibit recovery of the developmental costs of implementing syndicated exclusivity and indicated that decoders used in satellite reception would not selectively black out programs in over 200 markets.[118]

There is an exception to syndicated exclusivity called *significant viewing*. It is often evident in small communities where several stations on a cable system will run the same syndicated program. This is permitted because of significantly viewed signals that, although technically distant signals, are nonetheless legally carried by local cable systems. Since each of those three stations may be in a different market, each has *market exclusivity* to that program, and each may carry it.

13.4.3 Sports Blackout

The FCC has also imposed nonduplication rules on sports broadcasts. A TV station's live broadcast of a sporting event may not be carried simultaneously by cable systems in the station's market unless all tickets to the event have been sold.

The FCC has also imposed nonduplication rules on sports broadcasts. The rules stem from a fear that local sporting events may not be televised if fans stay home to watch them on television. The sports blackout rules prohibit cable systems from carrying the broadcast of a live sporting event that is taking place in the community to which a station is licensed if all of the tickets have not been sold.[119] The rules apply only to cable systems with more than 1,000 subscribers.

DISCUSSION QUESTIONS

1. What are the shortcomings of the FCC's policy on children's programming?
2. Can an acceptable definition of a "child" in terms of age be adopted when considering children's programming?

---

[115] 3 F.C.C.R. 5288.
[116] 890 F.2d 1173 (1989).
[117] *Id.* at 1179.
[118] Syndicated Exclusivity Requirements for Satellite Carriers, 68 Rad. Reg. 2d (P&F) 1172 (1991).
[119] 47 C.F.R. § 76.67.

3. A critic of the FCC's rule against airing hoaxes said that the rule was not necessary since 99.9 percent of radio stations weren't likely to violate the rule. At what point should the FCC enact a rule that regulates content?

4. If a radio station shock jock acquires substantial audience ratings, are the ratings an indication of marketplace acceptance of the content that should outweigh program review by the FCC?

5. Distinguish between payola and plugola.

6. Discuss the problems of having a safe harbor for indecent content that begins at 10 P.M.

7. Should a safe harbor for indecent material exclude morning drive time? Why or why not?

8. How many complaints about an allegedly indecent programming item should be required before the FCC begins its process to determine if the material violates FCC rules? Should multiple complaints, for example, from pressure groups, be counted as separate complaints?

9. To what extent do children have rights in choosing programs they want to hear or view?

10. Even though the FCC evaluates allegedly indecent content after the fact, the Commission nevertheless makes decisions about the appropriateness of program content. How is this action justified?

11. In *FCC* v. *Pacifica Foundation*, the majority opinion maintained that the First Amendment protection of broadcasting could be limited because broadcasting is uniquely accessible to children. Does limiting the presentation of indecent material on radio infringe on the First Amendment interests of adults to hear the same material, or do adults have other alternatives that excuse the limitation?

12. Is a popular song simply entertainment, or do such songs serve a purpose/function in society? If so, what purpose/function(s) do songs serve?

13. Do you believe that indecency must constitute actual use of a word that describes a sexual or excretory activity, or is innuendo sufficient to be considered indecency?

SUGGESTED READINGS

Emord, J. W. "The First Amendment Invalidity of FCC Content Regulations." *Notre Dame Journal of Law, Ethics & Public Policy* 6 (1992): 93.

Eysenck, H. J. *Sex, Violence, & the Media.* New York: Harper, 1978.

Lipschultz, Jeremy Harris. "Conceptual Problems of Broadcast Indecency Policy and Application." *Communication & the Law* 14 (June 1992): 3.

National Association of Broadcasters. *Lotteries & Contests: A Broadcasters Handbook.* 3rd ed. Washington, DC: NAB, 1990.

Palumbo, Michael J. "Has the Marketplace Failed the Children: The Children's Television Act of 1990." *Seton Hall Legislative Journal* 15 (1991): 345.

"Regulation of Indecent Radio Broadcasts: George Carlin Revisited—What Does the Future Hold for the Seven 'Dirty' Words?" *Tulane Law Review* 65 (Nov. 1990): 131.

Reiss, G. A. "Indecent Speech on the Air, the FCC and the First Amendment: An Update," *Columbia University Journal of Law and Arts* 15 (spring 1991): 435.

Smith, F. Leslie. "The Charlie Walker Case." *Journal of Broadcasting* 23 (spring 1979): 137.

Chapter

14

NETWORKS

Ever since the days of the Great Depression, the original "War of the Worlds" broadcast, and FDR's fireside chats, the networks have been a powerful force in the electronic media. First in radio, then in television, the networks have dominated prime time programming and advertising sales and revenues. In fact, network influence eventually became so overbearing that the FCC promulgated rules designed to limit network control over local radio and television stations and over the production and distribution of television programming. Even the Justice Department became involved, targeting the networks for antitrust action. This chapter will offer a brief discussion of the major networks, then summarize regulatory policies and court decisions affecting networks and their relationships with affiliated stations.

14.1 DEFINITION OF A NETWORK

A network is a program distributor that sends programs to interconnected outlets simultaneously.

Before we can discuss network regulations, we need to clarify precisely what we mean when we use the term *network*. All radio, television, and cable networks share certain characteristics. Each has varying numbers of interconnected outlets or affiliates that receive and typically carry the same programming simultaneously, either by wire connections or satellite. The term *network* is used in this chapter to refer to the organizations that feed programs to outlets or affiliates—ABC, PBS, CNN, or USA, for example—not the affiliated stations or cable outlets that carry the programs. The American Broadcasting Company feeds programming to local television stations across the country such as WBRC, channel 6, ABC's affiliate in Birmingham, Alabama. ESPN, a cable network, feeds its programs to cable systems nation-wide. Most of our discussions and nearly all the FCC's policies affecting networks apply only to the commercial television networks. In 1991, the FCC defined a "television network" as:

> [A]ny person, entity, or corporation providing on a regular basis more than fifteen (15) hours of prime time programming per week (exclusive of live coverage of bona fide news events of national importance) to inter-connected affiliates that reach, in aggregate, at least seventy-five (75) per-cent of television households nationwide; . . .[1]

The definition is intended to include whoever controls or owns the network. The FCC excluded from the definition all public or noncommercial and non-English-speaking networks as well as networks involved in the direct sale of products and services. Technically these are networks, but they are exempted from most of the restrictions placed on ABC, CBS, NBC, and to a much lesser extent FBC (Fox Broadcasting Company). The reason for the exemption is that only the three largest commercial television networks listed above have been perceived as exercising excessive influence over affiliates and program production and distribution.

It is important to keep in mind that since the networks are not licensed, the FCC has less direct authority over network programming than it does over local stations. Early regulations affecting network policies actually placed restrictions on local affiliates. You may wonder, therefore, how the Commission can adequately enforce restrictions placed on the networks. Regulatory leverage can be found in two places. First, in addition to affiliates, the networks each have stations that they actually *own and operate*. These stations are commonly referred to as *O & O's* (meaning owned and operated by the network). Most O & O's are highly profitable VHF stations in top-10 markets. The FCC has been allowed to condition license renewal of O & O's on whether the networks accept and follow whatever constraints are placed upon them. So, if the network fails to abide by FCC rules the O & O's can be fined or even lose their operating licenses.

The FCC also has leverage over the networks through their affiliated stations. Local television stations across the country, like WBRC, which carry ABC's programming but are not owned and operated by the network, must adhere to FCC policies. If ABC should choose to defiantly violate FCC polices, WBRC could be fined or even lose its license. It is unlikely, of course, but a defiant network could find itself with no stations on which to air its programs.

The Commission can also regulate networks by placing restrictions *directly* on affiliates. The prime-time access rule (EMG 14.3.3.3), for example, restricts the amount of prime-time programming a network can air by prohibiting affiliates from carrying more than three hours of prime-time network programming each evening. Of course, as we will see later on in discussions of the FCC's fin-syn rules, the Commission can still exert some direct authority over networks.

---

[1] 6 F.C.C.R. 3094 (1991).

As you read about network regulations, keep in mind that the ascent of cable television has resulted in significant declines in programming shares and overall influence of the commercial television networks. As a result, the FCC has rescinded many of the rules designed to limit network power. Still, most FCC network regulations are directed toward the major television networks.

14.2   DEVELOPMENT OF THE NETWORKS

By the early 1930s the networks dominated the broadcast industry. Rapid growth in the cable industry led to a proliferation of cable networks in the 1980s.

Network broadcasting began even before Congress had established the Federal Radio Commission. The first network broadcast occurred when stations WEAF in New York and WNAC in Boston were connected in January 1923 for a saxophone solo originating in New York. Less than a decade later networks would become such a force in the broadcast industry that the FCC would pass rules specifically designed to curb their influence.

14.2.1   First Broadcast Networks

The first network, NBC, began offering programming in 1926 and eventually operated three networks simultaneously. CBS became a legitimate competitor to NBC by 1930, and the Mutual Broadcasting System was formed in 1934. ABC was formed in 1943 after NBC was forced to sell one of its three networks.

In 1923, AT&T ran the first permanent network line. It connected stations WEAF in New York and WMAF in South Dartmouth, Massachusetts. By the end of 1924, 26 stations had joined the AT&T network, which by then stretched from coast to coast. Several years later AT&T sold off its broadcast interests to RCA. Under the leadership of board chairman Owen Young and vice president and broadcast expert David Sarnoff, RCA formed the National Broadcasting Company, which began operation on November 15, 1926. By 1927, NBC was operating three separate networks of stations. The NBC red network was derived mainly from stations previously owned by AT&T. The weaker blue network consisted mainly of former radio group stations.[2] NBC's Pacific network operated on the West Coast until 1928, when lines were completed across the nation.

The organization that eventually became CBS was originally established to provide programming to radio stations without having to rely on music licensed to ASCAP. When Sarnoff and NBC refused their programming service, a new network was formed. After a slow start, CBS gradually became a genuine competitor to NBC

---

[2] It is generally believed that the colors "red" and "blue" as names for the networks came from the red and blue pencils used by NBC engineers to map out the interconnections of stations across the country.

when William S. Paley purchased controlling stock and took over leadership of the network in 1928. By 1933, CBS boasted over 90 affiliates and the two networks combined owned 17 stations, most of which were full-power, unlimited-time operations. In fact, as early as 1931, the networks accounted for about half of all profits in the radio industry.[3] Network dominance of radio eventually led to the chain broadcasting rules, the first FCC rules directly affecting networks. As we will see later, those rules played a direct role in the formation of the third major broadcast network, the American Broadcasting Company. ABC, essentially a spin-off of NBC, suffered through a slow and rocky start in radio and later in television.

The Mutual Broadcasting System was formed in 1934 and eventually worked out affiliation agreements with almost 20 percent of the nation's radio stations. But Mutual was formed as a program-sharing cooperative and never exerted as much influence over its affiliates or the industry as did the other networks. In fact, many Mutual stations *were* affiliates of NBC or CBS, and many were low-power stations in rural markets with smaller audiences.

14.2.2 Public Broadcasting Networks

The FCC has exempted PBS from most regulations affecting the three major television networks.

The Public Broadcasting Service (PBS) was formed in 1969 by the Corporation for Public Broadcasting, which was chartered by Congress in the Public Broadcasting Act of 1967. PBS was created to provide interconnection of public stations for simultaneous airing of programming. The radio counterpart to PBS, National Public Radio (NPR), was formed in 1970 to serve noncommercial educational radio stations. The rules and regulations affecting commercial networks discussed in this chapter have never applied to public broadcast networks.

14.2.3 New Television Networks

A fourth commercial television network, the Fox Broadcasting Company, was formed in 1987. Six years later Warner Brothers announced formation of a fifth network.

Just as cable penetration surged to an all-time high and the number of cable programming services increased dramatically, Australian media tycoon Rupert Murdoch purchased Twentieth Century Fox Film Corporation and Metromedia's six independent television stations and formed the Fox Broadcasting Company. Fox recruited a lineup of independent stations and launched its prime-time programs in 1987. Because of a desire to protect this new source of television programming

---

[3] Christopher Sterling and John Kittross, *Stay Tuned: A Concise History of American Broadcasting*, 2d ed. (Belmont, CA: Wadsworth, 1990) 105–115.

diversity, the FCC has defined Fox as an "emerging" network and exempted it from some regulations affecting the other commercial television networks.

By 1993, Warner Brothers and Paramount had announced plans to form new commercial television networks. Warner Brothers' decision was apparently sparked, in part, by an interest in maintaining an outlet for programs produced by its own production houses once ABC, NBC, and CBS are allowed in the domestic syndication market (EMG 14.3.7.2).[4]

14.2.4 Radio Networks Today

Although radio networks offer a wide variety of news, talk, and music programming, FCC regulations affecting radio networks have been eliminated.

When television was introduced in the 1940s the networks began to move popular prime-time programs from radio to the new visual medium. By the mid-1950s, most radio stations had switched to music formats and the networks' influence over the radio industry had rapidly dissipated. Still, networks continue to provide music, news, and talk programming to commercial and public radio stations across the country. ABC controls six full-service networks and CBS operates two networks and a program syndication unit. NBC's radio networks as well as that of the Mutual Broadcasting System are now owned by Westwood One, which also operates two talk radio networks, Talknet and The Source. Other talk and music format networks distribute their programming via satellite to radio stations around the country. Despite the high number of network services offering a wide variety of programming, radio networks are no longer the target of FCC regulations.

14.2.5 Cable Networks and New Delivery Systems

The rules and regulations affecting the television networks have not been applied to cable, low power television, or state and regional news networks.

Most network development in the past two decades has occurred in the cable industry. As the number of homes connected to cable television increased, so did the number and diversity of cable networks. By the mid-1980s, the number and diversity of cable networks had increased dramatically. Today, networks such as USA, CNN, The Home Shopping Network, ESPN, and MTV are transmitted by cable into millions of homes across the nation.[5] Cable and satellite systems also offer premium or pay networks such as Cinemax, The Disney Channel, and Showtime, pay-per-view networks including Playboy at Night and Viacom's Viewer Choice, and superstations such as WTBS, WGN, and WOR. The emergence of cable networks

---

[4] Joe Flint, "Warner Unveils a Fifth Network," *Broadcasting and Cable*, 30 Aug. 1993, at 14; Steven McClellan, "Paramount Network Adds Five Stations," *Broadcasting & Cable* 7 March 1994 at 14.

[5] For a comprehensive listing of cable networks, *see* Susan Tyler Eastman, *Broadcast/Cable Programming: Strategies and Practices*, 4th ed. (Belmont, CA: Wadsworth, 1993) 245–364.

has prompted some federal legislation (EMG 14.3), but the FCC has not passed cable network regulations similar to those affecting the television networks. Similarly, the FCC has no regulations specifically restricting programming by low-power television or state and regional news networks. In fact, the rapid development of cable and other electronic media delivery systems and programming services has contributed to the elimination of some regulatory constraints on the major television networks (EMG 14.3.7.1).

14.3 GOVERNMENT REGULATION OF BROADCAST NETWORKS

The three major regulations specifically targeting networks are the chain broadcasting rules, the prime-time access rule, and the financial interest and syndication (fin-syn) rules.

Most of the policies affecting networks have been formulated out of concern about (1) network dominance over radio or television program production and distribution, (2) contractual agreements that restricted local affiliates' discretion in scheduling programming and required long-term affiliations with the networks, and (3) a desire to help independent stations gain access to quality programming.

14.3.1 Chain Broadcasting Rules

The chain broadcasting rules were adopted because the FCC believed the radio networks had become too heavy-handed in dealing with local radio affiliates. Today, the chain broadcasting rules, which apply only to television, restrict network-affiliate agreements, prohibit dual network operations and network control of station rates, and prohibit stations from using network sales representatives.

Before we discuss the chain broadcasting rules it is important to point out that "chain broadcasting" is just another way of saying "network broadcasting." A chain of stations is a network of stations sharing common programs. A "group" of stations, on the other hand, operates under common ownership.

The original chain broadcasting rules were adopted in 1941. The FCC's primary goal was to limit the power and influence exerted by the networks over local radio affiliates. As radio programming gravitated to television and affiliate relationships between television stations and networks began to proliferate, the FCC applied most of the chain broadcasting rules to network dealings with the new medium.

The chain broadcasting rules withstood a challenge in 1943 in *NBC* v. *United States*, which is discussed in detail in Chapter 9 (see EMG 9.2.5). The Court not only upheld the right of the FCC to regulate network-affiliate agreements but also issued a powerful endorsement of a broad FCC authority to regulate radio in the public interest.

Interestingly, one of the original network rules actually led to the formation of a new network. The *dual network* rule prohibited any one company from operating two separate networks in the same market. The rule was directed squarely at RCA, which was operating its red and blue networks in many of the nation's largest markets. As a result of the new restriction, RCA sold its blue network in the summer of 1943 to Edward J. Noble, principal owner of the Life Savers Company. In that same year Noble formed the American Broadcasting Company. Ironically, the FCC granted a waiver of the very same rule when ABC began operation of four specialized radio networks in 1967.[6]

Another of the original rules prohibited networks from owning two stations in one market. Since ownership restrictions are covered in separate FCC regulations (EMG 7.1.3), the chain broadcasting rules no longer address this issue. One other original rule has been abolished. The FCC had placed a maximum limit of two years on network-affiliate contracts. The two-year rule was applied to television in 1945, then repealed altogether in 1989.[7] The Commission concluded that the limit was no longer necessary and possibly counterproductive to the goal of protecting local affiliates and offering developing networks greater access to programming outlets. The decision was also based on the FCC's perception of a significant potential public benefit in allowing networks and affiliates to determine their own appropriate term of affiliation. By 1977, the FCC had eliminated all the chain broadcasting rules as they applied to radio.[8]

In their current form, the chain broadcasting rules provide that no license shall be granted to any television station that engages in any of the following seven practices:

1. *Exclusive Affiliate Agreements:* Licensees are not permitted to enter into any agreements, express or implied, with any network under which the station is discouraged or prevented from acquiring programs from any other national or regional network.[9]
2. *Territorial Exclusivity Agreements:* Licensees are also prohibited from entering into network agreements that prevent or hinder any other station in the same or another community from airing programs offered by the network that are not broadcast by the affiliated station. An affiliate may contract for rights to first airing of network offerings, but may not prevent another station from carrying programs it has refused.[10]
3. *Option Time Agreements:* Licensees are not allowed to enter into agreements that allow the networks to exercise "options" over when particular programs are aired. This means stations control their own programming schedules, not the networks. Stations cannot be coerced

---

[6] 11 F.C.C.2d 163 (1967).
[7] 4 F.C.C.R. 2755 (1989).
[8] 63 F.C.C. 2d 674 (1977).
[9] 47 C.F.R. § 73.658(a).
[10] 47 C.F.R. § 73.658(b).

into clearing airtime whenever the network wants to use a particular time slot.[11]

4. *Rejection Agreements:* Licensees are prohibited from entering into agreements that prevent or hinder the stations from (a) refusing any network program that the station reasonably believes is unsatisfactory, unsuitable, or contrary to the public interest, or (b) preempting a network program and replacing it with a program of greater local or national importance.[12]

5. *Dual Network Operations:* The same rule that forced RCA to sell its blue network is still in effect today. Licensees are not permitted to affiliate with any network organization that maintains more than one network of stations. This rule does not apply if the networks are not operated simultaneously or if there is no substantial overlap in the areas served by the stations composing the network.[13]

6. *Network Rate Controls:* No licensee is allowed to enter into any kind of agreement that prevents or hinders the station from fixing or altering its rates for the sale of nonnetwork broadcast time.[14]

7. *Network Agency Representation:* Stations are not permitted to use networks or any organizations under the direct or indirect control of networks as representatives for the sale of nonnetwork broadcast time if the station has any kind of affiliation with that network. The rule does not apply to stations licensed to networks or subsidiaries of networks.[15]

14.3.2   Rules Protecting Independent Stations

FCC rules give independent television stations first choice of network programs not broadcast in a market by a regular affiliate.

These rules apply when (1) the market has two stations that are regular affiliates of a major network, (2) the market also has one or more VHF or UHF stations that are not affiliates of a major network, and (3) the technical facilities of the nonaffiliated station are reasonably comparable to those of the regular affiliates. When these conditions exist, network affiliates cannot broadcast certain types of programs from an unaffiliated network until the independent stations in the market have been offered and have rejected the programs. The types of programs include:

1. any evening program, until the independent station has either accepted 15 hours per week of such programs or accepted a lesser amount and indicated that it wants no more;

---

[11] 47 C.F.R. § 73.658(d).
[12] 47 C.F.R. § 73.658(e).
[13] 47 C.F.R. § 73.658(g).
[14] 47 C.F.R. § 73.658(i).
[15] 73 C.F.R. § 73.658(i).

2. any sports programming aired on the networks between 12 noon and 7 P.M. on Saturdays, Sundays, and holidays;
3. any program broadcast after 11 P.M. local time (10 P.M. in the central time zone) that is a continuation of a program started earlier and carried by the independent station;
4. any program aired after 7 P.M. (6 P.M. central) that is a continuation of a sports program begun earlier on the independent station;
5. *any* program presented in the same week by the independent station.

Suppose, for example, a market consists of station A, an ABC affiliate, station B, a CBS affiliate, and station C, an independent. Suppose further that Station A decided to refuse ABC's news program *20/20* and broadcast a local *Bowling for Dollars* program every Friday evening instead. Station B, a CBS affiliate, could not contract for and broadcast *20/20* until after Station C, the independent, had first choice at accepting or rejecting the program. The restriction would not apply if the independent had already accepted 15 hours of such programs or indicated that it wanted no more.

The FCC also prohibits network affiliates from carrying evening programming, or weekend or holiday sports programming from any other network that has an affiliate in the market until the programming has been offered to and rejected by the independent stations.[16]

14.3.3   Prime-Time Access Rule

The prime-time access rule, in its various forms, has limited the amount of network programming local affiliates may carry.

By the 1960s, television had completely supplanted radio as the dominant electronic mass medium. The networks, just as they had with radio 30 years earlier, quickly gained control of television programming. The major networks' programs dominated prime-time schedules, and "off network" series, or network programs once broadcast in prime time, were carried by affiliates and independents in time slots throughout the day.

14.3.3.1   *Prime-Time Access Rule I (PTAR I)*

The first prime-time access rule created one hour of access time by prohibiting local affiliates from carrying network programming for more than three hours during prime time.

By 1965, a concerned FCC had issued a notice of proposed rule making that would set limits on network programming during prime-time viewing hours. Four years later, an influential study and report by the Arthur D. Little Corporation sug-

---

[16] 47 C.F.R. § 73.658(2)(3)(4).

gested a need to increase competitive sources of programming. Because of the dominance of the networks, high-cost prime-time syndicated programming had virtually disappeared, and nonnetwork programming offered by stations increasingly consisted of programs that had once run on the networks.

One year after the Little Report, in 1970, the Commission instituted the first *prime-time access rule* (PTAR I). It is sometimes suggested that the primary justification for PTAR I was to promote more local, as opposed to network, programming. If this was the FCC's primary objective, it was not articulated until the rules were revised several years later. In handing down PTAR I the Commission announced three major objectives: (1) curtailing stations' dependence on networks for programming, (2) encouraging new sources of production and distribution, and (3) increasing diversity of programming sources. During the 1960s almost every key prime-time program was network produced, and the number of first-run syndicated programs had decreased in other time periods as well. The FCC argued that by increasing the motivation for producing syndicated programming, the overall supply of programs would increase. It was believed that this would result in greater programming diversity and provide greater programming flexibility for independent and UHF stations. Only when the rules were revised in 1975 did the Commission suggest that the cleared access times should be used for programming to meet local needs.[17]

The restrictions PTAR I placed on network affiliates were simple and straightforward. No station would be allowed to carry network programming for more than three hours per day between 7 and 11 P.M. local time (6 and 10 P.M. in the central time zone). Under the new rule most stations would reduce network programming by one hour each evening. The time no longer used by the network was referred to as *access time*. The prohibition included new programs and programs in syndication that were previously aired on a network (off-network programs). The rule applied only to stations in the top 50 markets where there were three or more commercial television stations.

PTAR I included several exemptions. Stations carrying network coverage of fast-breaking or on-the-spot news events, live sports events, or political broadcasts by legally qualified candidates for public office were allowed to stay with the network until the exempted programming was concluded.[18]

The prime-time access rule was immediately challenged and upheld by an appeals court. The case, *Mt. Mansfield Television* v. *FCC,* also dealt with the financial interest and syndication rules and will be discussed later (EMG 14.3.4.1).[19]

14.3.3.2 *Prime-Time Access Rule II (PTAR II)*

In PTAR II the Commission reduced access time to one-half hour each evening and specified the access time period as 7:30 to 8:00 P.M. (eastern time). Prime-time access was completely eliminated on Sunday.

---

[17] Competition and Responsibility in Network Television Broadcasting, 23 F.C.C.2d 1825 (1970).

[18] 23 F.C.C.2d 382 (1970).

[19] Mt. Mansfield Television v. FCC, 442 F.2d 470 (1970).

The revised version of the rule was passed in 1974,[20] but in *National Association of Independent Television Producers & Distributors* v. *FCC*, the court prohibited the Commission from placing the modifications into effect before September 1975.[21] Independent producers had successfully argued that the FCC had allowed inadequate time for the industry to adapt to the changes. The court had been convinced that programs already in production on the basis of PTAR I would be unfairly jeopardized by the more liberal restrictions of PTAR II.[22] Understandably, with access time cut in half, the demand for independently produced programming would be cut in half. Producers feared the new rule would leave them with large inventories of unmarketable programs.

14.3.3.3   *Prime-Time Access Rule III (PTAR III)*

PTAR III increased access time back to one hour and specified prime time to be 7 to 11 P.M. (eastern time). The rule applies only to the top 50 markets and offers exemptions for public affairs and other types of programs.

The courts' reaction to PTAR II influenced the FCC to modify the rule again in 1975, this time successfully. PTAR III became effective September 8, 1975, and is still in effect today. The restrictions, summarized below, are similar to PTAR I with some additional exemptions:

1. Commercial television stations owned by or affiliated with a national television network in the 50 largest television markets[23] can air no more than three hours of network or off-network programming during prime-time hours.
2. Prime-time hours are designated as 7–11 P.M. in the eastern and pacific time zones, and 6–10 P.M. in the central and mountain time zones.
3. PTAR III exempts, on nights other than Saturday, (a) network and off-network programs designed for children aged 2 to 12, (b) public affairs programming, and (c) documentaries.
4. PTAR III also exempts feature films and special news programs dealing with fast-breaking news events. The exemption for political broadcasts was revised to include broadcasts on behalf of legally qualified candidates for public office as well as those broadcast by candidates themselves. Regular network news broadcasts are exempted up to a half hour if adjacent to a full hour of continuous local news or locally produced public affairs programming.
5. PTAR III also exempts reasonable runovers of live broadcasts of sporting events, not including postgame analyses or summaries. Also exempted are

---

[20] 44 F.C.C.2d 1080 (1974).

[21] National Ass'n of Indep. Television Producers & Distributors v. FCC, 502 F.2d 249 (1974).

[22] 25 F.C.C.2d 318 (1973). *See also* 47 C.F.R. § 73.658(k).

[23] The top 50 markets were determined by using average prime-time audience ratings for all stations in the market according to the Arbitron Television Markets and Rankings Guide. Since 1975, the Commission has used Arbitron survey data to determine the 50 largest markets.

network broadcasts of international sporting events, New Year's Day college football games, or other special network programming when the network devotes an entire evening to the same programming.

In PTAR III the FCC clearly emphasized the importance of airing programming responsive to community needs and interests. The Commission informed stations that they would be expected to use some access time for such programming.[24]

Once again the modifications were challenged in court.[25] The National Association of Independent Television Producers & Distributors argued, in part, that the exemptions for particular types of programs represented an unconstitutional regulation of programming content. The court disagreed, stating that the authority of the FCC to interest itself in the types of programs broadcast by licensees has consistently been upheld by the courts. The court upheld the major changes adopted in PTAR III, concluding that the rules did not constitute an unlawful restraint on free speech. The court also held that the prime-time access rules were not so dismal a failure that they were arbitrary, capricious, or contrary to the public interest. Still, the court, in a decision that in certain parts reads more like a television program review than a court decision, did not paint a very positive picture of the impact of the prime-time access rules:

> The result has been, as could have been expected to some degree, that it is largely the cheaper productions, daytime fare, that have been put into the cleared prime time slots. What was not intended by the Commission was the monotony of the product. A kind of Gresham's law seems to operate in first-run syndication—the cheaper tending to run the dearer out of circulation. The fact is, as the Commission concedes, that the degree of diversity in programming has been disappointing.[26]

Nonnetwork program producers and syndicators may disagree with the court. Without PTAR there would be much less opportunity for programs such as *Wheel of Fortune, Jeopardy!, Inside Edition*, and *Entertainment Tonight*, which are typically aired during access time. The quality of the programs may well be debated, but without the access hour, the 7–8 P.M. time slot (EST) could potentially be saturated with first-run network or off-network programming.

In 1989 the FCC permanently waived the prime-time access rules for the Home Shopping Networks (HSN I and HSN II). The waiver also exempted the parent company, Home Shopping Network, Inc., from a rule prohibiting any company from operating two separate networks. The Commission justified the waiver on the basis that HSN was not involved in the production, acquisition, or distribution of programs to commercial stations to be broadcast during access periods.[27]

---

[24] 50 F.C.C.2d 829 (1975).
[25] National Ass'n of Indep. Television Producers & Distributors v. FCC, 516 F.2d 526 (1975).
[26] *Id.* at 533.
[27] 4 F.C.C.R. 2422 (1989).

FCC commissioners are currently contemplating repeal of the prime-time access rules. The tremendous growth of cable television has altered the perception of the major broadcast networks as being totally dominant and a significant threat to free and open competition in the programming industry.

14.3.4   Financial Interest and Syndication Rules

The financial interest and syndication rules prohibited networks from syndicating or having any financial interests in programs other than first-time exhibition rights on the network. The FCC virtually eliminated the rules in 1993, declaring them ineffective and no longer necessary.

Providing local affiliates with an hour of prime-time access addressed only one dimension of the problem. Networks could still dominate the syndication market because of the sheer quantity of programs to which they owned rights. The *financial interest and syndication* (fin-syn) rules, adopted in 1970, served to complement the prime-time access rules by placing severe restrictions on network involvement in the syndication market.

Fin-syn rules are relatively simplistic. Most importantly, the 1970 fin-syn rules prohibited the major television networks from syndicating programs. They could, of course, purchase exhibition rights to a program to air it during prime time. But in doing so they were not allowed to demand or negotiate financial interest or any kind of rights to syndicate the program *after* its run on the network was completed.

If a program was originally produced by the network (also referred to as produced "in-house") and shown during prime time, the network could *sell* the syndication rights to an independent syndicator, but the network could retain *no financial interest* in profits generated by the program once in syndication. For example, one of the most successful prime time-network programs ever was *M*A*S*H*, originally produced by Twentieth Century Fox. The program made millions for CBS, airing in prime time from 1972 to 1983. In fact, the final episode of *M*A*S*H* was the most-watched program in history. The series has also been highly successful in syndication, but CBS has been allowed no financial involvement in the syndication rights. Those rights are controlled by Twentieth Television Corporation, the syndication arm of Fox.

It is quite common for a successful network prime-time program to be attractive for syndication, especially to independent stations, many of whom are constantly searching for competitive programming. Audiences seem willing to watch episodes of top programs repeatedly. But more importantly, television stations often engage in a practice called *program stripping* in which off-network syndicated programs are scheduled at least five times a week, often over an extended period of time. Generally, only the more successful prime-time series have generated enough episodes to sustain a syndication run of sufficient duration. Former network successes such as *All in the Family, The Cosby Show, Hawaii Five-O,* and *Happy Days* have seen enormous success in syndication. But these programs also illustrate a major concern of the FCC. Even today many non-prime-time syndicated programs are ones originally aired during prime time by the major networks. This serves to fuel arguments over the extent to which the Commission's goal of programming source diversity—a goal of both prime-time access *and* fin-syn rules—was ever achieved.

Of course, like most governmental policies the fin-syn rules contained additional stipulations that will be spelled out shortly. But the rules still had one primary objective—to restrict network control over programming by limiting financial involvement in the syndication business. It was clearly the FCC's intent that the rules would lead to an increase in the number of different program producers and thus, an increase in diversity of programming.

Specifically, the 1970 fin-syn rules prohibited networks from (1) domestic syndication of any program, (2) international syndication of any program other than ones produced by the networks, and (3) acquisition of any right or financial interest in any programming, other than a right to first-run exclusive showing on the network.[28]

14.3.4.1 *Mt. Mansfield Case*

In the 1971 *Mt. Mansfield* case, a U.S. court of appeals upheld the financial interest and syndication and prime-time access rules.

In the *Mt. Mansfield* case the petitioners had asked the court to strike down both sets of rules for two principal reasons. First, it was argued that the prime-time access rules constituted a direct restraint on free speech and violated the First Amendment. The undue restraint, they argued, violated First Amendment rights of three groups:

1. network distributors, since their programming products were banned during access time periods;
2. licensees of local network affiliates, whose freedom of choice of programming was restricted; and
3. the viewer, who was denied a chance to watch the network programming.

The court said that the FCC's intent was to encourage diversity of programming and correct a situation where only three organizations (the major networks) controlled prime-time programming. Therefore, the court ruled that the prime-time access rule acts to *fulfill* rather than violate First Amendment principles.

The petitioners also argued that the FCC had no authority to pass the fin-syn rules because they placed restrictions on networks instead of licensees and were, therefore, outside the jurisdiction and authority of the FCC. The court disagreed, holding that fin-syn and prime-time access rules were within FCC authority so long

---

[28] 23 F.C.C.2d 382 (1970). The rules were adopted after a six-year study on competitive forces in television programming, lengthy proceedings, and a report by the Arthur D. Little Company that detailed network dominance. The prime-time access rule was adopted during the same proceedings.

as they were reasonably related to the FCC's responsibilities to regulate television broadcasting[29] (see Box 14.1).

14.3.4.2   *Viacom* v. *FCC*
In the *Viacom* case the court ruled that the financial interest and syndication rules did not apply to nonbroadcast uses of programs.

The fin-syn rules were clear enough regarding the networks' ability to acquire financial interests in broadcasting or syndicating programs. But what about *non-broadcast* uses of programs? What if a network wanted to purchase rights to programs to be carried over a cable network or distributed by way of videotape or videodiscs?

In June, 1981, the FCC ruled that the fin-syn rules did not bar networks from acquiring such nonbroadcast interests in television programs. CBS had begun production and distribution of videocassettes and was prepared to distribute videodiscs and get involved in cable programming. Accordingly, CBS wanted to acquire nonbroadcast rights to programs produced by public and foreign television stations.

Viacom asked the court to overturn the FCC ruling, arguing that the Commission essentially had amended the fin-syn rules without following proper rule-making procedures. In *Viacom* v. *FCC* the appeals court disagreed, holding that the FCC's ruling was an interpretation, not an amending of the fin-syn rules. Furthermore, the court explained that cable and videodisc technologies were not fully developed when the fin-syn rules were adopted, and there was simply nothing in the rules preventing networks from acquisition of nonbroadcast interests.[30]

14.3.5   Antitrust Action against the Broadcast Networks
The methods used by the three major television networks to contract television programming rights resulted in antitrust action by the U.S. government. The cases were resolved when the networks signed consent agreements restricting dealings with program producers and with each other.

Concern over network programming practices was not limited to the FCC. In 1972, the Department of Justice filed antitrust suits against ABC, CBS, and NBC. Back in the early 1940s the networks tried to argue that the FCC was not authorized to enforce regulations based on antitrust law. The argument lasted only until 1943 when the Supreme Court, in its *NBC* v. *United States* decision, ruled that the Commission can pass and enforce antitrust regulations so long as they serve the public interest.[31]

RCA tried a different approach. A deal had been worked out in the mid-1950s whereby RCA would give $3 million and a Cleveland VHF station to Westinghouse

---

[29] Mt. Mansfield Television v. FCC, 442 F.2d 470 (1971).
[30] Viacom v. FCC, 672 F.2d 1034 (1982).
[31] NBC v. United States, 319 U.S. 190 (1943).

BOX 14.1   Prime-Time Access and the First Amendment

The *Mt. Mansfield* court rejected the petitioners' arguments that the prime-time access rule violated the First Amendment rights of networks, licensees, and viewers. Although it was also rejected, CBS, one of the litigants in the case, presented an interesting analogy in its argument to the court. CBS suggested that the prime-time access rule was analogous to a policy that would prohibit newspapers in the nation's 50 largest cities from devoting more than a certain percentage of space to stories obtained from national sources. In other words, if the government can limit local television affiliates from carrying national network programming for more than three-fourths of their prime-time schedule, why would it not be permissible to prohibit newspapers from publishing more than three-fourths of their stories from national news sources?

The court was not impressed. The analogy, argued the court, failed to consider two important principles:

1. that the airwaves are scarce (the scarcity rationale), or the argument that controls on the broadcast media are justified because the airwaves are limited; and,
2. that there is no unabridgeable First Amendment right of every individual to speak or publish.

The second principle was based on reasoning from the *Red Lion* decision (EMG 11.5.1), which established that the public's First Amendment rights—not the broadcasters' (including the networks and affiliates)—are paramount. The restraints were justified, according to the court, because they were designed to open up the market and create greater diversity of programming to better serve the public interest.*

---

* Mt. Mansfield Television v. FCC, 442 F.2d 470 (1971).

---

in exchange for a Philadelphia television station. There had been allegations that RCA had threatened to deny NBC affiliations to all Westinghouse stations unless the deal was agreed to. When the U.S. Department of Justice stepped in to reverse the deal, RCA argued that the Justice Department had no jurisdiction because the FCC had already approved the sale.

The Court, in *United States* v. *Radio Corporation of America*, held that the FCC's approval was based only on whether the transfer of control was in the public interest. The sale, and other network business, therefore, was still subject to review by the Justice Department to determine whether antitrust laws had been violated.[32]

---

[32] United States v. Radio Corp. of America, 358 U.S. 334 (1959).

The 1972 antitrust suits against the networks charged that the network programming practices that prompted the FCC to pass the fin-syn and prime-time access rules were monopolistic. Specifically, the government accused the three networks of requiring independent producers of television programs to sign away rights to their programs in order to obtain exhibition contracts with the networks.[33] If this was happening, in order for independent producers to get programs televised during prime time they would be forced to give up syndication rights and other financial interests in subsequent off-network broadcasts of the programs. For example, suppose an independent producer named "Bestshows Inc." produced a program entitled *Diane's World*. Bestshows negotiates exhibition rights with ABC and the program becomes a smash hit. Under the old rules, Bestshows could have been forced to sell ABC its syndication rights to *Diane's World* or face never having the program shown at all. As a result, ABC ends up with the prime-time exhibition rights *and* profits from the program's run in syndication.

The Justice Department also accused the networks of excluding from prime-time broadcast any program in which they had no ownership interest, refusing to offer programming time to advertisers, and controlling the price paid for exhibition rights to motion picture films distributed by nonnetwork distributors.

In 1976, NBC settled its antitrust suit out of court by signing a consent agreement with the government. The Justice Department then issued what is called a *consent decree*. A consent decree in an antitrust suit is a negotiated settlement between the government and a business. It allows the business to settle an antitrust suit without having to admit to any actual wrongdoing. Once approved by a judge, a consent decree has the full force of the law.

In this consent agreement NBC agreed to stay out of domestic syndication and stop acquiring financial interests in programs other than first-run rights of exhibition on the network. The agreement also prohibited reciprocal arrangements in which NBC would purchase exhibition rights to a program produced by CBS or ABC on the condition that they purchase similar rights from NBC.[34]

In 1980, ABC and CBS signed similar agreements.[35] The three original consent decrees, in part, paralleled restrictions placed on the networks by the FCC's financial interest and syndication rules.

14.3.6 1983 Tentative Decision

In 1983, with network influence decreasing, the Commission decided to phase out the financial interest and syndication rules. However, after intense lobbying by Hollywood producers and pressure from the White House and Congress, the FCC dropped plans to eliminate the rules.

---

[33] An exhibition contract is one that allows the network to show or "exhibit" its programs through its affiliated stations in exchange for a sum of money paid to the program producers. For example, suppose NBC wanted to obtain exclusive exhibition rights to the syndicated *Montel Williams Show*. NBC would enter into a contract with Viacom, producer of the program, to purchase exhibition rights.

[34] United States v. National Broadcasting Co., 449 F. Supp. 1127 (1978).

[35] United States v. CBS, 45 Fed. Reg. 34,463 (1980); and United States v. ABC, 45 Fed. Reg. 58,441 (1980).

As cable television prospered and the FCC fostered the deregulatory era of the 1980s, sentiment against the fin-syn rules resulted in efforts to have them repealed. In 1983, the FCC issued a statement suggesting that the fin-syn rules were, if anything, impeding instead of enhancing competition in programming. The 1983 statement proposed radical changes in the rules that would have eventually brought about their repeal. The Commission had concluded by 1983 that the networks had lost whatever monopolistic power over programming they once had, and that the fin-syn rules had actually served a negative function. The rules, according to the Commission, were effectively blocking entry of new firms into the production business, since independent producers could not sell syndication rights to their programs to the networks.[36]

Following the 1983 statement, independent program producers in Hollywood and elsewhere lobbied the FCC to reconsider. With Congress and the Reagan administration joining in the effort, the FCC succumbed, and efforts to change the rules were dropped. It was the emergence of the Fox network later in the decade that forced the Commission to once again consider the viability and effectiveness of the fin-syn rules and ultimately adopt changes.

14.3.7   1991 Fin-Syn Rules

In 1991 the Commission relaxed restrictions on the networks by adopting the following new fin-syn regulations.

1. All fin-syn regulations on non-prime-time programming were eliminated.
2. Networks were allowed to acquire financial interest and domestic and international syndication rights in outside (nonnetwork) produced programming. However, these rights had to be negotiated within 30 days *after* a license agreement was reached with the producer to show the program on the network.
3. Networks were allowed to syndicate outside produced programs internationally. All domestic syndication still had to be handled by an independent distributor.
4. Networks were allowed to produce first-run syndicated programs, but syndication still had to be handled through an independent distributor.
5. Networks were allowed to engage in domestic and international syndication of in-house productions, but in-house productions were limited to 40 percent of the network's prime-time schedule.[37]

The changes were seen as a compromise by many in the programming industry. The new rules did offer the new limit on exhibition of in-house productions, but the changes were otherwise more modest than what the networks had wanted. It made little difference because just 19 months later, the 1991 fin-syn rules were remanded to the Commission by a U.S. court of appeals.

---

[36] Tentative Decision and Request for Future Comments, 94 F.C.C.2d 1019 (1983).
[37] Evaluation of the Syndication and Financial Interest Rules, 6 F.C.C.R. 3094 (1991).

14.3.7.1   *Schurz Communications v. FCC*

In 1992, a U.S. court of appeals tossed out the 1991 fin-syn rules. The court gave the Commission 120 days either to provide proper justification for the rules or to write new ones. The court ruled that given changes in the industry, the FCC had failed to justify the fin-syn rules.

The *Schurz* court never questioned the right of the FCC to promulgate rules regulating the networks. What the court objected to was the manner in which the 1991 rules were formulated. Specifically, the court held that the FCC never fully justified the new rules, given changes in the industry since the original rules were adopted and the Commission's own arguments for their repeal in the 1983 tentative decision just a few years earlier.[38] The court, as shown in Box 14.2, also scolded the Commission for ignoring substantive objections raised by numerous parties during the rule-making process.

The court also took it upon itself to summarize key changes that had occurred in the industry since the 1970 rules were established:

1. Networks had lost significant audience shares, primarily as a result of the expansion of cable television.
2. The networks were now buying only about 7 percent of the total video and film programming produced annually, down from 20 percent in 1970.
3. The networks now controlled only about 12 percent of total television advertising revenues.
4. There was now a fourth network, the Fox Broadcasting Company.
5. The number of independent stations had increased significantly since 1970.
6. In part because the fin-syn rules had made program production a riskier enterprise, there were 40 percent fewer producers of prime-time programming than in 1970.

The court also speculated that the 1991 rules would do more harm than good. How, the court asked, could it help a producer to be forbidden to sell programming to a class of buyers (the networks) that may be the highest bidders? And, if diversity of programming was a goal of the rules, the more likely result was that the smallest, weakest, and newest production firms would not be able to bear the high risk of production, especially in a market weakened by removal of the networks. The court was also perplexed with the about-face taken by the FCC since the 1983 statement, which had acknowledged the networks' loss of influence and proposed a phasing out of fin-syn rules.

Interestingly, the court also objected to the FCC's treatment of the Fox network. Under the 1991 rules, Fox, with its own production facilities as well as the

---

[38] Schurz Communications v. FCC, 982 F.2d 1043 (1992).

BOX 14.2   The *Schurz Communications* Decision: A Reprimand for the FCC

In its *Schurz* decision, the court clearly reprimanded the FCC for ignoring arguments presented by interested parties during formulation of the financial interest and syndication rules. The court reminded the Commission that it is not enough that FCC rules be rational:

> [T]he agency must examine the relevant data and articulate a satisfactory explanation for its action including a "rational connection between the facts found and the choice made." . . . The new rules flunk this test. The Commission's articulation of its grounds are not adequately reasoned. Key concepts are left unexplained, key evidence is overlooked, arguments that formerly persuaded the Commission and that time has only strengthened are ignored, contradictions within and among Commission decisions are passed over in silence.*

---

* Schurz Communications v. FCC, 982 F.2d at 1057 (1992).

---

entire library of Twentieth Century Fox, was allowed to supply its affiliates with no more than 14 hours of prime-time programming per week. Otherwise, all fin-syn rules would apply to Fox. The court suggested that this only served to lessen competition and was especially troublesome to the court, since many Fox affiliates were UHF stations that had historically operated at a competitive disadvantage.

Finally, the *Schurz* court admonished the FCC for never defining what it meant by diversity in programming. Diversity could mean *source diversity*, or sources of program production. Or the term could refer to *outlet diversity*, or distribution outlets, namely television stations. A third form of diversity is actual *program diversity*, or the variety and heterogeneity of programs. The FCC, according to the court, never distinguished among the types of diversity or explained the interrelationship among them.

14.3.7.2 *Repeal of the Financial Interest and Syndication Rules*

In April 1993 the FCC abolished most of the restrictions on network acquisition of financial interest and announced a two-year expiration of all syndication rules.[39] Within weeks lawsuits were filed in several federal courts to have the 1993 rules set aside.

---

[39] The financial interest and syndication rules cannot be unilaterally abolished by the FCC. Before the rules could be eliminated, antitrust consent decrees (EMG 14.3.5) signed by the networks must be lifted.

The 1993 rules allow the television networks to acquire financial interests and syndication rights to all *outside produced* network programming.[40] This means the networks can purchase financial interest and syndication rights in and profit from the syndication runs of prime-time programs such as *Roseanne, Murphy Brown,* and *Seinfeld* once they enter the syndication market.

The networks still cannot actually syndicate any programs themselves, at least not in the domestic market. Syndication must be handled by independent syndicators regardless of whether the program was produced independently or by the networks. There are exceptions. Networks can own rights to and syndicate all non-prime-time and all nonentertainment programming. The new rules also remove all financial interest and syndication restrictions on foreign markets for all the networks.

The networks are still prohibited from acquiring financial interest in or being involved in first-run syndicated programming, unless the program is solely an in-house production. Even then, the network can acquire financial interest but cannot be involved in actual syndication of the program.

The 40 percent limit on the amount of in-house programming a network may carry in its prime-time schedule was eliminated. The Commission concluded that the cap was no longer necessary, since the new rules prohibited the networks from syndicating programs domestically. Without the ability to syndicate, the Commission reasoned, the networks would be less motivated to produce and saturate prime-time schedules with their own programs.

The 1993 rules retained the *antiwarehousing rule*. This rule requires a network to release and allow syndication of any program for which it holds syndication rights *four years* after the program's debut on the network or within *six months* of the end of the program's network run, whichever comes first. The rule is designed to prevent networks from stockpiling programs, a practice that could effectively block independent stations from obtaining competitive programming.

Fox Broadcasting Company, which the FCC described as "emerging," is totally exempted from all fin-syn rules regardless of the number of hours of prime-time programming provided. The Commission did not want to suppress development of new networks or any other alternative sources of programming.

The final provision of the new rules calls for all remaining fin-syn restrictions to expire two years after the date on which the antitrust consent decrees signed by the networks over a decade ago (EMG 14.3.5) were lifted. The two-year period is seen as a sunsetting interval. Interested parties will be given an opportunity to present arguments to the Commission six months prior to the expiration date, but the FCC made it clear that the burden of proof will be on those seeking to retain the remaining fin-syn rules. Accordingly, the consent decrees were substantially modified in 1993 to allow the new FCC fin-syn rules to take effect. The modifications removed court restrictions preventing networks from (1) acquiring financial interests in nonnetwork uses of television programs produced by nonnetwork produc-

---

[40] Outside produced programming is programming that is not produced by a network. It includes programs produced by any independent program supplier.

tion houses, (2) engaging in domestic syndication, and (3) conditioning the purchase of network rights to programs on the purchase of other network interests.[41]

14.4   RESTRICTIONS ON CABLE AND SATELLITE NETWORKS

> Under the new cable law, exclusive contracts between cable program suppliers and cable operators are eliminated except in cases where the FCC finds them to be in the public interest.

Satellite and cable network operators have not been the focus of specific FCC policies. Exceptions have included syndicated exclusivity and network nonduplication rules (EMG 13.4.2 and 13.4.1) and waivers granted to two cable networks regarding the prime-time access rules (EMG 14.3.3). But recent antitrust action by the Justice Department and the Cable Television Consumer Protection and Competition Act of 1992 have combined to have a potentially significant impact on cable networks. The new law forbids cable operators from entering into exclusive arrangements with program suppliers. In other words, program producers—including those affiliated with cable operators—will now have to offer programming to DBS, wireless, and other multichannel services on the same terms as those offered to cable operators. It was the refusal of cable programmers to make their shows available to satellite and wireless cable operators that prompted the antitrust action. On June 9, 1993, seven of the largest cable operators signed an agreement to share programming and pay almost $5 million to settle the antitrust action against them.[42]

This could have a considerable impact on satellite and cable programming because a significant amount of cable programming is produced by the companies signing the agreement, most of which are *vertically integrated*. Vertical integration means that the same company produces cable programming and owns cable systems. An excellent example of vertical integration is Viacom International Incorporated (also discussed in EMG 14.3.4.2). Viacom, a large cable system owner, also owns cable programming networks including, for example, Nickelodeon and MTV.[43] It

---

[41] Evaluation of the Syndication and Financial Interest Rules, 8 F.C.C.R. 3282 (1993): Joe Flint, "Networks Win, Hollywood Winces as Fin-syn Barriers Fall," *Broadcasting & Cable* November 22, 1993: 6, 16.

[42] John Lippman, "Cable Pact Gives Upstarts a Shot at $21 Billion TV Pie," *Los Angeles Times*, 10 June 1993, home ed., at D1.

[43] Viacom originated when the prime-time access rules (EMG 14.3.3) put the major broadcast TV networks out of the syndication business. CBS spun off its domestic syndication arm to CBS stockholders, forming the basis for Viacom. In 1987, National Amusements, owner of a large chain of movie theaters, bought out Viacom. Viacom continued to handle program syndication (including *The Cosby Show* and *All in the Family*) but greatly expanded operations to include ownership of cable systems, satellite cable networks, and radio and television stations. Viacom has also produced movies, prime-time television series, and miniseries, and engaged in programming and cable ventures overseas. In 1994 Viacom increased its market influence even more by entering a tentative agreement to purchase all interests of Paramount Communications.

would be of obvious benefit to Viacom to withhold Nickelodeon and MTV from DBS operators and other competitors in a market in order to offer the services exclusively on its cable systems. Under the new cable law and terms of the antitrust agreement, vertically integrated companies such as Viacom *must* offer their program services to competing satellite delivery systems and wireless cable operators. The vertical integration provision of the 1992 cable act was upheld in 1993 by a U.S. district court in *Daniels Cablevision* v. *United States.* Cable operators had argued that the restrictions on the ability of programming services to offer special rates and conditions of delivery would reduce cable systems' incentives to carry them. The court rejected this notion, as well as the argument that without the ability to negotiate exclusive arrangements the cable companies would be unable to create innovative programming packages for consumers.[44] The court ruled that the new restraints were content neutral and served a substantial governmental interest.

Clearly, this could mean a boost for the newer technologies. The new cable law also prohibits cable operators and other multichannel services from being forced to acquire financial interest in programs as a condition of having the programs carried on their systems.[45]

14.5   PROGRAM EXCLUSIVITY RULES

The FCC has a couple of rules designed to protect local over-the-air television stations from competition from cable systems. The rules differ from others described in this chapter in that they place restrictions on cable operators, not on the networks.

The *network nonduplication rules* (also called network exclusivity rules) prohibit cable operators from bringing in a distant signal that duplicates a local station's programming. For example, if a local CBS affiliate carries *60 Minutes,* no cable system serving the station's market may offer the program on any channel (other than that of the local station). The Commission passed the rules to protect local broadcasters from having audiences for their programs split between two channels.

In 1990, the FCC reinstated the *syndicated exclusivity rules.* These rules, discussed in greater detail in Chapter 13, prohibit cable systems from duplicating syndicated programming of over-the-air local stations that have purchased exclusive rights to those programs (EMG 13.4.2).

DISCUSSION QUESTIONS

1. To what extent are the chain broadcasting rules necessary in the 1990s? Do local television affiliates need protection from the networks? In what way? Which rules should be kept and which are no longer necessary?

---

[44] Daniels Cablevision v. United States, 835 F. Supp. 1 (1993).
[45] Cable Television Consumer Protection and Competition Act of 1992, 102 Pub. L. No. 385 (1992).

2. Assess the impact of the prime-time access rules. Assume you are a current FCC commissioner. Would you argue to keep or eliminate PTAR? Have the rules actually led, as the FCC hoped, to greater programming diversity? Do you agree with the court's opinion in the *National Association of Independent Television Producers* case?

3. Should the networks be allowed to purchase financial interest in "all" programming? Why or why not?

4. To what extent should the commercial television networks be allowed in the syndication market? What dangers are there in repealing the syndication rules?

5. Why did the Justice Department file antitrust suits against the networks? Would you advocate lifting the consent decrees? Why or why not?

6. Discuss the impact of the consent decrees signed in 1993 by major cable operators on the marketability of satellite and wireless cable systems.

7. Why might you advocate that special exemption from PTAR and fin-syn rules be given to the Fox network?

8. Discuss the implications of the *Schurz* decision. Why was the court so critical of the FCC? What was the court's reasoning regarding the basic First Amendment issues?

9. How much control should be placed on vertically integrated cable entities? What kinds of controls are appropriate?

10. Discuss the methods by which rules affecting networks are actually enforced.

SUGGESTED READINGS

Bagdikian, Ben H. *The Media Monopoly.* 2d ed. Boston: Beacon, 1987.

Barnouw, Erik. *Tube of Plenty: The Evolution of American Television.* Rev. ed. New York: Oxford UP, 1982.

Friendly, Fred W. *Due to Circumstances Beyond Our Control.* New York: Random, 1967.

Halberstam, David. *The Powers That Be.* New York: Knopf, 1979.

Hayton, Paula Brown. "Just Another Episode in Syndex Regulation." *Entertainment Law Journal* 12 (1992): 251.

Krattenmaker, Thomas G. "Prime Time Access Rule: Six Commandments for Inept Regulation." *Communication-Entertainment Journal* 7 (1984): 19.

Paper, Lewis J. *Empire: William S. Paley and the Making of CBS News.* New York: St. Martin's, 1987.

Rosencrans, Suzanne. "The Questionable Validity of the Network Syndication and Financial Interest Rules in the Present Media Environment." *Federal Communications Law Journal* 43 (1990): 65.

Sterling, Christopher H., and John M. Kittross. *Stay Tuned: A Concise History of American Broadcasting.* 2d ed. Belmont, CA: Wadsworth, 1990.

Chapter 15

LIBEL, PRIVACY, AND INTELLECTUAL PROPERTY

The rules and regulations set forth by the FCC and the Communications Act are not the only legal concerns of the electronic media. Radio and television stations, wireless cable and cable systems, and satellite system operators must—just like their print media counterparts—adhere to laws and court decisions affecting libel, invasion of privacy, and copyright. A good percentage of litigation involving these areas of law is related in some way to programming. A lawsuit is possible every time a radio talk show host or morning drive disc jockey calls somebody a name or levels an accusation, or whenever a television or cable network newscaster reveals embarrassing information about a government official or any other person. And the electronic media must constantly monitor programming content to make sure no copyrighted material is programmed without first obtaining rights.

In this chapter we will discuss legal questions that are pertinent to all mass media. What kind of statements constitute libel? Precisely what must a plaintiff do to win a libel case against a media defendant? How does the law protect citizens against media intrusions into their private affairs? What types of mass media works are covered under copyright law?

Answers to these questions are found in libel and privacy law, which is promulgated and enforced mainly at the state level, and comes under the general heading of "tort" law.[1] On the other hand, copyright law is regulated by federal statute—the Copyright Act of 1976.

---

[1] A *tort* is a civil or private wrong committed against an individual, as opposed to a criminal wrong. A personal tort such as libel or invasion of privacy involves injury to a person's reputation or feelings as opposed to bodily harm or damage to property. For a comprehensive discussion of torts *see* William L. Prosser, *The Law of Torts,* 3rd ed. (St. Paul, MN: West, 1964).

This chapter is a review of the legal guidelines and relevant court cases affecting libel, invasion of privacy, and copyright law. Each section will include discussions of relevant court cases involving the electronic and print media.

15.1   LIBEL LAW

Although many libel suits are dropped or dismissed before trial, an increasing number conclude with costly settlements.

The threat of libel litigation has become increasingly troublesome for electronic media. True, most libel suits are resolved before the case ever reaches trial, but settlements are often costly, and even when media defendants win libel cases the legal costs soar into the many thousands of dollars. Losing a libel case can mean financial catastrophe. A 1991 report by the Libel Defense Resource Center (LDRC), a nonprofit information clearinghouse, showed that media defendants lost 70 percent of libel cases that made it to juries in the 1980s.[2] A more recent report indicates that the number and amount of damage awards to libel plaintiffs appear to be on the increase. The average award of $9 million in 1990 and 1991 was six times that of the previous decade.[3] It was in 1991 that a jury awarded the largest libel judgment in U.S. history—$58 million—to Texas district attorney Vic Feazel, who was falsely accused by WFAA-TV in Dallas of taking bribes to fix drunk driving and drug possession cases. The station ultimately settled with Feazel for a lesser, undisclosed amount.[4] In early 1993 a New York appellate court upheld an $18.5 million judgment (later reduced to $15.5 million) against Buffalo television station WKBW for incorrectly associating a restaurant owner with organized crime.[5]

Cable programmers have also suffered losses. The Home Shopping Network was forced to negotiate a settlement after a Florida jury awarded GTE $100 million in libel damages. HSN had accused the phone company of causing the loss of half its incoming calls during March of 1987.[6] And newspapers are not immune from escalating damage awards. In 1992 a trial judge upheld a $34 million jury award against the *Philadelphia Inquirer*. The newspaper had accused a former prosecutor of quashing a homicide investigation as a personal favor.[7]

---

[2] Libel Defense Resource Center, "New Study Charts Dramatic Increase in Large Libel Awards against the Media; Other Trends Unfavorable to Libel Defendants Noted in Latest Two-Year Update of Decade-Spanning Survey," (LDRC Press Release, September 26, 1991), in Kent R. Middleton and Bill F. Chamberlin, *1993 Update to The Law of Public Communication*, 2d ed. (New York: Longman, 1993) 13–14.

[3] *New York Times*, "Libel Case Awards Found Increasing," 20 Sept. 1992, final ed., at sec.1, 34.

[4] *Id.*

[5] Prozeralik v. Capital Cities Communications, 188 A.D.2d 178 (1993). *See also* Peter Viles, "Largest TV Station Libel Verdict Upheld," *Broadcasting*, 15 Feb. 1993, at 9.

[6] Barry Meier, "A Hard Look at Home Shopping's Family Ties," *New York Times*, 26 Apr. 1993, late ed., at D1.

[7] *Philadelphia Inquirer*, 10 Sept. 1992, late ed., at A1.

The multimillion dollar awards have certainly not discouraged potential libel litigants from filing suits. Washington apple growers have filed a $150 million libel suit against CBS for a *60 Minutes* segment on potential dangers of the pesticide Alar. Television celebrity Oprah Winfrey and her fiance Stedman Graham have sued a Canadian tabloid for more than $300 million for publishing what they call false allegations that Graham had performed homosexual acts with a cousin. Former *Tonight Show* personality Ed McMahon sued the *Star* tabloid for $5 million for alleging that he drank heavily during a flight to London and stumbled off the plane. Even British prime minister John Major filed a libel suit, this one against two British magazines for reporting that he had an affair with a caterer.

In times past, media defendants could take solace in the fact that jury libel damage awards were often later reduced. But the 1991 LDRC report indicated that the number of judgments against media defendants that were ultimately reduced, reversed, or vacated has dropped by 50 percent.

15.1.1   Nature of Libel Law

Although most defamatory messages disseminated via broadcast stations are spoken, defamation on radio and television is considered libel, the more serious and costly form, rather than slander.

Traditionally, libel has been distinguished from slander in that libelous communications are written, slanderous ones are spoken. Obviously, a listener cannot read written comments on a radio receiver, and rarely is information written out on television. So, you might assume that defamatory comments in a newspaper come under the scope of libel law, and the same comments on a radio, television, or cable program would be treated as slander. This was true until about 1950 when the courts began to eliminate the distinction between libel and slander for the electronic media.

The distinction had been based on two principal assumptions:

1. Written defamations are potentially more harmful, especially since they possess a *permanence of form*, meaning that written materials can be passed from person to person indefinitely. Radio waves, on the other hand, radiate from the transmitting tower and can be received only once. Radio libel, therefore, was considered to lack the durability possessed by written libel.[8]

2. Written comments have traditionally been interpreted as being more deliberate or intentional. It seemed only right that penalties for a

---

[8] This assumption fails to take into account that broadcast messages can be recorded on audio- and videotape and passed from person to person. Of course, there were no videotape recorders prior to 1950 and most audio recording equipment was owned and operated by radio stations and other businesses and commercial establishments.

deliberate act of defamation should be more harsh than for an impromptu or accidental "slip of the tongue" slander.

The distinction was first challenged in 1934 when a New York court ruled that defamation occurring in motion pictures would be treated as libel.[9] For broadcasters, the distinction was partially discarded in the 1947 case *Hartmann* v. *Winchell*. The court held that radio broadcast slander constituted libel, but only if the defamatory comments were read from a script. The *Hartmann* decision would ultimately be interpreted more broadly because of a compelling concurring opinion written by Justice Stanley H. Fuld:

> When account is taken of the vast and far-flung audience reached by radio today—often far greater in number than the readers of the largest metropolitan newspaper . . . it is evident that the broadcast of scandalous utterances is in general as potentially harmful to the defamed person's reputation as a publication in writing.[10]

Still, almost three years after *Hartmann*, a federal judge refused to consider televised defamatory comments as libel even though a U.S. government employee had been blatantly accused of being a Communist on NBC's *Meet the Press*.[11]

It was not long, however, before libel decisions involving radio and television began to reflect Fuld's perspective. One classic example involved an ABC television network variety program aired in the mid-1950s called *The Stork Club*. During one episode, a New York City restaurateur accused another of financial instability, saying, among other things, "I wish I had as much money as he owes." In the libel suit that followed, a New York court, relying on Fuld's logic, set aside the distinction between libel and slander and held that the capacity for harm is just as great for comments that are broadcast as for those published in a newspaper.[12] Although some courts later side-stepped the issue by using the term *defamacast*,[13] the distinction between libel and slander for electronic media had virtually disappeared by the 1980s.

The argument that print media messages possessed greater permanence of form was challenged by an Alabama court in 1980. A reporter for WALA-TV had accused an advertising and public relations firm of reneging on a contract with the city of Mobile. The Alabama court declared the defamation to be libel, pointing out that WALA aired the story over 40 times during an 11-month period.[14]

---

[9] Brown v. Paramount Public Corp., 240 A.D. 520 (1934).

[10] Hartmann v. Winchell, 73 N.E.2d 30 (1947).

[11] Remington v. Bentley, 88 F. Supp. 166 (1949).

[12] Shor v. Billingsley, 158 N.Y.S.2d 476 (1956).

[13] American Broadcasting–Paramount Theatres v. Simpson, 106 Ga. App. 230 (1962).

[14] *See* First Indep. Baptist Church of Arab v. Southerland, 373 So. 2d 647 (Ala. 1979); and Gray v. WALA, 384 So. 2d 1062 (Ala. 1980).

Today, any defamatory message originating on radio or television is treated as libel.[15] A 1985 California court ruling suggests that the same is true for other electronic media as well. The case involved a comedy routine by comedian and actor Robin Williams in which he joked about there being no wines marketed specifically to blacks. He went on to suggest one, giving it the name "Reggie" with an expletive attached,[16] and proceeded to ridicule both the idea and the proposed wine. The routine was shown on pay cable television (HBO) and was later distributed on audiotape and record albums under the title "Throbbing Python of Love" and on videotape that was also made available for rental.

A California wine distributor named David Rege filed a libel suit against Williams, claiming that his wine could be confused with Williams's imaginary one and that the routine had incorrectly associated his wine with black consumers. The court ruled resoundingly that Williams's comical comments could not give rise to a cause of action for libel because they could not reasonably be taken seriously. The court also denounced the plaintiff's arguments as racially discriminatory and repugnant. The court did, however, address the fact that various media, including cable television, records, and audio- and videotape were involved in distribution of the Williams monologue. The court concluded that the new technologies had rendered the electronic media distinction between libel and slander obsolete.[17]

Unfortunately for the student of libel, there is no uniform law of libel laid out in a federal statute or even in the common law. Each state has its own laws determining what constitutes a libelous action, what must be demonstrated by a plaintiff in order to win a libel case, and what defenses are available to the defendant. Some commonalities do exist, however, and the courts have established clear precedent regarding several aspects of libel law.

It should also be noted that libel cases involving media defendants are handled differently from those involving private communications such as letters of recommendation or credit references. The principles of law and court decisions discussed in this chapter apply only to cases involving the mass media.

15.1.2 Elements of Libel: The Plaintiff's Burden of Proof

To win a libel suit, the plaintiff must show defamation, publication, identification, and fault.

This means that a libel plaintiff must establish that he or she has been identified and defamed in a media publication, and that the defamation has damaged his or her reputation. Plaintiffs must also establish that the medium is at fault, and in some

---

[15] Matherson v. Marchello, 100 A.D.2d 233 (1984).

[16] The spelling of the wine became a matter of dispute. Williams claimed the spelling of his imaginary wine would be "Reggie." The full name Williams attached to his imaginary wine was "Reggie, Motherfucker [sic]." The plaintiff spelled his name, wine distributorship, and wine store "Rege," which he claimed had four different pronunciations.

[17] Polygram Records v. Rege, 170 Cal. App. 3d 543 (1985).

cases must prove that the defamatory communication is false. The burden of proof on any libel plaintiff is heavy, but the burden on public officials and celebrities is even greater.

15.1.2.1 Defamation

Defamation is communication that harms a person's reputation, subjects a person to hatred or ridicule, or causes a person to be socially ostracized.

One element of proof for a libel plaintiff is that *defamation* has occurred. Since the determination of what constitutes defamation evolves from state common law, the definition of "defamation" varies widely from state to state. Generally, defamation is a communication that causes harm to an individual's (1) reputation, (2) ability to enjoy social contact with others, or (3) ability to work or engage in business practices. In *Keller* v. *Miami Herald Publishing* a Florida court defined defamation as communication that "tends to subject one to hatred, distrust, ridicule, contempt, or disgrace."[18] Any statement or other communication that places a person in a highly unfavorable light such that he or she is shunned by others or suffers occupational damage of some kind would likely be considered defamatory.

A few states have adopted what is called the *innocent construction rule*. Under this rule, if there is a way to construe a statement in a nondefamatory manner, the courts will interpret it that way.

The law is consistent and quite clear on one matter. The damage caused by a defamatory communication need only occur to the plaintiff's reputation, or what other people "think" about the plaintiff. It may help justify a more substantial damage award, but to win a libel suit the plaintiff does not have to prove any actual personal injury or damage other than that related to reputation. One Ohio court even ruled that a city cannot sue for libel because a city, unlike a person, has no reputation to be damaged. The case involved an ABC report that had erroneously included Grafton, Ohio, among a list of cities with hazardous chemical dumping sites.[19] The courts have stipulated that a plaintiff's reputation must be damaged among a significant group of reasonable persons in a community, and not just one or a few persons or a group that is not representative of the community.

As explained in Box 15.1, defamatory messages broadcast on television or carried on a cable network or satellite service are not necessarily spoken or written statements or comments. Pictures can defame as easily as words, and in some cases the person defamed is never explicitly mentioned. For example, in a 1977 ABC documentary entitled "Sex for Sale," voice-over comments about street prostitution were accompanied by shots of three women walking down a street. When one of the women sued for libel, the court agreed that her appearance could be construed in a defamatory manner.[20] Of course, libel may also occur if a picture or video

[18] Keller v. Miami Herald Publishing Co., 778 F.2d 711 (1985).
[19] Grafton v. ABC, 435 N.E.2d 1131 (Ohio App. 1980).
[20] Clark v. ABC, 684 F.2d 1208 (1982).

BOX 15.1   Libel and the Electronic Media

In this text the term *communication* or *message* will be used instead of *comment* or *statement* when referring to defamatory messages. This is because defamation in the visual media is not limited to verbal statements. Although the majority of libel suits are based on written or spoken comments, defamation can also occur in a photograph or any other source of video. This kind of "visual" defamation most often occurs when pictures, sometimes the wrong ones, are placed beside unflattering headlines, cutlines, or stories, or when newscast video shows a person not actually involved in the story being discussed. The pictures themselves send messages that could serve as the basis for a libel suit.

---

segment distorts a scene in any way, whether by unusual camera angles or editing techniques.

A number of federal courts have held that in television defamation cases, the audio and video should be considered together, since the visual medium allows interpretations that cannot be ascertained through a mere reading of a transcript.[21] The courts have argued that it is the juxtaposition of the audio and video that conveys the intended meaning.[22] But a 1993 appeals court decision seems to contradict this ruling. The case involved a well-publicized child custody dispute between Eric Foretich and his ex-wife, Dr. Elizabeth Morgan, a prominent Washington plastic surgeon. Morgan had spent 25 months in jail rather than reveal the whereabouts of the couple's daughter or give visitation rights to Foretich as directed by the court. Foretich had sued CBS and each of his two wives over charges made on the television program *People Magazine on TV* that he had sexually molested his two daughters. The trial court dismissed the suit, but Foretich argued on appeal that the judge erred by refusing to view a videotape of the program. The appeals court disagreed, holding that Foretich failed to demonstrate any additional defamatory inference that might be drawn from the video, nor did he identify any error in the written transcript of the program. The court concluded that failure to view the tape was insignificant.[23]

15.1.2.1.1 Libel Per Se
Communications that are defamatory on their face are referred to as libelous *per se.*

Words such as *criminal, communist, liar,* and *whore* are so universally interpreted as defamatory that they could clearly damage a person's reputation. These words and most of the communications discussed in this chapter are libelous *per se*

---

[21] Silvester v. ABC, 650 F. Supp. 766 (1986).
[22] Lasky v. ABC, 631 F. Supp. 1015 (1986).
[23] Foretich v. CBS, 619 A.2d 48 (1993).

because no surrounding context or other facts need be considered in determining whether the messages are defamatory.

15.1.2.1.2   Libel Per Quod

Communications that have defamatory meaning only when other facts are considered are called libelous *per quod*.

Suppose a radio talk show host claims that a particular local citizen owns stock in a company that markets and distributes sexually oriented but not obscene adult literature. Such a statement would not be libelous per se, as long as the materials were not falsely described as pornographic or obscene. But what if it turns out that the citizen identified is also an evangelical minister? What if, as a result of the broadcast, the minister is repudiated by his church? A jury may well find these statements to be libelous *per quod.*

That is what happened when a Spokane, Washington, newspaper simply published in its records section that a local citizen named Philip Pitts was divorced from his wife. This was in fact true, but the divorce had actually been granted 14 months before the publication, and Pitts had been remarried for some time. The court concluded that the article led friends and acquaintances of Pitts to believe that he was a bigamist. He was awarded $2,000.[24]

Similarly, when female author Pat Montandon was the only guest on a program for which *TV Guide* included the description "From Party Girl to Call Girl," the court ruled that by implication readers could have perceived Montandon as having been a prostitute. She was awarded $251,000.[25]

Some states require plaintiffs to carry a heavier burden of proof and to demonstrate specific monetary losses in cases involving libel per quod. However, since the burden of proof for libel plaintiffs has increased over the last 30 years, the legal distinction between communications deemed libelous per se and libelous per quod is less significant than a few years ago.

15.1.2.1.3   Categories of Defamatory Communications

Five common categories of defamatory communications are those involving criminal activity, sexual slurs, other personal behaviors and characteristics, politics and religion, and business dealings.

1. *Communications Involving Criminal Activity:* Perhaps the most common type of defamatory communication involving mass media occurs when an individual is linked to some kind of criminal activity. Falsely accusing a person of almost any kind of crime is likely to be considered libelous.

Some journalists think that use of the word *alleged* will avoid libel suits, even if a story falsely identifies a person as a criminal suspect. To say an individual is "alleged to have committed vandalism" may be journalistically correct, but if the

---

[24] Pitts v. Spokane Chronicle Co., 63 Wash. 2d 763 (1964).
[25] Montandon v. Triangle Publications, 45 Cal. App. 3d 938 (1975).

wrong person is identified, the statement is still likely to be libelous. A jury awarded one woman $300,000 after San Diego station KCST-TV mistakenly identified her as an alleged prostitute. The woman had actually testified at a grand jury hearing about police involvement in a prostitution ring, but a KCST reporter pulled her name from a newspaper article and called her the actual suspect.[26]

Libel plaintiffs involved in misidentifications still have to prove that the mistake occurred due to negligence. When KWTV in Oklahoma City identified the wrong person as a suspect in a robbery case, the court excused the error. The court reasoned that the prompt reporting of matters of public interest serves a "paramount societal need."[27] Despite the mistake, the court concluded that the station had exercised due care.

But station KYW in Philadelphia lost a libel suit after broadcasting the name and place of business of an individual implicated in a car-towing racket. The court ruled that the station should have known that an appeals court had overturned the man's conviction prior to the broadcast.[28]

In 1993, a New York appellate court upheld a $15.5 million libel award to a person falsely identified as a *victim* of a crime.[29] Two Capital Cities properties, WKBW-TV and WKBW radio, had falsely identified Buffalo restaurant owner John Prozeralik as the victim of a mob-style abduction and beating at a Cheektowaga, New York, motel. The court was influenced by the fact that another Buffalo station had correctly identified the actual victim the morning *before* the WKBW broadcasts. The court called the mistaken linking of Prozeralik to organized crime an act of "groundless speculation and conjecture."[30] The large award was upheld despite the fact that both stations issued retractions upon discovering the mistake (see Box 15.2).[31]

2. *Sexual Slurs:* A quick way to get involved in a libel suit is to falsely accuse someone of rape, incest, child molestation, public nudity, adultery, prostitution, or other form of sexual misconduct. Courts have also ruled that falsely referring to someone as impotent, a homosexual, or a rape victim is defamatory.

3. *Other Personal Behaviors and Characteristics:* Courts have also determined that communications suggesting that an individual is dishonest, immoral, cowardly, foolish, financially irresponsible, or stupid are defamatory. The same goes for associating a person with a contagious or otherwise dreadful disease, such as hepatitis, AIDS, leprosy, or mental instability. Singer Whitney Houston filed a $60 million libel suit against the *New York Post* for falsely publishing that she had been hospitalized in Miami for taking an overdose of diet pills.[32]

[26] O'Hara v. Storer Communications, 231 Cal. App. 3d 1101 (1991).
[27] Benson v. Griffin TV, 593 P.2d 511 (1978).
[28] Purcell v. Westinghouse, 191 A.2d 662 (1963).
[29] Prozeralik v. Capital Cities Communications, 188 A.D.2d 178 (1993).
[30] *Id.* at 182–183.
[31] A group of news organizations has petitioned New York's highest court of appeals to have the large award set aside. *See* Alan Pergament, "Libel Verdict Draws Media Fire," *Buffalo News*, 20 May 1993, city ed., at television section 6.
[32] Harry Levins, "People," *St. Louis Post-Dispatch*, 1 July 1993, five star ed., at 6A.

BOX 15.2   Retractions: Necessary But Not Always Effective

Anytime a news organization makes a false and potentially demeaning statement about an individual or group, a retraction is essential from a professional and ethical perspective and may even inspire a potential libel plaintiff not to file suit. On the other hand, retractions often have little influence on a court once a suit is filed. In *Prozeralik* v. *Capital Cities*, WKBW-TV, once the mistaken identity was discovered, broadcast the following retraction:

"Tonight, we have developments on two fronts in the abduction that ended yesterday in a Cheektowaga motel. First, the victim is not, and I repeat, is not, John Prozeralik, the operator of John's Flaming Hearth Restaurants." The newscaster went on to clearly identify the actual victim, another Buffalo restaurant owner.*

Despite the strongly worded retraction, Prozeralik was awarded over $15 million in damages.

---

* Prozeralik v. Capital Cities Communications, 188 A.D.2d at 182 (1993).

---

4. Politics and Religion: Any communication that falsely associates an individual with a controversial organization such as the Communist Party, the Neo-Nazis, or the Ku Klux Klan will likely be considered libelous. It can also be libelous to accuse someone of spy activity or question the person's patriotism. To merely suggest that one has been expelled from a particular church or religious order can be considered defamatory. Keep in mind that the defamatory communication must damage the individual's reputation. It is for this reason that courts have typically not held even distasteful racial slurs such as "spic" or "nigger" to be defamatory.[33]

5. Communications Involving Business Dealings: Any communication that damages an individual's ability to conduct business may be considered defamatory. Professionals and self-employed persons can sue for libel if they are accused of offering inferior service or conducting business in a fraudulent, incompetent, deceptive, or unethical manner.

Businesses can initiate libel suits as well as individuals, but only for damage to the reputation of the corporation as a whole, not to individuals within the corporation. Businesses can sue if associated with any of the practices described above, or for allegations that the business is financially unstable. As explained in Box 15.3, a single incorrect communication about a business often will not provide the basis for a successful libel suit.

15.1.2.1.4 Trade Libel.   Another type of libel involving business is called *trade libel* or *product disparagement*. The issue in a trade libel suit is whether the prod-

---

[33] *See* Raible v. Newsweek, 341 F. Supp 804 (1972), Ledsinger v. Eurmeister, 318 N.W.2d 558 (1982), and Rambo v. Cohen, 587 N.E.2d 140 (1992).

BOX 15.3   The Single Mistake Rule

Some states have adopted what is called the *single mistake rule*. Under this rule, the courts will forgive communications that falsely attribute a one-time error to a business or professional person. For example, it might not be libelous to incorrectly report that a local hamburger franchise sold tainted meat on a given day. But it is clearly defamatory to falsely assert that a pattern of such service has occurred.

---

uct or service of the business has been defamed, not the business itself. A California court defined trade libel as "an intentional disparagement of the quality of property, which results in a pecuniary damage to the plaintiff."[34] To win a trade libel case the plaintiff must establish all elements of proof required of any other libel plaintiff and must also prove that sales of the product or service were harmed and that the defamation occurred with malice (EMG 15.1.4). After *Consumer Reports* magazine reported that Bose speakers sent sound wandering "about the room," the Bose Corporation sued and was able to prove to the court that sales had dropped. The engineer conducting tests on the speakers had actually been told by listeners that the sound tended to move "along the wall in front of and between the speakers."[35] Bose still lost its libel suit because the court was not convinced that the magazine *knew* it was publishing a falsehood by changing the phrase.

15.1.2.2   Publication
Publication occurs when one or more persons other than the plaintiff or defendant see or hear the communication.

A libel plaintiff must also prove that *publication* has occurred. Since publication occurs when even one person other than the plaintiff or defendant sees or hears the communication, publication is not an issue in most media libel cases. Even the smallest AM daytime radio station has an average audience reach of at least one person, so publication is most often assumed in cases involving electronic media. It is important to understand how the word *publish* is used in the context of libel law. In other contexts it is used only in reference to printed material. In libel terminology, publication also refers to presentation of subject matter on radio, television, cable, or satellite. Therefore, any defamatory remarks made on radio, television, or cable are considered to be "published."

15.1.2.3   Identification
A successful libel suit must establish that the plaintiff has been identified in the communication.

---

[34] Erlich v. Etner, 224 Cal. App. 2d 69 (1964).
[35] Bose Corp. v. Consumers Union of United States, 508 F. Supp. 1249 (1981), *aff'd*, 466 U.S. 485 (1984).

Since many libelous communications use the plaintiff's name or picture right along with defamatory comments, establishing identification is often a simple matter. But sometimes identification occurs more indirectly. The courts have ruled that publication of a person's name or picture is not required to establish identification. In the most important libel case ever, *New York Times* v. *Sullivan*, the actual name of the plaintiff, Police Commissioner L. B. Sullivan, was never mentioned.[36] In another case a libel judgment was won where the plaintiff, accused of being caught in a "compromising spot" with the wife of a Palm Beach socialite, was identified only through a combination of facts that directed attention to his status as a former FBI agent.[37]

Complete identification of persons involved in news stories can help avoid libel suits. The now-defunct *Washington Star* newspaper avoided a libel judgment when it identified the murderer of Dr. Michael J. Halberstam as Jerry Summerlin, 22, of the 550 block of Dana Place, N.W., Washington, D.C. Another Washington resident named Jerry Summerlin claimed that he was wrongfully identified in the story as the murderer. The court disagreed, holding that the identification was sufficiently detailed to avoid confusion, especially since the plaintiff was not 22 years old and did not live at the same address. But what if the newspaper reporter had accidentally looked up and reported the plaintiff Summerlin's address or had been supplied his middle name by a police officer? If either had been published, the plaintiff would have likely established identification.

Groups of persons can be identified in defamatory communications and sue for libel, but only if the group is small enough that individual group members could be associated with the defamatory communication. The question is, how large a group is too large? The courts are a bit unclear on this. In the often-cited libel case *Neiman-Marcus Co.* v. *Lait*, the court attempted to establish some guidelines. A book had stated that the store's nine models were high-priced prostitutes, the 25 "salesmen" were fairies (meaning homosexuals), and the "salesgirls" were prostitutes. The court held that identification did occur for the salesmen and models, but with 382 saleswomen, it would be difficult to associate the allegations with any one individual. The court said that when a group is that large, identification does not occur even if the defamatory language suggests inclusion of all members.[38] However, even in small groups, if the communication is not all-inclusive and defames only one or a few of the group's members, the courts have ruled that no unnamed individual can establish that identification has occurred.[39]

On the other hand, the Oklahoma Supreme Court held in 1962 that unnamed individuals were identified when a magazine accused the University of Oklahoma football team of using amphetamines to increase aggressiveness. A jury had awarded a fullback on the team who was never named in the article a $75,000 libel judg-

---

[36] 376 U.S. 254 (1964).
[37] Hope v. Hearst Consolidated Corp., 294 F.2d 681 (1961).
[38] Neiman-Marcus Co. v. Lait, 107 F. Supp. 96 (S.D.N.Y. 1952).
[39] Arcand v. Evening Call, 567 F.2d 1163 (1977).

ment. The University of Oklahoma carried around 60 players on its football squad when the article was published.[40]

Identification is less likely when the numbers get above 100. After selling off his interests in the Kentucky Fried Chicken fast-food chain, Colonel Harland Sanders described the chicken served by the chain as a "damn fried doughball stuck on some chicken," and the gravy a combination of "wallpaper paste" and "sludge."[41] The new owners of KFC sued for libel, but the court ruled that no one restaurant out of the 5,000 nationwide could have been identified.[42]

15.1.2.4   *Fault Requirement*

The private libel plaintiff must also establish that the communication was false and was published with negligence.

Even if a plaintiff is able to establish defamation, publication, and identification, a libel suit cannot be won unless *fault* is successfully attributed to the media defendant. Precisely how this is done varies from state to state and depends on whether the plaintiff is a public or private person (EMG 15.1.5.2). Still, the fault requirement is the most difficult to satisfy and is the principal issue in the majority of libel cases.

For most people who are neither prominent in the community in which they live nor prominently involved in issues relevant to a defamatory communication, the plaintiff must only demonstrate that the communication was published with *negligence.* This has been interpreted by the courts to mean (1) published without exercise of reasonable care, or (2) published with behavior not typical of a reasonably prudent person in the same occupation. For example, it might be considered negligent if a radio news reporter made no attempt to verify information that turned out to be false, especially if the information was obtained from a questionable source.[43]

In 1986, the Supreme Court ruled that in addition to negligence, private plaintiffs must also prove that the defamatory information is false—if the communication involves a matter of public concern.[44] In effect the Court has created a two-step process for establishing fault. The plaintiff must first prove the statements are false, then establish that they were published negligently. Public officials and certain other prominent persons have a much higher burden of proof, as we will see in the next section.

15.1.3   *New York Times* v. *Sullivan*

In the *Sullivan* decision the Supreme Court ruled that public officials must prove actual malice in order to win a libel suit. The Court said that communications

---

[40] Fawcett Publications v. Morris, 377 P.2d 42 (Okla. 1962).

[41] Kentucky Fried Chicken v. Sanders, 563 S.W.2d at 8–9 (1978).

[42] *Id.* at 8.

[43] Kent R. Middleton and Bill F. Chamberlin, *The Law of Public Communication*, 3rd ed. (New York: Longman, 1994) 138.

[44] Philadelphia Newspapers v. Hepps, 475 U.S. 767 (1986).

published with reckless disregard for the truth or with knowledge of falsity are published with actual malice.

The circumstances for this case arose out of protests against racial inequalities at Alabama State College in Montgomery. In March 1960, an advertisement entitled "Heed Their Rising Voices" was published in the *New York Times*. The ad had been paid for and signed by 64 persons, black and white, many of whom were prominent. The ad proclaimed that thousands of southern Negro students were engaged in nonviolent demonstrations in affirmation of their right to live in human dignity as guaranteed by the U.S. Constitution but were "being met by an unprecedented wave of terror" and that "after students sang 'My Country Tis of Thee' their leaders were expelled," and that truckloads of police surrounded the campus.[45]

Montgomery's commissioner of police, L. B. Sullivan, although never mentioned by name, claimed that he was libeled by derogatory and false references to the police. There were factual errors in the ad. The police never really surrounded the campus. The students actually sang the National Anthem and were expelled for demanding service at a lunch counter, not for the singing demonstration. The ad also falsely stated that the dining room door was padlocked and that students refused to register. The *Times* ad manager had failed to check the facts because the ad came from a reputable firm and contained the signatures of prominent persons.

Under what is called *strict liability* libel law, a legal approach in effect in Alabama and other states at that time, it was much easier to win a libel suit against the mass media. All the plaintiff had to do was establish publication and identification and prove some kind of damages. This meant that no matter how careful reporters and editors might be, they would likely lose a libel suit if a plaintiff could demonstrate some damage as a result of a news story. Indeed, under strict liability the jury awarded Sullivan $500,000 damages.

On appeal the U.S. Supreme Court tossed out the strict liability approach and reversed the lower court decision. The Court, with Justice Brennan writing the opinion, established three fundamental changes in libel law.

1. The Court changed the meaning of libel per se. Previously, statements were libelous *per se* if they accused a public official of misconduct. The defendant assumed the burden of proof to establish that the statements were either true or fair comment based on truth. Otherwise, the court would presume what is called common law malice (or ill will toward the plaintiff) and award both compensatory and punitive damages (EMG 15.1.7). The *Sullivan* decision established that even statements libelous per se deserve some First Amendment protection if related to discussion of public issues.

2. The Court ruled that the First Amendment allows some false statements to be made in heated debate over the public conduct of public officials.

---

[45] New York Times v. Sullivan, 376 U.S. at 256–257 (1964).

Otherwise, the Court reasoned, a chilling effect stifles free and open discussion.

3. The Court held that in order to win a libel suit, public officials must prove that statements were published with *actual malice*. Actual malice was defined as published with *knowledge of falsity*, or with *reckless disregard for whether the statement was true or false*.

A libel plaintiff does not have to prove actual malice beyond a reasonable doubt, the standard used in criminal trials. Actual malice is established by the "preponderance of evidence" test used in other civil litigation. The Supreme Court concluded that the *New York Times* had, at worst, been negligent in publishing the advertisement. The lower court decision and damage award was overturned.[46]

15.1.4 Courts and Actual Malice

Since the *Sullivan* decision the courts have attempted to clarify the meaning of "reckless disregard for the truth" and "knowledge of falsity."

The *Sullivan* decision greatly shifted the burden of proof to the plaintiff. To win a libel suit, a public official would have to prove publication, identification, defamation, and actual malice. Practically speaking, public officials could no longer collect damages for libel just because a defamatory communication was false, even if it could be proven false.[47] What this accomplished was the establishment of a constitutional defense in libel suits. Previously, media defendants were at the mercy of individual state statutes or common law decisions in state courts. After *New York Times* v. *Sullivan,* mass media were afforded First Amendment constitutional protection to which state laws and court decisions must conform. In 1967 the Supreme Court extended the actual malice standard to other types of prominent persons[48] in *Curtis Publishing* v. *Butts*.[49]

Subsequent decisions have helped clarify the meaning of the two definitions of actual malice. In *Garrison* v. *Louisiana* the Court suggested that "knowledge of falsity" means defamatory communications are published with a "high degree of awareness of their probable falsity."[50] In *St. Amant* v. *Thompson* the Court suggested that "reckless disregard" means that the defendant entertained "serious doubts about the truth of the defamatory comments."[51] In 1985, a U.S. court of

---

[46] The *New York Times* v. *Sullivan* decision also placed editorial advertising on higher constitutional ground than other advertising. It would be another 10 years before commercial advertising would receive First Amendment protection. *See* Bigelow v. Virginia, 421 U.S. 809 (1975) and Virginia State Bd. of Pharmacy v. Virginia Citizens Consumer Council, 425 U.S. 748 (1976).

[47] New York Times v. Sullivan, 376 U.S. 254 (1964).

[48] The distinction between public officials, public persons, and private persons is discussed in EMG 15.1.5.2.

[49] 388 U.S. 130 (1967).

[50] Garrison v. Louisiana, 379 U. S. 64 (1964)

[51] St. Amant v. Thompson, 390 U.S. 727 (1968).

appeals offered the following examples of what would be considered reckless disregard:

1. A journalist deliberately slants and ignores evidence contrary to the false premise of the story.
2. A journalist is, in the opinion of the court, out to get the plaintiff.
3. The journalist's notes contradict the published statements of interviewees.
4. The mass medium refuses to retract the story or publish a letter written by the plaintiff in response to the story.[52]

In 1989, the Supreme Court ruled that the Hamilton, Ohio, *Journal News* libeled a municipal judge candidate, Daniel Connaughton. After having endorsed Connaughton's opponent, the *Journal News* reported that Connaughton had used dirty tricks during the campaign, including offers of jobs and a Florida vacation for help in discrediting his opponent. The paper also reported that an aide to Connaughton had accepted money in exchange for disposing of minor criminal charges. The charges were ultimately determined to be either misleading or unfounded, so when Connaughton lost the election he sued the newspaper for libel.

The Supreme Court ruled that the newspaper published the charges with reckless disregard for the truth because it intentionally failed to conduct a thorough investigation and ignored available evidence that raised doubts about the charges. Specifically, the Court expressed dismay that the newspaper failed to interview key witnesses or listen to a tape recording directly related to the charges. The Court upheld an award of $200,000.[53]

15.1.4.1 *Talk Radio and Reckless Disregard*

The FCC does not require talk radio programmers to use a delay system to prevent defamatory and other types of undesirable comments from being broadcast. The courts have disagreed on how use or nonuse of a delay system affects libel suits.

The emergence of talk radio has created a number of legal concerns for station operators, not the least of which is the threat of libel suits. As a result many stations use a delay system during call-in broadcasts that allows screening of callers' comments several seconds before they are broadcast and provides an opportunity to delete any comments that are questionable. The FCC once considered, then rejected, a proposal to *require* stations airing talk programming to use delay systems.[54] The courts have also generally avoided rendering decisions that could be interpreted to require their use.

---

[52] Tavoulareas v. Washington Post Co., 759 F.2d 90 (1985).
[53] Harte-Hanks Communications v. Connaughton, 491 U.S. 657 (1989).
[54] 39 F.C.C.2d 1038 (1971).

In 1976, a Wyoming court ruled that a mandate to use tape delay would re-strict public debate and force censorship.[55] An anonymous caller to Wyoming sta-tion KFBC's *Cheyenne Today* talk program charged that a former insurance com-missioner had been discharged because of dishonesty. The subsequent libel suit was premised on the argument that KFBC's failure to use a tape delay system met the constitutional standard of reckless disregard for the truth. The court disagreed, holding that any such ruling would

> impose an obligation upon radio broadcasting companies which would in-hibit in a substantial way, the free and robust nature of public debate. The impact of censorship would not fall upon the broadcaster's words and ideas; instead it would be applied to the opinions and ideas of those mem-bers of the public who elected to participate in this kind of public forum.[56]

A Louisiana appeals court reached the opposite conclusion in 1971.[57] WBOX in Bogalusa was sued for libel after a caller to the station's *Call and Comment* program suggested that a local physician, a drug store manager, and a restaurant owner were involved in illegal drug trafficking. The court ruled that radio stations have the duty to prevent callers from making defamatory comments. The court said that allowing such comments to go out over the air was comparable to the station receiving defamatory information from an anonymous source and broadcasting the material with no attempt at verification:

> The direct broadcast of such anonymous defamatory material, without the use of any monitoring or delay device, is no less reprehensible in our judgment. The publication, in either event, is done by the station, and we find that there is the same reckless disregard for the truth in each instance.[58]

The court also said that WBOX, by not using a tape delay, "placed itself in a position fraught with the imminent danger of broadcasting anonymous unverified, slander-ous remarks based on sheer rumor, speculation, and hearsay."[59]

Radio and television personalities are at some risk when they joke about indi-viduals in a manner that could be considered defamatory. A Maryland jury decided that a joke told by Baltimore radio personality Johnny Walker was not only not funny, it was libelous. The joke was aired in the context of a blizzard that struck Baltimore in 1979 during which there was considerable civil unrest including the

---

[55] Adams v. Frontier Broadcasting, 555 P.2d 556 (1976).
[56] *Id.* at 557.
[57] Snowden v. Pearl River Broadcasting Corp., 251 So. 2d 405 (1971).
[58] *Id.* at 410.
[59] *Id.* at 411.

looting of commercial establishments. Walker, on his *Little News in the Morning* program, typically made impromptu comments about current events. Following a story about a knee injury suffered by a local black television commentator, Walker said something to the effect of, "Wonder how he hurt his knee. Probably fell down carrying a TV during the blizzard last week, right?"[60]

The court concluded that Walker acted with reckless disregard in showing no concern whether his statement would be considered by reasonable listeners as true. The court added that Walker should have known his comments would be believed by some. No credit to his listeners, but on a previous occasion the switchboard at Johns Hopkins Hospital was swamped with calls after Walker announced that the late Elvis Presley had registered at the hospital.[61]

15.1.4.2 *Proving Knowledge of Falsity*

To establish knowledge of falsity the plaintiff must demonstrate knowledge of what a public official or other prominent defendent was thinking when the defamatory communication was written, produced, or published.

Libel plaintiffs find it difficult to prove that defamatory communications were published with knowledge that they were false. Carol Burnett was apparently able to do so when the *National Enquirer* published a story suggesting she had been loud and boisterous and had spilled wine in a Washington restaurant. After determining that there were conflicting accounts of the evening, the court ruled that the *Enquirer* reporter probably knew the story was false.[62]

One reason that knowledge of falsity is so difficult to prove is that it presumes knowledge of what was in the mind of a libel defendant when the defamatory communication was published. In *Herbert* v. *Lando* the U.S. Supreme Court ruled that a public official or other prominent plaintiff can inquire into a reporter's state of mind and into the entire news editorial process in order to establish actual malice. In practical terms, this means that libel plaintiffs have the right to question media defendants about any doubts regarding the veracity of published communications and about conversations with other reporters and editors as a story is shot, edited, written, or planned. Herbert had sued CBS producer Barry Lando for $45 million after a *60 Minutes* story accused him of fabricating war crimes.[63]

In 1993, a jury decided that *New Yorker* magazine writer Janet Malcolm libeled psychiatrist Jeffrey Masson by publishing inaccurate and defamatory quotations. However, a federal judge ruled that the case against Malcolm had to be retried because the jury could not agree on a damage award.[64] The Supreme Court had

---

[60] Since no recording was made, the precise wording of the comment is not known. It was also contested whether the comment was immediately followed by canned laughter.

[61] Embrey v. Holly, 429 A.2d 251 (1981).

[62] Burnett v. National Enquirer, 144 Cal. App. 3d 991 (1983).

[63] Herbert v. Lando, 441 U.S. 153 (1979). *See also* Hatchard v. Westinghouse Broadcasting Co. 532 A.2d 346 (1987).

[64] Masson v. New Yorker, 960 F.2d 896 (1992).

remanded the case for reconsideration, ruling that even when direct quotes were knowingly altered, actual malice was not established unless the alterations resulted in a significant change in the meaning of the statements.[65] The judge also ruled that the new trial would not involve the *New Yorker* because Malcolm worked as an independent contractor and Masson had failed to prove that the magazine *knew* that the quotations had been altered.

15.1.5   Public Officials

> The distinction between public and private persons is critically important because only public persons, including public officials, have to prove actual malice to win a libel suit.

But what kind of people are included within these broad categories? A Norwalk, Connecticut, police patrolman found out he was a public official after a citizen wrote a letter to the local newspaper calling him abusive and suggesting that he twisted her arm excessively and treated her as a common criminal. As a public official he was required to prove actual malice—which he was not able to do—in order to collect libel damages.[66]

15.1.5.1   *Defining Public Officials*

The courts have generally considered two types of individuals to be public officials: (1) anyone who is elected to public office, and (2) anyone who is a government employee.

Most courts have ruled that government employees, to be considered public officials, must occupy some position of leadership. In *Rosenblatt* v. *Baer*, the Supreme Court said that a public official is any government official who has or is perceived by the public to have control over the conduct of government affairs.[67] Obviously, mayors, city council members, and police commissioners are public officials. But the courts have also ruled that police traffic officers, firefighters, school board members, supervisors of public operations such as recreation areas, persons with control over the expenditure of public funds, and persons who have previously held public office are public officials.

Public official plaintiffs are required to prove actual malice only when the defamatory communication involves (1) the official conduct of the plaintiff, or (2) the overall fitness of the plaintiff to serve as a public official. Clearly, the range of matters concerning fitness to serve in office can be broad and could include issues related to the private life of an official such as use of drugs, or immoral or unethical behavior.

---

[65] Masson v. New Yorker, 498 U.S. 808 (1991). Since the trial ended without a unanimous verdict the district court declared a mistrial in 1993. *See* Masson v. New Yorker, 832 F. Supp. 1350 (1993).

[66] Moriarty v. Lippe, 294 A.2d 326 (1972).

[67] Rosenblatt v. Baer, 383 U.S. 75 (1966).

15.1.5.2 Distinguishing Public and Private Persons

In *Gertz* v. *Welch* the Supreme Court ruled that only public officials and people who deliberately become involved in matters of public concern have to prove actual malice.

In 1971 the Supreme Court handed down what for a short time looked to be another landmark libel decision. News reporters at Philadelphia radio station WIP had referred to magazine distributor George Rosenbloom as a "smut peddler." Despite the fact that a judge had ruled that materials the police had confiscated from Rosenbloom were not obscene, the station reported that he was distributing obscene material. Rosenbloom sued for libel and won a six-figure judgment.

In a plurality decision the Supreme Court overturned the judgment, holding that the *New York Times* actual malice standard should be applied to all persons, public and private, when the speech involves matters of public interest.[68] The decision would have rendered the distinction between public and private persons superfluous in many libel cases, but only three years later *Rosenbloom* was essentially overturned by the truly landmark case, *Gertz* v. *Welch*.[69]

When Chicago attorney Elmer Gertz agreed to represent the parents of a Chicago youth shot by police, the ultraconservative John Birch Society's *American Opinion* magazine attacked him unmercifully. The magazine called Gertz "Leninist Elmer Gertz" and "Communist-fronter Gertz," and referred to him as a member of the "Red Guild."[70] The latter was a derogatory reference to the National Lawyers Guild, whose members had defended persons accused of being Communists during the McCarthy red scare era[71] and who were opposed to the more conservative American Bar Association. The magazine also charged that the police had prepared a file on Gertz when in fact no such file ever existed. It was obvious, therefore, that false statements were made. Gertz sued the publisher, Robert Welch, for libel.

It should be noted that Gertz was prominent nationally among attorneys, was the author of several books, magazine articles, and radio plays, and had even helped write the Illinois state constitution. He had also gained notoriety by receiving a commutation of the death sentence for Jack Ruby, the man who in 1963 shot and killed Lee Harvey Oswald in the Dallas police station. The lower courts had ruled that Gertz was a public figure and would have to prove actual malice to win his libel suit, but the Supreme Court overturned the decision and repudiated the *Rosenbloom* decision. The Court held that *only public officials and people who become involved in matters of interest by their own choosing* have to prove actual malice. The Court also proclaimed a rather narrow definition of a public person:

---

[68] Rosenbloom v. Metromedia, 403 U.S. 29 (1971).

[69] Gertz v. Robert Welch, Inc., 418 U.S. 323 (1974).

[70] *Id.* at 326.

[71] During the early 1950s, U.S. Senator Joe McCarthy of Wisconsin used fear of communism to gain notoriety. He did so by accusing U.S. government personnel of being or having been Communists. Although most of his accusations were groundless, McCarthy was a master at using news media to publicize his accusations and build a power base. As a result, many persons were blacklisted and their careers ruined.

Absent clear evidence of general fame or notoriety in the community, and pervasive involvement in the affairs of society, an individual should not be deemed a public personality for all aspects of his life.[72]

Although Gertz was well known among attorneys and certain others, he had not, according to the Court, sought or achieved general fame throughout the community. In fact, the Court noted that none of the jurors had ever heard of him. The *Gertz* Court reasoned that private persons require greater protection against media, since they have little or no access to media channels for refutation of false or otherwise derogatory comments.

15.1.5.3   *Two Types of Public Persons*

All-purpose public persons have to prove actual malice in any libel suit. Vortex or limited public persons must prove actual malice only when the libel suit is directly related to an issue in which they are involved.

Following the *Gertz* decision, the courts seemed to recognize two types of public persons, defined as follows:

1. *All-purpose public persons* are those who have achieved widespread notoriety and who exercise general power or influence and occupy a position of continuing news value. Examples of all-purpose public figures include celebrities such as Michael Jackson, Dan Rather, or Jane Fonda. It would be up to the courts, but high-profile celebrities such as Oprah Winfrey and sports superstars such as Michael Jordan would also likely be included. All-purpose public figures must prove actual malice in any libel suit.

2. *Vortex (limited) public persons* are those who have voluntarily thrust themselves into discussion of a public controversy with specific intent to affect the outcome of that controversy. Vortex public persons must prove actual malice *only* in defamation suits directly related to the voluntary activity. For libel suits affecting all other aspects of their lives, they are private persons. An example of a vortex public person would be a local citizen circulating petitions for or against a proposed ordinance, or a major league baseball player discussing issues related to the player's involvement in baseball. As explained in Box 15.4, the courts have used a three-part test to establish whether a plaintiff is a vortex public person.[73]

The Supreme Court seems reluctant to define libel plaintiffs as "involuntary" public figures. When Russell Firestone, heir to the Firestone Tire fortune, obtained

---

[72] Gertz v. Robert Welch, Inc., 418 U.S. at 352 (1974).

[73] Waldbaum v. Fairchild Publications, 627 F.2d 1287 (1980).

BOX 15.4   Vortex Public Persons: A Three-step Test

In the 1980 case *Waldbaum* v. *Fairchild Publications*, a U.S. court of appeals summarized the three steps necessary to determine whether a plaintiff is a vortex public person.* The court must:

1. define the precise controversy involved;
2. determine the plaintiff's role in the controversy;
3. determine if the defamatory communications were germane to the plaintiff's participation in the controversy.

If the plaintiff's role was performed involuntarily or the libelous communications were not germane to the controversy, the plaintiff is not likely to be considered a vortex public person.

---

* 627 F.2d 1287 (1980).

---

a divorce from his wife Mary Alice, *Time* magazine published a brief notice that said he was granted the divorce on grounds of extreme cruelty and adultery. Adultery was in fact not mentioned in the divorce decree. When Mary Alice sued for libel, *Time* claimed that she was a public figure. Indeed, she was prominent, a socialite so frequently covered by the news media that she maintained a clipping service to keep a record of her publicity. The divorce itself had generated substantial media coverage, including press conferences conducted by Ms. Firestone. The Supreme Court, however, ruled that Mary Alice Firestone was not a public figure because she did not thrust herself into the public eye regarding a public controversy in order to influence any particular outcome.[74]

In *Hutchinson* v. *Proxmire*, Hutchinson, a behavioral scientist, had received a $500,000 grant to study animal aggression. Senator William Proxmire, convinced the grant was a waste of money, criticized the funding agencies and suggested that Hutchinson had "made a monkey out of the American taxpayer."[75] Hutchinson sued for libel damages, claiming the comments had damaged his ability to obtain grants and his standing among colleagues. The Supreme Court ruled that Hutchinson was not a public figure, since he had never sought any kind of prominence. Even if questionable expenditure of public funds was considered a public controversy, Mr. Hutchinson was involved only because of the senator's comments.[76]

In *Wolston* v. *Reader's Digest*, Wolston sued the magazine for accusing him of being a Russian spy. *Reader's Digest* argued that he was a public figure because he had previously made headlines by refusing to testify before a grand jury investigat-

---

[74] Time Inc. v. Firestone, 424 U.S. 448 (1976).
[75] Hutchinson v. Proxmire, 443 U.S. at 116 (1979).
[76] *Id.* at 111.

ing spy activities. The Court ruled that Wolston was not a public figure because he had not thrust himself into a public debate.[77]

The Supreme Court has never made a declarative ruling on whether public persons remain public over a long period of time, but lower courts have held that they do as long as any new defamation pertains to the issue with which public person status was first achieved. A New York court ruled that Roy Cohn, assistant to Senator Joseph McCarthy in the early 1950s red scare era, was still a public figure in 1980. NBC had broadcast a program titled "Tail Gunner Joe," which Cohn claimed held him up to public ridicule and damaged his reputation.[78]

15.1.6 Defenses against Libel Suits

Media defendants have successfully used seven defenses in libel suits: statute of limitations, truth, absolute privilege, qualified privilege, consent, opinion and fair comment, and neutral reportage.

Although plaintiffs in libel suits have a considerable burden of proof, defendants still must actively construct a defense to help bring about a favorable verdict. The determination of which defenses will be most effective depends on the source, circumstances, and context of the alleged defamation.

15.1.6.1 *Statute of Limitations*

In most states, plaintiffs must file libel suits within two years of the alleged defamatory publication.

Whatever the time period, a statute of limitations defense is a certain winner so long as there is no dispute over the exact date of publication. Most states adhere to the *single publication rule*. This means that only the initial publication is considered when determining the exact date of publication. In other words, the clock does not start over every time a newspaper or magazine is resold or displayed. The rule does not apply to new editions of a newspaper and is not much help to broadcast and cable newscasters, since most news stories are repeated at least once. Each follow-up newscast or update that repeats the defamation constitutes a new publication that starts the clock again.

15.1.6.2 *Truth*

Since the burden of proof is on the plaintiff to prove that defamatory communications are false, defendants are usually not forced to use truth as a defense in libel suits. Still, any media defendant who can establish truth is likely to win a libel suit.

Most libel suits against the media involve either public plaintiffs or issues of public concern. Since the *Sullivan* and *Hepps* decisions have significantly shifted

---

[77] Wolston v. Reader's Digest, 443 U.S. 157 (1979).
[78] Cohn v. NBC, 414 N.Y.S.2d 906 (1979); *aff'd* 430 N.Y.S.2d 265 (1980).

the burden of proof to plaintiffs in these cases, truth is used as a defense less often than it was before 1964. When a truth defense is pursued, a media defendant does not have to prove that every detail of a story is true in order to establish truth.

Of course, one would expect truth to be most effective as a defense when the communication is actually true. If the communication is true, libel litigation is less likely even if the message is extremely negative and damaging to an individual.

15.1.6.3 *Absolute Privilege*

Public officials and certain other persons have absolute protection against being sued for libel for any statements made during official proceedings.

You may be surprised to learn that in some situations false and damaging statements can be made about an individual or corporation without exposing the speaker to any risk of a libel suit. For example, any statement made by a government official acting in an official capacity is privileged. However, in *Hutchinson* v. *Proxmire* the Supreme Court made it clear that comments, if they are to be protected, must be made during *official* deliberations. The Court ruled that Senator Proxmire's criticisms of Hutchinson's research were protected if made on the Senate floor during official deliberations, but protection did not extend to his office or to appearances on television talk shows.[79]

The absolute privilege protection is intended to ensure free and open discussion and debate in the formation of public policy. The privilege extends to most levels of government and includes comments made by judges, attorneys, witnesses, and other participants in judicial proceedings. The privilege exists even if the statements are made with ill will, knowledge of their falsity, or reckless disregard for whether they are true or false.

15.1.6.4 *Qualified Privilege*

In most states, the media cannot be sued for libel when broadcasting or otherwise publishing fair and accurate summaries of legislative, judicial, executive, or other governmental proceedings. The protection also extends to records and documents related to official proceedings.

The privilege afforded mass media is called "qualified" because it does not provide absolute protection for the media. For example, journalists are not protected if reports are published with common law malice (with ill will or intent to harm). Also, in most states qualified privilege applies only to fair, balanced, and reasonably accurate summaries of official proceedings. Reports based on any sealed or secret documents, or trial proceedings such as depositions that are not part of the official record are likely not protected. Reports of arrests may not be protected until the police have officially charged an individual with a crime. Still, qualified privilege is a critically important protection for the media. It allows journalists to report on even

---

[79] Hutchinson v. Proxmire, 443 U.S. at 111 (1979).

controversial government proceedings without fear of libel litigation if the reports are accurate and balanced and made without malice of any kind.

15.1.6.5 Consent

Consent is effective in libel suits only in the unlikely event that the plaintiff consented to publication of defamatory communications and had (or should have had) substantial knowledge of the details of the communication prior to publication.

Although rarely available to defendants, consent, if obtained in writing, is an effective defense in libel suits. Some states recognize what is called *implied consent*. This occurs when a news reporter confronts the plaintiff before broadcasting or otherwise publishing defamatory charges and asks for a response. If the charges are denied, the reporter has the right to report the charges along with the denial. Also, if a plaintiff agrees to talk to the media about the allegations, consent may be assumed.

15.1.6.6 Opinion and Fair Comment

Statements of opinion and communications containing loose, figurative, or hyperbolic language have traditionally received more protection against libel suits than statements of fact. However, in *Milkovich* v. *Lorain Journal* the U.S. Supreme Court ruled that there is no separate constitutional protection for statements of opinion.

Although potentially defamatory comments could fall into either category, there is a distinction to be made between "opinion" and "fair comment." Whereas fair comment as a defense evolved through common law, the courts have recognized a constitutional protection for opinion.

By definition, opinions are judgments or appraisals made by journalists, commentators, or talk show hosts, and are not intended as factual declarations. Many states require that opinions be based on statements of fact, but the facts themselves do not have to be published along with the defamatory communication. Underlying facts may be commonly known or otherwise available to the listener, viewer, or reader. If an opinion is stated with malice of any kind, the opinion protection is nullified.

Supreme Court Justice Lewis Powell, in his *Gertz* v. *Welch* opinion, stated, "There is no such thing as a false idea" and said that opinions should be protected regardless of the injury they may cause.[80] Despite a later declaration by the Court that these arguments were indeed dicta[81] and that the issue was still up to the states, the *Gertz* decision has often been cited as lower courts have protected statements of opinion.[82]

---

[80] Gertz v. Robert Welch, Inc., 418 U.S. at 339 (1974).

[81] You may remember from Chapter 1 that dicta are statements made by a judge in an opinion that do not have direct bearing on the legal issue in question. Powell's comments are considered dicta because the *Gertz* decision did not involve statements of opinion.

[82] Miskovsky v. Oklahoma Publishing, 459 U.S. at 923 (1982).

The breadth of protection can be extensive. In protecting opinion, courts have allowed such characterizations as sleazebag,[83] sloppy and irresponsible,[84] fascist,[85] scab,[86] and horse's ass.[87] The protection also extends to critical comments and reviews of plays and other artistic performances. Near the turn of the century the *Des Moines Leader* blasted a vocal trio called the Cherry Sisters in a scathing review:

> Their long skinny arms . . . swung mechanically and (after a while) waved frantically at the suffering audience. The mouths of their rancid features opened like caverns, and sounds like the wailing of damned souls issued therefrom. . . . Jessie, the only one who showed her stockings, has legs with calves as classic in their outlines as the curves of a broom handle.[88]

Despite the caustic language, the review was ruled fair comment.

The opinion and fair comment defenses are certainly not absolute. When KNXT-TV, a CBS affiliate in southern California, aired a videotape of the arrest of an auto shop owner who failed to give required written estimates for repairs, a California court ruled that the story was protected as fair comment. The court noted, however, that if the story had aired nationally the protection may not have applied, since the local shop owner's arrest would not have been of national public interest. In its investigative report the KNXT news team had requested estimates from the shop owner. The bill was $160 despite the fact that, aside from a bad spark plug, another mechanic had already judged the car to be in good working order.[89]

In *Greenbelt* v. *Bresler*, the Supreme Court permitted a reporter's use of the term *blackmail* in covering a heated debate over a zoning change request. Charles Bresler, a real estate developer, had sought the zoning change so that he could build a high-rise apartment complex. When he offered to donate land for a new school if the change was granted, an opponent charged that the offer amounted to blackmail. The Court ruled that readers could reasonably interpret the reporter's use of the term *blackmail* to be one person's opinion of Bresler's offer.[90]

After Boston television reporter John Cole was fired by WBZ-TV, a newspaper quoted a spokesperson for the station who had referred to Cole's reporting as "bad," and "sloppy and irresponsible." Cole sued the station, but the court ruled that the comments were protected statements of opinion.[91]

[83] Henderson v. Times Mirror Co., 876 F.2d 108 (1989).
[84] Cole v. Westinghouse Broadcasting Co., 435 N.E.2d 1021 (1982).
[85] Buckley v. Littell, 539 F.2d 882 (1976).
[86] Old Dominion Branch No. 496, Nat'l Ass'n of Letter Carriers, AFL-CIO v. Austin, 418 U.S. 264 (1974).
[87] Blouin v. Anton, 431 A.2d 489 (1981).
[88] Cherry v. Des Moines Leader, 86 N.W. 323 (1901).
[89] Rollenhagen v. City of Orange, 116 Cal. App. 3d 414 (1981).
[90] Greenbelt Coop. Publishing Co. v. Bresler, 398 U.S. 6 (1970).
[91] Cole v. Westinghouse, 435 N.E.2d 1021 (1982).

In another case involving Boston media, a magazine described a television sportscaster as the worst sportscaster in Boston. A Massachusetts court ruled that the comments were protected, especially given the context of the article. It had appeared in the magazine's annual "best-worst awards" edition.[92]

In *Ollman* v. *Evans* the court attempted to provide a basis on which to distinguish between statements of fact and opinion. The case resulted from an editorial appearing in the *Washington Post* and other newspapers that accused University of Maryland professor Bertell Ollman of wanting to use the classroom to convert students to Marxism and prepare them for a Marxist revolution. The editorial also quoted an unnamed political scientist as saying that Ollman lacked status within the profession. Following publication of the article the University of Maryland board of trustees refused a search committee recommendation that Ollman be appointed chair of the Department of Government and Politics. Ollman sued the *Post* for libel, and the case was ultimately heard en banc by the D.C. Circuit Court of Appeals.[93] The court decided, in a not-so-compelling 6-5 vote, that the statements were protected opinion. As explained in Box 15.5, the decision also provided a test to help distinguish fact from opinion.[94]

The viability of opinion as a libel defense was substantially diminished by the U.S. Supreme Court in 1990. Following the outbreak of a brawl at a wrestling match, the Maple Heights (Ohio) High School wrestling team had been placed on probation. The *Lorain Journal* had accused the coach, Michael Milkovich, of inciting the riot by inspiring students to attack opposing fans. The newspaper also claimed that Milkovich had lied at a hearing on the incident.

The Supreme Court decided that use of the word *lied* was not "loose, figurative, or hyperbolic language." To the contrary, the Court concluded that the words communicated rather clearly that Milkovich had committed perjury. In his majority opinion, Chief Justice Rehnquist argued that there is no separate constitutional privilege for assertions of opinion. Reluctant to completely eliminate protection for pure opinion, the Court proposed a two-part test to distinguish protected from unprotected defamatory statements:

> Step One—*determine whether the comments are verifiable*
>
> Step Two—*determine whether a reasonable reader would think that the article implies defamatory facts*

News stories and other communications using loose, figurative language would continue to receive protection.[95] Some legal experts argue that despite the two-part test the *Milkovich* decision has severely limited the opinion defense and will, therefore, produce a chilling effect on journalists and other commentators, since any

---

[92] Myers v. Boston Magazine, 403 N.E.2d 376 (Mass. 1980).

[93] An en banc decision is one made by all judges of a particular U.S. Circuit Court of Appeals as opposed to the usual panel of three judges.

[94] Ollman v. Evans, 750 F.2d 970 (D.C. Cir. 1984).

[95] Milkovich v. Lorain Journal, 497 U.S. 1 (1990).

BOX 15.5   Distinguishing Fact from Opinion: A Four-Factor Test

In his decision in the case *Ollman* v. *Evans*, Judge Kenneth Starr offered the following four-factor test to help the courts distinguish fact from opinion.*

1. *Common Usage*: What do the words mean? Do they have definite, commonly accepted meanings or are they ambiguous and open for interpretation? The more ambiguous the language, the less likely the words will be construed as fact.
2. *Verifiability*: To what extent can the statements be objectively proven true or false?
3. *Linguistic Context*: What do the words appear to mean when considered in the context of the entire article? For example, the comments about Professor Ollman were made in an editorial column on the editorial page of the newspaper. Any reasonable person should presume that comments made in such contexts are more opinion than fact.
4. *Social Context*: What do the words appear to mean when considered in the broader social context? For example, the reference to blackmail in *Greenbelt* v. *Bresler* originated in a heated debate over a controversial zoning request.† News reports of comments made in such contexts have been afforded somewhat more protection.

---

* Ollman v. Evans, 750 F.2d 970 (D.C. Cir. 1984)
† Greenbelt Coop. Publishing v. Bresler, 398 U.S. 6 (1970).

---

statement capable of being proven true or false will be actionable as libel.[96] As for Milkovich, he settled his case in 1991 for an amount estimated to be over $100,000.

Following the *Milkovich* decision, the Supreme Court remanded a $4 billion libel suit against ABC's *20/20* program. In a segment called "Save the Elephants," aired on March 12, 1987, Arthur Jones, a wealthy businessman and inventor of the Nautilus exercise machines, was accused of being insensitive to the plight of elephants he had relocated from Africa to his estate in Ocala, Florida. The animals were in the process of being widely dispersed, a process described on the program as a "fate worse than death." The program clearly intimated that dispersement was detrimental to the health and welfare of the elephants. Jones contended that the program portrayed him as a liar, a cheat, dishonest, an animal abuser, a hypocrite, and a wacky screwball. The district court had ruled that the statements could not be reasonably interpreted as defamatory and that many were protected as nonactionable

---

[96] John B. Cromer, "Milkovich v. Lorain Journal Co.: This Opinion May Stifle Yours," 20 Cap. U. L. R. 497 (1991).

opinion. The Supreme Court, following the *Milkovich* decision, remanded the case for further consideration. The appeals court concluded that since the program had been judged to be nondefamatory, the question of whether the *20/20* statements were protected opinion was moot.[97]

15.1.6.7   *Neutral Reportage*

Some courts have recognized a neutral reportage privilege that allows journalists to accurately report comments made by public persons even if there is doubt about the truthfulness of the comments.

The neutral reportage privilege is granted only when the following elements are established:

1. The story must be newsworthy and typically should involve a public controversy. The controversy cannot be media instigated.
2. The defamatory comments must have been made by a responsible person.
3. The individual libeled must be a public figure or a public person.
4. The reporter must accurately report the libelous comments and present opposing viewpoints.
5. The reporter must be impartial.

A famous neutral reportage case involved the use of the pesticide DDT. The *New York Times* published an article that quoted Audubon Society officials as accusing scientists of being paid to lie and act as spokespersons for the pesticide industry. Some scientists named in the article were contacted and had denied the charges. Courts had previously established that such denials give the reporter reason to believe the charges are false.

A U.S. court of appeals ruled that the Constitution protects a journalist who publishes accurate, unbiased reports of accusations against public figures even if the journalist has doubts about their veracity. According to the court's decision:

> What is newsworthy about such accusations is that they were made. We do not believe that the press may be required under the First Amendment to suppress newsworthy statements merely because it has serious doubts regarding their truth.[98]

The Supreme Court has declined several opportunities to make a definitive ruling on neutral reportage, so the defense is not recognized in many states. It should be used as a libel defense with caution.

In most cases media defendants attempt several angles of defense. CBS advanced three defenses—opinion, truth, and absence of actual malice—in a suit

---

[97] Jones v. ABC, 961 F.2d 1546 (1992). *See also* 694 F. Supp. 1542 (1988).
[98] Edwards v. National Audubon Soc'y, 556 F.2d 113 (1977).

brought by a tobacco company, and failed on all three. On a news perspective program Chicago station WBBM-TV, owned by CBS, had broadcast that Viceroy, a cigarette manufacturer, was engaged in a strategy to attract young people to smoking. Viceroy was accused of projecting "the cigarettes as an invitation into the adult world . . . as an illicit pleasure, a basic symbol of the growing-up maturity process."[99] As for CBS's three defense arguments, the court ruled that (1) the commentary contained statements of fact, not protected opinion, (2) the comments were not truthful, since an FTC report mentioned in the report was not fairly summarized, and (3) the comments were broadcast with actual malice, since a CBS employee destroyed relevant documents while the litigation was pending. Viceroy was awarded a $3 million judgment.[100]

15.1.7   Types of Damages

Successful libel plaintiffs are allowed to collect compensatory, presumed, and punitive damages.

A libel plaintiff can establish all the elements of proof necessary to win a libel suit and still be awarded no money unless damages can be proved. Three broad categories of damages are available—compensatory, presumed, and punitive.

15.1.7.1   *Compensatory Damages*

Compensatory damages, also called actual damages, are paid for injury to the defamed person's reputation, for mental anguish, and for monetary losses.

An injured party does not have to prove specific damages to collect compensatory damages. The courts require only that the plaintiff provide sufficient evidence of mental anguish, suffering, or humiliation.

Special damages are awarded if the plaintiff does prove specific monetary losses. Special damages are not awarded for any kind of mental anguish or humiliation.

15.1.7.2   *Presumed Damages*

Presumed damages can be awarded to public officials and public persons only when the communication is libelous per se and actual malice is established.

Presumed damages are awarded under the assumption that some type of damage is presumed to have occurred whenever someone is libeled. In 1985, the U.S. Supreme Court ruled that when defamatory statements do not relate to matters of public concern, private persons can collect presumed and punitive damages without establishing actual malice.[101]

---

[99] Brown and Williamson Tobacco Corp. v. Walter Jacobson and CBS, 827 F.2d at 1123 (1987).
[100] *Id.* at 1119.
[101] Dun & Bradstreet v. Greenmoss Builders, 472 U.S. 749 (1985).

15.1.7.3 *Punitive Damages*

Punitive damages are awarded by juries in order to punish the mass medium involved in the defamation. Punitive awards can total many millions of dollars.

In some states, private plaintiffs suing for defamatory communications that do not deal with issues of public concern must establish common law malice to collect punitive damages. Since *Gertz* v. *Welch*, all other plaintiffs must prove *New York Times* actual malice.

The awards for punitive damages can be astronomical, but are quite often reduced by the court. A few states disallow punitive damage awards altogether, and there is widespread concern that huge punitive awards in libel cases create a chilling effect on journalists and other commentators.

The 1978 "Miss Wyoming," Kimerli Jayne Pring, was awarded $25 million in punitive damages along with $1.5 million in compensatory damages because of an article in *Penthouse* magazine. She claimed the article, which suggested a fictional Miss Wyoming could make men "levitate" during sexual intercourse, made her appear to be sexually promiscuous and immoral.[102] The judge reduced the punitive award to half the original amount but deliberately kept it above the $10 million worth of libel insurance carried by *Penthouse*. An appeals court later reversed the entire decision, holding that the article could reasonably be interpreted only as pure fantasy.[103]

15.2 LAW OF PRIVACY

The right of privacy is most often defined as (1) *the right to be left alone*, and (2) *the right to be free from unwarranted publicity*. Privacy law in most states is divided into four broad categories: appropriation or commercialization, intrusion, dissemination of private facts, and putting a person in a false light. More recently, courts have also awarded damages for intentional and negligent infliction of emotional distress.

Invasion of privacy, much like libel, has become a significant legal problem for the mass media. In the first place, privacy is becoming a somewhat extinct commodity in modern society. Computerized record keeping has resulted in the availability of data banks containing huge quantities of information on individuals and businesses. Computerized cable systems offer "upstream capacity" that allows subscribers to use cable service for home security and other services but could also allow dissemination of certain information—such as whether they are at home at a given time—that subscribers might prefer to keep private. Satellite technology and electronic news-gathering capabilities allow television stations to broadcast live

---

[102] Pring v. Penthouse International, 695 F.2d at 441 (1982).
[103] *Id.* at 438.

sound and video from almost anywhere, and when this technology is combined with widespread use of private video camcorders, the potential for intrusion into private matters is increased dramatically.

The Constitution never mentions a right to privacy, but in the 1965 case *Griswold* v. *Connecticut* the Supreme Court recognized a constitutional basis for an individual's right to be free from undue governmental influence. In *Griswold* the Court overturned a Connecticut law prohibiting the sale of contraceptives on the basis that it unduly interfered in the lives of married couples.[104]

The origin of a right to privacy can perhaps be traced back to an 1890 *Harvard Law Review* article by Boston attorney Samuel Warren and his former Harvard Law School classmate, Louis D. Brandeis, who would eventually become a Supreme Court justice. Even back then Warren and Brandeis were concerned about the manner in which "mechanical devices" allowed intrusions into the private lives of citizens.[105] They advocated that the courts recognize a right to privacy.

Whether that right is constitutionally protected became a principal issue during the 1987 confirmation hearings of rejected Supreme Court nominee Robert Bork and is a central issue in the controversy over women's abortion rights. In the landmark abortion decision *Roe* v. *Wade* the Supreme Court said that even though the term is not mentioned in the Constitution, "the Court has recognized that a right of privacy, or a guarantee of certain areas or zones of privacy, does exist under the Constitution."[106] Courts have now interpreted the right to protect individuals from a variety of privacy invasions.

As noted in the presummary to this section, courts generally recognize four types of invasion of privacy: appropriation or unwarranted commercialization, privacy intrusion, dissemination of private facts, and putting a person in a false light. All four types are recognized in most states, either by statute or by common law.

15.2.1 Appropriation or Unwarranted Commercialization

> Appropriation is the using of a person's name, picture, photograph, likeness, or any aspect of the person's personality without permission to achieve some commercial advantage or profit.

Appropriation goes back to 1903 when the New York state legislature passed an appropriation statute in response to the case *Roberson* v. *Rochester Folding Box*. Abigail Roberson had suddenly discovered widespread use of her picture advertising a brand of flour. She sued but lost because there was no statute protecting individuals from such practices. So, the New York legislature passed a statute re-

---

[104] Griswold v. Connecticut, 381 U.S. 479 (1965).
[105] Samuel Warren and Louis D. Brandeis, "The Right of Privacy," 4 *Harv. L. Rev.* 193 (1890).
[106] Roe v. Wade, 410 U.S. 113 (1973).

quiring consent before a person's name or likeness could be used in a commercial manner.[107]

The courts have generally allowed the use of names and photographs of individuals involved in newsworthy events such as car crashes, riots, and robberies. Names and photographs may also be used in feature stories, but journalists should make certain that no false or demeaning impressions are created. For example, a television news feature on the use of libraries by young persons may include shots of identifiable children and still not constitute appropriation. But if the feature deals with a more controversial topic such as parents' neglect of children's nutritional needs, the same shots may be actionable under other types of invasion of privacy or even libel law.

If the purpose of a communication is clearly commercial, the courts are less lenient with the media. For example, a court ruled in 1980 that it was clearly appropriation when a company started selling portable toilet seats using television superstar Johnny Carson's famous intro "Here's Johnny."[108] But commercialization does not have to be so obvious. When *Playgirl* magazine published a sketch of a man resembling Muhammad Ali sitting in a boxing ring, the court ruled that Ali's likeness was improperly commercialized. The sketch had included the description "the Greatest," a signature statement often used by Ali.[109] And when a Jacqueline Kennedy Onassis look-alike model was used by Christian Dior in an advertisement, Onassis successfully sued for appropriation. The ad featured the model, dressed to look like Onassis, along with several actual celebrities.[110]

Public figures and celebrities such as Ali and Onassis have additional protection under what is called the *right to publicity*. This gives celebrities the right to control use of their names, likenesses, pictures, voices, or any distinct feature or talent they possess. The right is recognized as a "property right," which means that unlike appropriation, the right of publicity may continue even after the death of the celebrity. State laws vary widely regarding this right, so many issues regarding the right to publicity are unsettled. One matter that has been settled is that a singer's right to publicity is violated when his or her voice is imitated for commercial purposes. Ford Motor Company was ordered to pay entertainer Bette Midler $400,000 for airing a commercial in which her voice was imitated. The singer had been asked to perform her hit song "Do You Want to Dance" for the ad. When Midler refused, one of her former backup vocalists was hired to imitate her voice. A number of people testified that they believed the voice in the commercial was Midler's.[111]

In 1993, the Supreme Court refused to overturn a $2.5 million award to singer Tom Waits, whose distinctive, raspy singing voice was intentionally imitated in a radio commercial for SalsaRio Doritos. Waits, known to be strongly opposed to the

---

[107] Roberson v. Rochester Folding Box Co., 171 N.Y. 538, 64 N.E. 442 (1902).
[108] Carson v. Here's Johnny Portable Toilets, 498 F. Supp. 71 (1980).
[109] Ali v. Playgirl, 447 F. Supp. 723 (1978).
[110] Onassis v. Christian Dior, 472 N.Y.S.2d 254 (1984).
[111] Midler v. Ford Motor Company, 849 F.2d 460 (1988).

endorsement of products by artists, was so well imitated that an alternative recording was considered by the producers of the commercial due to concerns over a potential lawsuit. Punitive damages were awarded because the jury found that the defendants had, in addition to misappropriating Waits's voice, acted with "oppression, fraud, or malice."[112]

The Supreme Court, in *Zacchini* v. *Scripps-Howard*, ruled that "the broadcast of a performer's entire act poses a substantial threat to the economic value of that performance."[113] The case resulted when WEWS-TV in Cleveland broadcast a 15-second segment showing performer Hugo Zacchini being blasted out of a cannon, even though he had asked that the segment not be aired. The Court concluded that the act was the performer's professional property and that the broadcast threatened its economic value, since those who saw it on television might be less likely to go and see the performance in person.

In appropriation suits, promotional programming will likely be considered commercial. During a "Dialing for Dollars" game on KTFX-TV in Salt Lake City the station broadcast the name and phone number of a local resident. The resident subsequently received a number of prank phone calls—some rude and threatening—from KTFX viewers who happened to hear the number. A Utah court ruled that such promotional use of an individual's name and phone number violates state law prohibiting any use of a person's identity for advertising purposes.[114]

It is typically not considered appropriation to include shots of identifiable people in brief promotional messages. Station KATU-TV in Portland, Oregon, used shots of an automobile accident victim receiving medical care in a promotional advertisement for an upcoming special report on emergency medical services. The *only* use the station made of the shots was promotional, since the station never ran a story on the accident. The victim, who was shown bleeding and in obvious pain, sued for invasion of privacy. The court ruled that the advertisement did not invade his privacy, since his appearance was only incidental to the station's purpose of promoting the program.[115]

The use of file footage or file photographs in a promotional manner is also not considered appropriation. In *Booth* v. *Curtis Publishing, Holiday* magazine had published a picture of actress Shirley Booth, star of the 1960s television show *Hazel*, swimming at a resort in the West Indies. When the picture was published a second time purely to promote the magazine, Booth sued for appropriation. The court ruled that the picture was designed only to illustrate the quality and content of the magazine, and that Booth's appearance was only incidental to that purpose.[116]

[112] The jury also awarded damages because of the likelihood that radio listeners would be misled into believing that Waits had endorsed Frito-Lay's products. This constitutes a violation of the Lanham Act as discussed in EMG 15.3.14. Frito-Lay, Inc. v. Waits, 113 S. Ct. 1047 (1993); Waits v. Frito-Lay, Inc., 23 U.S.P.Q.2d (BNA) 1721 (1992).
[113] Zacchini v. Scripps-Howard Broadcasting Co., 433 U.S. 562 (1977).
[114] Jeppson v. United Television, 580 P.2d 1087 (Utah 1978).
[115] Anderson v. Fisher Broadcasting Co., 712 P.2d 803 (1986).
[116] Booth v. Curtis Publishing, 15 A.D.2d 343 (1962).

15.2.2 Privacy Intrusion

Privacy intrusion occurs when one intentionally intrudes—physically or by technological or any other means—on the seclusion, private affairs, or concerns of an individual. Generally, events occurring in public places can be recorded and published, but use of zoom lenses or powerful microphones to gain access to otherwise private places or events would likely be considered privacy intrusion.

What comes to mind when most people think of invasion of privacy is really what is called *privacy intrusion* or simply *intrusion*. Intrusion is actionable in most states if the intrusion would be highly offensive to a reasonable person. The mass media do not really find themselves as defendants in intrusion cases that often, especially when compared to libel or other forms of invasion of privacy. But certain practices can increase the risk of litigation and should be avoided.

Electronic media journalists must be particularly cautious in gathering information in private places. The increasing sophistication of news-gathering technology only increases the temptation to snoop around and capture events and interactions that are private. Microphones can now pick up conversations from considerable distances, and telephoto lenses allow photographers to zoom in on otherwise secluded, private areas. Tape recorders and cameras are so small that they can easily be concealed. It should be noted that it does not matter how important or newsworthy a story is if intrusion occurs. Newsworthiness does not make private property public and is not an effective defense in a privacy intrusion suit.

Although ethically questionable, it is not illegal in some states for journalists to conceal recorders and surreptitiously tape conversations, as long as they identify themselves as journalists. But it is illegal to use camera zoom lens and directional microphone technology to gain access to and record what would otherwise be private interactions. A general rule is that only those events and interactions that can be clearly seen or heard in a public place may be listened to, photographed, and recorded.[117] If gaining access requires use of technology—even something as simple as a stepladder—surveillance and/or recording of communications may constitute intrusion.

Sometimes even matters occurring in public cannot be broadcast or otherwise published. The subject matter must still be newsworthy or the individuals involved may sue for dissemination of private facts, which we will discuss in the next section. The point is that privacy intrusion cannot occur in public places. Whatever occurs in public is public, and the act of photographing, recording, broadcasting, or publishing it does not make it private. Spectator John Neff found this out when *Sports Illustrated* published a photograph of him standing in a crowd at a Pittsburgh Steelers football game with his trousers unzipped. The court, influenced somewhat by the fact that Neff had encouraged the photographer to take his picture, ruled that his privacy was not invaded because he was photographed in a public place.[118]

---

[117] Jaubert v. Crowley Post-Signal, 375 So. 2d 1386 (La. 1979).
[118] Neff v. Time, Inc., 406 F. Supp. 858 (1976).

John Jacova did nothing to encourage his appearance in a television news story on a gambling raid. Jacova was innocently standing in the cigar shop of Miami's Casablanca Hotel when police rushed in with television cameras close behind. In an evening newscast he was clearly visible standing against a wall talking to officers, and viewers could have concluded that he was a suspect. But the court held that a television station—just like a newspaper, newsreel, or other communication medium—"has a qualified privilege to use in its telecast the name or photograph of a person who has become an 'actor' in a newsworthy event."[119]

15.2.2.1 *Recording Telephone Conversations.*

To tap someone's telephone is not only an invasion of privacy, it is also a violation of the federal wiretap statute.[120] Although it is illegal to intercept telephone conversations, it is not illegal in most states for one participant in a conversation to record or transmit the conversation to a third party, with or without the knowledge of the other participant. Federal Communications Commission policies are more restrictive. Any person interacting via telephone with broadcast station personnel must be notified if the conversation is to be taped for broadcast.[121]

15.2.2.2 *Intrusion into Public and Private Places*

Journalists may commit intrusion when they remain on private property or inside business establishments when asked to leave by the occupant or owner. The legal wrong of intrusion occurs when the act of intrusion is committed, not when material obtained is broadcast or otherwise published.

The distinction between public and private places is not always so clear. One point that is clear is that journalists who enter private property should leave if asked to by any legitimate owner, occupant, or management authority on that property.

15.2.2.2.1 *Intrusion and Private Dwellings*

A journalist must obtain permission to gather information or shoot video inside a private dwelling. Gaining access to a home through misleading or surreptitious methods is considered an act of intrusion. However, a homeowner who consents to an in-home interview with media representatives may have no expectation of privacy.

In most circumstances a private home is a private place. When *Life* magazine reporters Jackie Metcalf and William Ray went to the private home of A. A. Dietemann to investigate rumors of medical quackery, they did so under the pretense of being patients. They also concealed a camera and eavesdropping equipment. Ray took photographs as Dietemann conducted an examination of Metcalf,

---

[119] Jacova v. Southern Radio and Television Co., 83 So. 2d 34 (1955).
[120] Omnibus Crime Control and Safe Streets Act of 1968, 18 U.S.C. § 2510–2520.
[121] 3 F.C.C.R. 5461 (1988).

who had falsely complained of a lump on her breast. As Dietemann issued his diagnosis—that Metcalf had consumed rancid butter some 12 years earlier—the entire conversation was transmitted to a recorder in a nearby car occupied by a health inspector and representative of the district attorney's office. *Life* later published the pictures and an account of the incident in an article on medical quackery.

A U.S. court of appeals was unimpressed with the reporters' journalistic savvy or the involvement of health and other public officials. The court ruled that the reporters had committed intrusion because they entered Dietemann's private home and used a hidden microphone and camera.[122] In its decision the court said:

> The First Amendment is not a license to trespass, to steal, or to intrude by electronic means into the precincts of another's home or office. It does not become such a license simply because the person subjected to the intrusion is reasonably suspected of committing a crime.[123]

Despite his arrest for medical quackery, Dietemann was awarded $1,000 in damages.

It should be noted that the *Dietemann* court held that it was not a crime to publish the pictures. The legal wrong occurred when Dietemann's private property was intruded upon, not at the time of publication.

ABC was sued after former *20/20* reporter Geraldo Rivera and an executive producer arranged an interview with a woman who claimed an Ohio judge was exchanging lenient criminal sentences for sexual favors. Sandra Boddie agreed to the interview but asked not to appear on camera. ABC hid a camera and recorded the interview anyway and even broadcast a segment on *20/20*. Boddie's suit included charges of invasion of privacy and violation of federal wiretap law.

A federal appeals court ruled that since Boddie consented to the interview no intrusion had occurred, even though the camera and recorder were concealed and she claimed to be unaware that the recording was being made.[124] The court rejected the notion that a person could have any expectation of privacy when talking to a reporter for a major television network. The wiretap claim was at first upheld, since the microphone had transmitted a signal to third parties listening in a nearby van. But the court ultimately concluded that Congress never intended for wiretap statutes to be actionable against media defendants engaged in news gathering unless the journalists themselves had committed a crime or tort.[125] The *Boddie* decision should not be taken as an unrestricted green light for journalists, but it does show how distasteful news-gathering techniques can be, yet still remain inside the letter of the law.

---

[122] Dietemann v. Time, Inc., 449 F.2d 245 (1971).
[123] *Id.* at 249.
[124] Boddie v. ABC, 731 F.2d 333 (1984).
[125] Boddie v. ABC, 694 F. Supp. 1304 (N.D. Ohio 1988).

15.2.2.2.2   Doctrine of Conversion

Under the doctrine of conversion, a journalist who accepts and files documents obtained by another through intrusion has also committed intrusion.

Given the court's position in *Dietemann,* what if the "sting" had been carried out by persons not associated with *Life* magazine? What if an individual commits a definite act of intrusion, illegally obtains documents, and then turns them over to a reporter who broadcasts or otherwise publishes the stolen information?

That is precisely what happened when documents were removed from the office of Senator Thomas Dodd of Connecticut. The documents, containing evidence of misappropriation of campaign funds, were removed, photocopied, and returned to Dodd's files. Copies were given to journalists Drew Pearson and Jack Anderson. The court ruled that the individuals who entered the office and photocopied the documents had committed intrusion but refused to rule that publication of the information was an act of intrusion, even though the journalists *knew* the documents had been stolen. Senator Dodd had argued that journalist Pearson should be held liable through what is known as *conversion,* or the unauthorized exercise of ownership rights over another's property. The court ruled that conversion had not occurred because the documents had no property value, and because the journalists received only photocopies of the original documents, which were promptly returned to Dodd's files.[126] Had the journalists accepted the original documents and placed them in their own files, they would likely have committed an act of conversion.

15.2.2.3   Intrusion and Business Establishments

Places of business may be public or private places. Generally, journalists may stay if invited, but should promptly leave any business establishment when asked to do so by the owner or other legitimate authority.

As part of a crackdown on prostitution, Chicago undercover cop Arlyn Cassidy set out to investigate one of the city's massage parlors. After paying $30 for what was billed as a "deluxe" lingerie modeling, Cassidy watched as the model changed garments several times. He also made suggestive remarks and physical advances before arresting the woman for solicitation. Little did Cassidy know that the local ABC outlet, WLS-TV, had placed news cameras behind a one-way mirror and taped the entire encounter. Cassidy claimed his privacy was invaded but the court disagreed, holding that (1) the film crew was not in a private home, but in a public business, (2) Cassidy was a public official acting in an official capacity, and (3) the television news crew had been invited into the business.[127]

The law is unclear regarding privacy intrusion and news gathering inside restaurants. Journalists should typically expect a restaurant to be a private place, public only for the purpose of eating dinner, and promptly leave if asked. As part of an

---

[126] Pearson v. Dodd, 410 F.2d 701 (1969).
[127] Cassidy v. ABC, 377 N.E.2d 126 (1978).

investigation into health code irregularities, WCBS-TV reporters stormed into the fashionable Le Mistral restaurant in New York with cameras rolling. The sudden appearance of cameras in the dining area sent customers scurrying about and even ducking under tables. The camera crews persisted despite repeated demands from management that they leave. The court ruled that such entry without permission, and after being asked to leave, was an invasion of privacy.[128]

A similar situation occurred when reporters from WROC-TV in Rochester, New York, were invited to accompany Humane Society investigators to a home in which cruelty to animals was suspected. The reporters entered and photographed the home despite protests from the occupants. The court ruled that such uninvited and unpermitted entry into a private home is an invasion of privacy.[129]

15.2.2.3 *Implied Consent and Common Custom and Usage*

Under the doctrine of implied consent, persons who are involved in newsworthy events are considered by the courts to have given implied consent to be photographed and identified in news stories. Likewise, the doctrine of custom and usage allows journalists to enter private property so long as they leave upon request. These doctrines are not recognized in all states and do not offer absolute protection to journalists against intrusion suits.

On September 15, 1972, fire destroyed the Jacksonville, Florida, home of Klenna Ann Fletcher, killing her seventeen-year-old daughter. Mrs. Fletcher, who was out of town, learned about the fire and loss of her daughter the next day by reading the newspaper and viewing photographs published therein. The photographs, which included a silhouette of where the girl's body had been, were taken by a newspaper photographer at the request of a fire marshal who had run out of film.[130]

The court rejected Fletcher's charges of invasion of privacy:

> The law is well settled in Florida and elsewhere that there is no unlawful trespass when peaceful entry is made, without objection, under common custom and usage.[131]

Since media defendants have also lost privacy suits in similar circumstances, it should be emphasized that the doctrines of implied consent and custom and usage offer questionable protection for journalists. The doctrines did not protect an Orlando television station news crew that accompanied police on a midnight raid of a private boarding school suspected of abusing students.[132] Students and teachers were roused from their beds during the raid. Photographers roamed freely through-

---

[128] Le Mistral, Inc. v. CBS, 61 A.D.2d 491 (1978).

[129] Anderson v. WROC-TV, 441 N.Y.S.2d 220 (1981).

[130] Florida Publishing v. Fletcher, 340 So. 2d 914 (1977).

[131] *Id.* at 916.

[132] Green Valley School v. Cowles Broadcasting, 327 So. 2d 810 (Fla. App. 1976).

out the dormitory shooting video, some allegedly after police searches had left rooms in total disarray.

The court held that the doctrine of custom and usage does not give journalists a right to participate in night raids:

> To uphold (the television station's) assertion that their entry upon (the school's) property at the time, manner, and circumstances reflected in this record was ... within the "common custom and usage in Florida" could well bring to the citizenry of this state the hobnail boots of a Nazi storm-trooper equipped with glaring lights invading a couple's bedroom at midnight with the wife hovering in her nightgown in an attempt to shield herself from the scanning TV camera ... [A] law enforcement officer is not as a matter of law endowed with the right or authority to invite people of his choosing to invade private property and participate in a midnight raid of the premises.[133]

A Wisconsin court ruled against WMTV-TV in Madison, Wisconsin, and station photographer Bryan Brosamle, who entered private property while riding in a police squad car. The police had been summoned because gunshots had reportedly been fired at boys riding bicycles near the property. The property owner had assumed Brosamle was a police officer and never asked him to leave. The Wisconsin court ruled that custom and usage does not allow journalists to enter private property and gather news without permission, even if accompanied by police.[134]

15.2.2.4 *Limits of Aggressive Journalism.*

There are no laws preventing journalists and photographers from aggressive and persistent pursuit of critical information and exclusive photographs. But when freelance photographer Ronald Galella went too far the courts demonstrated willingness to protect individuals from outrageous surveillance techniques. Galella had aggressively stalked and photographed Jacqueline Kennedy Onassis. On one occasion he circled her in a motorboat so closely she feared being cut by the propeller. On another, he jumped from behind a wall and startled her son, John Jr., into falling off his bicycle. The court judged his behavior to be overzealous and restrained him from going within 150 feet of Ms. Onassis.[135] Galella was later held in contempt of court for violating his restraining order.[136]

15.2.3 Dissemination of Private Facts

The media can be sued in some cases where true and accurate information is disseminated. The courts have held that dissemination of private facts occurs when

---

[133] *Id.* at 819.
[134] Prahl v. Brosamle, 295 N.W.2d 768 (Wis. Ct. App. 1980).
[135] Galella v. Onassis, 353 F. Supp. 196 (S.D.N.Y. 1972).
[136] Galella v. Onassis, 533 F. Supp. 1076 (S.D.N.Y. 1982).

media publish information that is (1) private, (2) highly offensive to a reasonable person, and (3) not of legitimate concern to the public.

In the first section of this chapter we dealt with problems created when mass media are accused of publishing false and defamatory communications. But the media are at risk of being sued in some cases where information that is published is accurate, but private.[137] The courts have defined "private facts" as those "so intimate and so unwarranted" that they "outrage the community's notion of decency."[138] For example, a prominent plastic surgeon who displayed before-and-after photographs of a facial lift patient was found to have revealed private facts. Dr. Csaba Magassy had shown the photographs during a "Creams versus Plastic Surgery" clinic at Garfinckel's Department Store and on a local Washington, D.C., television station.[139]

Lifetime Cable Network and the BBC agreed to settle a private facts suit filed by Eric Foretich after his daughter Hilary was shown demonstrating, using anatomically correct dolls, how Foretich allegedly sexually abused her. The controversial segment was part of the documentary "Hilary in Hiding" based on a long-standing custody dispute that also resulted in libel litigation (EMG 15.1.2.1).

15.2.3.1 *Establishing That Facts Are Private*
Private facts have been defined by the courts as those that are not of general interest to the public and are not a matter of public record or in the public domain.

No plaintiff can win a private facts suit unless the information disseminated is clearly private. Courts have determined that each of the following is *not* private:

1. Events that take place in a public place or in public view, such as an apprehension or arrest by the police,[140] or the act of standing in line to collect unemployment benefits.[141]
2. Information that is in the public record, such as information obtained regarding individuals' criminal records[142] or names of rape victims.[143] In *Florida Star* v. *B.J.F.*, a newspaper published the identity of a rape victim after a reporter obtained the name from the Duval County, Florida, sheriff's office. The release of the name violated the sheriff's office policies, and publishing the name violated both the newspaper's own policies and an eighty-year-old Florida statute preventing publication of rape victims' names. The U.S. Supreme Court ruled that the First

---

[137] William Prosser, *Restatement (Second) of Torts* § 652D (1977).
[138] Sidis v. F-R Publishing Corp., 113 F.2d 806 (1940).
[139] Vassiliades v. Garfinckel's, 492 A.2d 580 (1985).
[140] Harrison v. Washington Post, 391 A.2d 781 (1978).
[141] Cefalu v. Globe Newspaper, 391 N.E.2d 935 (1979).
[142] McCormack v. Oklahoma Publishing Co., 613 P.2d 737 (Okla. 1980).
[143] Cox Broadcasting Corp. v. Cohn, 420 U.S. 469 (1975); Florida Star v. B.J.F., 491 U.S. 524 (1989).

Amendment protects media against privacy suits when names of rape victims are obtained through public records. The Court refused to protect publication of *all types* of truthful information, but held that rape is a matter of public significance. In 1993 a Florida appeals court ruled that the same statute involved in the *B.J.F.* case violated the First Amendment rights of the *Globe*, the national tabloid that had revealed Patricia Bowman's name after she accused William Kennedy Smith of rape in West Palm Beach.[144]

3. Information that is in the public domain. For example, Oliver Sipple, who saved President Ford from a would-be assassin, lost his privacy suit against newspapers that identified him as gay because the courts concluded it was already well known that he was a gay activist in the San Francisco area. It should be noted that the court also ruled that Sipple and facts about him were newsworthy because he had been involved in thwarting the assassination attempt.[145]

15.2.3.2 *Establishing That Facts Are Highly Offensive*
Photographs and other communications that offend basic decency and are not newsworthy may be considered by the courts to be highly offensive.

Even when events occur in places as public as a county fair, they could still be considered private facts if they are judged to be highly offensive. For example, as a woman walked past an air jet in an Alabama county fair fun house her dress blew over her head, exposing her legs and underwear. A photographer just happened to get a picture of the incident, and it was published in the local newspaper. The woman was identified in the photograph because her children could be seen at her side. She won a $4,000 judgment because the court ruled the photograph was offensive to modesty and decency and had no legitimate public interest.[146]

A classic example of offensive information involved a *Time* magazine story about a woman with an eating disorder that caused her to lose weight even though she ate constantly. *Time* went to the hospital, snapped her picture, and published a story that referred to her as the "starving glutton." The court ruled that the article was an invasion of privacy because (a) the right to privacy should include the right to privately obtain medical treatment at home or in a hospital, (b) the story was highly offensive to any reasonable person, and (c) publication of the woman's name was not newsworthy, since the disease was not contagious and she was not a threat to the public.[147]

---

[144] "Court Upholds Reversal of Victim Identification Statute," 17 *The Brechner Report* 1 (1993), ed. Charles N. Davis, U of Florida.

[145] Sipple v. Chronicle Publishing Co., 154 Cal. App. 3d 1040 (1984).

[146] Daily Times Democrat v. Graham, 162 So. 2d 474 (Ala. 1964).

[147] Barber v. Time, Inc., 159 S.W.2d 291 (Mo. 1942).

15.2.3.3 Establishing That Facts Are Not of Legitimate Concern to the Public

The courts have established newsworthiness as a solid defense in private facts cases.

In 1982, the *Cocoa Today* newspaper won a private facts suit against plaintiff Hilda Bridges, whose photograph appeared in the newspaper. Bridges had been held hostage in the apartment of her estranged husband, who forced her to disrobe to help discourage an escape. She eventually was able to run outside, covered only by a small dish towel. The towel covered her front, but the picture appearing in the newspaper did reveal her hips and clearly showed that she was nude. The court ruled against Bridges, holding that the picture captured a newsworthy event that was in the public interest.[148]

The newsworthiness defense applies to a broad range of circumstances. Obviously, information obtained from public documents or official proceedings is usually protected. The newsworthiness defense also persists over a long period of time, even if the information has been forgotten or all public records are expunged. The defense protects the use of spot news stories such as automobile accidents[149] and arrests,[150] and the information does not even have to involve hard news. The newsworthiness defense can also be used in cases dealing with information that is deemed "strange" or otherwise of interest to the public.[151]

Consent to publish is also a defense against private facts suits so long as consent is given voluntarily and by the correct person and is sufficiently broad to cover the type of media dissemination involved. Consent to use pictures or information in one medium or context does not necessarily mean use is allowable in other media or contexts.

15.2.4 Putting a Person in a False Light

False light cases against the electronic media involve newscasts, photographs, and other program segments that have led to some kind of inaccurate interpretation of individuals shown or described. The two main types of false light are *false statements or distortion* and *fictionalization*.

False light invasion of privacy is actually quite similar to libel. Whenever programs, pictures, articles, or books have resulted in some kind of false or distorted perception of an individual, false light litigation is possible. The *Saturday Evening Post* provided an excellent example of false light when it published the photograph of a young girl who had been knocked down by an automobile. The picture appeared beside the caption "They Ask To Be Killed" in an article on pedestrian care-

---

[148] Cape Publications v. Bridges, 423 So. 2d 426 (Fla. App. 1982).
[149] Kelley v. Post Publishing Co., 98 N.E.2d 286 (Mass. 1951).
[150] Williams v. KCMO Broadcasting Div., 472 S.W.2d 1 (1971).
[151] Virgil v. Sports Illustrated, 424 F. Supp 1286 (1976).

lessness. In fact, the girl was not at fault. The car had run a stop signal. The girl was awarded $5,000 for being portrayed in a false light.[152]

Before a plaintiff can win a false light suit against a media defendant, three elements of proof must be established:

1. the information responsible for the false light must be highly offensive to a reasonable person;
2. the information must be widely disseminated; and
3. fault must be demonstrated.

In false light suits, proof of fault usually requires proof of *New York Times* actual malice, meaning knowledge of falsity or reckless disregard for truth or falsity. But the courts have not ruled conclusively on this and a few states allow private plaintiffs the lesser burden of proof of negligence.

Obviously, while there are similarities between libel and false light litigation, there are critical differences. Libel law requires only one person to receive a defamatory message but private facts must be widely disseminated. In this respect false light is similar to the dissemination of private information invasion of privacy, discussed previously. Libel law requires plaintiffs to prove damage to reputation, but private facts plaintiffs must show only that the information is highly offensive to the reasonable person.

Despite the differences, many of the defenses available to the media are the same for libel and private facts suits. As stated previously, in most states media defendants in both types of suits are protected by the First Amendment, meaning that public plaintiffs have to prove actual malice to win libel *and* private facts cases. Some states restrict litigants to one charge or the other, but it is common for plaintiffs to pursue both libel and private facts claims in suits against media defendants.

False light can occur in a variety of forms and contexts but is most easily divided into two main categories:

1. *false statements* or *distortion*, and
2. *fictionalization*.

15.2.4.1 *False Statements or Distortion*

The most common type of false light litigation involves what is referred to as distortion or false statements. This most often occurs when pictures and/or statements are used out of context or with critical information omitted.

Television news reporters should be especially cautious when using file footage to cover stories on sensitive topics. WJLA-TV in Washington, D.C., found this out while doing a story on a new treatment for genital herpes. As the reporter said "For the twenty million Americans who have herpes, it's not a cure," the camera zoomed in tightly on a woman who happened to be standing on the corner. The

---

[152] Leverton v. Curtis Publishing, 192 F.2d 974 (1951).

woman sued for private facts invasion of privacy and the court ruled that the close-up shots clearly supported the inference that she had herpes.[153]

Photographs can create false light problems for newspapers as well. Coal miner Sue Crump won a false light suit when a newspaper used her picture to illustrate a story dealing with harassment of females in the mining industry. The article cited examples of women having been stripped and greased and of another dangled from a water tower. The court ruled that readers could have falsely assumed that Crump had been similarly harassed.[154]

CBS lost a false light suit in 1979 because of a video segment aired on *60 Minutes*. The court ruled that the segment created a false impression that Pennsylvania hunter Clare R. Uhl was shooting birds that were already on the ground, a notion deemed highly offensive to residents of areas with large numbers of wild birds.[155]

15.2.4.2   Fictionalization

Fictionalization occurs when otherwise true stories are embellished or recreated inaccurately, or when characters portrayed in a work intended as fiction come too close in resembling actual people.

The *Cleveland Plain Dealer* lost a fictionalization suit for publishing an article about the 1967 collapse of the Silver Bridge across the Ohio River.[156] The accident killed 44 persons, including the husband of Margaret Cantrell. While doing a follow-up story several months after the tragedy, reporter Joseph Eszterhas visited the Cantrell home only to find Ms. Cantrell away. But Eszterhas proceeded to write the story as if she had been there, greatly exaggerating the effects of the accident on the family. He reported that Cantrell refused to talk about the incident and described her as living with her children in poverty and wearing "the same mask of non-expression she wore at the funeral."[157] The court ruled that the reporter knowingly and recklessly engaged in calculated falsehoods and clearly depicted the Cantrell family in a false light. The case could have offered the Supreme Court a chance to clarify whether private persons would have to prove actual malice to win false light litigation. But as it turned out, the court saw the *Plain Dealer* article as such an obvious example of knowing falsehood and reckless disregard that the plaintiff's burden of proving negligence or actual malice would have been easily met.

The *New York Times* actual malice standard was first applied to false light cases in *Time* v. *Hill*. In 1952, James Hill and his family were held hostage in their home for 19 hours by three escaped convicts. The family was terrified but suffered no physical harm during the ordeal. The convicts were captured soon after leaving the Hill house. A novel based on the incident led to production of a Broadway play, which likewise inspired a 1955 *Life* magazine article entitled "True Crime Inspires

---

[153] Duncan v. WJLA-TV, 106 F.R.D. 4 (1984).
[154] Crump v. Beckley Newspapers, 320 S.E.2d 70 (W. Va. 1984).
[155] Uhl v. CBS, 476 F. Supp. 1134 (W.D. Pa. 1979).
[156] Cantrell v. Forest City Publishing Co., 419 U.S. 245 (1974).
[157] *Id.* at 248.

Play." There was only one problem. The novel and play had embellished the incident, adding episodes of violence and a verbal sexual assault on one of Hill's daughters. *Life* followed suit, publishing pictures to illustrate violent scenes involving a son and a daughter. Hill, offended by the sensationalism of the *Life* article and the new threat to his desired anonymity, sued for invasion of privacy. A jury awarded him $75,000, but the Supreme Court reversed the decision, holding that when the information involved is a matter of public interest, false light plaintiffs must prove actual malice to collect damages.[158]

Television docudramas have resulted in several fictionalization suits. NBC has been a defendant in two such cases. First, the network lost a fictionalization suit to naval officer Kenneth Strickler, who was aboard a commercial airliner that had to ditch in the Pacific Ocean in 1956. In a dramatization of the accident, Strickler was falsely portrayed out of uniform, smoking a pipe and cigarettes, and directing prayer groups.[159]

Another NBC docudrama, "Judge Horton and the Scottsboro Boys," harshly portrayed a woman who 20 years earlier had accused nine black men of rape. Despite a paucity of evidence, all nine were found guilty and sentenced to death by all-white juries in Alabama. The telecast, which dramatized reversals of some of the verdicts, portrayed Victoria Price Street as a perjurer and referred to her as a "whore." NBC, which had been led to believe and had even announced that Street was dead (and therefore unable to sue), had not carefully checked the accuracy of facts portrayed in the docudrama.

The network was able to convince a U.S. court of appeals that Street was a public figure, given continuing public interest in the rape case. But NBC settled with Street out of court after the Supreme Court agreed to hear the case.[160]

Works intended as pure fiction but based too closely on actual people and events may also face fictionalization litigation. In one case, author Gwen Davis Mitchell lost a libel-privacy suit because her book *Touching* too closely paralleled the work of plaintiff Paul Bindrim, a licensed clinical psychologist.[161] Bindrim had conducted a number of nude therapy sessions, some of which included Mitchell, who had signed an agreement never to write articles about or otherwise disclose the nature of the sessions. Mitchell had altered facts and events of the sessions. The therapist was described in a manner totally different from Bindrim, and the book was spiced a bit with sexually explicit language that had not occurred during the sessions. Unfortunately for Mitchell, the embellished segments justified a court finding of actual malice. Since she attended several sessions, it was obvious to the court that she was aware of the falsity of the descriptions. The jury awarded Bindrim $75,000 damages.[162]

---

[158] Time, Inc., v. Hill, 385 U.S. 374 (1967).

[159] Strickler v. NBC, 167 F. Supp. 68 (1958).

[160] Street v. NBC, 645 F.2d 1227 (1981).

[161] This case was handled by the courts as a libel case even though the book was a fictionalized account of Bindrim's therapy sessions.

[162] Bindrim v. Mitchell, 155 Cal. Rptr. 29 (1979).

15.2.5   Infliction of Emotional Distress

Infliction of emotional distress has been defined by the courts as conduct so out-rageous and so extreme that it goes beyond all possible bounds of decency.[163]

Public figures sometimes file suit against the media claiming intentional inflic-tion of emotional distress in cases where they seem less likely to win a libel or invasion of privacy suit. Still, the burden of proof on the plaintiff is quite high. First, the conduct of the mass medium must clearly be outrageous. For example, Kimberly Foster lost her emotional distress suit because merely being shown on television working out in a spa with uncombed hair and wearing old sweatpants was not considered outrageous.[164]

A different decision was reached in a case involving Orlando television station WESH. The station had broadcast shots, including a close-up, of the skull of a six-year-old child abducted three years earlier. The family, just returning from memo-rial services for their daughter, happened to flip on the television just as the story aired. The trial court dismissed the case, but an appeals court held that reasonable persons in the community could find the airing of the photograph so outrageous as to be intolerable and beyond the bounds of decency. WESH ultimately settled the case out of court.[165]

The burden of proof for public plaintiffs in emotional distress cases was in-creased significantly in *Hustler Magazine* v. *Falwell*. The magazine had published an advertisement parody that portrayed prominent minister and political activist Jerry Falwell as having engaged in a drunken, incestuous affair with his mother in an outhouse. The Supreme Court noted that the ad parody was tasteless and repugnant in the eyes of most but was protected by the First Amendment because it involved ideas and opinions about a public figure. The court held that public figures and public persons may not recover for intentional infliction of emotional distress with-out showing that the publication contains a false statement of fact that was made with actual malice.[166]

15.2.6   Actual Physical Harm

A U.S. court of appeals decision involving *Soldier of Fortune* magazine suggests that publication of information that leads to actual physical harm may not be pro-tected.[167] The magazine's problems began with publication of a classified ad sent in by unemployed Vietnam veteran Michael Savage. The ad read, "Gun for Hire: 37-year-old professional mercenary . . . Discreet and very private. Body Guard, courier

---

[163] *Restatement of Torts* § 46(d) (1965).
[164] Foster v. Livingwell Midwest, Inc., 865 F.2d 257 (1988).
[165] Armstrong v. H&C Communications, 575 So. 2d 280 (1991).
[166] Hustler Magazine v. Falwell, 485 U.S. 46 (1988).
[167] Braun v. Soldier of Fortune Magazine, 757 F. Supp. 1325 (1991). *See also* 113 S.Ct. 1028 (1993), and 968 F.2d 1110 (1992).

and other special skills. All jobs considered."[168] Savage later admitting killing Atlanta resident Richard Braun and wounding his son after receiving a response to the ad.[169] Braun's sons sued for wrongful death and the court held *Soldier of Fortune* liable for failing to foresee grave consequences of its advertisements. The court awarded the Braun family a $4.3 million damage verdict, which was upheld by the Supreme Court in 1993.

15.3 COPYRIGHT LAW

The U.S. Constitution grants Congress the power to protect copyrights. Original works of authorship are protected under the Copyright Act of 1976. The Lanham Act of 1946 protects trademarks.

Article 1, Section 8 of the U.S. Constitution gives Congress the power "to promote the Progress of Science and useful Arts, by securing for limited Times to Authors and Inventors the exclusive Right to their respective Writings and Discoveries." This was included in the Constitution not to make people wealthy but to encourage creative activity and innovation. Protection is necessary so that copyright owners can have some expectation of reward for creative behavior. The Constitution protects inventions, which fall under the domain of patent law, and writings, which are protected by federal copyright statute.

Congress passed the first copyright legislation in 1790. The act was revised in 1909, and the current legislation, the Copyright Act of 1976, went into effect on January 1, 1978. The act can be found in Title 17 of the *U.S. Code*, § 101–118.[170]

In 1988 the United States formally signed on to the international *Berne Agreement*, formally known as the Berne Convention for the Protection of Literary and Artistic Works, which originated in 1886. The Berne Agreement is designed to help prevent violation of copyright and outright piracy of works on the international level. Congress has since revised the Copyright Act to adhere to all obligations of the international agreement.[171]

The Copyright Act specifically protects "original works of authorship fixed in any tangible medium of expression."[172] The term *fixed* means that a work, under the authority of the author, is sufficiently embodied in a copy or recording so that it can be observed, comprehended, reproduced, or otherwise communicated for more than a brief period of time. A radio station promotional jingle is fixed when it is recorded on audiotape. A television program is fixed as soon as it is recorded on videotape. Any live audio or video program is fixed as long as a copy (recording) is made simultaneously with the transmission. A book or other printed work is fixed

---

[168] Braun v. Soldier of Fortune Magazine, 757 F. Supp. at 1327 (1991).

[169] Savage and his two accomplices were convicted and sentenced to prison.

[170] The citation for the *U.S. Code Annotated* is 17 U.S.C.A. § 101–118.

[171] Berne Convention Implementation Act of 1988, Pub. L. No. 100-568, § 13.

[172] 17 U.S.C.A. § 102.

BOX 15.6   Types of Works That Can Be Copyrighted

Fixed works of authorship that can be copyrighted include the following:

1. Literary works
2. Musical works, including the lyrics
3. Dramatic works, including music
4. Pantomimes and choreographic works
5. Pictorial, graphic, and sculptural works
6. Motion pictures, television programs, and other audio-visual works
7. Sound recordings

---

as soon as its pages emerge from a printer or typewriter. As shown in Box 15.6, the Copyright Act is explicit about what types of works can be protected.[173]

15.3.1   Concept of Originality

The courts have determined that *originality* is the most important criterion in determining whether a work may be copyrighted. Determining whether a work is truly original is often most difficult, especially when dealing with music and works involving historical fact. Generally, to win a copyright suit a plaintiff must establish that an infringing work is not original but is substantially or strikingly similar to the copyrighted work.

To be copyrighted, a work must first and foremost be original. The concept of originality means that the work is solely the work of the copyright owner, created through his or her own effort, and not derived or copied from the work of others. Interestingly, in most cases there is no requirement that the work be especially innovative, unique, or groundbreaking.

The burden of proof on the plaintiff in a copyright suit is heavy, and the courts often give any benefit of the doubt to the accused. In 1986 Monica Sheehan and Luis Rojas developed an idea for a television game show involving music and music video trivia. They intended to market the game, which was to be named "Laser Blitz" (or "Video Blitz"), to MTV. Sheehan and Rojas wrote rules and an overall format for the show, drafted artwork illustrating sets and props, and prepared a schematic drawing of audio-visual features. MTV turned down "Laser Blitz," but later began airing a program called *Remote Control*, which Sheehan and Rojas claimed was virtually identical in sequence, structure, style, and rules.

The court agreed with the plaintiffs that "Laser Blitz" was an original work because it contained a number of unique attributes but concluded that it was not sufficiently similar to *Remote Control* to constitute copyright infringement. In fact,

---

[173] 17 U.S.C.A. § 102.

it was those same attributes that made "Laser Blitz" original—particularly the proposed use of an operable laser gun requiring skill as opposed to a mere prop resembling a remote control in the MTV program—that convinced the court that *Remote Control* was not a copy of the plaintiff's program.[174]

Originality is often the principal issue in suits involving musical compositions. In 1965, the British rock group Gerry and the Pacemakers recorded "Don't Let the Sun Catch You Crying." The song was written by the group's lead singer, Gerrard Marsden. A copyright suit was filed by composer Joe Greene, who in 1946 had written a song with the same title except for the word "Cryin" in place of "Crying." While Greene argued that Marsden's song copied the lyrical theme and underlying musical phrase of his song, Marsden denied ever having even heard Greene's song. The court, in a typical ruling involving the question of originality, ruled that despite similarities, the two songs were not so strikingly similar to establish that copying had occurred.[175]

15.3.2   Originality and the Protection of Ideas

Copyright protects only the work itself, not the *idea* of the work or the *facts* behind it.

Although cartoon characters on the Hanna Barbera NBC cartoon series *The Snorks* were similar to those in an unpublished, copyrighted work titled *Snorkie Snorkel vs. Simon Shark*, by Shirley Evans, a federal district court ruled that there was no copyright violation. First, there was no evidence that Hanna Barbera had ever seen Evans's work, but the court held that sharing the idea of an undersea world was "a far cry" from establishing striking similarity.[176]

Evans's unsuccessful attempt to protect the idea of an undersea world of characters illustrates a major principle stated in the Copyright Act:

In no case does copyright protection for an original work of authorship extend to any idea, procedure, process, system, method of operation, concept, principle, or discovery, regardless of the form in which it is described, explained, illustrated, or embodied in such work.[177]

When Pulitzer Prize–winning *Miami Herald* reporter Gene Miller collaborated on a book with a woman who was kidnapped and held in an underground box for seven days, he assumed his work was protected. However, despite the fact that negotiations with Universal Studios for movie rights to his book had broken down, the studio proceeded to produce a docudrama about the ordeal anyway. Miller sued for copyright violation, but a U.S. court of appeals ruled that only the manner in which

---

[174] Sheehan v. MTV, 22 U.S.P.Q.2d (BNA) 1394 (1992).

[175] Northern Music Corp. v. Pacemaker Music Co., 147 U.S.P.Q. (BNA) 358 (1965).

[176] Evans v. Berrie & Company, 681 F. Supp 813 (1988).

[177] 17 U.S.C.A. § 102.

Miller had presented the ideas in his book was protected and not his research or the facts surrounding the incident. Miller had estimated that he spent some 2,500 hours researching and writing the book.[178]

In *Alexander* v. *Haley*, author Margaret Alexander argued that Alex Haley's book *Roots*, on which the classic television mini-series was based, was extracted from her novel *How I Wrote Jubilee*. The court recognized similarities but held that most dealt with matters of historical or contemporary fact. The court said Alexander's copyright was not violated even if Haley had been made aware of the facts in question by reading Alexander's book.[179]

15.3.3   Rights of Copyright Owners

Copyright owners control the following aspects of their work: reproduction, derivative creation, distribution, and performance.

Copyright law bestows on owners of copyrights exclusive rights to:

1. reproduce the copyrighted work in copies or sound recordings;
2. prepare derivative works based on the original;
3. distribute copies or sound recordings of the copyrighted work to the public for sale or other transfer of ownership, or by rental lease, or lending; and
4. publicly perform (or display as the case may be) literary, musical, dramatic, choreographic, audio-visual, sculptural, and other works, including the individual frames of motion pictures.

15.3.4   Duration of Copyright

Copyright lasts for the life of the author plus 50 years. For businesses, a copyright lasts for 100 years from the date of creation or 75 years from the date of copyright.

Since the rights to an original work outlast the life of the author, a copyright can obviously be willed to the owner's heirs. Works already copyrighted when the 1976 act was passed are protected for a total of 75 years.

15.3.5   Registration and Notice of Copyright

Copyrighted works should be registered and identified by the appropriate copyright symbol. A copyrighted work is technically protected even if the work is not registered and no notice is affixed, but an owner may not file suit against an infringer unless registration requirements are fulfilled.

---

[178] Miller v. Universal City Studios, 650 F.2d 1365 (1981).
[179] Alexander v. Haley, 460 F. Supp. 40 (1978).

BOX 15.7   Copyright Notices

A copyright notice consists of the following three elements:

1. The symbol © (the letter *c* in a circle), or the word *copyright* or the abbreviation *copr.*
2. The year of the first publication of the work. For compilations or derivative works containing previously published material, the year of the first publication of the work should be listed.
3. The name and owner of the copyrighted work, or an abbreviation through which the name can be recognized, or a widely known alternative name of the owner.

The notice appearing on sound recordings consists of the following three elements:

1. The symbol ℗ (the letter *p* in a circle).
2. The year the sound recording was first published.
3. The name and owner of the copyright as stipulated in #3 above.

Works may be registered for copyright by completing a form available at the Copyright Office, Library of Congress, Washington, D.C. 20559, and submitting a copy of the work (two copies of published works) along with a $10 registration fee. Whenever possible, a copyright notice should be affixed to all copies of a copyrighted work. The content of copyright notices is summarized in Box 15.7.[180]

Failure to register and deposit copies can result in a $250 fine, and the fine can be as high as $2,500 for willful and repeated failure to comply with ownership registration requirements. Moreover, a copyright owner cannot sue for infringement until the work is registered.

Failure to affix a notice is also likely to result in what are called "innocent infringements" for which the owner has little recourse. Anyone who innocently picks up a work and makes copies cannot be sued for copyright infringement if the work has no notice affixed and the person had no idea the work was protected. The courts do allow limited recovery of profits in some cases of innocent infringement.

15.3.6   Remedies for Copyright Infringement

The remedies for infringement of copyright include *injunctions, impoundment,* and *recovery of actual or statutory damages.* Criminal copyright infringement, the deliberate violation of copyright for financial gain, may result in fines and prison terms.

---

[180] 17 U.S.C.A. § 401.

The owner is entitled to seek infringement remedies whenever a copyright is violated. The following remedies are available:

1. *Injunctions*: Often the owner will have the violator served with an injunction, or a court order to cease and desist in whatever activity is causing the infringement.
2. *Impoundment and Disposition of Infringing Articles*: The court can have any copies of the copyrighted work impounded or destroyed. This means that expensive equipment such as audio and video recording and editing equipment can be confiscated.
3. *Damages*: The owner is entitled to collect monetary damage awards.

Two types of damages may be awarded, actual and statutory. *Actual damages* can be collected to cover losses caused by the infringement, including attorney's fees and any profits gained by the infringer. In *Sheldon* v. *Metro-Goldwyn*, the movie *Letty Lynton* was produced by Metro Goldwyn even though negotiations with Sheldon to obtain rights to the script had broken down. Sheldon was awarded $118,000 in damages from the profits of the film, even though he had asked for only $30,000 for the rights to the script. Plaintiffs such as Sheldon are entitled only to profits earned by the attraction of the story (or the copyrighted work) itself, not that of the actors' talent and box office appeal with which Sheldon (or the copyright owner) had nothing to do.[181]

Statutory damages, according to the Copyright Act, allow the owner to collect, instead of actual damages, a sum of not less than $250 or more than $10,000 as the court considers just. If the copyright owner bears the burden of proof and the court determines the infringement was deliberate, statutory damages may go as high as $50,000.

Criminal copyright infringement occurs when a court finds an individual has deliberately violated a copyright for commercial or private financial gain. Such violations carry penalties of up to one year in prison or $10,000 in fines, or both. The penalty for violating copyrights of sound recordings is even more severe, calling for fines up to $25,000 and one year imprisonment for the first offense, and $50,000 and up to two years for the second offense.[182]

15.3.7 Two Elements of Proof Necessary to Win a Copyright Suit

To win a copyright suit a plaintiff must demonstrate that:

1. the infringing party had *access* to the copyrighted work, and
2. the infringer did indeed *copy* the copyrighted work, which requires a demonstration of *substantial or striking similarity* to the copyrighted work.

---

[181] Sheldon v. Metro-Goldwyn, 309 U.S. 390 (1940).
[182] 17 U.S.C.A. § 506.

As discussed previously, copyright plaintiffs must prove at least a substantial similarity between the two works. Some courts require the more rigorous proof that the two works are "strikingly similar."

15.3.7.1 Access to Copyrighted Work

A copyright plaintiff must prove that the alleged infringer had reasonable access to the work.

It would, of course, be difficult for one to copy an original work to which he or she has had no access. But whether an alleged infringer has had reasonable access to a particular work is often difficult to establish. Author Sonya Jason failed in her attempt to convince the court that writers of the film *Coming Home* had seen a copy of her book *Concomitant Soldier*, which had a similar plot. Only a few copies of the manuscript had been circulated, but Jason argued that one copy could have fallen into the hands of one of the film's screenwriters. The court held that access could not be established by such a "bare possibility."[183] Songwriter Lloyd Chiate tried to argue that Stevie Wonder's hit song "I Just Called to Say I Love You" was a copy of Chiate's "Hello It's Me, I Just Called to Say." The court concluded that Chiate never established that Wonder had access to his song, even though Wonder co-wrote the song with a friend of Chiate's. It surely helped that the court seemed convinced that Wonder composed his song first.[184] A similar suit against the singing group The Bee Gees, for their song "How Deep is Your Love," was rejected by the courts for failure to establish that the alleged infringers had access to the copyrighted works.[185]

15.3.7.2 Substantial or Striking Similarity to the Copyrighted Work

The burden of proof on the plaintiff in a copyright suit goes beyond merely establishing similarities between the infringing work and the copyrighted work. The plaintiff must prove that the infringing work is strikingly or substantially similar. This usually means the two works must be similar in a number of ways.

Lisa Litchfield claimed that the motion picture *E.T.* copied her musical play *Lokey from Maldemar*. Her copyright suit was dismissed because the court perceived a lack of substantial similarity between the dialogue, characters, and mood of the two works.[186] The court reached the same conclusion when Warner Brothers tried to argue that ABC's *The Greatest American Hero* too closely paralleled the *Superman* movies.[187] Both characters could fly and possessed other superhuman powers including X-ray vision, long-distance hearing, and the ability to resist bullets. Both acquired their power when they donned leotards and a cape, and both

---

[183] Jason v. Fonda, 526 F. Supp 774 (1981).
[184] Chiate v. Morris, 972 F.2d 1337 (1992).
[185] Selle v. Gibb, 741 F.2d 896 (1984).
[186] Litchfield v. Spielberg, 736 F.2d 1352 (1984).
[187] Warner Brothers v. ABC, 523 F. Supp. 611 (1981).

used the powers to fight evil. Despite the similarities, the court concluded that the characters were too dissimilar to establish substantial similarity. The ABC hero, Ralph Hinckley, was described as an ordinary man who was comically inept. Hinckley was small and thin, informally dressed, and his personal life was constantly in shambles. The court, on the basis of these and other characteristics, called him the "antithesis" of *Superman* and ruled that to win its suit Warner Brothers would have to prove that the "concrete expression" of *Superman* was copied.[188] In the opinion of the court, it obviously was not.

Universal Studios was able to demonstrate substantial similarity when a film entitled *Great White* too closely resembled the movie *Jaws*.[189] As in the Greatest American Hero case above, there was no dispute over the fact that the ideas were similar. But the court ruled that *Great White* went much further, citing similarities between the basic story points, the major characters, the sequence of events, and the development and interplay of characters. Both movies had extensive dialogue between a "salty English-accented skipper" and a shark expert, and in both the skipper is eaten by the shark, which is later killed by dynamite detonated by the shark expert.[190]

The courts have established that copyright violations can occur unintentionally and even unconsciously. Intentional or not, it is still a violation. In 1976 a federal district court ruled that singer-composer and former Beatle George Harrison violated copyright with his song "My Sweet Lord." Bright Tunes Music had argued that several musical phrases resembled an early sixties hit song called "He's So Fine." Harrison vehemently denied any influence of the Bright Tunes song on his. The judge ruled that the two songs were substantially similar even though he was convinced that Harrison was not conscious of the fact that he was using a musical phrase contained in "He's So Fine."

The court also held that access was established by the fact that top hit records are by definition publicly disseminated. "He's So Fine" was a popular recording in the United States and was also a top hit for several weeks in Harrison's homeland of England.[191] Using this same reasoning, plaintiffs filing suits involving radio, television, and cable programs would not find it difficult to establish access, since wide public dissemination is virtually assured.

15.3.8   Work-for-Hire and Copyright

The U.S. Supreme Court has established that the copyright for a work-for-hire belongs to the employer, not the artist creating the work. However, employers cannot control copyrights to works produced by independent contractors and freelance artists.

The Copyright Act of 1976 states that *work-for-hire* shall be any work produced by an employee while working "within the scope of his or her employment"

---

[188] *Id.* at 616.

[189] Universal City Studios v. Film Ventures International, 543 F. Supp. 1134 (1982).

[190] *Id.* at 1137.

[191] Bright Tunes Music Corp. v. Harrisongs Music, 420 F. Supp. 177 (1976). The ultimate award in this case was extremely complex. For an explanation see ABKCO Music, v. Harrisongs Music, 944 F.2d 971 (1991).

or any work "specially ordered or commissioned" if the parties sign a written agreement as such.[192] In work-for-hire situations the author, writer, composer, photographer, or producer does not own and cannot acquire the copyright to the work produced, no matter how original. The rights belong to the employer.

Congress never defined "employee" or "employment," but in the 1989 case *Community for Creative Non-Violence* v. *Reid* the U.S. Supreme Court ruled that freelance artists and independent contractors are not employees in the traditional sense. James Earl Reid had accepted a directive by the CCNV, an organization dedicated to eliminating homelessness, to produce a sculpture commemorating homeless people. When Reid completed the sculpture as promised, both parties applied for a copyright. The Supreme Court settled the dispute by concluding that Reid was an independent contractor—not an employee. He had supplied his own tools, worked without daily supervision, had absolute freedom of hours, and was assigned no additional projects by CCNV. The Court then offered a test for determining whether a hired party is an "employee" who, as such gives up all rights to work produced. The test is summarized in Box 15.8.[193]

BOX 15.8   The *Reid* Test: Determining Whether a Hired Party Is an Employee

In *Community for Creative Non-Violence* v. *Reid*,* the Supreme Court ruled that the following factors should be considered in determining whether a hired party is an employee:

1. the skill required,
2. the source of the tools and instruments used to create the work,
3. the location of the work,
4. the duration of the relationship between the parties,
5. whether the hiring party has the right to assign additional projects to the hired party,
6. the extent of the hired party's discretion over when and how long to work,
7. the method of payment,
8. the hired party's role in hiring and paying assistants,
9. whether the work is part of the regular business of the hiring party,
10. whether the hiring party is in business,
11. the provision of employee benefits and the tax treatment of the hired party.

---

* 490 U.S. 730 (1989).

---

[192] 17 U.S.C.A. § 101.

[193] Community for Creative Non-Violence v. Reid, 490 U.S. 730 (1989).

In 1992 a computer programmer failed the *Reid* test. While employed by a small firm to handle computer operations, Cornell engineering graduate Clifford Aymes created a software package to manage retail records. Aymes worked alone with semiregular hours, received no health or other benefits, and no payroll taxes were deducted. However, because Aymes used company hardware and was occasionally assigned to other projects, the work was judged to be for hire.[194]

The *Reid* test has implications for electronic media. Suppose a cable television employee, also a highly skilled photographer and editor, uses cable system editing equipment to produce a documentary on crime in the community. Who would control rights to the work? With the increasing utilization of computers in video productions, copyright battles will likely emerge over software produced by specialists for various production purposes. In any event, it is best for persons who create original works not to involve an employer in any way if ownership of copyrights is desired.

15.3.9   Fair Use

To determine whether a particular use of a copyrighted work is considered a fair use, the Copyright Act of 1976 specifies that the following factors be considered:

1. the purpose and character of the use, including whether such use is commercial in nature or for nonprofit educational purposes;
2. the nature of the copyrighted work;
3. the amount and substantiality of the portion used in relation to the copyrighted work as a whole; and
4. the effect of the use upon the potential market for or value of the copyrighted work.[195]

The courts have ruled that newsworthiness is an effective defense in fair use cases.

The law allows limited use of copyrighted materials without permission under certain conditions. Under the *doctrine of fair use* such practices as reproducing copyrighted material in comparative ads, photocopying articles from periodicals, and making tape recordings from your favorite compact disc may not be considered violations of copyright law.

In what is considered a landmark fair use case, the *Nation* magazine was found to violate Harper and Row's copyright by publishing an article entitled "The Ford Memoirs: Behind the Nixon Pardon." Harper and Row had purchased rights to publish a book containing President Ford's memoirs and had negotiated a $25,000 deal with *Time* to allow the magazine to publish excerpts just before the book went on sale. The *Nation* article scooped both *Time* and Harper and Row by publishing

---

[194] Aymes v. Bonelli, 980 F.2d 857 (1992).
[195] 17 U.S.C.A. § 107.

critical passages from the memoirs, including verbatim quotations explaining Ford's pardon of President Nixon.[196]

Nation argued that the publication was fair use because of the newsworthiness of the information. The U.S. Supreme Court disagreed, holding that the public's interest in expedient dissemination of news does not outweigh copyright concerns, especially when one party has purchased rights to first publication. The Court concluded that (1) *Nation's* purpose in publishing the article was a commercial attempt to scoop the other publishers; (2) the publication of direct quotations served as the "dramatic focal point" of the article; and (3) the *Nation* article caused obvious damages to Harper and Row, given that *Time* canceled its deal once the article was published.[197]

Newsworthiness has been used successfully as a defense in other fair use cases. In 1968, Bernard Geis Associates attempted to purchase rights to a film of President Kennedy's assassination. Amateur photographer Abraham Zapruder was taking home movies of the president as the shots were fired at the motorcade. Geis Associates wanted the Zapruder film to produce pictures for their book *Six Seconds in Dallas. Life* magazine, which had paid $150,000 for rights to the film, refused, but charcoal sketches were produced from a duplicate and published in the book anyway. *Life* sued, but the court decided that the publication was a fair use because of strong public interest in information about the Kennedy assassination. The court stated that pictures could have been obtained from other sources anyway and that the book was marketable because of the theories it advanced, not because of the sketches.[198]

Protection has also been extended to television stations covering newsworthy events, even if official coverage has been licensed to a competitor. A U.S. court of appeals refused to halt WCVB-TV's coverage of the Boston Marathon even though another Boston station had purchased rights to televise the event. The court rejected the argument that viewers might be confused about which station was officially authorized to carry the race.[199]

15.3.9.1 *Fair Use as a Defense: Use with Caution*

Fair use is not a viable defense in a copyright suit if the use is determined to be commercial.

Television, radio, and cable programmers should exercise caution whenever using audio or video segments of any kind from an outside source. During a 1990 episode of *Good Morning America*, ABC aired a segment on Mackinac Island in Michigan. The segment included 38 seconds of video that ABC producer Donna Vislocky had obtained from the Mackinac Island Chamber of Commerce. After

---

[196] Soon after taking office following Nixon's resignation, President Ford pardoned Nixon of any and all possible criminal activity associated with the Watergate scandal. The pardon was handed down in the summer of 1974 before Nixon was ever charged with any specific criminal act.

[197] Harper and Row v. Nation Enterprises, 471 U.S. 539 (1985).

[198] Time, Inc. v. Bernard Geis Assoc., 293 F. Supp. 130 (1968).

[199] WCVB-TV v. Boston Athletic Ass'n, 926 F.2d 42 (1991).

screening the first 10–12 minutes of the 18-minute video, Vislocky selected the shots she wanted and never saw the end credits, which contained a copyright notice. After the segment aired, the copyright owner sued for willful infringement. ABC argued that it was a privileged fair use and that airing the segment at worst amounted only to an innocent infringement.

The court rejected the fair use defense, holding that the use, occurring as it did within a *Good Morning America* segment, was commercial.[200] This being so, the impact of showing the video on the marketplace was assumed to be significant. The court also noted that ABC used the best scenes, or the heart of the video. ABC's innocent infringement argument was also rejected because Vislocky "failed to conduct even a routine fast-forward review of the entire tape—which she admitted at her deposition would have taken no more than a minute—to ascertain whether there was a copyright notice" on the tape.[201]

Obviously, what is considered fair use by media professionals, scriptwriters, or even college professors may differ from the manner in which courts interpret the Copyright Act. In 1991, a federal court held that Kinko's, a nationally franchised photocopying business, infringed rights of publishers by copying journal articles and book chapters for professors' course readings. Despite the obvious educational purpose, the court ruled that such copying without permission was not a fair use and awarded a total of $500,000 damages to several publishers.[202]

15.3.9.2   *Parody and Fair Use*

The fair use doctrine offers protection for parody as long as the parody does not adversely affect the market value of the copyrighted work. The courts have extended First Amendment protection to parody.

On May 20, 1977, a skit on the NBC program *Saturday Night Live* made fun of a New York City public relations campaign by having cast members sing the words "I Love Sodom" to the copyrighted tune of "I Love New York." The court ruled that use of the music was fair use, since it did not interfere with the marketability of the protected work.[203]

Parody protection extends to commercials as well. When portions of a new Coors beer commercial were previewed on the syndicated program *Entertainment Tonight*, the Eveready Battery Company sought a court injunction to halt airing of the ads. The commercials parodied Eveready's successful "Energizer Bunny" ad campaign by having actor Leslie Nielsen wear fake rabbit ears, teeth, and a tail and beat a drum displaying the Coors Light logo. Nielsen even exited the commercial with a voice saying "Coors Light, the official beer of the nineties, is the fastest growing beer in America. It keeps growing and growing. . . ." Eveready claimed copy-

---

[200] Hi-Tech Video Productions v. Capital Cities/ABC, 804 F. Supp. 950 (1992).
[201] *Id.* at 958.
[202] Basic Books v. Kinko's Graphics Corp., 758 F. Supp. 1522 (1991).
[203] Elsmere Music v. NBC, 623 F.2d 252 (1980).

right and trademark infringement, but the court, despite the substantial similarity between the two works, ruled that the commercial was protected parody.[204]

Not all parody is protected by the First Amendment. A U.S. court of appeals made this abundantly clear in a 1993 decision involving television star Vanna White.[205] White had filed an appropriation suit against Samsung Electronics because a commercial for the company featured a robot dressed in a wig, jewelry, and clothes in a manner that resembled White. As the robot stood in front of a "Wheel of Fortune" game board a caption read, "The longest-running game show. 2012 A.D." The ad attempted to humorously suggest that the show would go on even after White was replaced by a robot. The court ruled that depite the parody, the commercial had misappropriated her identity.[206]

Rap singer Luther Campbell (also known as Luke Skyywalker) was sued for violating copyright after recording what he alleged was a parody of the late singer and songwriter Roy Orbison's song "Oh Pretty Woman." Campbell's rap song "Pretty Woman," which was recorded by his group 2 Live Crew, uses the same music but substitutes for Orbison's adjective "pretty" with such negative descriptions as "big hairy" and "two timin" and suggests that the woman has a baby as a result of being out with another man. Campbell argued that the shocking nature of the lyrics satirized Orbison's original song and society as a whole.[207]

The appeals court ruled that the 2 Live Crew version violated copyright because it was primarily commercial, it copied a substantial portion—including the heart—of the original work, and it could have damaged the market value of the song. The Supreme Court overturned the decision in 1994, however, holding that the lower court overemphasized Campbell's profit motive since most parody could be perceived as proprietary. Justice Souter, who wrote the opinion for the Court, said that Campbell was entitled to a trial since parody deserved much the same protection as other forms of commentary. Souter argued that the 2 Live Crew version could be interpreted as commentary on the naiveté of an earlier time (Orbison's version was a top hit in 1964). Parody, according to Souter, would have to be examined on a case-by-case basis to determine if fair use protection should be extended.

The Court's decision was far from a complete victory for 2 Live Crew. The Court held that Campbell would still have to prove that no more of the original work was used than was necessary to establish the intended commentary, and that the new version had not damaged the market value of Orbison's or any future version of the song.[208]

15.3.9.3 *Fair Use and Videotape Recorders*
The U.S. Supreme Court has ruled that home VCR recording of television programming is a fair use.

---

[204] Eveready Battery Co. v. Adolph Coors Co., 765 F. Supp. 440 (1991).
[205] White v. Samsung Electronics, 989 F.2d 1512 (1993).
[206] *Id.* at 1518–1519.
[207] Acuff-Rose Music v. Campbell, 972 F.2d 1429 (1992).
[208] Campbell v. Acuff-Rose Music, 114 S. Ct. 1164 (1994).

In the early 1980s, just as the sale and use of videotape recorders (VCRs) had increased dramatically, a U.S. court of appeals ruled that VCR distributors were liable for copyright infringement if the VCRs were used to record broadcast programming off the air. Universal Studios had sued Sony, hoping to ultimately curtail the recording of copyrighted programming. The decision, which advanced the notion of a vicarious liability for distributors, would have devastated the VCR market. But in 1984 the Supreme Court, in *Sony* v. *Universal Studios*, issued what is called the "Betamax" decision, which overturned the lower court. The high court ruled that Universal would have to prove that VCR owners would use the machines to make unauthorized copies of copyrighted materials and that Sony *knew* such use would occur when the VCRs were sold. The Court, rejecting the notion of vicarious liability, ruled that home VCR recording of television programming for entertainment purposes was a fair use because such recording would not damage the market value of the programming.[209]

A video store can purchase videotapes of television and cable programs, concerts, and movies and rent them to the public under what is called the *first-sale doctrine*. The doctrine is not specifically set forth in the Copyright Act but the courts have interpreted the act to allow such practice as long as the tapes were originally purchased legitimately.[210]

15.3.10   Copyright and the News

News events and the fact that they happen cannot be copyrighted, but the language and literary style of news stories can be protected.

As far back as 1918 the courts have protected news reports. In that year the U.S. Supreme Court, in *INS* v. *Associated Press*, ruled that competing news services could not pirate the news from Associated Press.[211] This kind of unfair competition is called *misappropriation*, and involves the inappropriate use of material acquired as the result of the "expenditure of labor, skill, and money."[212] The Court also said that news facts could not be copyrighted. This would allow a competitor to use facts presented on a radio, television, or cable newscast as tips to produce a story of its own, but even this use is misappropriation if the infringer has produced the story after expending no effort or investigation of its own. This means that radio and television stations and cable operators cannot "steal" news from a newspaper or any other print or electronic medium. Some 45 years after the *INS* decision a Pennsylvania court issued an injunction against radio station WPAZ in Pottstown, Pennsylvania, for reading stories from the local newspaper, the *Pottstown Mercury*.[213]

---

[209] Sony Corp. of Am. v. Universal Studios, 464 U.S. 417 (1984).
[210] United States v. Atherton, 561 F.2d 747 (1977).
[211] International News Service v. Associated Press, 248 U.S. 215 (1918).
[212] *Id.* at 239.
[213] Pottstown Daily News Publishing Co. v. Pottstown Broadcasting Co., 411 Pa. 383 (1963).

CBS ran into copyright problems by getting into too big a hurry to broadcast information about Charlie Chaplin upon his death on Christmas Day in 1977. Actually, the network had been working on a biographical sketch for some time and had previously attempted to obtain the rights to Chaplin film clips. When Chaplin died, CBS used the clips without permission and finished the project. When the owner sued for copyright infringement and unfair competition (EMG 15.3.14), CBS claimed First Amendment news reporting privilege. The court ruled that CBS had misappropriated the "skill, expenditures and labor" of the plaintiffs for "commercial" gain and awarded damages totaling over $700,000.[214]

A 1991 Supreme Court decision may have cast some doubt over just how protected individual news stories are. In *Feist Publications* v. *Rural Telephone Service* the Court ruled that the names, addresses, and telephone numbers in a telephone book are facts, not original compilations protected by copyright. The key to the Court's decision was that the telephone listings lacked originality, the most important criterion of protectability.[215]

In *CNN* v. *Video Monitoring Services* the listing of telephone numbers, names, and addresses was judged comparable to the listing of facts in a news story. Video Monitoring Services (VMS) was providing clients with copies of video segments recorded from numerous programming sources nationwide, including CNN. CNN sought and received a U.S. district court injunction forcing VMS to stop recording and selling segments of its programming, and a copyright battle was on.

The U.S. Court of Appeals, Eleventh Circuit, ruled that news stories, interviews, and weather reports presented within newscasts constitute preexisting, collected, and assembled materials that are basically factual—much like the telephone book listings in the *Feist* decision.[216] An original work is created, according to the court, by the selection, coordination, and arrangement of stories into a newscast. In overturning the injunction, the court cited a strong public interest in dissemination of information:

> In a society where the free flow of and access to ideas is mandated by the First Amendment, it would be particularly pernicious to allow the news media, cloaked in the privilege of the First Amendment, to thwart such access and to control such flow under the title of a copyright owner.[217]

Despite this ruling, almost a year later the Ninth Circuit Court of Appeals concluded that AVRS, a "news clipping service," did infringe copyrights by marketing videotapes of news segments from Los Angeles television stations. The segments that spawned the litigation contained raw footage of an airplane crash and a train wreck, both shot by an independent news service and licensed for use by the television stations. The court, confirming an earlier court opinion that news clipping

---

[214] Roy Export Co. v. CBS, 672 F.2d 1095 (1982).
[215] Feist Publications v. Rural Telephone Service Co., 111 S. Ct. 1282 (1991).
[216] Cable News Network v. Video Monitoring Services of America, 940 F.2d 1471 (1991).
[217] *Id.* at 1484.

services were "unabashedly commercial,"[218] rejected AVRS's fair use defense. Interestingly, AVRS made the same arguments as the court in the *CNN* decision, namely that the video clips were not original works and that the public's First Amendment right of access to newsworthy events precludes copyright infringement. Both arguments were rejected and the court awarded $20,000 in damages.[219]

15.3.11   Copyright and Cable Television

> The Copyright Act of 1976 defines the retransmission of broadcast signals as a copyright infringement. But the act also confers on cable operators a compulsory license that grants them permission to retransmit signals through payment of a fee instead of the purchase of rights to each individual program retransmitted. The amount of the fee is determined by copyright arbitration royalty panels convened by the librarian of Congress.

Cable system operators have traditionally received special treatment from Congress and the courts regarding copyright law. For one thing, the rights to much of what is transmitted over a cable system have already been obtained by local television stations and programming networks. Should cable companies have to purchase them again? In 1968 the U.S. Supreme Court ruled that they did not. In *Fortnightly* v. *United Artists* the Court ruled that retransmission of television programming was not a "performance" (EMG 15.3.12) and thus did not violate copyright.[220] Even when systems began importing signals from around the country the Court held firm that cable operators did not have to purchase rights to retransmitted programming.[221]

Change was imminent, however. For one thing, broadcasters were unhappy about having to pay programming royalties only to have cable systems pick up and retransmit their programming for free, and even collect a fee from subscribers.

Congress changed everything by passing the Copyright Act of 1976, which defined retransmission of broadcast signals as a copyright infringement. However, instead of requiring cable operators to purchase rights to all retransmitted programming, the act grants them a *compulsory license*. The compulsory license requires cable operators to pay royalty fees twice a year. This allows them to retransmit copyrighted programming. The amount of the fee is based on the cable system's gross revenues and the number of distant signals carried.

On December 17, 1993 President Clinton signed into law the Copyright Royalty Tribunal Act of 1993.[222] The act eliminated the Copyright Royalty Tribunal (CRT) which had been responsible for setting royalty fees and distributing payments but was perceived by many as performing too few functions to justify its $1 million annual budget. Establishment, collection, and distribution of royalty fees as

---

[218] Pacific and Southern Co. v. Duncan, 744 F.2d 1490 (1984).
[219] Los Angeles News Serv. v. Tullo, 973 F.2d 791 (1992).
[220] Fortnightly Corp. v. United Artists, 392 U.S. 390 (1968).
[221] Teleprompter Corp. v. CBS, 415 U.S. 394 (1974).
[222] 107 Stat. 2304 (1993).

well as enforcement of all rules and regulations of the CRT was turned over to copyright arbitration royalty panels to be convened by the librarian of Congress.

In 1980, the FCC complicated cable copyright matters a bit by eliminating limits imposed on cable operators regarding the carriage of distant signals. Three years later the CRT raised the royalty fees for distant signals to the current level of 3.75 percent of a cable operator's basic revenues for each distant signal carried. Cable operators filed suit in protest, but the new rates were upheld in *National Cable Television Association v. CRT.*[223] Some cable operators subsequently ceased carriage of some distant signal superstations such as WGN, WOR, and WTBS.

15.3.12 Music Licensing

In order to use any copyrighted music in programs, commercials, or for any other purpose, electronic media operators must obtain public performance rights. Rights are obtained mainly from three organizations: American Society of Composers, Authors, and Publishers (ASCAP), Broadcast Music Incorporated (BMI), and the Society of European Stage Actors and Composers (SEASAC).

Sometimes programmers and advertising agencies contract directly with composers to obtain original music, but the rights to the vast majority of music you hear on radio and television are owned by composers and music publishers. If any copyrighted music, live or recorded, is broadcast, performance rights must be obtained. Public performance, discussed in Box 15.9, includes use of music in commercials, public service announcements, and promotions. Broadcasters must also purchase *synchronization rights* in order to combine copyrighted music with video segments to produce commercials or other video packages.

BOX 15.9 Public Performance of Music

Public performance of music includes any live performance of copyrighted music and the playing of recorded music whether on phonograph records, tapes, or compact discs. The term *public* has been interpreted broadly. It includes playing music in shopping malls, aerobic exercise and dance studios, skating rinks, hotels, and of course, on radio and television stations. The courts have defined public performance so broadly that it includes virtually any commercial use of music, but smaller business establishments have been allowed to play radios and recorded music as long as the sound systems are not too sophisticated.

The purchase of sheet music or a tape or compact disc allows the purchaser to perform or play the music privately but does not grant permission for public performance rights or cover the royalty fees.

---

[223] National Cable Television Ass'n v. Copyright Royalty Tribunal, 724 F.2d 176 (1983).

Rights to use music are obtained for a fee. The amount paid by broadcasters is determined by the amount of music programmed and the market size of the station. Failure to pay royalty fees can result in stiff penalties. Radio station WKND in Windsor, Connecticut, was fined $23,000 (or $1,000 for each infringement) for continuing to play compositions owned by ASCAP after the station's licensing agreement with the organization had expired. ASCAP had monitored WKND for four days and recorded 23 separate ASCAP compositions played by the station.[224]

15.3.12.1 Blanket License

The *blanket license* is a practice whereby a licensing organization offers use of all music compositions in its repertory for a negotiated fee.

For television stations, the blanket license allows the broadcast of any music contained in syndicated programs as well as locally produced programs and commercials. The fee is typically based on gross revenues of the station. The fee is distributed to the composers and music publishing companies. The licensing agencies, under a 1941 consent decree, cannot force a programmer to purchase a blanket license as the only means of obtaining music performance rights.

The major television networks also have blanket licenses to cover music contained in their programs. Negotiation of music rights in the cable industry has proven difficult, as we shall discuss shortly. In 1991, HBO settled a year-long battle with BMI by agreeing to pay 15 cents per subscriber for performance rights.

In 1985, the U.S. Supreme Court let stand an appellate court ruling that the blanket license was not an unreasonable restraint on trade. A group of local television station owners had filed suit against ASCAP in hopes of having blanket licensing replaced by a process that would leave the acquisition of licensing rights up to program suppliers. In *Buffalo Broadcasting* v. *ASCAP* the court upheld the blanket license. The court ruled that since television stations could still seek other means of licensing, the blanket license did not restrain buyers or sellers from negotiating for the licensing of performance rights.[225]

A similar suit was filed against BMI by the National Cable Television Association (NCTA), Black Entertainment Network (BET), and the Disney Channel (TDC). The cable plaintiffs argued that cable programming services had no choice but to acquire the blanket license from BMI because syndicated programming contained BMI-licensed songs. The plaintiffs pointed out that syndicated programs comprise a large percentage of overall cable programming and cable operators are prohibited from deleting any segments of programs, including those containing music.

The court's decision was similar to that in *Buffalo Broadcasting*. The court once again upheld blanket licensing, holding that cable operators have other means of obtaining performance rights for syndicated programming. Three alternative means were discussed in both cases:

---

[224] Boz Scaggs Music v. KND Corp., 491 F. Supp. 908 (1980).
[225] Buffalo Broadcasting Co. v. ASCAP, 744 F.2d 917 (1984), *cert. denied*, 469 U.S. 1211 (1985).

1. *Source Licensing*: the program producers/suppliers obtain rights;
2. *Direct Licensing*: the rights are obtained by programmers directly from composers and music publishers;
3. *Per Program Licensing*: a modified form of blanket licensing whereby rights are obtained for a fee paid to a licensing agency based on programs containing that agency's music.

BMI offered a fourth alternative that was not warmly received. They suggested that cable operators could merely refrain from playing any music licensed to BMI. Broadcasters and cable operators and programmers had previously suggested that direct licensing and per program licensing were not attractive or realistic alternatives.

The BMI decision came as a double dose of bad news to The Disney Channel and BET. The court ruled that the two cable programmers infringed music copyrights by continuing to use BMI music without paying royalty fees after negotiations with BMI had broken down. Statutory damages were assessed to the tune of almost $2 million for TDC and $225,000 for BET.[226]

15.3.12.2 *Music Licensing and Retail Establishments*

Large retail stores, restaurants, and other commercial establishments must pay licensing fees in order to play copyrighted music to enhance the commercial attractiveness of their businesses.

What if a business simply plays a radio or displays a television receiver? Radio and television stations have already obtained performance rights, so one might expect that a retail business could play a radio station's signal or display a television receiver inside the establishment without running afoul of copyright laws. This is true, but only partially.

In 1982, the Supreme Court let stand a lower court ruling that playing radio broadcasts of copyrighted music in Gap clothing stores did constitute copyright infringement. The court concluded that Gap stores, which average 3,500 square feet, are too large to transmit broadcast signals without requiring sound systems more elaborate than those used in private homes. The court advised the retailer to subscribe to a music service.[227]

Keep in mind that the court was not concerned about infringement of the broadcasters' rights. Broadcasters would never object anyway because they want their signals publicly retransmitted. It is the music within the broadcasts that creates the problem.

Smaller establishments, like George Aiken's Chicken, a fast-food restaurant in Pennsylvania, may be able to get away with what the Gap stores were doing. So long as the receiving equipment is comparable to that in a private home, establishments may receive what is called a *homestyle exemption*. Aiken's establishment utilized a

---

[226] National Cable Television Ass'n v. BMI, Inc., 772 F. Supp. 614 (1991).
[227] Sailor Music v. Gap Stores, 668 F.2d 84 (1981).

radio and four ceiling-mounted speakers. The Supreme Court, in a ruling made just before changes in the federal copyright law, concluded that such transmission did not constitute public performance so there was no need for Aiken to obtain performance rights.[228] However, the Copyright Act of 1976 defined "performance" and "public performance" so broadly that the Court's rationale in the *Aiken* case may no longer be applicable.

In the 1991 case *BMI* v. *Claire's Boutiques*, a U.S. court of appeals ruled that under the new Copyright Act definitions the restaurant owner in *Aiken* clearly performed the works in question. But the court was quick to say that Congress never intended for such performance—utilizing an ordinary radio or television receiver in public—to be an infringement, since such use of copyrighted work is so minimal. The court was also concerned about the impact of a decision banning such retransmission, given the huge number of establishments engaged in the practice. The court then offered factors to consider in determining whether an establishment has infringed copyright. They include:

1. size of the establishment;
2. noise levels in the areas where the transmission is made audible or visible; and
3. the extent to which the receiving apparatus is augmented to improve the quality of the transmission in public areas.[229]

In 1992, BMI tried to argue that one retailer, Edison Brothers, operated so many stores that the homestyle exemption should not apply. Edison Brothers was operating about 25,000 stores including Size 5-7-9 Shops, Jeans West, and J. Riggins. The court rejected BMI's suit, concluding that the number of stores made no difference. The court stressed once again that type of equipment was equally as important as the size of the establishment.[230]

15.3.13   Satellite Transmissions and Copyright

It is perfectly legal to own a satellite dish and receive unscrambled transmissions for private viewing. Although infringements are numerous, it is a violation of copyright to receive and display satellite transmissions to customers in pubs, restaurants, hotels, and motels.

Congress specifically exempted the manufacture, distribution, sale, and use of satellite dishes for private viewing from otherwise stringent prohibitions against the interception of satellite transmission. The exemption does not apply to scrambled (encrypted) programming, and it does not allow commercial establishments to use

---

[228] Twentieth Century Music Corp. v. Aiken, 422 U.S. 151 (1975).
[229] Broadcast Music Inc. v. Claire's Boutiques, 949 F.2d 1482 (1991).
[230] Edison Bros. Stores v. BMI, 954 F.2d 1419 (1992).

satellite dish programming to attract customers to their establishments.[231] Even the reception and transmission of satellite programming to prison inmates is prohibited.[232]

The restrictions also apply to hotels and motels that use dishes to pick up satellite transmissions, including those of subscription television services (STV), and offer the programming to guests without paying copyright royalties.[233] The courts have also held that sports "blackout" policies prohibit pubs and other establishments from televising sporting events in markets included in the blackout.[234]

Even though the law seems clear to the lay observer, the courts have been inconsistent in dealing with individuals who make and distribute descramblimg devices. The Communications Act states:

> Any person who manufactures, assembles, modifies, imports, exports, sells, or distributes any electronic, mechanical, or other device or equipment, knowing or having reason to know that the device or equipment is primarily of assistance in the unauthorized decryption of satellite cable programming ... shall be fined not more than $500,000 for each violation, or imprisoned for not more than 5 years for each violation, or both.[235]

The Electronic Communications Privacy Act, a 1986 amendment to the Federal Wiretap Act, also prohibits the intentional manufacture, assemblage, possession, or sale of any electronic, mechanical, or other device "primarily useful for the surreptitious interception of wire, oral, or electronic communications."[236] The act calls for fines of up to $10,000 and prison terms of up to five years, or both. The amendment was added not long after the so-called Captain Midnight incident in which an Ocala, Florida, satellite dish retailer deliberately interfered with an HBO transmission.[237]

Despite the seemingly obvious intent of the legislation, when one company was accused of apparently doing what the laws prohibited—modifying satellite television receivers to allow descrambling—a federal district court dismissed the charges. The court, interpreting the statutes narrowly, argued that the devices made by the company were not necessarily "primarily" used for surreptitious interceptions, and that the term *electronic communications* did not necessarily mean "satellite transmissions."[238] If it did, Congress should have specified so, according to

---

[231] Quincy Cablesystems v. Sully's Bar, 650 F. Supp. 838 (1986).

[232] Sioux Falls Cable Television v. State of South Dakota, 838 F.2d 249 (1988).

[233] ESPN v. Edinburg Community Hotel, 735 F. Supp. 1334 (1986); American Television and Communications Corp. v. Floken, Ltd., 629 F. Supp. 1462 (1986).

[234] National Football League v. McBee & Bruno's, 792 F.2d 726 (1986).

[235] 47 U.S.C. § 605(e)(4).

[236] 18 U.S.C. § 2512(1)(b).

[237] "Captain Midnight Regrets His Methods," *Tampa Tribune*, 24 July 1986; final ed.; at 7B.

[238] United States v. Hochman, 809 F. Supp. 202 (1992).

the court. Other federal district courts have handled cases with nearly identical alleged violations of the same statutes and rendered guilty verdicts.[239]

Home Box Office was successful in a copyright infringement suit against Shaun Kenny, who advertised, promoted, and sold descrambling kits. Kenny would also install the device for customers who mailed in circuitry boards and paid a $39 (cash only) fee. Kenny had even organized a "descrambling summit" in the British West Indies during which he taught and sold instructional videotapes describing how to descramble satellite signals. In 1990, a federal appeals court enjoined Kenny from further manufacturing, installing, importing, or distributing descrambling devices. The court assessed a $20,000 statutory damage judgment, and awarded the plaintiffs over $450,000 in requested attorney fees and court costs.[240]

In 1987, NBC filed a copyright suit against the Satellite Broadcast Networks (SBN), a company that picks up and scrambles broadcast signals from local television stations and retransmits them by satellite across the nation.[241] Home satellite dish owners pay a fee to receive the signals unscrambled. NBC claimed that SBN, by redistributing the signal of Atlanta affiliate WXIA, infringed on the network's copyright. SBN responded that NBC and its affiliates had no choice but to allow secondary transmission because satellite delivery systems, just like cable systems, operated under a compulsory license.

Despite a Copyright Office ruling that a facility must both receive and transmit signals from within the same state to qualify for a compulsory license, the court ruled that SBN should be considered a cable system:

> [T]o conclude that SBN cannot be a cable system because of its geographic reach would be to prevent those in sparsely populated areas from receiving the quality television reception technology can provide.[242]

The court based its remarks on the fact that cable systems find it economically unfeasible to wire homes in areas with fewer than 40 households per square mile. According to the court, SBN's secondary transmissions were permissible under FCC rules and did not infringe upon NBC's copyright. In 1988 Congress provided a compulsory license to satellite services such as SBN.[243]

15.3.14 Unfair Competition

Unfair competition is the passing off of one's goods or services as those of a competitor. It includes but is not limited to the misuse of a competitor's name, symbol, slogan, or device. Businesses are protected against unfair competition by the Lanham Act of 1946 and by the courts through common law.[244]

---

[239] United States v. Splawn, 982 F.2d 414 (1992); United States v. Hux, 940 F.2d 314 (1991).

[240] Cable/Home Communication Corp., v. Network Productions, 902 F.2d 829 (1990).

[241] NBC v. Satellite Broadcast Networks, 940 F.2d 1467 (1991).

[242] *Id.* at 1471.

[243] 17 U.S.C.A. § 119.

[244] 15 U.S.C.A. § 1125(a).

In 1986, a group of corporate executives planning to launch a fourth commercial television network decided to call it the Fox Broadcasting Company. Use of the term *Fox* would allow them to take advantage of the high recognition of its sister corporation, Twentieth Century Fox. There was only one problem. A "Fox Broadcasting Company" already existed, and operated station WIBF-FM in Pennsylvania. Copyright law offers little or no protection of names, trademarks, or station slogans, so the WIBF interests sued for *unfair competition* and *trademark infringement*. After a brief discussion of these two areas of law we will return to see what happened in the case *Fox Broadcasting* v. *Fox Broadcasting*.[245]

Unfair competition has been defined as "anything done by a rival in the same business by imitation or otherwise designed or calculated to mislead the public in the belief that, in buying the product offered ... for sale, they were buying the product of another manufacturer."[246] In other words, unfair competition is palming off one's goods as those of a competitor. Trademark law, discussed in the next section, really deals with a type of unfair competition.

The law clearly applies to electronic media. For example, a television station that intentionally misleads the public into confusing its newscasts with those of a more successful station is engaging in unfair competition. The key to unfair competition is whether the public is misled or caused to be confused in some way regarding rival companies' products and services.

A plaintiff can establish an unfair competition claim by proving two elements:

1. *Secondary Meaning*: The plaintiff is required to show that the meaning conjured up by a name, slogan, or trademark goes beyond the ordinary meaning with which it is normally associated. Further, the meaning conjured up must be the plaintiff—the actual manufacturer or producer of goods or services claiming unfair competition. In radio, for example, secondary meaning might imply a mental association between a slogan such as "Power 104" and the radio station using the slogan. Secondary meaning is established if listeners associate the slogan with the station itself but not if it only conjures up the station's operating frequency (104 mHz).

   How about the phrase "it's the real thing?" Secondary meaning has been established because the slogan is strongly associated with the soft drink Coca-Cola.

   Now we can return to the *Fox* v. *Fox* case. The court acknowledged that WIBF used "Fox Broadcasting Company" on stationery and coverage maps, but not on the air, at least not until the other "Fox" arrived on the scene. The court concluded, therefore, that WIBF listeners would not conjure up thoughts of WIBF when hearing "Fox Broadcasting Company," so no secondary meaning was established.[247]

---

[245] Fox Broadcasting Co. v. Fox Broadcasting Co., Civil Action No. 86-4989 (E.D. Pa. 1986).
[246] B.V.D. Co. v. Kaufmann & Baer Co., 272 Pa. 240 (1922).
[247] Fox Broadcasting Co. v. Fox Broadcasting Co., Civil Action No. 86-4989 (E.D. Pa. 1986).

2. *Likelihood of Confusion*: A business charging unfair competition must also establish that a practice or use of a name, slogan, or trademark will cause the public to confuse the products or services of the two companies involved. For this to have occurred in the *Fox* case, the public would have to have confused programming offered by WIBF, a local radio station formatting primarily religious and foreign language programming, with that offered by a new commercial television network. The court considered this highly unlikely and dismissed charges against the television Fox.[248]

A similar case arose when two Chicago radio stations both began to include "107" in on-air slogans and station identifications. One station operated on 107.5 MHz, the other 106.7.[249] In the suit that followed the court concluded that, in this case, the primary meaning conjured up in the minds of the public when hearing "107" was the stations' position on the dial, not the stations themselves. Both were allowed continued use of the slogans.[250]

15.3.15   Trademarks

The Lanham Act of 1946 allows manufacturers and merchants to protect trade-marks so that their products can be distinguished from others.[251] A *trademark* is a word, name, symbol, device, or a combination thereof used to identify and distinguish one company's goods or services from those of a competitor.

The term *service mark* is sometimes used instead of *trademark* when referring to the sale, advertising, or promotion of products or services. The term *mark* is used in place of "trademark" and "service mark." The courts in recent years have used all three terms interchangeably.[252] Trademarks, as discussed in Box 15.10, are registered with the federal government. Only distinctive or nongeneric marks can be registered. Generic terms such as *biggest, love,* and *restaurant* cannot be registered, but some terms otherwise not distinctive can be registered if they acquire a secondary meaning as discussed in the previous section.

A successful plaintiff in a trademark suit can collect for damages, illegal profits resulting from the infringement, attorney's fees, and court costs. Trademark law, therefore, offers a business substantial protection against piracy of its business identity. One simply cannot go into business with a new product called Baby Ruth Bars or form a new cable network called ESPN even if the letters stand for something other than Entertainment and Sports Programming Network. It would also violate

---

[248] *Id.*

[249] It is interesting that neither of the stations was operating on either of the two frequencies (106.9 and 107.1) close enough to claim use of "107" in its marketing.

[250] Walt-West Enter. v. Gannett Co., 695 F.2d 1050 (1982).

[251] 15 U.S.C.A. § 1125(a).

[252] Walt-West Enter. v. Gannett Co., 695 F.2d at 1054.

BOX 15.10   Registration of Trademarks

Trademarks are registered with the federal government through the U.S. Patent and Trademark Office in Washington, DC.

Registered trademarks are indicated with the symbol® (the letter *R* in a circle), and the phrase "Registered in the U.S. Patent and Trademark Office," or an abbreviation thereof.

---

trademark law to refer to your product by Coca-Cola's slogan "the real thing" or form a new musical group called the Rolling Stones.

You would also have trademark problems if you began a singing or entertainment career calling yourself "Sting" or "Whoopi Goldberg," even though the real names of those entertainers, Gordon Sumner and Karen Johnson, are very different from those they have assumed professionally. The same principle would apply to the radio air name "The Greaseman," because it is already used by radio personality Doug Tracht.

The infringement does not have to be so obvious. Despite the decision in the "FM 107" case discussed previously, radio station call letters and marks such as "power rock" and "your oldies station" can be registered and protected. In *Pathfinder Communications* v. *Midwest Communications* the court offered strong protection for radio station call letters through trademark laws. Radio station WMEE, in Fort Wayne, Indiana, brought action against a station in nearby Decatur, Indiana, that had begun to use the call letters WNCZ. Despite the obvious differences, the court concluded that the two sets of call letters sounded too similar over the air and that listeners would likely confuse the two stations, especially since WNCZ was in the process of boosting its signal into Fort Wayne. The court noted that "WMEE" was a strong, established mark, and in fact was the most-listened-to station in the market according to the latest Arbitron surveys. Also, both stations were FM but only WMEE was stereo. The court determined that WMEE would be damaged if listeners tuned to WNCZ, thinking they were listening to WMEE, and became upset about the inferior sound quality.[253]

The names of television programs can also be registered. An unauthorized book entitled *Welcome to Twin Peaks* was found to be a copyright and trademark infringement. The publisher had not received permission to publish the detailed summaries of episodes of the program or to use the *Twin Peaks* program title trademark.[254]

Trademarks are protected even if the violator alters the mark somewhat. A T-shirt heat transfer company was found to have infringed on the well-known trade-

---

[253] Pathfinder Communications Corp. v. Midwest Communications Co., 593 F. Supp. 281 (1984).
[254] Twin Peaks Productions v. Publications Int'l, 778 F. Supp. 1247 (1991).

mark of Hard Rock Cafe by distributing transfers bearing a "Hard Rain Cafe" design similar to the Hard Rock Cafe trademark.[255]

Trademark protection is not extended to all uses of particular words or elements composing a trademark. In March 1990, an ad campaign designed to promote two new Canada Dry beverages used the expression "your new main squeeze" in both radio and print ads. The radio ad said in part, "just got hitched to a new main squeeze—the light, clean, refreshing taste of lemon. . . ." A company that distributed fruit juices under the registered trademark "Main Squeeze" claimed trademark infringement and unfair competition. The court ruled that Canada Dry was using the words in their ordinary as opposed to their special trademark meaning, so the commercials did not constitute a trademark infringement.[256]

Using a registered trademark in a telephone survey is also not a trademark infringement. The popular music group New Kids on the Block sued for trademark infringement when two newspapers conducted polls about the group. One paper, *USA Today*, asked readers to phone a 900 number to select the most popular member of the group. The profits, which totaled $300, went to a charity. The New Kids group argued that use of its name was a trademark infringement because readers might infer that the group authorized the poll and because money spent on the 900 call might be money not spent on New Kids merchandise. The court ruled that there was nothing misleading about the polls and that "trademark laws do not give the New Kids the right to channel their fans' enthusiasm (and dollars) only into items licensed or authorized by them."[257]

DISCUSSION QUESTIONS

1. Discuss whether you believe that print libel has more "permanence of form" than electronic media libel. Do you think that defamatory communications made in newspapers, magazines, and books are more damaging than those made on radio, television, cable, or satellite communications? Why or why not?

2. Discuss the fault requirement of plaintiffs in libel suits. What types of practices might be considered negligent? On the basis of fault, to what extent do callers to radio talk shows pose a libel threat to licensees? How do the courts define actual malice?

3. What types of communications are protected by the opinion/fair comment defense? Explain when the defense can and cannot be used.

4. Suppose you are a local television news investigative reporter who wants to take a camera crew into a local restaurant that has been accused of serving tainted or spoiled food. You arrive, cameras rolling, and the owner immediately asks you to leave. Instead, you keep shooting and run a story with video of the inside of the restaurant including patrons on the evening news. Does the First Amendment protect you from an invasion of privacy suit? What legal wrongs have you possibly committed?

---

[255] Hard Rock Cafe Licensing Corp. v. Pacific Graphics, 776 F. Supp 1454 (1991).
[256] The Citrus Group, Inc. v. Cadbury Beverages, 781 F. Supp. 386 (1991).
[257] New Kids on the Block v. News America Publishing, 971 F.2d 302 (1992).

5. What kind of invasion of privacy is committed by showing video of recognizable children at a local playground in a story about parental child abuse? What must a plaintiff do to win such a suit?

6. In *Time* v. *Hill*, the Court ruled that the Hill family could not collect damages for invasion of privacy. Why not? What does this tell you about media news coverage or other use of information about people caught up in newsworthy events?

7. What must a plaintiff do to prove that an electronic medium has infringed on a copyright? How do the courts go about determining whether a work is truly original? Does a copy have to be made deliberately?

8. Explain how the doctrine of fair use works as a defense against a copyright infringement suit. Discuss various electronic media practices to which fair use would be relevant.

9. Can CNN take news out of *USA Today* and read it over the air? Why or why not? What if a CNN reporter uses the facts in the *USA Today* article as the basis for a story?

10. What major issues with regard to music licensing face the electronic media today? Is the "blanket license" a fair method of obtaining rights? Should stores, motels, and sports bars and pubs be allowed to play or show radio or television programs containing music to their customers?

11. Suppose you manage a contemporary hit, rock music radio station that needs some good promotional spots. You hire a local singer who imitates the singer Sting to sing about your station to the tune of "Every Breath You Take," a hit recording by the group Police back in the early 1980s. What kind of legal problems might your station encounter?

SUGGESTED READINGS

Andrussier, Sean E. "The Freedom of Information Act in 1990: More Freedom for the Government; Less Information for the Public." *Duke Law Journal* 41 (1991): 753.

Forer, Lois G. *A Chilling Effect: The Mounting Threat of Libel and Invasion of Privacy Actions to the First Amendment.* New York: Norton, 1987.

Geik, Iris C. "Direct Broadcast Satellite and the Determination of Authors' Rights under the Berne Convention: Lucy in the Sky without Rights?" *Suffolk Transnational Law Journal* 2 (1992): 563.

Hartnick, Alan J. "A Copyright Aspect of Cable Regulation." *New York Law Journal* 207 (1992): 5.

Hopkins, W. *Actual Malice: Twenty-five Years after Times v. Sullivan.* New York: Praeger, 1989.

Lasswell, Bryan R. "In Defense of False Light: Why False Light Must Remain a Viable Cause of Action." *South Texas Law Review* 34 (1993): 149.

McLean, Deckle. "Public Versus Private Figure Determination under Gertz." *Communications and the Law* 14 (1992): 31.

Miller, Jermone K. *Video Copyright Permissions: A Guide to Securing Permission to Retain, Perform, and Transmit Television Programs Videotaped Off the Air.* Friday Harbor, WA: Copyright Information Services, 1989.

Performance Rights in Sound Recordings. Washington, DC: Government Printing Office, 1978.

Sanford, Bruce W. *Law and Privacy: The Prevention and Defense of Litigation.* New York: Harcourt, 1985.

Smith, Gerald R. "Of Malice and Men: The Law of Defamation." *Valparaiso University Law Review* 27 (1992): 39.

Streeter, Thomas. "Broadcast Copyright and the Bureaucratization of Property." *Cardozo Arts and Entertainment Law Journal* 10 (1992): 567.

Tanner, Craig Phillip. "Self-Censorship: The Unfortunate Result of Masson v. New Yorker Magazine, Inc.'s Altered Quotation Test." *University of San Francisco Law Review* 27 (1993): 515.

Wells, James A. "Modern Technology and the Conflict Between Copyright and Free Speech: The Application of Copyright Law to Television Newscasts." *West Virginia Law Review* 95 (1992): 247.

Chapter

16

REPORTING EFFORT

As you can see from our discussions of libel and privacy in the previous chapter, a considerable number of laws, policies, and court decisions are of particular relevance to journalists and other media professionals involved in the gathering and dissemination of news. With the emergence of CNN and other cable networks featuring news and information services, the expansion of news segments on local television in the early evening and on networks during late night hours, and the proliferation of news and information stations on AM radio, news has clearly become a principal source of programming and a critical revenue base for electronic media. In this chapter we will focus on three topics primarily related to news. First, we will look at the extent to which journalists have access to information held by governmental agencies. The Freedom of Information Act (FOIA) will be a particular focus of discussion. Second, we will summarize court cases and laws respecting the free press–fair trial conflict, once again emphasizing relevant cases involving the electronic media. Finally, we will look at the practice of allowing cameras in the courtroom.

16.1   ACCESS TO GOVERNMENT INFORMATION

The Freedom of Information Act requires federal agencies to provide access to documents that are in the public interest. The sunshine laws require state and federal agencies to open most meetings to the public.

Ever since the military and political failures in Vietnam and the illegal and unethical behavior of government officials during the Watergate scandal, there has been greater demand for access to government information and openness in official meetings. Federal and state courts, Congress, and state legislatures have all influenced the extent to which governmental agencies must release information to the public and the press. A limited constitutional right of access was granted by the Supreme Court in a landmark decision in 1980, and other federal and state courts have rendered decisions that help define the limits of access to government information.

16.1.1   Access to Government Information and the Courts

In July of 1979 the Supreme Court handed down its decision in *Gannett* v. *DePasquale.* The decision concerned and even shocked proponents of greater public and press access to governmental documents and proceedings, as well as those advocating an open trial process. In a plurality decision in which five separate opinions were written, the Court ruled that the press and public have no right of access to pretrial hearings.[1] Perhaps even more disturbing was the Court's argument that the Sixth Amendment—which guarantees the right to a *speedy and public trial*—simply did not apply to the press.

16.1.1.1   *Richmond Newspapers Decision*
In *Richmond Newspapers* v. *Virginia* the U.S. Supreme Court ruled that the press and public have a First Amendment right to attend criminal trials.

The concern generated by *Gannett* v. *Depasquale* was dissipated in 1980 when the Supreme Court issued its landmark *Richmond Newspapers* decision.[2] Sixth Amendment aside, the Court ruled that the First Amendment gives the press and public access to trials.

The case involved a defendant whose murder conviction had been overturned because a blood-stained shirt had been improperly admitted into evidence. After two subsequent mistrials—one because a juror had read and discussed newspaper accounts of the previous trials with other prospective jurors—the judge ordered the next trial closed, banning everyone other than witnesses while they testified. The *Richmond Newspapers* successfully appealed the order.

The extent to which the *Richmond Newspapers* decision grants access to other types of governmental proceedings is still debated. In his concurring opinion Justice Stevens seemed to advocate a more generalized right of access:

> Today . . . for the first time, the Court unequivocally holds that an arbitrary interference with access to important information is an abridgment of the freedoms of speech and press. . . . I agree that the First Amendment protects the public and the press from abridgment of their rights of access to

---

[1] Gannett v. DePasquale, 443 U.S. 368 (1979).
[2] Richmond Newspapers v. Virginia, 448 U.S. 555 (1980).

information about the operation of their government, including the judicial branch; . . .[3]

The Court also ruled that since a courtroom is a public place, the judge's order closing the courtroom had violated the public's right to peacefully assemble.

Since the *Richmond* decision, the Supreme Court has made a number of rulings that have guaranteed greater access to the criminal process. In 1984, the Court ruled that the public has a First Amendment right of access to the voir dire (EMG 1.5.3) process.[4] Two years later the Court extended that right of access to preliminary hearings.[5] The Court also struck down a Massachusetts law that required judges to close trials involving sex crimes when the victim was a minor. The Court used the following two-step test in deciding the case:

1. Have the place and process historically been open to the press and public? The Massachusetts court concluded there was considerable historical precedence for an open courtroom.
2. Does public access play a significant and positive role in the functioning of the process involved? The Court concluded that public access was essential to proper functioning of the judicial system.[6]

16.1.1.2 *Press Access and the Federal Courts*

While the Supreme Court has offered no further elaboration of its *Richmond Newspapers* decision, the high court has ruled that the press has no more access to government agencies and functions than the general public. Lower courts have denied the press any privileged access to various public and semipublic places.

Several key access decisions have involved law enforcement. In the 1974 case *Pell* v. *Procunier,* California prison officials argued that media coverage given to three inmates accused of killing a prison guard had contributed to instability and a breakdown of discipline within the prison. The Court ruled that the First Amendment provides no right of access for the press to interview prison inmates.[7]

More stringent restrictions were upheld in 1974 in *Houchins* v. *KQED.*[8] The case evolved after San Francisco television station KQED had run a story about a reported suicide at the Alameda County, California, jail in Santa Rita. The story included a quote from a psychiatrist who claimed that conditions at a portion of the jail called "Greystone" had contributed to illnesses in some of his patients. Greystone was also allegedly the scene of rapes, beatings, and unhealthy physical conditions. When KQED asked permission to take cameras into Greystone, Sheriff Thomas Houchins essentially banned reporters from his jail. Under Houchins's poli-

---

[3] *Id.* at 583–584.
[4] Press Enterprise Co. v. Superior Court of Cal., 464 U.S. 501 (1984).
[5] Press Enterprise Co. v. Superior Court of Cal., 478 U.S. 1 (1986).
[6] Globe Newspaper Co. v. Superior Court, 457 U.S. 596 (1982).
[7] Pell v. Procunier, 417 U.S. 817 (1974). *See also* Saxbe v. Washington Post, 417 U.S. 843 (1974).
[8] Houchins v. KQED, 438 U.S. 1 (1978).

cies, journalists were limited to once-a-month tours, but even then Houchins allowed no contact with inmates and no cameras or tape recorders.

KQED persuaded a lower court to issue an injunction lifting Houchins's ban, but the injunction was overturned by the Supreme Court. In his majority opinion Chief Justice Burger argued that the news media had no generalized right of access:

> The public importance of conditions in penal facilities and the media's role of providing information afford no basis for reading into the Constitution a right of the public or media to enter these institutions, with camera equipment, and take moving and still pictures of inmates for broadcast purpose. This Court has never intimated a freedom of access guarantee of a right of access to all sources of information within government control.[9]

Burger repeated the Court's ruling in *Procunier* that the media have no right of access any greater than that of the general public. Burger also said that information on prison conditions could be obtained by other means.

Several lower court decisions have helped define the federal courts' perspective on access. When Robert Sherrill, a reporter for the *Nation* magazine, was denied a White House press pass in 1966, he claimed a First Amendment right of access. The Secret Service considered Sherrill a security risk after learning of his conviction for assaulting the press secretary of the governor of Florida, who later referred to Sherrill as "mentally unbalanced."

A U.S. court of appeals ruled that access to the White House could be denied, but only for compelling reasons.[10] "Clearly," the court said, "protection of the President is a compelling, even an overwhelming, interest...."[11] The court did stress, however, that restrictions on journalists should be no more stringent than necessary, and ordered the Secret Service to publish its criteria for determining who may be denied a press pass and to explain to Sherrill in writing why he was denied.

In 1988, a U.S. court of appeals struck down a Washington law banning exit interviews of voters within 300 feet of a polling place. The court objected to the distance imposed, holding that such a broad ban would prohibit *all* exit polling and not just that which was disruptive. The bill had been prompted by concern that exit polling had a detrimental effect on the democratic process in that citizens who knew the likely winners in some races would not bother to vote at all.[12]

Another court ruled in 1971 that once an agency's records had been released to one media representative they could not be denied to another. The Davenport, Iowa, police had rather obviously discriminated against the underground newspaper *Challenge* by continually refusing access to files, affidavits, and investigative reports that were regularly made available to other journalists. The court said that it was not up to the police to make de facto decisions regarding which news organiza-

---

[9] Houchins v. KQED, 438 U.S. at 1 (1978).
[10] Sherrill v. Knight, 569 F.2d 124 (1978).
[11] *Id*. at 130.
[12] Daily Herald v. Munro, 838 F.2d 380 (1988).

tions were and were not legitimate and that this was precisely the kind of abuse that open records acts were designed to prevent.[13]

City officials are also prohibited from making access decisions on the basis of gender. In one of the first examples of women reporters demanding the same access afforded to males, *Sports Illustrated* reporter Melissa Ludtke sought and was denied access to the New York Yankees locker room during the 1977 World Series. Officials claimed that the presence of women would interfere with the personal privacy of the players, so Ludtke was forced to wait in a stadium tunnel for players to be escorted out for interviews. This obviously put Ludtke at a substantial competitive disadvantage to male reporters who were privy to comments and interviews inside the locker room. The court acknowledged the privacy concerns, but ruled that since Yankee stadium is city-owned, denial of access on the basis of sex violated Ludtke's rights to due process and equal protection under the law.[14]

16.1.2   Freedom of Information Act (FOIA)

The Freedom of Information Act requires disclosure of all federal government records not applicable to one of nine categories of exemptions.

If you go back all the way to the Administrative Procedure Act of 1946, government agencies were not really required to divulge much information. All the agency had to do was show "good cause" why particular information should remain secret, and the courts would back up most any justification given. Things began to change in 1966 when President Lyndon B. Johnson signed the first Freedom of Information Act. The act was intended to ensure greater public access to government information, but it remains a matter of dispute whether the original act resulted in significant increases in access. However, the act was amended in 1974 and 1976, and by 1986, when Congress passed the Freedom of Information Reform Act, access to information had become the rule to which exceptions had to be made in order for an agency to refuse disclosure.[15]

The Freedom of Information Act is based on the fundamental premise that the public should have access to government records unless there are compelling reasons why the records should be withheld. The act requires government officials to disclose government documents unless they apply to any one of nine categories of exemptions (EMG 16.1.2.3). Despite this, during the 1980s the trend was to broaden the scope of the exemptions and to increase the number of records classified as secret.

16.1.2.1   *Defining Government Agencies*

A government agency is defined in the act to include "any executive department, military department, Government corporation, Government controlled corpora-

---

[13] Quad-City Community News Service v. Jebens, 334 F. Supp. 8 (1971).
[14] Ludtke v. Kuhn, 461 F. Supp. 86 (1978).
[15] Freedom of Information Reform Act of 1986, 100 Stat. 3248 (1986).

tion, or other establishment of the executive branch of the Government (including the Executive Office of the President), or any independent regulatory agency."[16]

This includes, of course, the Federal Communications Commission, the Federal Trade Commission, and the Securities and Exchange Commission. The act does not apply to the following:

1. the president or any immediate staff members;
2. the Congress;
3. the federal courts; or
4. private corporations.

The act applies to documents, films, videotapes, computer printouts, disks, and tapes. A major factor in determining what is or is not covered is whether the record is capable of being reproduced.

The Supreme Court mandated a broadened scope of FOIA in 1989 by ruling that agencies are required to disclose requested documents even if the information contained in them is available elsewhere.[17] One implication of the decision is that agencies must provide access to state and local documents contained in centralized computer banks instead of forcing reporters and others to research the files of each state, county, or municipal agency individually.

In the 1980 case *Kissinger* v. *Reporter's Committee for Freedom of the Press,* the Supreme Court ruled that mere location of documents at an agency does not mean that they are controlled by the agency or fall under FOIA guidelines. Syndicated columnist William Safire had requested the State Department to turn over notes of Henry Kissinger's telephone conversations, but Kissinger had made the calls and notes while working at the White House. The Court concluded that the documents were White House, not State Department, records. The Court also said that in the event documents have been removed before an FOIA request is made, the agency does not have to provide access.[18] This decision raised some concern that agencies would be able to purge files in the event unwelcome requests seem imminent.

The act does not apply to information gathered by private organizations, even if the government pays for the study. In the 1980 case *Forsham* v. *Harris,* for example, the Supreme Court allowed the Department of Health, Education, and Welfare to withhold research data from a group interested in the study of diabetes. The group wanted access to raw data possessed by the Department of Health, Education, and Welfare that had been collected by private physicians and scientists working under $15 million in federal grants. Even though the U.S. government funded the research, a governmental agency engaged in some supervision of the research, and a governmental agency used the findings to assist in policy formulation, the

---

[16] 5 U.S.C.A. § 552 (f).
[17] Tax Analysts v. Department of Justice, 845 F.2d 1060 (1988).
[18] Kissinger v. Reporter's Comm. for Freedom of the Press, 445 U.S. 136 (1980).

Court ruled that HEW did not technically have control of the data and did not have to provide access.[19]

The opinions of agency employees or their thoughts about matters of public interest are not considered records. For example, a news reporter or any other private citizen can request access to copies of a proposed FCC rule, but there is no right of access to the opinion of an FCC commissioner or other staff member regarding the rule.

16.1.2.2   Fee Restrictions and Timeliness of Response.

Agencies may charge a fee for delivery of records, but the fees must be "limited to reasonable standard charges for document search, duplication, and review."[20] The news media, as well as noncommercial interests such as scientific or academic institutions engaged in research, are exempted from paying fees other than duplication costs. The news media exemption has resulted in disputes over just what constitutes a news medium. For the most part the courts have defined "news media" rather broadly. In 1987, the FBI tried to argue that a Canadian newspaper did not qualify for the waiver because it provided news outside the United States. A federal district court, in *Southam News* v. *Immigration and Naturalization Service,* ruled that any organization that gathers information of potential interest to the public and disseminates a distinct summary of that information is eligible for the fee waiver.[21]

Agencies are also prohibited from requiring advance payment unless the requester has established a history of poor payment or the agency has estimated that the costs will exceed $250. Agencies must comply with FOIA requests within 10 days or notify the requester of reasons for the delay. Those whose requests are ultimately denied must be notified of the right to appeal.

16.1.2.3   Exemptions to FOIA

The Freedom of Information Act lists nine categories of records that agencies may, under certain conditions, withhold. The exemptions allow, but do not require, that documents be withheld. Sometimes individuals or businesses file suit to block the release of particular records. Such cases are referred to as *reverse FOIA suits.*

Whether a particular record applies to a particular exemption has been the focus of a great deal of FOIA litigation. What follows is discussion of the nine exemptions (listed in Box 16.1) and related court cases.

16.1.2.3.1   Exemption One: National Security Information

Any records that are ordered to be kept secret by the president of the United States in the interest of national defense or foreign policy and are classified as such may be withheld.

---

[19] Forsham v. Harris, 445 U.S. 169 (1980).

[20] 5 U.S.C.A. § 552(a)(4)(ii).

[21] Southam News v. Immigration and Naturalization Serv., 674 F. Supp 881 (1987).

BOX 16.1   FOIA Exemptions

1. National Security Information
2. Agencies' Internal Rules and Practices
3. Matters Specifically Exempted from Disclosure by Statute
4. Trade Secrets of Other Confidential Business Information
5. Interagency or Intra-agency Memoranda or Letters
6. Personnel and Medical Files
7. Law Enforcement Records
8. Information Related to Banks
9. Geological and Geophysical Information

National security information is divided into three classes as follows:

1. *Top Secret:* information, the unauthorized disclosure of which could be reasonably expected to cause *exceptionally grave damage* to the national security;
2. *Secret:* information, the unauthorized disclosure of which could reasonably be expected to cause *serious damage* to the national security;
3. *Confidential:* information, the unauthorized release of which could reasonably be expected to cause *damage* to the national security.

An agency may use Exemption One to justify withholding documents only if in compliance with classification procedures established by the relevant executive order. Ever since the Reagan administration issued a new classification order in 1982, it has been easier for governmental agencies to classify documents.[22] Even before 1982 the courts had refused to question the validity of particular classifications or interfere with the classification process. In the 1973 case *EPA v. Mink*, Congresswoman Patsy Mink had requested documents used by the Nixon administration in selecting a site for nuclear testing. The cite chosen was Amchitka Island in Mink's home state of Alaska, but the documents had been classified as secret. Mink filed an FOIA suit to have the documents released, but the Supreme Court ruled that the courts lacked authority to review classification decisions made by the executive branch.[23]

16.1.2.3.2   Exemption Two: Internal Rules and Practices
Exemption Two provides protection for matters that are related solely to the internal rules and practices of the agency. The exemption pertains only to those records that are not of interest to the public.

---

[22] 47 Fed. Reg. 14,874 (1982).
[23] EPA v. Mink, 410 U.S. 73 (1973).

When federal prison inmate Michael Crooker filed an FOIA request for a training manual for agents entering the Bureau of Alcohol, Tobacco, and Firearms (ATF), the bureau denied access to portions of the manual. Since the manual explains ATF procedures including how agents conduct surveillance on people and automobiles, ATF agents argued that disclosure would help criminals evade the law. A U.S. court of appeals ruled in 1981 that the sections could be deleted because of the need to balance the interest in access to government information with the need to maintain the effective operation of federal agencies.[24] The balancing test had also been used in 1976 in *Department of the Air Force* v. *Rose*.[25] Student editors of the *New York University Law Review* had asked for summaries of honors and ethics hearings to provide information for an article on discipline at the service academies. The Air Force refused to hand over the records even with the names of participants deleted. The Supreme Court ordered their release, holding that the information was not merely internal and that Exemption Two did not allow the withholding of documents of genuine public interest. The Court again noted that the exemptions require a balancing of the public's interest in access to the requested information with the agency's interest in withholding it.

16.1.2.3.3 Exemption Three: Matters Specifically Exempted from Disclosure by Statute

Congress has specifically exempted a number of records from FOIA, including IRS documents and certain records held by the General Accounting Office, the CIA, and the Census Bureau.

Exemption Three is supposed to allow agencies to withhold only those records specifically identified by the statute. Advocates of open records argue, however, that statutes are sometimes used to justify withholding documents that legally should be revealed.

16.1.2.3.4 Exemption Four: Trade Secrets or Other Confidential Business Information

Exemption Four is designed to prevent the government from disclosing valuable and private commercial information that it has collected from businesses. The act never defines trade secrets, but the courts have said they include information, formulae, and patterns and devices that may offer a business an advantage over competitors.

Governmental agencies control a wide assortment of information about businesses. In 1979, concern over the release of commercial information increased when the Supreme Court handed down its decision in *Chrysler Corp.* v. *Brown.* Chrysler had tried to block the release of employee records at automobile assembly plants in Delaware and Michigan. The automaker made two principal claims. First, it

[24] Crooker v. Bureau of Alcohol, Tobacco & Firearms, 670 F.2d 1051 (1981).
[25] Department of the Air Force v. Rose, 425 U.S. 352 (1976).

feared release of the records would reveal important trade secrets. Second, there was concern that competitors would use affirmative action employment data contained in the documents to recruit minority employees away from Chrysler.

The Supreme Court ruled that FOIA did not authorize private interests from which information is obtained to block an agency from releasing that information. It was in the *Chrysler* decision that the Court ruled that exemptions to FOIA permitted, but did not require, agencies to withhold information.[26]

16.1.2.3.5   Exemption Five: Interagency or Intra-agency Memoranda or Letters

Exemption Five allows agencies to withhold working papers, staff reports, memoranda, and studies generated in the process of policy formation or decision making.

In *United States* v. *Weber Aircraft*, the Court ruled that confidential information gathered in an investigation of an air crash is protected by the exemption. The Air Force had refused to release information obtained through confidential interviews after Captain Richard Hoover's F-106B suffered engine failure and crashed. Hoover, who was seriously injured, sued the manufacturers of his ejection equipment, who in turn demanded access to all Air Force documents regarding the case. The Air Force turned over everything except the confidential information. The Court, in 1984, upheld the Air Force's refusal, citing the importance of confidentiality in assuring frank and open discussions to help solve agency problems and formulate policy.[27]

One year earlier, the Supreme Court, in *FTC* v. *Grolier*, also ruled that Exemption Five applies to working papers prepared by attorneys in a lawsuit, so long as they are not already routinely made available to litigants under the rules of civil procedure. The FTC had filed suit against Grolier for allegedly using deceptive sales practices to peddle encyclopedias. The Court protected the attorneys' papers even though the lawsuit had been dismissed before the FOIA request was even placed.[28]

The exemption does not apply to just any working documents. In 1982 the FBI was told to hand over a report (with names deleted) about an alleged incident in which an FBI infiltrator into the Ku Klux Klan had shot a civil rights worker and committed other illegal acts. The court held that Exemption Five would protect against dissemination of opinions and recommendations on which FBI decisions were based, but not factual aspects of the report.[29]

16.1.2.3.6   Exemption Six: Personnel and Medical Files

Exemption Six protects individuals against government disclosures of diseases, problems of drug abuse or alcoholism, marital problems, religious affiliation, and any documents applicable to a vaguely defined category that Congress labeled

---

[26] Chrysler Corp. v. Brown, 441 U.S. 281 (1979).
[27] United States v. Weber Aircraft, 465 U.S. 792 (1984).
[28] FTC v. Grolier, Inc., 462 U.S. 19 (1983).
[29] Playboy v. Justice Dep't, 677 F.2d 931 (1982).

"similar files." The exemption is intended to protect citizens against disclosures that would clearly constitute an unwarranted invasion of personal privacy.

The U.S. Supreme Court, in the 1982 case *U.S. Department of State* v. *Washington Post Co.,* held that the phrase "similar files" could be interpreted broadly by agencies. The Court held that any information about a specific individual, including whether that person was a U.S. citizen, could apply.[30] However, in *Department of the Air Force* v. *Rose* the Court ruled that information should be exempt only if the agency's interest in withholding it outweighs the public's interest in having it disclosed.

16.1.2.3.7 *Exemption Seven: Law Enforcement Records*

Information compiled for law enforcement purposes is exempt to the extent that disclosure of such information could reasonably be expected to (a) interfere with enforcement proceedings; (b) deprive a person of the right to a fair trial; (c) constitute an unwarranted invasion of personal privacy; (d) disclose the identity of a confidential source; (e) disclose techniques and procedures for law enforcement investigations or prosecutions, or disclose guidelines for law enforcement investigations or prosecutions if such disclosure could reasonably be expected to risk circumvention of the law; or (f) endanger the life or physical safety of any individual.[31]

In 1986 Congress amended the FOIA to make it clear that law enforcement officials could also withhold documents whenever

1. the subject of the information is unaware of a pending criminal investigation and disclosure of the existence of the records could interfere with the criminal process;
2. the request involves information supplied by an informant whose identity may be revealed by disclosure of the documents; or
3. the documents involve FBI files related to foreign intelligence, counterintelligence, or international terrorism.[32]

In 1982, the Supreme Court revealed an inclination to protect law enforcement records as broadly as possible. Journalist Howard Abramson had filed an FOIA request for FBI files on anti–Vietnam War activists. Abramson was investigating whether the Nixon administration had used the FBI to collect information on political adversaries. The FBI ultimately turned over some documents but withheld others, including a critical memorandum from former FBI director J. Edgar Hoover to a key White House aide.

A primary issue before the Court was whether the FBI should be forced to disclose a document that was not prepared for law enforcement purposes. The

---

[30] United States Dep't of State v. Washington Post Co., 456 U.S. 595 (1982).

[31] 5 U.S.C.A. § 552(b)(7).

[32] Freedom of Information Reform Act of 1986, 100 Stat. 3248 (1986).

Court ruled that it was the information on the document that should be protected, not the document itself. Although the memorandum to the White House was not intended for law enforcement, the information was originally *collected* for law enforcement purposes, thus the FBI was correct in refusing disclosure.[33]

The Supreme Court ruled in 1989 that Exemption Seven may be used to refuse disclosure of law enforcement files even if the information was *not* originally collected for law enforcement purposes. A corporation doing business as a defense contractor had been accused of fraudulent practices and wanted documents controlled by the Defense Contract Auditing Agency (DCAA). DCAA refused based on Exemption Seven, even though the information was originally provided to the Department of Defense before the allegations of fraud and as part of a routine audit, not as part of any law enforcement investigation. The Court upheld DCAA, concluding that there was no requirement that the information be compiled within any time frame, and that Congress had provided the exemptions to allow a proper balancing of the interest in access to information and the government's need to prevent disclosure of certain information.[34]

The Supreme Court dramatically increased the scope of Exemption Seven in the 1989 case *Department of Justice* v. *Reporters Committee for Freedom of the Press*. In a unanimous decision the Court ruled that FBI rap sheets on private individuals are *categorically* exempt from disclosure under FOIA.[35] The case evolved due to an investigation by CBS correspondent Robert Schakne into the relationship between Medico Industries, a company with defense contracts, and bribery allegations against a former Pennsylvania congressman. Schakne wanted FBI rap sheets on four brothers in the Medico family, three of whom were deceased. The Bureau handed over files on the three deceased brothers but claimed that release of records on the living brother would constitute an unwarranted invasion of privacy.

The Court reasoned that some compilations of personal information are so private that they should never be disclosed regardless of the public interest in the information. The Court then offered two additional perspectives that provided public records advocates more bad news. First, the Court indicated that a balancing of interests in freedom of information and personal privacy was necessary only in cases dealing with types of documents not categorically exempted.[36] Rap sheets, according to the Court, were categorically exempted. Second, the Court held that when release of information might reasonably be expected to invade the privacy of an individual, only those records that contain information about *government operations* should be disclosed. The court also expressed concern regarding the increasing use of centralized data banks, where information that may threaten personal privacy can be accessed and disclosed in an instant.

---

[33] Federal Bureau of Investigation v. Abramson, 456 U.S. 615 (1982).

[34] John Doe Agency v. John Doe Corp., 493 U.S. 146 (1989).

[35] By "categorically" exempt the Court meant that all examples of that particular category of documents, namely police rap sheets, were exempt from disclosure on FOIA. There would, therefore, be no case-by-case analysis or balancing of interests.

[36] Department of Justice v. Reporters Comm. for Freedom of the Press, 489 U.S. 749 (1989).

16.1.2.3.8   *Exemption Eight: Information Related to Banks*
Exemption Eight pertains to any information regarding the condition, operation, regulation, or supervision of financial institutions.

This exemption was born out of concern that disclosure of sensitive banking and other financial information could have a detrimental effect on consumer confidence in banks and other financial institutions.[37]

16.1.2.3.9   *Exemption Nine: Geological and Geophysical Information*
This exemption is intended to prevent disclosure of valuable oil and gas well drilling information.

Exemption Nine is obviously designed to protect sensitive proprietary information. The exemption is rarely of concern to mass media.

16.1.3   Federal Privacy Act of 1974

The Federal Privacy Act prohibits federal agencies from disclosing information about a person without written permission of the individual to which the record applies, unless the information is subject to disclosure under FOIA. The Privacy Act authorizes individuals to review and copy any personal information about themselves contained in agency files and to request amendments to any portion of the record believed to be inaccurate or incomplete.

It was obvious by 1974 that individuals needed protection from governmental misuse of the huge quantities of personal information collected and stored in agency files. Prompted by this concern and the realization that advances in computer technology had exacerbated the problem, Congress passed the Privacy Act of 1974.[38] The act not only protects individuals against governmental disclosure of personal information, it also gives them the right to request access to files containing personal information. The agency must either comply with the request or inform the individual of the reasons for noncompliance and procedures for a judicial review of the request.[39]

In 1984, Congress passed legislation to assure that whenever any information was subject to both FOIA disclosure and the Privacy Act, the information could be disclosed.[40] Still, the Privacy Act offers individuals considerable protection from disclosure because agencies often withhold information when unsure whether a particular document is subject to the invasion of privacy exemption.

---

[37] 5 U.S.C.A. § 552(b)(8).
[38] 5 U.S.C.A. § 552b.
[39] 5 U.S.C.A. § 552(d).
[40] 98 Stat. 2211–2212 (1984).

16.1.4   Access to Government-Controlled Property

Electronic media professionals are free to enter public property, shoot video, record events, and even snoop around as long as no electronic devices are used to facilitate eavesdropping into otherwise private areas. However, earthquakes, fires, explosions, plane crashes, and even traffic accidents transfer control of otherwise public property to police or fire officials.

Public property is just that, public. The sudden occurrence of an emergency situation, however, can render even the most public of places off limits to everyone, including the news media. In many areas authorities liberally allow the media access to sites of emergencies, but whenever asked to leave, news media personnel should be aware that there is no First Amendment or other right of access to scenes of emergencies.

Some municipalities have passed laws providing special rights of access to newsworthy events. The city of San Diego, for example, has an ordinance allowing the police to close off areas whenever a menace to public health is created by flood, storm, fire, earthquake, explosion, accident, or other type of disaster. However, the ordinance specifically prohibits denial of access to such closed areas to duly authorized representatives of any news service, newspaper, or radio or television station or network, unless their presence interferes with emergency operations.

The ordinance did not keep Steven Leiserson, photographer for San Diego's KFMB-TV, from getting arrested and spending some time in jail. On September 25, 1978, a commercial airliner collided with a small plane and crashed into a San Diego neighborhood killing all persons on board and several on the ground. Leiserson arrived on the scene shortly after the crash and shot videotape for about 30 minutes. However, a rumor quickly spread among officials at the scene that the crash may have been a criminal act designed to assassinate a public official on board. On that basis police began to clear what they thought might be a crime scene, and Leiserson was asked to leave. He insisted on staying and was arrested and booked for failing to comply with a lawful order of a police officer. There was never any accusation that Leiserson was hindering emergency operations or tampering with crash site evidence in any way and the charges against him were eventually dropped, but not before the news photographer had spent a few hours in jail and some $40,000 in attorney's fees.[41]

A similar incident occurred following a Midwest Airlines crash near Milwaukee in 1985, only this time the crash occurred on airport nonpublic property and there was no ordinance like the one in San Diego giving journalists legal access to sites of emergencies. In fact, the airport media guide explicitly stated that no media personnel were allowed to enter nonpublic areas of the airport without an authorized escort.

The crash site had been quickly sealed and secured by officials, but a WTMJ-TV station wagon made its way through a police roadblock by following an emergency

---

[41] Leiserson v. City of San Diego, 202 Cal. App. 3d 725 (1988).

vehicle. As law enforcement officials approached the car, news photographer Peter King disembarked, jumped a fence bearing a "No Trespassing" sign, and began to shoot videotape. Police ordered him to leave, and upon his refusal he was arrested and later found guilty of disorderly conduct.[42]

In 1981, the quest for access to the president of the United States and to the White House pitted what was then an upstart cable news network, CNN, against ABC, CBS, NBC, President Ronald Reagan, his chief of staff and several other top administration officials. CNN had filed a lawsuit claiming that its constitutional rights were violated when the three television networks were granted favored status in covering certain White House events. Whenever space was limited, White House policy was to allow admission to one television crew of five persons, rotated among ABC, NBC, and CBS. After CNN filed suit, the White House turned the selection process over to the television news organizations. Not surprisingly, a consensus plan never emerged, so the White House announced that future pools would not include the television media. The television news organizations immediately sought and received a court injunction against Reagan, Chief of Staff James Baker, and Deputy Press Secretary Larry Speakes. The injunction, issued by a U.S. district court, ordered the White House to stop the total exclusion of television news representatives from participating in pool coverage of White House events.

In making its decision the court used the following four-part test that is often employed by the courts when a party seeks an injunction:

1. Is there a substantial likelihood that the remedy sought by the party seeking the injunction will succeed?
2. Will the party seeking the injunction suffer irreparable injury if it is not granted?
3. Does the threatened injury to the party seeking the injunction outweigh the damage the injunction itself will cause to parties opposed to court intervention?
4. Is granting the injunction in the public interest?

The court sided with the news organizations after concluding that all four prerequisite questions were answered affirmatively.[43]

A different kind of access to the White House was sought during the Watergate scandal. When it was discovered that President Nixon had taped conversations in the Oval Office, the Watergate special prosecutor sought access to the tapes, the content of which was ultimately a major factor in Nixon's decision to resign. In 1974, the Supreme Court ordered Nixon to honor the prosecutor's subpoena to turn over the tapes.[44] The Court concluded that

---

[42] City of Oak Creek v. King, 436 N.W.2d 285 (1989).
[43] Cable News Network v. ABC, 518 F. Supp. 1238 (1981).
[44] United States v. Nixon, 418 U.S. 683 (1974).

neither the doctrine of separation of powers nor the generalized need for confidentiality of high-level communication, without more, can sustain an absolute, unqualified Presidential privilege of immunity from judicial process under all circumstances.[45]

Once the tapes were made available to the courts, electronic media representatives wanted access to them as well. In fact, Warner Communications requested copies of the tapes in order to duplicate, broadcast, and even sell copies to the public. The print media were less interested because during the trials of several Nixon administration officials the court had provided transcripts of the tapes, which were played as evidence.

The Court, rejecting Warner's request, held that while courts have recognized a general right of access to court documents, that right is not absolute. Since the tapes had been played in the courtroom and transcripts had been provided, the Court concluded that Warner had no common law right of access to obtain the actual recordings.[46] The Court also held that Warner had no more First Amendment right of access to the tapes than the general public, and that any requirements of access under the Sixth Amendment were satisfied by the fact that the Watergate trial was among the most publicized ever.[47]

16.1.5   State Access Laws

State open records laws typically stipulate broad definitions of agencies and records. As a result, a large percentage of state, county, and municipal documents are subject to disclosure.

In addition to the federal Freedom of Information Act, each of the 50 states has passed laws requiring access to public records held by state, county, and municipal agencies. Common law also provides limited access to state and local records. State access statutes have defined and classified records in such a manner that agencies and the press and public have considerable guidance as to which records are applicable.

Most states base justification for open records laws on the principle that open government is essential to a democratic society. The Arkansas Freedom of Information Act states:

[T]he proper functioning of a democratic society is dependent upon the public being informed at all times with respect to the operations of gov-

---

[45] *Id.* at 683.

[46] "Common law" was defined in EMG 1.1.3 as law created by judges as they render decisions on questions of law not covered by statutes. For this reason common law is also called "judge-made law." In this case a "common law right of access" would be one granted by judges in previous court decisions.

[47] Nixon v. Warner Communications, 435 U.S. 589 (1978).

ernment, and public officials shall at all times be held accountable for their public actions and conduct; . . .[48]

It is common for states, especially those passing or amending open records law recently, to define *records* broadly. The Arkansas statute defines records as "writings, recorded sounds, films, tapes, or data compilations in any form" and includes "all records maintained in public offices or by public employees within the scope of their employment. . . ."[49] In 1992, the Kentucky Supreme Court ruled that a letter written by the University of Kentucky to the NCAA in response to allegations of basketball recruiting violations was a public record.[50] In states such as Florida, which have adopted a broad definition, the law applies to computerized records.[51]

Of course, Arkansas and all other states have statutes specifically exempting certain records such as those pertaining to law enforcement investigations, state income tax, medical records, trade secrets, and student scholastic records. In many states courts have ruled that the exemptions must be interpreted narrowly.[52]

In most states agencies find it difficult to circumvent the law by arguing that they are not really "agencies" under the law. The manner in which *agency* is defined by the states is discussed in Box 16.2.

In many states, when educational institutions make top-level hires, records related to the search process must be made public. Universities prefer to keep the names and resumes of applicants confidential when hiring a new president or chancellor. The reasoning is that highly qualified persons in high-level or prestigious positions elsewhere may never apply because they prefer not to have their application and resumes made public. Despite this potential, courts have forced a number of universities, including Arizona State University[53] and Texas Agricultural and Mechanical University,[54] to disclose search-related records. On the other hand, a Florida court ruled that the state's public records law did not apply to records related to a search for a new dean at the University of Florida law school.[55]

Most states allow any person, corporation, citizen group, or other organization access to records, and journalists are provided no greater access than anyone else. Most states require no reason be given to gain access to state and local records.

---

[48] Ark. Stat. Ann. § 12-2801(10) (1967).
[49] Ark. Stat. Ann. § 12-2803 (Supp. 1985).
[50] University of Ky. v. Courier Journal, 830 S.W.2d 373 (1992).
[51] Matthew D. Bunker, Sigman L. Splichel, Bill F. Chamberlin, and Linda M. Perry, "Access to Government-Held Information in the Computer Age: Applying Legal Doctrine to Emerging Technology," 20 *Fl. St. U. L. Rev.* 543 (1993).
[52] Lamon v. McCord, 432 S.W.2d 753 (1968).
[53] Arizona Bd. of Regents v. Phoenix Newspapers, 806 P.2d 348 (1991).
[54] Hubert v. Harte-Hanks Texas Newspapers, 652 S.W.2d 546 (1983).
[55] Marston v. Wood, 425 So. 2d 582 (1982).

BOX 16.2   Definition of an "Agency"

In most states, what constitutes an "agency" is defined broadly and includes any agency supported by or receiving public funding. Kentucky's public records act, for example, includes in its definition of "public agency" every state or local government officer, state department, division, bureau, board, commission and authority, every legislative board, commission, committee and officer, every city and county governing body, council, school district board, special district board, municipal corporation, court or judiciary agency, and any board, department, commission, committee, subcommittee, ad hoc committee, council or agency, and any other body that is created by state or local authority in any branch of government or that derives at least 25 percent of its funds from state and local authorities.*

   In Arkansas, the state supreme court has applied the state's access laws even to obscure "agencies such as a voluntary association to regulate extra-curricular activities of high schools, an athletic conference, and a voluntary organization of educational institutions."‡

---

* K.R.S. 61.870(1).
‡ Lawrence W. Jackson, "Arkansas Freedom of Information Act: Working Papers and Litigation Files of Attorneys Hired by Public Entities are Subject to Disclosure," 13 *U. Ark. Little Rock L. J.* 731 (1991).

16.1.6   Government in the Sunshine Laws

Federal and state sunshine acts require that meetings of government agencies—even those consisting of as few as two members—be announced in advance and conducted openly. Most states allow some meetings to be held in closed "executive" sessions.

In 1976 Congress passed the Government in the Sunshine Act. The purpose of the act was to assure openness in government by requiring agencies to keep meetings open to the public. The act pertains to most government agencies and to every portion of every meeting unless otherwise exempted. The exemptions to the Sunshine Act are similar to those of FOIA.

   The federal Sunshine Act applies to agencies and subdivisions of agencies consisting of as few as two persons. Under the act, agency members may not jointly conduct or dispose of business without announcing the time, place, and subject matter of the meeting, whether it is open or closed, and the name and phone number of the person designated to provide information about the meeting. The announcement must be published in the *Federal Register* at least one week in advance. The time and place of the meeting can be changed only if the change is announced at the earliest practicable time. The subject matter and whether the meeting will be open or closed can be changed only after a majority of agency members decides no earlier announcement was possible and votes accordingly and the decision and votes are promptly announced. If a meeting is closed, the reasons and relevant exemptions must be cited.[56]

Although the provisions vary widely, all 50 states have also passed some form of a government in the sunshine law. Most require advance notice of the time, place, and subject matter of agency meetings. As with open records laws, many states define *agency* as any governmental body that receives or is supported by public funds. Some states actually list the agencies to which the law applies.

What actually constitutes a meeting varies among the states. In some states, a majority of agency members must be present, but in a few, the statute applies even if only two members are holding a discussion regarding agency business—even in a rest room.[57]

Most state statutes require that any business accomplished at a meeting that does not meet the provisions of a sunshine act is typically nullified. Most states also provide for penalties when open meetings laws are violated. Although prosecution of state and local agency members is rare, some states provide for criminal penalties if open records laws are knowingly violated.

Once an action is filed against a state or local agency, the courts are often quick to uphold sunshine act provisions. For example, a Missouri court ruled in 1984 that private meetings of an annexation study commission in St. Louis violated open meetings laws.[58] In 1979, a Florida court ruled likewise regarding individual discussions between the Orange County school superintendent and board members concerning school zone redistricting and the transfer of students. The superintendent wanted to develop a working plan before holding a public meeting in order to avoid any public uproar that might occur over the redistricting.[59]

A Florida judge advised agency members in his state not to take chances. He recommended that whenever a member is unsure about whether a gathering is in violation of sunshine laws, he or she should "leave the meeting forthwith."[60]

At least one court decided not to interpret sunshine laws too broadly. A judge ruled that the county commissioners in Lincoln County, Colorado, did not violate open meetings laws by closing the meeting room door to shut out distracting noise.[61]

Most state sunshine acts allow some meetings to be closed. Often referred to euphemistically as *executive sessions*, closed meetings usually involve sensitive matters such as agency personnel matters, labor negotiations and collective bargaining sessions, real estate transactions, security matters, or consultations with respect to litigation.

---

[56] 5 U.S.C.A. § 552(b).
[57] Acker v. Texas Water Comm'n, 790 S.W.2d 299 (1990).
[58] MacLachlan v. McNary, 684 S.W.2d 534 (1984).
[59] Blackford v. School Bd. of Orange County, Fla., 375 So. 2d 578 (1979).
[60] City of Miami Beach v. Berns, 245 So. 2d 38 (1971).
[61] Allen v. Board of County Comm'rs, 497 P.2d 1026 (1972).

16.1.7   Access During Wartime

> The U.S. government has drastically decreased news media access to battlefield locations and information about hostilities. The Department of Defense required news media representatives to pool resources during the Persian Gulf War.

One result of the quick cessation of hostilities in the Persian Gulf War was the resolution of a court case before the court was forced to consider a major constitutional issue: To what extent do the news media have a right of access to information and battlefield locations during wartime? During the Vietnam War the news media were allowed to roam about, shoot, write, and report from most anywhere the war was fought. Content was virtually unrestricted as well, aside from prohibitions against reporting anything that might endanger troops or threaten the national security.

Things had changed drastically by the time U.S. forces invaded Grenada in October 1983, and Panama in December 1989. And when the Persian Gulf War erupted in early 1991, the U.S. military handed down guidelines severely restricting the content of news reports and the ability of the news media to gain access to the war and related information. Most notably, the Department of Defense (DOD) instituted pooling arrangements whereby only a selected "pool" of representatives of the various media were allowed access to battlefield sites.

The pooling arrangements set off intense competitive battles among the media to be included among those selected. The DOD announced that its principal criteria for selection would be (1) whether the medium principally served the American public and (2) whether a long-term presence covering Department of Defense operations had been established.[62] Those that did not meet the criteria were not eligible to be in the pool. Since pool members were required to share information *only* with others in the pool, selection for the pools became essential to gaining access to critical information about the war. Reporters were forbidden to roam about on their own. The official policy was to detain and return to headquarters any media representatives detected on the front lines without a military escort. DOD claimed the pools served to balance the media's desire for "unilateral"[63] coverage with DOD's goal of maintaining operational security, protecting the safety of the troops, and preventing media interference with military operations.

Access to the Persian Gulf War battlefield was the principal issue in *Nation Magazine* v. *U.S. Department of Defense*.[64] *Nation* magazine, along with several other print and radio interests, filed suit against the DOD, Joint Chiefs of Staff chair Colin Powell, DOD spokesperson Pete Williams, and President George Bush. The plaintiffs claimed that the pooling arrangements infringed their First Amendment rights by limiting access to the battlefield. A separate action was filed by Agence France-Presse (AFP), a French news wire service that had been excluded from the

---

[62] CENTCOM Pool Membership and Operating Procedures, Department of Defense, January 30, 1991. (The rules were revised several times throughout the conflict.)

[63] The term *unilateral coverage* was used by DOD to represent the opposite of *pooled coverage.*

[64] Nation Magazine v. U.S. Dep't of Defense, 762 F. Supp. 1558 (1991).

pool. DOD, with agreement of all parties involved, consolidated the two cases in February 1991.

Together the plaintiffs raised two fundamental issues:

1. To what extent can the military limit access to battlefield sites?
2. To what extent did the DOD treat the various media unequally?

The DOD's primary defense was effective. It claimed the issues had become moot when the pooling requirements and other restrictions were lifted at the end of the war.[65] The court agreed in part, but concluded that while minor changes in language would occur, a similar pooling arrangement would likely be instituted in the future, creating a similar conflict. Therefore, the court decided to discuss the primary issues in the case and in doing so, offered insight into how pooling arrangements might be considered by courts in the future.

First, the court said that in order to obtain an injunction against the DOD, the plaintiffs must establish that the pooling arrangement created a genuine "threat of imminent, specific, and irreparable harm."[66] The court declined to make such a ruling in the present case, since the war had ended, rendering the issue moot.

The court refused to consider plaintiffs' access claims for the same reason, noting that a court should not "define the outer constitutional boundaries of access" in the abstract, with no specific restrictions in force.[67] But the court did reject the notion of unlimited access as unreasonable in wartime and expressed some impatience with the plaintiffs for not offering a compromise procedure:

> There is little disagreement, even from plaintiffs, that DOD may place time, place, and manner restrictions on the press upon showing that there is a significant governmental interest. Yet, when asked at oral argument about how the government may design appropriate non-content based regulations ... counsel for the *Nation* responded, "Fortunately, I don't have to make that decision."[68]

With that the court concluded that the access claims lacked sufficient focus and dismissed the complaint.

Even though the court offered but a glimpse of how future courts might handle cases involving pooling arrangements, it seems the burden of proof is clearly on the news media to demonstrate that specific and irreparable harm is caused by the arrangements if there is any hope of establishing a right of access to battlefield locations.

---

[65] The same defense was used and accepted by the courts in *Flynt v. Weinberger,* 762 F.2d 134 (1985), a case dealing with press restrictions during the Grenada invasion.

[66] Nation Magazine v. U.S. Dep't of Defense, 762 F. Supp. at 1569 (1991).

[67] *Id.* at 1572.

[68] *Id.* at 1574.

16.2 PROTECTION OF NEWS SOURCES

Most state and federal courts grant journalists a limited privilege to withhold the names of news sources. A number of states have liberal shield laws offering journalists protection from having to reveal sources or hand over information, audio- or videotapes, or other news items.

Journalists have for years argued for an absolute right to protect the confidentiality of news sources and information gathered for news purposes. The reasoning is logical and somewhat compelling. If sources can be assured that no one other than the journalist will ever know who they are, they are more likely to offer information. On the other hand, this kind of information, as well as audio- and videotapes and photographs, can often provide critical evidence for law enforcement to facilitate the arrest and prosecution of criminal suspects. Of course, the same information might provide the basis of acquittal for an innocent defendant. Courts, therefore, must often balance First Amendment rights of reporters with Sixth Amendment rights to a fair trial, or the public interest in the arrest and efficient prosecution of criminals.

Reporters contend that information available from confidential news sources is often obtainable from no other source, and may provide critical verification of facts that justify publication of a story. One need only reflect on the alleged importance of "Deep Throat," a confidential source of information on the Watergate scandal for *Washington Post* reporter Bob Woodward. Journalists also argue that being forced to divulge information regarding sensitive matters—particularly those related to criminal activity—compromises a reporter's ability to cultivate sources and effectively gather information.

The problem for journalists is that the courts have never established an absolute right to protect news sources. In this section we discuss the extent to which protection is offered to journalists by:

1. state courts through *common law,*
2. *state statutes,* and
3. the *First Amendment* and interpretations of the case *Branzburg* v. *Hayes.*[69]

16.2.1 Protection through Common Law

Courts have generally refused to grant a common law privilege for reporters to withhold information.

Courts throughout the nation have the authority to extend considerable, though certainly not absolute, protection to journalists who are under subpoena to reveal information, including identification of sources. Whatever protection they

---

[69] 408 U.S. 665 (1972).

have extended, however, has been limited. What often happens is that a judge will decide that the public interest is better served by obtaining the information from a journalist rather than protecting any limited First Amendment rights. The courts have been considerably more willing to extend a privilege not to testify to journalists subpoenaed in civil cases, so long as the reporter or news medium is not a party to the case.

16.2.2   Protection through State Statutes

State statutes offer greater protection for journalists than common law, but many states have no shield laws at all. Of those that do, some offer protection only to journalists working for the print media.

About half of the states have adopted some kind of shield law protecting journalists from being forced to reveal information. Some statutes are narrowly drawn, offering journalists protection only with respect to confidentiality agreements with sources. The Pennsylvania statute, for example, states:

> No person engaged on, connected with, or employed by any newspaper of general circulation or any press association or any radio or television station, or any magazine of general circulation, for the purpose of gathering, procuring, compiling, editing or publishing news, shall be required to disclose the source of any information procured or obtained by such person, in any legal proceeding, trial or investigation before any government unit.[70]

The precise wording of a state shield law may not be a good predictor of how it will be enforced. The Pennsylvania courts, for example, have interpreted the wording of the statute above so broadly that information gathered by reporters and even tape recordings been protected:

> The common and approved meaning or usage of the words "source of information" includes documents as well as personal informants. . . . "Source" means not only the identity of the person, but likewise includes documents, inanimate objects and all sources of information.[71]

Some states offer protection only when a reporter has specifically promised confidentiality to a source. Other states, such as Nebraska, protect any information obtained in the news-gathering process as well as journalists' "notes, outtakes, photographs, film, tapes, or other data."[72] The Nebraska act also specifically protects journalists against search warrant invasions unless the journalists themselves are suspected of a crime.

---

[70] 42 Pa. Cons. Stat. Ann. § 5942(a) (1982).
[71] In re Taylor, 193 A.2d 181 (1963).
[72] R.R.S. Nebraska § 20-145.

The electronic news media are perhaps less protected than their print counterparts. A few states protect newspaper reporters but exclude journalists working for radio and television. The distinction may be made because electronic media journalists do have a commodity that is quite attractive to law enforcement officials—actual audio- and videotape recordings of suspects and criminal activity.

The case of Bradley Stone, a photographer for a Storer Broadcasting station in Detroit, serves as an excellent example. After the murder of an off-duty Michigan state trooper was linked to gang members, Stone persuaded several gang members to appear on camera as long as no faces were shown and their identities were never revealed. The members even threatened Stone with bodily harm should he breach their agreement.

Problems for Stone apparently began when one gang member told police investigators that the persons responsible for the murder were among those videotaped. Making Stone's tapes even more appealing, eyewitnesses had informed authorities that they could identify the assailants if they saw them in a photograph. Stone was subpoenaed to appear before a grand jury and to bring his tapes with him. He refused.

Michigan's shield law offered Stone no protection because at that time it excluded television reporters. The courts declined to protect him either. A U.S. court of appeals ruled that even if there was a qualified privilege that might preclude Stone from having to testify, it would likely be overridden by the compelling public interest in prosecuting a murder suspect.

The court also upheld the Michigan statute's exclusion of the broadcast media, ruling that since no fundamental right to protect news sources existed, the law does not deny electronic journalists equal protection under the law. The court even suggested that the availability of visual identification evidence from the electronic media might serve as justification for a distinction between print and electronic media in state shield laws.[73]

Following the Stone case the Michigan legislature revised its shield law to read as follows:

> A reporter or other person who is involved in the gathering or preparation of news for broadcast or publication shall not be required to disclose the identity of an informant, any unpublished information obtained from an informant, or any unpublished matter or documentation, in whatever manner recorded, relating to a communication with an informant . . .[74]

The statute does not apply to cases involving crimes punishable by life imprisonment if the information sought is essential to the case and other means of obtaining the information have been exhausted.

---

[73] Michigan v. Storer Communications, 397 N.W.2d 244 (1986). *See also* Storer Communications v. Giovan, 810 F.2d 580 (1987).
[74] Mich. Comp. Laws § 767.5a.

The Pennsylvania shield law has also extended protection to electronic media reporters, but contains an exception requiring radio and television stations to keep recordings, transcriptions, kinescope film, or certified written transcriptions available for inspection for at least one year following a broadcast or telecast.[75]

16.2.3 First Amendment Protection: *Branzburg* v. *Hayes*

> In the *Branzburg* decision, a majority of the Supreme Court refused to grant journalists a First Amendment privilege to withhold sources and information. Justice Stewart's dissent, however, suggested a qualified privilege for reporters that has been widely accepted by lower courts.

Branzburg v. *Hayes* is actually a consolidation of three cases, all involving journalists' refusals to appear before grand juries to disclose information about possible criminal activity. Paul Branzburg, a reporter for the *Louisville Courier Journal*, defied court orders to testify about possible drug trafficking. Branzburg had written an article in which he said he had actually observed illegal drug use, and Kentucky's shield law did not apply to journalists who personally witnessed crimes. *New York Times* reporter Earl Caldwell refused to testify or provide notes or audiotapes of interviews with members of a militant organization called the Black Panthers. The Black Panthers were being investigated regarding possible assassination plots. Paul Pappas, the lone electronic media journalist, also refused to testify about Black Panther activities. Members of the group had allowed Pappas to enter a barricaded store during riots in New Bedford, Massachusetts. Pappas agreed to talk about what he had seen and heard outside, but not inside, the store.

All three journalists argued that the First Amendment protected them from being forced to disclose confidential information. But in a 5-4 decision, a majority of the U.S. Supreme Court rejected a First Amendment privilege for journalists. In his majority opinion Justice Byron White said that the public interest in law enforcement should not be overridden by any burden placed on news gathering by forcing journalists to testify before grand juries. White was not convinced that significant numbers of potential sources would refuse to talk just because reporters might be forced to appear before grand juries.

Justice Potter Stewart disagreed, and in an influential dissenting opinion argued that reporters have a First Amendment right not to be forced to testify unless the government could demonstrate the following:

1. probable cause to believe that a reporter has information that is clearly relevant to a specific violation of law;
2. that information sought cannot be obtained by any other means less destructive of First Amendment rights; and
3. a compelling and overriding interest in the information.

---

[75] 42 Pa. Cons. Stat. § 5942.

Stewart's dissent in *Branzburg* has proven to be somewhat more influential than the majority opinion. Although countless variations have appeared, Stewart's three-part test has been utilized in state and federal court decisions across the nation. Most courts have accepted a qualified First Amendment privilege for reporters. A typical example is *United States* v. *Burke*, in which a U.S. court of appeals threw out a subpoena served on *Sports Illustrated* reporter Douglas Looney. Looney had refused to testify about an interview with a key witness in a basketball point-shaving scheme at Boston College. The court ruled that the defendant failed to prove that the testimony would provide information essential to the case, or that it could not be obtained from other sources.[76]

Some courts have relied on the majority decision in *Branzburg* to uphold contempt citations issued to reporters. Four South Carolina journalists were held in contempt for refusal to testify about a case against state legislators who allegedly accepted bribes to secure votes on a bill to legalize a form of gambling known as parimutuel betting. A U.S. court of appeals held that *Branzburg* refused to recognize a reporter's privilege not to testify in criminal proceedings, even if the information is obtained during news gathering.[77] The court added that "the reporters have no privilege different from that of any other citizen."[78]

16.2.4 Journalists in Defiance: Court-Ordered Decisions

Reporters have demonstrated a willingness to go to jail before violating a confidentiality agreement with a news source.

In a famous case involving the *New York Times*, reporter Myron Farber spent 40 days in jail. Farber's research had been instrumental in the arrest and prosecution of Dr. Mario E. Jascalevich for the murder of patients in a New Jersey hospital in 1965 and 1966. Jascalevich, who was accused of injecting relatively healthy patients with overdoses of a muscle relaxant, subpoenaed Farber's notes on the grounds they were necessary to prove his innocence. Farber refused, and the trial judge found him in contempt of court. Farber was fined $1,000, plus an additional $1,000 a day, and sentenced to six months in jail. The *Times* was fined $100,000 plus an additional $5,000 a day. On appeal, the New Jersey Supreme Court ruled, based on its interpretation of *Branzburg*, that journalists have no First Amendment privilege to ignore a court subpoena. The court refused to balance competing interests in the case, and even argued that an *in camera*[79] inspection of Farber's notes would not be a violation of New Jersey's shield law.[80] Farber eventually spent 40 days in jail and was released only after Jascalevich was acquitted.

---

[76] United States v. Burke, 700 F.2d 70 (1983).
[77] Shain v. Long, 978 F.2d 850 (1992).
[78] *Id.* at 852.
[79] In camera, defined in EMG 1.5.3, means in the judge's chambers or in a courtroom with the public excluded.
[80] In re Farber, 394 A.2d 330 (1978).

More recently, *Stuart News* reporter Tim Roche served 18 days in the Martin County, Florida, jail. Roche refused to comply with a court order to disclose who gave him copies of confidential documents related to termination of parental rights and juvenile dependency. The controversy began in 1988 when a three-year-old girl was tortured and beaten to death in the home of her mother and stepfather, Cheryl and Carl Puffinberger. Following the stepfather's conviction and 10-year sentence for aggravated child abuse, Cheryl Puffinberger was declared unstable and unfit, and a sealed order was issued terminating her parental rights to a second daughter, still an infant. Despite the fact that all relevant documents were closed to public inspection, a story written by Roche appeared in the *Stuart News* on May 30, 1990, the day after the order was handed down.

A subpoena was issued requiring Roche to disclose his sources. He refused, so the court held him in criminal contempt and sentenced him to 30 days in jail.

On appeal, the Florida Supreme Court ruled that a reporter does have a qualified privilege to protect the names of sources. But the court also said that the privilege is not absolute and may sometimes give way to a greater purpose, such as the societal interest served by the need to keep certain proceedings private and confidential. Using a balancing approach, the court ruled that the public interest served by maintaining confidentiality of juvenile dependency and parental rights termination proceedings outweighs the reporter's and newspaper's First Amendment rights of access to the information.[81]

Balancing conflicting interests can lead to a compromise in the demands a court places on a news medium. In June 1991, WMAQ-TV, the NBC affiliate in Chicago, broadcast an interview with Henry Leon Harris, a key government witness in an ongoing racketeering and narcotics conspiracy trial. Some of what Harris said during the WMAQ interview apparently conflicted with what he had said under oath. The defense in the case then issued WMAQ a subpoena demanding any and all taped interviews with Harris, including outtakes (sections of the interview that were not broadcast). NBC handed over the portions of the interview that were broadcast, but agreed to allow access to the outtakes only for an in camera court review. The network claimed, among other arguments presented to the court, that public disclosure of the outtakes would destroy their future journalistic value, thus depriving NBC of its editorial discretion in whether to use other portions of the interview. The defense argued that its interest in receiving a fair trial overrode any First Amendment interests of NBC.[82]

The court, influenced by what seemed to be additional inconsistencies on the outtakes, acknowledged the value of videotape as "unique bits of evidence that are frozen at a particular place and time," and attempted to strike a middle ground.[83] Instead of forcing NBC to hand over the outtakes, the court ordered the court reporter to prepare transcripts of the tapes and turn the scripts over to the defense.

---

[81] Roche v. Florida, 599 So. 2d 1279 (1992).
[82] United States v. Bingham, 765 F. Supp. 954 (1991).
[83] *Id.* at 959.

This procedure, according to the court, "minimizes . . . the intrusion on NBC's news gathering rights and acknowledges NBC's proprietary rights" to the outtakes.[84]

Plaintiffs in civil cases have met with some success in forcing news media disclosures. On September 11, 1991, an article in the *Sun* tabloid quoted unnamed sources as making uncomplimentary comments about comedian Rodney Dangerfield. One, for example, described Dangerfield as "blotto" with a couple of naked women in a hotel room strewn with vodka bottles. Dangerfield filed a libel suit. Realizing actual malice would be impossible to establish without the opportunity to analyze the credibility of the Sun's sources, he asked the court to demand disclosure of their names. The court granted Dangerfield's request, but the *Star* claimed First Amendment privilege and ignored the court order.

A U.S. district court ruled that Dangerfield (1) had a compelling interest in the names, since he would be required to prove actual malice, (2) had exhausted alternative sources of obtaining the names, and (3) was not forwarding a frivolous or unmerited claim. These conclusions tipped the balance in favor of disclosure.[85]

In *Bell* v. *City of Des Moines*, however, the plaintiffs failed to establish even one of the three *Branzburg* criteria. The plaintiffs had requested outtakes from a videotape recording of a suicide that occurred in 1986 as several observers, including Des Moines police officers and a WHO-TV news crew, looked on. The plaintiffs argued that the tape would help prove that the victim's suicide could have been prevented by police, since his gun was not initially loaded and he could have been apprehended.

WHO agreed to turn over segments of the video used on the evening newscast, but not the outtakes. The Iowa Supreme Court ruled that the plaintiffs fell short of establishing that the tapes were essential to the case, that the information could not be obtained from other sources, or that alternative sources of information were even sought.[86]

16.2.5   A Broken Promise: Do Reporters Have to Keep Promises Made to Sources?

> The U.S. Supreme Court has ruled that the First Amendment does not give reporters the right to break promises of confidentiality if the promises would otherwise be enforced under state law.

What happens if a journalist simply breaks the promise of confidentiality with a source even before a court or other authority forces any kind of disclosure? That is essentially what happened to Dan Cohen, a public relations consultant and spokesperson for 1982 Minnesota Independent-Republican gubernatorial candidate

---

[84] *Id.* at 960.

[85] Dangerfield v. Star Editorial, 817 F.Supp. 833 (1993). *See also* Star Editorial v. U.S. Dist. Court, 7 F.3d 856 (1993).

[86] Bell v. City of Des Moines, 412 N.W.2d 585 (1987).

Wheelock Whitney. On a promise of confidentiality, Cohen offered news reporters a "hot tip" on Marlene Johnson, the Democratic-Farmer-Labor candidate for governor, just five days before the election. The information turned out to be legal documents showing the candidate had been convicted of petit theft and arrested for unlawful assembly. The latter offense occurred during a protest over minority hiring practices and the theft conviction, later vacated, was for leaving a store with $6 worth of sewing items.

Some media reported the story without divulging the source, but two newspapers, after considerable deliberation, published Cohen's name as part of the story and indicated his connection to the Whitney campaign. Cohen, who was immediately fired from his job, filed suit against the two newspapers for fraudulent misrepresentation and breach of contract. The trial court rejected the newspapers' First Amendment arguments and found for Cohen, who was awarded $200,000 compensatory and $500,000 punitive damages. The Minnesota Supreme Court reversed the decision, holding that Cohen had not established either claim, but the court speculated whether Cohen may have a claim under Minnesota's promissory estoppel law.[87]

The U.S. Supreme Court reversed the Minnesota Supreme Court, holding that the First Amendment "does not confer on the press a constitutional right to disregard promises that would otherwise be enforced under state law."[88] The case was remanded back for reconsideration. On remand, the Minnesota Supreme Court used the promissory estoppel grounds to reinstate the $200,000 compensatory award to Cohen.[89]

16.2.6   Privacy Protection Act

The Privacy Protection Act protects journalists by prohibiting law enforcement and other government officials from serving search warrants on the news media except in certain circumstances.

In 1971, a California district attorney, after seeing pictures of a student takeover of the administrative offices at Stanford University published in the *Stanford Daily*, obtained a warrant to search the newspaper for evidence to help identify those involved. The warrant authorized a search of all film, negatives, and prints relevant to the takeover. The newspaper claimed that the search violated its First, Fourth, and Fourteenth Amendment rights.

The Supreme Court disagreed, holding that the Constitution allows searches, without warning, of persons who are not criminal suspects, so long as there is reason to believe evidence of a crime can be found. Journalists reacted with con-

---

[87] Promissory estoppel law in its most basic form requires that if one person makes a promise to another it must be kept, particularly if the promise induces actions involving third parties. The law holds the person making the promise liable for any consequences of the promise.

[88] Cohen v. Cowles Media Co., 501 U.S. 663 (1991).

[89] Cohen v. Cowles Media Co., 479 N.W.2d 387 (1992).

BOX 16.3   The Privacy Protection Act

The 1980 Privacy Protection Act prohibits government officials engaged in criminal investigations from serving search warrants on the news media except in the following circumstances:

1. There is probable cause to believe that a news media representative has committed or is committing a crime relevant to the materials sought.
2. There is reason to believe that immediate seizure of the material is necessary to prevent a death or serious bodily injury to a human being.
3. The materials relate to classified information, the national defense, or restricted data.

---

cern that inappropriate and even harassing searches could be conducted under the guise of legitimate criminal investigations. Some states passed statutes to provide journalists some measure of protection. As indicated earlier, Nebraska law prohibits searches of news media facilities unless a news representative is suspected of a crime. In 1980, Congress passed the Privacy Protection Act, which restricts the ability of government to serve search warrants on journalists[90] (see Box 16.3).

16.3   COVERING THE COURTS

The courts have struggled to find effective remedies to combat excessive publicity before and during trials.

Advanced technologies have allowed electronic media journalists to provide intimate, immediate, and thorough coverage of the criminal process. Television and radio journalists can now report live from a crime scene, a district attorney's office, or a courthouse. And cameras inside the courtroom offer television viewers a front-row seat to observe courtroom proceedings.

16.3.1   Pretrial Publicity

Excessive pretrial publicity places an extra burden on the court to ensure that a defendant's right to a fair trial is not violated. Judges are sometimes forced to issue restrictive orders or to delay or move trials, and the jury selection process may also be more complicated.

---

[90] 18 U.S.C.A. § 793(ff). *See also* 42 U.S.C.S. § 2000aa (1993).

The Sixth Amendment grants criminal defendants the right to a trial by an impartial jury. High profile trials involving William Kennedy Smith, Oliver North, Manuel Noriega, and Mike Tyson dramatically illustrate how news coverage of the criminal process has complicated protection of this right. Even on the local level, media coverage often saturates the community with information about a crime, the criminal investigation, and courtroom proceedings.

16.3.1.1 *Remedies Available to the Courts*
The courts have six major remedies available for dealing with excessive publicity before and during a trial: continuance, change of venue, voir dire, change of venire, sequestering, and overturning the conviction.

Most of the remedies available to the court are preventive measures designed either to avoid seating anybody on the jury who has been exposed to prejudicial information or to shield the jurors who are selected from exposure to prejudicial information. The remedies most often used are as follows:

1. *Continuance*: The judge delays or postpones the trial for a specified amount of time. This is sometimes requested by the defense in order to prepare a motion or appeal designed to deal with pretrial publicity.
2. *Change of Venue*: In this case the trial is moved to another location, where it is hoped there has been less publicity about the case.
3. *Voir Dire*: As we explained in Chapter 1, this is the process of interviewing potential jurors to decide which to seat on the jury. Many factors go into jury selection, but with respect to pretrial publicity, the goal is to identify and exclude persons who may have been unduly exposed to or influenced by information about the case. Any such persons may be challenged by attorneys for the defense and dismissed. Through what are called "peremptory challenges" (see Box 16.4), attorneys may also dismiss a certain number of potential jurors just on suspicion of exposure to unfavorable publicity about a client.
4. *Change of Venire*: You may remember that the venire is the pool of potential jurors. When a change of venire occurs, another entire pool of prospective jurors is selected and the process is started over again, including the voir dire.
5. *Sequestering*: Sequestering is isolating a jury, sometimes for days, to ensure they receive no information during the trial.
6. *Overturning the Conviction*: This is, of course, a last resort, and one used when, in the opinion of an appeals court, all other remedies still do not provide the defendant a fair trial.

16.3.1.2 *Pretrial Publicity and Overruling Criminal Convictions*
The courts have overturned criminal convictions due to pretrial publicity, but the Supreme Court has ruled that jurors do not have to be completely ignorant of the facts of a case.

BOX 16.4   Challenges During Jury Selection

During the jury selection process attorneys may challenge prospective jurors and have them dismissed from the jury pool. Two commonly used types of challenges are:

1. *Challenge for Cause*: This is a challenge to a juror for which some reason for the challenge is given. For example, it may be determined that the juror has been exposed to a considerable amount of media coverage about the case at hand. If the judge accepts the challenge, the juror is dismissed. Attorneys can have any number of challenges for cause.
2. *Peremptory Challenge*: This is a challenge to a juror for which no reason has to be given. A particular prospective juror, for example, may simply strike the defense in a negative way. Attorneys are allowed only a limited number of peremptory challenges, with the maximum number varying from state to state.

The first time that the Supreme Court overturned a state criminal verdict on the basis of pretrial publicity was in 1961 in the case *Irvin* v. *Dowd*.[91] Leslie Irvin had been charged with a series of murders near the city of Evansville, Indiana. Shortly after his arrest, police and prosecutors issued a press release announcing that Irvin had confessed to each of the murders. Media coverage grew increasingly extensive, saturating the community as Irvin was indicted and the court attempted to seat a jury. A change of venue was granted the defense, but under Indiana law that meant moving only to an adjacent county where media coverage had been virtually the same. During the four weeks of voir dire the defense filed for two additional venue changes and eight motions for continuances, but all were denied. Irvin was tried, convicted, and sentenced to death.[92]

The Supreme Court unanimously ruled that Irvin's Sixth Amendment rights were violated and that he should be granted a new trial. The court determined that considerable pretrial publicity and a deep pattern of prejudice throughout the community was clearly reflected in the fact that 8 of the 12 jurors thought Irvin was guilty before being seated.

In *Rideau* v. *Louisiana* the Supreme Court reversed a murder conviction partly on the basis of presumed juror bias resulting from the broadcast of a film of the defendant confessing to the crime.[93] Rideau, accused of bank robbery, kidnapping, and murder, had confessed during a 20-minute interview session with the

---

[91] Irvin v. Dowd, 366 U.S. 717 (1961).
[92] Interestingly, after all the hype and attention given to Irvin and the case, only nine days after sentencing he managed to escape from the county jail. He was recaptured in Michigan soon thereafter.
[93] Rideau v. Louisiana, 373 U.S. 723 (1963).

local sheriff. The entire interview, including the confession, was filmed and subsequently shown on a local television station on three consecutive days. In overturning the conviction the Supreme Court noted that 3 of the 12 jurors admitted during voir dire to having seen the film:

> [W]e hold that it was a denial of due process of law to refuse the request for a change of venue, after the people of Calcasieu Parish had been exposed repeatedly and in depth to the spectacle of Rideau personally confessing in detail to the crimes with which he was later to be charged.[94]

Other cases have provided insight into how the courts interpret and deal with pretrial publicity. Jack "Murph the Surf" Murphy lost his appeal to the Supreme Court to overturn a robbery and assault conviction because members of the jury learned from the news media that he was a convicted felon. Murphy attracted greater than usual attention because of his flamboyant lifestyle and his part in the 1964 theft of the Star of India sapphire from a museum in New York. The Court concluded that mere exposure to such facts does not necessarily prejudice a juror into a guilty verdict.[95]

In *Patton* v. *Yount* the high court ruled that jurors do not have to be totally ignorant of the facts surrounding a case. The essential criterion, according to the Court, is whether a potential juror can make an impartial decision based only on the facts presented in the courtroom.[96] In 1991, the Supreme Court ruled that during voir dire, prospective jurors do not even have to be *asked* about the specific content of media exposure.[97]

16.3.2 Publicity During the Trial

> After the highly publicized Lindbergh baby kidnapping case the American Bar Association adopted Canon 35, which contained strict guidelines for media coverage of trials and advocated a ban on cameras in the courtroom. During the 1970s rigorous standards were adopted and states gradually allowed electronic media equipment back in the courtroom. In 1981, the Supreme Court ruled that camera coverage of trial proceedings does not violate a defendant's right to a fair trial.

Electronic media coverage of trials got off to a bad start. Until the 1970s state and federal courts pretty much prohibited television news personnel from bringing cameras into the courtroom. Judges, many lawyers, and the ABA were very much opposed to having radio and television reporters using any kind of equipment to cover trials. Canon 3A(7) of the ABA's code of judicial ethics recommended that judges prohibit microphones and cameras except in specified situations, none of which provided for live broadcast or other public dissemination. Canon 3A(7) su-

---

[94] *Id.* at 726.
[95] Murphy v. Florida, 421 U.S. 794 (1975).
[96] Patton v. Yount, 467 U.S. 1025 (1984).
[97] Mu'Min v. Virginia, 111 S. Ct. 1899 (1991).

perseded the even more restrictive Canon 35, which stated that the presence of electronic media equipment would be a major distraction. Canon 35 had been adopted two years after the 1935 trial of Bruno Hauptmann, who was convicted of the abduction and murder of the two-year-old son of Charles Lindbergh.[98] The trial received unprecedented coverage because Lindbergh had attained hero status by being the first person to fly nonstop across the Atlantic Ocean. Hundreds of reporters had packed the courtroom and surrounding hallways as the trial proceeded. Although disruptions were apparently kept to a reasonable minimum, the case generated sufficient concern that the ABA added Canon 35 to its code of ethics.[99]

16.3.2.1 *Estes* v. *Texas*

After the *Estes* case, most states banned television coverage of courts altogether.

The 1965 Supreme Court decision in *Estes* v. *Texas* closed courtroom doors to cameras a little tighter. Over the objections of the defense, the judge had permitted cameras in preliminary hearings and during the trial of accused swindler Billy Sol Estes. The cameras and crews were, according to some, disruptive, and four jurors were selected for the trial despite having watched the pretrial hearing on television. The Supreme Court ruled that televising the trial violated Estes's right to a fair trial. The Court said that cameras in the courtroom presented four major threats:

1. they serve as a distraction and create an uncertain impact on juror prejudice;
2. they have a negative impact on the quality of witness testimony;
3. they place additional burdens on the judge; and,
4. they cause mental and perhaps even physical harassment of defendants.

Three dissenting justices expressed doubt whether Estes had really been deprived of a fair trial, and even Justice Brennan, who wrote the majority opinion, said that the decision should not be interpreted as prohibiting television cameras at all trials.[100]

16.3.2.2 *Sheppard* v. *Maxwell*

In *Sheppard* v. *Maxwell*, the U.S. Supreme Court overturned a murder conviction. The Court criticized the trial judge for failure to control the media during the trial and held that the jury should have been shielded from media publicity.

One year after the *Estes* decision the Supreme Court reversed another conviction, this time because of extensive publicity before *and* during the trial. On July 4, 1954, the wife of physician Sam Sheppard was found dead in her Bay Village, Ohio,

---

[98] State of New Jersey v. Hauptmann, 180 A. 809 (1935).

[99] For a more complete discussion of the Hauptmann case and restrictions on the use of cameras in the courtroom, *see* Richard B. Kielbowicz, "The Story Behind the Adoption of the Ban on Courtroom Cameras," 63 *Judicature* 14 (1979).

[100] Estes v. Texas, 381 U.S. 532 (1965).

the trial. There was only one point during testimony that the judge asked the camera operator to desist in an activity that the judge perceived to be distracting. Otherwise, all prescribed procedures were followed and there were no distracting incidents.

The improvements can be attributed to the guidelines laid out for coverage of Florida courtrooms and those imposed by the judge. The rules allowed only one camera, one camera technician, and no artificial lighting. Audio had to be picked up from the existing courtroom system, and broadcasters were forced to pool coverage if more than one organization wanted access. No equipment could be moved during the trial, not even to change film, videotape, or lenses, and recording of conferences between parties during the trial was prohibited. The judge at all times had complete discretionary power to terminate coverage.

Today, most states allow some camera coverage of the courts and the federal courts have experimented with camera coverage of civil proceedings. Coverage has even reached the point where an entire cable network (Court TV) carries nothing but court proceedings, commentary on trials and legal matters, and other programming related to courts.

16.3.3   Restrictive Orders and Prior Restraint

Gag orders are imposed by the courts to prohibit trial participants and the news media from disclosing the content of legal proceedings.

Gag orders have been used since the 1960s to prohibit trial participants and the news media from disclosing what goes on during legal proceedings. Gag orders are often initiated by judges, but sometimes parties to the litigation request and are granted various types of injunctions against disclosing certain information. Usually a judge will specify in a gag order precisely which topics cannot be discussed.

16.3.3.1   *United States* **v.** *Dickinson*

In the *Dickinson* case the U.S. Supreme Court ruled that the First Amendment does not allow journalists to disobey court-imposed gag orders.

The *Dickinson* case illustrates how reporters should not respond to a gag order. The conflict began when a U.S. district court judge issued a gag order prohibiting the media from publishing or broadcasting information about an upcoming preliminary hearing. The hearing was being held to determine whether there was sufficient evidence to prosecute a civil rights activist accused in 1971 of conspiring to murder the mayor of Baton Rouge. The judge feared that evidence submitted at the hearing, some of which would probably not be admissible during the trial, would be so highly prejudicial and incriminating that a fair trial might never be possible.

Larry Dickinson and Gibbs Adams were covering the hearing for the Baton Rouge *Star Times* and the *Morning Advocate*. After touching base with their editors, both journalists defied the gag order and published detailed stories about the hearing. Each was held in contempt and fined $300.

A U.S. court of appeals ruled that the gag order was, as Dickinson and Adams had argued, a violation of the reporters' First Amendment rights. The court reasoned that a restraining order cannot be based on mere speculation regarding fear of prejudicial information, especially when it is unclear whether a suspect will even be brought to trial. The court also concluded that there was a compelling need for the public to be informed of these proceedings, and that alternative remedies, such as continuance and change of venue, were not considered.

Despite the ruling, the court said the First Amendment does not give reporters the right to disobey a judge's order. The fines were remanded to the district court so the judge could reconsider. He did so, and once again fined each reporter $300. On appeal, the court upheld the fines, suggesting that Dickinson and Adams should have requested a hearing or appealed the judge's gag order, but not simply ignored it.[107]

16.3.3.2 *Nebraska Press Association* v. *Stuart*

In *Nebraska Press Association* v. *Stuart* the Supreme Court ruled that gag orders could be imposed only under certain circumstances.

In 1975, the tiny town of Sutherland, Nebraska, was the scene of the gruesome murder of six members of one family. The next day police arrested a neighbor of the victims, twenty-nine-year-old handyman Erwin Charles Simants, and the media quickly descended from all directions on the small town. It was soon learned that Simants had confessed to the murders.

The judge, seeking to protect Simants's chances of a fair trial, quickly issued a restraining order prohibiting news organizations from reporting (1) the fact that Simants had confessed or anything about his confession, (2) any other statements made by Simants, including information contained in a note written the night of the murders, and (3) any medical or laboratory information regarding possible sexual assaults on some of the victims. The judge even prohibited the media from reporting the fact that a gag order was in effect.

The U.S. Supreme Court unanimously struck down the restrictive order, holding that gag orders as a prior restraint may be constitutional in some cases, but should be imposed only as a last resort, and only then if the following three conditions were met:

1. There must be actual or very probable wide-spread prejudicial publicity.
2. There must be no other effective means available—continuance, change of venue, or voir dire, for example—that will control the effects of prejudicial publicity without imposing prior restraints.
3. There must be reasonable confidence that the gag order will work.

[107] United States v. Dickinson, 465 F.2d 496 (1972).

The Court ruled that the gag order in this case was inappropriate because only the first of the three test criteria was established.[108]

16.3.3.3 *Seattle Times* v. *Rhinehart*

In *Seattle Times* v. *Rhinehart* the U.S. Supreme Court ruled that litigants in civil suits do not have a First Amendment right to disseminate information obtained through the pretrial discovery process.

The *Seattle Times* had acquired information as part of the process of defending itself in a libel suit. Keith Rhinehart, spiritual leader of a religious group, was suing the paper for publishing, among other things, that he had entertained inmates at a nearby prison by awarding between $35,000 and $50,000 in cash prizes during an extravaganza featuring a chorus line of girls who shed their clothes and danced. The paper also said Rhinehart had accepted fees from individuals in return for putting them in touch with dead relatives and had sold magical stones that he had expelled from his body.

Rhinehart asked for $14 million in damages, so the *Times* sought and received access to the names of all the group's donors and members to help determine whether damages had indeed occurred. The judge then issued a restraining order prohibiting the newspaper from publishing the information.

In hearing the newspaper's appeal the Supreme Court focused on one principal issue: Do litigants in civil suits have a First Amendment right to disseminate, before the trial, information obtained through the pretrial discovery process?[109] The Court ruled that they did not, especially since the same information could be published if it had been obtained from another source. The restrictive order was upheld.[110]

16.3.3.4 *News-Journal Corporation* v. *Foxman*

In *News-Journal* v. *Foxman* a gag order was upheld. However, the court forced the judge who issued the order to be specific about to whom the gag order applied. The court also placed a limit on the duration of the order.

A bizarre criminal case in Daytona Beach, Florida, resulted in what would be considered a comprehensive restrictive order. Konstantinos Fotopoulos had been charged with murder in the death of a man he had allegedly hired to murder his wife, who was shot while she slept but survived. He was also charged in the death of another man, Kevin Ramsey, who was tied to a tree and shot in an execution-style murder. Fotopoulos had recorded Ramsey's murder on a videotape that was confiscated by police.

---

[108] Nebraska Press Ass'n v. Stuart, 427 U.S. 539 (1976).

[109] The pretrial discovery process occurs after a suit is filed but before the actual proceedings as attorneys for the plaintiff and defendant acquire information about the case at hand. Some information can be obtained forcibly through court-issued subpoenas.

[110] Seattle Times Co. v. Rhinehart, 467 U.S. 20 (1984).

Media coverage and public attention to the case was already extensive when on December 20, 1989, a re-enactment of the two murders was shown on the television program *A Current Affair*. Nine days later the judge issued a restrictive order prohibiting any persons with anything to do with the case, including police department employees, from talking to the news media about the case.

The Florida District Court of Appeals denied a petition from the *Daytona Beach News-Journal* to have the order quashed. The court did demand modifications in the order, including establishment of a narrower time limit. The court reasoned that there would be no reason for the order after the jury had been selected. The court also narrowed the scope of the order by eliminating the phrase "and all persons affiliated therewith" regarding various participants in the trial process. The court determined that the phrase was too vague to describe precisely who was affected by the order.[111] The *News-Journal* appealed again, but before the appeals court had rendered a decision a change of venue had been granted. Fotopoulos was tried, convicted, and sentenced to death. The appeals court later refused to rule that the order was inappropriate. The court did say that the First Amendment rights of the *News-Journal* were not violated because despite the order, its reporters were allowed to attend and report on all court proceedings.[112]

16.3.3.5   *United States* v. *Noriega*

The U.S. Supreme Court has held that there is a heavy presumption against the use of prior restraints on the media. Despite this, a prior restraint was placed on CNN in the *Noriega* case.

Before discussing the *Noriega* case it is important to note that the courts have consistently maintained that prior restraints placed on the media create serious threats to First Amendment freedoms. In 1971, the U.S. government attempted to restrain publication of a massive, classified study of U.S. involvement in Vietnam. The Supreme Court ruled that the government could not block publication of the information that came to be known as the "Pentagon Papers." The reason offered by the Court was a heavy presumption against prior restraint.[113]

A prior restraint placed on the Cable News Network was the focus 20 years later in *United States* v. *Noriega*. The case evolved after CNN managed to obtain tape recordings of telephone conversations between Panamanian dictator Manuel Noriega and his attorney. The calls were made to and from Noriega's jail cell in Miami following his arrest in the aftermath of the U.S. invasion of Panama. Defense attorneys moved quickly to prevent CNN from broadcasting any portion of the tapes.[114] On November 8, 1990, U.S. District Court Judge William Hoeveler granted a temporary restraining order, noting that prior restraint was justified despite the

---

[111] News-Journal Corp. v. Foxman, 559 So. 2d 1227 (1990).
[112] News-Journal Corp. v. Foxman, 939 F.2d 1499 (1991).
[113] New York Times Co. v. United States, 403 U.S. 713 (1971).
[114] Despite the fact that CNN is a cable television network that does not "broadcast," both the defense attorneys and the judge consistently used the term in relation to CNN's programming.

rigorous standards set forth in the three-part test established in the *Nebraska Press* case.

CNN fared no better with the U.S. court of appeals, which ruled that the First Amendment interests of the press and public would best be served if CNN turned over the tapes immediately so that the court could examine the content and render a more informed decision on the injunction.[115]

On November 18, 1990, the Supreme Court effectively upheld the restraint by refusing to review the case, so CNN turned the tapes over to the court.[116] CNN had already directly defied the court order and aired a portion of one of the tapes.

Ironically, after reviewing the content of the conversations, the court ruled that CNN could now legally broadcast the tapes. Perhaps even more ironically, CNN chose not to do so. Journalists contend that even temporary restraining orders can be as effective as permanent restrictions because the news value of information seldom outlasts the court proceedings, particularly when going through the appeals process.

A few weeks after the restraining order was lifted, a group of media representatives including Miami television station WPLG, *USA Today*, the *Miami Herald*, and broadcast stations owned by the Post-Newsweek Corporation asked the court for access to the transcripts of the tapes. The court, despite objections from Noriega's attorneys and CNN, made the transcripts available:

> CNN asks the court to defer not to its right to publish an exclusive story, but rather to its "right" to prevent the public, if it so wishes, from gaining access to information of public concern. Though the court respects CNN's right not to publish, it nonetheless declines to accord CNN such absolute and unfettered control over access to information which, in the court's discretion, should be made available to the public.[117]

The *Noriega* case is something of an aberration from an otherwise consistent rule of law that the burden of proof on the government in prior restraint cases is heavy. Still, the case illustrates that prior restraints can be issued against media. And, aside from obvious First Amendment implications, a prior restraint that is enforced even for only a brief amount of time can render otherwise newsworthy information useless to an electronic media news organization.

DISCUSSION QUESTIONS

1. To what extent do you think the First Amendment grants the news media access to prisons and sites of accidents and other emergencies? How does your position differ from that of the courts?

---

[115] United States v. Noriega, 917 F.2d 1543 (1990).
[116] United States v. Noriega, 752 F. Supp. 1037 (1990).
[117] *Id.* at 1045.

2. Should corporations and businesses be allowed to win reverse FOI suits in which they take action to block state, local, and federal agencies from disclosing documents to the media that may reveal "inside" information? Why or why not?

3. Discuss reasons why the FBI and other law enforcement agency rap sheets should and should not be exempt or subject to FOIA disclosure.

4. Assess the effectiveness of state open records and open meetings laws.

5. Explain the impact of *Branzburg* v. *Hayes* on the right of journalists to withhold information and names of sources from government officials. Be sure to distinguish between the majority and minority opinions in the decision.

6. In the event the Department of Defense again imposes the pooling arrangements used in the Persian Gulf War, how do you think the courts will respond to a First Amendment challenge from a news service not selected for the pool?

7. Suppose that you were Tim Roche, and you just received a sealed court document containing information about parental abuse that, if revealed, might save a young child from potential abuse. Do you write the story? Why or why not? How would you expect the court to respond?

8. Explain and assess the three-part test advanced in the *Nebraska Press Association* case. Under what conditions would a gag order be upheld by the courts? How about if a television station is preparing to broadcast video of an actual murder and a confession by the defendant? Would a gag order be upheld?

SUGGESTED READINGS

Braverman, Burt A., and Wesley R. Heppler. "A Practical Review of State Open Records Laws." *George Washington Law Review* 49 (1981): 720.

Clemens, Jennifer A. "Administrative Law: Freedom of Information Act Exemption Seven is Broadened." *Journal of Corporation Law* 16 (1991): 963.

Freedom of Information: A Compilation of State Laws. Washington, DC: GPO, 1978.

Freidman, Sophia R. "Sixth Amendment—The Right to an Impartial Jury: How Extensive Must Voir Dire Questioning Be?" *Journal of Criminal Law and Criminology* 82 (1992): 920.

Goldstein, Bruce D. "Confidentiality and Dissemination of Personal Information: An Examination of State Laws Governing Data Protection." *Emory Law Journal* 41 (1992): 1185.

Guidebook to Freedom of Information and Privacy Acts. 2d ed. New York: Boardman, 1986.

Hernon, Peter. *Federal Information Policies in the 1980's: Conflicts and Issues.* Norwood, NJ: Ablex, 1987.

Jaspin, Elliot, and Mark Sableman. "News Media Access to Computer Records: Updating Information Laws in the Electronic Age." *Saint Louis University Law Journal* 36 (1992): 349.

Murray, David J. "Troubled Skies Ahead for the Freedom of Information Act." *Western State University Law Review* 19 (1991): 325.

Rogalski, Heather A. "The Pentagon v. the Press: Is the Pool System a Solution to the Conflict?" *Bridgeport Law Review* 13 (1992): 107.

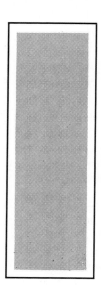

INDEX